RISK MANAGEMENT IN HEALTHCARE INSTITUTIONS

LIMITING LIABILITY AND ENHANCING CARE

Florence Kavaler, MD, MPH, MS

Professor and Chair of the Department of Health Policy and Management,
School of Public Health
State University of New York
Downstate Medical Center
New York, New York

Raymond S. Alexander, MBA, MS

President and Principal
Alexander, Wollman, & Stark
Philadelphia, Pennsylvania

JONES & BARTLETT
LEARNING

World Headquarters
Jones & Bartlett Learning
5 Wall Street
Burlington, MA 01803
978-443-5000
info@jblearning.com
www.jblearning.com

Jones & Bartlett Learning books and products are available through most bookstores and online booksellers. To contact Jones & Bartlett Learning directly, call 800-832-0034, fax 978-443-8000, or visit our website, www.jblearning.com.

Substantial discounts on bulk quantities of Jones & Bartlett Learning publications are available to corporations, professional associations, and other qualified organizations. For details and specific discount information, contact the special sales department at Jones & Bartlett Learning via the above contact information or send an email to specialsales@jblearning.com.

Risk Management in Healthcare Institutions: Limiting Liability and Enhancing Care, Third Edition is an independent publication and has not been authorized, sponsored, or otherwise approved by the owners of the trademarks or service marks referenced in this product.

Some images in this book feature models. These models do not necessarily endorse, represent, or participate in the activities represented in the images.

The authors, editors, and publisher have made every effort to provide accurate information. However, they are not responsible for errors, omissions, or for any outcomes related to the use of the contents of this book and take no responsibility for the use of the products and procedures described. Treatments and side effects described in this book may not be applicable to all people; likewise, some people may require a dose or experience a side effect that is not described herein. Drugs and medical devices are discussed that may have limited availability controlled by the Food and Drug Administration (FDA) for use only in a research study or clinical trial. Research, clinical practice, and government regulations often change the accepted standard in this field. When consideration is being given to use of any drug in the clinical setting, the health care provider or reader is responsible for determining FDA status of the drug, reading the package insert, and reviewing prescribing information for the most up-to-date recommendations on dose, precautions, and contraindications, and determining the appropriate usage for the product. This is especially important in the case of drugs that are new or seldom used.

Production Credits
Publisher: Kevin Sullivan
Acquisitions Editor: Amanda Harvey
Editorial Assistant: Rebecca Myrick
Associate Production Editor: Sara Fowles
Senior Marketing Manager: Elena McAnespie
V.P., Manufacturing and Inventory Control:
  Therese Connell

Composition: Lapiz, Inc.
Cover Design: Kristin E. Parker
Cover Image: © Anteromite/ShutterStock, Inc.
Printing and Binding: Edwards Brothers Malloy
Cover Printing: Edwards Brothers Malloy

Library of Congress Cataloging-in-Publication Data
Kavaler, Florence.
Risk management in healthcare institutions : limiting liability and enhancing care / Florence Kavaler,
  Raymond S. Alexander.—3rd ed.
    p. ; cm.
Rev. ed. of: Risk management in health care institutions. 2nd ed. c2003.
Includes bibliographical references and index.
ISBN 978-1-4496-4565-6 (pbk.)
I. Alexander, Raymond S. II. Kavaler, Florence. Risk management in health care institutions. III. Title.
[DNLM: 1. Health Facility Administration—United States. 2. Risk Management—ethics—United States.
  3. Risk Management—methods—United States. WX 157 AA1]
362.1068—dc23

                                                              2012022168

6048

Printed in the United States of America
16 15 14 13 12   10 9 8 7 6 5 4 3 2 1

Contents

Part I   Risk Management Administrative Issues   1

1   Risk Management: An Institutional Imperative   3

Raymond S. Alexander and Florence Kavaler

9 A Primer on Medical Malpractice   243

Arthur S. Friedman

Part III   Managing Risks in Other Healthcare Venues   423

About the Authors

Florence Kavaler, MD, MPH, MS, is Professor and Chair, Department of Health Policy and Management, and Associate Dean for Research Administration at the School of Public Health, State University of New York, Downstate Medical Center, in New York City. She was formerly Professor of Preventive Medicine and Community Health at the College of Medicine, State University of New York, Downstate Medical Center, and Principal Clinical Coordinator, IPRO, in New York.

Dr. Kavaler was formerly Assistant Surgeon General (Rear Admiral), Director of the U.S. Public Health Service Hospital, Staten Island, New York; Study Director, Milbank Memorial Fund Commission for the Study Higher Education for Public Health; and Assistant Commissioner for Health and Medical Insurance Programs, NYC Department of Health. She serves in various Medical Director positions at CapitolCare (Blue Cross HMO in Washington, D.C.), SANUS in New York and New Jersey (New York Life HMO), and MetLife HMO in New York (Metropolitan Life Insurance Company).

She is a member of the NYS Health Department Board for Professional Medical Conduct, and former Chair of the NYS Education Department Board for Medicine and continues to serve.

Dr. Kavaler earned a BA from Barnard College, an MD from the College of Medicine at State University of New York, Downstate Medical Center, an MS in biostatistics, and an MPH from Columbia School of Public Health. She is a Diplomate (CHCQM) of the American Board of Quality Assurance and Utilization Review Physicians. She held a license as a nursing home administrator in New York and a license as a healthcare risk manager in Florida.

Dr. Kavaler was formerly President of the Institute of Medical Law, Inc., a seminar company, and President of Medical Network Managers, Inc., a healthcare consulting firm. Her consultation skills capitalize on extensive experience in public policy, hospital administration, ambulatory care services, health insurance HMOs, long-term care, and malpractice analysis.

Dr. Kavaler is a respected educator and funded researcher and is well published. Her articles address areas of medical care evaluation in multiple settings, administrative public policy dynamics, and research activities in drug addiction, foster child health care, hospital cost control, aging, public health, and history of medicine. Recent books include: *Computers in Medical Administration; Higher Education for Public Health; Foster Child Health Care;* and *Cost Containment and DRGs: A Guide to Prospective Payment.*

Raymond S. Alexander, MBA, MS, is the President and Principal in the firm of Alexander, Wollman, & Stark, a healthcare consulting and search firm based in Philadelphia, Pennsylvania. Mr. Alexander has spent the majority of his career in hospital administration, having served as the CEO of Mt. Sinai Medical Center in Milwaukee, Wisconsin, as well as in administrative positions at Beth Israel Medical Center and Montefiore Medical Center in New York City, and most recently held the position as the President and CEO of Albert Einstein Medical Center in Philadelphia. He was one of the founders of a consortium of hospitals that later became Premier Alliance.

During the course of his career, Mr. Alexander served as Assistant Commissioner for Health and Medical Insurance Programs for the New York City Department of Health. He was also a member of the Governor's Health Policy Task Force in Wisconsin, and was Vice Chairman of the Hospital Association of Pennsylvania and then served as Chairman Elect. He has been the past chairman of the Board of the Martin's Run Life Care Community and continues to serve on the Board of Directors. He has published 36 articles in areas of management and public health and has taught at the Medical College of Wisconsin, Columbia University, and the Wharton School at the University of Pennsylvania. He has been a Fellow in the American College of Healthcare Executives and the Public Health Association.

Mr. Alexander holds bachelor's and master's degrees in business administration from Dartmouth College and a master's degree in hospital administration from Columbia University.

Current clients include academic medical centers and teaching hospitals throughout the United States.

Contributors

Torrance Akinsanya, MPA, CPHQ, is currently the Senior Associate Administrator for Quality Management and Regulatory Affairs at SUNY Downstate Medical Center, University Hospital of Brooklyn. She has over 30 years of leadership experience in various healthcare positions because of her expertise in quality and accreditation management for hospitals. Previously, she served with the New York City Health and Hospitals Corporation as Deputy Executive Director, at Harlem Hospital Center, where she was responsible for quality management, regulatory affairs, and administrative responsibilities for 17 departments, including a Certified Home Health Agency. Formerly she was Associate Hospital Director at Queens Hospital Center in Queens, New York for 5 years with responsibilities for regulatory affairs and hospital operations. While there she served as Clinical Assistant Professor at Adelphi University where she lectured to Graduate MBA students on Hospital Operations. An article on her experience with the program was published in the *Journal of Healthcare Administration*. Ms. Akinsanya currently serves as the Treasurer and Secretary of the New York Association of Healthcare Quality and also serves on the Leadership Council of the National Association of Health Care Quality. She is an active member of several healthcare leadership organizations and lectures periodically on the topic of healthcare regulatory affairs.

Ms. Akinsanya obtained a bachelor's degree in psychology from Hunter College, CUNY, and holds a master's degree in public administration from C.W. Post College of Long Island University with a concentration in healthcare administration, and an Executive Management Certificate from New York University Wagner School of Public Administration. She is a certified professional in healthcare quality (CPHQ) and a registered health information technologist.

George Allen, PhD, CIC, CNOR, is Director of Infection Control at the State University of New York, Downstate Medical Center, and Clinical Assistant Professor at State University of New York College of Health Related Professions. Dr. Allen served as a member of the editorial board of the *AJIC Journal* and as a Guest Editor for issues in *Perioperative Nursing Clinics* in 2008 and 2010. He currently serves on the editorial board of the *AORN Journal* to which he contributes a monthly column. Dr. Allen is board certified in infection control and perioperative nursing. He was educated at the City University of New York, Medgar Evers College (BSN), Central Michigan University (MSA), and Kensington University (PhD, public administration).

Michael H. Augenbraun, MD, is Professor of Medicine at SUNY Downstate College of Medicine. He is also Professor in the Department of Epidemiology in the SUNY Downstate School of Public Health. He is currently the Chief of the Infectious Diseases Division at SUNY Downstate and serves as the Hospital Epidemiologist at University Hospital of Brooklyn. He graduated from the University of Rochester School of Medicine, completed an internal medicine residency at North Shore Hospital, Queens, and Memorial Sloan Kettering, New York, and a fellowship in infectious diseases at SUNY Downstate Medical Center. Dr. Augenbraun is on the Editorial Board of *Sexual Transmitted Diseases*, and is a reviewer for *Journal of Infectious Diseases, Clinical Infectious Diseases*, and other medical journals. He is a member of the American College of Physicians and the Infectious Disease Society of America. Dr. Augenbraun is a funded researcher in the areas of sexually transmitted infections, HIV, and hepatitis, and is well published in the medical literature. He is board certified in both internal medicine and infectious diseases.

Karen E. Benker, MD, MPH, is Associate Dean for Community Public Health Affairs at SUNY Downstate School of Public Health and Associate Professor in the department of Health Policy and Management. She teaches courses in hospital management and in access, cost, and quality of health care. In 2011, Dr. Benker was recognized at SUNY with the Chancellor's Award for Excellence in Faculty Service. After graduating from Pomona College, she completed her MD degree at the University of Southern California School of Medicine. She completed an internship in medicine and pediatrics at Lincoln Hospital, NYC, and then practiced as a primary care physician at Kings Country Hospital Center, Brooklyn, New York. At the NYC Department of Health, she conducted studies on the deaths of preschoolers from abuse and neglect and served as director of programs for homeless families and chemically dependent mothers. Other research followed, with the renowned medical anthropologist Anna Lou DeHavenon, on health outcomes of pregnant homeless women, leading to a successful suit reforming New York City policies on providing emergency shelter to this group of women. As medical director of the employee health service at Woodhull Hospital and Mental Health Center she instituted policies to prevent the nosocomial spread of chickenpox. Subsequently, she became an HIV Clinical Scholar in Clinical and Policy Studies at SUNY Downstate and an attending in the HIV program. In the SUNY Department of Family Practice, she became medical director of the first Community Health Center of Downstate. Dr. Benker has board certification in both family practice and in preventive medicine, a Certificate in Geriatrics from the Consortium of NY Geriatrics Education Centers, and a certificate from Rutgers Summer School of Alcohol and Drug Studies.

Alvin M. Berk, PhD, has been Interim Vice President for Facilities at SUNY Downstate Medical Center since 2004, where he is responsible for design and construction, facilities operations, and environmental health and safety. Prior to this appointment, he served as Director and Assistant Vice President for Management Systems, and, from 1987 to 1995, as Assistant Vice President for Information Services. Dr. Berk has a concurrent appointment as Assistant Professor of Health Policy and Management in the SUNY Downstate School of Public Health. His prior teaching experience prior to Downstate includes the NYC public schools, and courses at Brooklyn College and Fordham University. Dr. Berk is active in civic affairs, and has chaired a Brooklyn community board since 1989. He has written extensively on governmental issues for local media. He is a member of the American Society for Healthcare Engineering (ASHE) and the National Fire Protection Association (NFPA). After receiving his BA from Queens College, New York, he earned a PhD in psychology at the City University of New York.

Thomas M. Bodenberg, PhD, is Director of Decision Support and Data Management at SUNY Downstate Medical Center. In addition, he has served as an advisor to the Chancellor of the State University of New York on public health issues facing New York State. His specialties include data-driven strategic planning, program evaluation, outcomes research, and quality management and performance improvement. Prior to SUNY Downstate, he was a Senior Thought Leader with the Conference Board in New York City. He has also held full-time academic appointments at Boston University and the University of Massachusetts. Dr. Bodenberg holds BA and MBA degrees from the University of Chicago, and a PhD from Boston University.

Jean G. Charchaflieh, MD, MPH, DrPH, is Associate Professor of Anesthesiology at Yale University School of Medicine, New Haven, Connecticut. He is a Fellow of American College of Critical Care Medicine (FCCM); a Fellow of the American College of Chest Physicians (FCCP); a Diplomate of the American Board of Anesthesiology (ABA) with Special Qualifications in Critical Care Medicine (CCM); and a Diplomate in Neurocritical Care from the United Council for Neurological Subspecialties (UCNS). His doctor of medicine degree is from Aleppo University in Syria; his research fellowship in anesthesiology was at Massachusetts General Hospital and Harvard Medical School; his anesthesiology residency was at Loyola University Medical Center; his critical care fellowship was at Memorial Sloan-Kettering Cancer Center; and his neuroanesthesia fellowship was at SUNY Downstate Medical Center, Brooklyn, New York. Subsequently, he received an MPH with a major in community health sciences (Urban & Immigrant Health) and a DrPH with a major in health policy and management from SUNY Downstate Medical Center School of Public Health. He is a member of the Beta Iota Chapter of the Delta Omega Society, a national honorary public health society, and is the author of dozens of peer-reviewed publications and book chapters.

Alice L. Epstein, MHA, FASHRM, DFNAHQ, is a Risk Control Liaison for CNA Financial Corporation in Chicago, Illinois. She has more than 30 years of consulting, clinical, and operational experience serving diverse clients in the healthcare industry and is author of multiple chapters in multiple textbooks focusing on healthcare risk management. Her areas of specialty include heathcare risk and quality management consulting, risk management program development, research, educational programs, product liability consulting, and strategic planning services. She is a member and Fellow of the American Society of Risk Management and the National Association of Quality Assurance. Ms. Epstein received an MS in hospital and health administration from the University of Alabama.

Arthur S. Friedman, JD, is in the private practice of law, specializing in criminal defense and litigation of healthcare related issues. In his more than 30 years of legal experience, he has been Special Assistant, New York Attorney General in the Office of the Special Prosecutor for Medicaid Fraud; Senior Attorney for the U.S. Department of Health and Human Services; Vice President and General Counsel to the New York and New Jersey HMO affiliates of the Metropolitan Life Insurance Company; and consultant to various healthcare organizations, including Blue Cross of New York. Mr. Friedman received his law degree from Brooklyn Law School (New York).

Steven J. Greenblatt, JD, served as Director of Labor Relations at the SUNY. Downstate Medical Center for 16 years and is currently Director of Workforce Training and Development as well as Acting Affirmative Action Officer. Previously, he managed thousands of disciplinary investigations, trials, and appeals as Deputy Inspector General of the New York City Department of Sanitation. He has successfully mediated various workplace disputes and investigated numerous claims of discrimination in several New York State agencies. He taught business law and personnel management and conducts training in the psychological contract, sexual harassment prevention, cultural sensitivity, and performance management, as well as speaks on employment law–related topics such as fraud prevention in healthcare and substance abuse testing. Mr. Greenblatt was a trial and appellate attorney in the Bronx County District Attorney's Office; and then Law Secretary to the Administrative Judge, Bronx County, Criminal Part; and then Appellate Counsel to more than 20 counties' District Attorneys as Director of the Criminal Justice Appellate Reference Service for the N.Y.S. Division of Criminal Justice Services. Mr. Greenblatt holds a JD degree from New York Law School and a master's in labor law from New York University School of Law.

Gary H. Harding, BS, BMET, is a Consulting Biomedical Engineer with more than 30 years of consulting and clinical experience in serving diverse clients across the globe in the healthcare industry. Mr. Harding is the author of multiple chapters in multiple textbooks focusing on patient safety applications in clinical services and biomedical engineering. His areas of specialty include professional liability management, corporate strategic planning/performance analysis, product development and liability consulting, accident investigation, forensic engineering, educational programming, and FDA consulting assistance in new products, government regulations, and product recalls. He graduated magna cum laude from Temple University with a BS in Biomedical Engineering Technology with additional training in Law and Social Policy from Bryn Mawr College. Today, Mr. Harding splits his time between his professional activities and his humanitarian and community service activities, for example, as the President of a Habitat for Humanity Affiliate.

Kathie McDonald-McClure, JD, is a partner at Wyatt Tarrant & Combs LLP law firm, Louisville, Kentucky, and a member of Wyatt's Health Care Practice Service Team. She draws upon her long legal career in the healthcare industry to advise healthcare providers in a variety of regulatory risk areas. Her focus areas include, among others, the Anti-Kickback Statute, Stark Law, False Claims Act, Medicare reimbursement systems and secondary payor rules, clinical trials, HIPAA/HITECH, and making a "meaningful use" of electronic health records. She also consults on risk management and liability insurance matters, drawing upon her experience as the VP of Liability Claims for Kindred Healthcare, the largest diversified provider of post-acute care services in the United States. She is the editor of the HITECH Law Blog, which reports on legal developments regarding financial incentives for healthcare providers who make meaningful use of a certified electronic health record and HIPAA privacy and security requirements. Dr. McDonald-McClure obtained her JD from the University of Louisville Louis D. Brandeis School of Law in 1985. She studied business administration and marketing at both Murray State University and the University of Louisville, obtaining a bachelor of science in business administration with highest honors in 1982.

Kevin M. McLaughlin, CPCU, MAS, is director of Professional Liability at Marsh and McLennon Agency LLC, New Jersey. He has a broad range of knowledge in the healthcare field on issues such as HIPAA, credentialing and privileging, billing and coding, E&O, captive formation and self-insurance, contract issues (including construction, leases, events, insurance and environmental exposures), peer review, and vicarious liability. Much of this experience was attained by engaging with hospitals, nursing homes, physician groups, allied health care, medical products and manufacturers, including research companies. Additional experience is with advertising agency, bank and other large commercial account clients. Mr. McLaughlin also managed a unit that handled hundreds of individual physicians, acted as consultant on two worker's compensation captives and as Director of a unit for two hospital-based captives. He has been teaching classes on risk management and insurance as adjunct faculty at Seton Hall and Fairleigh Dickinson University for the past 25 years. He also taught classes for hospital risk managers on behalf of the Institute of Medical Law, Inc, NYC and at Hofstra University and the University of Maryland. Mr. McLaughlin attained a BA degree in business administration from Seton Hall, a master of administrative sciences from Fairleigh Dickinson University on a Fellows Scholarship, a CPCU degree from the Insurance Institute of America and a degree in risk and insurance from the College of Insurance, New York. He has instructed classes as Adjunct Faculty at Seton Hall and FDU on Risk Management and

Insurance for the past 25 years. He also presented information to Hospital Risk Managers on behalf of The Institute of Medical Law at SUNY, Hofstra and the University of Maryland.

David Metz, MPA, is Principal of MediSyn, a healthcare consulting group. He is an insurance, financial, and health services executive and educator with over 30 years of public and private sector experience in administration, managed care, medical education, employee benefits, and risk management (LHCRM). Formerly, he was President and CEO of CapitalCare, Inc; Vice President of Blue Cross and Blue Shield of the National Capital Area; CEO of the George Washington University Health Plan; Vice President of Operations and Finance of the Georgetown University Community Health Plan; and Senior Vice President for Insurance and Financial Services for the National Rural Electric Cooperative Association. In New York City, he served as Assistant Commissioner of Health for Communicare and as Health Insurance Advisor to the budget office. He has held academic appointments at Schools of Medicine at UNC Chapel Hill, Georgetown, George Washington University, and the Columbia University School of Public Health. Mr. Metz earned a BA from Queens College, NY and an MPA from New York University.

Kathleen E. Powderly, PhD, CNM, is the Director of the John Conley Division of Medical Ethics and Humanities at the SUNY Downstate Medical Center. She is Vice Chairperson of the Kings County Hospital Center/University Hospital of Brooklyn Ethics Committee and serves as clinical ethicist at KCHC, UHB and UHB at LICH. Dr. Powderly teaches clinical ethics to students and practitioners in medicine, nursing, public health, and allied health. She is on the ethics committees of the American College of Nurse-Midwives and the University Faculty Senate of SUNY, as well as on the IRB of Public Health Solutions. She is a Fellow of the New York Academy of Medicine and has been an Adjunct Associate at the Hastings Center. Dr. Powderly was educated at Niagara University (BS, nursing), Yale University (MSN, maternal-newborn nursing/nurse-midwifery), and Columbia University (MPhil, PhD). Her PhD is in sociomedical sciences.

Robert Stanyon, MS, BSN, CPHRM, FASHRM, has a risk management consulting practice in Hackensack, New Jersey. He is formerly the Vice President for Risk Management at FOJP Service Corporation in New York City where he was responsible for selected risk management programs for the hospitals and agencies of the UJA/Federation of New York. He is a former board member and past president of the Association for Healthcare Risk Management of New York, has chaired the Online Education Task Force of the American Society for Healthcare Risk Management, and has been a member of the editorial review board for the *Journal of Healthcare Risk Management*. His published writings include risk management issues in electronic medical records systems, online distance learning for healthcare professionals, managing nursing error, and issues associated with the compassionate re-use of pacemakers in the third world. He had overall responsibility for the design and management of distance learning courses for over 5,000 attending physicians, residents, and nurses in the Federation system and assisted in the development of an online course in the interpretation of fetal monitoring tracings for obstetrical clinical staff. He received bachelor's and master's degrees in microbiology from Syracuse University and the University of New Hampshire and his associate's and bachelor's degrees in nursing from Quinsigamond Community College and Saint Peter's College. He is a Fellow of the American Society for Healthcare Risk Management and a certified professional in healthcare risk management (CPHRM).

Amy Wysoker, PhD, RN, APRN, BC, is a professor in the Department of Nursing at the C.W. Post Campus of Long Island University, School of Health Professions and Nursing. She is an academic that has taught in various universities. She is also an adjunct faculty member for the Lienhard School of Nursing at Pace University, School of Health Professions, Doctor of Nurse Practitioner Program. She teaches ethical, social, legal, and professional issues in both undergraduate and graduate programs. Dr. Wysoker is a certified clinical specialist in psychiatric mental health nursing and is in private practice as a psychiatric/mental health consultant and a medical-legal nurse consultant. Her publications include ethical and legal issues in psychiatric nursing. She has received a BS (in nursing) from SUNY College of Nursing, an MA (nursing) from New York University, and a PhD (nursing) from Adelphi University.

Introduction to the Third Edition

It has been over a decade since the publication of the second edition of *Risk Management in Healthcare Institutions*. In this period of time, healthcare delivery has dramatically changed, creating new issues and challenges for healthcare professionals. The field of risk management has grown infinitely more complicated and complex, and problems that could not have been previously imagined are facing today's professionals. Patient safety and quality have been elevated to the highest level, with executives with this title reporting directly to the CEO and to the Boards of Directors. The Institute of Medicine's landmark report, "To Err is Human: Building a Safer Health Care System," and the more recent report, "Crossing the Quality Chasm," brought the issues clearly into focus.

Let us look at the dramatic changes that have occurred in the healthcare field and their impact on patient safety and quality. Certainly the passage of the Affordable Care Act will have wide ranging implications, particularly the focus on the electronic health record. The implementation of the electronic health record has made record keeping more efficient but has run into resistance from older physicians and caregivers who have not grown up with the technology, creating a "digital divide." Also, the expense of conversion from written medical records has slowed the migration into the new paradigm. Certainly, risk management professionals need to be conversant with the technology and its incumbent problems and employ it into the monitoring and reporting systems. Exposure to hackers poses a real threat. In Utah, some 780,000 records were breached, and in South Carolina, 228,000 records were improperly transferred to an employee's email account.

The past 10 years have seen changes in the physician's relationship with hospitals. Many more physicians are giving up practices with the attendant headaches and joining physician groups associated with hospitals. Along with this trend is the employment of Hospitalists to provide primary care to hospitalized patients. No longer do physicians in practice make rounds, but rather shift this burden to the Hospitalists. Orienting and sensitizing these groups to the safety and quality issues becomes an important challenge to today's risk manager.

Along with the growth of hospital employed physicians is the trend of hospital mergers and acquisitions and the increasing move to corporate models for the healthcare system. Competition has led to business practices that were once the province of industry. Marketing and advertising has grown to be a significant budget item in an effort to attract patients who bypass physicians to gain access to prestigious centers. The smaller hospitals are less able to compete in the marketplace and as a result are not able to access the capital markets for growth and development. Merging cultures of different healthcare organizations is very difficult and fraught with problems. Clearly, patient safety and quality are at risk as new financial and organizational models are developed.

The Affordable Care Act has the potential to equal, if not surpass, the creation of Medicare and Medicaid. Its implications on the delivery and financing of health care will affect every hospital and health system in the country. It has and will drive many institutions to formulate accountable care organizations (ACOs). As of this printing, there are some 40 ACOs in formation, involving many large medical centers with over 15,000 physicians. Setting standards and quality measures for these organizations poses new and uncharted problems. As this movement spreads, the challenges to maintain quality and safety loom as new problems.

Coupled with this movement is the growth of the internet and online access to healthcare information that was previously available only to professionals through textbooks. Consumers have become increasingly more sophisticated and aware of healthcare threats. Contemporary patient safety and quality initiatives need to take this into account when untoward events occur. There will be tough questions raised and patients will demand satisfaction.

Another significant change has been the proliferation of caregivers in the healthcare setting. Nurses, physician assistants, patient navigators, and aides have assumed a greater role in patient care. This, coupled with the advent of hospitalists, creates layers of care that are at best very confusing to the patient. The more professionals who come in contact with the patient, the greater the risk of untoward events. The use of checklists and adherence to protocols becomes critical in the new healthcare environment.

The public's increasing demand for accessible health care has resulted in a shortage of physicians, particularly in the primary care specialties such as geriatrics and family practice. As a result, new medical schools are being formed at an unparalleled rate. As of 2012, there were over a dozen new medical schools at various stages of organization. Finding enough internship and residency training slots is becoming a greater challenge and puts a strain on the academic medical centers that need to balance an educational experience with the service that the house staffs provide. Restrictions on the number of hours that trainees can work further exacerbate the problem. The impact on quality and safety needs to be carefully monitored as the training programs are initiated and developed.

Academic health centers are not immune from the issues listed above. Many of the larger centers are involved with mergers and acquisitions to bolster their teaching programs and their bottom line. The use of technology starts at the larger centers. Such techniques as robotic surgery, proton beam therapy, and organ transplants all carry significant risks. Staff need to be well trained and aware of the risks inherent in each of these therapies. Cutting edge care can have great benefits as well as significant side effects.

The national Hospital Engagement Networks (HENs) is expected to take the quality and safety movement to a new level. The project is funded by the Centers for Medicare & Medicaid Innovation as part of the national Partnership for Patients Initiative. The program has lofty goals, attempting to reduce the number of hospital acquired infections by 40% and reduce readmissions by 20% by the end of 2013. These goals present a unique challenge to the healthcare system.

This book offers leaders of healthcare institutions, from board members to CEOs to medical staff members and other key leaders, the latest information on risk management. In view of the amount of material in the book, it is clear that this has not been a solitary effort. The authors want to acknowledge the contributions of consultants and experts who have written many of the chapters, and we want to express our deep appreciation for their contributions.

We appreciate the continuing support of our previous contributors who effectively updated their special interests and added more recent references.

In addition, we welcome the new contributors whose chapters highlight the expanding scope of risk management and new venues such as ambulatory care, office-based surgery, and telemedicine.

Of particular merit, we recognize the meticulous and efficient administrative, technical, and research activities of Francine Benjamin, MS, and also the support of Lois Hahn in the preparation of the manuscript.

It is our experience in the healthcare field in government and the private sector, in policy making and administration, and in a variety of care venues, which has provided us with the appreciation of the magnitude of the scope of risk management and the opportunity to present this field in this book.

Florence Kavaler, MD, MPH, MS
Raymond S. Alexander, MBA, MS

PART 1

Risk Management Administrative Issues

CHAPTER 1

Risk Management: An Institutional Imperative

Raymond S. Alexander and Florence Kavaler

THE EVOLUTION OF RISK MANAGEMENT

Following the insurance crisis of the 1970s, the Institute of Medicine issued a landmark report entitled *To Err Is Human: Building a Safer Health Care System.* Two large studies, conducted in Colorado and Utah and in New York, revealed that adverse events occurred in 2.9% and 3.7% of hospitalizations, respectively. It was also found that more than half of these events resulted from medical errors that could have been prevented.[1]

When these data are extrapolated to the 35,527,377 admissions to U.S. hospitals, it appears that more than 1 million medical errors could occur in a year, implying that more than 140,000 Americans die each year from medical errors—more than from motor vehicle accidents. It is estimated that the national cost of preventable events ranges between $17 billion and $29 billion.

Although controversy swirls about the data presented in the report, many healthcare professionals would argue that the actual number is less important than the fact that no one needs to die needlessly or suffer from preventable medical errors (see **Box 1-1**).

> **Box 1-1   Deaths of Nine Alabama Patients[2]**
>
> Nine patients died at Alabama hospitals due to an intravenous supplement that was found to be contaminated by bacteria. Ten other patients who received the supplement were also sickened by the bacteria, *Serratia marcescens,* which is commonly found in water. State officials attribute the source to a pharmacy that compounded the solution.

A *New York Times* article dated January 6, 2012, indicated that hospital employees recognize and report only one out of seven errors, accidents, and other events that harm Medicare patients while they are hospitalized, according to a study conducted by the U.S. Department of Health and Human Services. Even after hospitals investigate preventable injuries and infections that have been reported, they rarely change their practices to prevent repetition of adverse events.[3]

According to the Agency for Healthcare Research and Quality (AHRQ), the number of people treated in U.S. hospitals for illnesses and injuries from taking medications jumped 52% between 2004 and 2008—from 1.2 million to 1.9 million. More than 53% of hospitalized patients treated for side effects and other medication-related injuries were 65 years and older.[4]

In a state that requires reporting of wrong-site surgery, statistics from June 2004 to December 2008 revealed there were 427 reports of near misses (253) or surgical interventions started (174) involving the wrong patient (34), wrong procedure (39), wrong side (298), and/or wrong part (60). Eighty-three patients had incorrect procedures done to completion. Actions involving surgeons contributed to 92 cases. Other factors cited in wrong-site surgeries were site markings, patient positioning, and unverified consents (see **Box 1-2**).[5]

Box 1-2   Wrong Patient Got Kidney Transplant[6]

The University of Southern California Hospital halted kidney transplants in January 2011 after a kidney was accidentally transplanted in the wrong patient. The patient who received the wrong kidney escaped harm because the kidney happened to be an acceptable match. The hospital shut down its program after realizing the error.

The Joint Commission Center for Transforming Healthcare collaborated with eight hospitals that perform more than 130,000 procedures annually to determine why wrong-site surgery continues to occur. They found the following root causes:[7]

- Lack of intraoperative site verification when multiple procedures are performed
- Ineffective hand-off communication or briefing
- Primary documentation not used to verify the patient procedure, site, and side
- Site mark(s) removed during prep or covered by surgical draping

- Time-out process occurs before all staff are ready
- Time-out performed without full participation
- Time-outs do not occur when multiple procedures are performed by multiple providers in a single operative case

It is critical to monitor any adverse events from both a quality and a legal standpoint. The University of Michigan Health System[8] developed a proactive risk management program based on "common sense" as defined by a group headed by a former trial lawyer. The program stressed improved patient safety, accountability, and communication. The University of Michigan Health System does not wait for litigation to happen, but rather follows these principles:

- Quick and appropriate compensation where inappropriate care causes injury
- Vigorous defense of medically appropriate care (see **Box 1-3**)
- Reduction of patient injuries by learning from mistakes (see **Box 1-4**)

These principles have improved patient safety, lowered liability costs, reduced the organization's total number of claims, and improved patients' experiences.

Box 1-3   Alarm Fatigue[9]

Death attributed to "alarm fatigue" at the University of Massachusetts Memorial Medical Center has pushed the hospital to intensify efforts to prevent nurses from tuning out warning alarms. Nurses exposed to a cacophony of beeps may no longer hear them or begin to ignore them. A 60-year-old man died in the intensive care unit after alarms signaling a fast heart rate and potential breathing problems went unanswered for nearly an hour, according to state investigators.

Stanford University Medical Center,[11] in contrast, works with an outside contractor, and has its own captive liability company. The cornerstone of its safety initiatives comprises technology and online education that facilitates communication between patients and physicians.

The Joint Commission on Accreditation of Healthcare Organizations (JCAHO, now known as The Joint Commission) promulgated safety standards that took effect on July 2, 2001. The critical areas of these standards related to (1) providing leadership, (2) improving organizational performance, (3) information management, and (4) patients' rights. The update of September 2011 once again stressed leadership in the safety and quality of care, to include the following:[12]

- A culture that fosters safety as a priority
- The planning and provision of services that meet the needs of patients
- The availability of resources for providing the care
- The existence of competent staff and other providers
- Ongoing evaluation and improvement of performance

The governing body is pinpointed as having the ultimate responsibility for this oversight. Notably, a proactive risk assessment can help correct problems, mitigate risks, and reduce the likelihood of experiencing adverse events.

In the Institute of Medicine report entitled *Crossing the Quality Chasm,* it is noted that the U.S. healthcare system does not provide consistent, high-quality care to all people, creating this so-called chasm.[13] Given the growing complexity of healthcare delivery, the system has fallen short in its ability to apply the new technology into safe practices. As more advances occur, it may be even less prepared to respond to the challenges ahead. Variation affects almost every key performance measure of the Institute of Medicine's six key dimensions of a good healthcare system: effectiveness, efficiency, safety, satisfaction, access, and equity.

A recent study indicated that 10% of physicians and nurses have taken dangerous shortcuts in providing care. That percentage represents roughly a threefold increase since the 2005 publication of the study entitled *Silence Kills.* Safety tools such as protocols, perioperative briefings, checklists, and SBAR (Situation, Background, Assessment, and Recommendation) are being implemented to counteract this risk. Systems thinking about safety has been the biggest reason for the success of hospitals in this regards, according to the National Science Foundation Center for Health Organization.[14]

RISK MANAGEMENT DEFINED

Risk management for healthcare entities can be defined as an organized effort to identify, assess, and reduce, where appropriate, risks to patients, visitors, staff, and organizational assets. Another definition states that risk management is a program designed to reduce the incidence of preventable accidents and injuries to minimize the financial loss to the institution should an injury or accident occur.[15]

From a managed care viewpoint, the risk management definition can be expanded to encompass a comprehensive rationale:

> Risk management is the process of assuring that covered persons (members) receive all of the healthcare services they need, to which they are entitled under the contract, no more and no less, at the most cost-effective level possible by reducing or eliminating untoward incidents (occurrences) that might lead to injury or illness of patients, visitors, or employees.[16]

Untoward or adverse outcomes tend to yield a broad spectrum of possible explanations. A research scientist argued that there was no such thing as a medical accident. As a caveat for the doctors, he quoted from Shakespeare's Julius Caesar: "The fault…is not in our stars, but in ourselves." He concluded that more precise medical terminology would help physicians reduce harm: "Accident conveys a sense that bad outcomes are to be explained in terms of fate and bad luck rather than a set of understandable, and possibly changeable, antecedents."[17]

PROGRESSIVE STEPS IN THE RISK MANAGEMENT PROCESS

In straightforward terms, risk management is the protection of assets. Risk management personnel usually accomplish this goal by following four steps in progression or combination: risk identification, risk analysis, risk control/treatment, and risk financing.[7] In slightly different wording, the risk management process can move from (1) identifying exposures to accidental loss that may interfere with an organization's objectives, to (2) examining feasible alternative risk management techniques for dealing with these exposures,

to (3) selecting the best risk management techniques, to (4) implementing the chosen risk management techniques, to (5) monitoring the results of the chosen techniques to determine effectiveness. Arguing that this risk management process needs refinement to reflect reality, Burlando[18] opts for the 5i system, a measured application of five descriptors:

- Investigate: observe or study by close examination and systematic inquiry
- Inform: present in material form
- Influence: affect or alter by indirect or intangible means
- Interpret: explain or tell the meaning of; present in understandable terms
- Integrate: form or blend into a whole; unite with something else

Furthermore, Burlando declares that the mission of risk management "is to select, coordinate and efficiently apply interdisciplinary skills to harmful uncertainties which may diminish the future value of public, private or personal resources."

Risk Identification

Risk identification involves the collection of information about current and past patient care occurrences and other events that represent potential losses to the institution. In alphabetical order, such risks can be identified as antitrust violations, breach of contract, casualty exposure, defamation, embezzlement, environmental damage, fraud and abuse, general liability, hazardous substance exposure, professional malpractice, securities violations, transportation liability, and worker's compensation. It is vital to realize that risk identification is not a one-time static analysis. Instead, the identification of possible liability risks—such as unexpected treatment outcomes, patient complaints about care, and adverse events that did, or could, cause harm—must be an ongoing process. Early warning data can be obtained through security reports, quality assessment studies, accreditation and/or licensure surveys, and patient complaints. Risk managers should receive a steady stream of information from specific departments, such as when attorneys seek chart information from medical records in preparation for a suit; billing offices, following up on delinquent statements, hear aggravated complaints; volunteers hear complaints because patients do not regard them as employees; and quality assessment activities yield data connected with their screening and review procedures. Furthermore, statistical data from insurers can identify those high-risk individuals and services involved in the payment of claims.

Risk Analysis

Risk analysis entails the evaluation of past experience and current exposure to eliminate or limit substantially the impact of risk on cash flow, community image, and employee and medical staff morale. The seriousness of the risk must be considered in terms of the probable severity to the individual and to the organization, the number of people possibly harmed, and the likelihood and/or frequency of occurrence. Closed claims data are most helpful in gaining an insight into the evaluation of current risks. A priority of high-risk activities for the risk manager logically develops from risk analysis information.

Risk Control/Treatment

Risk control and/or treatment is the organization's response to significant risk areas, as well as its rejoinder to limit the liability associated

with incidents that have occurred. It is the most common function associated with risk management programs. Loss control activities within an institution should not be viewed as a single formal program, because of the varied interrelated and overlapping elements. Often, loss control activity is equated with safety management, as their basic objectives are similar. At times, the quality assessment functions also cloud the specifics of loss control. It is not unusual for a loss/risk control program to be a collaborative effort involving risk management, quality assessment, and safety management. Ideally, a risk control/loss management program should categorize the potential liability problems into four areas: bodily injury, liability losses, property loss, and consequential losses. **Figure 1-1** illustrates some elements of risk exposure. Note that the healthcare organization's governing board and the chief executive officer (CEO) are responsible for the overall risk control system. In the second circle surrounding the board and the CEO are the administrative personnel who implement the programs. Specific elements in the third and fourth circles illustrate bodily injury, liability losses, property loss, and consequential losses.

A variety of methods and a combination of techniques are used for controlling the risks: risk acceptance, exposure avoidance, loss prevention, loss reduction, exposure segregation, and contractual transfer.

Risk Acceptance

Essentially, risk acceptance means that the facility decides not to purchase insurance against specific adverse events because the risk cannot be avoided, reduced, or transferred. In addition, the probability of loss is not great and the potential fiscal consequences are within the institution's capabilities to resolve.

Figure 1-1

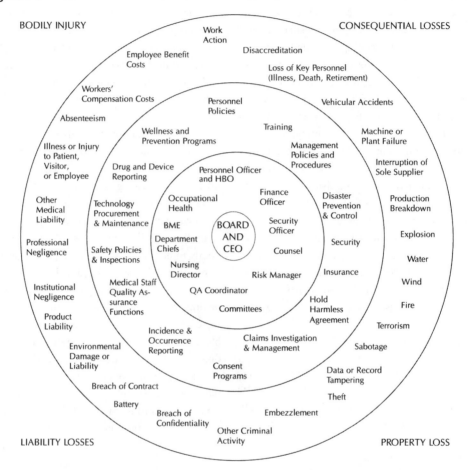

BODILY INJURY

CONSEQUENTIAL LOSSES

Work Action

Disaccreditation

Employee Benefit Costs

Loss of Key Personnel (Illness, Death, Retirement)

Workers' Compensation Costs

Personnel Policies

Vehicular Accidents

Absenteeism

Training

Machine or Plant Failure

Wellness and Prevention Programs

Management Policies and Procedures

Illness or Injury to Patient, Visitor, or Employee

Drug and Device Reporting

Personnel Officer and HBO

Interruption of Sole Supplier

Other Medical Liability

Technology Procurement & Maintenance

Occupational Health

Finance Officer

Disaster Prevention & Control

Production Breakdown

BME

Security Officer

Professional Negligence

Safety Policies & Inspections

Department Chiefs

BOARD AND CEO

Security

Explosion

Counsel

Water

Institutional Negligence

Medical Staff Quality Assurance Functions

Nursing Director

Risk Manager

Insurance

Wind

QA Coordinator

Committees

Hold Harmless Agreement

Fire

Product Liability

Terrorism

Incidence & Occurrence Reporting

Claims Investigation & Management

Environmental Damage or Liability

Sabotage

Consent Programs

Data or Record Tampering

Breach of Contract

Theft

Battery

Breach of Confidentiality

Embezzlement

Other Criminal Activity

LIABILITY LOSSES

PROPERTY LOSS

Exposure Avoidance

After he investigated a hospital's major liability losses, a consultant advised: "Eliminate the emergency room!" In theory, exposure avoidance aims to rid the institution of the service, personnel, or equipment that may cause the loss, or to advise the institution never to be involved in providing the service or program at all.

Loss Prevention

Using early detection and investigation, risk managers examine medical records, incident reports, patient complaints, and patient billing to

pinpoint loss prevention areas. Some losses in specific services can be prevented by the involvement of medical and ancillary staff in educational programs and preventive maintenance. Some sources even advise keeping the patient fully informed of all mishaps, thereby relying on the satisfied patient not to sue the institution.

Loss Reduction

Although loss prevention activities may be undertaken, loss reduction is also pursued in most institutions. It involves the management of claims and ensures that all records are preserved and that all personnel are prepared in the event of a loss. Settlements and releases conclude loss reduction efforts. Without abandoning high-risk services, loss reduction or minimization aims to control adverse events by focusing on activities such as staff education, revisions of policy, and procedures.

Exposure Segregation

Administrators can decide to separate out or to duplicate the specific offending services, personnel, or activities identified as exposure risks to the institution. Risk managers can suggest intensive control actions; for example, to reduce medication errors in a hospital, all pharmaceuticals can be disbursed from a central location. If the problem appears to be the distance between medication source and delivery, satellite pharmacies can be established on selected floors.

Contractual Transfer

A facility can transfer or shift the risk to the organization that provides the service through insurance or contract. This practice allows the institution to provide a high-risk service while avoiding liability loss. If a contracted company operates the emergency room of a hospital, the facility avoids risk by ensuring that the contract includes the assumption of all risk by the contractor. Although private insurance premiums can be used to handle contractual liability coverage, the facility may still be responsible for selecting a qualified contractor.

Risk Financing

Appropriate indemnification of risk requires a comprehensive prospective and retrospective organizational analysis of the direct expenditures associated with quantifying and funding losses and risk management activities. Financing choices include self-insurance, commercial insurance coverage, insurance premiums, and funding for any related risk management activities and liability payouts. While risk financing may be the responsibility of the institution's or agency's financial office, risk managers can make a valuable contribution to the deliberations by communicating effectively with the finance department, using terminology that finance personnel can understand.

RISK MANAGEMENT ACTIVITIES ___

An examination of the eight minimal components of a risk management program, as defined by the American Society of Healthcare Risk Management (ASHRM), engenders a fuller understanding of a risk management program:[19]

1. There must be a designated, trained, and experienced risk manager who must obtain at least eight hours of continuing risk management education annually.
2. Risk managers must have access to all necessary credentialing, management, and medical data.
3. Institutions must commit the necessary resources to risk management through a written policy statement that is adopted by the governing body, medical staff, and administration.
4. Facilities must have a system in place for the identification, review, and analysis of unanticipated adverse outcomes.
5. Organizations must have the means to centralize risk management data and to share and integrate data collection and analysis with other clinical and administrative departments.
6. Periodically—at least annually—risk managers must provide the organization's governing body with a report that reviews and evaluates risk management program activity.

7. Risk managers must ensure that medical-staff and new-employee educational programs on minimizing patients' risks and addressing high-risk clinical areas are provided.
8. Risk managers must forward information on individual practitioners, such as malpractice claim history, knowledge of adverse outcomes, and incident reporting data, to the committees that evaluate the competency of medical staff.

Strictly from a business-oriented approach, risk management aims to accomplish three major functions:

- Reducing the organization's risk of a malpractice suit by maintaining or improving the quality of care
- Reducing the probability of a claim being filed after a potentially compensable event (PCE) has occurred
- Preserving the institution's assets once a claim has been filed

Without doubt, risk management includes quality assessment and related activities, such as medical staff credentialing, occurrence screening, incident reporting, and peer review. In addition, it seeks to promote effective communication and a positive attitude between patients and staff, and to make patients less likely to sue for malpractice.

Physicians agree on three ideal attributes for a professional risk manager: the ability to present facts rather than feelings, the ability to be concise in writing about or stating the situation, and the wherewithal to understand the facts and to respond to critical questions. In contrast, nurses identify three common qualities of a good risk manager: a demonstrated willingness to listen, an understanding of the other person's responsibilities and problems, and a team approach to problem solving that involves asking input from others in forming solutions. These responses lead to the conclusion that a risk manager's basic skills must include the art of persuasion, the expertise to be a keen listener, and knowledge about team building.[20] Importantly, risk managers must realize that the board of directors or governing body is part of the team, even though that directorate is not the immediate supervisor.

Legislative and regulatory mandates also guide risk management activities to focus on preventive maintenance of equipment and devices, on patient safety measures, and on enhancing the safety of employees and visitors. Examples of such measures include ensuring that equipment is clean, properly calibrated, and in good repair; that a nurse call system is functional; and that security personnel patrol well-lighted parking lots and hallways.

CLASSIFICATION OF RISK LIABILITIES

Risk events include a multitude of sins: untoward incidents occurring to patients (clients), employees, or visitors; use of inadequate equipment or procedures to perform a task; use of improperly trained or qualified individuals to perform a task; improper manufacture of a product; and contamination or pollution of the environment. Failure to perform a service may prevent the achievement of a desired outcome or lead to an undesired outcome, may cause harm or injury, and may result from an error of omission or commission. Some specific examples of risk events, classified by type, include the following:

- *Property risks:* structural damage, vehicular accidents, technological obsolescence, theft, sabotage, production breakdown, and consequential losses

- *Casualty/liability risks:* professional negligence (PCEs and adverse patient occurrences), worker's compensation, directors and officers liability, environmental liability, and product liability
- *Employee benefit risks:* cost of benefit plans, disability claims, and Employee Retirement and Income Security Act (ERISA) violations

Risks can be identified through the use of records and files, flowcharts, personal inspections, expert consultations, surveys, questionnaires, and financial statements. Risk analysis considers the frequency and severity of the loss as related to profit, stable earnings, growth, continuous operation, legal requirements, and humanitarian concerns. A comparative assessment combines cost–benefit analyses with frequency of risk events and with populations affected to yield a weighted risk analysis. Interestingly, people may accept a new technology with perceived injury risks or reject a technology because of a minimal risk of injury. Medical care generally may be devoted to problems that are relatively minor. Because the viability of the institution is at stake, efforts must be made to evaluate and weigh the risk to preserve assets and to restrict the loss.

RISK RED FLAGS _____

One or more "red flags" in connection with a patient's care should alert healthcare providers to take actions to remedy the situation. Appropriate care and treatment should be provided, and patient records should reflect that care. In addition, the risk management department should be notified. Some specific red flags are highlighted here:

- *Treatment conditions:* poor treatment results, repetition of the problem, lack of follow-up care, and equipment malfunction
- *Patient relations:* dissatisfied patient, antagonistic patient or family members, complaining relatives, patient discharged against medical advice, intimidated patient, poor physician–patient relationship, and poor staff–patient relationship
- *Practice management:* poorly maintained medical records, lack of critical policies and procedures, and excessive volume of patients
- *Conduct of staff:* acting outside the scope of training, lack of qualified supervision, performance of a procedure for the first time without supervision, outspoken or rude behavior, personality conflict, and poor physician–staff relationship

RISK MANAGEMENT TOOLS _____

Prompt identification of injuries and accidents to patients, visitors, and staff members has been a primary concern of risk management programs since they were first implemented in hospitals. In this manner, institutions address potential problems and correct their causes before they can occur again. In addition, administrators can take immediate action to avoid or lessen the cost of a lawsuit. Three systems are used to accomplish prompt identification: incident reporting, occurrence reporting, and occurrence screening.

Incident Reporting

Incident reporting systems were developed to identify events that were not consistent with the routine operation of the hospital or the routine care of particular patients or visitors, such as malfunctioning equipment or medication errors. **Box 1-5** illustrates the use of an incident reporting system.

More recently, incident reporting systems have incorporated computer technology. Calgary General Hospital (Alberta, Canada) devised a computer program that identifies five major incident categories: falls, medication errors, treatment/procedure errors, assaults, and computer errors.[22] Another computer system focuses on the early identification of patterns and trends in the "how" and "why" of untoward events. Coded vulnerability indicators include the following specific options: system failure (22 choices); diagnostic tests (12 choices); consultation (28 choices); documentation (37 choices); patient rapport (7 choices); clinical conduct (50 choices); human factors (14 choices); and a miscellaneous narrative section. Analysis of the adverse events yields an awareness of and a basis for improved clinical practice and professional risk avoidance.[23]

Reporting systems rely on facility personnel to recognize and report an incident to a risk manager, a quality assurance coordinator, or a member of the management team. The reports tend to focus on treatment procedures, medication, intravenous and blood errors, infections, birth injuries, falls, burns, and equipment problems that could result in claims against the

organization. By themselves, the reports do not offer a complete picture of the number of incidents that occur in a facility. According to some estimates, incident reports identify only 5% to 30% of adverse patient occurrences at a hospital. Staff may not report incidents for several reasons: lack of understanding of what a reportable incident is, fear of punitive action, concern that incident reporting exposes them to personal liability, reluctance to report incidents involving physicians, lack of time for paperwork, and lack of knowledge about the results that an effective incident reporting system can achieve. Only the person who witnessed the incident, or first discovered it, should file and sign an incident report. Anyone else with first-hand knowledge of the event should file a separate report. Critically, anyone filling out an incident report should keep in mind that the written report will be available to lawyers, and any admissions or accusations could be damaging to the reporting individual as well as to the employer. Thus there are several dos and don'ts regarding the filing of an incident report:[23]

- *Do* record the details in objective terms, describing exactly what was seen and heard, and nothing else: Jones writes that she found Mrs. Smith on the floor beside the bed, not that she fell.
- *Do* describe which actions were taken at the scene, such as helping the patient back into bed, assessment findings, and any instructions to the patient.
- *Do* document the time of the incident, the name of the doctor notified, and the time notified, and have the supervisor review the report.
- *Don't* include names and addresses of witnesses, even if the form requests such information. Such data make it easier for

attorneys to sue the institution. Check with the supervisor before supplying this information.

- *Don't* file the incident report with the patient's chart. Instead, send the incident report to the person designated by the organization to collect and review such matters.
- *Don't* admit liability or blame or identify others as responsible. Obviously, this incrimination could be harmful to the agency if a lawsuit ensues.

Occurrence Reporting

Some states and insurers require or encourage institutions to develop lists of specific adverse patient events (APEs) or adverse patient occurrences (APOs) that must be reported by staff, physicians, or both—that is, occurrence reporting. APOs could include maternal or infant death, a surgical patient's unplanned return to the unit, or an allergic reaction to medication. Although the lists vary at the discretion of the organization, the insurers, or the states, specifying the reportable events increases the APO identification process by 40% to 60%. Because this system depends on individuals for reporting, however, many incidents still may not be written up. To promote better reporting, some states grant immunity from legal action to persons who provide or evaluate risk management information. In addition, efforts have been made to protect against the possibility that documents generated by the risk management program will become public information.

Occurrence Screening

Occurrence screening systems identify deviations from normal procedures or expected treatment outcomes and may be used in both risk management and quality assessment. An occurrence screening system uses criteria to identify APOs but does not rely on staff members to report the adverse events. Typical examples of APOs that can be identified using such a system include transfer from a general care unit to a special care unit, nosocomial infection, and unplanned return to an operating room. Medical record analysts or trained data screeners systematically review patient records using the prespecified criteria to discover APOs. Peer reviewers then determine whether a deviation from acceptable standards of care actually occurred. Such screening can be conducted during or after the patient care, or at both times. An estimated 80% to 85% of APOs can be identified by occurrence screening—a much higher percentage than obtained through incident reporting systems. Furthermore, a risk management program that combines occurrence screening with review of other data sources, such as incident reporting, infection surveillance, antibiotics use review, and medical staff peer review, can identify 90% to 95% of APOs—a greater proportion than any individual method can identify.

RISK AND QUALITY OF CARE

Any risk management process may sound harsh and lead to the conclusion that the healthcare industry is adopting a businesslike, bottom-line approach without consideration for the humane aspects of providing care to people in need. This perception is not accurate, although even charitable and well-meaning organizations must, of course, maintain financial viability to continue their worthwhile endeavors. Significantly, governmental and voluntary nonprofit healthcare agencies must compete with proprietary healthcare providers in an open marketplace. That fact is a major stimulus that compels all healthcare providers to reduce their losses and to attract patients to the services being offered. For this reason, risk management by healthcare institutions becomes an integral tool of sound management. It is possible, however, that some patients covered by different insurance programs may receive differential care (see **Box 1-6**).

Box 1-6

Of great concern is the fact that premature death directly resulted from confirmed quality problems in 53 (7.4%) of 706 Medicare, patients and in 42 (27.2%) of 154 Medicaid patients. These deaths were avoidable and were directly due to departures from accepted standards of medical care. Also of concern is the fact that readmission occurred in 60 Medicare patients and 18 Medicaid patients, resulting from confirmed quality-of-care problems during the previous admission.[24]

These connections are affirmed by the accreditation standards of The Joint Commission (TJC). Every applicable institution that seeks TJC accreditation must show substantial compliance with several standards that apply only to the quality-of-care and patient safety aspects of risk management:

- A hospital's governing body must provide resources and support for the quality assurance and risk management functions related to patient care and safety.
- A hospital's chief executive officer, through the management and administrative staff, must ensure appropriate medical staff involvement in and support for the following:
  - The identification of areas of potential risk in patient care and safety
  - The development of criteria for identifying cases with potential risk regarding patient care and safety, and evaluating these cases
  - The correction of problems in patient care and safety identified by risk management activities

- The design of programs to reduce risks related to patient care and safety
- A hospital's management must establish and maintain operational linkages between risk management functions related to patient care and safety, and quality assurance functions.
- A hospital's management must ensure that existing information relative to the quality of patient care is readily accessible to both the quality assurance and the risk management functions.

RISK MANAGEMENT/QUALITY ASSURANCE FUNCTIONS AND ACTIVITIES

In 1980, the American Hospital Association (AHA) formed the Interdisciplinary Task Force on Quality Assurance and Risk Management to define the relationship between hospital risk management (RM) and quality assurance (QA). A causal connection exists between risk management, the quality of care, and quality assurance programs. A quality–risk continuum has been identified, and quality assurance and risk management programs must work together to achieve their own goals. Four dicta emerge from the quality–risk spectrum:

- Quality control is the process of assuring that standards are met. The objective is 100% met, or zero defects.
- Risk control ensures that losses due to property, casualty, or employee benefit risks are prevented, reduced in frequency and/or severity, or transferred.
- Quality control is doing what you want to do: meeting standards.
- Risk control is not doing what you do not want to do: preventing errors.

RM and QA Comparisons

Risk management and quality assurance are two activities whose functions sometimes overlap. When that overlap occurs, their purposes and methods are almost indistinguishable. An examination of RM and QA leads to the relevant conclusion that a close working arrangement between the two activities is unavoidable. Integrating RM and QA, where feasible, could achieve the following results:

- Maximization of the use of limited resources
- Elimination of duplication because the data sources for both activities are the same
- Creation of a means for developing new solutions to problems
- Facilitation of the development of training programs
- Improvement of the budget process by identifying and consolidating budget requirements for both activities

One TJC requirement mandates that hospitals seeking approval have programs that link risk management with quality assurance. A review by the U.S. Congress Office of Technology Assessment (OTA) concluded that the QA–RM link "may promote quality-enhancing rather than wasteful defensive medicine."[25]

ADMINISTRATION OF RISK MANAGEMENT PROGRAMS

Goals and Prime Objectives

A risk management system aims to identify, evaluate, and reduce risks to patients, visitors, employees, and professional staff involved in the provision of healthcare services. There should be a written description of the program, periodic revisions and review, and amendments when changes are made. All federal, state, and local legislation and regulations should be complied with and documented. Incidents such as fires, equipment malfunction, poisoning, strikes, disasters, and termination of vital services should be reported to the proper authorities.

With the help of a risk management committee responsible to the Board of Directors, Mt. Sinai Hospital (Toronto, Canada) identified three objectives for its risk management program:[26]

1. To reduce the frequency of preventable adverse occurrences that lead to liability claims
2. To reduce the probability of a claim being filed after an adverse event has occurred
3. To help control the costs of claims that do emerge

Initiatives integrated into this risk management program included acting on the risks identified in the recommendations of a coroner's jury, in departmental reports, in incident analysis, in occurrence reporting, and in a claims summary database.

Responsibilities of a Risk Management Committee and Coordinator

Because a risk manager's activities involve the entire institution and all its programs and services, the responsibilities can evolve into a long, overwhelming list of tasks.[27,28] Many tasks overlap with other units and are cooperative in nature. Grouping the responsibilities delineates the descriptive scope of a risk manager's job.

**Purpose, Accountability, and
Authority Functions**

- Coordinate and carry out risk management activities in line with the program objectives
- Secure written statements affirming the support of the governing body, the administration, and the medical staff for the risk management program
- Describe the organizational reporting lines and the relationships between the risk manager and the rest of the institution
- Prepare a written statement detailing the involvement of every department and service and its responsibilities in risk management activities
- Provide for the flow of information among quality assurance, credentialing, peer review, and any risk management committee
- Monitor all incidents related to patient care
- Define the responsibility to recommend and implement corrective actions
- Prepare a statement assuring the confidentiality of all data collected for the risk management program

Specific Functions

- Review the potentially compensable events (PCEs)
- Investigate the PCEs
- Analyze and pinpoint trends in PCEs
- Report appropriate PCEs to the insurance carrier
- Assist in the resolution of conflicts among patients, physicians, and institution to avoid claims
- Settle claims, obtaining liability releases, at the authority level approved by management
- Adjust or write off bills as necessary within authority approved by management
- Maintain files of all lawsuits

- Ensure protection of records and other evidence
- Prepare the necessary material and people for a legal defense under the guidance of the insurance company and defense counsel
- Represent the institution in legal proceedings within defined parameters
- Assist and monitor the activities and charges of the defense counsel
- Provide risk management support/input to appropriate medical staff and institutional committees
- Act as the institution's resource for risk management topics
- Prepare reports to the board, the healthcare system, management, and other entities as directed
- Comply with applicable regulatory codes and professional standards
- Provide risk management education for institutional personnel, medical staff, and residents
- Maintain professional competence through participation in seminars, conferences, and so on, and through membership in appropriate professional societies
- Develop the annual risk management budget
- Determine general, short-term, and long-term objectives
- Evaluate the program regularly and update it as necessary

Functional Relationships

- Biomedical engineering in regard to new products, equipment involved in PCEs, record keeping, and risk management alerts
- Quality assurance in regard to PCEs, professional staff, and incidents
- Safety/fire/disaster committees
- Employee health services

Risk Management Committee

Programs should include a risk management committee to assist in prioritization of risk reduction activities and to act as a liaison to the various professional staffs in the hospital. A typical risk management committee has a physician chairman, as well as representation from the major medical and surgical services, the nursing department, the technical staff (biomedical engineering, radiology, respiratory services, clinical laboratory), and the quality assessment department, plus the risk manager. One or more members of the governing body and hospital counsel may be members. A risk management committee reviews key risk-exposure information: all claims; all state-reported incidents; internal incidents of concern because of either the extent of injury or the potential for injury; emerging treads in delivery of care that present new avenues of exposure; and any other issues or events that may occur, or be averted, that may have the actuality or potential of leading to a heavy loss of financial resources or good reputation. Having a mix of clinical and technical personnel on the committee provides for multifaceted examination of loss potential and risk exposure of any situation. This committee reports to the medical staff, governing body, and administration and frequently serves as the primary source of ongoing education on loss prevention in a facility.

The goals of the risk manager and the administration in working within this committee are to facilitate information flow among various departments and services and to provide a central focus for collaborative loss control and risk reduction actions.

Responsibility of the Governing Body

A commitment, including accountability, to an institution-wide risk management program must be adopted in a written governing board policy. Governing body bylaws should include mechanisms for the approval of medical staff bylaws, including the appointment and reappointment of physicians. A mechanism must be established for reporting risk management activities to the board. If possible, a governing body member should be appointed to any risk management advisory group or committee.

Under the guidance of the governing board, one risk manager suggested that "chaos theory" offers an opportunity to enhance risk management. Chaos theory is "based on the simple principle that order can be found in disorder."[29] This theory concentrates on events that do not adhere to established principles, are unpredictable, do not result in a rational aftermath, and appear to disregard a lucid explanation. At a minimum, chaos theory provides a few buzzwords for risk managers. At most, this theory presents a unique prototype that has direct application to the risk management process. Five chaos theory concepts forge links to risk management practices:

1. Predictable patterns exist in apparent random events, because the nature of risk is universal; only the scale changes. Risk managers change their perspectives to study the larger universe, examine parallel systems, and avoid the isolation of increasing specialization.

2. A sensitive dependence on initial conditions may exist. Small initial events need to be studied and related to larger outcomes. Could the minuscule wind from a butterfly's wings cause severe weather changes elsewhere in the world?

3. Risk managers usually deal with apparently discrete or chance events. Over time, specific patterns begin to materialize as the random repetitive behavior produces information. Risk managers need to know where

to look for this information and extract the relevant data to apply in their activities.

4. Risk managers must comprehend the intricate interconnected network of forces and external influences that determine the variety of eventual outcomes. Predictably, these forces include the institutional values, goals, and rules, such as a smoke-free workplace, a policy of hiring the handicapped, or a mandate to recycle waste products.

5. To move from the conspicuous and make connections to the improbable, risk managers must adopt new ways of looking for risks using a combination of intelligence and perspicacity.

SPECIFIC RISK MANAGEMENT FUNCTIONS

Incident Identification, Reporting, and Tracking

An identification and reporting process must exist to identify any circumstance or occurrence that may prove injurious to a patient or that may result in an adverse outcome to a patient. Mortality, morbidity, infections, complications, errors in diagnosis, transfusions, results of treatments, and unimproved cases other than those related to the natural course of disease or illness should be reviewed. Each institution must define and list what constitutes a reportable incident and transmit that information to all employees and all regulatory bodies. A management system should include these elements:

- A time frame within which incidents must be reported
- Designation of the individual to receive incident reports

- Requirement that any employee or medical staff appointee who is aware of an incident must report it to the appropriate person
- The sharing of information, at a minimum, between quality assurance and risk management

The success of the program depends on the risk management staff's skill in obtaining relevant information. In any risk management program, the keystone to information gathering is the incident report. Originally designed by the insurance industry, this report is the mainstay tool for risk assessment in all risk management programs in all industries.

Incident report forms are usually custom-designed for a healthcare facility by the risk management department, taking into consideration the type of information and the amount of detail for any event that need to be collected for adequate computer tracking. To foster use of this form, most risk managers prefer to sacrifice detail in favor of quick notification of an incident. Incident report forms should be devised so that they are unlike any other forms used in the facility, and they should be easy to complete. User-friendly forms have frequently occurring incidents listed in alphabetical order, with a check-off box, allowing space for a brief description of any detail the reporter thinks may be relevant to the situation. Some facilities include a space for physician's comments if the event required medical intervention. On prompt notification of a serious event or situation, risk management staff can conduct their own investigation immediately and institute any needed loss control measures simultaneously.

Routing of the incident report must be clearly defined. In some facilities, the report is sent immediately to the risk management office. In most hospitals, if a report is completed by nursing staff, it is routed through nursing administration before being transmitted to the risk manager. An industry standard for transmitting the incident report is no later than 24 hours, with telephone notification to the risk manager as soon as possible after any serious injury or other significant event. A combination of user-friendly forms, staff education, and feedback through risk management trend reports will encourage information flow that meets or exceeds the standard of 4.5 incident reports per licensed bed per year.

Incident reports can be categorized by type of event and severity of situation for computer tracking purposes. A severity index or scale might be based on the type of injury or the type of breach of procedure. Using a scale of 0, 1, 2, or 3, the 0 represents "no injury" whereas 3 may be an injury requiring significant "therapeutic intervention," or a significant "breach of procedure" such as giving medication to the wrong patient. This information can easily be developed into a graphic report to accompany the risk manager's analysis and recommendations of loss exposures and risk activities as reported in monthly, quarterly, and annual reports to the safety committee, the quality assessment committee, and the CEO and finance officer.

State-Mandated Incident Reporting

Some states have recognized the utility of risk management programs for the identification of major areas of patient vulnerability within the healthcare system and mandate the reporting of "incidents" to a state regulatory agency, although details of such requirements vary considerably from state to state. New York mandates reporting of hospital staff strikes; disasters or emergency situations affecting hospital operations; termination of any vital services in the hospital, such as telephone, laundry services, and pest control; and poisoning occurring within a hospital. When the peer-review process finds that the standard of care was not met and a patient death or impairment of bodily function unrelated to the normal disease process occurred, the incident must also be reported to the state Health Department. In addition, events requiring police or other legal notification are reportable in New York. In contrast, Massachusetts mandates quarterly and annual reporting of adverse patient events to the Board of Registration in Medicine. Events that are reportable in Massachusetts are defined as incidents of patient harm or death as an outcome of medical intervention. Meeting the standard of care is implied, but not explicit, in the regulations, leaving facilities to make their own interpretations as to whether an incident is reportable. Both New York and Massachusetts reserve the right to conduct an on-site review of any incident, including examination of the credentials of any personnel involved in an event.

Other states have legislative mandates for risk management programs. These state regulations relate to the administration of a risk management program, investigation and analysis of identified risks, education programs, patient grievance procedures, and confidentiality of risk management data. Obviously, it is incumbent on risk managers to be aware of the specific legislation that applies in their own states. Risk managers and quality assessment professionals can use statewide statistical data to compare the type and severity of events by region or type of healthcare facility to "improve" modalities of care.

Incident Review and Evaluation

The incident review and evaluation process must provide for the following responses:

- Investigation of all incidents, even if no injury results
- Identification of trends among incidents
- Referral of incidents and trend summaries to be evaluated to determine whether further action is necessary
- Referral of incidents requiring further action to the appropriate institutional individuals, departments, services, and committees

Actions to Prevent Recurrence of Incidents

Any actions taken by quality assessment, peer review, or medical staff committees regarding referred identified problems must be documented in a written record. These actions can be classified using the acronym PACED: preventive, administrative, corrective, educational, and documentary.[30]

- *Preventive* activities could include a patient relations program; an employee newsletter; a formal safety and security program; a community input effort; and ongoing planning, coordination, and review functions.
- *Administrative* actions relate to an active process, involvement of department heads, and a formal philosophy regarding administration.
- *Corrective* activities focus on the encouragement of problem identification, the monitoring of problem situations, the existence of internal audit functions, and the expeditious resolution of problems.

- *Educational* programs concentrate on creating an interdepartmental educational services unit, upgrading medical and technical skills, having a patient education program, and maintaining records of educational activities.
- *Documentary* activities include attention to personnel files, financial records, medical charts, regulatory requirements, and written policies and procedures.

The following examples identify a host of work area concerns that could be involved in risk management actions:

- Hazards at work
- Fire safety
- Disaster plans
- Electrical safety
- Central services safety
- Employee/patient safety
- Nursing safety
- Malpractice/legal liability
- Medical staff
- Anesthesia personnel
- Surgery personnel
- Surgical suite hazards
- Surgery and anesthesia
- Nursing treatment
- Dietary safety
- Housekeeping safety
- Pathology safety
- Respiratory safety
- Radiology/laser safety
- Nursing/pharmacy errors
- Nursing and law

Internal Documentation

Institutions must maintain complete files of all risk management documentation, along with malpractice liability coverage documentation, individual malpractice case files involving the institution, and records of all expenses involved in safety programs to reduce or eliminate patient injuries. Documentation should be contained in the recorded minutes of appropriate bodies, as well as in reviews of credentials and personnel files of staff.

Credentialing and Privileging

Professional staff credentialing aims to ensure that institutions are staffed only by qualified individuals and that those individuals' performance is maintained at an acceptable level. Credentialing activities consist of a complete review of the licenses, education, and training of all applicants seeking appointment or employment. In addition, physicians must regularly have their privileges updated. This process of recredentialing involves an evaluation by the institution of the physician's clinical experience, competence, ability, judgment, and demonstrated performance in specified functions, such as open heart surgery, before any reappointment. Specifically, a profile of each physician and dentist must be compiled from at least the following data sources:

- Morbidity and mortality review
- Blood utilization review
- Safety committee review
- Peer review organization data
- Medical care evaluations
- Incident report review
- Liability claims data
- Continuing education programs and training
- Utilization review
- Infection control review
- Surgical case review

- Tissue review
- Medical record review
- Complaints
- Prescription review
- Medical case review

In addition, hospitals are mandated under the Healthcare Quality Improvement Act of 1986 to make inquiries to the National Practitioner Data Bank concerning each physician, dentist, and others. Queries directed to the Federation of State Medical Boards, individual state medical boards and societies, and the insured's malpractice insurance carrier will provide additional information on adverse professional actions, discipline, and sanctions. The federal legislation also mandates reports to the National Practitioner Data Bank of disciplinary actions or dismissals of medical staff from hospitals and institutions based on peer-review activities and adverse situations.

In terms of risk management, credentialing and privileging are critical because they represent the primary mechanism available to hospitals, agencies, managed care organizations, and other institutions to help ensure that only competent personnel are employed and that those providers perform only those clinical duties and procedures for which they are deemed clinically competent. This evaluation process, in turn, reduces the likelihood of the occurrence of any negligent acts that could result in a claim against the organization. A facility or agency with a nonexistent or ineffective credentialing or privileging process could find itself in an indefensible position if a malpractice claim were filed, as the absence of such a process might indicate that the institution was negligent in ensuring that it employed only competent healthcare providers.

Patient Complaint Program

A copy of the "Patient's Bill of Rights" should be given to each patient on admission and be available in the patient's own language. These rights should be posted in conspicuous areas throughout the institution or agency. A formal written program for addressing patient complaints must be established, along with documentation of any action taken to resolve grievances. All complaints must be investigated promptly and thoroughly. Patients must be provided with the name and phone number of the representative designated to respond to such complaints. Representatives, in turn, must treat complaining patients with dignity, courtesy, and due regard for their privacy while providing information about the following:

- Whom the patient may contact regarding the complaint
- Whom the patient may contact if dissatisfied with the resolution
- Procedures for investigating the complaint
- When the patient can expect a verbal or written response or resolution to the complaint

Tracking patients' complaints and identifying trends in those complaints should be routine and reported to the risk management and other committees as necessary.

Risk Management Education

Risk management education should be included in orientation and annual in-service training programs for all institutional employees and professional staff in the following areas:

- Organization and goals of the risk management program
- "Patient's Bill of Rights"
- Patient relations and complaint program

- Incident-reporting program
- Reporting responsibilities for alleged professional misconduct
- Safety program and department-specific safety practices.

Several insurance companies sponsor risk management seminars for physicians and nurses, providing them with continuing medical or nursing education credits. Core educational units fall into four categories. Opening with the perceived reasons for the malpractice problem, the seminar first covers the public patient, plaintiff attorneys, laws, the standard of care, and the role of physicians in iatrogenic injuries and defensive medicine. Second, the seminar focuses on loss prevention strategies, including rapport between physician and patient, communications, satisfaction, informed consent, office staff strategies, relationships between physician and hospital, and medical record documentation. Third, the seminar highlights litigation awareness, emphasizing the dos and don'ts if physicians are sued. Finally, arbitration details the alternate dispute resolution forum, the binding legal resolution, and the advantages and disadvantages of each method. In theory, these seminars may prevent claims, conserve the institution's financial resources, prevent patient injury, and improve the quality of patient care delivered.

Insurance Companies and Risk Management

Insurance companies offer their insured institutions a variety of risk management services, including consultation, educational programs, publications, closed-claim studies, and computer software packages. Consultations between insurance company representatives and institutional risk management personnel aim to help the organization minimize the risk of malpractice claims. Services may include claims auditing, chart review, policy review, and evaluation of specific clinical areas. Individual insurance company personnel may spend time in loss prevention and loss control activities. In filling this role, these individuals keep up-to-date with changes in laws and standards of practice having implications for facility liability, including lessons learned from cases involving actual losses and case-law decisions. Sometimes, the problem is a misunderstanding of the insurance policy.

Educational services seek to help organizations minimize the frequency and severity of malpractice claims. Programs can be provided in several formats, including national, regional, local, and institutional seminars and individualized focused training workshops. Seminars allow representatives of all the insured organizations to meet and discuss clinical, administrative, and legal risk management issues. Focused workshops give individual risk managers a more in-depth examination of issues that directly affect their specific facility. Companies may offer formal certificate programs for risk managers in areas such as an overview of risk management, risk exposure identification and evaluation, or functions of risk management. Each course may consist of self-study, specified readings, study questions, and projects. At the end of each course, participants may be tested and evaluated by qualified faculty.

Publications are designed to aid the insured institution to manage and reduce its liability risk. This kind of material ranges from pamphlets on a single issue to workshop proceedings to multivolume books to a combination of mass-media approaches. Often, insurance companies publish and distribute regular newsletters, case alerts, and bulletins. Available videotapes, audiotapes, films, and slide presentations may deal with topics such as malpractice in the emergency department, medication errors, and minimizing risks in surgery.

Claims are studied continuously by the insurance companies. A database of open and closed claims filed against their insured organizations and individuals is routinely analyzed to identify lessons learned, so that future claims can be avoided. Professional liability representatives periodically analyze claims to identify factors that may have caused their submission. These factors are evaluated jointly by insurance company representatives and institution officials in an effort to correct the situations that led to the claims. This process is facilitated by computer reports that pinpoint the frequency and severity of malpractice claims.

While insurance companies do not require a prescribed risk management program, the surveys of the agency or institutional program and the results of the data analysis may reflect the adequacy of this program and lead to variations in the premiums charged. Continuing professional liability coverage may be conditional on implementing corrective action based on recommendations for improvement in the program or in specific situations that can cause liability.

Dos and Don'ts of Risk Management: A Claims Perspective

Small things that hospital employees, departmental supervisors, and medical staff members do—and don't do—can have a significant impact on the frequency and severity of claims made against a hospital. Risk management experts urge hospitals to enforce dos and don'ts relative to documentation, product malfunction, contracts, confidentiality, and conflicts (see **Box 1-7**).

Box 1-7   Dos and Don'ts of Risk Management

DOCUMENTATION[31]

- *Do* follow all policies and procedures pertaining to documentation.
- *Do* document any changes in the patient's status, attempts to contact the patient's physicians or family members, and other activities relevant to the patient's care. The absence of such documentation makes defending a medical malpractice action against the hospital difficult. In the words of one plaintiff attorney, "If it's not in the chart, it never happened."
- *Do* complete documentation entries contemporaneously. If changes or updates are necessary, they should be documented in a timely manner, with the date, reason for the change or update, and the initials of the person making the change included.
- *Don't* alter records out of fear of litigation or disciplinary action. Altered records discovered by a plaintiff attorney can make a case practically indefensible.
- *Don't* make changes to documentation days after an event occurs. Outline in memo form the situation surrounding the need for a change and discuss it with the hospital risk manager.

PRODUCT MALFUNCTION

- *Do* contact the risk management department whenever a product malfunctions, regardless of the perceived consequences at the time of the malfunction.
- *Do* notify the manufacturer of the malfunctioning product as soon as possible.
- *Don't* return the malfunctioning product to the manufacturer after it has caused an injury.
- *Don't* discard the malfunctioning equipment, product, or disposable accessories. Instead, store it in a secure location until the hospital's professional liability company can be notified. Without the product as evidence, securing a contribution from a manufacturer would be very difficult if the incident ultimately warranted settlement, and the hospital could be solely liable.
- *Don't* attempt to recreate the malfunction to discover what or how something happened. A report from an independent third-party investigation will be less credible if the product has been altered in any way.

CONTRACTS

- *Do* review all vendor contracts to ensure that the hospital is not exposed to additional risks.
- *Do* have all contracts reviewed annually by the hospital attorney.
- *Don't* sign a contract without reading it and understanding it first.

CONFLICTS

- *Do* keep conflicts involving physicians and the hospital out of the public arena.
- *Do* familiarize all hospital personnel with hospital policies and procedures that affect their daily jobs. Lack of knowledge of hospital policies is not a viable defense.
- *Don't* allow or engage in open criticism of health professionals' treatment of a patient. Any documented conflicts over patient care would not only make a case very difficult to defend, but could also raise the ultimate value of the judgment.
- *Don't* enact policies or procedures that are unrealistic. The hospital will be held to its stated policies and procedures as standards of care.

CONFIDENTIALITY

- *Do* hold professional discussions about patients in hospital settings, not in public areas.
- *Don't* discuss patients' problems outside of the hospital.

Computer Use in Risk Management

Next to an involved risk management committee, the most valuable asset for any risk management program is a one-gigabyte computer and all the software the risk management department can afford.

Although smaller agencies and facilities (those with fewer than 200 beds) can manage data for trend analysis manually, the need for long-term trend analysis of incidents, claims, equipment problems, and internal disasters (for example, floods occurring from broken pipes only on weekends) cannot be overemphasized. While many software packages are available that provide for central entry of data and specialized modules for RM, QA, or utilization review, the purchase decision should be based on a thorough analysis of the risk management data needs. Standard database software can be selected and customized to a particular program's needs at a significant savings over the special risk management packages available. In selecting software, the type of information that the risk manager will be analyzing and the type of reports that will be generated from the analysis are the key factors in making the purchase decision.

Data that risk management most frequently analyzes for trends include events involving patient injury, events leading to financial loss to the institution (floods, fires, theft), malpractice suits naming the facility, dates and allegations of malpractice suits filed against medical staff members (obtained on appointment and reappointment), and "indicators"—specific events with potential for patient injury or financial loss, such as a missing surgical consent, an antibiotic given to the wrong patient, a missing patient chart, or narcotic cabinet keys missing from the pharmacy. It is common to track hospital incidents and events by date, time, and location. Malpractice claims are usually tracked by date, allegation, person(s) involved, and damages requested, and are followed through the entire defense process, listing information collected and individuals deposed for the defense, to judgment, settlement, or dismissal of the case. The amount of the judgment or settlement is tracked, as are the expenses incurred. Any one of the many risk management packages currently on the market or one of the database software packages would handle this type of information quite readily.

TOWARD THE FUTURE

Usually, risk managers aim to reduce preventable adverse events, and to minimize financial loss to their organizations should such events occur. In a rapidly changing business environment, risk managers must be able to accurately determine where their healthcare organization is headed and effectively plan methods and techniques to mitigate the risks to their institutions. Within these goals, risk managers, along with everyone else, from top management to the lowest-level employee, appear to be involved in almost every aspect of the healthcare delivery system. Healthcare organizations that survive the constant turmoil in the industry will be abetted by an effective, strategic risk management program.

REFERENCES

1. Institute of Medicine, National Academy of Sciences. (1999). *To err is human: Building a safer health system.*

2. Sack, K., & Williams, T. (2011, March 31). Deaths of 9 Alabama patients are studied: All got intravenous supplement. *New York Times.* www.NYtimes.com/2011/03/31/us/31intravenous.html

3. Pear, R. (2012, January 6). Report finds most errors at hospitals unreported. *New York Times,* p. A12.

4. Lucado, J., & Elixhauster, A. (April, 2011). Medication-related adverse outcomes in U.S. hospitals and emergency departments. HCUP Statistical Brief #109. Rockville, MD: AHRQ. www.hcup-u.s.ahra.gov/reports/statbriefs/sb109.pdf

5. Clarke, J. R., Johnston, J., & Finley, B. S. (2007). Getting surgery right. *Annals of Surgery, 246*(3), 395–405.

6. Zarembo, A., & Girion, L. (2011, February 18). Wrong patient got kidney at USC. *Los Angeles Times.* LATimes.com/news/local/la-ne-use-kidney-20110218.0.5603801.story

7. Wrong site surgery. (2011, November). *Hospital and Health Networks,* pp. 35–37.

8. Boothman, R. C., Blackwell, A. C., et al. (2009, January). A better approach to medical malpractice claims? The University of Michigan experience. *Journal of Health & Life Sciences Law.*

9. Kowalczyk, L. (2011, September 21). Alarm fatigue a factor in 2nd death. *Boston Globe.* articles.boston.com/2011../30185391_1_alarm_fatigue_nurses-patients

10. Hamill, S. D. (2011, July 10). Entire UPMC transplant team missed hepatitis alert. *Pittsburgh Post-Gazette.* www.post-gazette.com/pg/11191/115-9219-455-0.5tmcmpid-news

11. Conway, J., & Federico, F. (2011, October 18). Respectful management of serious clinical events. *Institute for Health Care Improvement.* www.ihi.org/../Respectfulmanagementofseriousclinicalaeswhitepaper.us

12. The Joint Commission. (2011, September). CAMH Update 2.

13. Institute of Medicine, National Academy of Sciences. (2001, March). *Crossing the quality chasm: A new health system for the 21st century.*

14. McKinney, M. (2011, April 11). The more you look ... *Modern Healthcare,* p. 8.

15. Smith, D. G., & Wheeler, J. R. C. (1992). Strategies and structures for hospital risk management programs. *Health Care Management Review, 17*(3), 9–17.

16. Hinman, E. J. (1995). Risk management: An overview. Presentation notes for lecture for Institute of Medical Law, Inc., course on risk management.

17. Evans, L. (1993). Medical accidents: No such thing? *British Medical Journal, 307*(6917), 1438–1439.

18. Burlando, A. J. (1990). The 1990s: The decade of risk management. *Risk Management, 37*(3), 50–56.

19. Hagg, S. R. (1990). Elements of a risk management program. In L. M. Harpster & M. S. Veach (Eds.), *Risk management handbook for health care facilities,* (pp. 23–33). Chicago: American Hospital Publishing.

20. Hine, C. (1993). Doctors, nurses differ on RM communication. *National Underwriter, 97*(43), 10–11.

21. Clinical Skillbuilders. (1992). *Write better documentation.* Springhouse, PA: Springhouse Corporation.

22. Pesaud, D. D., & Dawe, U. (1992). Personal computers and risk management. *Hospital Topics, 70*(3), 11–14.

23. Hazen, S., & Cookson, J. (1990). A database tool for centralized analysis of untoward health care events. *Military Medicine, 155*(10), 492–497.

24. Nenner, R. P., Imperato, P. J., Silver, A. L., & Will, T. O. (1994). Quality of care problems among Medicare and Medicaid patients. *Journal of Community Health, 19*(5), 307–318.

25. U.S. Congress, Office of Technology Assessment. (1994). *Defensive medicine and medical malpractice* (OTA-H-602)(pp.32–33). Washington, DC: Government Printing Office.

26. Freedman, T. J., & Gerring, G. (1993). Focus on risk management. *Leadership, 2*(3), 29–33.

27. Murov, K. L. (1995). Implementation of a risk management program. An educational presentation for the Institute of Medical Law, Inc., New York Health Care Risk Management Program.

28. Monagle, J. F. (1985). *Risk management: A guide for health care Professionals.* Gaithersburg, MD: Aspen.

29. Burlando, T. (1994). Chaos and risk management. *Risk Management, 41*(4), 54–61.

30. Rowland, H. S., & Rowland, B. L. (1995). *Hospital risk management: Forms, checklists and Guidelines.* Gaithersburg, MD: Aspen.

31. MAG Mutual Insurance Company. (1994). *Hospital Risk Manager, 2*(3), 3.

CHAPTER 2

Regulatory Environment

Torrance Akinsanya and Thomas M. Bodenberg

STANDARDS AND RISK MANAGEMENT

Health care is one of the most regulated industries in the United States. A regulatory environment is generated by the establishment of standards by legislative acts, by regulations administered by official executive agencies, and by standards of professional organizations. Violations of the law and/or regulations or standards could considerably interrupt healthcare providers' revenue streams and even result in litigation, financial penalties, and incarceration for high-level management personnel. An understanding of the regulations is vital for individuals and institutions engaged in healthcare risk management.

A STANDARDS PRIMER

In a healthcare milieu, standards are statements concerning proper procedures and/or actions to be taken in given clinical or administrative situations. Using juxtaposed terms, standards can be created within the following boundary dimensions:[1]

- Explicit or implicit
- National or local
- Validated or consensual
- Used or ignored
- Periodically updated or static

Explicit standards, on the one hand, are written guidelines intended to ensure that everyone follows the same specific procedures in given clinical or administrative situations. Implicit standards, on the other hand, are usual and customary or based on collective experience but are unwritten, understood, assumed, or implied. Standards that are documented by scientific testing are verifiable and replicable; thus their validity can be authenticated. Consensual standards develop by mutual agreement among involved parties.

Government jurisdictions, professional associations, or voluntary organizations at national, state, or local levels may develop and promulgate standards that may be incorporated into codes of ethics or separate guidelines, or be embedded in legislation and regulations. Excellent standards may be in force when the precepts are first established, but without a dynamic process of periodic review and updating, standards can fall into disuse and be ignored. Standards may also be evidence based or promulgated through known facts.

PROMULGATION AND IMPLEMENTATION OF STANDARDS

Standards may be promulgated within four classifications: legal, regulatory, reimbursement, and practice guidelines. To compound matters further, there may be crossovers between the classifications (**Box 2-1**).

Box 2-1   Examples of Regulatory Interplay and Conflicts

- The Equal Employment Opportunity Commission (EEOC) wants to extend employment discrimination protection to obese people under the Americans with Disabilities Act (ADA) and the Rehabilitation Act of 1973.[2]
- The EEOC declared chronic obesity to be a protected category under the ADA. Obesity is defined as being twice the normal weight for one's size.[3]
- A jury awarded 5'2", 320-pound Bonnie Cook $100,000 for a discrimination violation of Section 504 of the Rehabilitation Act of 1973. A pre-hire physical exam by the Rhode Island Department of Mental Health, Retardation, and Hospitals found her "morbidly obese" and denied her a job.[4]
- Under three court decisions, obesity, sexual obsession, and tobacco smoke allergies do not amount to disabling conditions protected by law.[5]

Three particularly troubling areas for healthcare institutions illustrate the conflicting legislative interplay:

- Occupational Safety and Health Administration (OSHA) standards provoke conflicts with the Americans with Disabilities Act (ADA) relative to pre-employment medical examinations.
- Health insurance guidelines evoke interplay between the Employee Retirement and Income Security Act (ERISA) and ADA regarding health insurance plans that exclude or limit benefits for disabling conditions.
- State worker's compensation laws may conflict with the ADA by using examinations of the back to screen out injury-prone job applicants.[6]

LEGAL STANDARDS

Legislatively, standards have been required relative to a broad spectrum of healthcare issues, such as public health rules, disease-reporting requirements, utilization of immunizations, evidence-based care as in the case of treatment of specific disease entities, patients' rights, discharge planning, reporting of adverse events, worker's compensation, health insurance, and licensing of institutions, agencies, and professionals. Usually, legislation is followed by regulations issued by the appropriate executive department.

A judicial system provides the primary legal initiative for implementing standards. If disagreements arise, the parties involved meet in a courtroom to decide the issue before a judge and sometimes a jury. Subsequently, the decision of the court yields a basis in law for future actions. Statutes and court orders constitute the framework for the legal implementation of standards. These legal renderings provide the foundation for healthcare institutional policies relative to advance directives, living wills, informed consent, access to medical records, and information about practitioners.

FEDERAL MANDATES

Mandatory regulations cover a multitude of activities in the healthcare industry. For example, healthcare institution must meet the conditions of participation (COP) established by the federal Center for Medicare and Medicaid Services (CMS) before it can be reimbursed for treating people covered by the Medicare health insurance program. Like members of any other industry, healthcare providers must meet the mandates of federal regulations, such as those required by The Joint Commission (TJC) and OSHA. One official at a large hospital summed up the effect of federal regulations on the healthcare industry as follows:

> Although workplace regulations are serious, time-consuming and expensive, in the scheme of things, federal workplace regulation is not the worst thing.[7]

The sections that follow look at some examples of federal regulation of the healthcare industry.

Center for Medicare and Medicaid Services

The CMS has established regulations, standards, and conditions that govern how hospitals function in the United States. Its standards related to the delivery of care and the environment of care are enforced by local Department of Health agencies through unannounced inspections and reports. Noncompliance with CMS standards and conditions can result in a hospital being relegated to "immediate jeopardy to the life and safety of patients" status. Such situations require immediate remediation or a hospital is placed on a termination track for Medicare and Medicaid programs. Noncompliance may also result in individual and institutional penalties as well as litigation. To avoid this situation, hospitals are encouraged to establish quality management and risk management programs that will promote the internal identification and correction of serious noncompliant issues and to take the necessary corrective measures prior to regulatory agency inspections.

Hospitals are also regulated to provide patient advocacy and language interpretation programs for patients. Put simply, hospitals are required to communicate with all patients in a language they understand. These regulations are intended to provide patients with an opportunity to voice their concerns through ongoing communication with their healthcare providers. Hospitals are also required to have a patient relations department that advocates on behalf of the patient. The underlying concept of these programs is that increased communication can avert or reduce serious medical errors and reduce litigation and added healthcare costs.

Occupational Safety and Health Administration

Legislative mandates that apply to the workplace illustrate the complex spectrum of conceivable risk management activities in healthcare institutions, from addressing civil rights issues to regulating new areas such as employee pensions. OSHA-related laws and regulations have continued to evolve, thereby protecting the working public, yet creating substantial costs for implementation and increasing potential liabilities for businesses. However, enforcement agencies commonly negotiate settlements with employers even when not required by the regulation.

On a federal level, the Occupational Safety and Health Act of 1970 requires employers to furnish each employee with work and a workplace free from recognized hazards that can cause death or serious physical harm.

Figure 2-1   Examples of Regulatory Statutes, Descriptions, and Penalties[9]

OCCUPATIONAL SAFETY AND HEALTH ACT (OSHA)

Description

Requires employers to furnish each employee with work and a workplace free from recognized hazards that can cause death or serious physical harm.

Penalties

$5,000 to $70,000 for each willful violation; up to $70,000 for each repeat violation; up to $7,000 for serious, other-than-serious, or posting violation for each day of failure to abate hazard; abatement of hazard; imminent danger situations: $500,000 for a corporation, and $250,000 and/or six months imprisonment for an individual for a willful violation that results in death of an employee; one year imprisonment if prior conviction; $200,000 for an organization, and $100,000 and/or six months imprisonment for an individual for false statements in a required certified document.

DRUG-FREE WORKPLACE ACT (DFWA)

Description

Requires recipients of federal grants and contracts to take certain steps to maintain a drug-free workplace.

Penalties

Debarment; restraining order or injunction.

CONSOLIDATED OMNIBUS BUDGET RECONCILIATION ACT (COBRA)

Description

Provides for continued healthcare coverage under group health plans for qualified separated workers for up to 18 months.

Penalties

$100 per day for failure to comply with notice requirements; elimination of tax deductibility of plan contributions.

TITLE VII OF THE CIVIL RIGHTS ACT

Description

Prohibits employment or membership discrimination by employers, employment agencies, and unions on the basis of race, color, religion, sex, or national origin; prohibits discrimination against women affected by pregnancy, childbirth, or related medical conditions.

Penalties

$100 for each willful violation of posting requirements, unpaid wage, liquidated or punitive damages.

By itself, this law contains myriad regulations required of healthcare facilities that apply to accidents, blood-borne pathogens, drug testing for employees, ergonomics, hazard communication, infection control, inspections by OSHA, lasers, maintenance and sterilization of medical equipment, medical wastes, medication safety, radiation, record keeping, reproductive hazards, safety and health committees, self-audits, staff training, and violence in the workplace.[8] Furthermore, new rules can be adopted as the federal government emphasizes the enforcement of standards in the healthcare workplace. As of February 9, 1994, OSHA rules were put into place requiring facilities that use nonsolid prescription drugs, such as aerosols, liquids, and powders, to maintain material safety data sheets (MSDSs) for these drugs, and to use the MSDSs in training (see **Figure 2-1** and **Table 2-1**).

Table 2-1   Categories of Potential Hazards Found in Hospitals[10]

Hazard Category	Definition	Examples Found in the Hospital Environment
Biological	Infectious/biological agents, such as bacteria, viruses, fungi, or parasites, that may be transmitted by contact with infected patients or contaminated body secretions/fluids	Human immunodeficiency virus (HIV), vancomycin-resistant enterococcus (VRE), methicillin-resistant *Staphylococcus aureus* (MRSA), hepatitis B virus, hepatitis C virus, tuberculosis
Chemical	Various forms of chemicals that are potentially toxic or irritating to the body system, including medications, solutions, and gases	Ethylene oxide, formaldehyde, glutaraldehyde, waste anesthetic gases, hazardous drugs such as cytotoxic agents, pentamidine ribavirin
Psychological	Factors and situations encountered or associated with one's job or work environment that create or potentiate stress, emotional strain, and/or other interpersonal problems	Stress, workplace violence, shift work, inadequate staffing, heavy workload, increased patient acuity
Physical	Agents within the work environment that can cause tissue trauma	Radiation, lasers, noise, electricity, extreme temperatures, workplace violence
Environmental, mechanical/biomechanical	Factors encountered in the work environment that cause or potentiate accidents, injuries, strain, or discomfort	Tripping hazards, unsafe/unguarded equipment, poor air quality, slippery floors, confined spaces, cluttered or obstructed work areas/passageways, forceful exertions, awkward postures, localized contact stresses, vibration, temperature extremes, repetitive/prolonged motions or activities, lifting and moving patients

In late 1993, new guidelines for controlling the spread of tuberculosis (TB) were mandated, with particular attention given to the high risk of TB exposure in healthcare facilities and nursing homes. The federal Centers for Disease Control and Prevention (CDC) recommendations called for the use of improved masks, the use of ultraviolet light to kill airborne TB germs, ventilation standards, and tightened record keeping. New standards proposed in 1997 and 2002 have further expanded interest in TB-related risk assessment.[11]

OSHA indicated that healthcare facility hazards could be minimized in several ways: engineering and work practice controls, personal protective equipment, hepatitis B virus (HBV) vaccination, training and education, and appropriate use of signs and labels.[12] In 1993, OSHA reported 2,064 violations of the blood-borne pathogen regulations by healthcare industry organizations. This regulation was the most frequently violated standard in the industry that year. Specific blood-borne pathogen standards that were violated fell into five deficiency areas: exposure control plan (28%), methods of compliance (24%), communication of exposure to employees (23%), hepatitis B vaccination and post-exposure evaluations and follow-up (19%), and record keeping (6%).[13]

In 1991, OSHA published the Occupational Exposure to Blood-borne Pathogens standard in recognition of the significant health risk associated with exposure to viruses and other microorganisms that cause blood-borne diseases. Of primary concern are the human immunodeficiency virus (HIV), hepatitis B (HBV), and hepatitis C (HCV). In many patients, these diseases are fatal or chronically disabling.

The CDC reported 56 documented cases of occupationally acquired HIV infection in healthcare workers between 1985 and 1999, and an additional 136 cases of possible transmission. The agency also reported 8,700 cases of HBV infection in 1987, but only 800 new cases in 1995. Healthcare workers' risk of exposure to HCV is much higher than the risk of HIV, mostly because of the high frequency of HCV in the general population, which makes it a more significant threat through needlestick and sharps injuries.[14]

In 2000, the Needlestick Safety and Prevention Act (H.R. 5178)[15] was promulgated to specifically address the 600,000 needlesticks and other sharps injuries that occur each year. This revision of the blood-borne pathogens standard emphasizes the importance of reviewing institutions' exposure control plans annually, and of implementing engineering controls and use of safe medical devices such as retractable syringe needles, sliding needle shields, needleless connectors for IV delivery systems, self-blunting phlebotomy, and winged-steel needles.[16] Employee input into the plan and the selection of safe medical devices to be utilized is emphasized and requires documentation. Record keeping and a sharps injury log, along with maintenance of information on first aid, medical care, and subsequent follow-up of medical illnesses, are important aspects of reducing the sequelae of these injuries.

The Joint Commission has established standards related to National Patient Safety Goals (NPSGs) that include needlestick prevention and safety. These goals have added adherence to the federal Needlestick Safety and Prevention Act to the TJC accreditation process, which has speeded hospital compliance. TJC goals address issues such as improving the accuracy of patient identification; improving communication among caregivers; ensuring medication safety; preventing wrong-site, wrong-procedure surgery; and preventing hospital fires. Hospitals are required to establish processes and adopt CMS regulations to prevent adverse events that may be caused by noncompliance with these NPSGs.

Health Insurance Portability and Accountability Act of 1996

In 1996, President William J. Clinton signed the Health Insurance Portability and Accountability Act (HIPAA; Public Law 104-191).[18] This broad legislation deals with a wide set of health policy issues and mandates action that seeks to (1) ensure continuity of healthcare coverage for individuals when changing jobs; (2) improve the management of health information; (3) simplify the administration of health insurance; and (4) combat waste, fraud, and abuse in health insurance and health care. These rules—the first comprehensive federal standards for medical privacy—have affected virtually every doctor, patient, hospital, drugstore, and health insurance company in the United States.[19]

Title II of the HIPAA law (also known as Administrative Simplification) includes requirements for ensuring the security and privacy of individuals' medical information. The standards aim to maintain the right of individuals to keep information about themselves private. Hospital compliance is now required.

The regulations protect medical records and other "individually identifiable health information" (communicated electronically, on paper, or orally) that is created or received by covered healthcare entities that transmit information electronically. Covered entities include healthcare providers (such as hospitals), healthcare insurers, and organizations that process healthcare transactions on behalf of providers and insurers.

Individuals' medical records relating to their past, present, or future physical or mental health condition, the provision of health care, or the payment for such care are considered private and are protected under HIPAA.

Institutions engaged in the processing of electronic medical records and claims submissions are required to assess the potential risks to and vulnerabilities of the individual health data in their possession in electronic form, and to develop, implement, and maintain appropriate security measures. They must also document these security measures and keep them current.

The laws also specify standards for a "security matrix," which depicts a minimum level of security for electronic health information. Institution- and agency-wide attention needs to be focused on specifying authorization to access information, developing a contingency plan, reporting untoward incidents, and training employees on security and privacy concerns.

The HIPAA rules specify that information from a person's medical records cannot be disclosed to an employer unless the patient specifically authorizes the disclosure. Also, patients can review their medical records and request changes to correct errors, and researchers can use medical records to track an outbreak of disease if they strip the records of the patients' identities.

The rules set strict standards on using personal data from patients for marketing purposes. They prohibit drugstores from selling personal medical information to drug companies or other businesses that want to sell products or services. In the past, some drug companies have paid pharmacies for customer health information and used it to try to sell products to individuals with conditions such as osteoporosis, diabetes, or depression.

Enforcement, Compliance, and Penalties

OSHA attempts to control or shape the behavior of a regulated community through the enforcement of certain rules or commands monitored by compliance inspections, administrative adjudication, or the courts.

Obviously, employer compliance is influenced by the employer's awareness of the regulatory requirements. A randomly selected mail survey of almost 2,000 employers found that more than 50% reported little or no awareness of OSHA's Hazard Communication Standard (HCS) or were not knowledgeable about its key requirements.[20]

Significantly, the effectiveness of command-and-control regulation is influenced by the level of available regulatory resources and the sanctions for noncompliance. There are only approximately 2,000 compliance offices in the United States to enforce standards in more than 6.5 million workplaces. Historically, OSHA penalties have been inconsequential: The average penalty for a serious violation was $750 in fiscal year 1993; criminal sanctions are infrequent; and a conviction is rare. In comparison, the allowable legislative sanctions are quite severe. The maximum civil monetary penalties under OSHA are substantial (**Box 2-2**), ranging

---

Box 2-2

An Ohio children's hospital was cited and fined $21,250 for failure to require protective eye equipment where there was reasonable probability for injury . . . failure to use engineering and/or work practice controls to eliminate employees' exposure to hazardous substances . . . and failure to include the physical and health hazards of workplace chemicals in employee training.[23]

---

from thousands of dollars to $500,000, plus imprisonment in more severe cases.[21]

In addition to setting standards for the workplace, federal legislation affects individual healthcare providers. Seeking to improve the quality of health care, legislators have created some potentially high-liability risks for institutions that employ or contract with licensed healthcare practitioners.

Emergency Medical Treatment and Labor Act of 1986

The Emergency Medical Treatment and Labor Act of 1986 bars hospitals and physicians from ordering transfers of emergency patients or women in active labor until they are stabilized. "Dumping patients" through inappropriate transfers (**Box 2-3**), such as diverting patients via radio messages to ambulances or denying services to psychiatric patients, could incur fines of up to $50,000 per violation. Repeat offenders could be terminated from the Medicare program.[22]

Box 2-3

An uninsured patient arrived at the hospital in labor, with signs of fetal distress. She waited almost 12 hours without being admitted, was allegedly stabilized, and discharged. She returned 18 hours later, was transferred to a general hospital, underwent a cesarean section, and delivered an anemic baby who died within a few days. A federal court for Virginia ruled that the hospital had violated the anti-dumping statute, and that the baby had died as a direct and proximate cause of the hospital's negligence.[24]

Six hospitals have been terminated from Medicare participation since the law went into effect, but four of those have been recertified.

A report from the Public Citizens Health Research Group claimed that enforcement of the dumping law has lagged behind the increased complaints about the practice.[25] Extending the regulation, several courts have ruled that this law applies not only to patient dumping, but also to the more general allegations of inadequate care of insured patients.[26]

Mammography Quality Standards Act of 1992

Public Law 102-539 requires national uniform quality standards for mammography facilities, whether in a hospital, physician's office, mobile van, military base, or any other public or private enterprise. By October 1, 1994, all mammography facilities had to be certified by the Food and Drug Administration (FDA) or, alternatively, by the American College of Radiology. Facilities must apply for accreditation annually and submit to several procedures: a periodic review of clinical images; an annual survey by a medical physicist; and compliance with quality standards for equipment, personnel qualifications, quality assessment programs, record keeping, and reporting.[27–29]

Enhanced mammography regulations effective since April 28, 1999, are directed at ensuring that physicians and personnel are adequately trained and qualified to conduct mammography examinations and interpret mammograms. The requirements include reporting the results of mammograms quickly to physicians and patients (in lay terms) to avoid delay in follow-up testing and treatment.[30]

As of January 2012, almost 11,300 mammography units at 8,125 U.S. facilities had been accredited. Teaching hospitals must meet additional requirements for diagnostic residency training programs that specify the interpretation,

under direct supervision, of 240 mammographic examinations within six months of qualifying as an interpreting physician.[31]

Recent studies suggest that "radiologists are missing far more tumors than previously assumed." Physicians who interpret mammograms may be radiologists or other specialists, and their skills vary widely. Risk management opportunities exist for double-reading mammographies to uncover missed cancers and for physician failures to be interpreted appropriately. Federal emphasis has not been on the quality of physicians' practice, but rather on equipment design and performance characteristics (**Box 2-4**).[32]

Box 2-4   Radiology Lawsuits[33]

- Delayed diagnosis and failure to diagnose breast cancer are major causes of malpractice suits against radiologists.
- The most expensive claims are made against radiologists.
- The second most expensive claims are made against obstetrician/gynecologists and general surgeons.
- Most cases involve diagnostic issues rather than surgical or breast cancer treatment problems.

Safe Medical Devices Act of 1990

A report from the National Committee for Quality Health Care (NCQHC), a coalition of providers and manufacturers, urges mandatory federal FDA-like premarket review of emerging technology involving modified tests and treatments. From the viewpoint of its vested interest, the NCQHC seeks to curb inappropriate use of medical technology.[34] This group has recommended that medical and surgical procedures be required to demonstrate their clinical efficacy before being adopted outside the research setting. Currently, new drugs and devices must undergo rigorous

FDA premarket review, but no such requirements exist for emerging medical tests and treatments that do not involve a new product.[35] Critics of such requirements believe that a formal regulatory system could impede providers and delay access to promising new technology and procedures.

Responding to critics who have demanded speedier action, the FDA Modernization Act of 1997 allows many new devices to be marketed before they have undergone full-scale clinical trials. However, some devices have had little data available on their clinical efficacy and safety, and some manufacturers have submitted false data, hiding injuries, deaths, and malfunctions, and providing inadequate financial disclosures (**Box 2-5**).[36]

Box 2-5   Medical Device Failures

- A heart device lead used in 128,000 patients worldwide—the Riata, manufactured by Guidant—was said to cause death because some of its defibrillators could short-circuit. The internal wires also tended to break through the outer coating and cause electrical problems such as unintended shocks in some patients.[37]
- In 2007, Medtronic recalled a widely used lead called the Sprint Fidelis after reports emerged of the device cracking and failing in patients.[37]
- Pfizer and Shiley agreed to pay $10.75 million to settle claims and to monitor patients who had received a defective heart valve device.[38,39]
- Federal marshals impounded more than 2,000 sphygmomanometers from the Surgical Instrument Company of America because these devices allegedly had defective pressure gauges and leaking and torn inflator bladders.[40]
- Wire leads on 22,000 pacemakers manufactured by Telectronics Pacing Systems were declared a potentially lethal risk for patients with cardiac problems because of possible fractures in the wire leads, which could cause severe heart injury or death.[41,42]

Manufacturers of medical devices aver that liability concerns threaten their implant research activities. Since "there are no inert materials," the climate of litigation in the United States may "ultimately push device manufacturers to introduce their new devices in countries less prone to litigation."[43] Furthermore, in light of cost-containment restraints, healthcare organizations are considering the reuse of disposable medical devices. However, the FDA says that "providers that reuse disposable devices are liable for the products' safety and effectiveness."[44]

In the past decade, more than 2 million implanted devices have been recalled. Heart-device implants such as pacemakers, defibrillators, valves, and stents accounted for 800,000 (40%) of the recalls, and bone screws and plates for 470,000 units (23%). In addition, 66,000 breast implants and 27,000 penile implants were recalled. Use of recalled devices can have a catastrophic effect on patient care and patient outcomes. Best practices call for the use of computerized programs that notify end users of the recalled product with oversight by internal hospital committees.[45]

Risk managers must contemplate many possible causes of injury relative to medical devices: design defects, manufacturing defects, random component failure, packaging errors, user errors, idiosyncratic patient reaction, sabotage, faulty repair, or maintenance or calibration errors. Estimates attribute 50% to 80% of medical-device accidents directly to user error on the part of the patient, technician, physician, nurse, or other professional.[46]

Corporate giants in U.S. medical device production have been involved in regulatory sanctions invoked by the FDA.[47] In February 1994, for example, Siemens Medical Systems signed a consent decree stating that it had improperly manufactured certain devices, such as hearing aids, pacemakers, patient monitors, and ultrasound monitors. Siemens was granted time to correct the violations,[48] and by November 1994 the company had received approval from the FDA to resume marketing of its devices.[49]

Nearly 25 million Americans have one sort of implant or another, and medical devices continue to raise the specter of huge liability risks. For example, Sulzer Orthopedics of Austin, Texas, agreed to a $1 billion settlement in 2002 related to failed replacement hip joints. Boston Scientific Corporation faced more than 500 lawsuits from women who say they were injured by problems resulting from an implant to control incontinence.[50]

MedWatch

In June 1993, the FDA announced a new program, called MedWatch: The FDA Medical Products Reporting Program.[51] Because many health professionals do not routinely report adverse events, MedWatch was designed to encourage the voluntary reporting, by professionals and consumers,[52] of serious adverse events caused not only by medical devices, but also by biologics, dietary supplements, and drugs. Problems such as defective devices, inaccurate or unreadable product labeling, packing or product mix-up, contaminations or stability problems, and particulate matter in injectable products should be reported promptly.

Eight months after MedWatch was launched, 4,625 adverse events had been reported; 2,270 were drug reactions (64%) and 856 were device problems (20%). Pharmacists were the overwhelming source of reporting (2,531, or 55%), distantly followed by physicians (683, or 16%).

Importantly, many hospitals and physicians still do not report malfunctions of medical equipment as the law requires.[53]

Of concern to risk management, as many as 10% of hospital admissions in the United States are due to adverse reactions. If an adverse event occurs in the hospital, approximately two additional inpatient days, costing about $1,000 per day, are needed for the patient. Critically, as many as 75% of adverse drug reactions are preventable.[54] On a less positive note, a medical marketing trade journal alerted its readers in 1994 to the hidden negative aspects of MedWatch relative to their business concerns.[55]

On July 20, 2001, the FDA issued an advisory to hospitals and nursing homes concerning the misconnecting of oxygen delivery systems. From July 1997 to July 2001, the FDA received reports of 7 deaths and 15 injuries associated with such medical gas misconnections (**Box 2-6**).

Box 2-6   Medical Gas Mishaps[56]

- At the Hospital of St. Raphael's in Connecticut, two women died during diagnostic catheterization when they were given lethal doses of nitrous oxide instead of oxygen. A safety feature on the oxygen flow meter was missing.
- At a hospital in Ohio, two patients died after a medical gas deliverer used a wrench to disconnect the fitting on a vessel of nitrogen that he believed to be oxygen, and replaced it with an oxygen fitting.

Currently, there is also a proposal by the FDA for a new format for prescription drug product labeling, also known as the package insert. The current labeling has been criticized as being too lengthy, complex, and hard to use; the changes are designed to make the package insert more user friendly, in the hope of reducing medical errors.[57]

Baycol (Cerivastatin), a cholesterol-lowering drug, was pulled off the market by Bayer Corporation in response to 31 deaths due to severe rhabdomyolisis, an adverse muscle reaction reported to the FDA. At the time, more than 700,000 people were taking Baycol, which was approved in 1997.[58]

The CDC and the FDA have been investigating CryoLife Corporation after 27 people developed serious infections, and one died, after receiving soft-tissue implants processed by the company. Approximately 650,000 people each year in the United States have surgery involving soft-tissue implants, and CryoLife supplies 15% to 20% of the market. The company processes 70% of the nation's heart valves, and 90% of vascular tissue from human cadavers; it also supplies soft tissues such as tendons, ligaments, and cartilage for elective orthopedic surgery.[59]

Medical Waste Tracking Act of 1988

The Medical Waste Tracking Act of 1988 (MWTA) was a political response to the highly publicized hysteria over hypodermic needles that washed up onto the beaches of three states. Although the MWTA was a federal law, its mandates were limited to two years and applied only to Connecticut, New Jersey, New York, Rhode Island, and Puerto Rico. Participation was voluntary for any other state. The MWTA requires tracking of seven types of waste: cultures and stocks, pathological wastes, human blood and blood products, sharps, animal waste, isolation waste, and unused sharps. By 1991, when the MWTA expired, the problem had evaporated.

Regulations for hazardous waste, such as mercury or radioactive wastes, are also developed by the federal government. Potentially infectious medical waste, sometimes referred to as regulated medical waste, is generally covered by state regulations.

The MWTA required the Environmental Protection Agency (EPA) to investigate various treatment technologies available at the time for their ability to reduce the disease-causing potential of medical waste. The technologies that the EPA examined in 1990 included incinerators and autoclaves (both on-site and off-site), microwave units, and various chemical and mechanical systems. From the information gathered during this period, the EPA concluded that the disease-causing potential of medical waste is greatest at the point of generation and naturally tapers off after that point, thus presenting more of an occupational concern than a generalized environmental concern. Risk to the general public of disease caused by exposure to medical waste is likely to be much lower than the risk to the occupationally exposed individual.[60]

Environmental Protection Agency

Almost all medical waste is incinerated. The EPA promulgates regulations governing emissions from medical waste incinerations. The rationale of these regulations is to reduce substantially the amount of essentially harmful emissions from medical waste. In addition, many states have regulations that require the treatment of medical waste. Companies that handle medical waste are required to be certified, licensed, or regulated. Treated medical waste may be disposed of on solid landfills.

Although individual hospital incinerators are relatively small, an EPA report stated that, collectively, medical waste incineration by hospitals may be the largest source of airborne dioxin emissions in the United States.[61] Such emissions constitute a risk because the EPA has concluded that dioxin causes cancer in animals and is a probable human carcinogen. Hospitals use many disposable medical products typically made of chlorinated plastics. These waste materials, which have a high chlorine content, are burned, freeing the element during combustion to form dioxin. Often, medical waste incinerators lack technologies to reduce, control, and monitor toxic emissions into the air. Opponents of this method of waste disposal vehemently assert that medical waste should not be incinerated under any circumstances.[62] As of 1996, EPA regulations required hospitals using medical waste incinerators to eliminate toxic emissions and to monitor compliance. As a result, hospitals have changed the way they handle medical waste. In Florida, high-volume regional incinerators have replaced smaller on-site units. Since 1989, approximately 90 small hospital incinerators, representing 75% of Florida's total number, have shut down. In 1994, the Mayo Clinic in Rochester, Minnesota, opened a $10.6 million, state-of-the-art incinerator 10 miles north of the clinic. At this facility, advanced incineration technology is combined with an aggressive recycling program to reduce the volume of waste burned. This incinerator also accepts waste from other area hospitals.

Currently, more than 90% of potentially infectious medical waste is incinerated. In August 1997, the EPA promulgated regulations concerning emissions from medical waste incinerators (MWI). These regulations include (1) stringent air emissions guidelines for states to use in developing plans to reduce air pollution from medical waste incinerators built on or before June 20, 1996, and (2) final air emission standards for medical waste incinerators built after June 20, 1996. These guidelines and standards should substantially reduce MWI emissions. The EPA estimates that mercury emission

will decline by 94%, particulate matter by 90%, hydrogen chloride by 98%, and dioxin by 95%.

On June 24, 1998, the EPA entered into a voluntary partnership with the American Hospital Association (AHA) and its member hospitals to (1) virtually eliminate mercury waste generated by hospitals by 2005; (2) reduce overall hospital waste volume by 33% by 2005, and 50% by 2010; and (3) jointly identify additional substances to target for pollution prevention and waste reduction opportunities.[60]

Regulatory Implementation Mandates

Legislation allows governmental agencies to audit and survey healthcare facilities to determine whether each institution is abiding by regulatory standards. These audits and surveys can be accomplished through personal visits, written questionnaires, or telephone inquiries. They may be by appointment or random, without notice to the agency, such as by the state health department.[63]

Inspectors have the power to review the physical plant and the operations of facilities, and to examine documentation. Serious violations can result in a loss of a license to operate as well as in monetary fines. Risk managers must ensure that the organization is prepared at all times for an unannounced or unexpected audit or survey.

STATE LEGISLATION AND REGULATIONS

Historically, general health regulation has been a matter of local concern.[64] Healthcare facilities such as hospitals, skilled nursing facilities, intermediate nursing facilities, and managed care entities require a license before they can become operational. Individual professionals such as physicians, dentists, registered nurses, physical therapists, and psychologists must have a state license or state registration before they can render care to their clients.

Reacting to "oppressive healthcare regulations," in 1994 New York's governor revised 16 edicts, including those mandating on-site inspections, hospital social work departments, the education and experience requirements for emergency room staffs, the explanation to all patients of their rights, and the indicators for reporting adverse events.[65] A *New York Times* editorial labeled the plan "a modest easing of hospital regulations."[66] This action by a state governor follows the example set at the federal level of reducing the government's involvement in the regulation of industry. New Jersey legislators also considered reforming 25 years of a tight rein over healthcare facilities and services,[67] but not before flexing their regulatory power again (**Box 2-7**).

Box 2-7

Blue Cross/Blue Shield of New Jersey was fined $106,000 for setting up a string of family health centers without prior approval from the state health department. These centers were part of a $13 million network of 10 centers to serve 200,000 managed care policyholders.[68]

The sections that follow look at some examples of state regulation of the healthcare industry.

Licensure and Registration of Professional Institutions

State governments have always had the responsibility of licensing healthcare professionals and defining the parameters of their practices. All of the states' license professionals such as physicians, dentists, and registered nurses, but not all license or register providers such as physical and occupational therapists. Licensing or registration remains a state prerogative and is subject to change. In addition, legislation concerned with professional malpractice is embedded in state tort law that deals with civil and criminal injury and harm. **Box 2-8** raises a malpractice question and answers with a real example.

Box 2-8

Should an insurer deny malpractice coverage to a nurse who rendered a service that, under statute, is defined as "medical" practice? Nurse Valerie Tomlinson was suspended from the Royal Cornwall Hospital for operating on a patient.[69]

Smoke-Free Workplace

More than 40 states have enacted legislation to restrict smoking in public places, including healthcare facilities, and many states regulate smoking in the workplace. Civil court judges in California, Georgia, and Ohio have found that "battery," which usually entails touching people against their will, can apply to second-hand cigarette, cigar, or pipe smoke (**Box 2-9**).

Box 2-9

Bank receptionist Bonnie Richardson claimed that a colleague maliciously directed pipe smoke at her. She went to the hospital twice for severe headaches, nausea, and weight loss. She sued and won. A judge for the Georgia State Appeals Court declared: "Pipe smoke is visible. It is detectable through the senses and may be ingested or inhaled. It is capable of touching or making contact with one's person in a number of ways."[70]

Although many states and cities have adopted laws restricting smoking in public places, when it comes to enforcement, such laws are usually regarded as self-policing.[71] Efforts to eliminate the risk of secondhand cigarette smoke were stimulated by a 500-page 1992 report from the EPA that estimated 3,000 deaths occur each year from such exposure.[72] Even small amounts of smoke can endanger non-smokers and may double or triple their risk of heart disease.[73] Indoor air quality regulations are evolving to protect workers from various outdoor contaminants and to control microbial contaminants by routine inspection.[74,75]

Smoke-Free Environment

About one in five Americans still smokes, and smoking remains the leading cause of preventable deaths. Employees who smoke cost, on average, $3,391 more per year each for health care and lost productivity, according to federal estimates.[76]

Many states have enacted the Clean Indoor Air Act, which prohibits smoking in any indoor area of a place of employment. Hospitals are required to comply with this act by prohibiting smoking by patients, visitors, and employees. Regulations prohibit smokers from coming within 25 feet of the entrance to a building, including emergency entrances, and within 50 feet of loading docks. Each facility is required to have a Clean Indoor Act agent. An institution may facilitate compliance with the posting of signs and implementation of policies and procedures. Hospitals in Florida, Georgia, Massachusetts, Missouri, Ohio, Pennsylvania, Tennessee, and Texas, among others, stopped hiring smokers in the last year, and more are openly considering the option.

Violence Prevention

California passed a law requiring all hospitals to provide training and education in security measures. All hospitals were required to initiate violence prevention programs effective July 1995. This legislation was prompted by statistics revealing that almost 60% of the hospitals in the five largest cities in the state had reported attacks on staff, patients, and visitors.[77] Beefing up security was particularly critical for emergency rooms. A survey by the journal *Topics in Emergency Medicine* reported that 43% of hospitals experienced at least one physical attack per month on a medical staff member (**Box 2-10**).[78]

Box 2-10
Danbury Hospital in Connecticut was cited and fined by OSHA for failing to provide its employees with sufficient protection against workplace violence.[79] • In March 2010, a nurse was shot three times by an 86-year-old patient at the hospital. • Another 25 employees were forced to go on restricted duty because of injuries inflicted upon them by patients.

STATE-MANDATED RISK MANAGEMENT LEGISLATION

Several states have passed legislation or promulgated regulations requiring hospitals to implement risk management programs. In most of these states, risk management requirements are specifically designed to interrelate with other quality assessment initiatives in the hospital environment. Significantly, the requirements are made a condition for the hospital's licensure by the state. Generally, the mandates focus on preventing and controlling risk to patients, rather than on risks such as fire prevention, equipment maintenance, safety, and security. Preventive methods include a root-cause analysis (RCA) or in-depth analysis as to the cause of adverse events or medical errors. Common causes of medical errors include miscommunication and lack of communication during handoffs. Other high-risk causes may involve errors in medication or delays in diagnosis and delays in treatment.

Not every state mandates every risk management characteristic. Nevertheless, a framework has emerged for implementing a basic risk management program in all instances.

Risk Management Responsibility

Depending on the state, hospitals must assign risk management responsibility to a single risk management coordinator or to a committee. In some instances, states can choose between the two.

Governing Body Involvement

The CMS requires governing body involvement, whose emphasis ranges from ensuring that the governing body provides an adequate level of resources and support systems to a minimal requirement that the governing body formally approve a risk management and patient safety and quality plan with periodic updates. States can require that the governing board or hospital administrator receive reports on the risk management program. Reporting requirements vary from a general statement to specific language calling for quarterly reports. A few states mandate that a member of the governing body also be a member of the risk management and/or quality assessment committee.

Governing body involvement in risk management in adverse events involving transplant and organ donation is specifically required.

Risk Identification

Most states require systems to identify as well as report risks to patients. Legislative wording can be general, without establishing procedures, or it can be specific. Sometimes the legislation specifies the types of incidents to be reported by hospital staff, the patient grievance data required, and the additional quality assessment information demanded. Colorado, for example, commands its hospitals to submit for state approval a general description of the types of cases, problems, or risks to be reviewed, and the criteria to be used for identifying potential risks. Massachusetts's detailed requirements call for three risk identification methods: incident reporting, occurrence reporting, and occurrence screening. New York mandates reporting based on established criteria, with requirements for submission of completed RCA and corrective actions.

Risk Analysis

Legislative mandates for risk analysis can range from a general obligation to specifics such as what to include in such analysis (e.g., frequency and causes of injuries, time, place, persons involved).

Risk Management Education

State legislation can specify topics to include in risk management activities, can compel annual risk management education for designated staff, or can merely call for educational programs without giving a time frame. Examples of relevant subject matter include injury prevention, patient safety, principles and techniques of infection control, incident reporting or staff responsibility to report professional misconduct, legal aspects of care, causes of malpractice claims, patients' rights, improved communications, and topics related to employees' job responsibilities. Staff education can be mandated for all staff, for appropriate staff, or for staff engaged in patient care activities. One state excludes physicians from the education requirement. The CMS regulations require annual evaluation of risk management progress enforcement, to be carried out through local health departments.

Sharing of Information

Colorado obliges hospitals to coordinate all pertinent case, problem, or risk review information with other applicable institutional quality assessment or risk management activities. Maryland requires "a flow of information" among quality assessment, credentialing, peer review, and any risk management committees. North Carolina dictates "operational linkages" between risk management and other functions relating to patient care, safety, and staff performance. New York orders hospitals to review an extensive array of information, including quality assessment data, complaints, incident reports, and utilization review data, to identify problems in patient care. Massachusetts indicates that credentialing, quality assessment, risk management, and peer review functions should be strongly and thoroughly integrated. Many states have legislative requirements on credentialing information. Under CMS regulations, hospitals are required to consider a physician's ongoing practice performance upon reevaluation.

New York, Washington, Maryland, and Kansas specifically require that a quality assessment or peer review committee be responsible for acting to correct identified problems.

Patient Grievance Procedures

All patients are required to be given the Patient's Bill of Rights within four hours of admission to a hospital. In addition, breastfeeding mothers are required to be given a Mother's Bill of Rights in some states, such as New York. The Patient's Bill of Rights requires informed consent for medical treatment and informed consent for surgical and invasive procedures to be given to the physician of record. Lack of proper notification is often the cause for many medical malpractice litigation cases. In the event that a patient refuses treatment, a physician may treat the patient to save his or her life. Patients also have the right of privacy, the right to receive treatment information in their primary language, and the right to nondiscrimination.

Most states regard patient grievance data as an important element in their risk management requirements. Maryland detailed its mandates for a patient complaint program with four specific requirements:

- Risk management and quality programs must include a formal written program for addressing patient complaints.
- Patients must be given information about the program, including the name and phone number or address of a hospital representative whom the patient may contact to register a complaint.
- A hospital representative must treat the complaining patient with dignity, courtesy, and due regard for privacy, and must provide the patient with certain information about the complaint-handling process.
- A hospital representative must document the complaint and any action taken as a result of it and respond to the patient within seven days.

Massachusetts requires that all patients receive written notice of their rights within 24 hours of admission and be informed about how to file complaints. Alaska's general requirement orders the hospital to have a procedure to investigate, analyze, and respond to patient grievances related to patient care.

Immunity and Confidentiality for Providers of Risk Management Information

Seven states grant immunity from liability to those who provide information on adverse incidents; six provide for confidentiality. Immunity and confidentiality provisions have two goals: (1) to shield those who report or evaluate risk management information and (2) to protect privileged risk management records from subpoena, discovery, or other public disclosure.

Risk Management Follow-Up Procedures

Legislation and/or regulations may require a follow-up or review of a hospital's specific risk management actions and can include a summary report of risk management actions to the governing body. New York and Colorado oblige hospitals to institute a method for evaluating the effectiveness of actions taken to address risks or problems. Maryland mandates that hospitals establish an internal committee structure to conduct reviews and evaluations of risk management activities. Massachusetts obligates hospitals to create a system to ensure compliance with incident reporting requirements.

LOCAL CITY AND COUNTY LEGISLATION CONTROLS

Regulations and rules that affect risk management may be created at city and county levels. Although city and county legislative bodies often adopt and/or adapt federal and state requirements, local variants may exist. For example, a city health department may enact its own regulations, such as procedures for the reporting of tuberculosis or communicable diseases of a sensitive nature (e.g., positive lab results for sexually transmitted diseases), guidelines for sanitation and disposal of hazardous waste, restrictions on the transport of radioactive and nuclear materials through city streets, and the functions of patient advocates. Likewise, a county water department may set thresholds for purification chemicals added to drinking water or to be found in waste water. Building codes, fire safety regulations, and occupancy permits are generally a function of local government. A risk manager should be aware of the major laws and regulations at all levels of government.

REIMBURSEMENT REQUIREMENTS

Third-party insurers set their own standards for reimbursement to providers and to the insured parties. Usually, the insurers establish an indemnification system wherein the providers agree to reimbursement standards such as accepting whatever fee schedule the insurer establishes as the total payment, accepting predefined amounts for specific services but billing the patient for any differential from their regular fee, or agreeing to a discount off their usual and customary fee. Some variations on these standards involve a patient out-of-pocket copayment or coinsurance. Private insurance companies may also set their own standards for the types of services for which they will pay and for when the services are appropriate.

Managed care organizations negotiate their reimbursement fees with individual practitioners, with clinical groups, and with hospitals. Significantly, these reimbursement guidelines can include financial incentives or disincentives. On the one hand, if practitioners reduce their referrals and hospitalizations, they may receive a bonus from any surplus funds. On the other hand, if practitioners use too many resources in rendering care, the potential bonus could be reduced. Such financial awards or punishments must always be within the standards for quality of care that the managed care entity establishes. Despite their critics, health maintenance organizations (HMOs) and preferred provider organizations (PPOs) maintain that their subscribers receive whatever medical care is appropriate; no medically necessary care is denied. Serious arguments have erupted about the financial incentives in health care, and the money/care relationship raises liability issues in terms of risk management.

Obtaining reimbursement from public entities requires adhering to these entities, respective standards as well. Medicare is a federal insurance program, and its standards are uniform for the entire nation. Under this program, fees are calculated based on federal determinations. Medicaid, in contrast, is a combined federal/state/local financing program with 50 different standards as established by each of the 50 states. Each state also determines its own of reimbursement policies for the medicaid program.

Through a prospective payment system using a payment mechanism of diagnosis-related groups (DRGs), the federal Health Care Financing Administration (HCFA) requires that every Medicare patient be classified into one of the approximately 500 DRGs for the care-providing institution to receive payment for services rendered. Furthermore, the HCFA sets a length of stay for each DRG, and providers must explain why patients are remaining in the facility if the outside limit of the length of stay is exceeded.[80]

A resources-based relative value scale (RBRVS) is another potential reimbursement mechanism for services rendered by providers. The RBRVS aims to set fees for ambulatory care provided by physicians. Generally, the reimbursement relies on a written calculation of the relative value of specific procedures as compared to an initial base service. In essence, a price is set by agreement with the insurers, and standards are implemented to follow the rules. Violations could disqualify the facility or the caregiving individuals from providing care to people covered by that insurer.

Federal Medicare Incentives to Improve Quality of Care

The emergence of evidence-based medicine has been generally accepted since 1995 as essential to effective and safe medical practice.[81,82] These practices include administration of aspirin and beta blockers to patients with heart attack and heart failure smoking cessation advice for coronary patients, pneumococcal vaccinations given to pneumonia inpatients, proper antibiotics administered within proper time frames for surgical patients, and prompt percutaneous intervention among heart attack patients. The linkage to patient safety emerged due to the impact of two seminal works published by the Institute of Medicine entitled *Crossing the Quality Chasm*[83] and

To Err Is Human.[84] In addition, there has been a recent impetus to use evidence-based medicine to augment or replace the time-consuming practice of an evidence-based clinical trial.

Pay for Posting: The Deficit Reduction Act of 2003

Pay-for-posting had its origins in the Deficit Reduction Act of 2003.[85] The CMS, under the auspices of the U.S. Department of Health and Human Services (HHS) in collaboration with the Hospital Quality Alliance (HQA), the Agency for Healthcare Research in Quality (AHRQ), The Joint Commission, the National Committee for Quality Assurance (NCQA), and the American Medical Association (AMA), mandated that inpatient institutions submit for posting their adherence to process-based measures of health care.

Pay-for-posting is part of HHS's broader National Quality Initiative, which focuses on an initial set of 10 quality measures ("core measures") by linking reporting of those measures to the payments hospitals receive for each discharge. Hospitals that submit the required data receive

the full payment update to their Medicare DRG payments. Nearly all (98.3%) of the hospitals eligible to participate in this program are complying with the requirements of the provision. This high rate is due not only to the desire *not* to lose the full payment update, but also the posting on the HHS website "Hospital Compare."[86] In addition, many private payers use these core measures, along with other patient safety data, to evaluate hospitals for suitability of payment. The HHS program employs evidence-based medicine, along with other patient safety practices, to address the problems publicized in the Institute of Medicine publications (**Table 2-2**).

Several years after the implementation of the core measures, a set of measures covering the patient satisfaction domain was added to the pay-for-posting program. These measures looked at not only physician-to-patient and nurse-to-patient communication, hospital staff responsiveness, pain management, and discharge information, but also external situations such as quiet and cleanliness of the hospital. An overall rating of the hospital topped off the set of the component measures. These measures were also posted to HHS's "Hospital Compare" website.

Table 2-2   Set of Core Measures (Pay-for-Posting) for a Model Midsize Hospital in 2003

Core Measures	Hospital Performance	90th or More Percentile	State Average	National Average
Acute Myocardial Infarction	88%	100%	94%	92%
Aspirin at discharge	86%	99%	93%	96%
Beta blockers at arrival	78%	100%	84%	88%
Beta blockers at discharge	92%	95%	94%	93%
ACEI-ARBS for LVSD*	100%	100%	98%	95%
Heart Failure				
LVSD assessment	88%	90%	66%	77%
ACEI for AVSD*	92%	94%	79%	91%
Pneumonia				
Antibiotics within 4 hours	74%	89%	85%	84%
Oxygenation assessment	99%	100%	99%	99%
Pneumococcal vaccination	53%	100%	70%	68%

*ACEI-ARBS for LVSD: angiotensin converting enzyme inhibitors–angiotensin receptor blockers for left ventricular systolic dysfunction
*ACEI for AVSD: angiotensin converting enzyme inhibitors for atrial ventricular systolic dysfunction

Evolution from Pay-for-Posting to Pay-for-Performance

The years from 2005 to 2009 brought about three changes: a net expansion of process-based core measures, the retirement of measures that were "topped off" (i.e., those attaining 100% compliance), and the incorporation of new outcome measures. The process-based core measures included several surgical care improvement project (SCIP) points dealing with proper antibiotic administration, body hair shaving, and other issues. The new outcome measures were 30-day postdischarge mortality and 30-day postdischarge readmissions based upon Medicare-covered, age 65-plus discharges. These outcome measures, along with the patient satisfaction measures, were risk adjusted to make the outcomes as comparable as possible across institutions given differences in inpatient demography and comorbidity.

Value-Based Purchasing

What was notable about this new round of changes was that not only were hospitals required to post their performance on process and outcome measures, but also that these measures formed the basis for "value-based purchasing."[87] Value-based purchasing (VBP) is defined as a payment reform under which hospitals and other providers are given bonuses based on their performance against quality measures. Put another way, VBP includes any purchasing practice aimed at improving the value of healthcare services, where value is a function of quality and cost.[88]

The Patient Protection and Affordable Care Act of 2010[89] mandated that the CMS, starting with federal fiscal year 2013 (FFY 2013), hold back 1% of an institution's inpatient prospective payment system (IPPS) base operating payments

(called the VBP contribution percentage). This 1% is to be "earned back"—in part, in full, or in excess—by performance on selected core measures. In each subsequent year, this percentage will increase by 0.25%. The VBP program is self-funded; that is, the sum of monies earned by institutions in excess of the 1% withhold will equal the monies *lost* by institutions that do not meet the performance criteria to earn back the 1% withhold. For FFY 2013, the performance criteria will consist of several process and patient satisfaction measures. In FFY 2014, they will also include 30-day postdischarge mortality measures for principal diagnoses of acute myocardial infarction, heart failure, and pneumonia. This system is intended to pay for care that rewards better value and patient outcomes rather than volume of services.

Scores and Withhold Determination

Beginning in FFY 2013, the amount of "earn back" on the withhold will be determined by weighting the "process of care scores" (selected core measures) by 70%, and "patient experience of care scores" (i.e., patient satisfaction) by 30%. The "process of care" domain will consist of 12 measures: one covering myocardial infarctions—primary percutaneous intervention received within 90 minutes, one addressing heart failure discharge instructions, two addressing pneumonia, and surgical care accounts for the remaining measures. The "patient experience of care" domain will consist of eight measures covering communication, pain management, environmental conditions, and a summary rating. Each measure will earn from 0 to 10 points, with patient care potentially earning a "consistency score" that is also in the range of 0 to 10 points. All scores in each domain will be summed and weighted appropriately. The scores are based on two global criteria: *achievement* and *improvement*. The steps in deriving the scores are as follows:

1. A baseline period—from July 1, 2009, to March 31, 2010—will apply for the appropriate measures.
2. A performance period—from July 1, 2011, to March 31, 2012—will also apply to these measures.
3. The *achievement score* is calculated by comparing a hospital's current performance to all hospitals' baseline performance. If a hospital attains the benchmark (the mean of the top deciles—usually close to, if not equal to, 100%), it earns 10 points. If it falls within the achievement threshold (usually the 50th percentile of all hospitals' performance on that measure), it earns a score of 1 to 9, based on the performance between the threshold and the benchmark.
4. The *improvement score* for a measure is the improvement recorded based on performance in the performance period compared with the baseline period. The baseline for determining improvement points may actually fall below the achievement threshold; the improvement score is based on where the hospital stands at the end of the performance period relative to the benchmark.
5. The higher of either the achievement or improvement score is taken for each measure, then summed across the measures. This sum is weighted by 70% and called the *clinical process domain score.*
6. The *patient experience domain score* is calculated in a similar fashion, but the scoring is based on a "floor" (the lowest score nationally on a measure), the

threshold (50th percentile nationally) and the benchmark (95th percentile). If an institution does not earn any points either on the achievement or improvement dimensions (this applies if *no* score reaches the threshold), it can still earn up to 20 points for consistency; that is, points are awarded if an institution's scores are all better than the floor, and all approach the threshold.

The score is plotted on the *x*-axis of an approximately 45-degree line. The corresponding value on the *y*-axis is the VBP payment percentage. If this percentage is 100%, the institution receives all its contribution, or withhold. If it is greater than 100%, then it receives its contribution plus the percentage above 100%. If it is less than 100%, then it receives correspondingly less. The CMS reserves the right to adjust the slope of the VBP payment line according to budgetary factors.

For FFY 2014, the clinical process domain scores will be weighted by 45% instead of 70%. While the patient experience of care weighting will still be 30%, the remaining 25% will be based on an *outcomes* measure—namely, 30-day postdischarge mortality for Medicare patients with primary diagnoses of acute myocardial infarction, heart failure, or pneumonia. The risk-adjusted mortality rates will be compared via rank-ordering with all participating institutions nationally.

For example, for a midsize hospital based in the northeastern United States for FFY 2013 and FFY 2014, illustrative data may be derived from the "Hospital Compare" website.[86] This hospital has performed slightly under the national norm on the process of domain score, and relatively poorly on the patient experience of care score; however, it has earned consistency points. For FFY 2014, this institution will have earned outstanding scores on risk-adjusted mortality outcomes that are currently posted on "Hospital Compare" (**Table 2-3**).

1. *Total Performance Score.* This score reflects the change in weightings from FFY 2013 to FFY 2014. Despite lower scores on the first two domains, superior performance on the outcomes domain

results in a higher total performance score for FFY 2014.

2. *Linear Payout Function Factor.* The slope of the payout line, with the total performance score on the *x*-axis, and the VBP payment percentage on the *y*-axis. As scores are expected to improve nationwide due to monetary incentives, the slope will decrease, requiring even higher performance to maintain the same payback from the withhold.

Table 2-3 Value-Based Purchasing for a Model Midsize Hospital, Estimates for FFY 2013 and FFY 2014		
VBP Score Estimates	**FFY 2013 Program**	**FFY 2014 Program**
a. Process of Care Domain Score	42.73%	34.17%
b. Patient Experience of Care Domain Score	8.00%	7.00%
c. Outcomes Domain Score	Not applicable	93.33%
d. Total Performance Score (TPS) FFY 2013 = (a * 30% + b * 70%); FFY 2014 = (a * 45% + b * 30% + c * 25%)	32.31%	40.81%
Estimate Based on Most Recent "Hospital Compare" Data Posting		
e. Linear Payout Function Factor (slope of payout line—based on funds devoted)	2.43	3.07
f. VBP Payment Percentage (d * e)	78.48%	125.22%
VBP Contribution Amount		
g. Estimated Total Inpatient Prospective Payment System	$29,179,100	$29,646,000
h. VBP Program Contribution Percentage	1.00%	1.25%
i. VBP Program Contribution (g * h)	$291,800	$370,600
VBP Redistribution		
j. VBP Payout (i * f)	$229,000	$464,100
k. Net VBP Gain/(Loss)	($62,800)	$93,500

3. *VBP Payment Percentage.* The result on the *y*-axis.
4. *Estimated Total Inpatient Prospective Payment System Base Operating Payments.* The amount expected to be paid to the hospital by CMS.
5. *VBP Contribution Percentage.* The percentage withhold for that particular fiscal year; it is expected to increase annually.
6. *VBP Program Contribution.* The withhold.
7. *VBP Payout.* The VBP payment percentage (from the *y*-axis) times the withhold.
8. *Net Gain/Loss.* Payout minus the withhold.

The Future of Value-Based Purchasing

What lies in the immediate future? The diffusion of the electronic health record (with substantial financial incentives currently being provided for its implementation) should ease the identification of risk, and facilitate good performance in value-based purchasing. Moreover, there has been, and will continue to be, an evolution away from process measures to outcome measures. These value-based purchasing results have financial implications for reimbursement to the hospital. Improvement in the scores of these indicators will result in increases in the quality of care, financial benefit, and the reduction of risk.

FALSE CLAIMS

In reimbursement, "bundling" and "unbundling" refer to the manner in which services are billed. When care is rendered as a package with all the resources included in the billed amount, the services are said to be bundled together. Unbundled services are itemized and billed for separately.

Regulations need to be checked to determine whether revenue flow can be increased by unbundling individual items of care. Whereas inpatient care services may be bundled together in a set fee for each DRG, outpatient care may not be reimbursed in a similar fashion. To enable unbundling, facilities could convert selected inpatient services to outpatient services, assuming that such conversions were feasible and pose no harm to patients.

Anti-fraud activities of the federal government under the regulations of the False Claims Act (FCA) range from audits of hospitals, nursing homes, medical care organizations, and practicing health professionals to targeted medical care claims. It is estimated that there is a direct monetary return of $8 for each $1 invested in FCA enforcement activities.[90] To date, regulatory actions have, for example, resulted in a $30 million settlement with the University of Pennsylvania and a $5.3 million fine at Georgetown University.[91] Under July 1996 regulations for teaching hospitals, the federal government also started PATH (Physicians at Teaching Hospitals) audits (**Box 2-11**).

Box 2-11

Thomas Jefferson University paid $12 million to settle charges that faculty claimed reimbursement for patients treated by residents.[92]

The FCA allows the government, as well as private citizens, to sue individuals or companies that are defrauding the government, and to recover three times the damages plus additional penalties. In Pennsylvania, 11 hospitals and their consultants were charged with upcoding, unbundling, and rebundling Medicare claims to increase their reimbursement. Physicians or institutions found guilty of fraudcharges can be excluded from participation in Medicare, Medicaid, and other federal programs (**Box 2-12**).

> **Box 2-12 False Claims**
>
> - Good Samaritan Hospital agreed to pay $793,548 to settle allegations that it submitted false claims to federal health benefit programs for four years. Patients were made to appear worse off in the claims to create higher reimbursement rates.[93]
> - Tenet Healthcare Corporation paid almost $43 million to settle allegations of overbilling Medicare in 2007 for inpatient rehabilitation care when patients did not qualify for such an admission.[94]

The reward provision under FCA allows whistleblowers a 15% to 25% share of the total amount the government recovers. Whistleblowers are encouraged and protected, and could be employees or competitors. Lawsuits initiated by whistleblowers are called *qui tam* cases.

PRACTICE GUIDELINES

Voluntary regulatory programs, such as those operated by The Joint Commission, the National Committee for Quality Assurance, and board certification programs offered by professional specialty societies, have a decided impact on risk management considerations. Healthcare institutions may be denied reimbursement by government programs and third-party insurers if they are not accredited by The Joint Commission.[95,96] With the increased competition in the healthcare field, voluntary accreditation can be used in marketing and advertising activities, given that the public views such accreditation as evidence of high-quality care.

The Joint Commission's nationwide prominence in promoting high-quality health care has influenced most state regulatory agencies to accept its findings when considering accreditation and/or licensure applications. Third-party insurers rely on TJC decisions in reimbursement matters. On the federal level, HHS accepts TJC accreditation as evidence that the institution meets the Medicare conditions of participation. That recognition allows the provider to bill for services rendered to individuals having Medicare coverage.

Disturbingly, a 1992 validation sample by the federal HCFA of TJC-accredited hospitals revealed that one of three failed to meet Medicare/Medicaid standards. The October 1994 *Health Letter* of the Public Citizens Health Research Group reported that 57 (34%) of 167 hospitals failed to meet one or more of the federal conditions of participation. Profound questions can be raised about the safety and quality of care rendered at such facilities. This validation sample suggests that between 1,000 and 1,900 hospitals may have placed millions of patients at risk without timely intervention by The Joint Commission, raising serious questions as to whether government regulators should continue to rely on this organization for hospitals' accreditations.[97]

The Joint Commission sponsors accreditation programs for seven different types of health care: ambulatory health care, home care, hospice care, long-term care, psychiatric facilities, hospital care, and managed care. Each of these accreditation programs develops standards and uses a peer-based consultative and educational survey process to stimulate the provision of high-quality patient care. In addition, each accreditation program encompasses a variety of organizations and providers:

- Ambulatory care: clinics, surgery centers, college or university health services, community health centers, emergency care centers, group practices, primary care centers, and urgent care centers.
- Home care and hospice care: independent programs, home healthcare agencies, hospital-based programs, long-term care organizations, and psychiatric agencies. Areas covered include home visits by healthcare professionals, setting up equipment, education of family members providing care, homemaker services, drug administration in the home, personal services such as shopping, and support services such as lawn mowing.
- Long-term care: hospital-based care, freestanding care, nursing homes, rehabilitation centers, and custodial facilities.
- Psychiatric facilities: community mental health services, programs for the developmentally disabled, forensic psychiatric services, substance abuse programs, and psychiatric services.
- Hospital care: approximately 75% of the general and specialty hospitals in the United States accredited by The Joint Commission.
- Managed care: a variety of developing managed care entities, such as HMOs, PPOs, and individual practice associations (IPAs).

In recent years, a few prominent organizations have been granted "deemed status" by the federal government to conduct surveys. These surveys seek to determine whether hospitals provide timely, appropriate, and efficient care as well as qualifying institutions for federal government reimbursements.

Standards may be implemented within an institution, and apply only in that facility, through utilization management, quality assessment, and peer review. *Utilization management* tends to focus on the efficacious and effective use of resources. *Quality assessment* aims to ensure that the procedures followed abide by the internal standards and guidelines. For example, new criteria for reporting an occurrence as a sentinel event have been issued by The Joint Commission;[98] failure to comply with the reporting requirement will place the facility on accreditation-watch status. Incidents must be reported to The Joint Commission when a patient is affected by circumstances such as the following: an event resulting in an unanticipated death or major loss of function not related to the natural course of the patient's illness or underlying condition; suicide during continuous care; infant abduction or discharge to the wrong family; rape; hemolytic transfusion involving the administration of blood or blood products having major group incompatibilities; or surgery on the wrong patient or body part.

Peer review occurs in tissue committees, mortality conferences, infection control committees, and quality improvement committees.

In addition to these activities that implement standards, organizations usually have their own mandates regarding admissions, readmissions within a brief time period for the same condition, appropriate laboratory and diagnostic tests, repeated surgery for the same problem, length of stay, the process of care, and discharge planning (**Box 2-13**). Risk managers must be alert to any

---

Box 2-13

The Department of Veterans Affairs issued an advisory to its physicians recommending that they no longer perform arthroscopic surgery on the knee. A study by VA researchers concluded that it was no more effective than placebo arthroscopy.[99]

violations of internal standards, as they have a direct relationship to outside regulatory requirements. Most of these internal guidelines could have an impact on reimbursement from third-party insurers.

To complicate the situation, internal requirements may be duplicated by outside organizations. Notable examples include The Joint Commission, the Medicare and Medicaid programs, the Institute of Medicine, the Agency for Health Care Policy and Research, the National Committee for Quality Assurance, and a variety of specialty professional societies. Risk management programs can use these outside standards as the minimum on which to establish their internal guidelines. If internal standards are better than the outside guides, violations and penalties are less likely.

What If Practice Guidelines Are Not Met?

Failure to fulfill the legal obligation to provide a quality of care that meets professional standards constitutes a breach of standards. Although medical malpractice awards may occupy the mass-media headlines, the reality is that the majority of Americans do not sue their healthcare providers. Legislation, as noted in **Box 2-14**, has attempted to raise the mandated level of physician competence.

Box 2-14

A legislative bill sought to change the physician competence standard from requiring "a preponderance of credible evidence" to requiring "clear and convincing evidence," a tougher standard. A newspaper editorial noted that the doctors would move from the same standard that applies to lawyers to a more stringent level.[100]

Falls are the most common adverse event reported by healthcare institutions. An elderly patient may fall from a bed because its railings are missing, an employee or a visitor may slip on a wet floor when a warning sign is absent, and a nurse may be stuck by a needle if syringes are not disposed of correctly. All of these incidents are covered in the practice guidelines and training of healthcare workers—and all are preventable.

Hospital-acquired conditions such as pressure ulcers and catheter-related urinary tract infections are indicators of quality of care that have been a major target for reduction by hospitals in recent years. These adverse events contribute to the increased healthcare costs. In 2012, the federal government awarded $350 billion to 25 Hospitals in Engagement Networks under its Partnership for Patients Initiative. A 40% reduction in readmissions to hospitals is one goal of this project; the overall objective is to transform the culture of health care to one of prevention, thereby addressing the waste of resources in health care.

In the healthcare environment, potential damages from breaches of standards could include physical, emotional, social, and/or environmental harm. An individual could receive merely bumps and bruises, or could be permanently disabled or even die. Embarrassment, humiliation, and mental distress are typical allegations included under "pain and suffering" in lawsuits related to adverse events. Breakage and structural damages may also be involved. The damages envisioned appear to be limited only by the creativity of the people suing the healthcare facility.

A broad range of damage outcomes are possible, including censure, personnel action, monetary loss from fines, loss of individual practitioner privileges, facility closures and/or reductions, loss of licensure, loss of accreditation, a professional or criminal negligence lawsuit, imprisonment, loss of confidence in the facility, revenue stream disruption, mergers, bankruptcy, and corporate dissolution.

Ignorance of the Law Is No Excuse

Numerous complicated laws, regulations, and standards seriously affect the management of risks in healthcare institutions. Violations of these mandates can result in fines and penalties that could damage the healthcare facility's financial well-being. Risk management personnel help prepare for regulatory or voluntary inspections, maintain documentation relative to administrative and clinical issues mandated by good operations, and establish appropriate oversight of the medical care provided by the agency or hospital. To carry out these functions effectively, risk managers must initiate mechanisms to learn about all the laws, regulations, and standards, on federal, state, and local levels, and to implement risk prevention and control activities.

REFERENCES

1. Speigel, A. D., & Backhaut, B. H. (1980). *Curing and caring: A review of the factors affecting the quality and acceptability of health care.* New York: SP Medical & Scientific Books, pp. 22–27.
2. Joint Commission on Accreditation of Healthcare Organizations. (2001, October). *Device vise: Joint Commission enforcing OSHA needle mandate, hospital infection control.*
3. Allerton, H. (1994). Price per pound. *Training & Development, 48*(5),144.
4. Murphy, B. S., Barlow, W. E., & Hatch, D. D. (1994). Discrimination against the obese violates Rehab Act. *Personnel Journal, 3*(2), 35–36.
5. Moskowitz, E. (1994). In the courts: Am I disabled? *Hastings Center Report, 24*(3), 4.
6. Skoning, G. D., & McGlothlen, C. A. (1994). Other laws shape ADA policies. *Personnel Journal, 73*(4), 116–118.
7. Bain, D. P. (1989). *Initiatives in hospital risk management.* GAO/HRD-89-79. Washington, DC: Government Printing Office, pp. 6, 20–27.
8. Wilson, T. H. (1994). *OSHA guide for health care facilities.* Tampa, FL: Thompson Publishing Group.
9. Shikles, J. L. (1994). *Workplace regulation: information on selected employer and union experiences.* GAO/HEHS-94-138. Washington, DC: Government Printing Office, pp. 26–28, 42–44.
10. U.S. Department of Labor, Occupational Safety and Health Administration. (2001, November 20). *Hospital hazards.*
11. U.S. Department of Labor, Office of Public Affairs. (2002, January 14). *OSHA reopens tuberculosis rulemaking record.*
12. Udasin, I. G., & Gochfeld, M. (1994). Implications of the OSHA's blood-borne pathogen standard for the occupational health professional. *American Journal of Occupational Medicine, 36*(5), 548–555.
13. Thompson Publishing Group. (1994). Brochure for Wilson book (see reference 8), pp. 2–3.
14. U.S. Department of Labor, Occupational Safety and Health Administration. (2000). Congressional Testimonies: Blood-borne Pathogens (June 22, 2000). The Subcommittee on Workforce Protections House Education and the Workforce Committee, Statement of Charles N. Jeffress, Assistant Secretary of OSHA.
15. Needlestick requirements take effect April 18. (2001, April 12). OSHA national news release.
16. *NIOSH alert: Preventing needlestick injuries in health care settings.* Publication No. 2000-108.
17. Sentinel Alert. (2001, August). Preventing needlestick and sharps injuries. *Joint Commission on Accreditation of Healthcare Organization, 22.* http://www.TheJointCommission.org.
18. Health Insurance Portability and Accountability Act of 1996, Public Law 104-191, Title II, Subtitle F, Administrative Simplification and Privacy Provisions (28 December 2000). In: R. Pear, (2002, August 10). Bush rolls back rules on privacy of medical data. *New York Times,* p. 1.
19. Associated Press. (2002, August 4). Efforts abound to limit pharmaceutical marketing. *Home News Tribune,* (East Brunswick, NJ), p. E10.

20. Occupational Safety and Health Administration. (1991). *OSHA action needed to improve compliance with hazard communication standard.* GAO/HRD-92-8. Washington, DC: Government Printing Office.

21. Litvan, L. (1994). OSHA sharply increases fines for serious safety violations. *Nation's Business, 82*(9), 8.

22. COBRA: A summary of final regulations. (1995). *Hospital Risk Manager, 3*(4):1–2.

23. Bernstein, S. (1994). Advertising letter re Wilson book (see reference 8), p. 3.

24. Patient not formally admitted but "dumped" all the same. (1995). *American Medical News, 38*(9), 20.

25. McCormick, B. (1994). Dumping law enforcement lags. *American Medical News, 37*(42), 37.

26. Felsenthal, E. (1994, August 30). Patients skirt states' malpractice limits. *Wall Street Journal*, p. B2, col. 3.

27. Segal, M. (1994). Mammography facilities must meet quality standards. *FDA Consumer, 28*(2), 8–12.

28. Segal, M. (1994). Quality standards compliance for mammography facilities. *Journal of the American Medical Association, 272*(10), 763.

29. Fintor, L., Alciati, M. H., & Fischer, R. (1995). Legislative and regulatory mandates for mammography quality assurance. *Journal of Public Health Policy, 16*(1),81–103.

30. Mammography Quality Standard Act, Federal Register Notice, Direct Federal Rule. June 17, 1999.

31. Doctors falling short in mammogram skills. (2002, June 27). *New York Times* News Service.

32. In Denver, a mammogram team learns from its errors. (2002, June 28). *New York Times* News Service.

33. Breast cancer delayed diagnosis or failure to diagnose are a major cause of loss payments. *Dateline, MLMIC, 3,* 2.

34. Oberman, L. (1994). Group backs FDA-like review of tests and treatments. *American Medical News, 37*(40), 6–7.

35. Cohen, R. (1995, February 10). Medical device industry wants a private, European-type FDA. *Star-Ledger* (Newark, NJ), p. 3, col. 4.

36. Roane, K. (2002, July 29). Replacement parts. *U.S. News & World Report*, pp. 54–59.

37. Meier, B. & Thomas, K. (2012, April 19). Weak remedy for a heart device. *New York Times*, Business Day, p. B1.

38. Meier, B. (1994, July 2). Pfizer unit to settle charges of lying about heart valve. *New York Times*, p. A33, col. 1.

39. Meier, B. (1995, January 30). Defective implants can slip past FDA's checkpoints. *Staten Island Advance* (NY), p. B8, col. 1.

40. Rudolph, R. (1994, November 4). U.S. seizes blood pressure devices at firm cited for failing FDA rules. *Star-Ledger* (Newark, NJ), p. 71, col. 1.

41. Leary, W. (1995, January 16). Remedy sought for 22,000 patients with risk pacemakers. *New York Times*, p. A9, col. 1.

42. Leary, W. (1995, January 25). Government urges testing for pacemakers with wiring problem. *New York Times*, p. A13, col. 1.

43. Service, R. S. (1995). Liability concerns threaten medical implant research. *Science, 266*(4), 726–727.

44. Scott, L. (1995). Researchers test safety of medical device reuse. *Modern Healthcare, 25*(17), 78.

45. Cohen, R., & Orr, J. S. (2002, August 13). A hip-maker's billion dollar mistake. *Star-Ledger* (Newark, NJ), p. A1.

46. Bruley, M. (1991, December 6). *Investigating equipment-related accidents.* Presentation at the American Health Risk Management Association, New York.

47. Rudolph, R. (1994, November 8). Ousted J&J exec files suit to regain his post. *Star-Ledger*, (Newark, NJ), p. 24, col. 3.

48. Siemens unit in U.S. to halt some output to correct problems. (1994, February 25). *Wall Street Journal*, p. B8, col. 1.

49. Taylor, I. (1994, November 8). FDA clears the way for Siemens Medical. *Star-Ledger* (Newark, NJ), p. 45, col. 4.

50. Cohen, R., & Orr, J. S. (2002, August 11). Often the patient is the last to know. *Star-Ledger* (Newark, NJ), p. 9.

51. Kessler, D. A. (1993). Introducing MEDWatch: A new approach to reporting medication and device adverse effects and product problems. *Journal of the American Medical Association, 269*(21), 2765–2768.

52. Monitoring medical products: You can help. (1994). *People's Medical Society Newsletter, 13*(3):6.

53. Burton, T. M. (1994, May 2). Law concerning medical devices is often ignored. *Wall Street Journal*, p. B1, col. 3.

54. Horton, R. (1994). MEDWatch moves forward. *Lancet, 343*(8893), 285–286.

55. Dickinson, J. G. (1994). Hidden negatives in FDA's MedWatch efforts? *Medical Marketing & Media, 29*(3), 34, 36.

56. Hospital where 2 died says it failed to shut a gas line. (2002, January 19). *New York Times*, p. B5.

57. Food and Drug Administration, Office of Public Affairs. (2000, December 21). Physicians labeling proposal. *HHS News*.

58. http:/www.civilrights.com/baycol.html

59. Blakeslee, S. (2002, August 15). Recall is ordered at large supplier of implant tissue. *New York Times*, p. 1.

60. U.S. Environmental Protection Agency. (2002, June 24). Medical waste: Frequently asked questions. http://www.epa.gov/epaoswer/other/medical/mwfaqs.htm

61. Hearn, W. (1994). EPA calls hospital incinerators key dioxin emission source. *American Medical News, 37*(40), 19.

62. Charlton, A. (1995, April 16). Advisory panel voices opposition to incinerating medical waste. *Star-Ledger* (Newark, NJ), p. 40, col. 4.

63. Leusner, D. (1994, December 2). Coalition beats back legislation to replace state inspection of hospitals. *Star-Ledger* (Newark, NJ), p. 35, col. 1.

64. Johnsson, J. (1995). Supreme court lowers barrier to health reform. *American Medical News, 38*(19), 1, 28, 31.

65. Fisher, I. (1995, April 5). Pataki will lift some regulations for health care. *New York Times*, p. 1, col. 6.

66. A modest easing of hospital regulations. (1995, April 12). *New York Times*, p. A24, col. 1.

67. Leusner, D. (1995, March 19). Debate begins on easing health service rules. *Star-Ledger* (Newark, NJ), p. 21, col. 2.

68. Whitlow, J. (1995, February 8). Blue Cross fined $106,000 for failing to get clearance on HMO centers. *Star-Ledger* (Newark, NJ), p. 7, col. 1.

69. Who is a surgeon? (1995). *Lancet, 345*(8951), 663–665.

70. Woo, J. (1994, April 11). Blowing smoke around others may be battery. *Wall Street Journal*, p. B6, col. 6.

71. Rigotti, N. A., Stoto, M. A., & Schelling, T. C. (1994). Do businesses comply with no-smoking law? Assessing the self-enforcement approach. *Preventive Medicine, 3*(2), 223–239.

72. U.S. Environmental Protection Agency. (1992). *Respiratory health effects of passive smoking: Lung cancer and other disorders*. EPA/600/6-90/006F. Washington, DC: Government Printing Office.

73. Smoke said to take greater toll on nonsmokers. (1995, April 5). *New York Times*, p. A21, col. 1.

74. Murphy, B. S., Barlow, W. E., & Hatch, D. D. (1994). OSHA proposes indoor air quality regulations. *Personnel Journal, 73*(6), 32–35.

75. Swoboda, F., & Hamilton, M. M. (1994, December 4). No-smoking push ignites firestorm of controversy. *Star-Ledger*, (Newark, NJ), Sec. 3, p. 1, col. 1.

76. Sulzberger, A. G. (2011, February 10). Hospitals shift smoking bans to smoker ban. *New York Times*.

77. Dunkel, T. (1994). Newest danger zone: Your office. *Working Woman, 19*(8), 38–41.

78. Kahn, S. (1994). Risk of violence a chronic problem in many hospitals. *Business Insurance, 28*(37), 1, 12. Retrieved from www.NYTimes.com/2011/02/11US/11smoking.html

79. Spiegel, A. D., & Kavaler, F. (1986). *Cost containment and DRGs: A guide to prospective payment*. Owing Mills, MD: Rynd Communications.

80. OSHA faults hospital for workplace violence violations. (2012, April). *Hospital Security*. Retrieved from http://www.campussafetymagazine.com/channel/Hospital-security/News/2010/07/19/08

81. Haynes, R. B. (2006). Of Studies, syntheses, synopses, summaries, and systems: The 5s evolution of information series for evidence-based health care decisions. *Evidence-Based Medicine, 11*(6), 162–164.

82. Guyatt, G., Rennie, D., Meade, M., & Cook, D. (2008). *Users' guides to the medical literature: A manual for evidence-based clinical practice. (2nd ed.)*. New York: McGraw-Hill.

83. Institute of Medicine. (2001). *Crossing the quality chasm*. Washington, DC: National Academy Press.

84. Institute of Medicine. (2001). *To err is human*. Washington, DC: National Academy Press.

85. Centers for Medicare and Medicaid Services (CMS). (2003). Medicare Prescription Drug, Improvement, and Modernization Act (MMA Section 501(b)): Reporting Hospital Quality Data for Annual Payment Update (RHQDAPU).

86. U.S. Department of Health and Human Services. (n.d.). www.hospitalcompare.hhs.gov

87. Meyer, J., Rybowski, L., & Eichler, R. (1997). *Theory and reality of value-based purchasing: Lessons from the pioneers.* AHCPR Publication No. 98-0004. rockville, MD: Agency for Health Care Policy and Research.

88. Value-based purchasing, rules and regulations. (2011, May 6). *Federal Register, 76*(88), 2490.

89. H.R. 3590 (111th) Patient Protection and Affordable Care Act, 111th Congress, 2009–2010.

90. Meyer, J. & Anthony, S. (2001, October 1). Reducing health care fraud: An assessment of the impact of the False Claims Act. *Legislative and Policy Issues in the Year 2001: Legislative Update of the False Claims Act Legal Center.* http://www.tat.org/legislative.html

91. Phillips, J. R., & Cohen, M. L. (1997, February 10). How to avoid liability under the False Claims Act. *American Medical News.*

92. Compliance in Medical Research and Academic Centers Forum, St. Louis University School of Medicine, November 29–30, 2001. http://www.hcca-info.org/documents/acad-comp.pdf

93. Cohen, M. (2012, March 28). Good Samaritan Hospital claims it defrauded health program. *Baltimore Sun.*

94. Pelofsky, J. (2012, April 10). Tenet to pay almost $43 million to settle false claims. *Reuters.*

95. Altman, L. K. (1995, May 31). Federal official cites deficiencies at Harvard hospital. *New York Times,* p. A16, col. 1.

96. Altman, L. K. (1995, May 12). Hospital official resigns over drug overdoses. *New York Times,* p. A16, col. 1.

97. Thirty-four percent of The Joint Commission–accredited hospitals failed Medicare standards in 1992. (1994). *Medical Benefits, 11*(21), 11.

98. The Joint Commission sentinel event reporting detailed at E&A Conference. (1998). *AABB Weekly Report, 4*(25), 6–7.

99. Kolata, G. (2002, August 24). V.A. suggests halt to kind of knee surgery. *New York Times,* p. A9.

100. Rx for competence (editorial). (2003, November 19). *Star-Ledger* (Newark, NJ), p. 32, col. 1.

CHAPTER 3

Risk Management in Employment

Steven J. Greenblatt

We live and work in a litigious society.[1]

Box 3-1

In the healthcare workforce, race was cited in 2,934 (39.6%) bias claims, followed by 2,642 (35.7%) claims of "retaliation." Disability bias was alleged in 2,074 (28%) complaints, sex bias was alleged in 1,812 (24.5%) of complaints, age bias was alleged in 1,560 (21.1%) of complaints, and national origin bias was alleged in 794 complaints (10.7%). Violations of Title VII of the Civil Rights Act were alleged in 5,278 (71.3%) of all bias complaints filed in the healthcare sector.[2]

To insulate organizations, employees, patients, and the public from harm and liability, we must develop and enact policies and procedures in the workplace. The procedures by which an enterprise selects, appoints, promotes, demotes, disciplines, and separates employees often define its vulnerability to risk and litigation. Risk can emanate from a host of compliance issues across a broad range of areas, including age, color, disability, gender, race, and sexual orientation (Title VII of the Civil Rights Act). Various statutes impose obligations on employers (e.g., Consumer Credit Protection Act of 1968, Employee Retirement Income Security Act of 1974, Fair Labor Standards Act of 1938, Family and Medical Leave Act of 1993, Health Insurance Portability and Accountability Act of 1996, Immigration Reform and Control Act of 1986, National Labor Relations Act of 1947, Occupational Safety and Health Act of 1970, Sarbanes-Oxley Act of 2002). Despite well-publicized laws and regulations and notorious gaffes by healthcare employers over the years, history continues to repeat itself, and our litigiousness remains well fed.

LESSONS STILL TO BE LEARNED

Before a survey of trends in legal risk management is undertaken, incredulity is a key response to a review of several cases over the last few years. These examples serve as an instructive reminder of how easily employers can create liability and, conversely, how easily they can avoid it.

In January 2010, an assisted living center paid a $43,000 settlement to the Equal Employment Opportunity Commission (EEOC) to resolve a complaint wherein a Muslim housekeeper was fired rather than allowing her to wear her hijab (head scarf).[3] The employer chose to make the employee decide between her religious beliefs and her job.

Takeaway: Insensitivity to the employee's personal rights and needs proved costly, and rigidly bureaucratic adherence to dress standards prevailed over providing a simple accommodation.

One regional EEOC office estimates that one-third of the prospective plaintiffs who intend to file a complaint bring some sort of digital evidence—emails, text messages, live recordings.[4] The classic example of resort to electronic support for a plaintiff's case harkens back more than a decade to the 1996 Texaco case of race discrimination in which the company was embarrassed and had to pay in excess of $140 million in damages and other program changes.[5]

Takeaway: Training, enforcement of affirmative action policies, and an equal playing field would have avoided this costly humiliation.

Box 3-2

In 2004, Abercrombie and Fitch agreed to pay $40 million to class-action litigants (employees, would-be employees, and minority job candidates) who claimed they had been dissuaded from applying for positions. The company also paid $10 million in costs, changed its marketing, and agreed to desist from creating a predominantly white sales staff.[6]

In an age discrimination complaint, an absence of management documentation supporting the personnel changes relating to the plaintiff and willful indifference—if not active participation—by upper management in a scheme to pare the workforce that created a hostile working environment through allegations of poor performance of older workers, supported punitive damages in an award totaling almost $2.5 million.[7]

Takeaway: Integrity in management and conscientious documentation ensure ethical and justifiable decisions.

Healthcare employers that accede to patients' requests or demands for white caregivers will be found liable for race discrimination.[8] The current trend is to emphasize patient satisfaction, but it may not take precedence over discriminatory demands.

Takeaway: Prioritizing customer preferences over the maintenance of a hostile working environment will result in liability.

In 2009, the California Supreme Court upheld compensatory damages of $500,000 and punitive damages of almost $2 million for reprehensible conduct by a supervisor. The manager told an employee who had been diagnosed with a medical condition that she was "disgusting" because she dug her nails into her arms as a result of a nervous disorder, criticized her body odor (which was caused by medication she was taking for a panic disorder) in front of coworkers, and ostracized her by ignoring her greetings and not including her when the supervisor brought in specialty food items, holiday trinkets, or travel souvenirs. Upper management knew of this treatment and did not respond to the employee's complaint, constituting "management malfeasance."[9] It is often said in such cases that Title VII of the Civil Rights Act, which prohibits recognized types of illegal discrimination, is not a civil code.

Takeaway: Tolerance of harsh or relentless incivility can result in liability for discrimination.

Two nurses, who were responsible for quality assurance and regulatory compliance, anonymously reported a physician to the state medical board, alleging that he had sutured a rubber scissors tip to a patient's finger, used an unapproved olive oil solution on a patient with a highly resistant bacterial infection, failed to diagnose appendicitis, and conducted a skin graft in the emergency room without surgical privileges. They did not name the patients in their complaint, but referenced patient numbers. Winkler County Memorial Hospital in Texas terminated the nurses' employment. In an unprecedented case, the physician persuaded his friend, the sheriff, to obtain a search warrant and found the anonymous allegations on their computers. The nurses were indicted for misuse of official information, but a jury held in their favor after only one hour of deliberations. The hospital settled the case with the nurses for $750,000. The hospital was subject to administrative fines for violations of Texas laws regarding the regulation of hospitals from the Texas Department of State Health Services based on its on-site investigation pursuant to the nurses' complaints.[10]

Takeaway: Miscreants must be recognized and their incompetence and manipulation stopped. Employers must resist knee-jerk responses to employees who report alleged wrongdoing in good faith.

Cases of this nature abound, even though they are easily avoided through prudent and reasonable management. Employers need to refocus their responses in an age where supervisors abuse their authority and employees know their rights. An examination of several current banner issues of liability follows.

WRONGFUL DISMISSAL OR DISCHARGE

A rapidly growing area of employer liability centers on allegations of wrongful dismissal or discharge. Approximately 65% to 70% of the workforce are considered "employees at will," meaning that "an employer may dismiss an employee hired for an indefinite period of time for any reason or no reason at all without incurring

liability to the employee."[11] The Minnesota Court of Appeals, in *Stagg v. Vintage Place, Inc.,*[12] held that when an employee handbook includes a specific progressive disciplinary policy, an employee's at-will status is modified and some job security is presumed.

Nevertheless, an employer may not discharge an employee for an unlawful reason, such as racial discrimination. Historically, employers had broad powers to dismiss employees who were employed at will (i.e., without any contract). Those guidelines permit termination of an employee for a bad reason, a good reason, or no reason at all.[13] In recent years, however, courts and state legislatures have whittled away at this previously untouchable doctrine. Exceptions to the employment-at-will rule have been expanding based on a variety of legal concepts, including claims in contract, torts (civil wrongs), and the fact that a particular termination violates public policy (e.g., termination after whistleblowing in defined statutory instances,[14] or covered health and safety matters, or retaliation).[15]

A number of courts have found an implicit contract assurance of job security in employer communications such as employer policies, handbooks, oral assurances, industry customs, employer conduct, and the duration of employment. Most frequently, the claim is based on a personnel manual or handbook.[16] A disclaimer in an employee handbook may, in some cases, override other provisions that appear to recognize proprietary rights in an employee.[17] Although courts do not always find that these documents establish contracts between an employer and its employees, employment contracts have been inferred from them in some instances; the more detailed the document's descriptions of disciplinary procedure, the more likely it will be found to be an implied contract.[18] Furthermore, courts have used the legal concept of an implied covenant of good faith and fair dealing to find an existing contractual relationship restricting an employer's decisions to dismiss an employee.[19]

Employees cannot be terminated in violation of public policy, even at-will employees. To make a valid claim for such a violation, the employee must present clear and convincing evidence that he or she engaged in an act encouraged by public policy, or refused to act in a way prohibited or discouraged by public policy,[20] and that employer retaliation for this act was the factor motivating the discharge. To qualify as a discharge in violation of public policy, the issue at stake must affect the public at large, not just the individual employee. Moreover, the public policy relied on must be unambiguous; in some jurisdictions, it must be based on a statute. Statutes cover wide-ranging public policies including discharge or discipline for exercising statutory rights based on FMLA, worker's compensation, pregnancy, disability, gender, and sexual orientation; these laws vary by state and among smaller government entities. In some states, termination in violation of public policy exposes the employer to punitive damages. The wide-ranging potential for liability is not clearly defined, as illustrated in cases where violations of certain public professional ethics codes serve as a basis for such liability.[21]

SEXUAL HARASSMENT AND GENDER DISCRIMINATION

Sexual harassment in healthcare workplaces presents a unique challenge as a result of the intimate nature of patient care as well as the physically close working environment of healthcare workers. As in most workplaces, the existence of a power differential also creates a clear and present danger.

"Hostile environment" sexual harassment occurs when conduct has the purpose or effect of unreasonably interfering with a person's work environment based on actions or word with a sexual connotation.[22] "Quid pro quo" sexual harassment emerges when conduct causes a "tangible employment action" or a change in terms and conditions of employment based on a refusal to comply with a supervisor's sexual demands.[23] The key is the existence of a tangible employment action; under *Faragher v. City of Boca Raton*,[24] an employer is vicariously or per se liable for sexual harassment when such a situation exists. Where no such adverse employment action occurs, the employer may defend itself based on a bifurcated affirmative defense: (1) It exercised reasonable care to prevent and correct any sexually harassing behavior (generally assumed to mean having a written and promulgated policy with training and promptly and thoroughly investigating claims of which the employer receives cognizable notice[25]) and (2) the employee failed to bring the complaint to the employer's attention. Healthcare employers must exercise conscientiousness to preserve this defense; notice of potentially actionable behavior has been recognized in the filing of a complaint, the oral recital of a complaint to a supervisor or a person empowered to investigate, the service of a summons, or pervasive sexual harassment in the organization (the employer "knew or should have known about the conduct").[26] Anecdotally, it appears that hospitals often serve as the foci for claims—many meritorious—of sexual harassment.

In 2009, Flushing Hospital Medical Center was found vicariously liable for the sexual harassment of a nurse by an attending physician

Lutheran Medical Center in Brooklyn, New York, ignored the complaints of eight nurses who claimed that a physician in the hospital's Employee Health Center engaged in inappropriate medical exams and asked invasive questions during the pre-employment process. When the hospital did not respond to their complaints, the nurses sought relief from the EEOC, which interviewed many nurses who had been recently hired. The EEOC determined that the physician, who eventually lost his license to practice medicine in New York, engaged in similar conduct on a continuing basis. The hospital settled the matter in 2003 for $5,425,000 distributed to 51 nurses and instituted reforms to deter future violations. The new chief executive officer (CEO) initiated training for employees, an anonymous hotline, female chaperones for all employment-related exams, and a rule prohibiting breast and gynecological exams in pre-employment screening.[27] This expensive lesson could have been averted if the corporate culture had been one that was committed to upstanding conduct and did not gloss over rank-and-file employees' concerns.

when its medical director, who had allegedly witnessed the errant physician spinning her around and trying to force a kiss onto the plaintiff nurse, and who was subsequently chosen to handle the investigation and correct any improprieties, took no action. Moreover, the plaintiff alleged that the doctor had assaulted her at other times and that his proclivities were well known to hospital management, which did nothing to curb his behavior. After a jury trial, the plaintiff was awarded $8 million in damages, plus $5.5 million in punitive damages. The first award was reduced to $750,000, and the punitive damages were dismissed because the hospital—under the direction of the same medical director—obtained the doctor's resignation within four days of the plaintiff's written

complaint.[28] This case illustrates that turning a blind eye to unfiled charges amplifies liability but that prompt action upon receiving actual notice may facilitate diminution of damages, especially where, as here, the hospital was "teetering near financial ruin." Nonetheless, the "blind eye culture" that prevails in many hierarchical hospital settings can contribute to the prevalence of such claims.

The Flushing Hospital message was not transmitted to Brigham & Women's Hospital in Boston. In the latter facility, a physician was victimized by other physicians, putting into perspective the notion that liability can arise only when the relative power of the parties is plainly disparate. A jury awarded a neurosurgeon $1 million based on a hostile sexual environment, $600,000 for retaliation, and more than $1.3 million in attorneys' fees and tortious interference with advantageous relations; the Federal First Circuit Court of Appeals affirmed the awards in total.[29] The court also termed the conduct of one doctor "blatantly sexist and offensive." Its recital of some of the facts and its conclusions are instructive:

2002–03: Day ignores Tuli at conferences by stating, "[L]et's ask the spine guys, Eric and Marc, what they think," and omitting her despite the fact that she is also a spine surgeon.

2004: At a graduation dinner and in front of a female resident, Day asks Tuli, "Can you get up on the table to dance so you could show them how to behave."

2004: In the summer, Tuli attends a bachelorette party for a coworker and sees a blow-up doll with a picture of her face attached to it.

2004: Day makes comments on different occasions: "You're just a little girl, you know, can you do that spine surgery?" "Oh, girls can do spine surgery?" "Are you not strong enough to use the hand instruments?"

2005: In February or March 2005, with his arm on Tuli's back, Kim says, "Why don't we leave this place and go to the Elliott Hospital so I can give you an oral exam"; "I think you're really hot"; and "I imagine you naked."

2005: Early in 2005, Day sits in on Tuli's teaching conference and disagrees with Tuli's lecture. He does this more than once, and Tuli does not believe that he did so during male doctors' teaching conferences.

2005: Residents, who are supervised by Day as residency director, ignore Tuli's pages, fail to assist her on rounds, and fail to show up for clinical duties. In the summer, Tuli notices that she is given less-experienced, junior residents for her cases.

6/05: Tuli becomes aware of a hospital-affiliated party planned with "strippers and cages and beer kegs." Although it was supposed to celebrate the incoming chief residents, a new female chief resident was excluded. Day approves of the party and of outside funding for it.

2005: In September or October, Day and Tuli meet to clear the air, and Day says, "Our relationship is like that of lovers and you've cheated on me," with his hand on her arm; he also calls her "deranged." When she attempts to shake his hand at the end of the meeting around 10:00 P.M., he gives her a prolonged hug.

11/05: A resident throws Tuli into the scrub sink and then the garbage.

12/06: Kim states, "Oh, could you wear one of those belly dancing outfits and show us a dance?"

2007: Kim states that he would "like to have the opportunity to sexually harass" Tuli; Tuli observes him fondling a physician assistant at a department event.

5/07: Day looks in on Tuli's spine surgery and makes "some comment to the effect of whether [she] was able to do that case because [she] was a girl, are you sure you can do that, you're just a girl, something to that effect."

8/07: Day bars Tuli from spine oncology research, saying that he had "a guy in mind" for the job.

. . . Tuli also reported that Day had given her other prolonged hugs and had held her hand as they walked at work. She also testified that Day had questioned her authority in multiple teaching conferences and had made comments repeatedly about Tuli "being a little girl" and questioning whether she could do a "big operation"; the incidents noted here were particular examples of this recurrent behavior for which she could remember specific dates.

The "accumulated effect of incidents of humiliating, offensive comments directed at women and work-sabotaging pranks, taken together, can constitute a hostile work environment." *Tuli repeatedly complained about these acts, but the hospital did nothing to prevent their repetition* [emphasis added]. That Tuli managed to get her work done despite the harassment does not prevent a jury from finding liability. The jury was entitled to find that a hostile workplace had been tolerated and that the hospital was liable.

This case serves as a stark reminder that ignoring such disrespectful conduct will no longer pass muster. Allowing such conduct to continue with impunity invites litigation. The

Tuli case was exacerbated by the fact that an alleged harasser was directly involved in the credentialing process, buttressing his malevolent imprimatur on her professional aspirations; his input resulted in Tuli's referral for anger management and a requirement to obtain approval from the Physician Health Service, an outside agency that would evaluate her and recommend a course of action. These machinations should be red flags for any healthcare employer. Hospitals that directly employ physicians should take note.

According to the EEOC, Grays†Harbor Community Hospital in Aberdeen, Washington, failed to take appropriate action despite repeated complaints to upper-level management that a supervising pharmacist was sexually harassing at least four pharmacy technicians. The agency's investigation found that the supervisor made offensive sexual comments, inflicted details of his sex life and masturbation habits on the technicians, and showed explicit material from the Internet to the women. He also was known to approach a woman from behind to whisper in her ear, block her pathway, and rub her back, legs, and arms, the agency said. The hospital agreed to a $125,000 settlement in 2011.[30]

In response to complaints from 10 current and former employees, according to the EEOC, California's Garfield Medical Center allegedly retaliated or terminated the workers in lieu of taking action on their complaints. One male Admitting employee subjected them to inappropriate touching, propositions for sex, graphic discussions of sexual activities, obscene pictures, and comments regarding female body parts, including those of underage patients. He was not terminated for two years. As a result of this combination of alleged nonfeasance and malfeasance, in 2011 the hospital, without admitting

---

Box 3-4

A male nurse, who eventually was promoted to a supervisory position, made unwanted sexual advances and sexual jokes and innuendos to female colleagues and subordinates. Women who rejected the advances or complained about harassment were given more difficult job assignments and had their work performance unfairly disparaged. A nurse who made a written complaint detailing acts of alleged sexual harassment by the supervisor was fired the following day. Another woman was given a poor evaluation because she complained about harassment. The settlement terms required First Street Surgical Partners to pay $210,000 in relief to compensate three women who filed charges of discrimination with the EEOC. Additionally, $80,000 was distributed among other current and former employees and contract workers who may have been subjected to sexual harassment or retaliation, and the male nurse whose actions provoked complaints was permanently barred from working for First Street. The decree also required other corrective actions, including the demotion of the director of nursing, the hiring of a human resources specialist, and training designed to prevent future acts of sexual harassment or retaliation.[31] In this case, an unhappy corporate culture issue rears it ugly head once again.

---

any wrongdoing, agreed to pay the 10 women $430,000 and to establish a fund of another $100,000 for any unidentified victims.[32]

AIDS AND THE HEALTHCARE WORKPLACE

AIDS in the healthcare workplace has patient implications as well as inspires employment concerns. "Persons living with HIV/AIDS have to endure not only archaic attitudes that they present a health threat, but also moral disapproval of their behavior. Patients and coworkers often stubbornly hold onto these stereotypes."[33]

Due to the combination of fear and moral disapproval, workplace discrimination against those diagnosed with HIV is considerably greater than discrimination against other disability groups.[34] AIDS, however, is classified as a disability under the Americans with Disabilities Act and the Rehabilitation Act.[35]

Not much has changed with respect to AIDS in the healthcare workplace since the decision in *State University of New York v. David Young*.[36] In *Young*, a respiratory therapist intentionally injected the same needle into two patients, twice, thereby placing the already gravely ill patients at further risk of contracting AIDS or hepatitis. This egregious violation of patients' rights and the consequent exposure to transmission of disease were the primary motivations for the court to reverse the arbitrator's reinstatement of the employee and uphold the hospital's proposed penalty of termination.

The concern surrounding the contagiousness of AIDS continues to inflame healthcare employers' responses to employees with the condition, although the recent case law is sparse. In *Couture v. Belle Bonfils Memorial Blood Center*,[37] a phlebotomist in training disclosed that he was HIV positive, and management sought to place him in a different position, that of a product management technician, where the pay rate would be comparable. The plaintiff was not happy in the new position and sought to return to his phlebotomist role, but that was not made available. The plaintiff resigned. The court held that leaving the employ of the blood center was the plaintiff's choice; reassignment to an undesirable job may constitute an adverse, employment action, thereby triggering potential discrimination, but reassignment to a position to which the plaintiff initially consents but does not desire does not qualify. Because no adverse employment action had been taken, the court ruled, no discrimination had occurred. This case remains good law, but it should be considered in the context of other settled law that fear or aversion to a person who is an employee is not a satisfactory basis for taking adverse employment action; blind reliance on customer preference without some intervening bona fide occupational qualification will not survive judicial scrutiny.[38]

The wisest course for healthcare employers is to educate employees so as to dispel myths about the disease. This topic appears to meld naturally with the mandated annual review of universal precautions. Moreover, there are concerns, within the framework of informed consent, about whether HIV-infected physicians performing invasive procedures must disclose this status to patients.[39]

DUE PROCESS

Every healthcare employer will confront absenteeism, tardiness, negligence, insubordination, theft, falsification of records, or substance abuse at some point in time. Discipline or termination may be warranted in such cases. Fairness and predictability should govern any response if the employer wishes to avoid legal liability. "Due process" requires that there be (1) a clear rule against the misconduct; (2) a reasonable rule; (3) a thorough and objective investigation in which the employee has the opportunity to offer his or her side of the story; (4) notice of the charges and penalty sought; and (5) an opportunity to respond or appeal in some fashion. To achieve these zones of relative safety, employers usually apply progressive disciplinary rules that include ascending penalties where feasible. If these procedures are observed evenhandedly, the employer is in a strong position to defend itself against a claim of lack of due process. Note, however, that application of progressive discipline may subvert an employee-at-will status.

WORKER'S COMPENSATION

Worker's compensation is a mutually beneficial social insurance system whereby the employer agrees to underwrite an injured employee's medical costs and a significant portion of a worker's salary in exchange for the waiver of the employee's right to sue the employer.[40]

Worker's compensation is an expensive program that has not fully realized its potential. More than merely a shield for employers against employee lawsuits and a concomitant safety valve for injured workers, it can be used to avoid accidents and create a safer and more efficient workplace. This effort has generally not been undertaken,[41] to the detriment of struggling healthcare employers and injured workers. When one considers the overall costs of worker's compensation to healthcare employers,[42] it behooves them to reduce the associated costs through reasonable means.

Unfortunately, worker's compensation fraud is rather simple to perpetrate, and the surrounding circumstances tend to offer incentives to those who understand its lack of priority in many circles. For instance, many cases of "soft fraud" involve claiming false injuries, malingering, filing claims based on injuries actually received off the job, and inflating the alleged harm. The allure of these deceitful actions can be better understood in light of recent surveys. According to the Coalition Against Insurance Fraud, one in five American adults— approximately in 45 million people—says it

is acceptable to defraud insurance companies under certain circumstances, although four of five adults think insurance fraud is unethical.[43] Nearly one of four Americans says it is not unusual to defraud insurers (8% say it's "quite acceptable" to bilk insurers, and 16% say it's "somewhat acceptable").[44] This environment intertwines with the fact that "[m]any insurance companies unwittingly encourage fraud by paying suspicious claims rather than fighting them. Insurers sometimes reason that paying the suspicious or nuisance claim is less expensive than paying the legal fees to fight it. Insurers also fear fighting suspect claims for fear of paying multi-million dollar 'bad faith' lawsuits if they lose."[45] Because most companies carry worker's compensation insurance, their motivation to aggressively pursue wrongdoers is significantly diminished. Finally, worker's compensation fraud is viewed by those who engage in it as a low-risk activity because investigative conscientiousness is rarely implemented, and the eventual penalties are generally relatively lenient.[46]

Healthcare employers can reduce costs significantly through a determined return-to-duty program that detects credible red flags.[47] Their resolve should also be reinforced with investigations where is reasonable cause exists to believe that an employee has made a false claim. The workplace culture should be developed to encourage personal accountability for the team and individual goals. Supervisory training should inculcate the professional obligation to root out miscreants, and this responsibility should be explicitly included as part of supervisors' performance expectations. Using trusted medical providers to assess the genuine extent of objective medical injury buttresses these efforts, as does vigorous pursuit of disciplinary charges and, where appropriate, criminal sanctions. A clear deterrent effect has been observed in workplaces that target this misconduct.[48] Healthcare employers that fail to engage these tools relinquish an important source of morale and revenue.

RETALIATION

> *"Revenge turns a little right into a great wrong."* —German proverb

> *"Before you embark on a journey of revenge, dig two graves."* —Confucius

The unique quality of retaliation law arises because even when the underlying charge of discrimination or wrongdoing is not proved, because retaliation may still take on a life of its own. It can survive the defeat of a plaintiff's underlying claim and continues to represent a potential liability. Moreover, the claim of retaliation can be more easily proved, because retaliation does not require proof of repugnant racism, sexism, ageism, or other inherently revulsive form of employment practice, and the underlying elements of the claim are within every juror's life experience.

Box 3-5

A retaliation claim includes three elements: (1) the claimant engaged in protected activity-opposition or participation activity; (2) the employer took adverse action against the employee: and (3) a causal connection exists between the protected activity and the adverse employment action.[49]

This exposure is magnified when one considers that the EEOC received double the number of retaliation charges over the past decade compared to prior decades and more charges of retaliation than any other type of complaint. Today a claim is rarely lodged for any form of discrimination without appending a claim for retaliation. The offense in such cases can arise from any kind of discrimination—race, color, gender, sexual harassment, disability, age, religion, sexual orientation, and so on. Because many charges cross over several types of discriminatory acts, retaliation can also follow suit and replicate itself.

Plaintiffs often prevail in retaliation claims where they have not succeeded with respect to the primary claim of discrimination; that is, the secondary charge takes on a life of its own. The reasons for this counterintuitive result are not difficult to understand: Retaliation does not require proof of discrimination. More to the point, juries empathize with persons who are the subject of retribution and often reward them with generous damages,[50] occasionally (depending on the statutory provisions) punitive damages that can increase the employer's exposure.[51]

The reasons for this evolution are clear. People—perhaps, especially supervisors—are human, and the default response to claims of wrongdoing generally involves some knee-jerk reaction that provides the named wrongdoer with a sense of "evening up the score." Some supervisors resort to this behavior because they deliberately wish to create a hostile environment for the person making the charge; others may do so at a subconscious but nonetheless legally cognizable level. Recently, for example, UBS lost a verdict of $10.6 million based on sexual harassment claims that were met with retaliation.[52] The damages—$10 million for punitive damages, $350,000 for sexual harassment, and $242,000 for retaliation—would eventually be pared down to conform to the statutory cap for punitive damages of $500,000.

Unless supervisors are trained and then pointedly reminded at the point when an employee files a complaint that retaliation is not only prohibited but also an easy trap to fall into, the EEOC retaliatory count will continue to grow.[53] Employer liability is at risk if these steps are not adopted to ensure the vitality of a policy against retaliation.

In *Yanowitz v. L'Oreal USA, Inc.,*[54] a male manager of a cosmetics company, dissatisfied with the attractiveness of a female sales associate, instructed the associate's immediate supervisor to terminate her and "get [him] somebody hot." When he later returned and found that the inadequate sales associate was still working, he directed the immediate supervisor to an attractive blonde woman and instructed her to replace the dark-skinned sales associate with an employee who looked like the blond woman. She refused. This series of exchanges occurred shortly after the plaintiff had been named "Sales Manager of the Year," and she began to experience implied threats of termination, reformulation of how she should supervise her sales district, and an undermining of her managerial effectiveness. She left the company, claiming stress, and sued based on retaliation. The California Supreme Court held that the case should be heard by a jury because refusal to follow what the plaintiff reasonably believed was a discriminatory directive is protected conduct, and it affected the terms and conditions of her employment. The plaintiff did not have to utilize legal terminology or file a complaint to qualify for shelter from retaliation.[55] In 2005, this finding was an expansion of retaliation law; since then, the U.S. Supreme Court has further extended the reach of the prohibition.

The U.S. Supreme Court has recently ruled in several significant retaliation cases that have consistently expanded the rights of plaintiff-employees. According to the decision in *Burlington N. & Santa Fe Railway Co. v. White,*[56] retaliation occurs when a reasonable employee would have found the challenged action materially adverse, or if it might well have dissuaded a reasonable worker from making or supporting a charge of discrimination. The Court noted that this finding does not immunize the plaintiff from petty slights or minor annoyances that all employees experience: Snubbing and personality conflicts are not actionable. Conversely, changing a schedule of a mother with school-age children may qualify as non-petty and material; excluding someone from a weekly training lunch that fortifies professional advances might deter someone and qualify as retaliation. This standard clarifies and lowers the bar for employee-plaintiffs.

In *Crawford v. Metropolitan Board of Education of Nashville,*[57] after the plaintiff answered questions honestly in a sexual harassment investigation in which the new employee relations director was the target of investigation, she was subsequently charged with fraud and terminated from employment. So, too, incidentally, were two other witnesses who answered questions in the same inquiry. In essence, the Court decided that the plaintiff need not initiate her own complaint to be protected under Title VII of the Civil Rights Act. The Court held that merely answering questions in an internal investigation without filing a formal complaint is a protected activity. Eventually, the plaintiff received an award of $1.5 million. Employers should revise their policies if they do not explicitly cover all cooperative witnesses, and they should provide effectual shelter for those employees. This logic requires that healthcare employees remain vigilant when they conduct investigations, because under *Crawford,* witnesses are instantly transformed into potential plaintiffs if they participate in the process in good faith.

In a case brought pursuant to the Fair Labor Standards Act (FLSA), *Kasten v. Saint-Gobain Perf. Plastics Corp.,*[58] the Supreme Court determined that an *oral* complaint triggers insulation from retaliation. *Kasten* contended that he was terminated after complaining about the location of time clocks—specifically, that their placement prevented employees from earning credit for time donning and removing work clothes, a subject that is subsumed by the FLSA. He was terminated allegedly for failing to clock in and out after being warned. The language in the statute, "file any complaint," provides for a broad interpretation that was deemed to include verbal complaints. Federal and state statutes have minute variations that may allow for similar applications, so employers should regard all complaints, including "informal" grievances made to supervisors or managers, as potentially sheltering employees from retaliation.

Supporting another person who is a victim of sexual harassment is also protected conduct.[59] In the context of a substance abuse rehabilitation facility, this lesson was learned through costly litigation in which the compensatory damage award for emotional distress was reduced to $175,000 (from $764,000), the lost wages award was $421,657, the lost fringe benefits award was reduced to $11,658, and the punitive damages award was reduced to $200,000 (from $350,000). The differences, one can be certain, were made up in attorneys' fees.[60] Notably, the only thing the coworker did in *Mugavero* was to inform the supervisor that a coworker intended to bring a sexual harassment complaint against him, and she thereafter supported it. The supervisor responded by referring her to the New York State Office of Professional Discipline and terminating her. Retaliation complaints beckon.

In *Thompson v. North American Stainless LP,*[61] the Supreme Court greatly expanded the employer's potential exposure when it ruled that an adverse employment action against the fiancé of an employee who had filed a charge against her employer was cognizable retaliation. By hurting the fiancé, the employer was reaching the employee. Title VII prohibits any action that "well might have dissuaded a reasonable worker from making or supporting a charge of discrimination."[62] The Court's "zone of interest" analysis carries a powerful message; it holds that a plaintiff may not sue unless he or she "falls within the 'zone of interests' sought to be protected by the statutory provision whose violation forms the legal basis for his [or her] complaint,"[63] This language has already been interpreted to extend to a husband whose wife filed a disability discrimination complaint. Moreover, the husband worked for a company that was under contract to the original defendant, but the court in *McGhee v. Healthcare Services Group, Inc.,*[64] held that the two employers were intertwined; "[a]llowing employers to induce their subcontractors to fire the subcontractor's employees in retaliation for the protected activity of a spouse would clearly contravene the purpose of Title VII. It is effortless to conclude that a reasonable worker might be dissuaded from engaging in protected activity if she knew that her husband would be fired by his employer."[65] It has long been held that one who opposes discrimination need not be a member of the statutorily protected group to receive the protection of prohibitions against retaliation—a rationale that significantly broadens the number of prospective plaintiffs in retaliation cases.[66] Retaliation is laden with untold layers of potential liability.

Box 3-6

The best advice for employers is to take the following steps:

1. Create red flags to identify employees who may be subject to retaliation.
2. Advise the employee of the policy prohibiting retaliation, the recourse available, and clear directions on how to report it. Document this meeting.
3. Affected supervisors should be admonished not to treat the employee differently after the complaint comes to light. Employers must treat employees who complain cautiously; a good rule of thumb is to treat them similarly to those employees who do not complain about or oppose discrimination, as that fact is not supposed to enter into personnel decisions.
4. Any employment action should be documented with the reason why it is taking place and vetted by a manager who is not emotionally involved in the controversy, preferably someone who is not aware that a complaint has been lodged.
5. Should a supervisor engage in retaliation, or should coworkers take retaliatory measures, the employer must put a stop to those practices and take effective disciplinary action.

WHISTLEBLOWING

A related concern for all employers, especially healthcare employers, is whistleblowing. Many state statutes provide insulation from retaliation for whistleblowers if they fall within protected boundaries. Moreover, several new federal regulations waive the previously sacrosanct notion that the employee must first complain internally; that safety valve is now a thing of the past.

Several federal statutes create opportunities for potential whistleblowers. The Elder Justice Act, a part of the Patient Protection and Affordable Care Act of 2010,[67] requires every individual "employed by" or "associated with" a long-term care facility as an owner, operator, agent, or contractor to report a "reasonable suspicion" of a crime affecting residents or those receiving care. The broader False Claims Act[68] provides for substantial civil penalties for fraudulent claims for payment or approval by the federal government. The Department of Justice may obtain triple damages of the amounts billed and remove the provider as a Medicare or Medicaid participant.[69] The law derives much of its power from the *qui tam* provision that permits individuals who bring forth previously undisclosed and significant information of fraud under the statute to receive between 15% and 30% of the total amount recovered through their actions. This specification effectively concretizes the incentive to report. According to some authorities,[70] a significant portion of the fines imposed have been in the healthcare industry.[71] This development was not unexpected in light of the March 2010 Patient Protection and Affordable Care Act, which significantly broadened fraud and abuse exposure under the False Claims Act.[72] Anti-kickback provisions now fall under the False Claims Act, and other provisions apply to nursing homes, pharmaceutical manufacturers, and durable medical device makers. Any healthcare enterprise that directly or indirectly receives federal funds through Medicaid or Medicare must participate in compliance programs to minimize exposure.

Qui tam actions are essentially invitations to disgruntled or merely hard-pressed employees

Table 3-1	Whistle Blower Cases		
Facility	**Claim**	**Date**	**Amount Recovered by Government/Claimant**
Pfizer, Inc.	Off-market marketing of Bextra and kickbacks to physicians.	2009	$2,300,000,000/$51.500,000[80]
Nichols Institute Diagnostics	Faulty lab testing kits that led to overtreatment and unnecessary surgeries.	2009	$302,000,000, which includes $253 million to settle the *qui tam* lawsuit, $9 million to settle other civil lab claims, and $40 million to settle a felony criminal charge
Christ Hospital, Cincinnati, Ohio	Cardiologists at the hospital[81] were given time in an outpatient testing unit based solely on the amount of cath-lab revenues they generated for the hospital the previous year. Many of those procedures were billed to Medicare or Medicaid.	2010	$76,500,000/$23,500,000
Wheaton Community Hospital, Minnesota	From 1998 to 2004, the hospital admitted patients and kept others admitted in acute care when doing so was not medically necessary and then falsely billed Medicare for the cost of these admissions.	2010	$846,461/$203,150[82]
Veteran Affairs Medical Center, Northport, New York	Ran an unaccredited nuclear medicine program for three years.	2010	Program closed[83]
LSU Medical Center, Shreveport, Louisiana	Members of its medical school faculty billed Medicare for services they said were done by teaching physicians. The surgeries were actually done by residents—often without a teacher present.	2011	$700,000/$200,000[84]
25 hospital[85]	Unnecessarily kept kyphoplasty patients overnight.	2010	$101,000,000[86]

who have access to information that may not conform to strict federal guidelines. Almost $2 billion in settlements by the Department of Justice were the result of False Claim Act *quitam* actions in 2009[73]; of that amount, $1.6 billion involved healthcare. In 2010, the Department of Justice declared its battle against healthcare fraud to be a "top priority."[74] United States Attorneys' offices opened more than 1,000 new criminal healthcare fraud investigations in 2010 and filed criminal charges in 481 cases through the Health Care Fraud Prevention and Enforcement Action Team (HEAT)[75] One year earlier, in 2009, U.S. Attorney General Eric Holder and Secretary of Health and Human Services Kathleen Sebelius had announced the formation of HEAT[76] as a new effort with increased tools and resources and pledged a cabinet-level commitment to prevent and prosecute healthcare fraud.

Box 3-7

The mission of HEAT is: To marshal significant resources across government to prevent waste, fraud and abuse in the Medicare and Medicaid programs and crack down on the fraud perpetrators who are abusing the system and costing us all billions of dollars . . . To reduce skyrocketing health care costs and improve the quality of care by ridding the system of perpetrators who are preying on Medicare and Medicaid beneficiaries. . . . To build upon existing partnerships between [the Department of Justice and the Department of Health and Human Services], such as our Medicare Fraud Strike Forces to reduce fraud and recover taxpayer dollars.[77]

The federal government won or negotiated approximately $2.5 billion in healthcare fraud judgments and settlements, and it attained additional administrative impositions in healthcare fraud cases and proceedings. The Medicare

Trust Fund received approximately $2.86 billion during this period as a result of these efforts.[78] Treble damages, penalties, attorneys' fees, and possible imprisonment should be effective incentives for employers to follow the protocols.

Recent cases graphically illustrate the vulnerability of healthcare institutions and the incentive for employees with access to information to "blow the whistle" (**Table 3-1**). Healthcare employers should implement strategies to minimize the risks illustrated by these cases. One method is mandatory arbitration, a little used but court-approved process that circumvents costly litigation in the courts. Employee releases are also potential tools in certain cases to neutralize claims of employees leaving under a funded severance agreement.[79]

SOCIAL MEDIA

Facebook, YouTube, LinkedIn, and blogs are ubiquitous—and many employees use them, both at work and away from the worksite. Should employers be concerned? Given that the NLRA and similar state statutes, discrimination laws, and privacy/freedom of speech considerations[87] abound, the answer is a resounding "Yes."

Recruitment

Many employers look online for material posted by or about applicants. While this access may be tempting and may be fair game if the information is in the public domain, several employers have attempted to enter personal pages to obtain more insights.[88] This approach is inadvisable.

According to a 2010 survey by Jobvite,[89] more than 80% of employers either routinely or occasionally search for an online profile of job candidates. Another 13% utilize profiles provided by candidates. The overriding concern in these efforts is that the employer may discover information that is not germane to the job, such as membership in a protected class, disabilities, private associations, and political affiliations. Employers cannot "unring" this bell, and it portends potential claims of improper bias. Therefore, traditional recruitment techniques can be enhanced through use of email and other electronic correspondence, but a proactive methodology to ferret out tantalizing information on the Web will expose employers to liability without any corresponding benefit.

Employee Blogs and Commentary

If an employee blogs about problems at work or satirizes a senior leader, the employer will be inclined to look askance at such behavior and seek to bring an end to the activity or to the employee's tenure. Employees have a right to free speech, particularly when they are engaging in protected concerted activities.[90] The NLRB Advice Memorandum in Sears Holdings (Roebuck) (December 4, 2009) prohibited references by employees to confidential or proprietary information, sexual references, references to illegal drugs, and disparagement of company products or of competitors. The NLRB advised that these restrictions did not improperly restrict protected concerted activity under the NLRA, and it did not specifically reference social media. However, in *American Medical Response of Connecticut (AMR)*,[91] the National Labor Relations Board decided in late 2010 that where an employee who posted negative comments about a specific supervisor on her Facebook page was discharged after the posting and responding to other comments from coworkers about the same supervisor and related working conditions, the policy against speaking out in social media was too broad in the face of the statutory protections to engage in concerted activities. The *AMR* ruling therefore modifies the breadth of an employer's ability to circumscribe online or offline speech.

Some state statutes are even more restrictive and protect employees when they engage in lawful activities on their own time.[92] However, if employees pose for photos on a company airplane,[93] the resultant casting of the employer in a bad light may not be regarded as a protected activity. The laws that govern speech in the workplace are no different when applied to cyberspace.[94,95]

Employee Use of Social Media During Work Time

According to a 2011 survey by the Health Care Compliance Association and the Society of Corporate Compliance and Ethics,[96] 42% of respondent companies had disciplined employees for use of social media. With a policy that clearly delineates that use of company computers and time for personal messages constitutes theft of time or services, employers may discipline employees. However, the issue is how to determine whether an employee is abusing such access; information technology is available to assist in this effort. Although policies should advise that there is no expectation of privacy, monitoring employee usage without reasonable and specific cause carries many perils, including invasion of privacy and loss of trust.

Another seminal case that defines an employer's obligation vis-á-vis social media is

Blakely v. Continental Airlines,[97] in which the New Jersey Supreme Court held that an electronic bulletin board closely related to the workplace and beneficial to the employer, although not maintained by the employer, that contained defamatory statements about an employee resulting in a hostile work environment, created a duty for the employer to remedy that situation. Enabling access to online communication carries with it a responsibility to monitor its usage.

Bottom Line

Employers should create policies that clearly define what is permitted and what is not permitted during work hours. Confidential information must be defined and ruled out of bounds. Defamation should be prohibited. Moreover, harassment or visiting websites that contain questionable content should be strictly prohibited. Many of these sites can be filtered without danger of invading employees' privacy. To ensure that these policies are promulgated and understood, staff training should incorporate media policies and procedures.

BACKGROUND CHECKS

Negligent hiring is a legally recognized cause of action that requires a plaintiff to prove the following points:

- The subject was an employee
- The employee was incompetent or posed a foreseeable risk
- The employer knew or should have known about the incompetence or risk of the employee
- The employee caused an injury

- The negligent hiring was the proximate cause of the injury, bringing the employee into contact with the damaged party

In such a case, employers may be held directly liable (not merely vicariously liable) when an employee injures a third party and the employer knew or should have known of the danger (*Medical Assurance Company, Inc. v. Castro*).[98] Aside from the obvious wisdom of conducting background checks on prospective employees to avoid claims of negligent hiring,[99] many states *require* healthcare providers to do so.[100]

"Due diligence" consists of a background check to determine whether the applicant has a criminal record or other disqualifying personal history—but one should not stop there. This process includes checking for valid credentialing of persons who hold a license but has been extended beyond employees to other personnel whom a patient would assume is acting as an employee.[101] It goes beyond that technicality as well, to subsume moral or other impairments that may later surface to demonstrate that the employer did not adequately vet the candidate before putting the person in contact with patients, coworkers, or the public: The law requires, as does common sense and the duty of doing no harm to patients, a thoroughly documented risk-based exercise.[102] In addition, concerns must be addressed related to the Federal Sentencing Guidelines for Organizations,[103] which provide for fines higher than otherwise might be expected for federal crimes, including Medicare and even Medicaid fraud. The implementation of an effective compliance and ethics program[104] will mitigate those fines imposed when a violation is detected.

INCIVILITY AND VIOLENCE IN THE HEALTHCARE WORKPLACE _____

> **Box 3-8**
>
> In a study published in 2011, 57% of hospital workers witnessed disruptive behaviors by physicians and 52% witnessed disruptive behaviors by nurses; 32.8% of the respondents felt that the disruptive behavior could be linked to the occurrence of adverse events, 35.4% to medical errors, 24.7% to compromises in patient safety, 35.8% to poor quality, and 12.3% to patient mortality. Eighteen percent of employees reported that they were aware of a specific adverse event that occurred as a direct result of disruptive behavior.[105]

At the heart of many exposures to legal liability is the ever-present pressure to cater to physicians and other powerful revenue producers—as well as non-revenue producers—who are permitted to engage in uncivil conduct; inadequate response to such behaviors creates a hostile environment that is conducive to more disruptive conduct and violence.[106] The study titled "Silence Kills"[107] documented the effects on patient mortality and adverse events of climates of intimidation and bullying. The key findings in this study included the following:

- Eighty-four percent of doctors have seen coworkers take shortcuts that endanger patients.
- Eighty-eight percent of doctors work with people who show poor clinical judgment.
- Fewer than 10 percent of physicians, nurses, and other clinical staff directly confront their colleagues about their concerns.

The Joint Commission, in its Sentinel Event Alert,[108] set new goals and standards for healthcare workplaces to deal with those

> **Box 3-9**
>
> One nurse shared her personal story:
>
> It was morning rounds in the hospital and the entire medical team stood in the patient's room. A test result was late, and the patient, a friendly, middle-aged man, jokingly asked his doctor whom he should yell at.
>
> Turning and pointing at the patient's nurse, the doctor replied, "If you want to scream at anyone, scream at her."
>
> This vignette is not a scene from the medical drama *House*, nor did it take place 30 years ago, when nurses were considered subservient to doctors. Rather, it happened just a few months ago, at my hospital, to me.
>
> As we walked out of the patient's room I asked the doctor if I could quote him in an article. "Sure," he answered. "It's a time-honored tradition—blame the nurse whenever anything goes wrong."
>
> I felt stunned and insulted. But my own feelings are one thing; more important is the problem such attitudes pose to patient health. They reinforce the stereotype of nurses as little more than candy stripers, creating a hostile and even dangerous environment in a setting where close cooperation can make the difference between life and death. And while many hospitals have anti-bullying policies on the books, too few see it as a serious issue.[110]

wrongdoers who create intimidating work environments by creating a workplace that nurtures assertive communication. A continual stream of studies has documented this deleterious phenomenon where such a healthy corporate culture does not prevail.[109]

A national survey of physician and nurse executives[111] asked how many had observed or experienced these behavior problems from doctors or nurses in their organizations. The responses are shown in **Table 3-2**.

Table 3-2 Noted Behavior Problems	
Degrading comments and insults	84.5%
Yelling	73.3%
Cursing	49.4%
Inappropriate joking	45.5%
Refusing to work with a colleague	38.4%
Refusing to speak to a colleague	34.3%
Trying to get someone unjustly disciplined	32.3%
Throwing objects	18.9%
Trying to get someone unjustly fired	18.6%
Spreading malicious rumors	17.1%
Sexual harassment	13.4%
Physical assault	2.8%
Other	10.0%

In a 2008 study of 102 hospitals and more than 4,500 staff members,[112] the findings in **Table 3-3** were documented. The consequences of bad conduct and organizational malaise based on this study:

Table 3-3 Observers of Disruptive Behavior	
Who has seen doctors exhibit disruptive behavior?	
Staff overall	77%
Nurses	88%
Doctors	51%
Who has seen nurses exhibit disruptive behavior?	
Staff overall	65%
Nurses	73%
Doctors	48%

- Ninety-nine percent say disruptive behaviors lead to impaired nurse–physician relationships.
- Sixty-seven percent believe there is a link between disruptive behaviors and adverse events.
- Seventy-one percent believe there is a link between disruptive behavior and medical errors.
- Eighteen percent are aware of at least one specific adverse event that occurred because of disruptive behaviors; 20% of nurses responded in the affirmative, and 21% of administrators did so as well.

The lesson is clear: Healthcare employers oversee hierarchical bureaucracies that continuously operate in fast-paced and high-pressure situations that often create the opportunity to promote and perpetuate incivility. Ignoring the potential harm to patient care and to employee morale is done at your peril.

Physical violence in the healthcare workplace is also well documented.[113]

Box 3-10

The recent notorious cases of Michael Swango, M.D., and Charles Cullen, R.N., demonstrate the willingness of hospital administrators and educators to ignore clear signals of danger in the healthcare workplace to the mortal detriment of patients and coworkers.[114] Dr. Swango's patients had exceptionally high mortality rates and was ultimately convicted of killing patients in Ohio and New York. He was also convicted of falsifying his medical credentials, and the FBI is investigating him for up to 60 deaths. Mr. Cullen pleaded guilty to killing 29 patients and said he killed many more in New Jersey and Pennsylvania, often injecting Digoxin. He worked in hospitals and nursing homes, which often did not attempt to verify his credentials.

Healthcare employers are obligated to provide a safe workplace.[115] Nonetheless, approximately one-third of nurses have experienced workplace violence.[116] The Joint Commission issued a Sentinel Alert in recognition of the increase in crime and violent acts in the healthcare workplace.[117] It provided the following guidelines:

1. Work with the security department to audit the facility's risk of violence. Evaluate environmental and administrative controls throughout the campus, review records and statistics of crime rates in the area surrounding the healthcare facility, and survey employees on their perceptions of risk.

2. Identify strengths and weaknesses and make improvements to the facility's violence-prevention program.

3. Take extra security precautions in the emergency department, especially if the facility is located in an area with a high crime rate or gang activity. These precautions can include posting uniformed security officers and limiting or screening visitors (for example, wanding for weapons or conducting bag checks).

4. Work with the human resources department to make sure it thoroughly prescreens job applicants, and establishes and follows procedures for conducting background checks of prospective employees and staff. For clinical staff, the human resources department should also verify the clinician's record with appropriate boards of registration. If an organization has access to the National Practitioner Data Bank or the Healthcare Integrity and Protection Data Bank, check the clinician's information, which includes professional competence and conduct notes.

5. Confirm that the human resources department has ensured that its procedures for disciplining and firing employees minimize the chance of provoking a violent reaction.

6. Require appropriate staff members to undergo training in responding to patients' family members who are agitated and potentially violent. Include education on procedures for notifying supervisors and security staff.

7. Ensure that procedures for responding to incidents of workplace violence (e.g., notifying department managers or security, activating codes) are in place and that employees receive instruction on these procedures.

8. Encourage employees and other staff to report incidents of violent activity and any perceived threats of violence.

9. Educate supervisors that all reports of suspicious behavior or threats by another employee must be treated seriously and thoroughly investigated. Train supervisors to recognize when an employee or a patient may be experiencing behaviors related to domestic violence issues.

10. Ensure that counseling programs for employees who become victims of workplace crime or violence are in place.
    Should an act of violence occur at the facility—whether assault, rape, homicide, or a lesser offense—follow up with an appropriate response that includes the following measures:

11. Report the crime to appropriate law enforcement officers.

12. Recommend counseling and other support to patients and visitors to your facility who were affected by the violent act.

13. Review the event and make changes to prevent future occurrences.

Myriad studies have shown that violence in the workplace may be predictable because the perpetrators often state aloud precisely what they intend to do and to whom they mean to do it.

> [T]he killers do not just snap. An examination by *The New York Times* of 100 rampage murders found that most of the killers spiraled down a long slow slide, mentally and emotionally. Most of them left a road map of red flags, spending months plotting their attacks and accumulating weapons, talking openly of their plans for bloodshed. Many showed signs of serious mental health problems.
>
> But in case after case, the *Times* review found, the warning signs were missed: by a tattered mental healthcare system; by families unable to face the evidence of serious mental turmoil in their children or siblings; by employers, teachers and principals who failed to take the threats seriously; by the police who, when alerted to the danger by frightened relatives, neighbors or friends, were incapable of intervening before the violence erupted . . . The *Times* found that in 63 of the 100 cases (which involved 102 killers), the killers made general threats of violence to others in advance. Fifty-five of the 100 cases involved killers who regularly expressed explosive anger or frustration, and 35 killers had a history of violent behavior and assaults.[118]

Consequently, it behooves healthcare employers to take implicit threats and other disruptive behavior seriously.[119] Courts have supported reasonable employer decisions in this vein. In

Calandriello v. Tennessee Processing Center,[120] a highly secure facility that utilized retinal identification procedures learned that the plaintiff had improperly used the Internet at work to reformulate a company poster and place Charles Manson's face in place of an employee's face. He also used the company computer to view images of serial killers, assault weaponry, and other violent images. When the employer terminated the employee eventually, he appealed, claiming he was entitled to a reasonable accommodation based on diagnosed bipolar disorder pursuant to the Americans with Disabilities Act. The court, however, stated that the act does not require an employer to retain a *potentially* violent employee.[121] Along the same lines, in *Blackman v. New York Transit Authority,*[122] the Second Circuit Court of Appeals held that a transit worker's termination was proper when, after two supervisors had been shot to death by an ex-employee in whose termination they had participated, he stated that they got what they deserved. The Court noted, "It is clear . . . that a government official may, in certain circumstances, fire an employee for speaking—even on a matter of public concern—where that speech has the potential to disrupt the work environment."[123]

DEFAMATION

It is not news that employers are challenged when prospective employers of their staff members call seeking references. The dilemma is clear: Do you tell the truth and open yourself to a claim of defamation,[124] or do you sugarcoat the responses so as to shield yourself from liability? Equally clear is the principled response—to share all the gory details that you can support through documentation—although most employers choose instead to offer name, rank, and serial number as a matter of course to avoid this quandary. That reply, however, does not resolve the matter. Particularly in health care, when an employer has knowledge of predilections of employees that put patients at risk, neglecting or choosing to withhold that information opens an entirely new source of legal accountability. In *Davis v. Board of County Commissioners*,[125] the duty of former employers to prospective employers to disclose unfavorable information about an applicant was at issue. In *Davis*, supervisors at a detention center provided positive feedback about an ex-employee who had a history of sexual harassment. At the hospital that hired him, he was accused of sexual assault and sexual harassment. The *Davis* court held that when physical harm is foreseeable and the employer reveals the negative background, the previous employer can rely on a qualified privilege to shield it from liability.[126]

The best guidance an employer can follow is to limit disseminated information to facts that have been documented and have been subject to a signed release by the employee agreeing that the employer may share information, a signed settlement[127] with the employee, an empowering statute that shields an employer in defined circumstances often involving statements regarding patient care concerns in peer review,[128] or an arbitration decision; mere charges without more protection would likely not confer the qualified privilege to share information. One must factor in the notion that deliberate malice is often required for a finding of defamation. Opinions are often not held actionable, and while truth is always an absolute defense in defamation, this axiom relies on the ability to prove the veracity of a statement by clear and convincing

evidence.[129] There is no bar to a claim for defamation under a qualified privilege, so the risk for the employer will necessarily endure.

MICROINEQUITIES

Respect in the healthcare workplace is sometimes an elusive commodity. Surveys of disruptive physician conduct have revealed that nearly one-third of all nurses who left a hospital did so because of a disruptive physician.[130] More than 90% of the 1,200 individuals surveyed in one study had witnessed disruptive physician behavior, including yelling or raising the voice, disrespect, condescension, berating colleagues, berating patients, and use of abusive language. A survey of more than 2,000 pharmacists and nurses even more graphically demonstrates how physician behavior can stifle healthy communication and result in safety concerns.[131] Nearly half (49%) of the respondents said a history of physician intimidation altered the way they asked for clarifications about medication orders. Almost 70% said that at least once in the past year a physician had snapped, "Just give what I ordered," when asked for clarifications or questioned about a script.[132]

These microinequities are subtle—or not-so-subtle—statements and behaviors that have been characterized as "death by a thousand cuts." They have the effect of making others feel devalued or excluded, but fall short generally of legally cognizable discrimination.[133] The Joint Commission has recognized this communication threat and issued a Sentinel Event Alert on the subject.[134] Nurturing employees' voice,[135] thereby transforming the workplace into one where all employees may articulate their concerns without fear of retribution, is a salutary method by which to reduce employer risk.

Healthcare administrators who fail to implement meaningful measures to alleviate fear and silence in the workplace do so at their own peril, as well as their patients'.[137]

OTHER HIGHLY RECOMMENDED RISK MANAGEMENT STRATEGIES

As reflected in the discussion on microinequities, healthcare employers must hone their twenty-first-century leadership skills and tools. It is not sufficient to be reactive when risks rear their ugly heads; proactive tools are accessible and inexpensive. As the saying goes, "An ounce of prevention. . . ."

Healthcare employers should create a workplace culture that promotes genuine discussion and straightforwardness; it also nurtures employee engagement.[138] Engaged employees speak up and rarely file formal complaints; by definition, they are advocates for the organization and recommend it to friends and family.[139]

Conversely, those who work in a hostile environment often withdraw and engage in counterproductive behaviors.[141] In healthcare workplaces, bullying and other perceived inequities are often facts of life,[142] and their perpetuation largely negate employee dissatisfaction and amplify the potential for litigation.[143]

A climate of bullying and intimidation has also been documented to contribute to patient safety errors.[145] Just as patients are reluctant to sue physicians who display empathy and communicate well,[146] so, too, employees feel an affinity to leaders and organizations that treat them with respect and value their contributions; those employees find salutary methods to express their concerns in lieu of litigation.[147]

Managers and supervisors should engage in candid performance discussions, whether in the context of counseling sessions[148] or performance appraisals,[149] on both regular and as-needed bases. Employers that give prompt, evenhanded feedback are regarded as fair by employees and juries and courts,[150] and they set an organizational climate that is conducive to openness and transparency.[151]

Supervisory training and enhanced supervisory performance expectations can increase the utilization of these vital tools.

Fairness is part of the psychological contract that is shared by employees and employers. A significant breach in this unwritten agreement will often trigger latent litigiousness.[153] Employers should not be complacent if few complaints are made; healthcare employers face numerous litigation and nonlitigation perils as well, including compromised patient safety, disengagement, poor morale, and grievances.[154] In a 2005 poll, Gallup found that, despite the relative dearth of discrimination complaints, informal and undocumented perceptions of discrimination are much more common than employers might think; "unfiled" but nonetheless active and festering grievances are not statistically apparent but have their detrimental impact.[155] Nationwide, one in three African American employees perceives himself or herself to be the victim of racial discrimination.[156]

Most of the unfiled complaints[158] focused on perceived discrimination in promotion decisions and pay.[159] Numbers of complaints alone do not fully communicate the depth of feeling or possible hostility that an employee or a group of employees may be experiencing.[160] It therefore behooves employers in health care to reward employees who speak their minds.

REFERENCES

1. Healthcare workplace bias complaints jumped 21.7% in fiscal 2010, a record pace that outstripped the also unprecedented 15.9% rate of growth for bias complaints in the overall workforce, the EEOC said. Overall, EEOC fielded a record 99,992 private-sector workplace discrimination charge filings in fiscal 2010, which ended September 30. Healthcare workplace complaints represented 7.4% of all complaints filed in 2010, and grew from 6,078 charge filings in 2009, to 7,403 filings in 2010. Hospitals saw the number of complaints filed rise from 2,484 in fiscal 2009, to 2,945 in fiscal 2010, an increase of 18.6%, EEOC said.
2. Commins, J. (2011, January). EEOC healthcare bias complaints on the rise. *Health Leaders Media.* Retrieved from http://www.google.com/search?ie=utf-8&oe=utf-8&q=AIDS+discrimination+%22healthcare+workplace%22&rlz=1V4IPYX_enUS459US459
3. *Ahdaoui v. Ivy Hall Assisted Living* (Case No.: 1:08-CV-3067-BBM-SSC) (N.D.Ga.).
4. http://abcnews.go.com/Technology/secretly-recorded-work/story?id=13409126&page=1; *Roberts v. Texaco, Inc.,* 979 F.Supp. 2d 185 (S.D.N.Y. 1996).
5. http://www.nytimes.com/1996/11/17/us/size-of-texaco-discrimination-settlement-could-encourage-more-lawsuits.html?pagewanted=2; see also *Ingram v. Coca-Cola,* 200 F.R.D. 685 (Ga. 2001), wherein the company settled for $192.5 million for race discrimination. See the report of the task force monitoring this settlement at http://www.thecoca-colacompany.com/ourcompany/task_force_report_2005.pdf
6. See Greenhouse, S. (2004, November 17). Abercrombie & Fitch bias case is settled; CBS

News. (2009, February). The look of Abercrombie and Fitch. *60 minutes.* Retrieved from http://www.cbsnews.com/2100-18560_162-587099.html

7. *Saffos v. Avaya, Inc.,* http://law.justia.com/cases/new-jersey/appellate-division-published/2011/a3189-08-opn.html, 16 A.3d 1076 (N.J. Super. A.D. 2011). It is not insignificant for employers gauging risk exposure to note that the ultimate award of $2.5 million reflects a *reduction* from the original jury award of more than 75%. Juries are inclined to sympathize with worker-plaintiffs who are treated inequitably.

8. *Chaney v. Plainfield Healthcare Center,* 612 F.3d 908 (7th Cir. 2010). An agency that certified and assigned certified nursing assistancts paid $150,000 to settle charges that it used race in its assignment of personnel. *EEOC v. HiCare, Inc., dba Home Instead Senior Care,* No. 1:10-CV-02692 (D. Md. Dec. 10, 2010). In 2005, a chain of assisted living and senior centers paid $720,000 to settle charges that it screened out non-Caucasian applicants as potential employees because its general manager believed residents did not want them to enter their homes. *EEOC v. Merrill Gardens, LLC,* No. 1:05-CV-004 (N.D. Ind. Oct. 6, 2005). See http://www.eeoc.gov/eeoc/initiatives/e-race/ caselist.cfm#customer. In 2003, Abington Memorial Hospital in Philadelphia also allegedly instructed black personnel not to play a role in one patient's care delivery. See http://www.freerepublic.com/focus/f-news/994789/posts

9. *Roby v. McKesson,* 219 P.3d 749 (Cal. Sup. Ct. 2009). See *Niami v. Federal Exp. Print Services, Inc.,* 2010 WL 958045, *4+, 93 Empl. Prac. Dec. P 43,849+ (N.D.Cal. March 12, 2010) (adopting the *Roby* court's reasoning that management's personnel decisions that continue to send the hostile messages of the supervisor may be regarded as evidence of discrimination [here, based on a woman's sexual orientation]).

10. Sack, K. (2010, August 10). Texas nurses fired for alleging misconduct settle their suit. *The New York Times.* See also the trial transcript at http://texas-nurses.org/displaycommon.cfm?an=1& subarti-clenbr=538

11. *Stagg v. Vintage Place Inc.,* A-09-949 (Minn. Ct. App. 2010).

12. Id.

13. Despite the dubious proposition that someone can do something for no reason at all, the now famous (or infamous) iteration of employment at will encapsulates the power of employers to govern the workplace. Although employment at will expressly addresses employers' "absolute" right to terminate employees, it is about much more. Someone who has the power to terminate also has the power to do as he or she pleases with respect to all terms and conditions of employment. At its core, employment at will is about employer power and prerogative. Corbett, W. R. (2003). The need for a revitalized common law of the workplace. *Brooklyn Law Review, 69,* 91, 125–127. However, healthcare employers should not be led down the proverbial garden path: "[E]mployment at will provides employers far less freedom to discharge employees than appears at first blush, and it is vastly overrated in its value to employers. There are numerous exceptions to employment at will contained in federal and state statutes, tort theories such as wrongful discharge in violation of public policy, and contract concepts, among others." *Catholic University Law Review, 60*(615), 657 (2011), citing Sprang, K. A. (1994). Beware the toothless tiger: A critique of the Model Employment Termination Act. *American University Law Review, 43,* 849, 862–871.

14. For example, New York Labor Law § 740(2), the "whistleblowers' statute," provides, in relevant part, that an employer shall not take any retaliatory personnel action against an employee because such employee:
(a) discloses, threatens to disclose to a supervisor or to a public body an activity, policy or practice of the employer that is in violation of a law, rule or regulation which violation creates and presents a substantial and specific danger to the public health or safety . . .

15. *Crawford v. Metropolitan Government of Nashville,* 129 S.Ct. 846 (2009). In *State University of New York v. David Young,* 566 N.Y.S.2d 79 1991), the *employer* contested the employee's reinstatement as a violation of public policy and prevailed (the termination of an employee who placed patients in jeopardy was upheld, and an arbitrator's decision was struck down as in violation of public policy).

16. *Wooley v. Hoffman-LaRoche,* 491 A.2d 1257 (N.J. 1985). However, it may arise in other circumstances that do not require such a document, as in unfair

dismissal (wrongful discharge) or intentional infliction of emotional distress.

17. *Thomas v. MasterCard Advisors, LLC,* 901 N.Y.S.2d 638, 639 (1st. Dept. 2010).

18. *Woolley v. Hoffmann La Roche,* 491 A.2s 1257 (N.J. 1985).

19. *Bailey v. City of Wilmington,* 766 A.2d 477, 480 (Del. 2001) (describing situations in which this limit applies). But see *Kerrigan v. Britches of Georgetowne, Inc.,* 705 A.2d 624, 627 (D.D.C. 1997), affirming a trial court decision that a plaintiff employee was not protected by an implied covenant of good faith and fair dealing because "by definition [plaintiff]—as an employee at will, not under contract—had no basis for claiming breach of a "covenant."

20. For example, if a woman refuses to take part in a bawdy ritual while at an office party, and is disciplined or discharged, or if a disciplinary investigation commences and a witness requests the opportunity speak with an attorney and is discharged.

21. See *Madison Services Co. v. Gordon,* 2010 WL 3529588 (D. Colo.), citing *Rocky Mountain Hospital and Medical Service v. Mariani,* 916 P.2d 519 (Colo. 1996).

22. *Meritor Savings Bank v. Vinson,* 477 U.S. 57 (1986).

23. *Burlington Industries v. Ellerth,* 524 U.S. 742, 753–54 (1998).

24. Id.

25. *EEOC v. Cromer Food Services,* 2011 LEXIS 4279 (4th Cir. 2011).

26. *Indiana Civil Rights Commission v. Fireside Brewhouse,* http://www.in.gov/icrc/files/EMse10060256%281%29.pdf (2011); *Sandoval v. Amer. Bldg. Indus., Inc.,* 578 F.3d 787, 801 (8th Cir. 2009); see *Bennett v. Nucor,* 656 F.3d 802, 811 (2011) (racial discrimination).

27. See http://www.eeoc.gov/eeoc/newsroom/release/4-9-03.cfm; http://www.nytimes.com/2003/04/10/nyregion/brooklyn-sex-harassment-suit-is-settled-for-5.4-million.html; http://archive.eeoc.gov/litigation/settlements/settlement04-03.html

28. *Bianco v. Flushing Hosp. Medical Center,* 54 A.D.3d 304 (N.Y.A.D. 2 Dept. 2008). On remand to *Bianco v. Flushing Hosp. Med. Ctr.,* 2009 WL 2984842 (Trial Order) (N.Y. Sup. 2009); affirmed by *Bianco v. Flushing Hosp. Medical Center,* 79 A.D.3d 777 (N.Y.A.D. 2 Dept. Dec 14, 2010).

29. 656 F.3d 33 (1st Cir. 2011).

30. http://www.eeoc.gov/eeoc/newsroom/release/9-8-11b.cfm

31. http://www.eeoc.gov/eeoc/newsroom/release/9-8-11b.cfm

32. See *Becker's Hospital Review* at http://www.beckershospitalreview.com/hospital-management-adminstration/garfield-medical-center-in-california-settles-harassment-lawsuit-for-530k.html and http://www.eeoc.gov/eeoc/newsroom/release/11-16-11b.cfm

33. See, for example, *Doe v. Kaweah Delta Hosp.,* 2010 WL 5399228 (E.D. Cal.); the patient disclosed his AIDS diagnosis in the course of a hospital stay to a discharge planner who was also an acquaintance, and she allegedly spread the information to others; the plaintiff claimed he lost his beauty salon as a result.

34. See Conyers, L., et al. (2005). Workplace discrimination and HIV/AIDS: The National EEOC ADA Research Project. *Work, 25,* 37.

35. *Bragdon v. Abbott,* 524 U.S. 624 (1998). In *Abbott,* a dentist refused to treat an HIV-positive patient. Many courts nonetheless still apply an individualized approach to HIV/AIDS to determine whether the employee is, in fact, disabled under the statute. See Ravencraft, D. (2010). Why the "New ADA" requires an individualized inquiry as to what qualifies as a major life activity. *Northern Kentucky Law Review, 37,* 441. See 1973 Rehabilitation Act Section 504, 29 U.S.C. Section 794.

36. 566 N.Y.S.2d 79 (1991).

37. 151 Fed. Appx. 684 (10th Cir. 2005).

38. See, for example, *Silver v. North Shore University Hospital,* 490 F.Supp.2d 1346 (S.D.N.Y. 2007) (age discrimination based on a discriminatory mindset that outside funding sources would not favor persons older than 50 years of age); *CACI Premier Tech. v. Faraci,* 464 F.Supp.2d 527 (E.D.Va. 2007); *EEOC v. Hi 40 Corp.,* 953 F.Supp. 301 (E.D. Mo. 1996) (weight loss centers could not hire female counselors exclusively based on customer preferences); *Veleanu v. Beth Israel Medical Center,* 2000 WL 1400965 (S.D.N.Y.) (gender of the physician may be rationally related to patient preferences in obstetrics-gynecology and, therefore, is not discriminatory).

39. Iheukwumere, E. (2002). Doctor, are you experienced? The relevance of disclosure of physician

experience to a valid informed consent. *Journal of Contemporary Health and Policy, 18,* 373.

40. See, for example, Workers compensation program description and legislative history. *Social Security Administration Annual Statistical Supplement 2010.* Retrieved from http://www.ssa.gov/policy/docs/stat-comps/supplement/2010/workerscomp.html

41. See, for example, Leamon, T. B. (2009, September). Reducing occupational injury: The value and the challenge of determining the burden. Proceedings from *Use of Workers' Compensation Data for Occupational and Illness Prevention.* Retrieved from http://www.cdc.gov/niosh/docs/2010-152/pdfs/2010-152.pdf

42. See, for example, NYSIF announces 154 arrests, $16.6 million in fraud savings in 2009. Retrieved from http://ww3.nysif.com/AboutNYSIF/NYSIFNews/2010/NYSIF%20Announces%20 2009%20Anti%20Fraud%20Results.aspx. For the same period, according to the Department of Insurance, California's anti-fraud effort netted 682 arrests based on chargeable fraud of more than $370,000,000; http://www.insurance.ca.gov/0300-fraud/0100-fraud-division-overview/0500-fraud-division-programs/workers-comp-fraud/index.cfm

43. Four faces of insurance fraud. (2008). Retrieved from http://www.insurancefraud.org/four-faces.htm

44. Accenture, 2003.

45. Rose, R. (2009). Insurance fraud and workers compensation. *PLI/Literature, 796,* 317, 342.

46. See, for example, *Mtr. of Retz v. Surpass Chemical Co.,* 834 N.Y.S.2d 389 (3rd Dept. 2007); despite false claims of disability that were graphically disproved by surreptitious video surveillance, the claimant suffered only deprivation of benefits. In *Mtr. of Harabedian v. New York Hospital Medical Center,* 825 N.Y.S.2d 569 (3rd Dept. 2006), the plaintiff pleaded guilty to misdemeanor petty larceny in satisfaction of felony fraud charges for allegedly repeatedly obtaining reimbursements for medical-related expenses from her employer's carrier while also receiving payments for such expenses through her spouse's health insurance; she was declared ineligible for further benefits. To the same effect is *Robbins v. Mesivta Tifereth Jerusalem,* 874 N.Y.S.2d 638 (3rd Dept. 2009). Paying restitution often serves as the ultimate penalty. See *Mtr. of*

Dieter v. Trigen-Cinergy Solutions of Rochester, 787 N.Y.S.2d 499 (3rd Dept. 2005). Courts that impose sentences of probation and restitution for employees who work multiple jobs while collecting worker's compensation benefits do not ameliorate this atmosphere of leniency. See "New York Letter Carrier Who Lived Double Life Sentenced to Three Years' Probation" at http://www.uspsoig.gov/inv_health-care.htm

47. See Fulmer, S. Top 40 red flags which may indicate worker's compensation fraud. Retrieved from http://pursuitmag.com/top-40-red-flags-which-may-indicate-workers-compensation-fraud/

48. See the report of the Post Office Inspector General on anti-worker's compensation fraud efforts at http://www.uspsoig.gov/inv_healthcare.htm. The New York State Insurance Fund estimates that deterrence efforts present a return on investment of between 700% and 100%. See "Detecting Fraud" at http://ww3.nysif.com/SafetyRiskManagement/RiskManagement/LimitingLiability/DetectingFraud.aspx

49. See George, B.G. (2008). Revenge. *Law Review, 83,* 439, 467. ("The success of retaliation claims, as compared to the underlying complaint of discrimination, may be due in part to the more relaxed standard of 'discrimination.'"). Id. at 445.

50. *Houston v. Texas Southern Univ.* 2011 WL 31796 (S.D. Tex.).

51. Punitive damages are available where evil intent or motive or reckless or callous disregard for the protected rights of the employee is found. *Mendez. v. Starwood Hotels and Resorts Worldwide,* 764 F.Supp.2d 575 (S.D.N.Y. 2010); the jury empathized with the plaintiff and awarded punitive damages of $3 million for installing a hidden camera above the employee's workstation, but the award was reduced by the court to a nominal amount because the ratio of compensatory to punitive damages was 300:1; *Matusick v. Erie County Water Authority,* 774 F.Supp.2d 514 (W.D.N.Y. 2011).

52. The case results and details are at http://www.bloomberg.com/news/2011-05-04/ubs-unit-loses-10-6-million-sexual-harassment-jury-verdict-lawyer-says.html. *Ingraham v. UBS Financial Services Inc.,* 0916-CV-36471, Circuit Court, Jackson County, Missouri.

53. See supra, the *Tuli* and *Garfield Medical Center* cases cited under "Sexual Harassment."

54. 116 P.3d 1123 (Calif. 2005).

55. Many cases have since upheld opponents of discrimination under similar theories. See *Murphy v. Kirkland,* 930 N.Y.S.2d 285 (2nd Dept. 2011) (plaintiff opposed sexual harassment of another employee); *Sherrer v. Hamilton County Bd. of Health,* 747 F.Supp.2d 924 (S.D. Ohio 2010) (disability discrimination); *Mugavero v. Arms Acres,* 680 F.Supp.2d 544 (S.D.N.Y. 2010) (same as *Murphy,* supra).

56. 548 U.S. 53 (2006).

57. 129 S.Ct. 846 (2009).

58. 131 S.Ct. 1325 (2011).

59. *Murphy v. Kirkland,* 930 N.Y.S.2d 285 (2nd Dept. 2011).

60. *Mugavero v. Arms Acres,* 2009 WL 890063 (S.D.N.Y. 2009).

61. 131 S.Ct. 863 (2011).

62. Id. at 868.

63. Id. at 870.

64. 2011 WL 818662, 1 (N.D.Fla.).

65. Id. at 868.

66. See, for example, *Fogleman v. Mercy Hospital,* 283 F.3d 561 (3rd Cir. 2002) (the claim that the hospital terminated the employee because his father had filed a discrimination suit was cognizable under the Americans with Disabilities Act and the Age Discrimination in Employment Act); *Jackson v. Birmingham Bd. of Educ.,* 125 S.Ct. 1497 (2005) (permitting a man to make a claim for Title IX retaliation); *Sullivan v. Little Hunting Park, Inc.,* 396 U.S. 229, 90 S.Ct. 400 (1969) (wherein a Caucasian could sue for retaliation under 42 U.S.C. ß 1982 when he spoke out against discrimination against his black tenant). Merely naming another employee as a potential witness in an EEOC filing can confer protection. *EEOC v. Creative Networks,* 2008 U.S. Dist. LEXIS 103381 (D. Ariz. Dec. 12, 2008).

67. Pub. L. No. 111-148, 124 Stat. 119 (2010).

68. 31 U.S.C. sec. 3729-3733.

69. 42 U.S.C. § 1320a-7a.

70. Photopulos T. P., & Askew, G.W. (2008). Having your cake and eating it too: The (un)enforceability of releases on future qui tam claims. *Journal of Health and Life Sciences, 1,* 145.

71. In 2000, the Office of the Inspector General's (OIG's) $486 million settlement with Fresenius Medical Care Holdings, the nation's largest provider of kidney dialysis products and services, included the most comprehensive corporate integrity agreement ever imposed by the OIG. Other sizable 2000 settlements included $175 million with Beverly Enterprises, a nursing home chain, and $74.3 million with Anthem Blue Cross and Blue Shield of Connecticut. A current month-by-month listing of pending actions can be found at http://oig. hhs.gov/fraud/enforcement/criminal/index.asp and http://oig.hhs.gov/fraud/enforcement/cmp/false_claims.asp, and the majority of the charges are grounded in healthcare fraud. Many of the settlements were driven by self-reports, which reflects the real and potent authority of the OIG under the statute. One outcome was back pay and reinstatement for a victim of retaliation after reporting fraud. *U.S. ex rel. Nowak v. Medtronic, Inc.,* — F.Supp.2d—, 2011 WL 3208007 (Mass.). Such an outcome may not be anomalous in the future.

72. Patient Protection and Affordable Care Act (Pub. L. 111-148) (PPACA) and its companion, the Health Care and Education Reconciliation Act of 2010 (Pub. L. 111-152) (HERA).

73. Office of Public Affairs, U.S. Department of Justice. (2009, November 19). Justice Department recovers $2.4 billion in false claims cases in fiscal year 2009; more than $24 billion since 1986 [Press release]. Retrieved from http:// www.justice.gov/opa/pr/2009/November/09-civ-1253.html. A total of $2.4 billion was received altogether in that year; www.justice. gov/opa/pr/2009/November/09-civ-1253.html. The Department of Justice statistics include civil FCA settlements only; they do not include substantial criminal penalties or amounts awarded to the states under their false claims laws.

74. Id.

75. See http://www.stopmedicarefraud.gov/heatsuccess/index.html; http://www.hhs.gov/news/press/2011pres/01/20110124a.html

76. Department of Health and Human Services. (2009, May). Attorney General Holder and HHS Secretary Sibelius announce new interagency health care fraud and enforcement action team. Retrieved from http://www.hhs.gov/news/press/2009pres/05/20090520a.html

77. Department of Health and Human Services & Department of Justice. (2010, May). Health care fraud and abuse control program annual report for

fiscal year 2009. Retrieved from http://oig.hhs.gov/ publications/docs/hcfac/hcfacreport2010.pdf

78. Department of Health and Human Services & Department of Justice. Health care fraud and abuse control program annual report for fiscal year 2010. Retrieved from http://oig.hhs.gov/publications/docs/ hcfac/hcfacreport2010.pdf. In the three and a half years since its inception, Strike Force prosecutors filed 465 cases charging 829 defendants who collectively billed the Medicare program more than $1.9 billion; 481 defendants pleaded guilty and 48 others were convicted in jury trials, and 358 defendants were sentenced to imprisonment for an average term of nearly 44 months. http://www.codingnetwork. com/blog/post/health-care-fraud-and-abuse-control-program-annual-report-for-fiscal-year-2/

79. The employee should state explicitly in such a release that he or she is not aware of any violations of the law, or should specify those he or she is aware of. Whistling while they work: Limiting exposure in the face of PPACA's invitation to employee whistleblower suits. (2010). *Health Lawyer, 22,* 19, 24.

80. http://www.phillipsandcohen.com/2009/Bextra-whistleblower-case-leads-to-record-setting-Pfizer-settlement.shtml

81. The Health Alliance of greater Cincinnati and the Christ Hospital to pay $108 million for violating anti-kickback statute and defrauding Medicare and Medicaid. (2010, May). Retrieved from http://www. justice.gov/opa/pr/2010/May/10-civ-602.html

82. http://fraudblawg.com/2010/01/14/wheaton-community-hospital-violates-the-false-claims-act/

83. http://www.longislandpress.com/2011/12/01/whis-tleblower-feted-in-northport-hospital-case/

84. http://www.ktbs.com/news/27108735/detail.html

85. Seven individual hospitals' settlement amounts as of January 2010:

- Lakeland Regional Medical Center, Lakeland, Florida: $1,660,134
- Seton Medical Center, Austin, Texas: $1,232,956
- Greenville Memorial Hospital, Greenville, South Carolina: $1,026,764
- Health Care Authority of Lauderdale County and City of Florence, Ala., doing business as Coffee Health Group (formerly known as Eliza Coffee Memorial Hospital): $676,038

- Presbyterian Orthopaedic Hospital, Charlotte, North Carolina: $637,872
- St. Dominic-Jackson Memorial Hospital, Jackson, Mississippi: $555,949
- Health Care Authority of Morgan County—City of Decatur doing business as Decatur General Hospital, Decatur, Alabama: $537,893

http://www.phillipsandcohen.com/2011/ Hospital-Medicare-fraud-settlements-for-kyphoplasty-billing-bring-total-recovered-from-whistleblower-lawsuit-to-101-million.shtml

86. Ongoing Department of Justice investigation that began with a settlement for $75,000,000 with Medtronic Spine for counseling hospitals to admit patients undergoing the procedure overnight; see http://www.fcaalert.com/tags/kyphoplasty/

87. First Amendment/free speech concerns are not applicable to private employers.

88. Fake friending (gaining access to social networks through misrepresentation) and coerced friending (by supervisors whose requests may be perceived as coercive); *Petryol v. Hillstone Restaurant Group*, 2009 WL 3128420 (D.N.J. 2009).

89. http://recruiting.jobvite.com/news/press-releases/pr/ jobvite-social-recruiting-survey-2010.php

90. Under Section 7 of the National Labor Relations Act (29 U.S.C. § 151-169, NLRA), employees have the right to engage in concerted activity. Under Section 8 of the NLRA, it is an unfair labor practice for an employer to interfere with or restrain an employee in exercise of his or her rights.

91. Case No. 34-CA-12576 before the National Labor Relations Board.

92. See, for example, N.Y. LAB. LAW § 201-d(2)(c) (McKinney 2002) (prohibiting discrimination, refusal to hire, or termination of employees based on "legal recreational activities outside work hours, off of the employer's premises and without use of the employer's equipment or other property"); CAL. LAB. CODE § 1102.5(a) (2009); COLO. REV. STAT. § 24-34-402.5(1) (2008).

93. Simonetti, E. (2004, December 14). I was fired for blogging. *CNET.* Retrieved from http://news.cnet. com/I-was-fired-for-blogging/2010-1030_ 3-5490836.html. See *Simonetti v. Delta Air Line Inc.,* Case No. 1:05-CV-2321, Complaint filed (N.D. Ga. Sept. 7, 2005). The case was stayed after Delta

entered bankruptcy. Simonetti is considered "dooced"—fired for what she wrote in a blog. See Netlingo.com at http://www.netlingo.com/lookup.cfm?term=dooce

94. Of course, online information becomes available universally and is difficult, if not impossible, to retract.

95. Compare the termination of the sociology professor who was suspended for posting on her Facebook page in January, "Does anyone know where I can find a very discrete hitman? Yes, it's been that kind of day . . ." At a later date: "had a good day today. DIDN'T want to kill even one student. :-). Now Friday was a different story."

96. http://www.hcca-info.org/staticcontent/2011Social MediaSurvey_report.pdf

97. 751 A.2d 538 (N.J. 2000).

98. 302 S.W.3d 592 (Sup. Ct. Ark. 2009).

99. *C.R. v. Tenet Healthcare Corp.,* 169 Cal.App.4th 1094, 87 Cal.Rptr.3d 424 Cal.App. 2 Dist. (2009) (sexual abuse of patients).

100. See, generally, "Employee Background Checks Were on Many States' Lawmaking Calendars," 2003 State Legislation, Daily Labor Relations, Supp. Rep., No. 84, May 3, 2004 (S-5).

101. For example, *Jones v. Healthsouth Treasure Valley Hosp.,* 206 P.3d 473(2009) (wherein an independent contractor who worked in the hospital, a cell-saver technician, worked under "apparent authority" of the hospital and so gave rise to a claim of negligent hiring); in *Harrison v. Binnion,* 214 P.3d 473 (2009), a hospital was held by the Idaho Supreme Court to be potentially liable for credentialing a physician who had a history of substance abuse.

102. This baseline connotes more than merely interviewing an employee and reviewing his or her resume. It requires contacting references and former employers, for instance, if employment carries with it the authority to enter someone's living quarters or to provide intimate physical care. *Tallahassee Furniture Co., Inc. v. Harrison,* 583 So.2d 744 (Fla. App. 1 Dist., 1991). See N.Y. Corr. Law Sect. 752 (2) (McKinney 1987), allowing limited circumstances wherein employers can determine the risks of employing an ex-offender based on the correlation between the offense and the duties of the job, the interval since the offense, the age of the offender

at that time, and the gravity of the crime. See N.Y. Corr. Law Sections 750-53. All Medicare and Medicaid providers should be aware of the current focus of the Center for Medicare and Medicaid Services on vetting providers. See Dresevic, A., Romano, D. (2011, April). The Medicare enrollment process: CMS's most potent program integrity tool. *Health Lawyer, 23*(4), 1.

103. Sentencing Reform Act of 1984, Pub. L. No. 98-473, 98 Stat. 1987(codified as amended in scattered sections of 18 U.S.C. and 28 U.S.C.). These guidelines have been strengthened and impose affirmative responsibilities on boards of directors, including setting a corporate climate that encourages ethical conduct and compliance with the law. Supplement to Appendix C, Amendment 673, http://www.ussc.gov/Guidelines-/2010_guidelines/Manual_PDF/Appendix_C_Supplement.pdf (starting at page 102).

104. See Federal Sentencing Guidelines Manual § 8B2.1 (2009), for a full description of the components of such a program.

105. See Office of the Inspector General of the Department of Health and Human Services & America Health Lawyers Association. (2003, April). Corporate responsibility and corporate compliance: A resource for healthcare boards of directors. Retrieved from http://www.nhpco.org/files/public/040203CorpRespRsceGuide.pdf; see Department of Health and Human Services, Office of the Inspector General's Compliance Program Guidance for Pharmaceutical Manufacturers, 68 Fed. Reg. 23,731, 23,731 (May 5, 2003), for general guidance in healthcare.

106. Studies that support these conclusions abound. See American Hospital Association Resource Center. (2010). Workplace intimidation in the health care setting. Retrieved from http://www.ashrm.org/ashrm/.../WorkplaceIntimidationBibliography.pdf

107. The silent treatment. Retrieved from http://www.silenttreatmentstudy.com/. Key findings include: The 10 percent of healthcare workers who confidently raise crucial concerns observe better patient outcomes, work harder, are more satisfied, and are more committed to staying in their jobs.

108. Behaviors that undermine a culture of safety. (2008, July 9). *Sentinel Event Alert, 40.* Retrieved

from http://www.jointcommission.org/assets/1/18/SEA_40.PDF

109. See., for example, Halverson, D. (2010). Abuse in the medical workplace: Fact vs. myth. Retrieved from http://www.workplacebullying.org/2010/02/20/medical-workplace/; Felblinger, D. (2008). Incivility in the workplace and nurses' shame responses. *Journal of Obstetric, Gynecologic and Neonatal Nursing, 37*, 234–242; Hutton, S. & Gates, D. (2009). Workplace incivility and productivity losses among direct care staff. *American Journal of Nursing, 109*, 52–58 (patient and management incivility is more detrimental than coworkers); Rosenstein, A. & Naylor, B. (2011, March). Incidence and impact of physician and nurse disruptive behaviors in the emergency department. *Journal of Emergency Medicine.*

110. See Brown, T. (2011, May 7). Physician, heel thyself. *New York Times.*

111. Bad blood: Doctor–nurse behavior problems impact patient care. (2009, November/December). *American College of Physician Executives.*

112. Rosenstein, A. (2008). A survey of the impact of disruptive behaviors and communication defects on patient safety. *The Joint Commission Journal on Quality and Patient Safety, 34*, 464–471. Retrieved from http://www.mc.vanderbilt.edu/root/pdfs/nursing/ppb_article_on_disruptive.pdf

113. Gates, D. M. (2004). The epidemic of violence against healthcare workers. *Occupational and Environmental Medicine*, 649.

114. See Stewart, J. B. (2000). *Blind eye: The terrifying story of a doctor who got away with murder.* New York, NY: Simon and Schuster; Quirey, M. & Adams, J. (n.d.) National Practitioner Databank revisited: The lessons of Michael Swango, M.D. Retrieved from http://www.vsb.org/sections/hl/bank.pdf; Perez-Pena, R. et al. (2004, February 29). Through gaps in system nurse left trail of grief. *New York Times*; Leung, R. (2007, December 5). Did hospitals "see no evil"? *60 Minutes.* Retrieved from http://www.cbsnews.com/stories/2004/04/02/60minutes/main610047.shtml; A list of Charles Cullen's Victims. (2006). Retrieved from http://abclocal.go.com/wpvi/story?section=news/local&id=3954437

115. The Occupational Safety and Health Administration's guidance on prevention programs and response may be found at http://www.osha.gov/Publications/osha3148.pdf. In September 2011, OSHA issued new guidelines for investigation workplace violence incidents; see http://www.osha.gov/OshDoc/Directive_pdf/CPL_02-01-052.pdf

116. Campbell, J. et al. (2011). *Journal of Occupational and Environmental Medicine, 53*, 82–89. See Occupational hazards in hospitals." National Institute for Occupational Safety and Health. (2002). Retrieved from http://www.njha.com/ep/pdf/112200723511PM.pdf

117. Preventing violence in the health care setting. (2010, June 3). *Sentinel Event Alert, 45.* Retrieved from http://www.jointcommission.org/assets/1/18/SEA_45.PDF

118. Goodstein, L., & Glaberman, W. (2000, April 10). The well-marked roads to homicidal rage. See also Fessenden, F. et al. (2000, April 9). They threaten, seethe and unhinge, then kill in quantity. *New York Times;* "Of the 100 cases reviewed by *The Times,* 63 involved people who made threats of violence before the event, including 54 who threatened specific violence to specific people." See Atkinson, W. (n.d.). Keeping violent employees out of the workplace. *Risk Management.* Retrieved from http://www.rmmag.com/Magazine/PrintTemplate.cfm?AID=283

119. See Stewart, J. B. (2000). *Blind eye: The terrifying story of a doctor who got away with murder.* New York, NY: Simon and Schuster; Quirey, M., & Adams, J. (n.d.) National Practitioner Databank revisited: The lessons of Michael Swango, M.D. Retrieved from http://www.vsb.org/sections/hl/bank.pdf; Perez-Pena, R. et al. (2004, February 29). Through gaps in system nurse left trail of grief. *New York Times;* Leung, R. (2007, December 5). Did hospitals "see no evil"? *60 Minutes.* Retrieved from http://www.cbsnews.com/stories/2004/04/02/60minutes/main610047.shtml; A list of Charles Cullen's victims. (2006). Retrieved from http://abclocal.go.com/wpvi/story?section=news/local&id=3954437

120. 2009 WL 5170193.

121. Id. at 8 (italics added).

122. 491 F.2d 95 (2nd Cir. 2007).

123. Id. at 99.

124. An employee alleging defamation must show that the information concerned the employee, that it was

published or disclosed to others, that it is false, that it damages the employee's reputation, and that the employer either acted negligently or had malicious intent. If a hospital discharges an employee for incompetence, that is protected opinion if it can be substantiated with facts and documents upon challenge. *Doe v. White Plains Hospital Medical Center,* 2011 WL 2899174 (S.D.N.Y.). However, to maintain this protection from liability, the information can be published only to those with a need to know. See *Johnson v. Medisys Health Network,* 2011 WL 5222917 (E.D.N.Y. 2011).

125. 987 P.2d 1172 (N.M. 1999).

126. See also *Theisen v. Covenant Medical Center,* 636 N.W.2d 74 (Iowa 2001), wherein the court stated: A limited privilege applies to communications made in good faith on any subject matter in which the [person communicating] has an interest, or with reference to which he has a duty . . . if made to another person having a corresponding interest or duty, on a privileged occasion and in a manner and under circumstances fairly warranted by the occasion and duty, right or interest.

127. *Johnson v. C. White & Son, Inc.,* 2011 WL 761540 (D. Conn. 2011). See the Connecticut Supreme Court's recognition of the qualified privilege in *Miron v. University of New Haven Police Dept.,* 631 A.2d 847 (2007).

128. *Chudacoff v. Univ. Med. Ctr. of Southern Nevada,* 11 Cal. Daily Op. Serv. 7064 (9th Cir. 2011); *Ritten v. Lapeer Regional Med. Ctr.,* 611 F.Supp.2d 696 (E.D. Mich. 2009).

129. *Panghat v. New York Downtown Hospital,* 925 N.Y.S.2d 445 (1st Dept. 2011).

130. Rosenstein, A. (2002). Nurse–physician relationships: Impact on nurse satisfaction and retention. *American Journal of Nursing, 106*(6), 26–34. Cited in The Dun Factor. (2006, May/June). The six factors of communication risk. *Patient Safety and Quality Healthcare.*

131. From ISMP in Private Practice Success, September 2004.

132. See The Dun Factor, supra, fn. 130. Retrieved from http://www.psqh.com/mayjun06/dunsb1.html

133. See Rowe, M. (1990). Barriers to equality: The power of subtle discrimination to maintain unequal opportunity. *Employee Rights and Responsibilities Journal, 3,* 153. Retrieved from http://web.mit.edu/ombud/publications/barriers.pdf; Moynahan, B. (2009). Engaging employees: Pay attention to messages you're overlooking. Retrieved from http://www.workforcediversitynetwork.com/docs/Articles/Article_EngagingEmployees_Moynahan_3.09-3.pdf; Hinton, E. (2003, March/April). Microinequities: When small slights lead to huge problems in the workplace. *Diversity, Inc.* Retrieved from http://www.magazine.org/content/files/Microinequities.pdf

134. Issue 40: Behaviors that undermine a culture of safety. (2008, July 9). Retrieved from http://www.jointcommission.org/assets/1/18/SEA_40.PDF

135. See Gardezi, F. et al. (2009). Silence, power and communication in the operating room. *Journal of Advanced Nursing, 65,* 1390–1399.

136. How opportunities in the workplace and fairness affect intergroup relations. (2003). Survey conducted by the Center for Survey Research and Analysis at the University of Connecticut for the Level Playing Field Institute. The full report is available at http://www.lpfi.org/workplace/res_howfair.shtml

137. Silence kills. Retrieved from http://www.aacn.org/WD/Practice/Docs/PublicPolicy/SilenceKills.pdf. See also Vital Smarts. (2008). Eliminating cultures of silence. Retrieved from http://www.vitalsmarts.com/userfiles/File/pdf/PositionPapers/Cultures of Silence.pdf (wherein cases of a death at Baylor University Medical Center and one at Duke University Medical Center as a result of mismatched blood types during organ transplants were the result of people not speaking up and demanding that physicians engage in standard double-checking procedures). See Bleich, S. (2005). Medical errors: Five years after the IOM report. Commonwealth Fund. Retrieved from http://www.commonwealthfund.org/usr_doc/830_Bleich_errors.pdf; following up on Institute of Medicine. (2000). To err is human: Building a safer health system. Retrieved from http://www.iom.edu/~/media/Files/Report%20Files/1999/To-Err-is-Human/To%20Err%20is%20Human%201999%20%20report%20brief.pdf. For an in-depth case study of the impact of employee voice, see Rabkin, M., & Avakian, L. (2002). Enhancing patient care through enhancing employee

voice: Reflections on the Scanlon Plan at Boston's Beth Israel Medical Center. Retrieved from http://web.mit.edu/workplacecenter/docs/wpc0002.pdf

138. See, for example, Burris, E. R., & Detert, J. (2008). Quitting before leaving: The mediating effects of psychological attachment and detachment on voice. *Journal of Applied Psychology, 93*, 912. Nembhard, I., & Edmondson, A. (2006). Making it safe: The effects of leader inclusiveness and professional status on psychological safety and improvement efforts in health care teams. *Journal of Organizational Behavior, 27*, 941.

139. Social Knows Engagement Statistics. (2011, August). Retrieved from http://www.thesocialworkplace.com/2011/08/08/social-knows-employee-engagement-statistics-august-2011-edition/

140. See Fink, J. (2007). Unintended consequences: How antidiscrimination increases group bias in employer defendants. Retrieved from http://works.bepress.com/cgi/viewcontent.cgi?article=1000&context=jessica_fink and http://works.bepress.com/jessica_fink/1

141. The Joint Commission. (2008, July 9). Sentinel Event Alert: Behaviors that undermine a culture of safety, 40. Retrieved from http://www.jointcommission.org/SentinelEvents/Sentineleventalert/sea_40.htm. See the 2005 Silence Kills study at http://www.silenttreatmentstudy.com/silencekills/SilenceKills.pdf, and the Executive Summary at http://www.silenttreatmentstudy.com/Silent%20Treatment%20Executive%20Summary.pdf. See Institute of Medicine. (2004). *Keeping patients safe: Transforming the work force of nurses*. Washington, DC: National Academy Press.

142. Victims of bullying have been shown to suffer more adverse outcomes than victims of sexual harassment. Hershcovis, S., & Barling, J. (2010). Comparing victim attributions and outcomes for workplace aggression and sexual harassment. *Journal of Applied Psychology, 95*, 874.

143. See, for example, Yamata, D. (2007). Potential legal protections and liabilities for workplace bullying. Retrieved from http://www.newworkplaceinstitute.org/docs/nwi.web.bullying&law2.pdf

144. Id.

145. Rosenstein, A., & O'Daniel, M. (2008). A survey of the impact of disruptive behavior and communication defects on patient safety. *The Joint Commission Journal on Quality and Patient Safety, 34*, 464. Rosenstein, A. (2011). The quality and economic impact of disruptive behaviors on clinical outcomes in patient care. *American Journal of Medical Quality*; Rosenstein, A. (2010). Measuring and managing the economic impact of disruptive behaviors in the hospital. *Journal of Healthcare Risk Management, 30*, 20. See Tarkan, L. (2008, December 1). Arrogant, abusive and disruptive: A doctor. *New York Times*.

146. The link between patient satisfaction and malpractice. (2010, February). *Press Ganey*; Litman, R. S. (2009). Physician communication skills decrease malpractice claims. *ASA Newsletter, 73*(12), 20–21; Tallman, K. et al. (2007). Communication practices of physicians with high patient-satisfaction ratings. *Permanente Journal, 11*, 19; Return on investment: Reducing malpractice claims by improving patient satisfaction. (2007). *Press Ganey*. Retrieved from http://www.pressganey.com/Documents/research/hospitals/ROI%20Resources/Malpractice_Final_12-14-07.pdf?viewFile; Beyond patient satisfaction: How compassion creates loyalty. (2005). Interplay; Huntington, B., & Kuhn, N. (2003). Communication gaffes: A root cause of malpractice claims. *Baylor University Medical Proceedings, 16*, 16. Retrieved from http://baylorhealth.edu/proceedings/16_2/16_2_huntington.pdf

147. Tangirala, S., & Ramanujam, R. (2008). Employee silence on critical work issues: The cross-level effects of procedural justice climate. *Personnel Psychology, 61*, 37.

148. *Phillips v. Bowen*, 278 F.3d 103 (2nd Cir. 2002) (series of counseling sessions for Saratoga County Sheriff's Office employee upheld) (quoting *Smart v. Ball State University*, 89 F.3d 437, 442-43 (7th Cir. 1996); *Weeks v. New York State*, 273 F.3d 76 (2nd Cir. 2001); *McMillon v. Corridan*, 1999 WL 729250 (E.D. La. 1999). To the same effect is *Figueroa v. N.Y.C. Health and Hospitals Corp.*, 2007 WL 2274253 (S.D.N.Y. August 7, 2007).

149. See, for example, *Naik v. Boehringer Ingelheim Pharmaceuticals, Inc.*, 2010 WL 4702453 (C.A.7 (Ill.)).

150. In *Wayne v. Principi*, S.D.N.Y. March. 3, 2004 (Slip Opn.), the Department of Veterans Affairs prevailed in a retaliation case based largely on counseling

sessions; see also *Jack-Goods v. State Farm Mut. Auto. Ins. Co.,* Slip Opn., N.D.Ill. May 6, 2004 (counseling sessions, cited by the plaintiff-employee as evidence of racial and other discrimination, were held to be appropriate criticism of performance); *Ponniah Das v. Our Lady of Mercy Medical Center,* 2002 WL 826877 (S.D.N.Y. 2002) (criticisms that precede the protected activity are relevant to finding there was no causal nexus in retaliation claim); *Sims v. Health Midwest Physician Services Corp.,* 196 F.3d 915, 921 (8th Cir. 1999); *Riebhoff v. Cenex/Land O'Lakes Agronomy Company,* 1998 WL 901749 (Minn. App. 1998) (unpublished) (counseling sessions were held to be valid criticism of inadequate performance and defeated claims of age discrimination, retaliation, and defamation); *Mercado v. N.Y.C. Housing Authority,* 1998 WL 15 (disability); *Gasio v. Department of Navy,* 114 F.3d 1207 (Fed. Cir. 1997) (claim of wrongful discharge based on disrespectful conduct).

151. See Oakley, J. (2005). Linking organizational characteristics to employee attitudes and behavior. Northwestern University Forum for People Management. Bullying is three to four times more prevalent than sexual harassment according to the 2010 Workplace Bullying Institute Survey (http://www.workplacebullying.org/wbiresearch/2010-wbi-national-survey/). According to CareerBuilder.com, approximately one out of four victims of bullying complains to the human resources departments, but 62% of those people claim that nothing was done in response (http://www.careerbuilder.com/share/aboutus/pressreleasesdetail.aspx?id=pr632&sd=4%2f20%2f2011&ed=4%2f20%2f2099). In *Street v. U.S. Corrugated,* 2011 WL 304568 (W.D. Ky. 2011), five employees (three women and two men) sued, contending a turnaround expert was abusive to them (yelling, cursing, throwing objects, and making physical threats). Although they lost in court because the employer prevailed on an "equal opportunity" defense (i.e., the "expert" did not discriminate based on gender but treated everyone equally miserably), the employer apparently recognized a problem, and the expert was soon removed. Nonetheless, the employees had to do battle in court—an experience that they could not have regarded as positive—and the employer won a

Pyrrhic victory. For a study on verbal abuse of nurses, see Martin, A. et al. (2007). Nurses' responses to workplace verbal abuse: A scenario study of the impact of situational and individual factors. *Research and Practice in Human Resource Management.*

152. See Hastings, R. R. (2006, April). Minorities lack faith in promotion policies. *Society for Human Resource Management.* Retrieved from http://www.wshrma.org/newsletters/june2006.pdf

153. How opportunities in the workplace and fairness affect intergroup relations. (2003). Survey conducted by the Center for Survey Research and Analysis at the University of Connecticut for the Level Playing Field Institute. The full report is available at http://www.lpfi.org/workplace/res_howfair.shtml

154. Healthcare employers, under new pressure to meet patient satisfaction expectations, are also at risk when employees are not fully engaged. Sibson Consulting conducted its 2010 survey and found 52% of employees were engaged in 2009, compared with 47% in 2006 (http://www.sibson.com/publications/surveysandstudies/2009ROW.pdf). It defined "engaged" as one who know what to do and wants to do it. In December 2010, Blessing White found approximately 31% of employees engaged (http://www.blessingwhite.com/EEE__report.asp). See Fink, J. (2007). Unintended consequences: How antidiscrimination increases group bias in employer defendants. Retrieved from http://works.bepress.com/cgi/viewcontent.cgi?article=1000&context=jessica_fink and http://works.bepress.com/jessica_fink/1.

155. According to the Gallup data, 15% of all workers felt they had been subjected to some sort of discriminatory or unfair treatment. Among various racial/ethnic groups, 31% of Asians surveyed reported incidents of discrimination, the largest percentage of any ethnic group, with African Americans constituting the second largest group at 26%. Despite the incidents of discrimination experienced on the jobs, many employees chose not to file charges. Indeed, only 3% of the employees who filed charges at the EEOC were Asian/Pacific Islanders (http://www.eeoc.gov/eeoc/newsroom/release/12-8-05.cfm). These "unfiled" grievances have an impact that does lend itself to facile estimates.

156. See, for example, Three in ten African-American workers have experienced discrimination or unfair treatment at work. Retrieved from http://www.careerbuilder.com/share/aboutus/pressreleasesdetail.aspx?id=pr378&sd=6%2f19%2f2007&ed=12%2f31%2f2007; Ensher, E. et al. Effects of perceived discrimination on job satisfaction, organizational commitment, organizational citizenship behavior and grievances.

157. *Cincinnati Enquirer* poll at http://www.enquirer.com/editions/2001/09/04/loc_at_work_blacks_still.html

158. "The social costs of making attributions to discrimination may prevent stigmatized people from confronting the discrimination they face in their daily lives." Kaiser, C.R., & Miller, C.T. (2001, February). Stop complaining! The social costs of making attributions to discrimination. *Personnel and Social Psychology Bulletin, 27(2),* 254. Middle-class African Americans anticipate backlash from confronting discrimination; Feagin, J.R., & Sikes, M.P. (1994). *Living with racism: The black middle-class experience*. Boston: Beacon. In fact, in the study contained in "Stop Complaining!", "participants readily devalued an African-American man who attributed his failure to discrimination . . . participants thought he was a complainer . . . [I]t is stunning that this negative impression was created even when discrimination was certainly the cause of the failing grade" (pp. 261–262).

159. See Hastings, R.R. (2006, April). Minorities lack faith in promotion policies. *Society for Human Resource Management.*

160. Alternative dispute resolution mechanisms that carry insulation from retaliation have had notable successes: Crenshaw, W.D. (2011). Emerging applications for ADR. WL 284498; Morrison, G., & Robson, R. (2003, Spring). ADR in healthcare: The last big ADR frontier? *Conflict Resolution Quarterly.* Mandatory arbitration can also serve as a vehicle for resolution short of judicial proceedings: Stipanowich, T. (2010). Arbitration: "The new litigation." *University of Illinois Law Review, 201,* 1. These processes, however, must be infused with fairness, or else they will be perceived as employer-created tools to perpetuate inequitable treatment. See Hickox, S. (2010). Ensuring enforceability and fairness in the arbitration of employment disputes. *Widener Law Review, 16,* 101.

CHAPTER 4

Communications to Reduce Risk

Alice L. Epstein

Interactions between clinicians, and between clinicians and patients, and our ability to be understood are essential in the provision of quality care and patient safety. Informed consent, speak-up campaigns, preoperative surgical site verification, medication instructions, and family rapid response teams are promoted to improve patient safety. Communication skills are a basic tenet of all societies. Throughout history, the ability to communicate or inability to communicate has led to misunderstandings, wars, alliances, and treaties. Barriers to effective communication include the following:

- Lack of or poor listening skills
- Physical barriers
- Personal distractions

The ability to communicate depends on myriad factors. Intelligence, personality, age, and environmental factors (e.g., stress) all contribute to how well or how poorly we communicate. Studies have shown that lower-socioeconomic-status children have much more stress than their higher-status counterparts, although a 2012 study found that the lower-socioeconomic group does not have a higher propensity to litigate. Intelligence can be characterized as fluid or crystallized. Fluid intelligence is the ability to solve novel abstract problems on the spot; this type of intelligence diminishes with age. Crystallized intelligence, or knowledge of the world and how it works, increases as we grow older and gain more life experience. Crystallized intelligence is also clearly subject to education and to the increasing availability of information in today's society.[1]

In addition to intelligence, social situations, environment, income, opportunities, education, and biology influence our ability to communicate. Recognition of the constraints to communication and striving to mitigate and improve upon these factors pave the way to use communications in reducing risk and improving quality.

Extrapolating the findings of the National Research Council Committee on the Assessment of the 21st Century,[2] the following broad cognitive and affective skills are needed by healthcare clinicians:

- *Cognitive skills:* Nonroutine problem solving, critical thinking, systems thinking
- *Interpersonal skills:* Complex communication, social skills, teamwork, cultural sensitivity, dealing with diversity
- *Intrapersonal skills:* Self-management, time management, self-development, self-regulation, adaptability, executive functioning

Weel stated in 1983:

> With the increasing cultural pluralism of the United States, clinicians are more likely to encounter patients from a variety of socio-cultural backgrounds. Since this background influences the presentation of disorders and response to treatment, it behooves clinicians to possess guidelines for culturally appropriate practice. The answer is not necessarily in detailed knowledge of specific cultures. Rather, clinicians need to know how to consider language variations, the culture of their patients, and their own cultural backgrounds. Sensitivity to such issues may enhance the treatment of all patients.[3]

This premise of understanding patients within their societal demands and culture is paramount in managing risk.

According to some reports, medical schools are doing an inadequate job of facilitating medical students' understanding of patients' culture and the development of skills required for the provision of safe patient care. This includes an understanding of systems thinking, problem analysis, application of human factors science, communication skills, patient-centered care, and teaming concepts and skills.[4] Engaging the patient results in improved diagnostic ability, an understanding of the patient's perspective, and the development of a physician–patient partnership. Clinicians should listen to both what is said and what is not said, by observing body language, voice inflection, appropriateness of complaints, and nonverbal responses to questions.

The American Society of Healthcare Risk Managers[5] report that 100% of the time patients expect to receive the following treatment:

- Have their clinical care timely and impeccably documented
- Be listened to, taken seriously, and respected as a care partner
- Be told the truth—always
- Be supported emotionally as well as physically
- Receive high-quality, safe care

COMMUNICATION AND ITS IMPACT ON MALPRACTICE LITIGATION

History shows that physicians in the mid-1800s were targets of a great deal of malpractice litigation. Lawyers alleged that physicians did not provide due proper care, skill, and diligence. A review of the literature seems to indicate that the attitudes and behaviors of patients, lawyers, physicians, and judges have not changed significantly through the mid-1900s and continue in much the same vein today.[6] A major study analyzed 15 years of malpractice data for all physicians who were covered by a large professional liability insurer. Each year 7.4% of all physicians had a malpractice claim, with 1.6% having a claim leading to a payment. The proportion of physicians facing a claim each year ranged from highs of 19.1% in neurosurgery, 18.9% in thoracic–cardiovascular surgery, and 15.3% in general surgery to 5.2% in family medicine, 3.1% in pediatrics, and 2.6% in psychiatry.[7]

A national study of more than 7,000 American surgeons highlighted the toll that malpractice litigation takes on the emotions and quality of life of physicians. The frequency of malpractice lawsuits and the adverse associations with surgeons' mental quality of life, burnout, career satisfaction, and suicidal ideation can adversely affect surgeons' personal health.

Experiencing a malpractice lawsuit is associated with distress, including burnout and depression. Although the authors of this study were unable to determine whether burnout contributes to an increased risk of malpractice suits, they did note a previous study indicating a relationship between burnout and medical errors. Physician burnout can result in poor judgment in patient care decision making, hostility toward patients, adverse patient events, less compassion, and diminished commitment and dedication to productive, safe, and optimal patient care. It seemed intuitive to the authors to hypothesize a similar relationship between burnout and malpractice litigation.[8] Risk managers should be cognizant of the litigation history of the clinicians within their facility. Counseling programs, malpractice mentors, and peer support systems can provide assist for these stressed clinicians.

Patients sue for a variety of reasons—first and foremost, because they have suffered an injury from the healthcare system. Injuries occur as a result of what was done or not done to the patient. Of course, a patient may sue even if no injury has occurred, but these lawsuits are considered nonmeritorious. Unfortunately, even nonmeritorious lawsuits cost the healthcare clinician and organization thousands of dollars to defend. Patients taking legal action want greater honesty, an appreciation of the severity of the trauma they suffered, and assurance that lessons have been learned from their experience. Analysis of recent malpractice lawsuits indicates the principal reasons why patients sue have not changed over the years.

A seminal study on this issue was published in 1994.[9] The reactions of patients who experienced untoward adverse medical events remain much the same today. Of those interviewed:

- Ninety percent expressed anger.
- Eighty percent expressed bitterness.
- Fifty-five percent felt betrayed.
- Forty percent were humiliated.

Four main themes emerged from the analysis of reasons for litigation:

- *Altruism:* Prevention of similar incidents in the future to others
- *Rationalization:* Need for an explanation to know how and why the injury happened
- *Recompense:* Compensation for actual losses, pain and suffering, or to provide care in the future for an injured person
- *Accountability:* Admission of negligence from the staff or organization for their actions

Although the reasons why patients file lawsuits and how they feel following an untoward adverse event have not changed, the technology associated with communication has changed dramatically. How we communicate is dynamic and requires new skills and insight into the best methods to ensure effectiveness of these technologies. Telemedicine, for example, is transforming the traditional view of medicine. Patient assessments and evaluations are performed using the Internet through audio and video technology. Emergency departments are triaging patients online before they ever leave their homes. Texting and email are being used to connect patients and physicians. Healthcare consumers seeking advice are accessing the World Wide Web for health information. In addition, online social networks are part of the participatory process.

Technology is also available to track every medication, surgical sponge, medical supply, patient (including newborns), and staff member.

Wireless sensors can monitor even routine procedures, such as physician and nurse hand washing. Clinicians can access the vital signs of hospitalized intensive care patients via their smart phones, and obstetricians can monitor the uterine contractions and fetal heart rate of expectant mothers via their cell phones. Rather than having the intensive care unit be the sole place where frequent vital sign measurements are recorded, every hospitalized patient's heart rate and rhythm, blood pressure, and other vital signs will be monitored continuously by noninvasive wireless sensors. Risk managers need to facilitate development of communication skills for all clinicians that best utilize these technologies while not compromising patient care and the risk posture of the facility.

RESPECT AND CIVILITY

Disrespect is a common causal allegation when analyzing malpractice claims. Civility between healthcare providers is as important as civility and respect between clinicians and patients.[10] One of the most demoralizing events for any clinician is the occurrence of an unanticipated significant adverse clinical event. How healthcare providers and patients communicate during these trying times can significantly affect patient and provider outcomes. Multiple studies have been conducted to determine the effect of communication following adverse events. Overall, such studies have demonstrated that clinician communication provided in a timely manner with sincerity influences patients' responses to adverse events. "Confronting an adverse medical event collaboratively helped both patients and providers with patients' emotional, physical, and financial trauma, as well as minimized anger and frustration commonly

experienced."[11] Healthcare organizations and clinicians should consider the patient experience when developing training or evaluating processes in patient resolution.

Physicians and clinicians face the stressor of providing "correct" patient care, with all that entails, every day of their careers. They are subject to the frailties of existence, complexities of decision making, adequacy of training, and other complicating factors of life. Empathy, compassion, and care are the three basic moral tenets for all clinicians. Empathy is understood as "a mainly cognitive and morally neutral capacity of understanding." Compassion is the "emotional and virtuous core of the clinician." Care—an attitude as well as an activity—is regarded as the "intrinsically morally valuable" inclination to help and the activity involved in demonstrating that attitude. Empathic compassion care has been proposed as the balance between closeness and professionalism and the right form of attention to the person of the patient.[12] Empathic compassionate care combined with effective communication serves to improve the quality of care and minimize the risk that our differences bring to the situation. Personal and organizational communication strategies serve to enhance patient care.

CULTURAL SENSITIVITY

The complexity of the world is evident when examining the cultural differences of healthcare providers and patients. Providers have varying backgrounds, as do their patients. Once we accept the fact that we do not all think alike, we can strive to understand how our differences affect patient care.

More than half of the growth in the total U.S. population between 2000 and 2010 was due to the increase in the Hispanic population, which makes up 16% of the country's total population. The black population had the third-highest increase in its size, and accounted for 13% of the total population in 2010. The Asian population experienced the fastest rate of growth, with its share reaching 5% of the total population in 2010. The only major racial group to experience a decrease in its proportion was the white population, which fell from 75% to 72% of the total population. Minorities are expected to account for the majority of the U.S. population by 2042.[13]

Cultural destructiveness in patient care is evidenced through subjugation of the patient and denial or lack of respect for the patient's rights. Cultural incapacity is demonstrated through racism, maintaining stereotypes, and refusal to provide specific treatments or treat specific patients. Cultural blindness ignores differences, treats everyone the same, and does not acknowledge the cultural needs of the patient. Cultural sensitivity has as its fundamental underpinning the ability to overcome and embrace cultural differences and address how to deliver care in a manner that strives for the outcome that best meets the needs of the patient and does no harm.

The biopsychosocial model of patient-centered care and culturally sensitive practice was documented in medical literature as a scientific paradigm in 1977. This model strives for ethical neutrality to the extent that any scientific model or theory can achieve. For example, if the clinician wants to understand diabetes among Native Americans, this model suggests that the clinician needs to understand the social and cultural environment and the psychological impact that environment has on the individual, in conjunction with studying the genetics and the biochemistry of the disorder in that population.[14]

Thirty-five years after the introduction of this paradigm, studies continue to provide empirical support for the potential usefulness of the patient-centered culturally sensitive healthcare model.[15]

The Health Resources and Services Administration (U.S. Department of Health and Human Services) has an online website focused on provision of education and resources designed to assist healthcare providers in understanding and improving healthcare culture, language, and literacy. The agency views "effective health communication [as being] as important to health care as clinical skill. To improve individual health and build healthy communities, health care providers need to recognize and address the unique culture, language and health literacy of diverse consumers and communities."[16]

Georgetown University's National Center for Cultural Competence designed the Cultural Competence Health Practitioner Assessment at the request of the Health Resources and Services Administration. This self-assessment tool is intended to enhance the delivery of high-quality services to culturally and linguistically diverse individuals and underserved communities, as well as to promote cultural and linguistic competence as essential approaches for practitioners in the elimination of health disparities among racial and ethnic groups.[17] Professional medical associations, including the American College of Obstetrics and Gynecology, have also focused their efforts on improving cultural sensitivity of physicians.[18]

One should not presume that socioeconomically disadvantaged patients sue their healthcare providers more frequently than those who are more advantaged. A recent study reviewed medical and social literature regarding why patients tend to sue their physicians and found that poor patients tend to sue physicians less often than advantaged patients. The authors postulate that this difference may be related to a lack of access to legal resources and the nature of the contingency fee system in medical malpractice claims.[19] It is important not to dismiss the occurrence of adverse events that occur to socioeconomically disadvantaged patients as insignificant. Any adverse event is grounds for, and can result in, litigation, regardless of the economic status of the patient.

PATIENT EMPOWERMENT

Most cases of patient dissatisfaction stem from deficient communication on the part of healthcare entities and the clinicians, rather than from patients' personality quirks. The Joint Commission recognized the importance of patient empowerment in reducing medical mistakes in 2002. The Joint Commission, together with the Centers for Medicare and Medicaid Services, launched a national campaign to urge patients to take a role in preventing healthcare errors by becoming active, involved, and informed participants on the healthcare team.[20] The Speak Up program is copyright and reprint free, with no permissions required to use or copy the Speak Up materials. It advocates that patients have the right to know *when* something goes wrong with their care and *what happens* if something goes wrong during treatment. Topics and support materials on prevention of errors and infections are available for the following types of care:

- Ambulatory care
- Laboratory
- Long-term care
- Behavioral health care
- Home care

Such a program can be effective only when it is embraced by the healthcare entity and the clinicians. Best practice is to educate the staff to the basic elements of the program, reiterate to physicians and staff the importance of patient empowerment, provide the materials to patients, and review the materials with patients and family at admission and again at multiple intervals during the patient's stay or treatment. Simply leaving the brochures by the patient's bedside has negligible results. Patients are encouraged to speak up in the following situations:

- They have questions or concerns.
- They do not understand.
- They think they are about to get or got the wrong medicine.
- They think they have been confused with another patient.
- They think something does not seem right.
- They think their IV does not seem to be dripping right (too fast or too slow).

Patients have specific rights, some of which are guaranteed by federal law, such as the right to a copy of one's medical records, and the right to keep them private.[21] Many states have additional laws protecting patients. In 2003, the American Hospital Association (AHA) revised the its Patients' Bill of Rights with the Patient Care Partnership. The revised document was written in "plain language" in multiple languages to meet the health literacy needs of America.[22] It informs patients what they should expect during their hospital stay:

- High-quality hospital care
- A clean and safe environment
- Involvement in their care
- Protection of their privacy
- Help when leaving the hospital
- Help with billing claims

The AHA document sets patient expectations and clearly recognizes the importance of communication in providing these rights. How will the hospital communicate the level of care provided? What role does communication serve when involving patients in their care, their discharge, and their billing? The call for patient and family involvement in care is becoming louder every day. Clinicians, for example, are beginning to recognize that the subtlety of changes in a patient's condition is often best recognized by the patient or family. Developing an organizational response to these issues should be a collaborative effort, designed to protect patient rights while mitigating hospital risk.

The Bureau of Labor Statistics has projected job growth in many of the health professions over the next decade. The retirement of large numbers and a variety of health professionals is also anticipated to occur during this same time frame. Unfortunately, critical staffing shortages may contribute to communication problems and potentially to slow or ineffective responses to patients' conditions. According to the Bureau of Labor Statistics, of the 22 major occupational groups it monitors, health care represents one-third of the fastest-growing occupations through 2020. Employment in healthcare support occupations is expected to grow by 34.5% (well above the expected 14.3% growth rate for all job classifications), followed by personal care and services occupations (26.8%) and healthcare practitioners and technical occupations (25.9%). Registered nurses are expected to add the most employment (712,000), followed by home health aides (706,000), and personal care aides (607,000).[23] Employment of physicians and surgeons is projected to grow 22% from 2008 to 2018, much faster than the average for all occupations.[24]

Physician shortages are expected to reach 62,900 by 2015 and 91,500 by 2020.[25]

The physician shortage combined with federal and state government mandates to lower the cost of health care is leading to calls for additional midlevel clinicians (e.g., advanced practice nurses, nurse practitioners, and physician assistants) with greater scope of privileges. Communications designed to help patients understand the role of such midlevel clinicians should help mitigate risk concerns regarding clinician qualifications and responsibilities. Another response to the staffing shortages is the implementation of rapid response teams, designed to enable patients and family members to call for immediate help if they feel a patient is not receiving adequate medical attention. These teams were initially developed in 2006 in support of the Institute for Healthcare Improvement's 100,000 Lives Campaign. Empowering the patient and family to contact healthcare providers as they deem essential is a communication tool designed specifically to improve the quality of patient care and mitigate risk.

Patient empowerment should also include the right and freedom to complain or file a grievance about the patient's care or a healthcare provider without fear of retribution. A complaint is defined as an expression of dissatisfaction with some aspect of care or services. Most complaints have simple, obvious causes that can be addressed to the patient's satisfaction quickly at the level of service between the patient, hospital staff, and the department director. A grievance is a written or verbal expression of dissatisfaction with some aspect of care or service that has not been resolved to the patient's satisfaction, so that the patient desires that the complaint be addressed by investigation, review, and evaluation. Expressions of concern about quality of care should be considered grievances rather than complaints.

The complaint and grievance process is intended to ensure that patient and family concerns are investigated and appropriate actions are taken both to remedy the situation and to ensure that similar situations do not occur in the future. This process is fundamental to identification and management of risk. The ultimate responsibility for resolving patient grievances falls to the facility's governing body. Management should assume responsibility for the logistics and oversight of the patient grievance process. Patients should be informed at the time of admission or treatment of their right to file a complaint or grievance and should be provided a copy of the Patient Care Partnership pamphlet containing written information about how to address concerns and questions related to their care. Patient and family concerns and complaints should be addressed and resolved in a timely and appropriate manner.

HEALTH LITERACY

What if the patient can read at only the fifth-grade level or is illiterate? How does such a patient find his or her voice without embarrassment or fear of retribution? Health literacy is the degree to which individuals have the capacity to obtain, process, and understand basic health information. Health literacy means being able to follow instructions from a doctor, nurse, or pharmacist; manage a chronic illness; or take medication properly. According to the Institute of Medicine Report, 90 million people have difficulty understanding and using health information, and a 2006 study by the U.S. Department

of Education found that 36% of adults have only basic or below-basic skills for dealing with health material. Much of this difficulty is related to cultural diversity.

The U.S. Department of Health and Human Services, Health Resources and Services Administration, has developed an interactive online educational program and myriad tools and toolkits designed to improve health literacy through better design of patient educational materials and forms and clinicians' increased understanding of the issues.[26] All patient forms, educational materials, and discharge instructions should be assessed (measured) to ensure they are written in plain language at a level that is comprehensible by the general patient population. Analytic tools to measure the patient's health literacy include the Newest Vital Sign Test developed in 2005.[27]

Federal regulations require healthcare organizations to provide language services for those patients with limited English proficiency (LEP). Specifically, the National Standards on Culturally and Linguistically Appropriate Services in Health Care (CLAS standards), issued by the Office of Minority Health, detail what it means to provide adequate linguistic access services to LEP patients as proscribed in Title VI of the Civil Rights Act and Regulations. The act mandates language assistance and the provision of information and services in languages other than English to LEP individuals.[28] The Department of Health and Human Services issued guidelines on December 12, 2000, regarding the use of oral interpreters and the translation of written materials for use in facilities where a specific language is spoken by 10% or 3,000 people of the persons served.[29] A study published in 2010 indicated that 78% of hospitals were able to provide interpreters for the most commonly used second language within 15 minutes during business hours, but only 48% could provide interpreters in that time frame for their third most commonly used language. Hospitals were more challenged to inform patients of their right to linguistically accessible services. In fact, most hospitals did not meet the standard regarding use of competent interpreters; 62% reported that family members or friends of patients were used as interpreters, even though 70% of these hospitals had a policy prohibiting this practice. Most hospitals required that staff (79%) and contract (63%) interpreters undergo interpreter training, but ad hoc interpreters, such as volunteers and bilingual staff, usually did not. Finally, less than two-thirds of the hospitals had the following translated documents available in their most commonly requested language: advance directives, patients' rights, discharge instructions, and informed consent. Less than one-thirdof hospitals had these written documents available.[30]

Health literacy is an integral requirement within the Patient Protection and Affordable Care Act (ACA). The ACA adopted the National Library of Medicine's definition of health literacy: "the degree to which individuals have the capacity to obtain, process, and understand basic health information and services needed to make appropriate health decisions." The benefits of improving health literacy identified in the ACA include safeguarding patient rights through acknowledgment of the need for cultural competency and reduction of disparities. Moreover, the ACA notes that targeted health literacy innovations could improve health and reduce preventable hospitalizations. Provisions specifically applicable to healthcare providers include the following:

- Provider training on cultural competency, language, and literacy issues
- Patient information at appropriate reading levels
- Chronic illness self-management

CONSENT: INFORMED OR OTHERWISE

Informed consent implies a discussion of the hazards, risks, benefits, and alternatives (including nontreatment) for diagnostic tests and therapeutic procedures. As comprehensive as the informed consent process seems, the patient is not entitled to the entire body of medical knowledge. Valid informed consent is given by a person who has been informed, is competent, and has not been coerced. Consent given in the absence of information and competence, or in the presence of coercion, does not achieve these ends; hence, it is not valid. Informed consent is an interactive process between the patient and/or family, the physician or professional providing the treatment, and often nurses through education.

Although nurses are often required to obtain patients' signature on a consent form, in this specific act, they are merely getting the patients to sign the form acknowledging their informed consent. However, the nurse is in a unique position to ensure the validity of consent. Nurses do so both by enhancing patients' opportunities for becoming informed and by observing for signs of incompetence and coercion. Ofcourse, as with all communications, nurse and patient perceptions may differ regarding the practices of information giving, decision making, and informed consent.[31]

Informed consent regulations vary from state to state, in terms of the competencies of the patient, age, emergency care, research and clinical trials, type of procedure, and documentation requirements. The Center for Medicare & Medicare Service (CMS) has informed consent requirements that are applicable to all healthcare entities that receive federal reimbursement. CMS requires hospitals to ensure informed consent is obtained in a manner that is consistent with hospital policy. Its regulations list elements of what CMS considers a well-designed informed consent process:

The right to make informed decisions means that the patient or patient's representative is given the information needed in order to make "informed" decisions regarding his/her care ... Furthermore, it includes the patient's participation in the development of the plan of care, including providing consent to, or refusal of, medical or surgical interventions, and in planning for care after discharge from the hospital.[32]

According to CMS, a hospital's surgical informed consent policy should describe the following:

- Individuals who may obtain informed consent
- Procedures that require informed consent
- Circumstances in which surgery is considered an emergency procedure that can be undertaken without informed consent
- Circumstances in which a patient's representative may give informed consent
- The content of the informed consent form and instructions for completing it
- The process that will be used to obtain informed consent and document it in the medical record

- Mechanisms to ensure proper completion of the informed consent form and to ensure that the form is included in the patient's medical record before surgery (except for emergency surgery)
- The process for incorporating informed consent forms completed outside the hospital into the patient's record before surgery

Often physicians are wary of disclosing specific potential adverse side effects. The disclosure of potential risks and side effects may itself induce adverse effects through expectancy mechanisms known as nocebo effects, contradicting the principle of nonmaleficence. Research suggests that providing patients with a detailed enumeration of every possible adverse event—especially subjective self-appraised symptoms—can actually increase side effects. Describing one version of what might happen (clinical facts) may actually create outcomes that differ from what would have happened without this information. Thus the physician must determine how best to inform and educate the patient. It has been suggested that informed consent can be accomplished to minimize nocebo responses while still maintaining patient autonomy through "contextualized informed consent," which takes into account possible side effects, the patient being treated, and the particular diagnosis involved.[33] Risk managers should work with the medical staff in developing informed consent guiding principles to use within the healthcare facility.

PATIENT EDUCATION

An important part of the healthcare continuum is the patient's responsibility for self. Following discharge, the patient or the family becomes the activator of the next steps toward recovery. If the patient does not understand and buy in to what is expected of him or her, however, the prognosis for recovery is impaired. Healthy living is not the focus of this chapter, except in that it is the responsibility of the healthcare system to take reasonable steps to ensure patient education is provided in a manner that addresses cultural diversity and health literacy.

Patient noncompliance with therapeutic regimens is more the rule than the exception. Obviously, if harm results to the patient, litigation risk factors arise. Five communication techniques can improve adherence to the physician's instructions and reduce the risk of a lawsuit:

- Arrive at an agreed-upon physician/patient diagnosis through open discussion.
- Keep the regimen as simple as possible.
- Give the patient written instructions in understandable language.
- Motivate the patient with benefits, personal goals, and individual ability to achieve them.
- Discuss potential risks, possible side effects, and costs.

Barriers to patient education include lack of time, health literacy of the patient, fear of materials being used against the provider, skepticism of the patient's desire or ability to follow ever-changing standards and best practices, lack of adequate reimbursement, and the effects on the provider's personal life.

Access to the World Wide Web has increased the amount of health information available for consumers to use as a supplement to healthcare education materials usually available in physicians' offices, hospitals, and clinics. Support groups and alternative therapies can be explored in addition to resources for care. Nevertheless, because the Web is unregulated, not all information may be accurate. This poses a problem for professionals interacting with patients who have obtained dubious advice online or who have been in chat rooms whose quality is suspect. Technology can also be used in a positive fashion to provide customized patient educational handouts. In addition, professional disease-centered associations, governmental agencies, healthcare systems, and health insurance providers provide online resources available to the public. Integration of these resources helps to improve communication and expectations for patients surrounding their disease process, diagnostic tests, and treatments.

DISCLOSURE AND APOLOGIES

Patients conceive of errors broadly. What may be construed by a clinician as an anticipated potential side effect or adverse reaction may be perceived by the patient as an error. The severity assigned to errors also differs between patients and clinicians. Moreover, patients sometimes worry that clinicians might hide errors. Several professional associations have adopted disclosure guidelines that recognize the moral and ethical responsibility of disclosure to achieve the optimal clinical goal, while respecting patient autonomy. Improvements in the disclosure process enhance patient satisfaction, while promoting safe and high-quality care.[34] For instance, a culture of transparency to inform patients of harmful medical errors and offer compensation implemented by a tertiary care medical hospital system has demonstrated a reduction in legal claims by more than 25%. When this approach was implemented, the number of lawsuits and liability costs decreased and remaining legal issues were resolved much faster. The hospital system involved concluded it is possible to implement a disclosure-with-offer program without increasing liability claims and costs.[35]

Patients typically desire full disclosure of harmful errors that includes the following elements[36]:

- An explicit statement that an error occurred
- What happened—what the error was
- Why it happened—why the error occurred
- The implications for the patient's health
- How recurrences will be prevented—what will be done to prevent recurrences
- An apology

Physicians have a different take on disclosing errors, as they tend to define errors more narrowly than patients do. A Harvard study found that physicians agree in principle with full disclosure and want to be truthful, yet have difficulty in admitting to personal failure. There is a paternalistic concern that disclosure could further harm the patient and precipitate a lawsuit.[37] Multiple rationalizations for disclosing adverse events to patients exist, of which two are fundamental: (1) the ethical imperative, meaning that disclosure and honesty are the right thing to do to preserve your moral character, and (2) the need to preserve the patient–clinician bond of trust. From a malpractice or negligence perspective, disclosure wards off the allegations of concealment of error and, depending on the state, there may be a legal obligation to report an adverse event to a patient. Disclosure serves as the impetus that moves parties toward early settlement of a malpractice case, which can result in less money and time spent, reduced defense costs, and removal of the potential for an unfavorable jury verdict.

The American Medical Association's (AMA) medical ethics policy includes reference to the ethical responsibility to study and prevent error and harm.[38] The AMA endorses the offering of professional and compassionate concern toward patients who have been harmed, regardless of whether the harm was caused by a healthcare error. It recognizes that such communication is fundamental to the trust that underlies the patient–physician relationship, and may help reduce the risk of liability. An expression of concern need not be an admission of responsibility. When patient harm has resulted from an error, the physician should offer a general explanation regarding the nature of the error and the measures being taken to prevent similar occurrences in the future.

Every healthcare entity needs to develop a disclosure and apology policy and procedure. If something goes wrong, the patient has the right to an honest explanation and an apology. The disclosure, explanation, and apology should be made within a reasonable amount of time. Deciding what should be disclosed should be a joint decision, guided by policy. Most clinicians agree that clear-cut errors that affect patient care should be disclosed. The more difficult categories include the following:

- Errors that produce minor or transient harm
- Fatal errors
- Harmful errors in patients who are hopelessly ill
- Others' errors
- When someone else does not want the error disclosed

As soon as the adverse event is recognized, it is imperative that the clinician convey sincere concern and let the patient know the matter is being taken seriously, there will be an investigation, and the patient will be kept informed of its progress. Excessive information, promises, or apologies should not be offered immediately, as all facts are not yet known. A good response to the patient is, "Let me investigate and I will get back to you." This allows time for the clinician to communicate with the team. When discussing the event with the patient, a second person from the facility should be present as a witness to and part of the discussions.

Which criteria are used to select the "best" person to talk with the patient and family? Recognize the importance of a trusted advisor, who may not be the person who made the error, when choosing the best fit for the patient. Train some physicians to be skilled facilitators for others who may be lacking in the prerequisite communication skills. Have the attending physician take the lead if possible, but remain open to other options based on the situation. The facility representative who meets with patients should be in a position of authority, and excellent communication skills for this individual are imperative. He or she should be empathetic and respectful, capable of listening without becoming defensive, have adequate time to be present and listen, and be willing to follow up and continue the dialogue. The representative should have a clinical background sufficient for understanding clinical issues and communicating clinical concepts. Deciding who is the first and best person to engage the patient following a serious event should be decided mutually and collaboratively by the physician, nursing director, risk manager, and others. Patients are often reluctant to express dissatisfaction directly to their physician or nurse. Depending on the situation, their chosen emissary may be the bedside nurse, nurse manager, physician, risk manager, or representative of management.

It is important that all clinicians involved acknowledge the clinical event verbally and through documentation. Speculation should be kept to a minimum; facts and what is known to have occurred are more important. Disclosure and apologies should not wait until after root-causes analysis is complete. In addition, continue to follow the patient closely. Expressions of sympathy and apology should be sincere and for the event only, not for the causes of the event. The person apologizing should accept responsibility and take ownership of the issue/process. There should be a verbal commitment to the patient to evaluate and investigate.

The patient/family meeting should occur within 24 hours of identification of the event and should include the following behavior on the healthcare representatives' part:

- Determine what information the patient already has.
- Speak slowly and calmly; use simple language and not medical jargon. Do not rush, but rather be patient.
- Be straightforward, truthful, concise, and respectful.
- Discuss only facts known; do not speculate.
- Invite and answer all questions as honestly as possible.
- Listen without interruption.
- Explain what impact the event will have on the patient now and in the future.
- Describe steps being taken to mitigate the effects of the injury.
- Describe steps being taken to prevent a recurrence.
- Ensure that the patient and family understands the situation and the actions that will be taken.

During this meeting, it is important to validate the patient's and family's emotions. Compassion and remorsefulness can be perceived by others and a measure of sincerity is important.

- Ask if they need anything, and invite further questions now and later.
- Raise the opportunity for follow-up conversations.
- Assign a "contact" person for the patient and make a plan to get back to that individual.
- Keep the patient and family updated and obtain contact information.

This is not the time to blame others, a situation, or a process or to express or imply causations. Participants in the meeting should try not to be insensitive, misleading or mysterious, or defensive or angry. Communication styles that are sermonizing, haughty, condescending, patronizing, or authoritative should be avoided. Do not panic if a medical malpractice liability suit is threatened.

Disclosure laws and apology laws vary widely between states. A few states have no related legislation, such as New Mexico, Utah, and Wisconsin. A significant number of states have implemented legislation in this area, including, but not limited to, Arizona, California, Colorado, Idaho, Michigan, North Carolina, Texas, and Wyoming. Each state regulation varies, with some significant differences being noted. One of the most important differences is that an apology may or may not be construed as acknowledgment of a mistake or error. It is imperative that the risk management personnel and clinicians understand the differences between an expression of sympathy, condolence, commiseration, and compassion and a general sense of benevolence, as opposed to an apology. Know your state-specific laws and regulations before developing a facility policy.

PATIENT SATISFACTION

Patient satisfaction may be a measure not of what actually happened during the physician–patient encounter, but more of an individual's perception of what took place. Critics of patient satisfaction as an evaluative measure argue that patients lack the scientific background to evaluate care, the patients' health status may make them incapable of well-reasoned judgments, patients do not have a comprehensive grasp of their care, providers and patients have different goals, and definitions of quality care vary greatly. Patients seem to value the science of medicine (technical competence), art of care (attributes of caring), and amenities of care (comfort, courtesy, privacy, and promptness).

Strategic marketing by healthcare providers often aims to establish that their facilities' and providers' service quality and outcomes are the "highest," "best," and "superior." This is a risky undertaking from a risk management perspective. Facilities and clinicians rarely match up to these lofty attributes—and even if they do, when a serious adverse clinical event occurs, it proves challenging to defend why such a hallowed organization permitted an adverse event to happen. However, all attempts to satisfy patients should be undertaken, as this component of health care is viewed as a measure of quality.

Beginning in 2002, CMS partnered with the Agency for Healthcare Research and Quality (AHRQ), to develop and test the Hospital Consumer Assessment of Healthcare Providers and Systems (HCAHPS) survey. The HCAHPS survey was the first national, standardized, publicly reported survey of patients' perceptions of their hospital experience. While many hospitals have collected information on patient satisfaction for their own internal use, until HCAHPS there was no national standard for collecting and publicly reporting information about patients' experience of care that allowed comparisons to be made across hospitals locally, regionally, and nationally. In 2005, the Office of Management and Budget gave its final approval for the national implementation of HCAHPS for public reporting purposes. CMS implemented the HCAHPS survey in 2006, and the first public reporting of HCAHPS results occurred two years later.

Hospitals implement HCAHPS under the auspices of the Hospital Quality Alliance (HQA), a private–public partnership that includes major hospital and medical associations, consumer groups, measurement and accrediting bodies, government, and other groups that share an interest in improving hospital quality. Since 2007, hospitals subject to the Inpatient Prospective Payment System (IPPS) annual payment update provisions must collect and submit HCAHPS data to receive their full IPPS annual payment update. Non-IPPS hospitals, such as critical access hospitals, may voluntarily participate in HCAHPS. The Patient Protection and Affordable Care Act of 2010 includes HCAHPS among the measures to be used to calculate value-based incentive payments in the hospital value-based purchasing program, beginning with discharges in October 2012.[39]

Patient satisfaction assessment is a tool that can assist risk managers in understanding the risk posture of their patients. Expressed and perceived dissatisfaction should result in an investigation as to its potential and real causes. Health consumer advocates, also known as patient representatives, serve as a liaison between patients, families, hospital, and medical staff. They advocate for patients' rights, promote patient satisfaction, serve as point of contact for complaints and grievances, and serve as a resource and support for ethical issues.[40] If patients are never dissatisfied, then perhaps the healthcare entity is somewhat removed from litigation primarily on the basis of that satisfaction. Nevertheless, rarely are all of us satisfied all of the time. Once dissatisfaction and potential liability are identified, collaborative risk management activities should be initiated, as most problems are systemic and the result of interrelated and multicausal relationships.

GRADING AND RANKING HEALTH CARE

As a means to assess healthcare quality, consumers and the government are embracing report cards for healthcare entities. Consumers, patients, and clinicians have access to these comparative reports online. Medicare, for example, has long been deeply invested in measuring and comparative scoring of healthcare entities that receive government reimbursement and provides measurement data comparing the quality of services online.[41]

In early 2012, CMS began to display new quality measures based on MDS 3.0 nursing home resident assessments. These new quality measures will replace the quality measures that currently appear on Nursing Home Compare. CMS will resume calculating the Five-Star Overall Rating in late 2012; this system is designed to assist in comparing nursing homes. The CMS rating system is based on metrics identified in the Omnibus Reconciliation Act of 1987 (OBRA '87) and quality improvement campaigns. Ratings are derived from health inspections, staffing levels, and quality measures.

The Dialysis Facility Compare (DFC) program has been funded since 1999 and allows for the review and comparison of dialysis facility characteristics and quality information for all Medicare-approved dialysis facilities. Comparative measures include the number of patients with too-high and too-low anemia test results, adequacy of the dialysis, and measures to determine whether the patients achieve the expected length of life.

Hospitals have become the most recent entities subject to the CMS Compare system. Beginning in October 2012, Hospital Compare will include new surgical outcomes measures submitted on a voluntary basis by hospitals participating in the American College of Surgeons' (ACS) National Surgical Quality Improvement Program database. Current measures include patients' satisfaction, process of care measures, outcome of care measures, utilization of medical imaging, and patient safety.

Home healthcare agencies that receive government reimbursement and provide any or all of the following services are compared for quality: skilled nursing care, physical therapy, occupational therapy, speech therapy, medical social services, and home health aide services Quality measurements include the following metrics:

- How often patients improved
- How often staff checks patients for clinical indications
- Patient's level of pain
- Vaccinations/flu shots
- Risk of falls
- Depression risk
- Clinical improvement
- Patient education
- Urgent, unplanned care
- Hospital admissions

Ratings are available from a number of different sources. Since 1998, a privately owned enterprise has provided the public with data on hospitals and providers. Each year, this company determines risk-adjusted mortality and in-hospital complication rates to evaluate performance. To determine performance, it analyzes approximately 40 million Medicare discharges for a two-year period. Each hospital receives a quality-level rating across 27 procedures and diagnoses, ranging from pneumonia to heart failure to hip replacement.[42] An independent, nonprofit organization, "whose mission is to work for a fair, just, and safe marketplace for all consumers and to empower consumers to protect themselves,"[43] provides hospital ratings to help consumers compare hospitals based on patient experience and patient outcomes. Its ratings are derived from data on patient experience and outcomes gathered from public sources, including survey responses from millions of patients, data on infections and readmissions, federal government data related to patient experience and readmissions, and state-reported data on hospital-acquired infections. A major publication house ranks nursing homes, physicians, and hospitals annually. More than 5,000 hospitals, 10,000 physicians, and 15,000 nursing homes are ranked based primarily on governmental data, with list of the "best" published each year.[44] The Leapfrog Group is a voluntary program aimed at improving employer purchasing power by measuring a healthcare entity's healthcare safety, quality, and customer value. The intent is that those facilities that score high in these areas will be financially rewarded by those purchasing health care on behalf of their employees. A study of Leapfrog activities found that "hospitals that implemented patient safety practices endorsed by the

Leapfrog Group reported better quality of care and lower mortality rates," important factors in managing risk.[45]

Healthcare entities may also choose to participate with surveys conducted by voluntary measurement and accrediting bodies. Their participation results in a ranking or survey score based on data reporting and oftentimes an on-site assessment of practices and documentation. (Although accreditation may be technically "voluntary," many states require accreditation of certain types of healthcare entities for licensure.) Accreditation survey reports, including those from accrediting bodies, are often available for public viewing online. If this information is not available via the Internet, all the consumer need do is contact the accredited facility and request a copy of the survey report. Although the elements assessed by each accrediting body and methods of accreditation vary between the bodies, there are many similarities between them. Often the choice of which accrediting body the healthcare entity selects is based on price (cost of the survey and annual fees), perceived expertise of the surveyors, public and governmental acceptance of the organization, and marketing issues. There are three primary hospital accrediting bodies:

- Det Norske Veritas (DNV) Healthcare National Integrated Accreditation for Healthcare Organizations (NIAHOSM)
- Healthcare Facilities Accreditation Program (HFAP)
- The Joint Commission (TJC)

These organizations also provide accreditation for specialty facilities. Additionally, specialty accrediting bodies exist for specialty facilities including, but not limited to, home healthcare agencies, sleep centers, clinics, urgent care centers, and many more:

- Accreditation Association for Ambulatory Health Care (AAAHC)
- American Academy of Sleep Medicine (AASM)
- American College of Radiology (ACR)
- Accreditation Commission for Health Care (ACHC)
- Accreditation Commission for Home Care
- American Association of Ambulatory Surgery Facilities (AAAASF)
- COLA (previously known as the Commission on Office Laboratory Accreditation; now accredits all types of labs)
- Commission on Accreditation of Rehabilitation Facilities (CARF)
- Community Health Accreditation Program (CHAP)
- Continuing Care Accreditation Commission (CCAC)
- Healthcare Quality Association on Accreditation (HQAA)
- Pharmacy Compounding Accreditation Board (PCAB)
- URAC (previously known as Utilization Review Accreditation Commission; now accredits other types of organizations, such as health plans, managed care organizations, pharmacy benefit management organizations, and mail-service pharmacies)

A multitude of websites are available for consumer self-rating of hospitals, clinics, physicians, dentists, and other healthcare providers. The information posted on these sites is not vetted—that is, anyone can post information based on no measurable data—and primarily comprises patient satisfaction and dissatisfaction (i.e., personal opinion). Regardless of the basis for the rating, ranking, or opinions, it is imperative that all healthcare facilities and clinicians have a process in place to check the online information regarding their practice. Many of the organizations that publish such information permit an investigation into the data and allow the provider to respond to negative reports. Even if they do not, it is wise for the facility and clinician to know what is being said about them in public forums so that they are prepared to defend themselves when necessary, question the validity of the report, or correct their actions and practice to improve patient safety and quality. Many patients make decisions on which healthcare providers they utilize based on reputation and external rankings. Moreover, this information is often used when determining whether to mount a legal action against a provider.

Questions often arise regarding the validity or value of facility reporting and resultant rankings. A recent analysis of death rates was undertaken by reviewing the outcomes for Medicare patients with heart attack, heart failure, and pneumonia in the five years prior to the CMS launch of the Hospital Compare website and in the three years afterward. The analysis demonstrated that although individual hospitals' compliance with quality metrics for these conditions was satisfactory, the effort reduced the odds of a heart failure patient dying within 30 days by only 3%. Heart attack and pneumonia patients saw no improvement in their death rates. Seven years after the federal government started publicly reporting hospitals' performance on quality measures, evidence suggests that this transparency effort has not measurably improved patient outcomes.[46] Notably, outcomes related to process are difficult to interpret, and research has not clearly demonstrated correlations between some commonly used measures of structure and process and desirable outcomes. It behooves risk managers to "know their numbers" and ensure they accurately represent the care provided.

STRATEGIC CAVEAT

Risk managers must navigate the boundaries separating clinicians, regulators, accreditors, patients, and consumers as part of their communication challenge. Reducing risk through the improvement of communication requires the whole-hearted commitment of the healthcare organization, medical staff, and all employees. The programs noted in this chapter should not operate in silos, as they are effective only when part of a greater good. The cultural needs of all participants (patients and clinicians) should be addressed. Effective communications requires a global approach while recognizing the limitations and challenges of every group. In particular, satisfying all parties is not always possible. Competing priorities need to be addressed.

Under the health reform law now in force in the United States, hospitals must conduct a community needs assessment at least once every three years. Hospitals must make their assessments available to the public, and they must adopt strategies to meet the community health needs that are identified. This requirement creates opportunities to address cultural diversity, improve health literacy, and empower patients—all of which have an impact on reducing risk and improving patient safety.[47]

SOCIAL MEDIA CHALLENGES

Social media are the tools used by people to create social networks. Consumers, patients, healthcare entities, and physicians use social media to communicate and to learn. More than 300 social media sites currently exist, and reportedly 6.5 billion people use social media.[48] Social media interactions can be found on websites, blogs, forums, news, social media sites, and bulletin boards. Social media used for medical purposes include blogs, microblogs, file-sharing sites, chat rooms, message boards, online communities, and patient testimonials.

Consumer and Patient Use

Approximately 75% of Americans have access to and use an Internet connection point.[49,50] In 2010, 99 million U.S. adults reported having used social media resources for health-related purposes, up from 63 million in 2008 and 38 million in 2007. Studies conducted on the use of the Internet indicate the top reasons why people search for health information:[51–53]

- Specific medical treatment or procedure (80%)
- A medication (70%)
- Help make a self-diagnosis (58%)
- A physician or clinician (44%)
- Hospitals or other medical facilities (36%)
- On behalf of another individual (50%)

As a result of the information or tools they found online, consumers have challenged their doctor's treatment or diagnosis, asked their doctor to change their treatment, discussed information found online at a doctor's appointment, used the Internet instead of going to the doctor, or made a healthcare decision because of online information.[54]

According to Pew Center studies, peer-to-peer social media activities regarding healthcare accounts are conducted by as many as 34% of Internet users, or 25% of all U.S. adults.[55] Peer-to-peer online activities include the following:

- Reading someone else's commentary or description of experience about health or medical issues
- Consulting online reviews of particular drugs or medical treatments
- Searching for others who might have health concerns similar to theirs
- Posting comments, questions, or information about health or medical issues on a website
- Posting information about their experiences with a particular drug or medical treatment

Through such activities patients can be the source of patient confidentiality and privacy risks without being aware of that fact.[56] As they post or blog about their surgery, their roommate, nurses, and the food, they may compromise protected patient information—both their own and others'. Postings to social media websites are typically unencrypted and difficult to remove. Whether self-disclosed or disclosed by a third party, such information can cause the healthcare facility harm. The facility does not have control over what patients do with their own healthcare information, and there is no regulatory responsibility when it comes to patients posting their own heath information to social media sites. Therefore, these risks should be anticipated and mitigated. Patients and families should be informed of the sensitivity of patient data, the importance of not sharing it, and the facility's privacy policies.

Healthcare Organization Use

In a 2011 study of 3,300 marketers, 90% indicated that social media are important for their business and 93% indicated they were employing social media for marketing purposes. Mastering the marketing aspects of social media can take 6 hours or more each week; those with more years of social media experience spend even more time conducting social media activities. Only 28% of businesses surveyed are outsourcing some portion of their social media marketing. Marketing through social media is concentrated in email marketing, search engine optimization event marketing, and press releases.[57]

In today's healthcare industry, more than 20% of the hospitals in the United States have some kind of social media presence. Most hospitals use social media as an extension of their existing marketing and public relations plans. Posts and updates tend to revolve around themes such as sharing news about the organization and its services, sharing general medical news, highlighting the organization's community events, sharing "success stories," and doing basic customer outreach and engagement.[58] In 2010, the American Medical Association (AMA) issued a policy statement to help guide physicians in their use of social media.[59]

Data protection, security of information, risk of fraud, identity theft, reputation, and employment issues are only a few of the risks associated with such media. Thus the basic tenets of risk management should be applied to social media as well. All healthcare facilities and providers should develop and implement a social media policy and plan. The social media plan should identify who is authorized to use social media on behalf of the organization. An individual or group within the organization should be accountable for social media and have responsibility for posting content, monitoring usage and policy violations, and ensuring overall execution of the social media plan.

- Ensure that privacy policies specifically address the use of photos of patients, staff, volunteers, and visitors, and that use without authorization is prohibited.
- Establish a policy that defines whether and how the organization will reply via social media or other means to criticism, complaints, and compliments that appear on social media.

Employees may use social media to discuss their cases, patients, supervisors, the facility itself, the shifts they work, or their wages. Their discussions may be public, so patient confidentiality is always a concern. In-service education should include the role and rules of social media in the Health Insurance Portability and Accountability Act (HIPAA) privacy training. Offer examples of types of posts that should be avoided by employees in their personal time, such as posts that negatively portray the hospital or its services.

The organization should be aware of its social media presence, and should recognize such media as new sources of feedback and opportunities. This important communication tool can be used to connect with various types of audiences—the public, patients, and stakeholders. The organization needs to know what is being said about it and respond quickly (which in Internet time may be immediately following the post). Ongoing social media monitoring is a key component of any comprehensive Internet reputation management program. How is your facility represented and perceived in the world of social media? How does the facility know when, where, and how it needs to take action to protect itself?

Outdated information that is not current or reflective of the organization can be detrimental as well. The social media page and website should reflect the organization as it is today.

Misinformation or out-of-date information could be construed as misleading or fraudulent advertising. There is a reputational risk—which if challenged requires a very difficult recovery effort to countermand.

Social media also provide opportunities to improve the patient experience.[60] Such sites can contribute to longitudinal health and documentation, for example, by tracking a patient's progress, serving as a discharge advocate to take patients through the discharge process, and providing an after-care program for discharged patients. In addition, patients can engage with their social networking channels to stay in touch with family and friends while they are in the hospital.

Clinician–Patient Online Interaction

The AMA guidelines were developed for physicians, but are applicable to all online patent interactions and should be integrated into social media policy.[61]

- Refrain from posting identifiable patient information online.
- Use privacy settings to safeguard the clinician's personal information to the greatest extent possible, but realize that privacy settings are not foolproof and can be overcome.
- Monitor the clinician's Internet presence to ensure all information posted is accurate and appropriate. Social media monitoring can be conducted by in-house staff (although this effort is complex and time consuming) or by independent external sources.
- Maintain appropriate patient boundaries consistent with professional ethical guidelines.
- Separate personal and professional online content.

Vetting Online Information

Anyone can pose online as a doctor, an expert, or a researcher. Researchers from the London School of Economics study indicated only 25% of people surveyed said they check the source of online advice. This finding suggests that many people could be misled by inaccurate information, potentially putting their health at risk. Depending on websites visited, people with even common medical symptoms encounter numerous potential diagnoses, according to the study. "Relying on potentially inaccurate information could easily lead to people taking risks with inappropriate tests and treatments, wasting money and causing unnecessary worry."[62]

Providing more and better information about health may help empower individuals, but it is a challenge to ensure that online health information is of high quality and can be trusted. Not only is an ever-increasing amount of information available, but it can also be difficult to identify the source of website content or determine whether it has a link to commercial activity. The consequences of poor-quality information are serious, potentially leading to needless worry, unnecessary consultations, overuse of health services, and a delay in appropriate diagnosis. Online health information may also lead to false hope, unnecessary costs, and actions directly harmful to health due to recommendations for unproven, ineffective, or even deliberately bogus tests and treatments.

If healthcare organizations or clinicians plan to link to external websites, they should utilize resources that have been selected and evaluated for quality. The Medical Library Association has developed guidance to assist consumers in evaluating the legitimacy of Internet health-related websites. This guidance should be reviewed by healthcare entities that are posting links to external websites and documents to their own website.[63]

Evolving Risk of Social Media

Courts have yet to set precedents regarding appropriate use of social media use and abuse. Moreover, state laws and regulation in this area remain sparse.

In the past, employees have been fired for inappropriate use of social media and their cases brought before courts. Some were decided in favor of the plaintiff, while others were decided for the defense, and many settled out of court. The National Labor Relations Board has deemed that employees who post angry, often profane rants against their bosses and coworkers on the World Wide Web are protected by federal labor laws. It brought suit against 14 companies for terminating employees for these actions.[64]

Some companies ask job applicants to provide their social media passwords so they can review the applicant's online profiles. Questions have been raised about the legality of this practice, which is also the focus of proposed legislation in Illinois and Maryland that would forbid public agencies from asking for access to social networks.[65] Risk managers should ensure that at this time, with the lack of clear regulations and court decisions, pre-employment screening of social media profiles should be limited to information that is publicly available.

Social media activity has also been used in court as evidence. Although this practice is not yet well defined in the court system, the courts are aware of how easy it is to impersonate someone online and have established some basic principles for proving the reliability of social media evidence.[66] As with any evidence to be used in court, parties must be able to authenticate its validity.

Consumers are increasingly dependent on social networks to help them choose healthcare providers, determine a course of treatment, and manage their health risks. Healthcare providers need to embrace and adapt to this new technology, while acknowledging that there is a significant risk to engaging with social networks. As the regulatory environment becomes more defined and innovative organizations demonstrate measurable commercial value from social networks, increasing numbers of healthcare stakeholders are "expected to recognize and leverage this transformational technology's role in information acquisition and access. Social networks are a trend that could change the face of healthcare information sharing, providing new power for providers and patients alike."[67]

REFERENCES

1. Wargo, E. (2009, July/August). Intelligence and how to get it. *Association for Psychological Science Observer, 22*(6). Retrieved from http://www.psychologicalscience.org/observer/getArticle.cfm?id=2516
2. National Research Council. (2011). *Assessing 21st century skills: Summary of a workshop.* Committee on the Assessment of 21st Century Skills, Board on Testing and Assessment, Division of Behavioral and Social Sciences and Education. Washington, DC: National Academies Press. Retrieved from http://www.ncbi.nlm.nih.gov/books/NBK84218/
3. Moffic, H. S. (1983). Sociocultural guidelines for clinicians in multicultural settings. *Psychiatry Quarterly, 55*(1), 47–54.
4. Lucian Leape Institute. (2010, March 10). *Unmet needs: Teaching physicians to provide safe patient care.* Report of the Lucian Leape Institute Roundtable on Reforming Medical Education, Lucian Leape Institute at the National Patient Safety Foundation.
5. American Hospital Association & American Society for Healthcare Risk Management. (2009). *Risk*

management pearls to enhance communication in healthcare settings.

6. Spiegel, A. D., & Kavaler, F. (1997). America's first medical malpractice crisis, 1835–1865. *Journal of Community Health, 22*(4), 283–308.

7. Jena, A. B., et al. (2011). Malpractice risk according to physician specialty. *New England Journal of Medicine, 365,* 629–636. Retrieved from http://www.nejm.org/doi/pdf/10.1056/NEJMsa1012370

8. Balch, C. M. (2011, November). Personal consequences of malpractice lawsuits on American surgeons. *Journal of the American College of Surgeons, 213*(5), 657–667. Retrieved from http://download.journals.elsevierhealth.com/pdfs/journals/1072-7515/PIIS1072751511009781.pdf

9. Vincent, C., Young, M., & Phillips, A. (1994). Why do people sue doctors? A study of patients and relatives taking legal action. *Lancet, 343,* 1609–1613.

10. Silverman, B. C., et al. (2012). Lewd, crude, and rude behavior: The impact of manners and etiquette in the general hospital. *Psychosomatics, 53*(1), 13–20.

11. Duclos, C. W. (2005). Patient perspectives of patient–provider communication after adverse events. *International Journal of Quality Health Care, 17*(6), 479–486. Retrieved from http://intqhc.oxfordjournals.org/content/17/6/479.full

12. Gelhaus, P. (2012, January 24). The desired moral attitude of the physician: (III) Care. *Medical Health Care Philosophy.*

13. U.S. Census Bureau. (2011, March). Overview of race and Hispanic origin: 2010. *2010 Census Brief.*

14. Engel, G. L. (1977). The need for a new medical model: A challenge for biomedicine. *Science, 196,* 129–136.

15. Tucker, C. M., et al. (2011). Patient-centered culturally sensitive health care: Model testing and refinement. *Health Psychology, 30*(3), 342–350.

16. U.S. Department of Health and Human Services, Health Resources and Services Administration. (2012). Culture, language and health literacy. Retrieved from http://www.hrsa.gov/culturalcompetence/index.html

17. Georgetown University. (2012). *National Center for Cultural Competence's cultural competence health practitioner assessment.* Washington, DC. Retrieved from http://nccc.georgetown.edu/features/CCHPA.html

18. American College of Obstetricians and Gynecologists. (2011). Committee opinion no. 493: Cultural sensitivity and awareness in the delivery of health care. *Obstetries and Gynecology, 117*(5), 1258–1261.

19. McClellan, F. M. (2012, February 25). Do poor people sue doctors more frequently? Confronting unconscious bias and the role of cultural competency. *Clinical Orthopedics and Related Research.* Retrieved from http://www.springerlink.com/content/0524628700905vp3/fulltext.pdf

20. The Joint Commission. *Speak Up initiatives.* Oakbrook Terrace, IL: Auther. Retrieved from http://www.jointcommission.org/speakup.aspx

21. http://www.healthcare.gov/law/features/rights/bill-of-rights/index.html

22. American Hospital Association. (2003). *The patient care partnership: Understanding expectations, rights and responsibilities.* Chicago, IL: Auther. Retrieved from http://www.aha.org/content/00-10/pcp_english_030730.pdf

23. U.S. Bureau of Labor Statistics, Office of Occupational Statistics and Employment Projections. (2012, February 1). Economic news release: Employment projections: 2010–2020 summary. Washington, DC: Auther. Retrieved from http://bls.gov/news.release/ecopro.nr0.htm

24. U.S. Bureau of Labor Statistics. Occupational outlook handbook, 2010–11 edition. Retrieved from http://www.bls.gov/oco/ocos074.htm

25. Association of American Medical Colleges Center for Workforce Studies. (2011, November). 2011 state physician workforce data book. Retrieved from www.aamc.org/download/263512/data/state-data2011.pdf

26. U.S. Department of Health and Human Services, Health Resources and Services Administration. Health literacy. Retrieved from http://www.hrsa.gov/publichealth/healthliteracy/index.html

27. Weiss, B. D., et al. (2005). Quick assessment of literacy in primary care: The newest vital sign. *Annals of Family Medicine, 3*(6), 514–522. Retrieved from http://www.ncbi.nlm.nih.gov/pmc/articles/PMC1466931/

28. Officially, Title VI of the Civil Rights Act of 1964, U.S.C. 2000d et seq., and its implementing regulation at 45 CFR Part 80. *Federal Register, 65,* no.

169. Retrieved from http://www.hhs.gov/ocr/civil-rights/resources/specialtopics/lep/policyguidanced-ocument.html

29. U.S. Department of Health and Human Services, Office of Civil Rights. Limited English proficient (LEP). Retrieved from http://www.hhs.gov/ocr/civilrights/resources/specialtopics/lep/index.html

30. Diamond, L. C., et al. (2010). Do hospitals measure up to the national culturally and linguistically appropriate services standards? *Medical Care, 48*(12), 1080–1087.

31. Mahjoub, R., et al. (2011). Perceptions of informed consent for care practices: Hospitalized patients and nurses. *Applied Nursing Research, 24*(4), 276–280.

32. U.S. Department of Health and Human Services, Centers for Medicare & Medicaid Services, Center for Medicaid and State Operations/Survey and Certification Group. (2007, April 13). Revisions to the hospital interpretive guidelines for informed consent, Ref: S&C-07-17. Retrieved from http://www.cms.hhs.gov/SurveyCertificationGenInfo/downloads/SCLetter07-17.pdf

33. Wells, R.E., & Kaptchuk, T. J. (2012). To tell the truth, the whole truth, may do patients harm: The problem of the nocebo effect for informed consent. *American Journal of Bioethics, 12*(3), 22–29.

34. American College of Obstetricians and Gynecologists. (2012, March). Committee opinion no. 520. Committee on Patient Safety and Quality Improvement, Committee on Professional Liability. Retrieved from http://www.acog.org/~/media/Committee%20Opinions/Committee%20on%20Patient%20Safety%20and%20Quality%20Improvement/co520.pdf?dmc=1&ts=201203 04T2223105964

35. Kachalia, A., et al. (2000). Liability claims and costs before and after implementation of a medical error disclosure program. *Annals of Internal Medicine, 153*(4), 213–221.

36. Gallagher, T. H. (2005). Disclosing harmful medical errors to patients: A time for professional action. *Archives of Internal Medicine, 165*, 1819.

37. Powell, S. K. (2006). When things go wrong: Responding to adverse events: A consensus statement of the Harvard hospitals. *Lippincott's Case Management, 11*(4), 193–194.

38. American Medical Association. (2003, December). Opinion 8.121: Ethical responsibility to study and prevent error and harm. Retrieved from http://www.ama-assn.org/ama/pub/physician-resources/medical-ethics/code-medical-ethics/opinion8121.page

39. Center for Medicare and Medicaid Services. (2012, March 17). HCAHPS: Patients' perspectives of care survey. Retrieved from http://www.cms.gov/Medicare/Quality-Initiatives-Patient-Assessment-Instruments/HospitalQualityInits/HospitalHCAHPS.html

40. American Hospital Association & Society for Healthcare Consumer Advocacy. (2012). *From your patient advocate.* Chicago, IL: Auther. Retrieved from http://www.shca-aha.org/shca-aha/society/mission.html

41. Center for Medicare & Medicaid Services. (2012). Retrieved from www.healthcare.gov/compare

42. HealthGrades. (2011). Healthcare consumerism and hospital quality in America report. Retrieved from http://www.healthgrades.com/business/img/HealthcareConsumerismHospitalQualityReport2011.pdf

43. Consumers Union of U.S. (2011, June). How we rate hospitals: The basics. Retrieved from http://www.consumerreports.org/health/doctors-hospitals/how-we-rate-hospitals/the-basics/the-basics.htm

44. Health rankings & research. (2012). *U.S. News & World Report LP.* Retrieved from http://health.usnews.com/

45. Jha, A.K., et al. (2008). Does the Leapfrog program help identify high-quality hospitals? *Joint Commission Journal on Quality and Patient Safety, 34*(6), 318–325. Retrieved from http://www.leapfroggroup.org/media/file/CommonwealthFundreport_Jha.pdf

46. O'Reilly, K. B. (2012, March 19). Hospital report cards fall flat at improving patient outcomes. American Medical Association. Retrieved from http://www.ama-assn.org/amednews/2012/03/19/gvll0319.htm

47. Protecting consumers, encouraging community dialogue: Reform's new requirements for non-profit hospitals. (2010, May 5). *Community Catalyst.*

48. Smith, C. (2012, February 8). How many people use the top social media? *Digital Marketing Ramblings: The Latest Digital Marketing Tips, Trends and Technology.* Retrieved from http://expandedramblings.com/index.php/resource-how-many-people-use-the-top-social-media/

49. Internet World Stats. (2010). Internet usage and world population.

50. Pew Research Center Internet & American Life Project. (2011, August). Who's online: Internet user demographics. Retrieved from http://www.pewinternet.org/Static-Pages/Trend-Data/Whos-Online.aspx

51. Fox, S. (2011, February 1). Health topics: 80% of Internet users look for health information online. Pew Internet & American Life Project. Retrieved from http://www.pewinternet.org/~/media//Files/Reports/2011/PIP_HealthTopics.pdf

52. McDaid, D., et al. (2011, January 4). Untangling the Web. *Bupa Health Pulse 2010*. Retrieved from http://www.bupa.com/media/44806/online_20health_20-_20untangling_20the_20web.pdf

53. Fox, S., & Jones, S. (2009). *The social life of health information*. Washington, DC: Pew internet.

54. Manhattan Research. (2010, November 16). *Landmark study of U.S. consumer online health.*

55. Fox, S. (2011, February 28). *Peer-to-peer healthcare.* Pew Internet & American Life Project. Retrieved from http://www.pewinternet.org/~/media//Files/Reports/2011/Pew_P2PHealthcare_2011.pdf

56. McNickle, M. (2012, February 14). 5 patient-centered social media risks. *MedTech Media Healthcare IT News.* Retrieved from http://www.healthcareitnews.com/news/5-patient-centered-social-media-risks

57. Stelzne, M. A. (2011, April). 2011 social media marketing industry report. *Social Media Examiner.* Retrieved from http://www.socialmediaexaminer.com/SocialMediaMarketingReport2011.pdf

58. ECRI Institute. (2011, November). *Social media in healthcare: Healthcare risk control executive summary.* Plymouth Meeting, PA.

59. American Medical Association. (2010). AMA policy: Professionalism in the use of social media. Retrieved from http://www.ama-assn.org/ama/pub/meeting/professionalism-social-media.shtml

60. McNickle, M. (2010, January 12). 10 tips for optimal social media use. *MedTech Media Healthcare IT News.* Retrieved from http://www.healthcareitnews.com/news/10-tips-optimal-social-media-use

61. American Medical Association. (2010). AMA policy: Professionalism in the use of social media. Retrieved from http://www.ama-assn.org/ama/pub/meeting/professionalism-social-media.shtml

62. McDaid, D., et al. (2011, January 4). Untangling the Web. *Bupa Health Pulse 2010*. Retrieved from http://www.bupa.com/media/44806/online_20health_20-_20untangling_20the_20web.pdf

63. Medical Library Association. (2012, January 11). A user's guide to finding and evaluating health information on the Web. Retrieved from http://www.mlanet.org/resources/userguide.html

64. National Labor Relations Board. (2011, August 18). Acting general counsel releases report on social media cases: News release. Retrieved from https://www.nlrb.gov/news/acting-general-counsel-releases-report-social-media-cases

65. Employers ask job seekers for Facebook passwords. (2012, March 20). *Wall street Journal.* Retrieved from http://online.wsj.com/article/AP35b6fb378cc64062a3bceb87e17e2e03.html

66. 2011 Md. LEXIS 226, *Antoine Levar Griffin v. State of Maryland,* No. 74, September Term, 2010 Court of Appeals of Maryland 2011, MD Lexis 226, April 28, 2001 Filed.

67. Deloitte Center for Health Solutions. (2010). Issue brief: Social networks in health care: Communication, collaboration and insights. Retrieved from http://www.deloitte.com/assets/Dcom-UnitedStates/Local%20Assets/Documents/US_CHS_ 2010SocialNetworks_070710.pdf

CHAPTER 5

Financing Risk

Alice L. Epstein, David Metz, and Kevin M. McLaughlin

A risk exists if there is an event or action that can have a material effect on the financial or operational performance of the healthcare entity. The financial survival of a healthcare entity requires achieving the optimal balance between retaining risk and transferring risk. Sufficient funds or access to funds is required to ensure that adequate funds are available to finance the survival and recovery of the entity from a risk event, and to protect the ability of the healthcare entity to continue treating patients. Risk financing is, by common definition, the utilization of funds to cover the financial effect of unexpected losses or, simply put, to cover the costs related to unplanned adverse events. Sources of funds to pay for losses can be classified as internal (self-retention or a shared retention/captive program that uses collective funds from member organizations) or external (generally through the purchase of commercially available insurance).

EQUITABLE TRANSFER OF RISK

Insurance is defined as the equitable transfer of the risk of a loss from one entity to another, in exchange for payment. The amount charged to cover a specific dollar amount caused by the insured event is called the premium. The insurance transaction requires a payment to the insurer in exchange for the insurer's promise to compensate (indemnify) the insured in the case of a financial loss. The insured receives a contract, called the insurance policy, which details the conditions and circumstances under which the insured will be financially compensated.

The International Organization for Standardization (ISO) has developed principles, a framework, and a process to guide the management of risk. The standards (which are voluntary guidelines) emphasize the fact that management of risk must be tailored to the specific needs and structure of the particular organization. Risk financing is presented as a risk treatment activity to modify the risk.[1] An evaluation of the cost-effectiveness of the risk financing selection is paramount to the decision of which risk should be financed. Does the risk financing choice eliminate or reduce the cost of the risk to the healthcare entity? It is important to recognize that some losses or elements of a loss may be uninsurable, such as uninsured costs and damage to employee morale and the reputation of the organization.

How does the governing body determine its desired level of risk? It is essential that the healthcare entity leaders determine tolerance for risk and the desired balance of financial offense and defense. The risk that is right for one entity may not be right for another. There is no universal acceptance of risk level, although it is universally accepted from a business perspective that less risk may not always be better. The risk of an event—whether unexpected (such as a natural disaster or major regulatory change that is entirely beyond the healthcare entity's control) or an adverse clinical event that while unexpected in the individual circumstance was expected from an understanding of the industry—must be measured, evaluated, and planned for. The point of risk management is not to always reduce risk but rather to add value through the management of risk. "A balanced approach means taking [on] risk that is appropriate to the hospital's financial and competitive positions as well as financial goals and objectives, and that is consistent with the risk preferences of the board and management... [Application of this] strategy, which also informs all others, is clearly a joint responsibility of an organization's board and senior executives who are accountable for managing the organization in a manner that ensures achievement of strategic financial goals."[2]

FINANCIAL COSTS OF ADVERSE RISK _____

Included in the risk financing equation are the costs associated with identifying, minimizing, responding to, defending, and repairing the effects of an adverse event. Insurance, whether self-funded or commercially provided, is intended to cover associated costs. Loss of public or consumer confidence as a result of real or perceived safety concerns can lead to a significant loss of business and income.

Defense costs: Defense costs may exceed the settlement and may include lawyers' fees, court costs, transcription fees, and various other legal costs.

Settlement or judgment: Three types of awards may be bestowed: *general*, noneconomic loss such as pain and suffering; *specific*, such as medical bills or lost income; and *punitive*, such as punishment for acts considered reckless or unusually harmful by the courts.

Loss reduction: These costs are required to change work practices to avoid future losses.

Morale: Continuous losses cause employees to question work safety, the professionalism of the healthcare facility, and the management. Thus the institution may need to spend money to boost morale.

Opportunity costs: When a facility takes too long to decide on new projects or abandons them altogether, the opportunity dissipates and the institution incurs costs.

Although criminal actions can have ramifications of tremendous proportion, they are typically uninsurable. In some cases, unintentional criminal acts can be insured. Risk managers can address only imputed liability to the entity. Internal controls and procedures can deal with this type of exposure.

A COMPONENT OF RISK MANAGEMENT _____

Risk managers must identify their many areas of risk exposure and determine how best to manage their financial consequences. Identification of these various exposures is an organized process that relies on in-house adverse incident reports, patient safety data, quality improvement metrics, insurance company loss data, employee loss information, complaints, patient satisfaction survey results, financial reports, accreditation and licensure surveys, and professional literature. An appropriate risk management plan includes risk financing considerations. When formulating a plan, the risk manager must carefully evaluate the potential loss in terms of frequency of adverse events and the severity of their financial consequences. This analysis is central to the process of determining the most appropriate risk financing option.

Frequency refers to the number of times an event occurs and can be gauged in relation to any relevant period of time or area—per patient-day, per discharge, per year, per procedure in the emergency room area, per operating suite, or per intensive care unit. Risk areas of the entity should be studied both individually and comparatively over time, with some view of the facility's experience in relation to the experiences of other organizations. Typically, the most frequent adverse occurrences are of a minor nature, such as the loss of eyeglasses or false teeth. One of the difficulties in gathering accurate data is that such minor occurrences may go unreported. However, implementation of an occurrence screen procedure that requires employees to report specifically listed events may yield increased data about minor incidents. In essence, the "occurrence screen" is an integration of quality assessment and risk management.

Severity refers to the cost of the loss in dollars. Financial payouts can range from insignificant to catastrophic. A risk exposure that is infrequent and catastrophic can be one of the most difficult and time consuming to assess. Losses of that nature are difficult to plan for because their likelihood always seems remote and the size of the potential loss may distract attention from preventing other more prevalent, though less costly, potential losses.

Traditionally, a healthcare entity that experiences a combination of high-frequency and high-severity financial losses will find itself facing high costs and limited options. To counter these possibilities, risk managers must consider various risk management techniques, including high retentions, self-insurance, internal loss controls, claim procedures, and protocols. After selecting appropriate frequency and severity distributions, the actuary can set up a model to analyze various retention levels and run the simulation.

AVAILABILITY OF FUNDS

The decision to finance losses internally versus through external alternatives speaks to the fiscal health of the healthcare entity, its current and future investment income, credit/debit ratios, capital requirements, future expansion, availability of cash, governmental regulations, and risk appetite of the governing board. The availability of acceptably priced, external risk financing alternatives is a key factor in the cost/risk calculation and is influenced by the healthcare entity's claim experience, its risk exposures, and the insurance market's cycle, competition, and availability of reinsurance investment performance. External availability of funds and pricing follows insurance market cycles, commonly referred to as "hard" and "soft" markets.

A major insurance broker in a report analyzing the 2012 insurance market indicates that the 2011 rates (the price paid for insurance by the insured) for medical professional liability insurance typically stayed flat or decreased. The broker notes that many signs point to an increase in premiums in 2012, although a fair amount of competition among insurance carriers is likely to occur. The availability of funds (i.e., capacity) remained stable and sufficient in 2011. The broker's forecast calls for less capacity at the excess layer and intense scrutiny and risk review, which will likely lengthen the renewal process. It expects combined loss ratios for the medical professional liability market to begin to rise, although not dramatically (barring any significant industry events). Healthcare reform is changing the risk landscape, however, and the growth in the numbers of physicians employed by healthcare entities, will confound the risk equation; moreover, data security continues to grow as an area of exposure.[3]

Another major insurance broker indicates that healthcare reform will influence property and casualty insurance. Medical professional liability may experience changes as a result, due in part to the employment of physicians who will require more rigorous underwriting, based not just on the traditional specialty rating and loss review, but also on infection rates, readmission rates, and other quality indicators. According to this broker, in 2011 most of the major lines of coverage for the healthcare sector experienced no market changes, except for a late-year increase in property premiums. By comparison, in 2012, it expects to see flat to increasing pricing for healthcare entities. For medical professional liability, this broker anticipates that the current market will remain stable with some price reductions, while retentions, deductibles, limits, and coverage terms and conditions remain fairly stable.[4]

A third major insurance broker questions whether the paradigm of regularly revolving hard and soft markets can continue to exist in these economic times. It recognizes that after years of falling pricing, the insurance market has become more efficient, with profits being earned despite lower premiums. "The industry appears to be resilient, prudent, elastic, nimble, and smart." According to this broker, the changes in healthcare reimbursement will not threaten access to the capital that is available through the payment of premiums. Its report indicates that reinsurance pricing for property increased marginally in 2011 but forecasts that 2012 reinsurance pricing will climb higher. This organization views umbrella and excess pricing as firming but not hardening, although the insurance carriers are reportedly seeking price increases in the range of 5% to 10%.[5]

In summary, according to an international asset management, strategic advisory, and insurance research firm that reviews the industry on a quarterly basis, new challenges from a weak and changing economic recovery as well as health reform and increased competition will result in a modest increase in both exposure and premium price growth for both 2012 and 2013. This translates into good news for healthcare entities, which will find broad availability of insurance markets and capacity, albeit at a slight increase in price.[6]

PREDICTIVE ANALYTICS

A risk financing program should be sensitive to the financial condition of the healthcare entity, insurance market cycles, and changing economics. With increased competition and healthcare entities searching for the best value for their insurance funds, predictive analytics has attracted exponential interest from all organizations interested in funding loss exposures. Like any other businesses in a difficult economic environment, healthcare entities are tightening their expense ratio so that they can survive and even prosper. Increased costs to deliver health care, availability of funds, need for capital to meet ever-increasing technological advances, governmental regulations and societal expectations, and uncertainty in the economy direct how and when to spend funds on the financing of risk.

Once the risk manager has identified possible financial treatment of adverse events, the next step is to measure the effects of each treatment. Quantitative analysis measures the event's risk variables—for example, the event likelihood, impact, timing, coefficient of variation, and probability distribution. The qualitative analysis measures the event's impact on the healthcare entity's strategic goals, culture, and stakeholders. Improvement is accomplished through predictive analytics, which includes applications in behavioral economics, data visualization techniques, and text mining.[7]

Four analytical elements are necessary to evaluate the cost-effectiveness of the risk financing equation:[8]

- Actuarial analytics
- Customer analytics and distribution insight
- Claims analytics
- Risk analytics and compliance

Not every healthcare entity will engage fully in the use of these analytics. Nevertheless, it is important to understand how the results of predictive analytics affect the risk financing decision. Insurance carriers perform these analytics, as do risk retention groups and captives. Self-insured healthcare entities also engage in use of these analytics with the assistance of consultants and actuaries.

Actuarial analytics relies on the basic fundamental premise that the less significant the risk, the less funding that needs to be allocated to that risk. In the past, actuaries have heavily relied on univariate or one-way analysis for pricing and monitoring price efficiency. As the actuarial profession moves forward, its practitioners are using multivariate statistical techniques such as generalized linear modeling for assigning costs so as to develop a more

accurate, reflection of risk. The critical question in assigning predictive costs pricing is this: "Which risk factors or variables are important for predicting the likelihood and severity of a loss?"[8]

For example, a significant, positive correlation exists between the precipitous delivery of a high-risk neonate, the likelihood of a claim, and the lack of sophistication, technology, and specialty-trained physicians in the Level 1 hospital. Actuaries might use this knowledge to specify obstetrical professional liability costs by level of the hospital emergency department and nursery. As a result, the Level 1 hospital might have a higher cost of risk assigned to the potential delivery of a severely challenged newborn, keeping in mind that there should be a lower frequency of patients experiencing complicated deliveries than in hospitals with specialty obstetrics departments.

The potential for variation related to the frequency of adverse events as correlated to severity of adverse events is a complicating factor. "Although many risk factors that affect price are obvious, subtle and non-intuitive relationships can exist among variables that are difficult if not impossible to identify without applying more sophisticated analyses."[8] The risk financing decision algorithm weighs the probability of loss against the loss value. When the probability of loss is high, the decision may be to retain the loss, as the insurance markets may not insure the loss or will charge a high premium for doing so. If the healthcare entity does decide to retain the loss, its earnings and working capital must be capable of supporting the loss.

Claim payments and the management of claims are a significant expense in the risk financing equation. Effective management of the claims process is fundamental to the long-term sustainability of the risk financing selection. Claims analytics is the process of analyzing data at all stages in the claims cycle, including first notice of loss, payout, and subrogation. Managing the cost of claims means making the best decision as each new point in the claim continuum is reached. As a claim becomes more complex with additional information, the cost and loss adjustment expenses accumulate. Accurately forecasting the loss reserve and ultimately predicting the outcome of a claim is a challenge. Using analytics to calculate an accurate loss reserve amount and benchmark each claim based on similar characteristics can improve the loss reserve accuracy. Claims analytics utilizes historical loss data to forecast future losses at various retention levels. The loss data must incorporate changes to exposure and inflation.

INSURANCE MODELS

Almost every type of risk exposure can be covered under a self-funded insurance program or through a commercially available insurance program. Each model has its own set of operational, financial and tax-related benefits.[9] Commercially available insurance can be implemented quickly; its cost is fairly predictable, major exposures are usually covered, and the insurance company typically offers services that complement its insurance programs. Exposures not covered by the insurance carrier are not the carrier's responsibility or concern. If such events occur, the facility could still be exposed to substantial financial loss. In addition, part of the cost goes to insurance company expenses and profit.

Alternatives to the traditional insurance company programs include risk retention groups and captives. Self-funding may also be an option, but requires a significant amount of capital and reserves. Before choosing any insurance program, the healthcare entity should undertake a historical analysis of claims and premiums for a period of five years, if possible. This analysis should consider the time value of money and loss costs, both prospectively and retroactively. An appropriately trained and experienced actuary should be engaged when assessing funding levels and acceptable amounts of risk.

Self-funding options include, but are not limited to, the following:

- Self-funded programs require the healthcare entity to fund the insurance program, including the cost of operating the program (e.g., administration fees, stop-loss premium, and variable costs [the claims expense]). The program also pays the claims costs incurred. Typically, the entity purchases stop-loss insurance so that additional monies will be available if the claims costs exceed the catastrophic claims levels in the self-funded policy. The total cost of a self-funded program consists of the fixed costs, plus the claims expense, less any stop-loss reimbursements.

- Captives are owned by those (healthcare entities) they insure for the main purpose of funding the owner's risks. The owners actively participate in decisions influencing the captive's underwriting, operations, and investments. Captive insurance companies primarily (1) insure the risks of their owners and sometimes related or affiliated firms and (2) return underwriting profit and investment income. Essentially, a captive is an insurance carrier whose purpose is to underwrite insurance policies on behalf of its owner, in which the policyholders are the principal beneficiaries. Two basic types of captives are distinguished: single parent and group. A "single parent captive" is a subsidiary owned entirely by the parent. A single parent that provides risk financing only for the parent is called a "pure captive." A "broad captive" is owned by a single parent but also sells indemnity contracts to participating firms. In contrast, a "group captive" is owned by multiple firms and, therefore, usually meets the Internal Revenue Service (IRS) rules for accounting for the contributions as tax deductions. Captives are typically formed because the members believe their knowledge of their industry—in this case, health care—is superior to what the commercial insurance market can bring to the table. Consequently, they believe the captive will be a profit center.

- Risk retention/purchasing groups (RRG) are liability insurance companies that are owned by their members. A purchasing group consists of individuals or firms of like characteristics that share similar insurance needs. Risk purchasing groups are formed under the provisions of the federal Liability Risk Retention Act (LRRA) of 1986. The eligibility criteria for members of a purchasing group are set by the LRRA. Under the LRRA, the RRG must be domiciled in a state. Once licensed by its state of domicile, an RRG can insure members in all states. Because the LRRA is a federal law, it preempts state regulations, making it much easier for RRGs to operate nationally. As the name implies, these groups do not buy commercial insurance policies, but rather retain the risk within the group. In effect, the

members insure one another against liability claims and lawsuits. Because a risk retention group is an insurer, however, it may purchase reinsurance. The rates and policy forms of risk retention groups are not regulated, and risk retention groups are not covered by a guaranty association.

Review of the financial consequences of these programs is based on the philosophy of the healthcare entity. If the entity is fiscally conservative, a gradual approach should be used. Additional considerations involve portability, flexibility, services, and protection.

- *Portability:* For multistate organizations or networks, the portability feature is extremely important. If the insurance coverage is statutory in nature, such as worker's compensation or automobile liability, the ability to operate with a single insurance program in multiple states outside of conventional insurance is limited. States may require the insured to become licensed in each state for statutory coverage and to comply with all state laws. An alternative is to be "fronted" by a licensed insurance carrier, which would issue the policy and then reinsure with the self-insured program. Captives and their variations also can be used to address portability issues.
- *Flexibility:* Many financial programs, including some insured programs, require letters of credit or a bond to guarantee that the claims will be paid by the insured. Typically, the letters of credit must be collateralized. Often, programs require that each policy period have its own letter of credit or bond until all claims are liquidated. This mandate makes changing insurance carriers more difficult. Additionally,

there should be a consideration of whether there is flexibility when services are purchased individually.

- *Services:* Evaluation of the claim handling, investigation, claim payment, and loss control/risk management services is critical. Except for full insurance programs, the healthcare entity has an opportunity to choose the company, or third-party administrator, to service its claims or to perform loss control services.

Commercially available insurance is a contract between an insurance company and a business owner (healthcare entity). The purpose of the insurance is to minimize the owner's risks against losses through financial compensation, claims management, and risk control services. Insurance companies are rated based on their financial strength, assets, and ability to settle claims. Rating companies include A.M. Best, Standard and Poor's, Weiss Research, Duff and Phelps, and Moody's Investor Service.

RISK RETENTION

Regardless of the financial method used to fund risk, deciding how much risk to retain has important financial implications. The costs associated with adverse events can be significant and, regardless of the predictive models used, can greatly exceed expectations. Fundamental to this equation is understanding of the importance of knowing "not to risk a lot for a little." If the cost of internally insuring a risk with substantial limits of protection at a cost competitive with the commercial premium is not possible, then transferring the risk (i.e., buying true insurance) may be the best alternative, regardless of past retention levels or expected short-term premium savings. If the cost of insuring a loss is equal to

the costs associated with the risk, then the entity should consider retaining these losses. Retaining these risks may be approached through a large deductible, self-insured retention or by not purchasing a policy to cover the risk.

Estimating the total cost of risk (TCOR) to better determine retention levels requires analysis of three components:

- Costs of risk transfer (i.e., insurance premiums paid)
- Costs of risk retention (i.e., costs of claims that are absorbed and paid directly by the insured through deductibles or other self-insurance mechanisms)
- Administrative costs related to managing or controlling exposures to risk, and to managing claims once they occur)

TCOR is then analyzed against one or more of the following to determine cost-effectiveness:

- Annual revenues
- Net cash flow
- Number of days of cash on hand
- Budgeted TCOR
- Working capital
- Net worth

The best or optimal level of risk retention is not necessarily the one that produces the lowest combined cost of retained losses and excess premiums. Rather, it is the one that provides an acceptable compromise between the financial constraints, as measured by key financial indicators, and the hospital system's appetite for risk. Determining the extent to which financial requirements are violated and envisioning worst-case scenarios will aid in the evaluation process.... The appropriate retention level is the one that provides a comfortable fit with the organization's own appetite for risk while at the same time satisfying predetermined financial performance indicators. A disciplined methodology that properly quantifies financial exposure and downside risk implications will facilitate a more informed decision-making process.[10]

RISKS AND PERILS TO BE COVERED

A risk manager has the task of identifying exposures to loss and managing the potential effects of those exposures. This is a dynamic process that must be systematically approached on a recurring basis. The risk manager must understand each area of exposure. Obviously, this process is not a solo task; other professionals in administration and finance will be needed and should be available to assist in assessing the risks.

Automobile liability: Healthcare organizations may own their own vehicles for transporting supplies, equipment, patients, staff, or visitors. They may permit employees to use their own vehicles. Depending on the ownership of those vehicles, coverage may be available under the general liability policy, fleet policy, or hired and non-owned auto policy.

Aviation/aircraft liability: Injuries may be sustained while loading, transporting, or unloading aircraft. A general liability insurance policy excludes bodily injury arising from the loading or unloading of any aircraft.

Business interruption: Reimbursement of lost income may be necessary while the healthcare entity is being repaired or reconstructed from a covered peril so the entity can continue to pay bills related to utilities, staffing, and other overhead.

Business income and extra expense dependent on another: This coverage applies in the event that supply chain distributors and supply houses are unable to deliver supplies and/or medications. Losses can include continuing operation costs, overtime, rented equipment, and patient communication, among others.

Crime/fidelity: Employee dishonesty and theft including forgery, robbery, safe burglary, computer fraud, and wire transfer fraud may harm the firm's standing. Such risks may include theft by an employee as well as robbery or theft loss on and off the premises. Coverage can include audit costs and investigation expense.

Cyber-liability: All healthcare entities rely on computer-based systems and information networks for such tasks as billing, medical records, patient registration, marketing, and others. Breeches to these systems can result in extortion, business interruption, loss or damage to a network, e-theft, invasion of privacy, identity theft, and infection of others' networks. Coverage can include the costs to comply with applicable laws requiring the organization to notify its customers or users of a security breach that could potentially compromise private information.

Directors' and officers' (D&O) liability: Members of governing bodies and the entity they govern are at risk for the effects of their decisions. Coverage is afforded for the personal management decisions, misuse of assets, and errors or omissions of the members of the board of directors, the officers, and the chief executive of the healthcare organization. D&O coverage can be expanded to include additional administrative personnel. A D&O policy covers only nonphysical injury, and aims to protect against management errors and omissions.

Emergency evacuation: This coverage is associated with the costs of emergency evacuation of patients, visitors, and employees during a natural or human-made disaster. It can involve transportation, staffing, housing, family notification, and even advertising.

Employment practices: Coverage may be provided for alleged improper employment practices. Common accusations include sexual harassment, discrimination, hostile workplace, and wrongful termination.

Employee benefit liability: This coverage deals with errors or omissions in the administration of the employee benefits programs, including the extent of the lost benefit.

Employee injury and illness/worker's compensation: This coverage is statutorily required in all states. Coverage for statutory benefits as allowed by state law includes medical payments, indemnity, and legislatively mandated benefits and covers injuries to family members arising from the employee's injuries. In a healthcare setting, this form of risk management is considered critical coverage, as a disease could be transmitted from an employee to his or her family members.

Fiduciary liability: Financial injury may occur to others arising from an employer's acting in a fiduciary capacity. Most such damages arise from employee benefit plans. This coverage addresses risk exposures as a result of the handling of money for employees. It includes employee payroll deductions for pension plans, savings plans, and various employee benefit options. Exposures arise from the loss of funds or benefits.

General liability: This coverage focuses on injuries to third parties arising from operations.

Licensing board disciplinary proceedings: Coverage is needed for the defense of a licensed professional who is alleged to have violated his or her professional code of conduct or practice act before the practitioner's licensing board. There are associated fees and costs, including fines and penalties, resulting from the investigation and defense of a professional board action.

Media expense: Adverse publicity may result in the need to respond through responsive advertising or hiring a public relations professional to best deal with the situation to manage the public response.

Medical equipment breakdown: Equipment failure can result in costs associated with mechanical or electrical failure and related losses and damages, communication disturbance, debris and pollutant cleanup, fire control, and data restoration.

Medical waste pollution: Medical waste generated by the healthcare entity, such as specimens, blood, and items that possess sharp points, can accidently find its way into the mainstream waste, requiring the healthcare entity to clean up and remediate the waste and cover third-party damages caused by the accidental release of medical waste.

Patient confidentiality/privacy: Coverage for patient confidentiality or privacy breaches may include costs associated with an inquiry and investigation by state or federal authorities, including fines and penalties and defense of a Health Insurance Portability and Accountability Act (HIPAA) proceeding.

Peer review and medical staff credentialing: The facility may incur costs related to negligent peer review and credentialing allegations related to patient injury, Stark laws, competition, and racketeering.

Professional liability: This coverage deals with injuries to third parties arising from medical incidents. Liability typically arises from any and all services provided or not provided by an insured or someone for whom the insured can be held liable. A standard professional liability policy provides coverage when a patient is injured through the actions or lack of actions by healthcare entity staff as the injury relates to the clinical condition of the patient. Examples of patient injuries include the following:

- Nosocomial infections
- Burns to the patient as a result of a surgical fire
- Operating on the wrong side of the patient
- Medication errors
- Anesthesia complications causing injury

Property: Structures, their contents, and goods in transit may become damaged. For many institutions, physical property is their largest asset. Before examining insurance programs or alternatives, property insurance underwriters usually require basic information about buildings, contents, electronic data processing equipment, valuable printed material and documents, unusual property, personal property of others, boiler and other machinery, and business income. In large organizations, the insurance valuation of various types of property can be a very difficult task. An initial review must identify the types of property to be protected and the various risk exposures to be insured against. The following sections address each type of property individually.

- *Buildings:* Valuation of the physical plant is primarily a function of the total square footage and the cost per square foot. Generally, the cost per square foot is based on the type of construction, local labor costs, and safety features such as automatic sprinklers.
- *Construction activities:* Along with the building, any off-site property, property in transit, contractor's equipment, and installed equipment must have proper coverage. Because either the contractor or the building owner is responsible for these costs, the construction agreement should indicate acceptable coverage limits for automobile liability, worker's compensation, and general liability, naming the facility as an additional insured. If this is not done, the healthcare organization will be responsible for supplying the protection.
- *Contents:* Because the contents of buildings are so variable, this type of property is difficult to value, especially in a large facility. Physical contents of buildings include materials such as furniture, fixtures, and equipment. Disposable contents include inventories of medical supplies, spare parts, and housekeeping materials. Typically, the valuation of these contents is set at replacement cost.
- *Electronic data processing:* This property includes hardware and software, where valuation difficulty stems from the rapidly changing technology causing obsolescence in a short period of time.
- *Valuable papers, books, and documents:* These items includes the re-creation of critical documents such as medical records.
- *Personal property of others:* Such property consists primarily of leased equipment and the personal property of patients, guests, employees, and volunteers. Coverage includes the loss of patient property in the care, custody, and control of the facility or its employees.

INSURING AGREEMENTS

Insuring agreements state that the insurance company will pay those sums that the insured becomes legally obligated to pay. In other words, the law imposes an obligation on the insured. Further, the insurer responds to bodily injury or property damage inflicted upon a third party. Even if the lawsuit alleges uninsured acts along with a covered act, the insurance company has a "right and duty to defend" the healthcare entity. Inclusion of an insured act obliges the insurance company to defend the entire lawsuit, although the insurance company reserves the right to decide whether to settle or to defend. Exclusions enumerate the coverages specifically taken out of the contract, such as work-related injuries, pollution, aircraft, and automobile liability.

Because of the dynamic and complicated legal structure of a healthcare organization, the "named insured" can include the entity, its owners or active directors, officers and stockholders, employees, and real estate managers. A conditions section of the policy outlines the "named insured's" duties, rights, and responsibilities and the rights of the healthcare organization under the contract. Failure to properly review the conditions could mean restriction or denial of coverage when an event occurs.

A "consent" provision in an insurance contract identifies whether the insurance company needs the insured's consent to settle a claim. This clause obligates the insurance company to pay up to the covered amount of any pretrial settlement or post-trial judgment. If the insured refuses to settle, this entity is personally responsible for any judgment amount in excess of the proposed settlement.

Liability insurance differentiates between "occurrence" and "claims made" coverage. "Occurrence" policies cover all injuries that occurred during the policy period, regardless of when they were reported. "Claims made" policies cover injuries reported during the policy period that occurred after the policy retroactive date. An advantage of an occurrence policy is that it will cover all injuries during the policy period until the agreement is exhausted. A disadvantage is that medical malpractice claims may be made many years after the event. Any awards resulting from such claims are applied against dollar limits that seemed adequate at the time the insurance was purchased, which may prove inadequate at the time of award or settlement.[11,12]

PROTECTION FOR A RAINY DAY

Healthcare entities cannot continue to operate without positive cash flow and a positive or even profit-and-loss accounting. Risk managers can assist in protecting the financial assets of their organizations against devastating losses. A knowledge of the options and key areas of risk transfer and insurance helps build a comprehensive risk management program. Within healthcare entities, there are experts who can help with everything from overviews of insurance coverage, to department-specific risks and exposures, to an entire restructuring of the risk finance program. External resources and professionals include insurance brokers, insurance agents, consultants, actuaries, and numerous others who have expertise in specific aspects of healthcare risk financing.

The finances of the healthcare entity can be crippled by an uninsured or underinsured loss. Conversely, benefits can accrue through cost-effective improvements in the overall program. Employee morale increases as losses decrease. Operational efficiencies are realized when the healthcare entity's assets are properly protected. As complex as the risk management mission in financing and insurance is, the dynamic nature of the healthcare industry promises to lead to a higher level of sophistication with newer financial options to minimize losses.

REFERENCES

1. International Organization for Standardization. ISO Working Group on Risk Management, ISO 31000: (2009). *Risk management: Principles and guidelines.*
2. Kaufman, K. (2008, August 1). *Managing risk in a challenging financial environment.* Healthcare Financial Management Association.
3. Marsh. (2012, January 24). Navigating the risk and insurance landscape: United States insurance market report (2012). Retrieved from https://usa.marsh.com/LinkClick.aspx?fileticket=AIPswpflRbw%3d&tabid=1985&mid=10432
4. AON Risk Solutions. (2012). *2012 U.S. industry report, health care.* Chicago, IL.
5. Willis. (2011, October). *Marketplace realities: Solid footing and a foundation for growth, 2012.*
6. Conning. (2012, January). *Property-casualty forecast & analysis.* Hartford, CT.
7. Kallman, J. (2008, September 1). *RM 101: Financing risk retention, solution measurement, Vol. 55.* New York: Risk Management, Risk and Insurance Management Society.
8. SAS. (2012, January 3). The analytical P&C insurer: Using analytics to optimize business performance [white paper]. Cary, NC. Retrieved from http://www.sas.com/reg/wp/ca/40928
9. Self-Insurance Institute of America. (2012). *Captives and RRGs.* Simpsonville, SC. Retrieved from http://www.siia.org/i4a/pages/Index.cfm?pageID=4550
10. Daniels, G. L. (2010, July 1). Your hospital's strategy for managing total cost of risk. *Healthcare Financial Management.* Retrieved from http://readperiodicals.com/201007/2080606481.html
11. Stanovich, C. (2011, January). The increasingly complex CGL Policy. International Risk Management Institute. Retrieved from http://www.irmi.com/expert/articles/2011/stanovich01-cgl-general-liability-insurance.aspx
12. Austin, W. K. (2010, January). Property insurance resolutions for 2010. International Risk Management Institute. Retrieved from http://www.irmi.com/expert/articles/2010/austin01-commercial-property-insurance.aspx

CHAPTER 6

Ethical Issues for Risk Managers

Kathleen E. Powderly

There is an increased awareness of ethical issues in healthcare, and healthcare ethics is now incorporated into the curriculum in every healthcare educational program. Most hospitals have an ethics committee, although those committees may function at very different levels. A variety of forces have joined together to contribute to this increased awareness—patients' rights, advanced medical technologies, changing societal demographics, nontraditional family structures, changes in the doctor–patient relationship, disparities based on race or class, and dramatically increased economic burdens, among them.

Hospital risk managers will confront many ethical issues in their daily practice. They must be familiar with federal, state, and local legislation and may need to develop guidelines or policies for implementing applicable laws. Even where the law is clear, the nuances of patients, families, and illness scenarios often require consideration on a case-by-case basis. In other situations, there will be no law to apply and the risk manager will have to adapt measures to consider and resolve complex ethical problems. Working with the ethics process in place in the hospital will lead to better outcomes for patients and institutions.

This chapter discusses common ethical issues confronted by hospital risk managers, the process of healthcare ethics consultation, and the role of ethics committees, and provides examples of the complicated issues faced in today's healthcare institutions. Where appropriate, case law that is a matter of public record is used for illustration. In other cases, composites of cases faced in everyday practice are used to protect confidentiality.

ETHICS COMMITTEES

Role, Responsibilities, and Authority

Most American hospitals have one or more ethics committees. The number has increased dramatically as accrediting agencies such as The Joint Commission have begun to require attention to patients' rights and ethical issues during their institutional surveys.[1] The utilization and effectiveness of an ethics committee varies greatly from institution to institution and may depend on, and be a reflection of, its membership. If the ethics committee members are all upper-level administrators, for example, staff members, patients, and families of patients may be reluctant to ask the committee for assistance. At the same time, the committee needs to have participants who demonstrate credibility at high levels in the healthcare institution to be effective.

The precursors of hospital ethics committees were the dialysis committees of the 1960s,[2] as well as the committees on abortion and sterilization that existed for decades in Catholic hospitals. At the time when the Karen Ann Quinlan 1976 court decision[3] mentioned the use of the hospital's ethics committee, most hospitals did not have one. Ms. Quinlan happened to be a patient in a Catholic hospital in New Jersey that had an ethics committee to consider issues of abortion and sterilization. As the field of bioethics has grown, however, hospital ethics committees have become more common, and the use of ethics committees to consider complex cases has become a stronger recommendation. Federal government recommendations for ethics committees actually appeared in the Baby Doe regulations,[4] and infant care review committees have become common.

Ethics committees vary with regard to their placement in healthcare organizations. Some report to hospital administration; others report to the board of trustees, the medical board, or a specific clinical department. Where the committee sits in the organizational structure can have a dramatic impact on its effectiveness.

Ethics committees generally have three roles in healthcare institutions: education, policy development, and consultation. Committee members spend considerable time educating themselves, their hospital staff, patients, and the broader community served by the institution. This education includes a working knowledge of basic ethical principles and process, institutional policy relating to ethical and legal issues, and a basic understanding of the law as it applies to health-related issues in the particular geographical location.

Policy development related to ethical and/or legal issues also concerns ethics committees.

For example, the committee might develop a specific policy to implement the federal Patient Self-Determination Act (PSDA) or a state "do not resuscitate" (DNR) or surrogate decision-making law.[5,6]

Ethics committees often assume a consultation role in difficult cases. Usually, the bylaws of ethics committees allow a case to be brought to the committee by a patient, the patient's surrogate or family, the patient's physician or nurse, or anyone involved with the care of a patient. This might include the hospital risk manager, who may have become aware of a case that presents liability risks to the institution but that also includes ongoing difficult ethical dilemmas. Focusing on the liability risks only and not on the continuing needs of the patient and/or family may simply increase the institution's liability. Establishing trust in these situations and refocusing the discussion on the ongoing needs of the patient is in the best interest of both the patient and the institution.

Often, ethical dilemmas can be resolved by simply gathering together all of the involved individuals, including the patient or surrogate, and providing an objective, neutral committee or subcommittee to hear the concerns, facilitate communication, provide mediation, and clarify goals of treatment.[7,8] Sometimes the best option for the patient is identified; sometimes the "least bad" option is all that can be identified. This type of group deliberation may provide some comfort, especially if decisions are being made by a surrogate. With this approach, the surrogate can feel that he or she has been an integral part of a consensus without feeling burdened by the bottom-line responsibility.

The ethics committee's recommendations are advisory to the attending physician, not binding. Of course, this is true of all consultations (e.g., psychiatry, cardiology, neurology, or infectious disease). In some situations, the patient's physician or the institution's administration may be in the position of deciding whether to implement the committee's recommendations. Clinicians may decide that the recommendations violate their personal values, based on a conscientious objection, and may request that another clinician be assigned to the care of the patient; for example, a consensus that the patient should be withdrawn from a ventilator based on the patient's wishes or best interest might result in transfer of care to another physician if the attending feels this step violates his or her own values or religious beliefs.

Composition of the Ethics Committee

There is no single model for an ethics committee. Committees are generally interdisciplinary in nature and include physicians, nurses, social workers, allied health professionals, ethicists, and often a community member who is not an employee and can view matters objectively from the perspective of patients and their families. Some committees include representatives of the clergy, the hospital attorney, the hospital risk manager, and administrative personnel. In any specific case discussion, appropriate individuals with expertise not represented on the committee should be brought in as necessary.

One of the most important and unique aspects of an ethics committee is its interdisciplinary nature. Members should be chosen based on their expertise or interest and should not be appointed just to represent a particular constituency. A steady core of ethics committee members is really important to develop expertise and facilitate the group process. Many committees require ethics committee members to sign confidentiality agreements. Clinical departments may choose to have their own ethics committees, in addition to a hospital-wide ethics committee. Departmental committees are most common in departments of nursing, but they may also be found in medicine, pediatrics, and obstetrics/gynecology.

Some departments or professionals may feel more comfortable addressing issues within their own discipline, because they believe the problems are unique to their profession or department. This is a particularly common rationale for the existence of nursing ethics committees. Although these feelings are significant, a communication link must be maintained between the departmental committees and the overall institutional ethics committee, because issues may overlap. In planning educational programs, it makes sense to pool resources and to plan complementary programs.

Hospital risk managers are members of ethics committees in many institutions. Some committees include the hospital risk manager as an *ex officio* member without voting privileges; this individual also is generally not part of consult teams. Critics contend that sitting on a committee whose primary role is to protect the patient and serve as an advocate for patients' rights is a conflict of interest for the hospital risk manager, who is responsible for protecting the institution from liability. Putting the voting issue aside, an active communication link between risk management and the ethics committee is very appropriate. Cases that come to the ethics committee are, by definition, complicated. They may already have involved personnel with risk management, quality assurance, and palliative care responsibilities. Thus the risk manager may strongly suggest that the ethics committee get involved in a difficult case. Similarly, the ethics committee might consider alerting the attending physician to possible administrative issues or liability concerns and suggest contacting risk management for input. In cases brought before the ethics committee, there may be a need for the patient, patient's family, clinicians, and other members to understand the limits of the law and the hospital's perception of risk and liability—precisely the areas of a risk manager's expertise. A clinician may need to know if the hospital will support controversial decisions. Patients or family members may also need to understand the hospital administration's position on a deliberation. In addition, when a case is brought to the attention of risk management, coexisting ethical issues may be identified. Thus ethics committees and risk managers must work together. That having been said, the processes must remain distinct and separate.

ETHICAL GUIDELINES FOR RISK MANAGERS

To work with patients, families, and staff, it is important for risk managers to have a working knowledge of basic ethical principles and the ethical framework for decision making in health care. These principles and the process of decision making are discussed in this section.

Autonomy

Autonomy, or self-determination, is the core principle and bedrock of American bioethics. In the United States, the Constitution builds a framework of respect for individual rights, as long as the exercise of those rights does not infringe on the rights of others or endanger or harm others. In a country as heterogeneous and culturally pluralistic as the Unites States, ensuring autonomy can be quite a challenge. Adults have the right to make their own healthcare decisions, a change from former practice based on paternalism. In a paternalistic system, clinicians tell patients what to do, relying on what they think is right or best for them; patients do what they are told to do, without asking questions. Yet, a clinician's recommendations or decisions could be grounded in sound medical judgment or could be influenced by the clinician's own personal values or sense of what is right or wrong.

When decisions are based on a respect for autonomy, patients choose from the available options. From the clinician's perspective and values, the patient may make a "bad" decision. Despite the perception of others, individuals have the right to make bad healthcare decisions for themselves. The clinician, however, has an obligation to inform the patient in such a way that the patient can understand the available options, including no intervention or treatment where appropriate. Patients must be informed in a language and at an educational level which they can understand.

Respect for autonomy does not mean the patient can dictate treatment options the clinician is not comfortable with, nor does it preclude the clinician from offering information or an opinion about what he or she thinks the optimal options are for an individual patient. Providers also cannot force patients to be autonomous; some will defer their right to make decisions to surrogates (see **Box 6-1**).

The following illustrate dilemmas involving autonomy:

- The family of an elderly patient requests that she not be told of her terminal diagnosis because she would be upset, she would not be told in her "home country," and they want to protect her. This crisis can be avoided if we find out from the patient herself, upfront and before we have bad news, how she would like information handled.
- A 30-year-old Orthodox Jewish woman defers all of her medical decision making to her husband. This is extremely distressing to the obstetrics/gynecology staff, which has been trained to empower women and respect their decisions. The patient has the right to defer based on her culture and religion, and her choice should be respected, although she might be reminded periodically that she has chosen to defer and does have the right to make her own decisions.
- An elderly patient has gangrene of the lower extremity and refuses the recommended amputation She seems to understand what is going on, but not the life-threatening consequences of her decision. Her decisional capacity should be evaluated. Perhaps she had enough capacity to designate a surrogate. In the end, it is a tough decision to force amputation, although arguably in the patient's best interest. All of these cases must be evaluated individually.
- A woman who is the victim of domestic violence insists on not reporting the incident and going back to her husband, who is the abuser. There is no requirement for reporting in your state (this varies from state to state). The patient has the right to make this decision, and many advocates for victims of domestic violence would argue that she might be in more danger if he is reported.

Beneficence

In health care, beneficence is interpreted as the obligation to do good for patients. When there are no good options, the clinician should, at least, do no harm, as stated in the Hippocratic tradition of nonmaleficence.[9] At times, a clinician's sense of what is good for a patient is compromised by an autonomous patient's choices. When respecting the patient's wishes would cause harm, clinicians are not obligated to violate their own set of values and act against their desire to be beneficent. In such situations, clinicians are entitled to a conscientious objection. Although physicians cannot abandon a patient in an emergency, they can refer a patient elsewhere; clinicians can inform their superiors of their objections and ask that the patient be transferred to another provider (see **Box 6-2**).

Justice

The principle of justice dictates that people should be treated in an equitable, or fair, fashion. Justice is the ethical principle involved in dilemmas related to allocation of scarce resources or lack of access to health care or healthcare resources. There has been an increased focus on issues related to justice as the U.S. economy has experienced a dramatic downturn and the gap between those who have and those who have not has widened. Healthcare resources have become increasingly scarcer. In a "just" healthcare system, people would have access to the resources necessary to achieve a minimally acceptable level of health care. However, it is not clear that health care is a right, or an entitlement, in the United States, and the finite amount of healthcare resources is inequitably distributed.

While resource allocation is an important consideration on a societal level, clinicians are compromised when they have to allocate or deny access to healthcare resources at the

Box 6-2

These cases represent ethical dilemmas involving beneficence, which could be in conflict with autonomy or not feasible because of scarce resources.

- An obstetrician/gynecologist is caring for a patient who has vaginal bleeding and needs a D&C. The patient is a Jehovah's Witness and refuses blood transfusions, which are generally included in the presurgical consent process. She has the right to refuse; the physician also has the right to transfer her care to another provider. Institutions that care for large numbers of Jehovah's Witnesses often have nonblood programs that help to identify those clinicians who are comfortable with patients who refuse blood and those who are not. Cases involving adolescents and pregnant women who identify themselves as Jehovah's Witness are particularly challenging.
- A patient with metastatic disease is a candidate for a palliative procedure. She has a DNR order in place and refuses to suspend it. The anesthesiologist is not comfortable participating in the surgery, as an iatrogenic arrest may occur. This conflict is often alleviated if there is a thorough discussion with the patient or the surrogate regarding the place of DNR in the operating room.
- A proud, fiercely independent 85-year-old woman has had a stroke and can no longer care for herself. She insists that she wants to go home. Although she can make simple decisions, she does not want to accept the fact that she cannot go home. The patient refuses nursing home placement. These discharge planning dilemmas occur all the time. Unfortunately, there is inadequate home care and less than perfect nursing home options for many individuals. There is an ethical issue if the discharge plan is unsafe. While the nursing home option is safe, it is less than desirable. These situations strain the resources of the institution and exhaust providers. Good social work and patient relations departments can sometimes help to come up with the best option, but it may leave the patient and the staff feeling unhappy.

bedside. In reality, clinicians may have to struggle with how to apportion their time. Shortages of supplies or critical care beds must also be resolved. Some institutions are overwhelmed with a large number of undocumented immigrants who are not eligible for any reimbursement or with a large number of "boarders" because of the lack of skilled nursing facility beds. Over a considerable period of time, these allocation decisions and the associated stress can contribute to burnout in healthcare workers and can affect quality of care. However, a distinction should be made between insufficient resources for optimal care and situations where the resources are so scarce as to lead to an unsafe level of care. In the latter situation, the healthcare institution may be operating in an unethical or even an illegal fashion.

Ethical Standards for Decision Making

As indicated previously, autonomous adults have the right to make their own decisions, provided that they have decisional capacity. The standards that apply when they cannot participate in decision making are substituted judgment and best interest.

Decisional Capacity

Decisional capacity refers to individuals' ability to weigh the relative benefits, risks, or burdens of proposed interventions and their ability to make a decision. In contrast to a psychiatric or legal determination of competency, decisional capacity is a clinical judgment that the individual has the ability to weigh the benefits and risks of the particular decision he or she is being asked to consider at any given time. Importantly, an individual may have the capacity to make some decisions and not other, more complicated decisions, and/or may have capacity at some times and not at others. For example, elderly patients with dementia may be clearheaded at times and be able to understand and make simple choices. Sick elderly individuals facing difficult and complicated treatment decisions may understand that they do not have the capacity to make complex decisions but may be able to make simple decisions or designate a surrogate. Extremely sick patients or those undergoing surgery may temporarily lose their decision-making capacity and regain it after treatment or intervention.

Where possible, individuals who have enough decisional capacity to identify a healthcare agent or surrogate decision maker should be offered every opportunity to do so. In some difficult cases and where time permits, the risk manager should consider seeking a court-appointed guardian for difficult cases where the patient lacks capacity and there is no identifiable surrogate. Patients in this category are particularly vulnerable to either undertreatment, because there is no one to advocate for them, or overtreatment, because there is no one to request that treatment be stopped where appropriate.

Substituted Judgment

Substituted judgment applies when someone previously had the capacity to make his or her own decisions but has either temporarily or permanently lost that capacity. It seeks to determine what *this* individual would have decided, given *this* set of circumstances, based on what was important to the individual. Substituted judgment considers things such as culture, religion, lifestyle, life experience, and values. It is a very subjective judgment specific to this individual patient.

An advance directive can make substituted judgments much easier to achieve.[10] Living wills, healthcare proxies, and durable powers of attorney for health care are all forms of advance directives. It is important for the risk manager to be very familiar with the legally recognized forms of advance directives at the institution. A living will generally specifies a patient's wishes about medical treatment to prolong life and allows individuals to indicate what they would or would not want in specific situations. Most living wills focus on what the individual would not want and do not provide a lot of guidance on what they *would* want.

One of the problems with a living will is that the statements are often not clear in relationship to the particular situation at hand. What does it mean when individuals say they would not want to be on a ventilator, for example? They might not want to be maintained on a ventilator if they were in an irreversible, ventilator-dependent state. In contrast, they might not feel the same way about being on a ventilator for a few days after major surgery if their prognosis was good.[11] Because the patient lacks capacity when the advance directive is consulted, clinicians cannot have a conversation with the patient to clarify the meaning of the statements in the directive. Sometimes there is uncertainty about whether the patient would have changed his or her mind given the specific circumstances. In such circumstances, a surrogate decision maker, who is able to discuss the pros and cons of the specific interventions, is extremely helpful. Advance directives such as healthcare proxies and durable powers of attorney for health care allow for the designation of a surrogate decision maker, in addition to providing a vehicle for a living will component.

Healthcare organizations are required by federal law (PSDA) to ask on admission if patients have an advance directive and to give them information on how to do one in their jurisdiction if they have not.[12]

Despite all of our efforts to empower people regarding healthcare decisions, most hospitalized patients do not have valid advance directives when they are admitted. If they have decisional capacity and are not too sick, they may do one when admitted, but most do not. As a result, healthcare providers are often faced with difficult decisions to be made and no indication from the patient about what he or she would want. The identification of a surrogate decision maker who knows the patient will help providers make the best substituted judgment they can. Such a person may be able to inform the discussion with a clear sense of what the patient would have wanted based on conversations and experiences with the patient. If there were no specific conversations, the decision maker's relationship with the patient will help the clinicians to understand what the patient was like, how he or she lived life, what was important to the patient, and so on. This is far better than making decisions in a vacuum. As is often the case, the legal framework for identification of a surrogate and the process of surrogate decision making vary from state to state, and the risk manager must be familiar with applicable law in the local jurisdiction (see **Box 6-3**).[13,14]

Best Interest

The best interest standard applies when someone never had decisional capacity or when there is no way of knowing an individual's wishes. When a substituted judgment is not possible, the appropriate guideline is the standard of best interest, also known as the objective benefits/

> **Box 6-3**
>
> The following hierarchy of surrogate decision makers applies in New York State under the Family Health Care Decisions Act (2010):
>
> - Legal guardian with healthcare authority
> - Spouse or domestic partner if not legally separated
> - Adult child
> - Parent
> - Adult sibling
> - Close friend

burdens or "reasonable person" standard. Best interest applies for infants, children, and those persons with mental and/or developmental disabilities that have kept them from reaching decisional capacity. There is no means to determine what a particular infant or child would have done with no advance directive, no identifiable surrogate decision makers, and no established set of values. Thus caregivers must ask the following questions: What is in the best interest of this patient, given the current circumstances? What would a "reasonable person" choose to do under the circumstances? Making the decision "requires morally imaginative and empathetic efforts to enter the experimental world of such patients."[15] Despite the challenges, this determination should be as objective as possible, holding the best interest of the individual uppermost.

Informed Consent

Clinicians are obligated to provide autonomous adult patients with all the information they need, in a way that they can understand it, to allow them to make a fully informed decision. Patients must be given enough information to weigh the relative benefits and burdens or risks associated with the proposed intervention. Informed consent is a process, not just a signature on a consent form. While the signed consent form serves as documentation of the patient's understanding and consent, the process and dialogue between the clinician and patient are even more important and should be documented. Can desperately ill patients be expected to weigh all possible risks? Can patients absorb all the information they need to make an informed decision in one sitting? These are important considerations in the process of informed consent.

The legal doctrine of informed consent in the United States can be traced to the case of *Schloendorff v. Society of New York Hospital,* which was decided in 1914.[16] Ms. Schloendorff agreed to an examination under anesthesia for a fibroid tumor but did not agree to have the tumor removed. Her doctors, perhaps acting in a beneficent manner, removed the tumor anyway. She sued the hospital and lost on a technicality (she sued the hospital rather than the doctors and the court held that the nonprofit hospital could not be held liable for the actions of its employees). However, the language of Justice Cardozo's decision laid the groundwork for the legal doctrine of informed consent: "Every human being of adult years and sound mind has a right to determine what shall be done with his own body; and a surgeon who performs an operation without his patient's consent commits an assault for which he is liable in damages. (see **Box 6-4**)"

Conceptually, informing a patient about all possible risks associated with an intervention or treatment is overwhelming to clinicians. How does one determine the extent of the discussion to fulfill the obligations associated with informed consent? Clinicians and risk managers can be guided by the court decision in *Canterbury v. Spence:*

The discussion need not be a disquisition, and surely the physician is not compelled to give his patient a short medical education; the disclosure role summons the physician only to a reasonable explanation. This means generally informing the patient in nontechnical terms as to what is at stake: the therapy alternatives open to him, the goals expectably to be achieved, and the risks that may ensue from particular treatment and no treatment.[17]

Box 6-4

Mr. Canterbury consented to and underwent a laminectomy in 1958. Postoperatively, he fell and was subsequently paralyzed from the waist down. He consented to a second operation, but after that he "required crutches to walk, still suffered from urinal incontinence and paralysis of the bowels, and wore a penile clamp." In the court's decision there was a discussion of "true consent," or the obligation of physicians to disclose information to patients. Mr. Canterbury had not been warned about paralysis resulting from falls.

An expanded version of "true consent" in the court's decision provides guidelines for risk managers involved with the informed consent process:

True consent to what happens to oneself is the informed exercise of a choice, and that entails an opportunity to evaluate knowledgeably the options available and the risks attendant upon each.... The physician discharges the duty when he makes a reasonable effort to convey sufficient information although the patient, without the fault of the physician, may not fully grasp it.

Codes of Ethics

A code of ethics is one of the defining characteristics of a professional. Traditionally, the Hippocratic Oath conveyed a sense of the privileged roles and responsibilities of physicians over time. Almost every organization of healthcare providers has a code of ethics detailing the values, duties, and ethical responsibilities of their chosen professional membership. However, these codes of ethics contain broad aspirational statements that provide little assistance to the individual practitioner trying to interpret the applicability of the codes to specific clinical situations. Ethical codes are guiding principles, not directions for action in distinct situations. Although codes of ethics are open to interpretation, they remain important guidelines for healthcare professionals. The American Society for Bioethics and Humanities (ASBH) is currently working on a code of ethics for clinical ethics consultants.

Confidentiality

Every code of ethics emphasizes provider–patient confidentiality. Even though confidentiality is one of the most important obligations of healthcare providers and one that everyone agrees is important, it may also be one of the most commonly violated rules. Healthcare providers have an undeniable obligation to respect the privacy of all patients and to keep all information given to them in the strictest confidence. Unfortunately, anyone riding in the elevator or sitting in the cafeteria in a hospital can attest to breaches of confidentiality.

Violations of confidentiality are always ethically problematic. Such breaches are even more unethical if the information is serious, has the ability to stigmatize the patient, or could lead to discrimination. Certainly, a diagnosis of HIV seropositivity should be treated confidentially. There may be individuals, including healthcare providers, whom the patients may not wish to inform. Discrimination against people who are HIV positive, although illegal in many states and a violation of the Americans with Disabilities Act, does still exist. The Health Insurance Portability and Accountability Act (HIPAA) of 1996 was put into place to help protect confidentiality.[18] Although it has helped, its message about the importance of protecting information sometimes gets lost in the web of bureaucracy.

ETHICAL ISSUES IN EVERYDAY PRACTICE

There are many clinical situations in which a risk manager should have knowledge about ethical approaches to problem resolution and the resources available on site at the institution. Critics may contend that violations of ethical doctrines do not, in and of themselves, incur liability. Increasingly, however, professional organizations are publishing code of ethics that include current opinions with legal annotations—that is, liability arguments may be bolstered with data regarding ethical conflicts. The American Medical Association, for example, has published such opinions.[19] Ethical issues may arise in the provision of routine healthcare services such as decision making for adults with capacity, surrogate decision making, perinatal dilemmas, pediatric care, geriatric care, organ transplantation, and end-of-life choices. Some examples have been described previously; others will be discussed briefly in this section.

Perinatal Dilemmas

Perinatal issues constitute the most unresolved dilemmas in clinical ethics. While this is certainly true about abortion, it also holds for maternal–fetal conflicts and dilemmas in the neonatal intensive care unit (NICU).

Although certainly not without controversy, abortion is a constitutionally protected right in the United States.[20,21] Violence at abortion clinics, the debate over training residents in obstetrics/gynecology to perform abortions, and the current political debates over abortion and contraception are evidence of the continuing emotionally charged controversy related to this right. Risk managers should understand the law in their state regarding abortion, including access and consent issues.

In obstetrical care, maternal–fetal medicine remains highly charged with ethical predicaments. Clinicians practice as if they have two patients, the mother and the fetus, where only one of the patients speaks for herself. This emphasis on two patients was not always the case. In the nineteenth century, there was little discussion among physicians or midwives about the well-being of the fetus. Childbirth was dangerous for the mother, and little could be done for the infant, much less the fetus. During the twentieth century, childbirth became safer for the mother through the use of antibiotics, blood typing, cross-matching, and improved anesthesia. At the same time, technology evolved to allow for intervention directed at high-risk infants and fetuses. Ultrasound imaging allows for the visualization of the fetus and conveys a real sense of the fetus as an additional patient during the prenatal period.

Maternal–fetal conflicts arise only when the rights or behavior of the pregnant woman are not in the best interest of her fetus. Specific behaviors may provoke different emotional responses and ethical anguish in clinicians. A clinician may be able to accept the decision of a pregnant Jehovah's Witness to refuse a blood transfusion, on the basis of respect for autonomy. Clinicians may have much less tolerance for a pregnant woman addicted to crack cocaine (see **Box 6-5**).

Box 6-5

The following are examples of potential maternal–fetal conflicts:

- Abuse of illegal drugs or alcohol (which is legal but teratogenic)
- Refusal of a cesarean section indicated for maternal well-being and/or fetal distress
- Refusal of a necessary blood transfusion by a pregnant Jehovah's Witness
- Failure to adhere to a special diet by a brittle diabetic pregnant woman
- Demand to remove a cerclage at 30 weeks for maternal discomfort

---

A pregnant woman should not be treated any differently from other patients with respect to autonomy. Advocacy for the fetus requires a significant effort to help the pregnant woman understand the consequences if her behavior is not in the best interest of her fetus. On the one hand, some physicians would attempt to seek a court order if a pregnant woman refused a cesarean section necessary for fetal well-being. Even stronger motivation exists if the mother is also at risk, as in placenta previa. On the other hand, some physicians would attempt to get a court order but would not tie the woman down and operate without her consent, even with the court order. These clinicians hope that going to court reinforces, for the pregnant woman, their serious concerns and the seriousness of the situation. From an ethical perspective, it is an extremely serious matter to violate a woman's autonomy simply because she is pregnant (see **Box 6-6**).[22]

Case law is inconsistent and not particularly helpful in maternal–fetal conflicts. While some courts have intervened on grounds of fetal interest, others have refused to issue court orders.[23] In some cases, the patient has delivered while the court was still deliberating. The American College of Obstetricians and Gynecologists emphasizes respect for the wishes of pregnant women.

Box 6-6

Mrs. Angela Carder had been diagnosed with cancer as an adolescent, and it was in remission. She was warned that the cancer could be exacerbated by a pregnancy. Nevertheless, she became pregnant; the cancer reappeared and worsened. Early in her third trimester she was dying when a court ordered delivery of her fetus by cesarean section. Her neonate died after birth, and Mrs. Carder died shortly after the surgery. Surgery hastened her death by a few days. On appeal, the court reversed the earlier court's order, ruling that Mrs. Carder's autonomy dictated that her wishes be respected; she had not consented to the cesarean section. This was particularly an issue in her case because her fetus was at only borderline viability.

Decision making in the NICU raises profound ethical challenges. Prior to the regionalization of intensive perinatal care, clinicians and perhaps one or both parents made private decisions about imperiled newborns. Often, these decisions were not subject to public scrutiny or even to professional examination within a hospital. Imperiled newborns include premature infants, those with congenital abnormalities and genetic defects, and those who are very sick.

A landmark article about decision making in the NICU appeared in the *New England Journal of Medicine* in 1973.[24] In this article, Duff and Campbell argued that it is sometimes appropriate to withdraw or withhold life-sustaining treatment from seriously ill or anomalous newborns. They described a methodology employed in the NICU at Yale that attempted to achieve consensus regarding appropriate treatment for such newborns. All parties involved in the care of the baby, including the parents, were included in these discussions. The authors contended that it was sometimes appropriate to treat some of these severely compromised neonates less aggressively. Infants who were not treated aggressively were supported in a humane way during their dying days. In contrast, critics feared that nonaggressive treatment decisions could be problematic from a legal perspective and that grieving parents might not be in the best position to make such decisions for their children. An active debate regarding decision making in the NICU ensued among clinicians in pediatrics and neonatology. The Duff and Campbell model was an early example of the mediation model often recommended in current ethics consultation.

In the early 1980s, the federal government became involved in public policy regarding neonatal decision making, when the Baby Doe regulations were issued. On the basis of the Rehabilitation Act of 1973, these regulations established a telephone hotline and investigative procedures to deal with alleged discrimination against or inappropriate treatment of "handicapped" newborns. Although the regulations were overturned by the Second Circuit Court in the New York case of Baby Jane Doe, a public policy debate ensued. In addition, federal legislation was passed that required states receiving federal funds for child abuse and neglect prevention programs to create mechanisms to investigate suspected abuse or inappropriate denial of treatment for handicapped newborns.[25] Legislative amendments defined medically indicated treatment for newborns as "treatment, including appropriate nutrition, hydration, and medication, which in the treating physician's . . . reasonable medical judgment, will be most likely to be effective in ameliorating or correcting all such life-threatening conditions." Three exceptions are allowed in which treatment can be withheld: (1) infants who are irreversibly comatose; (2) infants for whom treatment would merely prolong dying, would not remedy all the infant's life-threatening conditions, and would be useless in ensuring survival; and (3) infants for whom treatment would be "virtually futile" and its provision would be inhumane. Many states used existing child abuse reporting measures to implement the federally mandated program. Risk managers should be aware of the specific procedures in their state.

Usually, parents are the appropriate decision makers for their children. They generally try to make decisions in the best interest of their children, and they live with the consequences of those decisions. However, parents need information from healthcare experts to make these difficult decisions. In addition, parents may be comforted if they have a sense that those caring for their infant agree with and support their decisions. Unfortunately child abuse and neglect statistics testify to the fact that not all parents strive to or are able to make decisions in the best interest of their children. In such rare cases, society has opted to protect the vulnerable child. Such situations occasionally arise with infants in the NICU. When parents are clearly not making decisions in the best interest of their child, an ethics committee should be consulted and ultimately a court order may be obtained. For example, parents could refuse to consent to surgery for an easily correctable gastrointestinal anomaly in an infant with Down syndrome. In other cases,

such as with anencephaly, aggressive treatment clearly is inappropriate. Most would agree that supportive care during the process of dying is the appropriate course for such infants. In the Virginia case of Baby K,[26] however, nonaggressive care was challenged. Baby K's mother demanded aggressive care for her anencephalic infant. Courts supported her request on the basis of legislation prohibiting discrimination against the handicapped and another law prohibiting "dumping" of patients from one hospital to another. Clinicians argued—unsuccessfully—that it was medically futile to treat Baby K. The U.S. Supreme Court refused to hear the case, and Baby K survived for more than two years.

Many patients in the NICU fall into a gray area where it is appropriate for clinicians and parents struggle to determine what is in the baby's best interest and to proceed accordingly. Many ethicists and clinicians believe that overtreatment, rather than undertreatment, is the major problem in the NICU. Fear of legal liability, a failure to understand legal requirements, the inability to accept the limits of technological medicine, and parents not wanting to accept these limitations and let go contribute to overtreatment.

Pediatric Care

Decision making for children is guided by the same ethical standard as for neonates: the child's best interest. Identifying those individuals who are optimally suited to determine the child's best interest and the parameters to use can present real dilemmas, however. Strict objectivity is a vital component of any choice.

Generally, parents are able to determine their child's best interest. As with neonates, parents must live with the consequences of their decisions for their children. To make fully informed decisions, parents require information from appropriate healthcare professionals. Children old enough to comprehend data about their health and proposed interventions should also be given information appropriate to their age and developmental level. Chronically ill children may be quite sophisticated about their health status and care. Although the legal decision-making authority generally resides with the parents, children should be given the opportunity to assent, if they are capable.[27] Particularly difficult situations arise when the patients are adolescents. They may have a high degree of understanding and disagree with the decisions of their parents. Some adolescents are considered emancipated or mature by virtue of living independently and/or becoming pregnant or having children of their own. In some circumstances, parents do not have the legal right to make healthcare decisions or their decision-making authority has been removed. This is another area where the law varies from state to state, and the risk manager must be aware of the applicable law in the local jurisdiction.

All states have mechanisms for the removal or suspension of parental custody when child abuse or neglect is suspected or verified. The state has an obligation to protect the potentially vulnerable child. In addition, healthcare providers have an obligation to report suspected child abuse or neglect. Although reporting violates confidentiality and may damage the provider–patient relationship, the protection of this vulnerable population warrants disclosure.

Religion is a variable that may influence the decisions parents make for their children. Freedom of religion is constitutionally protected, and parents are free to raise children as they see fit. Yet, sometimes religion interferes with what society perceives to be the best interest of children. Society may intervene and override the decisions of parents, such as when Jehovah's Witnesses refuse to consent to a blood transfusion for their child. When parents pursue nontraditional remedies or refuse surgery on the basis of their religious beliefs, clinicians or society may label the decisions "medical neglect." Communication with the parents and the child, as developmental level permits, is vitally important, whether or not a court order is pursued and granted.

Geriatric Care

Elderly people are quite vulnerable, and there is a heightened awareness of elder abuse in the United States. Risk managers must be aware of the legal requirements for reporting elder abuse in their jurisdiction. Elderly people can be victims of abuse from those caring for them in nursing homes, as well as in residential arrangements with relatives or friends. Many ethical dilemmas arise that are specific to nursing homes and group living situations.

A common problem for elderly patients in hospitals and nursing homes is the inappropriate use of restraints. Confused or senile elderly patients have a tendency to fall, and a fractured hip may result in a total loss of mobility for the patient as well as legal liability for the institution. Elderly patients who have capacity are prone to falls because they may fail to recognize their need for assistance and their limitations in certain situations. In this situation, restraining elderly patients may seem like a beneficent action. However, there is a clear limitation to the mobility and autonomy of patients restrained against their will. This is especially true when patients are restrained inappropriately or for the convenience of the staff. Because of restraint abuses, specific policies and protocols have been established, and emplacement of restraints often requires a doctor's order. Risk managers must be aware of administrative policies and legal guidelines, and work with staff to promote maximum safety for patients with minimal restriction of autonomy and mobility.

Frequently, elderly patients are ignored when healthcare decisions regarding them are made. Elderly individuals who retain their capacity must be allowed to make their own decisions and should be encouraged to prepare advance directives and to appoint surrogate decision makers. As indicated earlier in this chapter, many conflicts between autonomy and beneficence arise during discharge planning for elderly patients.

The appropriate use of limited healthcare resources for the elderly presents some quandaries. A large percentage of Medicare money is spent on elderly individuals in the last months of life. Ethicist Daniel Callahan has suggested reconsidering the allocation of resources to such patients.[28] In specific cases, the extension of life through technological intervention may be inhumane and, by some standards, unethical. In other situations, a reasonable quality of life may be maintained. There is no societal consensus on guidelines for the allocation of healthcare resources to the elderly; thus these situations must be considered on a case-by-case basis.

End-of-Life Choices

Difficult ethical dilemmas—including the right to refuse, or to request the withdrawal of, life-sustaining treatment—frequently occur at the end of life. Emotional debates about physician-assisted suicide and assisted suicide in general reflect concerns that healthcare institutions and professionals do not always adequately manage death and dying. Oregon voters approved a "Death with Dignity" law that empowers physicians to prescribe lethal doses of medication to terminally ill patients.[29] Other states have considered physician-assisted suicide bills. However, in 1997, the U.S. Supreme Court reversed lower court decisions in *Washington v. Glucksberg* and *Vacco v. Quill,* holding that there is not a constitutional right to physician-assisted suicide.[30] If pain were managed appropriately, perhaps chronically and terminally ill individuals, instead of contemplating suicide to escape a painful death or to avoid becoming a burden on their families, might recognize and consider alternatives. In recent years, there has been an increase in palliative care services and trained palliative care providers as part of a trend to address this issue. Although pain management has improved, some clinicians remain concerned that if they provide enough analgesics, such as morphine in a terminally ill cancer patient, they will expedite the patient's demise. From an ethical perspective, according to the principle of double effect, the intent of the intervention is of primary importance. A clinician prescribing morphine for the relief of pain is not doing so with the intent to kill, but rather to provide comfort. The goals of the treatment are critically important. Interestingly, if patients are allowed to self-administer morphine, they often use lower doses, because the anxiety associated with anticipating unrelieved pain is eliminated.

A properly designated surrogate decision maker should be able to consent to the withdrawal or withholding of life-sustaining treatment for an incapacitated adult. Surrogates and clinicians need to cooperate to form a substituted judgment or to determine what is in the patient's best interest, as discussed earlier.

Options available and the process to be followed in regard to end-of-life decision making differs among the states because of a U.S. Supreme Court decision that made this a state's rights issue and failed to establish a national standard.[31] The *Cruzan* decision allowed Missouri to maintain the most conservative standard in the United States regarding the withdrawal or withholding of life-sustaining treatment. The ruling enabled individual states to determine what constitutes "clear and convincing evidence" of a patient's wishes. In addition, the Court recognized artificially administered food and fluids as treatment subject to withdrawal under certain circumstances. That position was supported by the AMA (see **Box 6-7**).

Box 6-7

Nancy Cruzan, a woman in her twenties, existed for a number of years in a persistent vegetative state after a car accident. Her parents petitioned the court to allow the removal of a feeding tube from their daughter. In an attempt at substituted judgment, they based their request on what they believed Nancy would have wanted. In the only "right to die" case heard by the U.S. Supreme Court, the Court upheld the right of the state to determine, as narrowly or as widely as it chooses, what constitutes "clear and convincing evidence" of a patient's wishes. The parents' request was denied.

The case of Terry Schiavo reaffirmed the legal view that end-of-life care was a state's rights issue. Playing out in the media, the Schiavo case also raised issues about the choice of the appropriate surrogate, the patient's previously stated wishes, and artificial nutrition and hydration (see **Box 6-8**).[32]

Box 6-8

Terri Schiavo was 26 years old when she collapsed in cardiac arrest on February 25, 1990. She was resuscitated, but suffered profound cerebral anoxia. She went on to be diagnosed as being in a persistent vegetative state. Terri's husband and parents initially worked together to seek any intervention, including experimental interventions, that might help her to recover some function. After three years, however, her husband and parents became adversaries. Michael Schiavo had been appointed his wife's legal guardian and requested removal of her feeding tube based on what he believed to be her wishes. Terri's parents opposed the withdrawal of treatment based on their religious beliefs, which they believed were shared by Terri. There were multiple court battles, a review by Congress, and an attempt to bring the case to the U.S. Supreme Court. The Supreme Court did not hear the case and had previously determined (in *Cruzan*) that this was an issue for the state. All of the court decisions were won by Michael Schiavo. Terri Schiavo's feeding tube was removed and she died on March 31, 2005.

End-of-life decisions include choices about the management of pain, resuscitation, and the aggressiveness of interventions. While the goals of treatment for a terminally ill patient may be appropriately nonaggressive, each decision must be treated and documented separately. It may be appropriate to discuss a DNR order with the patient or surrogate while the patient is a candidate for palliative surgery or treatment in an ICU. In no case should the patient be denied nursing and basic supportive care by the clinicians on the care team. In contrast, the Baby K court ruling held that respiratory support for an anencephalic infant was "stabilizing care" within the meaning of federal law prohibiting patient "dumping." If such treatment was requested, the law did not allow an exception for comatose patients or medical conditions that could ultimately result in death.

Because no national end-of-life standard exists in the United States, risk managers must be familiar with the laws related to end-of-life decision making in their particular state. Within the parameters prescribed by law, dying patients and their families should be treated humanely and with dignity. Communication and documentation are vitally important at this time.

CONCLUSION

Although ethical behavior is not mandated by legislation, individuals may initiate lawsuits if they feel that healthcare providers made the wrong decision. In the face of complicated and perplexing patient care dilemmas, no "right choice" may exist, and varied rationales can justify the deliberate decision. Within a cost-containment milieu, healthcare providers may encounter high-risk liability potentials embedded in ethical considerations. Fixed-payment reimbursement schemes may promote "quicker and sicker" institutional discharges because money—not therapy principles—dictates early discharge. These cost-saving incentives can place healthcare professionals and institutions at risk when they violate professionally established ethical concerns about the patient–provider relationship.

Risk managers work to protect their institutions from legal liability. In many complex situations related to the provision of health care, the application of legal guidelines to the particular patient situation is not clear. Institutional policies and guidelines promoting ethical decision making, therefore, are vitally important and necessary to render optimal patient care. A risk manager needs to be familiar with basic ethical

principles as well as the law applicable at all levels of government. In addition, extensive communication among healthcare providers, ethics committees, institutional representatives, patients, and surrogates fosters ethical decision making and reduces legal liability for institutions. An ethics program in a healthcare institution is certainly a good risk management strategy.

REFERENCES

1. Governance Institute. (2009). *Leadership in healthcare organizations: A guide to Joint Commission Leadership Standards.*
2. Alexander, S. (1962, November 9). They decide who lives, who dies. *Life Magazine,* 103.
3. *In re Quinlan,* 355 A. 2d 657 (N.JU. 1976), cert. denied 429 U.S. 1992, 1976. *Star-Ledger* (Newark, N.J.) (1995).
4. 45 CFR 1340, DHHS Part IV. (1995, April 15). *Federal Register.*
5. H.R. 4449. Patient Self-Determination Act of 1990.
6. Swidler, R. N. (2010, June). New York's Family Health Care Decisions Act: The legal and political background, key provisions and emerging issues. *NYSBA Journal,* 18–27.
7. American Society for Bioethics and Humanities. (2011). *Core competencies for healthcare ethics consultation* (2nd ed.).
8. Dubler, N. N., Webber, M. P., Swiderski, D. M., & Faculty of the National Working Group for the Clinical Ethics Credentialing Project. (2009). Charting the future. *Hastings Center Report, 39*(6), 29–33.
9. Ahronheim, J. C., Moreno, J., & Zuckerman, C. (2000). *Ethics in Clinical Practice* (2nd ed.). Gaithersberg, MD: Aspen, pp. 1–98.
10. Brock, D. (1994). Advance directives: What is reasonable to expect from them? *Journal of Clinical Ethics, 5,* 57–60.
11. Teno, J. M., Lynn, J., Phillips, R. S., et al. (1994). Do formal advance directives affect resuscitation decisions and the use of resources for seriously ill patients? *Journal of Clinical Ethics, 5,* 23–30.

12. New York Public Health Law. (1990). Health care proxy, 2980–2994.

13. New York State Task Force on Life and the Law. (1992). *When others must choose: Deciding for patients without capacity.* Albany: Author.

14. 2010 N.Y. Laws ch. 8, A.7729-D (Gottfried et al.) and S.3164-B. (Duane et al.). Section 2 of Chapter 8 amends N.Y. Public Health Law (PHL) to create "Article 29-CC Family Health Care Decisions Act."

15. Fletcher, J. C., & Spencer, E. M. (1995). Incompetent patient on the slippery slope. *Lancet, 345*(8945), 271–272.

16. *Schloendorff v. Society of New York Hospital.* 211 N.Y. 125, 105 N.E. 92 (1914).

17. *Canterbury v. Spence,* 464 F. 2d 772, 785 (D.C. Cir. 1972).

18. www.hhs.gov/ocr/privacy

19. Council on Ethical and Judicial Affairs. (2012–2013). *Code of medical ethics: Current opinions with annotations.* Chicago: American Medical Association.

20. *Planned Parenthood v. Casey,* 112 S. Ct. 2791 (1992).

21. *Roe v. Wade,* 410 U.S. 113 (1973).

22. Minkoff, H., & Paltrow, L. M. (2006). The rights of unborn children and the value of pregnant women. *Hastings Center Report, 36*(2), 26–28.

23. *In re A.C.,* 533 A. 2d 611 (App. D.C. 1989); *In re A.C.,* 573 A., 2d 1235 (App. D.C. 1990).

24. Duff, R., & Campbell, A. G. M. (1973). Moral and ethical dilemmas in the special care nursery. *New England Journal of Medicine, 289*(17), 890–894.

25. 45 CFR 1340, DHHS Part IV. (1995, April 15). *Federal Register.*

26. Capron, A. M. (1994). Medical futility: Strike two. *Hastings Center Report, 24*(5), 42–43.

27. Leikin, S. L. (1992). Minors' assent or dissent to medical treatment. In *Making health care decisions, Vol. 3: Appendices: Studies on the foundation of informed consent.* Washington, DC: Government Printing Office, President's Commission for the Study of Ethical Problems in Medicine and Biomedical and Behavioral Research, pp. 175–192.

28. Callahan, D. (1987). *Setting limits: Medical goals in an aging society.* New York: Simon & Schuster.

29. Gesenway, D. (1995). Assisted suicide: It's the law in Oregon, but is it ethical? *ACP Observer, 15*(1), 12.

30. *State of Washington v. Glucksberg, Vacca v. Quill* No. 95-1858, and Supreme Court of the U.S. 521 US 793, 117 S. Ct. 2293 in same cases.

31. *Cruzan v. Director, Missouri Department of Health,* 110 S. Ct. 2841 (1990), 497 U.S. 262, 278 (1990).

32. Caplan, A. L., McCartney, J. J., & Sisti, D. A. (Eds.). (2006). *The case of Terri Schiavo: Ethics at the end of life.* Amherst, N Y: Prometheus Books.

CHAPTER 7

Assuring Safety and Security in Healthcare Institutions

Alvin M. Berk

Management of safety and security in a healthcare institution is crucial to controlling risk. A hospital experiencing a series of adverse incidents can incur penalties ranging from hefty fines to program disaccreditation and management turnover (see **Box 7-1**). Only an aggressive and well-organized safety and security risk management program can protect an institution, its employees, and its governing body. Such programs include the following steps:

- Assessing the risks facing the organization
- Assigning responsibility for their management
- Allocating the resources necessary to manage them
- Adopting policies and procedures to prevent risks
- Monitoring compliance with those policies and procedures

Since the terrorist attacks of September 11, 2001, and the contemporaneous anthrax incidents in Florida, New York, Washington, D.C., and Connecticut, several events have spotlighted and reshaped the safety and security risks facing healthcare institutions:

- Natural disasters such as Hurricane Katrina's 2005 devastation of New Orleans; the 2011 earthquake and tsunami that wrecked

---

Box 7-1

- The Parkland (Texas) Health and Hospital System was fined $20,000 by the state and $80,000 by federal agencies after 370,000 pills vanished from its facilities in 2007.[1]
- A Chicago hospital was fined $13,000 by the Occupational Safety and Health Administration (OSHA) in 2011 for improper hazardous waste handling.[2]
- A Brooklyn hospital was fined $48,000 in 2011 for hazardous materials violations ranging from improper asbestos removal to incorrect gas tank storage.[3]
- The Veterans Administration Hospital in White River, Vermont, was fined $372,254 in 2005 for improper handling and storage of hazardous waste.[4]
- Massachusetts General Hospital was fined $1 million in 2011 when an employee took documents containing confidential information about 192 patients and lost them on the subway.[5]

---

northeast Japan, echoed months later by a rare magnitude 5.8 quake on the East Coast of the United States and a much stronger one in Turkey; and, in the same year, by an unusually powerful tornado that destroyed a major regional hospital in Joplin, Missouri[6]

- Closer scrutiny of safety and security by the federal Center for Medicare & Medicaid Services (CMS) and by its largest accreditation partner, The Joint Commission (TJC), which promulgated detailed new standards in 2005 for hospitals' "environment of care"
- New rules in 2006 governing off-site and portable device access to electronic protected health information (EPHI), to update and strengthen the provisions of the Health Insurance Portability and Accountability Act of 1996 (HIPAA)
- Escalating risks to healthcare organizations from personal injury and information theft lawsuits

HOW REGULATION AND ACCREDITATION AFFECT RISK

Federal Medicare and Medicaid Requirements

Management of safety and security risk in any hospital accepting Medicare or Medicaid payment requires that the institution satisfy all conditions of participation (CoPs) promulgated by the CMS under Title XVIII of the Social Security Act. The portions of Title XVIII that are relevant to the management of safety and security risks are CoP §482.41, Hospital Physical Environment, and, for information management risks, CoP § 482.13, Patients' Rights.

Authorities Having Jurisdiction

All hospitals, regardless of whether they participate in Medicare, must comply with the rules of their respective state's Department of Health (DOH). Whether acting on behalf of CMS or on its own, the DOH is the primary authority having jurisdiction (AHJ) over a nonmilitary healthcare institution. Other AHJs typically include the local fire department, the local buildings or zoning department, the local environmental regulatory authority, and other state, county, and municipal agencies as applicable.

Accreditation

A hospital is "deemed" to be compliant with all CMS CoPs if it is accredited by one of the three independent organizations accorded "deemed status" by CMS. The oldest of these groups, The Joint Commission (formerly known as JCAHO), currently accredits approximately 19,000 healthcare programs in the United States.[7] Participating hospitals undergo a full TJC site survey approximately every three years, during which TJC nurses and physicians scrutinize clinical service delivery while engineers tour the facility, confirm staff knowledge of life safety procedures, examine equipment maintenance and inspection records, and determine whether all buildings conform to the applicable codes. The Joint Commission's review of records can extend to the date of the previous triennial survey.

A hospital also can expect a surprise visit from its accrediting agency if a "sentinel event" occurs (see **Box 7-2**),[8] or if a pattern of complaints emerges about clinical treatment or deficiencies such as dirty floors, broken doors, leaky ceilings, tepid water, or excessive noise. Even if the original complaints concerned clinical treatment, an visiting agency may notice something that prompts it to extend its scrutiny to the "environment of care." Thus an accredited hospital should be prepared for a safety and security inspection at any time.

Box 7-2

A sentinel event is an unexpected occurrence involving death or serious physical or psychological injury, or the risk thereof. Serious injury specifically includes loss of limb or function. The phrase, "or the risk thereof" includes any process variation for which a recurrence would carry a significant chance of a serious adverse outcome. Such events are called "sentinel" because they signal the need for immediate investigation and response.[9]

The Joint Commission's detailed "Environment of Care" standards cover safety and security, hazardous materials and waste, fire prevention, medical equipment, utilities management, and emergency management. TJC also promulgates standards for infection prevention and control. Two other CMS accreditation partners share "deemed" status with TJC: DNV Healthcare Inc. (DNV) and the American Osteopathic Association's Health Facilities Accreditation Program (HFAP). To healthcare professionals concerned with risk management, compliance with accreditation standards is essential.

The Difference Between Safety and Security

Safety and security are arguably different: Common safety principles can be applied across diverse healthcare facilities, while security planning must be site specific. Consequently, objections have been raised to a 2008 decision by TJC to combine safety and security under one set of standards.[10]

Sometimes, safety and security can conflict with each other, such as when a security supervisor decides to chain a secondary exit door at night and on weekends to prevent anyone from entering while the door is slowly closing behind someone who used it to exit. Such doors need to be clearly marked "Emergency Exit," placed under video surveillance, and fitted with alarmed "crash bars" to discourage their use. Under no circumstances should any exit door be chained or padlocked.

Other Surveys

A state department of health may schedule a "pre-occupancy survey" of any new or renovated facility or new major clinical equipment installation, such as a magnetic resonance imaging (MRI) device or computed tomography (CT) scanner. The DOH also may conduct a surprise inspection if it receives a serious credible complaint from a patient or patient's family. Like an unscheduled survey by an accrediting organization, a surprise DOH survey can extend beyond the subject of the complaint that prompted it. If the surveyors uncover serious safety or security deficiencies, this information could result in a finding that the healthcare facility is in violation of local law or of a CMS CoP. Either finding would place the institution at risk.

High-Risk Events

Despite full accreditation by TJC or another CMS "deemed" status organization, a hospital can be at risk of serious penalties if certain events occur and its remediation plan proves unsatisfactory. These "never" or "adverse" events include several that involve safety or security (see **Box 7-3**).[11] Several, considered by CMS to be "hospital-acquired conditions," will not be reimbursed. Some private payers have also adopted the CMS's nonreimbursement policy.[12]

Box 7-3   High-Risk Events

Safety-Related Hospital-Acquired Conditions
- Patient death or serious disability associated with electric shock, burn, restraints, or bedrails
- Patient death associated with a fall
- Any incident in which a line designated for oxygen or other gas intended for a patient contains the wrong gas or is contaminated by a toxic substance

Security-Related Hospital-Acquired Conditions
- Care ordered or provided by a person impersonating a physician, nurse, pharmacist, or other licensed healthcare provider
- The abduction of a patient of any age
- Sexual assault of a patient within or on the grounds of the facility
- Death or significant injury of a patient or staff from a physical assault that occurs within or on the grounds of the facility

Other Adverse Safety and Security Events
- Patient death or serious disability associated with patient elopement (disappearance)
- Patient suicide or attempted suicide resulting in serious disability, while being cared for in a healthcare facility

---

TECHNIQUES FOR MANAGING SAFETY AND SECURITY RISK

The techniques available for safety and security risk management resemble those for clinical risk. Such techniques include the following methods:

- A risk assessment estimate
- Failure modes and effects analysis (FMEA)
- Root-cause analysis (RCA)
- Technological redundancy
- Crew resource management
- Red rules[13]

Risk Assessment

Risk assessment starts by conducting an overall inventory of the safety and security risks facing a healthcare institution. The following major categories are covered:

- Patient safety
- Infection control
- Hazardous materials and waste
- Fire prevention
- Medical equipment and utilities management
- Disaster preparedness
- Information management

Once a risk is recognized, hospital leadership must estimate its severity and compare it with other risks to prioritize corrective efforts. A consistent methodology must be employed to calculate the risk level for each potential event. Using a simple ordinal scale (e.g., 1–5), a team of knowledgeable staff members will rate the event on (1) the severity of its impact, (2) its probability of occurrence, and (3) the organization's *lack* of preparedness to deal with it. These ratings are then multiplied to yield an overall risk score for the event, which can be compared with scores for other events. The event with the highest score can be presumed to pose the greatest risk to the healthcare facility. This method, however, is not without its critics.[14]

Failure Modes and Effects Analysis

FMEA is a structured method for examining any system, process, or complex array of equipment for risk of failure *before* it fails. An expert team studies each step or component, evaluates its weaknesses or defects, assigns it a risk score, quantifies the risk by multiplying ordinal ratings, and redesigns how the steps or components interact, so as to minimize the weakness of the overall system. Like root-cause analysis, FMEA was inspired by a landmark Institute of Medicine report entitled *To Err Is Human*.[15] FMEA embodies a basic principle of risk reduction: Complexity, such as that introduced by adding components, steps, or contingencies to a process, inherently adds to the risk of failure. This principle has been used to guide FMEA designed to reduce the risk of infant abduction from a hospital (see **Box 7-4**).[16]

Root-Cause Analysis

Complementing FMEA is RCA, a system-based analytic technique typically used *after* an adverse event occurs, to prevent its recurrence.[17] The Joint Commission requires that every sentinel event be subjected to an RCA. As with FMEA, RCA's core principle is that most mistakes happen not because of "individual recklessness," but because of "basic flaws" in the way a process or system is organized.[18]

RCA follows a rigorous prescribed format. It requires that an RCA team answer such questions as "What happened?", "Why did it happen?", and "What were the most proximate factors?", while conducting a detailed analysis of the processes involved (see **Box 7-5**).[19]

Like clinical mistakes, failed safety and security procedures and systems will benefit from performing a root-cause analysis. Why did a fire pump fail to work? Had it been tested? If not, why not? Had responsibility for testing been clearly assigned? Did the engineering unit have a backup plan if a scheduled test was missed? Had problems been correctly diagnosed? Were repairs done? Did the primary problem mask another defect? Was the pump beyond its useful life? Had the engineering staff informed senior management of this fact? Did management act in a timely fashion? Did the organizational structure interfere with prioritization of the need to replace the pump?

To discover opportunities for process improvement, RCA deliberately de-emphasizes the assignment of blame to individuals. For this technique to be successful, RCA participants must be confident that they will not be penalized for admitting human errors.

Box 7-5

From 1995 through mid-2010, The Joint Commission recorded 6,923 sentinel events in American hospitals. The most common were wrong-side surgery, suicide, postoperative complication, delay in treatment, and medical error. Assaults or homicides accounted for 4% of all sentinel events.[20,21]

Box 7-4   Use of FMEA to Prevent Infant Abduction

WakeMed is a two-campus, 629-bed hospital in Raleigh, North Carolina. Required by The Joint Commission to use FMEA to reduce risks, and with 7,800 births occurring at the facility each year, the hospital chose to apply FMEA to prevent infant abduction at its smaller, 114-bed campus. The FMEA team started by creating a flowchart detailing all steps involved in an infant's stay. Team members then "brainstormed" to identify what could go wrong ("failure modes") at each process step. They assigned a failure mode score to each step, based on (1) the severity of failure at that step, (2) the probability of that failure, and (3) the hospital's ability to catch the error before a patient was harmed. This produced a risk priority number (RPN) for each failure mode, and a total score for the multistep process. The steps with the highest RPN scores were targeted for redesign. The total RPN score went from 4,164 to 1,372—a 67% improvement.

Technological Redundancy

A common example of effective technological redundancy in hospitals is the provision of emergency electrical power to support emergency lighting, elevators, life safety equipment, and critical care equipment. Current disaster preparedness standards recommend that emergency power (EP) be available for these functions for up to 96 hours.

Typically, an EP system comprises three main components: a generator plant, a series of automatic transfer switches (ATSs) to transfer electrical load (lighting and equipment) from normal power to emergency power, and the circuitry to distribute that emergency power. When emergency generators are activated, lights and equipment will experience a momentary power switching interruption. This "blip" can prove disruptive in an operating room, a procedure room, or critical care areas where delicate equipment can be affected, (e.g., CT scanners and MRI machines). Best practices in such situations call for the use of an uninterruptible power supply to bridge the transition, usually by relying on rechargeable batteries and electronic circuitry to provide seamless power.

Ideally, an EP system should incorporate as much internal redundancy as possible. This practice will reduce the risk of equipment failure leading to adverse patient outcomes.[22]

Crew Resource Management

Crew resource management (CRM) is one of several human-error reduction strategies[23] that are available to reduce the risk of adverse incidents in a healthcare institution. A team-building technique originally developed to reduce air-crew errors, CRM "promotes and reinforces the conscious, learned team behaviors of cooperation, coordination, and sharing" by "creating an organizational environment where specific cooperative and communicative behaviors are defined."[24]

CRM can be employed to reduce risk in situations involving facility safety and security. Imagine a scenario in which an overnight-watch engineer responsible for rounding mechanical rooms to verify fan and pump operation notices that a key ventilation fan has failed, but lacks the parts or equipment needed to fix it. Typically, he or she would enter a work order for a work crew to repair the fan the next morning. Is this a sufficient response?

Using CRM, designated facilitators could present this hypothetical scenario to a multidisciplinary team comprising clinicians, engineering staff, and administrators. Team members would role-play to identify potential pitfalls in this scenario and suggest fault-tolerant alternatives. They might conclude that the engineer should inform nurses of the fan failure, just in case they did not notice a loss of air movement. They might suggest that nurses try to listen for signs of air movement upon entering a patient room. They might also suggest that the hospital administration invest in a computerized building information system to enable central monitoring of ventilation systems.

Because the CRM team would include members from a variety of disciplines and focus on process, the collaborative process would build teamwork, improve communication, and achieve a common understanding and broad "ownership" of the problem and its solution.

Red Rules

Originally developed to protect industrial production lines from critical errors, "red rules" are rules that cannot be broken under any circumstances.[25] In the clinical arena, reconciliation of the sponge count before closing a surgical incision and a time-out requirement before beginning an invasive procedure may be considered red rules. Enforcement of these rules requires that all employees be empowered to invoke them and halt "production" (i.e., surgical activity) until they are followed.

In the world of facility safety and security, wearing of personal protective equipment by maintenance staff could be a red rule, as could the prohibition against smoking in the operating room. Other red rules could call for everyone to wear a helmet in an active construction area or demand positive identification of visitors before admission to a postpartum nursing unit.

Some observers believe red rules can be overdone: "Relying on too many red rules can also lead to rule-dependent behavior in which practitioners do not feel obligated or permitted to think critically about patient care and safety outside the established rules."[26]

RECOGNIZING AND RESPONDING TO POTENTIAL ENVIRONMENTAL HAZARDS

The array of hazards affecting healthcare workers is extensive. OSHA, the federal agency that enforces workplace safety in all industries, lists the types of hospital-wide hazards shown in **Box 7-6**.[27] OSHA also provides extensive information on how to prevent and respond to these hazards.[28]

Hazardous materials and waste are inherent features of healthcare facilities. Pharmaceuticals, chemical reagents, sharps, soiled linens, and used wound dressings are all part of daily hospital life. Like other sources of risk, hazardous materials must be recognized before they can be managed. Three major categories of hazardous materials are subject to regulation:

- Biological (e.g., infectious waste)
- Chemical (e.g., pharmaceutical waste)
- Radioactive (e.g., isotopes)

In any hospital, management of hazardous materials must span the cycle from acquisition to disposal, with risk being evaluated and controlled at all steps. Management of hazardous materials requires participation by materials management staff, clinicians, and technical support personnel.

Each healthcare facility should develop and maintain a written plan for managing hazardous materials. According to The Joint Commission, such a plan defines "processes for selecting, handling, storing, transporting, using, and disposing of hazardous materials and waste from receipt or generation through use and/or final disposal."[29] It starts with an inventory of hazardous materials consistent with applicable law and regulation.

In most large institutions, biological materials are managed by the organization's infection control officer and infection control committee; chemical hazards are handled under the oversight of an environmental safety officer, and radioactive materials are managed under a radiologic safety officer. These functions require extensive training.

Occupational exposure to hazardous materials is regulated by OSHA or, in some cases, by a state agency dedicated to the OSHA mission. Extensive information about exposure to hazardous materials is published by OSHA and by the National Institute for Occupational Safety

Box 7-6   OSHA Healthcare Institution Hazards

OSHA Hospital-wide Hazards	Additional OSHA Hazards
Bloodborne pathogens • Standard • Human immunodeficiency virus (HIV), *Haemophilus influenzae* type B (HIB), and Hepatitis C virus (HCV)	Asbestos exposure Burns/cuts Carbonless paper Compressed gases
Electrical	Contaminated food trays
Ergonomics	Contaminated equipment
Fire hazards	Contaminated work environments
Glutaraldehyde	Dietary
Hazardous chemicals	Ethylene oxide gas (EtO)
Infection • Seasonal flu • Multidrug-resistant organisms (MDRO) • Methieillan-resistant *Staphylococcus aureus* (MRSA)	Foodborne disease Formaldehyde exposure Heat stress Laser hazards
Latex allergy	(Insufficient) lockout/tagout
Legionnaires' disease	(Lack of) machine guarding
Needlesticks	Musculoskeletal disorders—workstations
Noise	Laser plume
Mercury	Limited working space
Inappropriate personal protective equipment	Radiation exposure
Slips/trips/falls	Waste anesthesia gases
Stress	
Tuberculosis	
Lack of universal precautions	
Workplace violence	

and Health (NIOSH), a research program of the federal Centers for Disease Control and Prevention (CDC). Disposal of hazardous materials is regulated by the federal Environmental Protection Administration (EPA), or by its state counterparts, while transportation of such materials is subject to federal Department of Transportation rules.

Biologic Hazardous Materials: Infectious Waste Management

Typically, infectious waste is defined as "solid waste that contains pathogens with sufficient virulence and in sufficient quantity that exposure of a susceptible human or animal to the solid waste could cause the human or animal to contract an infectious disease."[30] In hospitals, residential healthcare facilities, diagnostic and treatment centers, and clinical laboratories, infectious waste generally consists of sharps (including hypodermic needles, syringes, scalpel blades, lancets, glass slides, and vials); human tissue, blood, and body fluids; microbiological laboratory waste; and tissue. In a facility conducting research, it may include blood or body fluids from animals carrying a zoonotic infectious agent.

When infectious waste becomes mixed with other materials, the aggregate must be treated as "regulated medical waste" (RMW).[31] Regulated medical waste must be clearly identified (hence, "red bag" waste), segregated from all other waste materials, and autoclaved or disposed of pursuant to the laws of the state in which it is generated and federal regulations.

All healthcare institutions generating infectious waste must implement an infectious waste management plan (see **Box 7-7**).[32]

Box 7-7

A comprehensive infectious waste management plan includes the following elements:

- Defines and designates those wastes to be considered and handled as infectious material
- Segregates infectious waste from noninfectious waste
- Establishes packaging standards for waste disposal
- Sets storage guidelines
- Specifies disposal methods
- Details contingency measures for emergency situations
- Arranges for staff education

Infectious waste is generated at many points during a hospital's operation. Each activity should be examined for risk using one or more of the techniques previously described.

Chemical Waste

Chemical wastes can be defined as any liquid, solid, or gaseous substances that are flammable, explosive, or toxic, or that can cause air and water pollution if released into the atmosphere, or that can produce an adverse physiological reaction. Examples of chemical wastes in hospitals include spent solvents, disinfectants, pesticides, and diagnostic chemicals; aerosol containers or gas canisters that may explode if incinerated or punctured; pharmaceutical waste; and wastes consisting of materials used during physical plant operation, such as refrigerants, petroleum products, and water treatment chemicals.

OSHA mandates that all employers make available to their employees information about the hazards associated with chemicals in the workplace.[33] The dangers posed by each chemical must be described on a material safety data sheet (MSDS), which also must state the chemical's properties and how it should be handled. Employee access to MSDSs is required by "right to know" laws.

A useful tool for quickly determining whether a chemical waste is classified as hazardous is the website maintained by the Healthcare Environmental Resource Center (HERC).[34] The HERC site also contains information about other hazardous materials, such as regulated medical waste, and provides links to relevant state regulations.

A hospital's hazardous materials management plan must include sections on chemical waste. One form of chemical waste, pharmaceutical waste, is generated at a healthcare facility by the following activities:

- IV preparation
- General compounding

- Spills/breakage
- Partially used vials
- Partially used syringes/IVs (if contaminated, they are considered biohazards)
- Discontinued, unused preparations
- Unused repacks (unit dose)
- Patients' personal medications
- Outdated pharmaceuticals

Like other chemical waste, discarded pharmaceuticals are considered a serious threat to the nation's water supply, through which they can be ingested by humans and animals. Accordingly, disposal of most drugs (but not of many chemotherapy agents) is regulated by the EPA through the Resource Conservation and Recovery Act (RCRA) of 1976.[35] The EPA has recently described best management practices for disposing of unused pharmaceuticals.[36] For a hospital, management of pharmaceutical waste is a complex challenge requiring expert leadership, ample resources, and cooperation by many parts of the organization.[37]

Another category of chemical waste is called universal waste. It comprises items that require careful handling, storage, and disposal, but do not qualify as chemical waste. Prominent examples include batteries, fluorescent bulbs, electronic equipment (including computers and monitors), and any mercury-containing equipment not found within one of the other categories. The organization's hazardous materials management plan must cover universal waste.

Radioactive Waste

Radioactive isotopes are commonly used in a variety of diagnosis and treatment methods. Well-known diagnostic examples include the use of radioactive isotopes of iodine, selectively taken up by the thyroid or used in intravenous imaging of the urinary tract; thallium, used to image blood uptake by heart muscle; and in positron emission tomography (PET) scans, the use of a radioactive glucose analogue called FDG.[38] Other isotopes are used therapeutically by radiation oncology specialists externally or through site-specific implantation (brachytherapy), or for systemic radiation therapy, in which a radioactive isotope is circulated throughout the body.[39]

Inasmuch as radioactive materials gradually lose their radioactivity, practitioners choose the clinically efficacious nontoxic isotopes that have the shortest "half-life," defined as the time it takes for a 50% decay in radioactivity to occur. Once used, a radioactive material must be safely stored until its radioactivity levels are safe and/or it can be safely transported to a licensed radioactive waste site.

After an isotope is used, it must continue to be managed. The principal components of a radioactive waste management plan deal with the following activities:

- Segregating wastes by physical form and, if possible, by isotope. Dry solids, aqueous liquids, animal carcasses, scintillation vials, and liquids with radioisotopes and hazardous chemicals (mixed wastes) should be segregated into separate containers.
- Packaging wastes according to their physical forms.
- Disposing, tracking, and removing wastes from where they were used.
- Storing the wastes on-site or off-site.

SECURITY

How to Prevent Intruders and Welcome Visitors

To survive in a competitive market, hospitals must present a warm, welcoming, and nonthreatening face to the public. They also must control visitor and employee access without creating long queues at entrances. Increasingly, hospitals are turning to high-tech solutions to manage visitor and employee egress. Employees can enter through automated turnstiles actuated by card swipe or proximity readers, while visitors and patients are greeted at a courtesy desk or a security station. Security officers can be garbed in slacks and blazers to soften their presence. Identification (ID) card–actuated entry portals also can prevent intruders from blending into a mixed stream of staff and visitors.

Academic medical centers, particularly in multihospital areas, present special challenges. Frequently, students and house staff train at a group of affiliated institutions, so as to ensure a diverse clinical experience. They may carry ID badges that lack the electronic code needed to use the staff entrance in all of those hospitals. If a hospital building is connected internally to a medical or nursing school, it may be impractical to equip all connecting doors with security features. Someone wearing a white coat may not be challenged until it is too late.

Protecting a healthcare facility against intrusion requires a multistep strategy. Depending on a facility's location, intrusion barriers should include perimeter controls, with a limited number of entry points and requirements for ID display, card swipe, or radio-frequency identification (RFID) chip recognition for all entering employees; a reception desk; creation of "security zones" to limit entry into high-risk areas; physical security devices (e.g., locked doors); an ID display requirement for all employees at all times; and extensive surveillance.[40]

Because interior security patrols are expensive, most institutions rely on perimeter controls to screen out would-be troublemakers. Without internal "zone" barriers, once an intruder gains entry, there is a risk that he or she will roam unchallenged until a target of opportunity presents itself: an open office door or an unattended notebook computer or cell phone. Unless sensitized to this risk by security management, many "civilian" hospital employees may be reluctant or fearful to confront a stranger, especially if that stranger is dressed like a physician (see **Box 7-8**).

Box 7-8

- The New Jersey Department of Health and Senior Services issued a cease-and-desist order to a young man who repeatedly donned a white shirt and stethoscope to gain field-level entry as an emergency medical technician (EMT) at football games.[41]
- A Florida woman dressed in scrubs so she could steal wallets and credit cards from a hospital's doctors and nurses.[42]
- In a Canadian incident, a woman wearing a stethoscope pretended to be a doctor, listening to the heartbeat of a critically ill patient and providing information on the patient's condition to her niece, who was visiting.[43]
- A 17-year-old man was arrested on felony charges of masquerading as a physician's assistant in a Florida emergency room in September 2011. Hospital officials called police about suspicions that he was an impostor. While working in the busy emergency room, the intruder performed CPR on a patient in cardiac arrest, performed physical examinations, and gave other forms of care to an undisclosed number of unsuspecting patients.[44]

Protecting Patient Valuables

Hospitals generally encourage patients to leave valuables at home—and virtually all institutions formally notify patients that the facility will not be responsible for lost or stolen items. Nevertheless, patients typically arrive with cell phones, keys, and wallets or purses containing cash, credit and debit cards, driver's licenses, and other important identification. Many bring eyeglasses and dentures; a few arrive with hairpieces and prostheses. Patients coming from inner-city areas where burglary is a concern may arrive with bags of clothing, personal computers, and cherished keepsakes. A hospital must have a plan to ensure that such personal possessions can be safeguarded during a patient's stay.

Typically, this effort involves offering patients access to secure lockers or safes, with all hospital-stored items inventoried, identified by the patient's medical record number, and recorded in the patient's chart. Despite the availability of lockable safes in many rooms, some patients prefer to keep their wallets or purses accessible in bedside cabinet drawers. During crowded visiting hours, an opportunistic thief—even one visiting another patient—can duck into a room while the occupant is out or distracted and empty a drawer in seconds. To some intruders, healthcare institutions also offer more than unguarded purses or laptops (see **Box 7-9**).

Box 7-9

- In 2003, an intruder entered a Florida hospital patient room, cut a morphine drip line, and walked off with the morphine and pump. Reportedly, the patient was too drowsy to notice.[45]
- In a notorious 2009 case in Milan, Italy, an intruder tried to gain access to the Italian prime minister's hospital room. He was stopped when he exited the elevator.[46]

Surveillance cameras cannot prevent this behavior. Video equipment is not ubiquitous and is sporadically monitored. Generally, only public areas such as corridors are equipped with security cameras. Even if a criminal incident is recorded, the recording proves more useful as evidence than as a means to apprehend a perpetrator (see **Box 7-10**).

Box 7-10

At several hospitals in Brooklyn, New York, intrepid thieves succeeded in entering unoccupied restrooms, shutting off the water supply to toilets and urinals, and dismantling pipes to remove automatic flushometers worth $200 to $400 each. According to the chief of security at one of the hospitals, several hundred flushometers were stolen before the criminals got caught in the act. Prosecutors were helped by video surveillance records showing one of them entering a restroom and then leaving, carrying a loaded backpack.[47]

Employee Theft

Not all hospital crime is committed by visitors. Thefts by employees frequently go unpublicized to preserve the hospitals' reputations. Nevertheless, employee theft in hospitals is a constant threat. Everything from drugs to laptops to expensive endoscopes and "mongo," marketable scrap metal, becomes a potential target in a busy institution, where tight budgets limit security coverage and employees think they know where surveillance cameras are located. Types of employee theft may include drug diversion, armed robbery, personal identification theft, fraud, computer theft, and pilferage (see **Box 7-11**).

Many hospitals hire "undercover" investigators to combat employee and visitor theft. Such programs are especially important in heavily trafficked urban medical centers.[49] Eventually, though, hospital staff may learn who the internal investigators are, undercutting their effectiveness in preventing employee crime.[50]

Infant Abduction

Infant abduction remains an infrequent but persistent problem in the United States, with the number of incidents each year basically holding steady since 1983. Abduction from hospitals, however, has decreased dramatically, dropping 50% between the period 1983–1992 and the period 1993–2006.[51] Altogether, 95% of abducted infants have been found.[52]

The plunge in abductions from hospitals can be attributed to tightened security procedures and improved technology—most notably, the use of RFID[53] (radio-frequency identification) chips that signal sensors whenever an infant is moved past the boundary of a protected area. Current practice attaches the RFID "tag" to the umbilical clamp in newborns, and uses a tag taped to the forearm for older children. This tag is sensitive to the child's body mass, and will actuate an alarm if improperly removed. When a sensor detects a baby being moved, best practice calls for a "lockdown," sealing all exit doors and actuating all interior magnetic locks, and a "Code Pink" announcement to alert staff.

Electronic monitoring systems must be highly reliable: A faulty system can fail to trigger an alarm; if it is oversensitive, it can generate a false alarm, leading to a loss of vigilance by staff.

Workplace Violence and Stress

In 2009, the U.S. Department of Justice reported that "approximately 572,000 nonfatal violent crimes (rape/sexual assault, robbery, and aggravated and simple assault) occurred against persons age 16 or older while they were at work or on duty, based on findings from the National Crime Victimization Survey (NCVS)."[54] Of these incidents, 10.1% occurred in general healthcare settings and another 3.9% in mental health settings. Among medical professionals, nurses were the group victimized most often. Unfortunately, the workplace violence rate probably is underreported: One study found that 44% of nurses do not report physical violence because it is just "part of the job."[55] The most commonly assaulted worker in the United States is a nurse's aide in a nursing home.[56]

Violence against workers is more common in health care than most private-sector industries. NIOSH reported that hospital workers were assaulted at a rate of 8.3 events per 10,000 workers, while the all-industry rate was 2 assaults per 10,000 private-sector workers.[57]

According to a survey of hospital security executives, hospital crime grew between 2005 and 2009.[58] Some of this crime may go unreported to police due to fear of adverse publicity.[59] Other reasons for underreporting cited in a separate survey of 3,465 emergency department (ED) nurses included the following:

- "The perception that reporting ED violent incidents might have a negative effect on customer service scores/reports
- Ambiguous ED violence reporting policies; fear of retaliation from ED management, hospital administration, nursing staff, or physicians for reporting ED violent incidents;

- Failure of staff to report ED violent incidents; the perception that reporting ED violent incidents was a sign of incompetence or weakness; lack of physical injury to staff;
- The attitude that violence comes with the job; and lack of support from administration/management."[60]

The growth in hospital violence, based on conclusions by the International Association for Healthcare Security & Safety, is attributable to a variety of factors:

- Increased gang activity
- Increased numbers of psychiatric patients seeking treatment in EDs because of closings of psychiatric facilities
- ED overcrowding, leading to long waiting times
- The growing use of alcohol and drugs by younger persons
- Open access, allowing uninvited visitors and weapons in the hospital without detection
- Use of community hospitals to treat violent prisoners
- Police taking persons arrested for alcohol and drug use offenses to emergency rooms for testing prior to formally charging them
- Increased unemployment
- The ubiquity of illness[61]

The pervasive presence of illness and injury in hospitals also causes high stress levels among staff members, who may resort to drug use as a coping mechanism. According to NIOSH, "Studies indicate that healthcare workers have higher rates of substance abuse and suicide than other professions and elevated rates of depression and anxiety linked to job stress."[62] But the stress felt by the family members of a seriously ill patient is even greater, occasionally leading to violence (see **Box 7-12**).

Box 7-12

In 2010, a man upset about news of his mother's medical condition opened fire in Johns Hopkins Hospital, wounding a physician before shooting his mother and himself.[63]

Others blame the increase in violence on health care's emerging role as a commodity, on the erosion of physician–patient relationships due to medical economics and specialization, and on societal incivility and the proliferation of weapons.[64]

Guns and Gangs

Hospitals must be prepared to treat victims of gang violence. Occasionally, a dispute follows a victim into an emergency room, along with the risk of gunfire and injuries to staff and bystanders.[65] To prevent this kind of violence, some emergency departments use fixed or hand-held metal detectors.[66–69] Unfortunately, guns also can become a concern for hospitals outside of the ED (see **Box 7-13**).

Box 7-13

- In 2011, a 53-year-old man whom police described as a disgruntled patient shot a 41-year-old transplant surgeon in an Orlando, Florida, hospital parking garage and then killed himself.[70]
- In Martinsburg, West Virginia, a woman fired a gun in a hospital parking lot before entering the facility.[71]
- In Brunswick, Georgia, a woman's licensed gun discharged accidentally in her hospital room.[72]
- In a bizarre episode in Sydney, Australia, healthcare workers found a loaded handgun concealed in the prosthetic limb of a 66-year old patient.[73]

Changing Roles When Dealing with Safety and Security

In complex healthcare organizations, the physicians, nurses, technicians, and administrative personnel who have well-defined roles in normal patient care delivery may find their relationships altered when safety and security are in the spotlight. For example, in a fire or hazardous materials incident, professional security officers may be designated as the first responders. An institutional safety officer and security officers will direct staff until fire fighters arrive. Nursing staff will control the evacuation of nonambulatory patients. Facilities workers will verify that fire protective systems are functional. Physicians, who are normally accustomed to being the leaders of patient care teams, may find themselves taking direction from others.

Frequently, the chiefs of hospital security departments have professional law enforcement agency experience. This factor enhances cooperation between the hospital and local police. It also imbues the security department with a professional law enforcement agency culture, which is useful both in general and in emergencies.

The Blurring Line Between Physical and Electronic Security

Physical security and information security techniques are merging as video surveillance incorporates artificial intelligence and high-tech access-control devices supplant traditional key-and-tumbler locks. Access to restricted areas or floors of a multilevel healthcare facility now can be controlled by centrally programmable keypads or card readers. Such locks can restrict access to predefined categories of personnel (e.g., to give only physicians, pharmacists, and nurses access to medical treatment rooms) and can be remotely reprogrammed to bar access to an employee who has been reassigned or terminated.

The ubiquity of cell phone cameras—as well as the possibility that cell phone signals will interfere with monitoring systems—has led many healthcare organizations to restrict cell phone use except in cafeterias and lounge areas. Nevertheless, smart phones carried by staff members as well as visitors make it easy to snap and distribute photos of patients without their knowledge or agreement. Even when cell phones are banned from patient care areas, risk of unauthorized photography remains (see **Box 7-14**).

> **Box 7-14**
>
> At Children's Hospital in Boston, a nurse recently discovered a webcam hooked up by parents in their child's hospital room, according to a report in *The Boston Herald*. The child's parents reportedly set up the camera so the child's favorite relative could see what was going on during the hospital stay. The incident raised questions about privacy issues.[74]

INFORMATION SYSTEMS

Today's hospitals depend to an unprecedented degree on computerized information systems and electronic communication. Since the 1960s, when the first computerized patient accounting and billing systems were introduced and clerks entered data on punch cards, healthcare information systems have evolved into powerful clinical tools, using hand-held devices to signal out-of-range lab results and flag incorrect drug doses and dangerous drug interactions. Such systems now can provide physicians and nurses with a "smart" template for patient history and physical examinations, and structure an instantly available comprehensive electronic medical record for all authorized providers.

Other information systems manage bed availability, register patients, optimize diagnosis-related groups (DRGs), track compliance requirements, manage physician credentialing, dispense medications, generate performance indicators, control diagnostic and therapeutic equipment, augment a surgeon's skills, manage ventilation systems, maintain inventories and order supplies, and perform a whole array of activities that formerly were the province of physicians, nurses, technicians, administrators, clerks, and pharmacists.

With their huge electronic stores of confidential employee and patient information such as dates of birth, parents' names, and Social Security numbers, hospitals are attractive targets for information thieves, perhaps second only to financial services companies, online merchants, and credit card issuers. Before hospitals began connecting to the Internet, computer printouts were the most common way for thieves to gain access to this kind of confidential hospital information. Until recently, in a typical hospital, computers were located in locked computing centers, and remote terminals and printers were protected in restricted areas behind nursing station counters or in accounting offices. Computer terminals were directly connected to mainframe computers by dedicated cables. Only a person with physical access, a valid password, and familiarity with arcane programming commands, could access information. Nevertheless, confidential employee and patient data could be compromised by employees who retrieved printouts containing names, dates of birth, Social Security numbers, and home addresses

from hospital computing systems. Unfortunately, this vulnerability persists (see **Box 7-15**).

Box 7-15
In 2010, a south Florida emergency room employee stole—and sold—printouts containing confidential ID information for 1,500 patients. The incident was the second major hospital identity theft in south Florida in two years.[75]

Unauthorized access to confidential information became marginally easier when computer terminals gave way to generic workstations and dedicated cabling schemes were supplanted by multipurpose internal networks. Risk increased further when hospitals connected with the Internet and started using commercial network infrastructure to send data across multihospital systems and to billing companies, third-party payers, health maintenance organizations (HMOs), and members of accountable care organizations (see **Box 7-16**).

Box 7-16
• In a 2011 incident, almost 20,000 Stanford University hospital patient records were exposed to public view over the Internet for nearly a year because a marketing agent for a billing contractor sent an electronic spreadsheet containing the data to a job prospect as part of a skills test.[76] • In another 2011 incident, Lawrence Memorial Hospital announced that credit card or bank check information associated with patient payments had been accessible on the Internet for more than a month.[77] • A Virginia Commonwealth University (VCU) server was infected in 2011 by a computer worm that may have caused the release of Social Security numbers and other personal data for VCU Health System employees.[78]

Confidential information can be protected against theft via the Internet by employing a software/hardware "firewall" to block selected data from entering or leaving the institution.[79] Such firewalls are effective but not impenetrable. They can be defeated by attaching "malware" to an email sent from outside to someone within the institution. If the recipient opens what usually is an innocuous-appearing attachment, the malware virus or worm it contains is now within the institution's firewall, where it can seriously compromise information security.

Alternatively, information may be compromised when someone smuggles a computer virus or worm into a hospital's internal network via an infected "thumb drive." Once inserted into a USB port on a networked computer within the hospital's firewall, such malware can enable unauthorized access to confidential information from outside. A hard disk also can carry such a virus (see **Box 7-17**).

> **Box 7-17**
>
> In 2011, Beth Israel Deaconess Medical Center notified 2,000 patients that some of their personal information may have been stolen when a computer service vendor failed to restore security settings on a computer before returning it to the hospital. The computer was found to contain a virus that sent patient medical record numbers, names, genders, and birth dates to an unknown location.[80]

The ease with which information can be accessed increases the importance of using encryption techniques to protect it. Hospitals frequently use virtual private networks (VPNs) as a cost-effective way to route protected patient information over a commercial Internet infrastructure. Unfortunately, despite many security features, VPNs can be breached; in 2010, four out of the 10 top data losses occurred in networks operated by healthcare organizations.[81] This vulnerability means that all patient information should be encrypted.

Information thieves need not possess sophisticated computer skills to gain access to confidential patient information. Hospital patients quickly become accustomed to providing their date of birth and Social Security number to hospital employees, which in turn makes them easy targets for a predatory hospital worker who wants to steal ID information (see **Box 7-18**).

> **Box 7-18**
>
> In Cranston, Rhode Island, an emergency department security guard was arrested for opening a retail store charge card using an ID stolen from an ED patient.[82]

The explosion in the use of healthcare computing systems has accelerated the migration of computer terminals from centralized nursing stations, where they are inaccessible to the general public, into patient rooms or corridors, where security control has to be electronically based. Workstations on wheels (WOWs) now dot the corridors of many hospitals. In other institutions, each patient room is fitted with its own workstation. All of these access points must be protected from unauthorized use. An authorized user can be verified by ID card swipe or by a proximity-detectable chip, thumbprint, or other high-tech recognition method. Passwords, which were once commonly jotted down on a sticky note left at a workstation, must now be changed regularly. All too often, however, laptops and home computers—frequently used by employees and consultants to analyze patient data—compromise the hospital-based protection schemes (see **Box 7-19**).

The Health Insurance Portability and Accountability Act

To define and protect the exploding body of electronic patient information throughout the United States, federal regulators have developed a set of standards collectively known as the HIPAA rules (see **Box 7-20**).

The rules stipulate that physicians, nurses, and administrators must master their principal features before being allowed to handle protected health information. Each healthcare institution must identify a privacy officer—typically a legal or compliance official—and a security officer—usually a high-level information systems expert, to work in concert to assure that HIPAA requirements are met.

Information security officers, as mandated by HIPAA, now protect a vast and complex information systems architecture—one where access to the huge databases holding patient information depends on other databases containing provider information, job descriptions, credentials, and employee records. All of these databases must be continually updated, usually at great cost to healthcare institutions.

Despite the best efforts of information security officers, information loss continues. Patient information breaches affecting 500 or more individuals are required by HIPAA to be chronicled by the U.S. Department of Health and Human Services (DHHS). The DHHS webpage has become widely known as the HIPAA "Wall of Shame." For 2009 and 2010, it listed more than 100 major breaches.[87]

FIRE SAFETY

According to the nation's preeminent fire safety organization, the National Fire Protection Association (NFPA), "municipal fire departments responded to an estimated 3,750 structure fires in medical, mental health, and substance abuse facilities annually" between 2003 and 2006. These fires caused one civilian death, 57 civilian injuries, and $26.9 million in direct property damage. Remarkably, this toll represented a 71% drop in healthcare facility structure fires between 1980 and 2008.[88]

The improvement in hospital and nursing home fire safety came as aging wood frame structures were slowly replaced by fire-resistant steel and concrete buildings, and as construction and health codes increasingly mandated specific provisions to inhibit fire ignition, confine flames and smoke, extinguish fires automatically, and warn building occupants of danger. Today, U.S. hospitals are required to comply with strict NFPA standards that shape regulation of fire suppression systems, fire barriers, smoke compartments, alarm and detection systems, and emergency exits and lighting; the materials used for ceilings, wall coverings, and curtains; and even how far a charting desk can protrude into a corridor (see **Box 7-21**).

Box 7-21 NFPA 101: Healthcare Facility Fire Safety Principles

- Fire-resistive construction
- Subdivision of spaces, known as compartmentation
- Protection of vertical openings
- Provision of adequate means of egress
- Provision of exit marking, exit illumination, and emergency power
- Limits on the use of interior finish materials
- Fire alerting facilities
- Control of smoke movement
- Protection of hazardous areas
- Adequate protection of building service equipment
- Control of fuel loads (i.e., combustible materials)
- Selected operational features

When these principles are correctly implemented, even a substantial fire can be confined while patients are protected in a safe area (see **Box 7-22**).

Box 7-22

Montefiore Medical Center experienced an extremely smoky fire in a basement cogeneration plant in 2011. The smoke was smelled in the ED and in several intensive care units (ICUs). Thanks to code-compliant construction and fully operational ventilation, detection, and alarm systems, a well-trained staff was able to quickly move patients to safety.[89]

Most fires in healthcare facilities originate in cooking equipment, contained trash, and electrical distribution and lighting equipment.[90] Cigarette smoking in hospitals has faded as a source of fires since this practice was widely banned as of December 31, 1993.[91] Nevertheless, illicit hospital smoking continues, albeit surreptitiously. In a recent inspection of a medium-sized hospital in Brooklyn, cigarette butts were observed in stairwells and mechanical rooms. Behavioral units frequently allow psychiatric patients to smoke as a therapeutic measure. Moreover, oxygen, which is commonly available in patient rooms, amplifies the danger from smoking (see **Box 7-23**).

Box 7-23

- A 2006 incident in Dallas, Texas, involved a patient who smoked in his hospital room while wearing an oxygen mask.[92] The fire engulfed his bed and caused more than 100 patients to be evacuated.
- In 2009, a female patient started a fire in her Orlando, Florida, hospital room that prompted patient evacuation.
- In 2011, fires in a South Carolina hospital[93] and a Tennessee nursing home[94] showed that the danger of cigarette smoking continues to imperil healthcare facilities.

The Tennessee nursing home incident demonstrated the importance of sprinkler systems, which extinguished that fire before it could spread. According to the NFPA, sprinklers have proved effective in 96% of the fires big enough to trigger sprinkler operation (see **Box 7-24**).

Box 7-24

A large Illinois hospital limited damage from a basement fire to $5,000 through the use of noncombustible materials in construction, smoke detector actuation of automatic doors and a sprinkler system, and an alarm automatically relayed to the local fire department. The fire was confined to the storage room, where a carelessly discarded cigarette had ignited pallets of toilet paper.[95]

Defend-in-Place

Immobilized patients cannot be easily evacuated in the event of a fire, especially from the upper floors of a multistory building, when, by code, alarm actuation automatically returns all elevators to the exit floor. Patients who are undergoing an invasive procedure or are in critical care may not be movable at all. Such patients are best protected through a "defend-in-place" strategy.[96] Given this reality, code requirements for new healthcare facility construction mandate the use of noncombustible materials, doors, and partitions that can withstand fire and smoke for up to two hours; elimination of all structural penetrations between adjacent "compartments," including doors and duct dampers that close automatically upon alarm system actuation; and complete smoke detection and sprinkler coverage.

When evacuation of a bedbound or otherwise immobilized patient to an adjacent compartment is an available option, success requires unencumbered corridors, careful planning, and extensive staff training. Beds and life support equipment must be easily movable by a single staff member. Nurses and other clinical staff must know whether life support equipment will continue to function when disconnected from normal power, and, if not, which procedures must be invoked.

Despite major advances in fire-resistant construction and mandated use of flame-resistant finishes and materials in healthcare occupancies, fire and smoke remain a hazard for patients. Doors must be wide enough to permit bedbound patients to be easily removed from their rooms. Corridors must be free of encumbrances such as trash barrels, dumpsters containing construction debris, or containers of documents intended for shredding, computer workstations, beds, chairs, and any other potential obstacle. Indeed, unnecessary corridor encumbrances are among the first hazards a survey team or fire inspector looks for when visiting a healthcare facility. Such obstacles represent one of the thorniest problems for hospitals that were designed decades ago, when there was no need to include storage space for confidential paper bins or today's essential portable devices, such as crash carts, WOWs, and medication dispensing carts.

Fire Safety Plans and Training

Good facility design and adherence to correct operating principles are not enough to ensure hospital fire safety. In addition, staff members must embrace their professional responsibility to protect and rescue patients, and must know how to act in event of a fire. To ensure this readiness and prevent panic, a well-developed fire safety plan and extensive staff training are essential. Each accredited U.S. hospital is required to develop and maintain a written fire safety management plan, which must include proactive processes for protecting patients, staff, and property.

These processes should be flexible. A healthcare worker may routinely move between several hospitals, each with its own physical characteristics, so it is essential for that worker to be able to understand basic fire safety principles while recognizing the specific needs of each facility. Awareness of exit and fire alarm pull station locations is crucial, as is familiarity with the institution's alarm format, which at one institution can be a "Code Red" announcement and at another can be a horn, bells, or gongs.

Typically, nurses, physicians, and others are taught to base their fire response behavior on the acronym RACE! (Rescue, Alarm, Confine, Extinguish/Evacuate!). Some hospitals consider strict adherence to RACE! too limiting. They reason that it takes no time for a nurse or doctor to shout "Fire!" or "Code Red!" while removing a patient from immediate danger. Once the patient is safe, the caregiver should run—not walk—to the nearest fire alarm pull station, typically located near an exit door or stair and always colored red, and activate the fire alarm system. Temporary employees and contractors must follow the same procedures. When these procedures are not followed, tragedy can ensue (see **Box 7-25**).

Box 7-25

A horrific fire in a private hospital in eastern India killed 94 people in late 2011 when hospital staff fled without evacuating patients from the smoke-filled building.[97] The 180-bed facility in Kolkata had been constructed with thick plate-glass windows, which hampered fire fighters from venting the building and rescuing patients. A West Bengal official said the hospital stored diesel and motor oil in the basement.

FACILITY DESIGN AND OPERATION

Architectural design can improve patient safety and reduce risk.[98–101] A comprehensive review of the impact of facility design on patient safety has identified several design principles and features that have been shown to improve patient safety:

- Single-patient rooms and ample use of acoustic insulating materials can minimize distractions and noise-induced stress.
- Standardized same-handed room design will foster consistent patient care techniques and speed emergency response.
- Placing the headwall and the toilet close to each other on the same wall will reduce the risk of patient falls.
- Adequate ventilation and air filtration can reduce the risk of infection.
- Individually controllable zoned lighting increases patient visibility and permits subdued lighting levels when desired.
- Seamless, washable surfaces reduce infection risk.[102]
- Prominent positioning of sharps receptacles and waterless hand cleanser dispensers will encourage staff use.
- Location of hand washing sinks near patient beds has been shown to increase hand washing, but sheer number of sinks has not.[103]

To verify these effects and to test the best methods to achieve them, the leadership of St. Joseph's Hospital in West Bend, Wisconsin, conducted a "national learning lab" to identify the best process to design and build an 82-bed acute care hospital around the improvement of patient safety. The top 10 design recommendations that emerged have since been embraced by many healthcare architects (see **Box 7-26**).[104]

Long before patient safety became an explicit goal of architects, sound facility design and operation were recognized as essential to a hospital's ability to protect patients, visitors, and staff. In addition to personal security and fire safety, a healthcare institution must manage risk associated with indoor air quality, water quality, water temperature, and construction projects.

Ventilation and Indoor Air Quality

Ventilation in a healthcare facility must minimize infectious risk. Contemporary ventilation standards have been informed by guidelines published by the CDC.[105] These guidelines stipulate that air-pressure relationships and frequency of air changes should vary throughout a healthcare facility. For example, a "clean utility (sterile supply) room" should be positively pressurized to minimize intrusion of airborne infectious agents, while a "soiled utility room," where contaminated bedding may be stored, should be negatively pressurized to prevent airborne pathogens from escaping into corridors.

Patient rooms also require special treatment. Newly constructed standard level-of-care patient rooms are ventilated with six air changes per hour (ACH), but older healthcare facilities may not attain this standard. The general principle guiding heating, ventilation, and air-conditioning (HVAC) design in a healthcare facility is that air should move from clean areas to dirty ones, and then should leave the building. If it contains airborne infectious agents, it should be filtered before being exhausted. Other prominent guidelines are summarized here:

- Immunocompromised patients should be placed in protective environment (PE) rooms, which are positively pressurized to prevent pathogen entry.
- Patients who may be shedding airborne pathogens (e.g., patients with tuberculosis) should be housed in negatively pressurized airborne infection isolation (AII) rooms. Both PE rooms and AII rooms typically have dedicated ventilation systems,
- In operating rooms, at least 20 air changes per hour are required, and all air must be taken directly from outside the building, subject only to filtration and temperature/ humidity regulation.
- High-efficiency particulate air (HEPA) filters can be selectively employed to further reduce airborne transmission of pathogens. Some HEPA filter units incorporate high-energy ultraviolet light sources to kill live pathogens.

Even in a well-designed facility, pressure gradients can change over time. Fans fail. Filters eventually become clogged, reducing airflow. A door chocked open or a window improperly sealed can disrupt pressure and airflow. A well-planned facility maintenance program is crucial to maintaining original design parameters and protecting patients against airborne infections.

Infectious agents are not the only airborne hazard affecting patients and staff members. Overall indoor air quality (IAQ) should meet outdoor standards. Contaminants such as smoke, pollen, mold spores and other particulates, carbon monoxide, carbon dioxide, nitrous oxide, sulfur dioxide, and volatile organic compounds (VOCs) can all trigger respiratory symptoms or nausea and contribute to other health problems.[106] Maintenance of satisfactory IAQ requires proper facility design and operation. Hospital air intakes should be located away from sources of pollutants such as driveways, parking areas, smokestacks, and generator exhausts. Filters should be incorporated into ventilation fans to screen out particulates, and a regular maintenance program is necessary to keep these filters clean. Laboratory fume hoods must operate properly to prevent VOCs and noxious chemical odors from disturbing patients and staff members.

Plumbing problems sometimes cause disturbing odors. Rotting organic material in a clogged drainage system can emit odors similar to those associated with mercaptans, the sulfur-containing odorants that natural gas suppliers add to odorless gas to make it detectable. These "sewer gas" odors may signal danger to anyone who smells them, even causing headache and nausea. An unused sink can become an odor

generator if its "P-trap"—the curved drain pipe beneath the sink—dries out and loses its ability to block sewage odors from escaping into the room.

External odors can infiltrate a healthcare facility through a ventilation system. Such odor complaints by employees have triggered OSHA inspections.[107] Because a single odor can affect many patients and staff members, it can generate multiple complaints. Repeated odor complaints can hurt a hospital's public relations, and, if communicated to an authority having jurisdiction or an accreditation group, can prompt an unannounced survey. In some instances, unexplained odors have forced hospitals to evacuate (see **Box 7-27**).

Box 7-27

- Almost 100 people were evacuated in November 2011 from Western Medical Center in Santa Ana, California, because of an unidentified odor.[108]
- Portions of a rural hospital in New York were evacuated in 2011 because smoke odors—probably from nearby wood stoves—frightened building occupants.[109]
- In 2007, an odor identified as a gas leak prompted an evacuation from a hospital in San Diego. The odor turned out to have come from a malfunctioning elevator.[110]

Water Quality

Legionella pneumophila, a gram-negative bacterium commonly found in garden soil, can cause pneumonia in immunocompromised patients. *Legionella* can appear in infectious concentrations in a healthcare facility's domestic hot-and cold-water systems, in water tanks, and in the mist produced by air-conditioning cooling towers. To avoid cases of Legionnaires' disease in transplant patients, patients with acquired immunodeficiency disease (AIDS), the elderly, and patients receiving radiation therapy, a healthcare institution will employ one or more preventive techniques, including the following:

- Reduction of breeding opportunities by using semi-instantaneous water heaters
- Systemic treatments of domestic water systems such as copper–silver ionization
- Injection of chlorine dioxide or monochloramine, exposure to ultraviolet light, and hyperchlorination
- Point-of-use filtration

In outbreak situations, water can be treated by superheating and flushing with or without hyperchlorination.

Hospitals should manage *Legionella* invasion as part of their infection control program. To do so, they may convene a multidisciplinary team of physicians, nurses, and engineering staff, led by an infection control practitioner (see **Box 7-28**).

Box 7-28

- Patients at a prestigious New York City hospital were warned in 2011 not to shower or use sinks or water fountains after one patient tested positive for Legionnaires' disease. All patients were provided with bottled drinking water and moist towelettes for washing until bacterial titers in the water supply could be restored to safe levels.[111]
- In a hospital in Miami, Ohio, delay in addressing water treatment allowed 10 cases of Legionnaires' disease to develop in early 2011.[112]

Water Temperature

State regulations governing permissible domestic hot water (DHW) temperatures in healthcare facilities vary widely. In a hospital or nursing home, DHW is required to be available at a distal outlet at temperatures warm enough for comfort and cool enough to prevent scalding (see **Box 7-29**).[113] To ensure that hot water throughout the facility meets these standards, engineers must produce it at higher temperatures to compensate for cooling during transmission to patient care areas. DHW piping systems can ensure immediate warm water at a faucet or shower head by circulating it continuously through supply-and-return loops located nearby.

Box 7-29

- A 90-year-old woman died in 2005 after being scalded in a nursing home bathtub in Canada.[114]
- In a 2011 incident in England, caregivers plunged an infant's foot into hot water, scalding the baby.[115]

Construction Hazards

During construction, healthcare facility renovations must be carefully controlled to minimize risk to everyone present at the site. At any construction site, workers are susceptible to risks such as noise, falling debris, fire, electric shock, eye damage, inhalation of VOCs or harmful dust, and numerous other hazards. At an active healthcare facility, construction-related precautions also must consider patients, visitors, and staff. Such precautions fall into two primary categories: interim life safety measures (ILSMs) and steps designed to prevent infection.

Interim Life Safety Measures

Renovations or repairs can temporarily compromise the integrity of structural partitions, block access to designed emergency egress paths, or hinder operation of fire alarm or suppression systems. When this happens, an institution must correct the deficiency as soon as possible. Until correction is accomplished, fire safety risks can be mitigated by implementing ILSMs. Typical ILSMs include increased fire surveillance by trained security or safety personnel, creation of temporary alternative exit paths, transfer of nonambulatory patients to secure locations, enhanced signage and other communications, and additional staff fire safety training.

The decision to institute specific ILSMs should be made through a formal life safety risk assessment, typically performed by a multidisciplinary team that includes the institution's safety officer, clinicians, administrators, security personnel, and project architects or engineers. The life safety risk assessment and mitigation plan must be carefully documented and periodically revisited to ensure that the selected ILSMs continue to be effective.

Infection Control During Construction

Infection control can be compromised by repair or renovation within an operating healthcare facility. Air-pressure relationships designed to limit the spread of airborne pathogens will change if ventilation systems or smoke barriers are temporarily disabled or modified. Most renovations and many repairs can generate dust. Dust-tight barriers should surround the construction site, which must be ventilated to yield a negative pressure zone within the site, thereby preventing dust from escaping.

Before any physical alteration or major repair is undertaken, it must be subjected to an infection control risk assessment (ICRA). The institutional infection control officer, working with clinicians, facilities personnel, and administrators, will determine the procedures needed to protect patients, visitors, and staff from infection during an alteration.

EMERGENCY PREPAREDNESS

Today's hospitals have been sensitized to the need for complete disaster readiness by the U.S. East Coast terrorist attacks of 2001 and the Madrid train bombings in 2004, and by natural disasters such as Hurricane Katrina's devastation of New Orleans in 2005, the major East Coast earthquake of 2011, a 2011 tornado that tore apart a major regional hospital in Joplin, Missouri, and Japan's earthquake and tsunami in the same year. Catastrophic events of such dimensions reminded hospitals that they must continually prepare for the unimaginable. Even smaller-scale incidents such as shootings in hospitals in Baltimore,[116] Chicago,[117] and Omaha, Nebraska,[118] remind us that healthcare institutions—ordinarily sanctuaries in a disaster—are themselves vulnerable to unpredictable danger.

The CMS and voluntary accrediting organizations have reacted to these perceived threats by stiffening the emergency preparedness standards for healthcare institutions. For hospitals and other institutions, emergency preparedness must contemplate how to prepare for a disaster that affects nearby communities and for a disaster that damages the institution itself. The plan must be an "all hazards" plan; it may contain sections for specific hazards, but its core, such as chain-of-command definitions, should be generic and consistent.

An effective emergency preparedness plan is not just a document. Rather, it is a total mode of behavior for a healthcare institution that centers on dedication of resources for emergency preparedness; designation of a command structure, including precise definition of roles and authority in a disaster; a culture of continuous training; frequent and carefully critiqued disaster drills to discover vulnerabilities and speed response; and constant updating of the plan to reflect changing risks and conditions.

What Is an Emergency?

Generally recognized categories of emergencies include the following:

- Bioterrorism emergencies (e.g., anthrax, smallpox)
- Chemical emergencies
- Mass casualties
- Natural disasters
- Radiation emergencies[119]

In a healthcare institution, many other situations also can constitute an emergency—generally any human-made or environmental event in which the medical needs of the community or the needs of the institution itself exceed the resources available. This definition implies that any internal event in a hospital or nursing home that threatens its ability to provide patient care can be declared an emergency. Such events can include a labor strike; a power failure; a steam plant shutdown; a loss of information systems, water, critical ventilation, or air conditioning; and a variety of other disruptive events (see **Box 7-30**). Additional disaster situations faced by hospitals can include communications and power failures, area water shortages and contamination, structural damage, hazardous materials exposure, facility evacuation, and resource allocation.[120]

The special challenges faced by America's 2,000 rural hospitals, many of which are old, isolated, and resource poor, may be even greater.[121]

The challenges hospitals face when dealing with a disaster include these tasks:

- Managing medical assessment, treatment, and continuing care in acute incidents involving large numbers of patients
- Effectively managing contaminated patients
- Recognizing, identifying, and managing consequences of bioterrorism
- Protecting employees, patients and their families, and anyone else within the facility
- Dealing with all of these tasks while continuing to provide everyday emergency care[122]

Disaster Planning

To prepare for a prolonged disaster, when roads and other transportation routes may be cut off, a hospital should have on hand sufficient fuel, water, and supplies to last for 96 hours. Even this supply will not be enough if the hospital's location or structure renders it susceptible to crippling damage from an earthquake, flood, or high winds. Supplies and utilities are only part of the picture, however: Every healthcare institution first depends on its human resources.

Physicians, nurses, and other essential healthcare workers may not be on-site when a disaster strikes, and they may not be able to return to the facility. In addition, the organizational cultures in most hospitals embrace deliberate and methodical consensus-driven and data-driven decision making. Emergencies, however, require a different approach: one in

Box 7-30   Possible Threats to Institutions

Security
- Bomb threat
- Civil disturbance
- Gang-related activity
- Hostage situation
- Infant abduction
- Location in high-crime area
- Terrorist attack, including nuclear, biological, chemical, and explosive threats (internal or external)
- Visiting or injured VIP
- Workplace violence

Utility Failures
- Central medical vacuum
- Central oxygen
- Electrical power
- Emergency generator
- Fire suppression/alarm system
- Heating, ventilation, and air conditioning
- Information system/computers
- Natural gas
- Overhead paging
- Security system
- Sewage
- Telephone/telecommunications
- Water main break

Geologic
- Snowstorm
- Earthquake
- Hail
- High winds
- Hurricane
- Ice storm
- Severe cold
- Severe heat/humidity
- Severe rainfall/flood
- Sinkholes
- Tornado
- Tsunami

Structural Threats
- Vehicle crash into facility
- Chemical (hazardous material) release (internal)
- Explosion (internal)
- Fire and smoke (internal)
- Flooding (internal)
- Gas leak (internal)
- Other structural damage to the building

Other
- Major vehicle crash (external)
- Hazardous material release or spill (external)
- Explosion (external)
- Fire and smoke (external)
- Flooding (external)
- Gas leak (external)
- Other mass-casualty incident
- Labor strike

which quick decisions must be made on the basis of imperfect or incomplete information—and often by individuals who may not constitute the organization's day-to-day leadership cadre. To deal with such contingencies, an emergency management plan must incorporate a command structure in which predefined job definitions and detailed task lists make it possible for available personnel, within the limits of their skills and training, to fill critical emergency functions.

These principles are embodied in HEICS, the widely adopted "hospital emergency incident command system" developed in California. HEICS, which has been continually refined since its creation, specifies a template for a durable and flexible command structure that provides several important benefits:

- A predictable chain of command
- Flexibility in different kinds of disasters
- Accountability for specific functions
- Thorough documentation of actions taken
- Common terminology to improve communication within and between organizations
- Flexibility and cost-effectiveness within organizations[123]

When a hospital disaster is declared, the institution's hospital command center (HCC) is activated and directed by an incident commander, who has overall responsibility for all activities. The incident commander may appoint other command staff personnel as needed to assist. The HEICS organizational structure features four main sections: Operations, Planning, Logistics, and Finance/Administration. Reporting to the Operations chief will be individuals responsible for the Staging, Medical Care, Infrastructure, Hazardous Materials, Security, and Business Continuity subsections. Other section chiefs cover all other essential hospital functions.[124]

HEICS (also known as HICS) is not a comprehensive emergency preparedness plan, but rather a tool to facilitate a plan's implementation. A complete plan must include specific departmental plans for each operational unit within the institution, and must address emergencies before they happen (mitigation and preparedness), once they have started (response), and after they have ended (recovery). In a healthcare facility, recovery must include restoration of both clinical and business functions.

The planning process itself must be carried out by a multidisciplinary Committee capable of representing all aspects of an institution's activities. The Emergency Management Committee should meet regularly and review all plan submissions and updates. The hospital command center should be activated periodically to discover procedural glitches, particularly in communications. Less often, an institution should participate in a broader planning exercise, teaming with local emergency response agencies to test interagency communication, adequacy of surge space and transportation, and impact of any mobilization on the surrounding community.

Despite these features, an emergency management plan may fail if it is based on faulty assumptions, or simply lacks imagination. The assumption that patients are safest when they remain in a hospital was discredited by Hurricane Katrina in New Orleans. One national healthcare leader has commented that evacuation from a healthcare facility threatened by a Category 5 storm should begin as long as three days ahead of its arrival (see **Box 7-31**).[125]

Finally, the same social media that present potential challenges for institutions wishing to maintain patient privacy have become valuable communications tools in mass disasters. Facebook, Twitter, and Ushahidi (in Kenya) have helped people share information during a crisis and were valuable in the massive earthquakes in Haiti and Chile and the tsunami in Japan. Members of the public used Twitter and Flickr during the Mumbai attacks in 2008.[129]

Disaster Plans for Information Systems Continuity

As computing systems have grown more powerful, healthcare institutions and practitioners have become almost totally dependent on computers for business functions and clinical support. This

Box 7-31

- Since Hurricane Katrina struck New Orleans in 2005, healthcare executives have worked closely with federal, state, and municipal officials to coordinate multihospital and nursing home evacuation efforts. Several years of preparation paid off: In August 2011, as Tropical Storm Irene was approaching New York City, several hospitals and nursing homes smoothly transferred their patients to inland facilities.[126,127]
- An executive vice president at MeritCare Hospital in Fargo, North Dakota, had to decide whether to evacuate 180 patients as the nearby Red River rose in March 2009. Realizing that other institutions would be competing for available ambulances and roadway space if mandatory evacuation was declared, patients were readied in advance with bags of medicines, checklists on their doors, and bar-coded triage bracelets on their wrists colored to indicate the type of transport required.[128]

factor vastly increases the importance of specialized disaster plans for information technology (IT). Yesterday's business continuity plans, which relied on manual record-keeping to bridge a multihour or multiday computer blackout, are being replaced by high-availability disaster recovery (HADR) systems,[130] which provide up to 99.9999% computing reliability, real-time data duplication, physically separated duplicate computing sites with independent emergency power, backup staffing, and networked communications topologies to eliminate disruptions from a severed cable or microwave link. The cost of HADR systems is enormous, because they imply duplication of data center costs, creation of communications network redundancy, and provision of emergency power for essential workstations.

SUMMARY

Like other risk management specialties, assuring safety and security in a healthcare institution requires anticipating the unprecedented and imagining the unimaginable. The continuing threat of global terrorism, emerging fluctuations in the frequency and severity of storms and tornadoes, the deterioration of America's utilities and transportation infrastructure, the aging of hospital buildings, and health care's increased reliance on computing and telecommunications systems are all factors that have raised the bar for healthcare safety and security risk managers, and will continue to do so. This growing risk has arisen in a climate of increasing regulatory and accreditation oversight. Some healthcare institutions have responded by staffing up their risk management units, often at an appreciable cost to the bottom line. Most hospitals have been forced to invest in safer and more secure facilities—a prudent strategy designed to control costs by reducing insurance premiums and litigation payouts.

As hospitals embrace new diagnostic and therapeutic techniques, including many involving new radioisotopes, reagents, and pharmaceuticals, each technological advance will add to the challenges faced by environmental managers. Hospital infection control standards will continue to become more stringent, raising the bar for indoor air quality and ventilation. If geopolitical developments increase reliance on coal for heating, hospitals may be forced to upgrade their ventilation systems to limit intake of hydrocarbon emissions and particulates. Noise control standards in patient rooms may become stricter. Clean water may become harder to assure as population growth, development, and disturbance of underground aquifers invade watersheds, and as distribution tunnels, mains, and plumbing systems continue to age.

Fear of terrorism will continue to spur security and disaster preparedness planning, as will concerns about increasing crime rates in harder economic times. Hospital disaster preparedness programs will increasingly contemplate floods and storms associated with climate change. Experiments with zoonotic agents such as the avian H5N1 influenza virus may force hospitals to reconsider their bioterrorism and pandemic precautions.[131]

Healthcare's growing dependency on wireless network and cell phone communication, as well as on computers to control building heating, ventilation, and air-conditioning systems, could prompt some institutions to extend their emergency power circuitry and prepare for disruptions from solar flares and electromagnetic pulse (EMP) incidents.[132] Many hospitals will invest in computing backup facilities and/or services, including those services based on "cloud computing."[133] Fire safety may be the sole area of safety and security in which risk is likely to diminish.

As new challenges to safety and security continue to emerge, healthcare professionals will be forced to spend more time and effort managing risk. The facility and operational enhancements they identify as essential—whether informally or by FMEA or root-cause analysis—will make their hospitals and patients safer. Some "best practices" will be adopted by peer institutions, and selected structural features and procedural improvements will be incorporated into accreditation standards and regulatory codes.

One pattern is clear: The difficulty, complexity, and cost of assuring safety and security in healthcare institutions will continue to grow. It will be a great challenge to the healthcare industry and its regulators and accrediting agencies to identify standards that yield meaningful improvements in safety and security, without jeopardizing the financial integrity of the institutions held to those standards.

REFERENCES

1. Zeeble, B. (2011, August 5). Parkland settles with federal agencies. *KERA News Roundup*. Retrieved from http://www.publicbroadcasting.net/kera/news.newsmain?action=article&ARTICLE_ID=1837176
2. St. Mary of Nazareth Hospital fined for mishandling chemical spill. (2011, March 30). *PR Newswire*. Retrieved from http://www.prnewswire.com/news-releases/st-mary-of-nazareth-hospital-fined-for-mishandling-chemical-spill-51676687.html
3. Morales, M. (2011, July 5). Interfaith Medical Center hospital in Bed-Stuyvesant fined for hazards. *NY Daily News*. Retrieved from http://articles.nydailynews.com/2011-07-05/local/29759434_1_hazardous-materials-osha-ted-fitzgerald
4. Deegan, D. (2005, August 5). Vermont-based Veterans Administration hospital cited and fined for improper handling and storage of hazardous waste. *US EPA News Release*. Retrieved from http://yosemite.epa.gov/opa/admpress.nsf/6d651d23f5a91b768525735900400c28/9373614c9a620d51852570cf007a2e46!OpenDocument
5. Mass General takes $1 million hit for losing 193 patient records. (2011, February 25). *Infosecurity Magazine*. Retrieved from http://www.infosecurity-magazine.com/view/16228/mass-general-takes-1-million-hit-for-losing-193-patient-records/
6. Sulzberger, A. J., & Stelter, B. (2011, May 23). A rush to protect patients, then bloody chaos. *New York Times*. Retrieved from http://www.nytimes.com/2011/05/24/us/24tornado.html?pagewanted=all
7. Joint Commission FAQ page. (2012). The Joint Commission. Retrieved from http://www.joint-commission.org/about/JointCommissionFaqs.aspx
8. Chufo, V. (2010, April 28). Riverside: Joint Commission makes unannounced site visit to look into complaint. *Daily Press*. Retrieved from http://articles.dailypress.com/2010-04-28/news/dp-local_riverside_0428apr28_1_health-care-organizations-joint-commission-complaint

9. Sentinel event. (2011). The Joint Commission. Retrieved from http://www.jointcommission.org/sentinel_event.aspx

10. Nesbitt, W. H. (2008, May 22). JCAHO proposed combining of safety & security under new EC standards a mistake. *Hospital Security Reporter.* Retrieved from http://www.thehospitalsecurityreporter.com/articles/08_0522.html

11. Never events. (n.d.). Agency for Healthcare Research & Quality. Retrieved from http://psnet.ahrq.gov/primer.aspx?primerID=3

12. Adverse events in hospitals: Overview of key issues. (2008). U.S. Department of Health and Human Services, Office of Inspector General. Retrieved from http://oig.hhs.gov/oei/reports/oei-06-07-00470.pdf

13. Karsten, M. (2011). Patient safety: Commitment versus compliance. *Nurse Leader, 9*(4), 47–49.

14. Cox, T. L., Jr. (2008). What's wrong with risk matrices? *Risk Analysis, 28*(2). doi: 10.1111/j.1539-6924.2008.01030.x. Retrieved from http://www.evira.fi/attachments/english/research_on_animal_diseases_and_food/risk_assessment/risk-matrices.pdf

15. Kohn, L., Kerrigan, J., & Donaldson, M. (Eds.) (2000). *To err is human: Building a safer health system.* Washington, DC: National Academy Press. Retrieved from http://www.nap.edu/openbook.php?record_id=9728&page=R1

16. Reichert, T. (2004). Applying failure modes and effects analysis in healthcare. Society of Health Systems Protection. Retrieved from www.iienet2.org/uploadedfiles/SHS/Resource_Library/Details/10_reichert.pdf

17. Patient safety: Conducting a root cause analysis of adverse events. (2009). Retrieved from http://www.rhqn.org/resources/Presentations/cont-ed/11-17-09/Adverse%20Event%20and%20RCA%20Conference%20Call%2011-17-09.ppt

18. Ibid.

19. Framework for conducting a root cause analysis and action plan. (2009, April). The Joint Commission. Retrieved from http://www.jointcommission.org/Framework_for_Conducting_a_Root_Cause_Analysis_and_Action_Plan/

20. Commission to review Hopkins hospital security after shooting. (2010, September 23). *The Baltimore Sun.* Retrieved from http://articles.baltimoresun.com/2010-09-23/health/bs-hs-hopkins-doctor-review-20100923_1_hopkins-officials-sentinel-events-joint-commission

21. Sentinel event data root causes by event type 2004—third quarter 2011. (2011). The Joint Commission. Retrieved from http://www.jointcommission.org/assets/1/18/Root_Causes_Event_Type_2004-3Q2011.pdf

22. Lavelle, J. (2011, September 9). Generators failed at two hospitals during blackout. *San Diego News.* Retrieved from http://www.signonsandiego.com/news/2011/sep/09/regional-hospitals-fully-operational-friday/

23. Rooney, J. J., Vanden Heuvel, L. N., & Lorenzo, D. K. (2002, September). Reduce human error: How to analyze near misses and sentinel events, determine root causes and implement corrective actions. *Quality Progress.* American Society for Quality. Retrieved from http://www.capapr.com/docs/reducing%20human%20error%20QP.pdf

24. Oriol, M. D. (2006). Crew resource management: Applications in healthcare organizations. *Journal of Nursing Adminstration, 36*(9), 402–406.

25. Anonymous. (2008, April 24). Some red rules shouldn't rule in hospitals. *ISMP Medication Safety Alert.* Retrieved from http://www.ismp.org/newsletters/acutecare/articles/20080424.asp

26. Ibid.

27. Hospital e-tool. (2011). U.S. Department of Labor, Occupational Safety and Health Administration. Retrieved from http://www.osha.gov/SLTC/etools/hospital/index.html

28. Hospital e-tool. (2011). U.S. Department of Labor, Occupational Safety and Health Administration. Retrieved from http://www.osha.gov/SLTC/etools/hospital/hazards/hazards.html

29. Comprehensive accreditation manual for hospitals. (2006). The Joint Commission. Retrieved from http://is.downstate.edu/is/jcaho/camh06/2006%20jcaho%20manual.pdf

30. Infectious waste vs medical waste. (2009, December 9). Wisconsin Department of Natural Resources. Retrieved from http://dnr.wi.gov/org/aw/wm/medinf/define.htm

31. Salkin, I., Krisiunas, E., & Turnberg, W. (2000). Medical and infectious waste management. *Journal of the American Biological Safety Association, 5*(2),

54–69. Retrieved from http://www.absa.org/abj/abj/000502Turnberg.pdf

32. Kavaler, F., & Spiegel, A. (Eds.) (2003). *Risk management in health care institutions: A strategic approach* (2nd ed.). Sudbury, MA: Jones & Bartlett.

33. Workers' rights. (n.d.). Occupational Safety and Health Administration. Retrieved from http://www.osha.gov/Publications/osha3021.pdf

34. Healthcare Environmental Resource Center. (n.d.). Retrieved from http://www.hercenter.org/

35. Summary of the Resource Conservation and Recovery Act, 42 U.S.C. §6901 et seq. (1976). United States Environmental Protection Agency. Retrieved from http://www.epa.gov/lawsregs/laws/rcra.html

36. Draft guidance document: Best management practices for unused pharmaceuticals at health care facilities. (2010, August 26). U.S. Environmental Protection Administration. Retrieved from http://water.epa.gov/scitech/wastetech/guide/upload/unuseddraft.pdf

37. Smith, C. (2007, April 17). *Managing pharmaceutical waste: A 10-step blueprint for healthcare facilities* [Presentation]. Retrieved from http://www.ohanet.org/SiteObjects/6F006F9A10C2D431388243EE89AF9377/waste_ppt.pdf

38. Fludeoxyglucose F18 injection. (2012). *RXList*. Retrieved from http://www.rxlist.com/fludeoxyglucose-drug.htm

39. Radiation therapy for cancer. (n.d.). National Cancer Institute. Retrieved from http://www.cancer.gov/cancertopics/factsheet/Therapy/radiation

40. Godfrey, P. (2011, October). Security in an open access environment. *Premium*. Retrieved from http://www.premium-me.com/s/security-in-an-open-access-environment

41. Halupke, K. (2007). Letter to Mr. Adam Zell. N. J. Department of Health and Senior Services. Retrieved from http://www.nj.gov/health/ems/documents/actions/07-c-034.pdf

42. Joyce, K. (2011, November 9). Women accused of stealing from hospitals and schools. *Fox35 News*. Retrieved from http://www.myfoxorlando.com/dpp/news/osceola_news/110911-women-accused-of-stealing-from-hospitals-and-schools

43. Stuffco, J. (2011, April 16). Family seeks answers over phony doctor. *CTV News*. Retrieved from http://www.ctv.ca/CTVNews/Canada/20110416/family-searches-in-fake-doctor-incident-110416/

44. Curtis, H. P. (2011, September 2). Cops: Teen posing as physician's assistant worked in Osceola hospital's ER. *Orlando Sentinal*. Retrieved from http://www.orlandosentinel.com/news/local/crime/os-teen-pose-physician-assistant-20110902,0,2130554.story

45. Associated Press. (2003, July 15). Intruder steals morphine from hospital patients. *St. Petersburg (FL) Times*. Retrieved from http://www.sptimes.com/2003/07/15/news_pf/State/Intruder_steals_morph.shtml

46. Squires, N. (2009, December 16). Silvio Berlusconi: Intruder overpowered outside hospital room. *The Telegraph*. Retrieved from http://www.telegraph.co.uk/news/worldnews/europe/italy/6825239/Silvio-Berlusconi-intruder-overpowered-outside-hospital-room.html

47. Dugan, T. (2011, November). Personal communication. SUNY Downstate Medical Center.

48. O'Brien, J. (2011, October 20). Hospital employee stole $800,000 in cash from patients' TV and phone payments, feds say. *The Post-Standard*. Retrieved from http://www.syracuse.com/news/index.ssf/2011/10/hospital_employee_stole_800000.html

49. Gray, R. (2010, October 5). How to create a hospital investigation unit. *Campus Safety*. Retrieved from http://www.campussafetymagazine.com/Channel/Hospital-Security/Articles/2010/10/Boston-Medical-Center-s-Investigation-Unit.aspx

50. Dugan, T. (2011, June). Personal communication. SUNY Downstate Medical Center.

51. Larue Huget, J., & Stein, R. (2008, September 6). Infant abductions: Down in hospitals, up in homes. *The Washington Post*. Retrieved from http://voices.washingtonpost.com/checkup/2008/09/infant_abductions_down_in_hosp.html

52. Burgess, A., et al. (2008). Nonfamily infant abductions, 1983–2006. *American Journal of Nursing, 108*(9), 32–38.

53. RFID. (2012). *Wikipedia*. Retrieved from en.wikipedia.org/wiki/Radio-frequency_identification

54. Harrell, E. (2011, March). Workplace violence, 1993–2009: Special report. U.S. Department of Justice. Retrieved from http://bjs.ojp.usdoj.gov/content/pub/pdf/wv09.pdf

55. Gerberich, S., et al. (2004). An epidemiological study of the magnitude and consequences of work related violence: The Minnesota Nurses' Study. *Occupational & Environmental Medicine, 61,* 495–503.

56. Gates, D. (2004). The epidemic of violence against healthcare workers. *Occupational & Environmental Medicine, 61*(8), 649–650. Retrieved from http://oem.bmj.com.newproxy.downstate.edu/content/61/8/649.1.full?ijkey=53a4bbfff31051b4d8b50d8bbfeb516abf315548&keytype2=tf_ipsecsha

57. National Institute for Occupational Safety and Health. (2002). Violence: Occupational hazards in hospitals. NIOSH publication 2002-101. Retrieved from http://www.cdc.gov/niosh/pdfs/2002-101.pdf

58. IAHSS Survey reveals healthcare statistics. (2010). International Association for Healthcare Security & Safety. Retrieved from http://www.pr.com/press-release/256209

59. Keely, B. (2002). Recognition and prevention of hospital violence. *Dimensions in Critical Care Nursing, 21*(6), 236–241.

60. Gacki-Smith, J., et al. (2009). Violence against nurses working in US emergency departments. *Journal of Nursing Administration, 39*(7/8), 340–349. Abstract retrieved from http://journals.lww.com/jonajournal/Abstract/2009/07000/Violence_Against_Nurses_Working_in_US_Emergency.9.aspx.

61. IAHSS Survey reveals healthcare statistics. (2010). Op cit.

62. Exposure to stress: Occupational hazards in hospitals. (2008). Centers for Disease Control and Prevention, National Institute for Occupational Safety and Health. Retrieved from http://www.cdc.gov/niosh/docs/2008-136/pdfs/2008-136.pdf

63. Friedman, E. (2010, September 16). Johns Hopkins Hospital: Gunman shoots doctor, then kills self and mother. *ABC News.* Retrieved from http://abcnews.go.com/US/shooting-inside-baltimores-johns-hopkins-hospital/story?id=11654462#.TsgNY1awVVo

64. Kelen, G., & Catlett, C. (2010). Violence in the health care setting. *Journal of the American Medical Association, 304*(22), 2530–2531, Retrieved from jama.ama-assn.org.

65. Nir, S., & Hartocollis, A. (2011, November 9). Gunman wounds nurse and guard at Bronx hospital. *New York Times.* Retrieved from http://www.nytimes.com/2011/11/10/nyregion/gunman-wounds-nurse-and-guard-at-bronx-hospital.html?_r=1

66. Ryan, J. (2011, July 13). Violence in the ER. *KUOW News.* Retrieved from http://www.kuow.org/program.php?id=23813

67. Nash Health Care adds metal detectors to emergency care center [Press release]. (2010, May 25). Nash Health Care. Retrieved from http://www.nhcs.org/press_releases/articletype/articleview/articleid/4

68. Amy, J. (2005, January 16). Hospital killing focuses security concerns. *The Mobile Register.* Retrieved from http://www.jrrobertssecurity.com/security-news/security-crime-news0025.htm

69. Sutherly, B., & Robinson, A. (2011, June 14). Hospital violence reportedly rising. *Dayton Daily News.* Retrieved from http://www.daytondailynews.com/news/dayton-news/hospital-violence-reportedly-rising-1184394.html

70. Shrieves, L. (2011, May 31). Rising violence shows hospitals should boost security, experts warn. *Orlando Sentinel.* Retrieved from http://articles.orlandosentinel.com/2011-05-31/health/os-hospital-security-20110531_1_american-hospitals-patient-parking-garage

71. Woman fires gun outside City Hospital. (2011). *The Journal.* Retrieved from http://www.journal-news.net/page/content.detail/id/565753/Woman-fires-gun-outside-City-Hospital.html?nav=5006

72. Gun goes off in local hospital. (2011, November 19). *Fox30 News.* Retrieved from http://www.fox30jax.com/content/actionlocal/story/Gun-goes-off-in-local-hospital/r0l_UunHHEqU8GatHeKxqQ.cspx

73. Phillips, L. (2011, November 20). Gun find in fake leg sends hospital in lockdown. *The Sydney Morning Herald.* Retrieved from http://www.smh.com.au/nsw/gun-find-in-fake-leg-places-hospital-in-lockdown-20111101-1msq5.html

74. New technology creates hospital security concerns. (2007, July 3). *HealthLeaders Media.* Retrieved from http://www.healthleadersmedia.com/content/TEC-90664/New-technology-creates-hospital-security-concerns.html

75. LaMendola, B. (2010, November 21). Identity theft ring breaches Holy Cross Hospital. *Sun Sentinel.* Retrieved from http://articles.sun-sentinel.com/2010-11-11/health/fl-hk-holy-cross-id-20101110_1_identity-theft-ring-patient-files-emergency-room

76. Sack, K. (2011, October 6). Patient data landed online after a series of missteps. *New York Times.* Retrieved from http://www.nytimes.com/2011/10/06/us/stanford-hospital-patient-data-breach-is-detailed.html?pagewanted=all

77. Smith, D. & Shaffe, N. (2011, November 7). Lawrence Memorial Hospital patients' credit card information compromised. *KCTV5 News*. Retrieved from http://www.kctv5.com/story/15981497/lawrence-memorial-hospital-patients-credit-card-information-compromised

78. Server security incident notification. (2011, November 12). Virginia Commonwealth University. Retrieved from http://wp.vcu.edu/securityincident/

79. Pickering, R. (2011). Internet firewall tutorial. *IPCortex*. Retrieved from http://www.ipcortex.co.uk/wp/fw.rhtm

80. Bray, H. (2011, July 18). Beth Israel reports potential data breach. *The Boston Globe*. Retrieved from http://www.boston.com/Boston/businessupdates/2011/07/beth-israel-reports-potential-data-breach/sLnihf9HOmBQDGc6GFCVTI/index.html

81. Phifer, L. (2011, January). Top 10 data breaches of 2010. *eSecurity Planet*. Retrieved from http://www.esecurityplanet.com/views/article.php/3921656/Top-10-Data-Breaches-of-2010.htm

82. McKinney, M. (2008, April 10). 4 accused of stealing IDs as part of cell-phone fraud. *Providence Journal*. Retrieved from http://news.providencejournal.com/breaking-news/2008/04/4-accused-of-st.html#.TuV3JlawVVo

83. Associated Press. (2011, November 4). U.C.L.A. Health System warns about stolen records. *New York Times*. Retrieved from http://www.nytimes.com/2011/11/05/us/ucla-health-system-warns-about-stolen-records.html?_r=1&ref=us

84. Clark, A. (2010, June 3). AvMed: Breach of customer data three times worse than reported. *The Gainesville Sun*. Retrieved from http://www.gainesville.com/article/20100603/articles/100609817

85. Health information privacy. (n.d.). U.S. Department of Health and Human Services. Retrieved from http://www.hhs.gov/ocr/privacy/hipaa/understanding/summary/index.html

86. HIPAA privacy rule and public health. (2003, April 11). *U.S. Centers for Disease Control Early Release, 52*, 1–12. Retrieved from http://www.cdc.gov/mmwr/preview/mmwrhtml/m2e411a1.htm

87. Breaches affecting 500 or more individuals. (2012). U.S. Department of Health and Human Services, Office for Civil Rights. Retrieved from http://www.hhs.gov/ocr/privacy/hipaa/administrative/breachnotificationrule/postedbreaches.html.

88. Flynn, J. (2009, February). Structure fires in medical, mental health, and substance abuse facilities. National Fire Protection Association.

89. Martin, D. (2011). Bronx hospital fire shows why emergency training is critical. *ASHE Advisory*. Retrieved from http://www.ashe.org/advocacy/advisories/2011/broxhospfire.html

90. Flynn, J. (2009). Op cit.

91. Fee, E., & Brown, T. (2004). Hospital smoking bans and their impact. *American Journal of Public Health, 94*(2). Retrieved from http://www.ncbi.nlm.nih.gov/pmc/articles/PMC1448226/

92. Patient's cigarette causes fire. (2006, July 15). *Lubbock Avalanche-Journal*. Retrieved from http://lubbockonline.com/stories/071506/sta_071506084.shtml

93. Vreeland, T. (2011, April 7). Smoker starts fire at Carolinas hospital system. *Carolina Live*. Retrieved from http://www.carolinalive.com/news/story.aspx?id=602623

94. Carpenter, J. (2010, July 8). Nursing home fire kills one, forces transfer of 27 residents. *The Herald News*. Retrieved from http://rheaheraldnews.com/story/1752

95. Jardin, J. (2002). Health care facilities. In R. E. Solomon (Ed.), *Fire and life safety inspection manual*. National Fire Protection Association. Retrieved from http://www.nfpa.org/assets/files/PDF/HCFacilitiesCh25.pdf

96. Ibid.

97. Polgreen, L., & Kumar, H. (2011, December 10). 94 die as private hospital in India burns. *New York Times*. Retrieved from http://www.nytimes.com/2011/12/10/world/india-hospital-fire-kolkata-west-bengal.html?scp=1&sq=india%20hospital%20fire&st=cse

98. Campbell, C. (2009, May 18). Health outcomes driving new hospital design. *New York Times*. Retrieved from http://www.nytimes.com/2009/05/19/health/19hosp.html

99. Reiling, J. (2008). Creating a culture of patient safety through innovative hospital design. In K. Henriksen, J.B. Battles, M.A., Keyes, & M.L. Grady (Eds.), *Advances in patient safety: New directions and alternative approaches. Vol. 2. Culture and Redesign*. AHRQ Publication No. 08-0034-2. Rockville, MD: Agency for Healthcare Research and Quality. Retrieved from http://www.ahrq.gov/downloads/pub/advances/vol2/Reiling.pdf

100. Reiling, J., Hughes, R. G., & Murphy, M. R. (2008). The impact of facility design on patient safety In R. Hughes(Ed.), *Patient safety and quality: An evidence-based handbook for nurses*. Rockville, MD: Agency for Healthcare Research and Quality. Retrieved from http://www.ncbi.nlm.nih.gov/books/NBK2633/

101. Naik, G. (2006, May 8). To reduce errors, hospitals prescribe innovative designs. *Wall Street Journal*. Retrieved from http://www.healthdesign.org/sites/default/files/news/To%20Reduce%20Errors,%20Hospitals%20Prescribe%20Innovative%20Designs.pdf

102. Reiling, J., Hughes, R., & Murphy, M. (2008). Op. cit.

103. Lankford, M., et al. (2003). Influence of role models and hospital design on the hand hygiene of healthcare workers. *Emerging Infectious Diseases, 9*(2), 217–223. Retrieved from http://www.ncbi.nlm.nih.gov/pmc/articles/PMC2901948/

104. Reiling, J. (2008). Op. cit.

105. Sehulster L., et al. (2004). *Guidelines for environmental infection control in health-care facilities*: *Recommendations from CDC and the Healthcare Infection Control Practices Advisory Committee (HICPAC)*. Chicago: American Society for Healthcare Engineering/American Hospital Association. Retrieved from http://www.cdc.gov/hicpac/pdf/guidelines/eic_in_HCF_03.pdf

106. Leung, M., & Chan, A. (2006). Control and management of hospital indoor air quality. *Medical Science Monitor, 12*(3), SR17–23. Retrieved from http://www.ncbi.nlm.nih.gov/pubmed/16501436

107. Author's personal knowledge.

108. Hospital in Santa Ana is evacuated after gas-like odor is detected. (2011, November 5). *CBS Los Angeles*. Retrieved from http://losangeles.cbslocal.com/2011/11/05/hospital-in-santa-ana-evacuated-after-gas-like-odor-is-detected/

109. Part of Carthage area hospital evacuated. (2011, November 5). *Fox 28 WNYF (Watertown, NY) News*. Retrieved from http://www.wwnytv.com/news/Part-of-Carthage-Area-Hospital-Evacuated-133308313.html

110. Natural gas odor prompts hospital evacuation. (2007, June 18). *San Diego News*. Retrieved from http://www.10news.com/news/13525001/detail.html

111. Memorial Sloan Kettering Cancer Center warns against its tap water after patient contracts Legionnaire's disease. (2011, September 18). *NY1*. Retrieved from http://manhattan.ny1.com/content/top_stories/147409/memorial-sloan-kettering-cancer-center-warns-against-its-tap-water-after-patient-contracts-legionnaire-s-disease

112. Legionnaire's outbreak largest in Ohio since 2004. (2011, March 10). *Dayton Daily News*. Retrieved from http://www.daytondailynews.com/news/dayton-news/legionnaires-disease-outbreak-largest-in-Ohio-since-2004-110

113. Mandell, A., et al. (1993) State regulation of hospital hot water temperature. *Infection Control and Hospital Epidemiology, 14*(11). Retrieved from http://www.jstor.org/pss/30149747

114. Law must require anti-scald device, inquiry judge told. (2005, December 3). *The Edmonton Journal*. Retrieved from http://www.canada.com/edmontonjournal/story.html?id=b85cf2df-f0f2-4a40-a6eb-cb1d1a1ee59e&k=96661

115. Six-day-old baby left with horrific burns after midwives plunged her foot into bowl of scalding water. (2011, June 13). *Daily Mail Reporter*. Retrieved from http://www.dailymail.co.uk/news/article-2002954/Stafford-Hospital-6-day-old-baby-left-horrific-burns-midwives-carlessness.html

116. Friedman, E. (2010, September 16). Johns Hopkins Hospital: Gunman shoots doctor, then kills self and mother. *ABC News*. Retrieved from http://abcnews.go.com/US/shooting-inside-baltimores-johns-hopkins-hospital/story?id=11654462#.TxJGBlZTadk

117. Associated Press. (2011, November 25). Suspect arrested in Chicago hospital gun death. *Fox News*. Retrieved from http://www.foxnews.com/us/2011/11/25/chicago-university-locked-down-after-gunman-shoots-woman-in-medical-center/

118. "Despondent" man killed by police in hospital confrontation. (2010, September 30). *KETV News*. Retrieved from http://www.ketv.com/r/25209323/detail.html

119. Emergency preparedness and response: Preparation for all hazards. (n. d.). Centers for Disease Control and Prevention. Retrieved from http://www.bt.cdc.gov/planning/

120. Ibid.

121. Gursky, E. (2004). Hometown hospitals: The weakest link? *The National Defense University*. Retrieved from http://www.dtic.mil/cgi-bin/GetTRDoc?AD=ADA476080&Location=U2&doc=GetTRDoc.pdf

122. Rubin. J. (2006). Recurring pitfalls in hospital preparedness and response. In J. H. McIsaac (Ed.), Hospital preparation for bioterror. Burlington, MA: Academic Press. Retrieved from http://www.homelandsecurity.org/journal/articles/rubin.html

123. Hospital Incident Command System (HICS). (2007). California Emergency Medical Services Authority, Disaster Medical Services Division. Retrieved from http://www.emsa.ca.gov/hics/

124. Ibid.

125. Larkin, H. (2006, May). 12-step disaster plan. *Hospitals & Health Networks*. Retrieved from http://www.hhnmag.com/hhnmag_app/jsp/articledisplay.jsp?dcrpath=HHNMAG/PubsNewsArticle/data/2006May/0605HHN_FEA_Preparedness&domain=HHNMAG

126. Herzenberg, M. (2011, August 26). Hurricane's approach forces hundreds to evacuate hospitals citywide. *NY1*. Retrieved from http://www.ny1.com/content/145880/hurricane-s-approach-forces-hundreds-to-evacuate-hospitals-citywide/

127. Inglesby, T. (2011, September 28). Progress in disaster planning and readiness since 2001. *Journal of the American Medical Association, 306*(12).

Retrieved from http://jama.ama-assn.org.newproxy.downstate.edu/content/306/12/1372.full.pdf+html

128. Fink, S. (2009, March 31). Disaster preparedness pays off in North Dakota. *ProPublica*. Retrieved from http://www.propublica.org/article/disaster-preparedness-pays-off-in-North-Dakota-20090331

129. Inglesby, T. Op. cit.

130. Quintero, D., et al. (2010). High availability and disaster recovery planning: Next-generation solutions for multiserver IBM power systems environments. *IBM Redbooks*. Retrieved from http://www.redbooks.ibm.com/redpapers/pdfs/redp4669.pdf

131. Fouchier, R., et al. (2012, January 20). Pause on avian flu transmission studies. *Nature Online*. Retrieved from http://www.nature.com/nature/journal/vaop/ncurrent/full/481443a.html

132. Electromagnetic pulse. (2012). *Wikipedia*. Retrieved from http://en.wikipedia.org/wiki/Electromagnetic_pulse

133. Ellis, J., & Razavi, A. (2011, May 6). Cloud computing or data center: How hospitals should analyze their health IT storage needs. *Healthcare IT News*. Retrieved from http://www.healthcareitnews.com/blog/cloud-computing-or-data-center-how-hospitals-should-analyze-their-health-it-storage-needs

PART 2

Managing Risks in
Clinical Services

CHAPTER 8

Patient Safety Tools: Integrating Quality and Managing Risk

Robert Stanyon

No challenge in risk management is more immediate than demonstrating that the risk management program makes a difference to the organization and its bottom line. This conclusion makes intuitive sense, but the objective evidence can be elusive to quantify. An evaluation process helps determine how well risk management is doing within the organization, while the processes of total quality management and continuous quality improvement enable institutions to make the transition to higher levels of performance and high reliability. Risk management focuses on an institution's exposure to financial loss. In minimizing this exposure, risk managers contribute to quality patient care by ensuring that hazards and injuries are less likely to occur. Enterprise risk management looks beyond the traditional risk silo and incorporates a larger view of exposure to loss that affects many other areas of the organization.

MEDICAL INJURIES ARE NEITHER NEW NOR UNCOMMON

Injury resulting from a medical procedure or event is nothing new. Kaiser Wilhelm II, as emperor of Germany and Prussia, was the architect of World War I. The young Kaiser suffered an Erb's palsy or similar condition at birth, during which chloroform anesthesia was used.[1,2] Today, Wilhelm's withered arm, hyperactivity, and emotional instability would certainly have resulted in a medical malpractice lawsuit. Even in 1859, the year of his birth, medical professional liability (malpractice) litigation already was an established process in the United States[3] (see **Box 8-1**). More recently, medical professional liability litigation has become an international phenomenon extending well beyond the United States to Canada,[5] New Zealand,[6] the Netherlands,[7] Sweden,[8] and such decidedly non-Western cultures as Japan where medical

---

Box 8-1   Medical Malpractice Has Been Around Awhile

Between 1840 and 1850, medical malpractice became a recognized cause of action in the U.S. courts. The most common cases were procedure related and resulted in poor medical outcomes. Prior to the 1840s, a physician would generally amputate a limb that had a compound fracture. As the century progressed, the improved training and experience of the best doctors resulted in attempts at realignment of these fractured limbs. The outcome often was an intact limb that was deformed. Gratitude did not always flow to the practitioner in these cases. Often, the best of them were sued.[3]

practitioners may face criminal prosecution for patient deaths related to medical care.[9,10] Not surprisingly, the threat of prosecution results in the practice of extreme defensive medicine.[11]

Modern medical knowledge and practice have conferred the extraordinary benefit of wellness on today's citizens, but medical accidents still happen. The Harvard Medical Malpractice Study estimated that roughly 1% of patients discharged from New York State hospitals were victims of medical negligence resulting in injury.[12] A larger number of patients experienced an injury not caused by negligence, but obviously resulting in patient dissatisfaction. This study concluded that injuries happen with significant frequency during hospitalization. Similar results were noted in studies conducted in Utah/Colorado[13] and Canada.[14] Although the number of adverse events varied, all of these studies showed very significant numbers of injuries. The New York and Utah/Colorado results were also used in the landmark Institute of Medicine (IOM) report, *To Err Is Human,* which publicized a range of 44,000 to 98,000 deaths attributable to medical error. Most recently, a new study conducted in a group of medical centers in Utah, Massachusetts, and Missouri indicated the number of adverse events during hospitalization may be 10 times greater than the rates found in the original New York and Utah studies. Of interest in this new study was the finding that the voluntary internal adverse event reporting systems used in hospitals "fail to detect most adverse events."[15]

Injuries and Lawsuits

Most of the injured patients in New York's Harvard study and the study in Utah and Colorado did not initiate a lawsuit. In fact, most of the actual claims did not result from adverse events caused by negligence.[16] Paradoxically,

many claimants who are not appropriate candidates for compensation seek redress for injuries in the courts. A later study reviewed the medicine practiced in 1,452 closed claims from five medical liability insurance carriers.[17] Importantly, most of the claims that paid significant damages did involve verifiable medical error. Claims not related to medical error were compensated at a significantly lower rate. The investigators concluded that reducing frivolous lawsuits would not significantly reduce the cost of "medical malpractice" to the healthcare system.

Some have argued that the increase in medical professional liability lawsuits bears some relationship to the number of new attorneys graduated from law schools each year[18] (see **Box 8-2**). We do know the cost of medical errors is high—$17.1 billion per year according to one recent estimate. This amount includes the medical and related costs to the patient and the healthcare system.[19] The cost of medical errors to the Medicare program alone was estimated to be approximately $8.8 billion for the years 2004–2006.[20]

Injuries happen, and so do lawsuits. The challenge for risk managers is to minimize the injury side of the equation. Current thinking assumes that a decrease in patient injuries will result in less medical professional liability litigation. Claims do require skillful management, but control of the future lies in prevention. Risk managers must be aware of the true cost of risk

Box 8-2   Supply-Side Medical Professional Liability

One rationale for the rapid rise in medical professional liability lawsuits could be the steady increase in the number of lawyers—approximately 45,000 new attorneys each year to fill a projected 30,000 legal jobs.[18] An oversupply of lawyers and generous awards from professional liability insurance coverage may create an incentive for professional liability litigation.

and the methods that may help prevent adverse events and lawsuits.

The Challenge of Prediction

If science and mathematics eventually permitted predictions about hazards and malpractice, risk management would be very different. Risk or hazard could be appreciated before the fact and eliminated before an adverse event. Importantly, predictive methods are statistical in nature. An equation cannot tell you that something *will* happen, only that there is an increased likelihood that it *might* happen. Such methods may be helpful in planning and program development, but bear in mind that events leading to professional liability claims are very rare and cannot be predicted with certainty.

Confounding prediction is the very nature of human interaction itself. For example, a patient who likes a particular practitioner is less likely to sue that physician in the event of a bad outcome.[21] To some extent, a physician's likability is determined by cultural attributes, although the reason could be as simple as giving a patient quality time. Cultivating a personal style acceptable to patients is an important loss prevention technique for today's physician. Physicians need to be enlightened, and the risk manager is in a unique position to identify those who may need help, because the risk manager knows which physicians have been sued and how frequently.

Predictive Models

Gibbons and colleagues developed a statistical model for predicting medical professional liability claims for individual physicians.[22] These investigators believed insurers could use this model to examine or "predict an individual's claim vulnerability." Among their findings:

- A sizable random physician effect exists.
- Risk of a claim increases for physicians between the ages of 40 and 60 years.
- Surgical specialists are at increased risk of a claim.
- Male physicians are at greater risk for a claim than their female colleagues.
- Following an initial claim, risk increases, particularly in the first year after the claim.
- Risk management education has beneficial effects on physicians with a prior claim history, particularly in anesthesiology and obstetrics/gynecology.

In addition, the researchers noted that even if the risk management education did not reduce the number of claims, the payout was often less because the education "may equip the physician to be a better defendant in the event of a claim."

How can this information be utilized? Should middle-aged male physicians in surgical specialties be targeted for intensive review and remedial education? Given the lag time between an adverse event and the receipt of a claim, it is likely that the damage or injury alleged in subsequent claims occurred prior to the arrival of the first claim. If a risk management program is to be proactive rather than reactive, the risk management activities to be emphasized must be planned in advance. Post-claim risk management education for professional staff seems like a good place to begin, but one should not expect to see immediate positive results from such a program.

Patient Safety and Medical Error Reduction

The Institute of Medicine (IOM) cited the results of the Harvard Medical Malpractice Study and others in calling for changes in the healthcare system that would improve safety for all patients.[23] The IOM's goal was to reduce the number of medical errors by 50%. There is disagreement about the actual numbers given in the report,[24,25] but not about the need to reduce the number of medical errors.

The importance of patient safety and medical error reduction is a unifying theme in risk management and quality management. Interventions to reduce error are given a high priority. For this reason, the publication of evidence-based information specific to clinical departments focusing on the efforts to reduce medical error is important.[26] Researchers agree that evidence-based data can validate some interventions, but not everyone agrees on the place for interventions that have not been tested by evidence-based methods.[27] For example, it seems common sense that to place a leading zero before a decimal point in a medication order will eliminate some medication errors. Any nurse who has transcribed medication orders knows this fact intuitively; an expensive study with statistical power would seem unnecessary. The risk manager, understanding these limitations, may find the Agency for Healthcare Research and Quality (AHRQ) report helpful in providing guidance for individual clinical departments.[26]

The Rand Corporation reviewed patient safety activities in four communities (Indianapolis, Indiana; Cleveland, Ohio; Seattle, Washington; and Greenville, South Carolina) and concluded that more work needs to be done, especially to develop a national capability to monitor changes in patient safety infrastructure and practices, along with their effects on a variety of stakeholders.[28] In the absence of such data, we will never know whether we have improved.

The National Quality Forum (NQF) has further refined its list of 34 evidence-based patient safety practices that are recommended for implementation at all hospitals. These practices serve as an excellent guide for review by the risk manager for designing programs and planning education sessions to improve patient safety.[29,30]

A question remains about how much we have improved since the original IOM report was publisher more than 10 years ago. The evidence seems to suggest that significant levels of preventable patient injury and death continue to occur in the U.S. healthcare system, comparable to the levels mentioned in the IOM report.[31]

For the risk manager, injuries resulting from adverse events are just one part of the total picture. To determine the success of a risk management program, all medical errors need to be accurately categorized and tracked.[32] A reduction in the number of errors would translate into measurable improvement. Finding error is almost impossible without a functioning error-reporting system. For such reporting to work, the institutional culture must foster blame-free disclosure of events.

Incident Reporting and Tracking Within the Organization

Occurrence or incident reporting is an essential activity for any organization, and the risk manager must be aware of what is reported and what its significance to the risk management program is—for example, whether there are any patient or staff injuries and what the exposures to any insurance and/or compensation program(s) are. Occurrence data must be collected, categorized, and tracked over time to assist in developing prevention programs.

Such a reporting system is necessary so that all incidents can be reviewed, and the more serious potentially compensable events (i.e., events that could lead to litigation) are examined more closely. Any event involving serious patient injury or death will also require a root-cause analysis (RCA) to determine possible causation as well as prevention measures that may be necessary to avoid recurrence of these events. Modern computerized reporting systems are capable of tracking various defined events, the individuals involved, the locations at which the events took place, and the appropriate follow-up activities and results. One such system, developed at Columbia Presbyterian Medical Center in New York and implemented at the Mount Sinai Medical Center, is the Medical Event Reporting System (MERS).[33] MERS is an online system for real-time reporting, tracking, and analysis of events. It also includes the ability to anonymously report near-miss events. Occurrence reports can be routed online to the appropriate individuals for review and can include the physician's assessment.

Healthcare-Acquired Conditions

The Centers for Medicare and Medicaid Services (CMS) now holds hospitals accountable for a specific list of healthcare-acquired conditions (HACs) for which no reimbursement will be provided to an organization for the care associated with the condition when it is acquired during the hospitalization.[34] Documentation of these conditions in the record, when present on admission (POA), is necessary for reimbursement to occur. The documentation requirement is burdensome but essential. The HACs must be managed appropriately by the healthcare organization regardless of the patient's reimbursement status.

The HACs are events that CMS believes should not happen. In addition, there are three "never events," for which reimbursement for the entire hospitalization will be denied; they are specifically related to surgery and should never occur: wrong patient, wrong site, wrong procedure. Risk managers need to ensure that HACs and "never events" are identified and tracked appropriately. The information needed to prevent these events should be a part of the risk management education program for staff.

The HAC list can change over time but included 12 categories for the year 2011:

- Foreign object retained after surgery
- Air embolism
- Blood incompatibility
- Pressure ulcer stages III and IV
- Falls and trauma
- Catheter-associated urinary tract infection
- Vascular catheter–associated infection
- Manifestations of poor glycemic control
- Surgical site infection, mediastinitis following coronary artery bypass graft
- Surgical site infection following certain orthopedic procedures
- Surgical site infection following bariatric surgery for obesity
- Deep vein thrombosis (DVT) and pulmonary embolism (PE) following certain orthopedic procedures

An AHRQ report analyzed HACs in selected community hospitals from 15 states in 2008. It revealed that almost 90% of HACs involved four categories: vascular catheter–associated infections, falls and trauma, catheter-associated urinary tract infections, and DVT/PE.[35]

AN OUNCE OF PREVENTION: COMMUNICATION _____

The importance of communication within the physician–patient relationship is clear: Physicians who use more effective communication techniques and spend a little more time with their patients are less likely to be sued,[36,37] and they include the patient in the decision making process.[38–41] The process of improving the understanding of the stakeholders (i.e., the patient and the physician) depends on mutual communication. Ideally the patient understands the risks, benefits, and alternatives of treatment, and the physician understands the "rich conceptualization of risk" entertained by the patient.[42] An important corollary to the findings in studies on this topic is that these simple communication skills can be learned by physicians to improve their practice climate.

Ultimately, a major contributor to medical professional liability risk is lack of patient satisfaction with the care delivered. How well did the provider communicate with the patient, and how interested or concerned was he or she with the outcome for the patient? The answer to this question may indeed be the best predictor for lawsuit avoidance.[43,44] Improving skills related to communication is a crucial loss prevention initiative for the risk manager.

Managing Expectations: Informed Consent

An important defensive strategy in health care is the informed consent discussion between the provider and the patient. When patients understand the risks, benefits, and alternatives for their treatment, they are better able to accept the outcome when it is not as expected. This understanding, may not obviate lawsuits but it can reduce the surprises and the upset that results. Informed consent is one of the tools used to facilitate a mutual understanding between the physician and the patient. The risk manager

must understand this complex process and incorporate the informed consent concepts into the proactive risk management education program. While the key element is the communication that occurs between the provider and the patient, the documentation of this conversation in the medical record is essential for treatment as it communicates what has occurred to other caregivers, to the billing process, and for legal purposes. For the risk manager, conducting a quality audit of the informed consent process in selected settings can be an important intervention to ensure adequate compliance.

For the individual patient, risks or hazards are more than statistics. They include a "fear factor," or a certain quantity of dread.[42] Patients do not want a complex process presented to them. Instead, they view risk in more concrete personal terms: How bad could it be and what are the odds that something bad will happen to me? A list of risks will need to be presented, but the patient will want to know when each of them could happen (e.g., during a procedure or a week later), and how permanent a negative result might be (e.g., resulting in death versus an infection that is easily treated with antibiotics).[45] Most patients want to know what their chances of hazard are—either as a statistical number derived from a population or as a relative value such as "poor" or "excellent." The challenge is to explain how one might be in the 1% risk group, rather than the 99% risk group.

When All Else Fails: Disclosure of Unanticipated Outcomes

Disclosure of unanticipated outcomes is mandatory in health care today. The Joint Commission (TJC) various state regulations, and the American Medical Association (AMA) all address the importance of informing the patient about outcomes of care that were not as expected. It is an important ethical issue but the question is not whether to disclose but rather how it should be done, who should be responsible, and what should be disclosed. Many organizations have discovered that not everyone is capable of handling this task well. Physicians and administrators need to understand how to organize and conduct disclosure to patients. It is particularly important for all staff to understand who will disclose, when it will be done, and exactly what will be disclosed. Having a well-defined process will avoid having someone who is well intentioned disclose fragmentary information at the wrong time. Often the risk manager can be helpful in organizing some aspects of this process, but the physician is usually the individual who will disclose an untoward event to the patient. Education for the professional staff can improve the quality of the disclosure process, and rehearsals can go a long way toward making it a better experience for everyone involved. The elements of disclosure cannot be left to chance. Knowing what to say can make the difference between an informed and understanding, if unhappy, patient or just a plain angry one. Good risk management begins with preparation.[46–48]

Disclosure of large-scale adverse events affecting multiple patients is a special case that requires specific planning and management to protect the patients and the reputation of the medical facility (see **Box 8-3**).[49–51]

One interesting study estimated the ultimate cost of paying for compensation related to medical professional liability for medical treatment injuries if providers were to disclose them to patients, presumably alerting patients such as those identified in the Harvard Medical

---

Box 8-3   Disclosure of Large-Scale Adverse Events: Every Risk Manager's Nightmare

On rare occasions, adverse events occur that may affect or harm relatively large numbers of patients. One such case, reported in 2003 at a medical center in Toronto, Canada, involved incomplete cleaning of prostate biopsy equipment over a period of about six years. There was no evidence that any of the more than 900 men had experienced an infection as a result of the procedure, but the hospital felt a duty to follow up and notify these individuals that they had potentially been exposed and offer them pathogen testing. There was no evidence of infection found during the follow-up testing but class-action lawsuit was filed for psychological harm during the waiting time for the test results. The hospital settled the suit without admitting liability for $1.2 million (Canadian) to 768 class members.[49,50]

Management of these events requires careful consideration and planning. Once an error has been confirmed, it should be disclosed, even though its full extent may not be appreciated at the time. Causal relationships should not be identified unless completely clear. A communication plan for patients should be in place to permit sharing of information and answering questions. Root-cause analysis should be led externally to ensure objectivity and results should be released to the public with a description of action taken to prevent a recurrence. Performance evaluations of the involved clinicians must be undertaken in a fair and unambiguous manner with the objective of improving patient safety.[51]

Malpractice Study who did not sue following an injury, that had suffered an injury as a result of their care. The real potential exists that there will be a large increase in litigation and cost with full disclosure. The study's Monte Carlo Simulation model predicted a 95% increase over current compensation costs. The median dollar amount of this increase amounted to $5.5 billion.[52]

INJURY REDUCTION: EVIDENCE-BASED PRACTICE

A number of initiatives using evidence-based interventions have transformed the practice of medicine and point the way toward a safer future for both patients and providers. Patients are rightfully concerned about the possibility of injury from medical error, but many remain unclear about what these risks are and how they are defined.[53] The Institute for Healthcare Improvement's (IHI) 100,000 Lives Campaign sought to reduce patient deaths by 100,000 over a period of 18 months, beginning in November 2004, using an evidence-based set of patient safety interventions.[54] The IHI enrolled more than 3,000 hospitals in the campaign and saved an estimated 122,300 unnecessary deaths. The campaign was declared a success. Importantly, the evidence-based interventions became a part of the participating hospitals' patient safety programs. One would think that patient injury and death would have declined in the wake of this initiative, but more recently the Consumer Union Safe Patient Project estimated that 10 years after the IOM report, preventable harm still accounts for more than 100,000 deaths in the United Staes each year.[55]

Other important studies, such as the Keystone ICU Project conducted in hospitals in the state of Michigan, demonstrated a significant reduction in central line–associated bloodstream infections (CLABSI) and ventilator-associated pneumonias (VAP) in the intensive care setting using a specific set of evidence-based interventions (see **Box 8-4**).[56] The success of this program was notable and these methods have been embraced by healthcare organizations nationwide.[56,57]

Risk managers need to be aware of evidence-based interventions within their healthcare organizations. These sources of data for monitoring are a valuable resource for the patient safety and risk management programs.

Box 8-4   Evidence-Based Procedures to Reduce Central Line–Associated Bloodstream Infections

The five evidence-based procedures recommended by the Centers for Disease Control and Prevention and utilized in the Michigan ICU study to reduce CLABSI:[56]

- Hand washing
- Using full-barrier precautions during line insertions
- Cleaning skin with chlorhexidine
- Avoiding the femoral site (if possible)
- Removing unnecessary catheters

ENTERPRISE RISK MANAGEMENT

Risk management was historically concerned with identifying financial exposures to the organization and establishing programs to negate or reduce their effect on that organization. A classic example is identifying of patient injuries leading to lawsuits that occur in an organization, quantifying the cost of these suits, and obtaining insurance to help manage the price of litigation. Prevention, in contrast, was generally left to the medical staff to manage. More recently, the concept of enterprise risk management (ERM) has changed the role of the risk manager in many ways.

ERM looks at the entire organization and the effect of risk, risk management programs, and interventions on the different components of an organization and its overall structure. These components, which are called domains or risk categories, define broad areas of risk. The board of directors, and senior executives' support is mission critical in an ERM framework.[58,59] Categories of risk or risk domains are broadly defined as follows:

1. *Operational/clinical risks* are related to the organization's core business and operations, including the clinical operations and outpatient services.
2. *Financial risks* are related to an organization's ability to earn, access, or raise capital as well as costs associated with risk transfer such as bonds and insurance premiums.
3. *Human capital risks* are related to recruitment, retention, and management of the workforce and include the worker's compensation program, employee turnover and absenteeism, union-related issues, and discrimination.
4. *Strategic risks* are related to the organization's growth and expansion plans, and include mergers and acquisitions, joint ventures, profitability, and financial performance, as well as customer/patient satisfaction.
5. *Legal/regulatory risks* are related to statutory and regulatory compliance as well as licensure and accreditation. The Joint Commission or related accreditation, compliance with Health Insurance Portability and Accountability Act (HIPAA) and Occupational Safety and Health Administration (OSHA) regulations, and Medicare conditions of participation are but a few examples.
6. *Technological risks* are associated with biomedical and information technology (IT) as well as equipment, devices, and telemedicine activities, among others. Today the emergence of the electronic health record, computerized physician order entry (CPOE) systems, picture archiving and communication systems (PACS) in radiology, and distributed information networks that connect widespread clinical operations are a few examples.
7. *Natural disaster/hazard risks* are related to unpredictable natural occurrences that result in physical loss of assets or reduction in their value. Such losses may also include related losses such as the cost of business interruption.

Decisions are made based on the simultaneous influence of a number of these areas acting together. As an example, the presence of birth injuries affects not only the medical professional liability insurance program, but also the details of management in labor and delivery including staffing and medical practice patterns. There may also be equipment issues, such as fetal monitoring capability, the readiness of the staff to use such equipment, and the ability to view the fetal monitoring patterns from remote locations. The financial issues go far beyond insurance and can affect the bottom line of the organization because of reduced patient admissions secondary to adverse publicity in the community. Marketing methods and materials may be called into question because of their potential for misunderstanding. Legal, regulatory, and accrediting considerations may have a direct effect on the organization's management of adverse events. The organization's policies on the management of labor and delivery, availability of sufficient expertise on a 24/7 basis, and, if something goes wrong, disclosure of adverse events to patients, along with many other details, will determine how well risk management can plan the defense of a lawsuit. If this sounds complicated, it is.

ERM is an organized way of managing risk that begins with the identification of risks and determination of their relative importance.[60,61] It is better to allocate resources to manage those risks that present the greatest exposure or have the potential to bring enhanced value to the organization. Once the risks and their relative priority have been determined, the processes for mitigation and management are developed. Which domains are affected, how they may be interrelated, and who will take responsibility for them are defined. Risks should be handled at the appropriate level, including at the level of the business unit, which would then report back through the enterprise chain. As in any scientific process, the results are monitored and the process is managed and revised as circumstances change over time.

Reports to the board of directors may be necessary to inform that group or one or more of its committees about risk management activities that affect the organization. This effort may include regular reports about professional liability claims and issues as well as reports concerning compliance with changing regulations, new patient safety initiatives, or management of unexpected occurrences. If there are any recommendations for action, these should be included as well.[62]

From a practical perspective, the concept of ERM divides an organization into areas of interest that may be separate but are interrelated. Areas such as risk management, quality management, human resources, marketing, medicine, nursing, finance, legal, regulatory and compliance, general counsel, senior management, and the board of directors all influence the management of risk. In some organizations, a chief risk officer[62] can gain an overview of these many areas and provide consistency in the management of events. In other cases, different individuals may have responsibility for these

areas but senior management provides the necessary coordination. A risk manager must be aware of the process and understand how he or she fits in to the structure so that information can be shared with the appropriate areas in an organized fashion. Some risks cannot be anticipated, such as the experience in preparing for the first H1N1 outbreak, the sudden appearance of a terrorist threat, or a cyberattack on the system's computers.

Whatever the structure, open communication and the ability to work together and in teams are critical to an organization's success today. The enterprise must be able to pull together disparate expertise to manage the large variety of hazards that may occur. The concept of value to the organization is an important underpinning for ERM. The strategies, plans, and interventions are prioritized based on the value that will be returned to the organization.

RISK MANAGEMENT PROCESS

Traditionally, the risk management process has defined the approach to problem solving and consists of five steps that are similar in other disciplines, such as quality improvement or nursing.[63] This process is a method for organizing the risk-related activities so as to ensure the best solutions are utilized. Knowledge of risk financing techniques is helpful to fully understand the concepts and alternatives. For example, selecting insurance as an option to cover a specified exposure requires an understanding of what insurance is and when it is appropriate. Similarly, an understanding of self-insured retention is important when commercial coverage may not be available for certain exposures.

The five-step risk management works like this:

1. Identify and analyze the exposures to loss.
2. Examine the feasibility of alternative techniques—for example, risk control to stop losses, risk financing to pay for losses.
3. Select the apparent best technique(s).
4. Implement the chosen technique(s).
5. Monitor and improve the risk management program.

In the last step, the program is evaluated as the particular operation, assumptions, and interventions are reanalyzed. Subsequent improvement of the process can follow this evaluation.

This same process is used within an ERM framework to identify the risks or exposures and to set priorities based on their relative importance or value to the organization, to determine which individuals or groups will manage and monitor these risks, and to plan how change will be managed over time.

QUALITY MANAGEMENT

"As a systems approach to preventing malpractice claims, organized risk management identifies, analyzes, and treats risks which quality assessment works to eliminate."[64] Historically, risk management and quality management were seen as separate disciplines with separate objectives. Today, a more integrated approach is seen as vital to the organization, shifting away from individual blame and accountability and toward a view that includes the concept of continuous improvement in healthcare. Solely blaming individuals for medical error misses the point and almost guarantees that mistakes will be repeated[65] (see **Box 8-5**).[66]

Box 8-5   Nursing "Error Equation"

In a series of articles beginning with one titled "Nursing Mistakes Kill, Injure Thousands: Cost-Cutting Exacts Toll on Patients, Hospital Staffs," Michael Berens of the *Chicago Tribune* made national headlines. This often-sensational series established a balance between the good and the less-than-good in nursing practice. Most importantly, inadequate staffing and insufficient training were singled out as important determinants in the "error equation." The hospital's cost-cutting strategies targeted its greatest expense—that of nursing. According to Berens, blaming individual practitioners would never have solved the problems in these hospitals. Rather, the fundamentals systems responsible for hiring, training, and retaining qualified nurses needed to be fixed.[66]

In the past, The Joint Commission defined quality assessment (QA) as a "formal, systematic program by which care rendered to patients is measured against established criteria."[67] The concept of QA has broadened considerably to encompass a management process for monitoring and evaluating quality issues, followed by changes in the healthcare system. This process has become known as quality management (QM). Ongoing monitoring of systems is necessary to ensure that problems are identified early and appropriate intervention is initiated. Inspection helps ensure improved quality and establishes thresholds for acceptability within a process. Under specific circumstances, oversight and disciplinary measures are necessary. There must be a mechanism for identifying dishonest or poorly performing practitioners. Sanctions or limitations in privileges may be necessary. Standards of care cannot be left to chance when a patient's safety is at stake. If health care is to improve beyond these artificial thresholds that discourage peak performance, the concept of quality improvement (QI) must be introduced.

After World War II, the modern quality movement began with the work of W. Edwards Deming in Japanese industry.[68] His 85-15 rule states: "When something goes wrong, 85% of the problem is related to systems failures; 15% is the fault of the people involved." This powerful concept rejects the traditional approach to problem solving that aims to identify those at fault and punish them. Although the threat of dismissal or of a poor evaluation can be motivational, the 85-15 rule posits that such interventions may not be the most effective way to solve a problem or to prevent its recurrence.

A better approach, total quality management (TQM), focuses on the system and not on the individual. Stratton urged management not to give employees the impression that they are responsible for the 15%.[69] Management must take responsibility for the entire problem, but employees may have a good idea of how to fix the process or system—the other 85% of the problem. Suggestion boxes have proved that it pays to ask employees. Three working premises about quality emerge:

- Quality is important and can be measured.
- People are a critical part of the solution and not necessarily the problem.
- Change is fundamental and always present, but change can be managed to improve any organization.

Kim discussed implementing TQM in the healthcare industry,[70] while Goonan described applications,[71] with an emphasis on clinical quality management, along with practical advice for establishing a TQM program.

Total quality management is a broad business concept that includes the continuous quality improvement (CQI) process. CQI initiatives occur simultaneously in many areas and are overseen and guided by the TQM process.

Lynn stated that TQM is the process that organizations use to improve their ability to satisfy customer expectations.[72] A key to understanding how TQM works in health care is the recognition of the central importance of the customer. In business, a customer buys services from a vendor and is free to choose to buy—or not to buy. Similarly, patients/customers of healthcare institutions can select services that meet their expectations and reject services that do not. This approach will be the measure of the healthcare organization's success in the future. The following fundamental beliefs form the basis of the TQM approach:[72]

- TQM is a positive strategy for growth and should be integrated into the organization's strategic business plan.
- Top management must be committed to and actively involved in the TQM process.
- TQM is a process, not a program.
- Quality improvement processes must be applied to all levels of the organization.
- Quality improvement benefits everyone, both internal and external audiences.

CHANGE MANAGEMENT: LEARNING FROM INDUSTRY

Toyota Production System

Many healthcare organizations exist in a competitive environment and need to show they are the best at what they do. To improve continuously requires a program that listens to the stakeholders, including patients, their families, clinical staff, nonclinical staff, students, administrators, and board members. Mechanisms must be implemented to tap into the expertise of all these individuals and improve the organization.

Toyota Motors of Japan has developed an impressive program to maintain and improve quality continuously. In this company, the focus is on the idea that anyone can stop production—that is, knowledge is not always in the possession of leaders. Open communication and a structure to manage change that involves everyone are key. Sharing knowledge across the organization about problems and their solutions reduces the chance of problems repeating themselves. A malignant feature of many organizations, including healthcare organizations, is the ever-present, often creative work-arounds that employees use to "work-around" a problem. As long as the work-around exists, the problem is never truly solved.[73]

As an example, Virginia Mason Medical Center in Seattle sent its executives and physician leaders to Toyota Motors in Japan to study the latter company's methods. When they returned, they reorganized many aspects of their system. One that stood out was the formation of rapid improvement teams that tackled processes needing improvement, thereby supporting quick constant change. Virginia Mason's patient safety alert process uses a 24/7 hotline for reporting problems and a "drop and run" commitment from senior leadership to respond to the reports and stop the processes that should not continue, much as can be done on a Toyota production line. Virginia Mason is on the front lines in setting an example for using Toyota Production System methods.[73,74]

In the end, it is the process for managing change that determines how successful your organization will be. Dr. Steven Speer, in his book *Chasing the Rabbit,*[75] has described four stages for process improvement, gleaned from the Toyota and Alcoa models, that will help in the development of a "high-velocity organization," one that outdistances the competition:

- *System design and operation:* The leaders, managers, and staff must understand the design and operation of the organization from the "ground up."
- *Problem solving and improvement:* All stakeholders respond to a crisis or challenge, then use a process called "swarming" to determine causation and contributing factors, and finally devise corrective measures. Swarming means rapidly bringing the individuals and resources together that can most effectively address the specific crisis or challenge. Root-cause analysis has a similar intent.
- *Knowledge sharing:* In this essential step, all members of the organization can learn from the mistakes of others and themselves. The intent is to share the details of the swarming step or the root-cause analysis as well as the improvement plan and any results that are available across all business units and locations,
- *Developing high-velocity skills in others:* This leadership development process at all levels completes Speer's blueprint for change by allowing organizations to reach a level of excellence and carry that capability into the future—the "high velocity" state.

In healthcare organizations, the threat of medical professional liability litigation as well as the demands of confidentiality and the regulatory chessboard make it difficult to share clinical improvement information across the organization following an adverse event. The organization faces real threats if confidentiality protections are lost when certain information is shared. This point presents a major block to organizational improvement (Knowledge Sharing is a key to Spear's/Toyota's third step), making it more difficult to learn from our clinical mistakes, near misses, and medical errors.[75] Healthcare organizations must find a way around this communication block if they are to reach the next level of excellence.

Lean Management System

The processes for improvement developed at Toyota and other corporations have given rise to the concept of Lean. Lean Management focuses on reducing waste and eliminating error in processes so that the work done contributes to the value of the organization and meets the needs of the customer. It begins with process analysis to identify steps within the systems that add value and those that do not. Eliminating or reducing those steps that do not add value is seen as the way to improvement, and is the beginning of Lean operations. Of course, this approach works only if an organizational culture of Lean thinking is developed—a challenge for leadership that begins at the top. All stakeholders should be involved in the redesign process to improve flow and eliminate waste. Modern healthcare organizations have multiple complex interdependent processes that are critical to their operations. Lean redesign involves a significant investment in financial and human capital to accomplish its objectives.[76,77]

Six Sigma, also developed in the industrial setting, takes a somewhat different approach; it focuses on eliminating causes of defects or error and minimizing variability in the manufacturing process. In the healthcare setting, it is used as a performance improvement method and utilizes statistical methods for analysis of success. Its objectives are similar to those of Lean Management Systems.[78]

Lean Management and High Reliability

These methods, which were originally developed in an industrial environment, have proved valuable in a number of healthcare settings. The Joint Commission president, Mark Chassin, has defined the goal in the healthcare quality journey as high reliability, which seeks to maintain patient safety at high levels over time.[79] Collective mindfulness is a key feature of successful organizations. It simply means that everyone at every level within the organization is aware that even small failures in safety can lead to devastating outcomes. Further, it is expected that deficiencies will be eliminated when they are identified and that the culture of the organization will promote safety owing to the realization that failures are possible at any time—a factor that results in enhanced vigilance. Chassin and Loeb suggest three requirements or changes that must be undertaken to reach these levels of reliability:[79]

- *Leadership* is the critical first step. This is a commitment from the very top for a long-term process requiring vision as well as resources. It defines this as a priority for all levels of leadership.
- *Safety culture* is necessary for organizations to avoid error. It means that individuals trust one another to do the right thing, including reporting unsafe practices or conditions without fear of reprisal. It also means that there is trust in the organization to fix those things that have been identified as unsafe.

- *Robust process improvement* includes the change management systems mentioned previously, such as the Toyota Production System and Lean Management, as well as Six Sigma, a quality process improvement methodology developed at Motorola in the 1980s to reduce error that has been used successfully in healthcare settings.

BARRIERS TO QUALITY MANAGEMENT INITIATIVES

The organizational culture of healthcare institutions may create obstacles to implementing patient safety and CQI initiatives.[80] Separation of administrative functions that are usually performed by nonclinicians from the medical functions performed by professional staff makes efforts to involve physicians in CQI more challenging. Physicians tend to focus their attention on patients and not on what they perceive to be administrative responsibilities, although the new generation of physicians seems more willing to take responsibility for the organization of health care. It is imperative for the success of CQI to help physicians understand how the process will benefit their patients. Furthermore, the hierarchical and bureaucratic structure of larger healthcare organizations makes the empowerment of the employees on CQI teams—a fundamental tenet of CQI thinking—even more difficult to achieve in such organizations. The barriers to establishing error-prevention programs in healthcare organizations include perceptions on the part of both staff and management that there is no time to step back from a situation and analyze it or that no one "owns" any of the processes in place. Other barriers include a lack of recognition or rewards for taking

problem-solving initiatives, attitudes of "this is the way it has always been done" or "nothing is ever done," and lack of vision or awareness of the desired end result.

To be successful, clinical improvement programs that involve changes in physicians' practice must involve the physicians who are affected. They need to feel that they are an integral part of the process and to know they have a stake in controlling the future. Training programs specifically for physicians can go a long way toward enlisting their cooperation and ensuring success of performance improvement initiatives.[81]

Another confusing factor for quality improvement participants may be the number of simultaneous programs in progress. A systematic approach with clear goals for each initiative and effective coordination of all projects is essential to avoid uncertainty.[81]

"Hot groups"[82] may allow an organization to bypass resistance to change. Hot groups are those that managers cannot control; individual members are self-motivated and see themselves as moving beyond their own limits. Neatly organized institutions often suffocate the initiative of this kind of group, but these groups are well worth cultivating as quality improvement teams. An entrenched cadre of middle management, resistant to change, may further hinder the quality improvement process.

Reminiscent of hot groups, an interesting approach to problem solving to accomplish organizational culture change called "positive deviance" was recently reported in a study from the Veterans Administration (VA).[83] There are always some individuals or groups in any organization who seem to have uncommon ability and leadership qualities to accomplish change and to reach objectives. The ability to use these positive deviants to accomplish safety objectives holds promise for making breakthroughs in performance. In the VA study, the researchers used positive deviance as a means to alter clinical practice and behaviors to reduce methicillin-resistant *Staphylococcus aureus* (MRSA) infections by making MRSA reduction everyone's responsibility. The program demonstrated a significant reduction in non-ICU MRSA infections over the nearly three-year period of the study.

CONTINUOUS QUALITY/PROCESS IMPROVEMENT

As a management tool, the concepts of continuous quality improvement and process improvement (PI) are an integral part of the thinking of healthcare administrators. CQI directs attention to the fundamental mechanism that drives a process or system being reviewed. Furthermore, CQI focuses on techniques to accomplish positive change by assessing a process that leads to an intervention.[84] In selected hospitals, CQI actions have decreased unnecessary intravenous catheter use,[85] improved preventive services in primary care,[86] decreased hospital costs for patients with chest pain,[87] and improved the timeliness of preoperative radiologic reports.[88] The success of the Keystone Project in reducing central line–associated bloodstream infections and ventilator-associated pneumonias in ICUs in Michigan is an outstanding example of a broad statewide initiative involving dissimilar sites to reach a common objective.[89] The Joint Commission Center for Transforming Healthcare's Hand Hygiene Project also used process improvement techniques to gain better control of hand hygiene (see **Box 8-6**).[90,91]

Box 8-6   TJC Center for Transforming Healthcare: Hand Hygiene Project

TJC Center for Transforming Healthcare, working with a group of eight hospitals, undertook a project to apply process improvement methods to increase compliance with hand hygiene principles. The group process contained the following steps:

1. Agree how to measure hand hygiene
2. Develop a measurement system with proven reliability
3. Determine baseline staff compliance—48% baseline compliance in this study
4. Identify the causes of noncompliance—15 causes identified in this study
5. Isolate each hospital's causes for noncompliance—each hospital had different causes for noncompliance in this study
6. Identify the "process owners" at each hospital who would monitor compliance over time and intervene when performance "deteriorated"

Approximately 16 months later, the hospitals were able to improve hand washing compliance to 81%. TJC has made tools available to its accredited organizations to assist them in similar hand hygiene improvement projects.[90,91]

Birnbaum discussed the use of sentinel events as an important component in managing the quality of care through CQI.[92] A sentinel event is a single occurrence of sufficient concern to trigger a systematic response. Parisi urged implementing a CQI approach to incident reporting as a means to improve healthcare systems and processes.[93] Regardless of the technique employed, evaluating the process after the intervention to further refine or change the strategy begins the cycle again. This cycle should be viewed as a spiral through time, rather than as a static circle. After each subsequent turn, the intervention will never be quite the same.

Quality Improvement Teams

In the improvement process, the quality improvement team (QIT) is the effector of change. Staff members appointed to a team should be the employees who actually do the work within the company or institution. A QIT should be of manageable size, with one member designated as recording secretary to ensure a written record of the group's proceedings. Traditional group dynamics theory suggests that the ideal team has 5 to 7, and generally no more than 10, members. A QIT may need to be somewhat larger to encompass the organization's various areas and disciplines. In addition, the team needs a leader to provide direction and vision for the group. In experienced groups that have developed a cohesive structure, any member can serve as the leader.

A facilitator, who is not a member of the QIT or part of the problem in the organization, acts in a guiding role when the team loses its focus or veers off track.[94] This key role combines the traditional task roles of clarifier, summarizer, and reality tester with the maintenance roles of harmonizer, consensus taker, and compromiser. The facilitator is primarily an observer and is in a unique position to provide feedback to the group regarding its progress or lack of progress. A QIT should meet regularly to carry out the CQI process.

With the prospect of numerous teams simultaneously moving in many directions, central guidance becomes necessary. There is a need to coordinate the QITs, to focus team efforts on strategic priorities, to transfer learning from one set of projects to another, and to focus quality improvement work on the organization's strategic priorities.[80] A steering committee should approve QIT projects and monitor the teams' progress. This committee can help remove obstacles to implementation and change.

CQI Questions

As a process, CQI implies that an organization knows what needs to be improved. If resources are limited, making the correct choice of targets may be unlikely. The following pertinent questions need to be asked:

1. Is there a corporate strategic plan or mission statement that sets the organization's general direction?
2. Which operations are fundamental or critical to the organization?
3. What are the needs of the external (community) and internal (employees, volunteers, attending physicians) customers? What do they expect from the organization?
4. How is the organization spending its money? Where is the money going? Can less be spent?
5. Which existing problems have been identified?
6. From current data, what can be done better and more efficiently?
7. Which activities would benefit from simplification? Which activities seem so complicated that it is obvious there must be a better way?
8. Where can the organization put its resources and expect a reasonable outcome or return, and what will bring value to the organization?

Undoubtedly, more than one problem will be isolated in the group's initial brainstorming session. Deming listed questions contributed by an executive of the Ford Motor Company to help a QIT start the process (see **Box 8-7**).[95]

Box 8-7   Initial QIT Questions[95]

Organizational Structure
- Where do specific departments fit into the total organizational structure?
- Which products and services does the organization provide?
- How does the organization provide these products and services? That is, which processes are used?
- What would happen if the organization (unit, section, department) stopped producing its products and services?

Individual Employees
- Where do you fit into your department? What is your job?
- What do you create or produce? That is, what are the results of your work?
- How do you do this? (Give a general description of what you do.)
- How do you know if you produce good results or poor results? That is, are there standards or criteria of good performance?
- If so, how were these standards established?

Customers
Immediate Customers
- Who directly receives the products or services that are produced? That is, who are the customers?
- How do customers use what is produced?
- What would happen if employees did not do their jobs correctly?
- How do employee efforts affect the organization's customers?
- How does the organization determine that the needs or requirements of its customers are not being met?

Intermediate and Ultimate Customers
- How far beyond the immediate customer can the organization trace the effect of what it does?

Organizational Suppliers
- How is work initiated (for example, assigned from boss, requested by customer, self-initiated)?
- Who supplies materials, information, services, and whatever else is needed to do your job (for example, boss, customer, coworker in the same group, people in other areas)?
- What would happen to employees if suppliers did not do their jobs?
- Do suppliers have performance standards?
- How do the efforts of suppliers affect the organization?
- How do suppliers discover that they are *not* meeting the organization's needs or requirements? Who works with them and fulfills obligations to them?

Those questions provided initial direction in thinking about what the organization's structure is, what the organization does, and where the individual team members fit into the organization, and they are directly applicable to healthcare institutions and agencies.

By focusing on the critical few objectives, rather than on the trivial many, this CQI review ensures that the organization's design for its future and direction is incorporated into the team's planning. Then, the quality improvement team can write its own mission statement to set its direction. Next, the team's goals and objectives must be developed. In particular, the objectives must be specific to the problem, and they must be measurable.[96]

A FOCUS ON THE CUSTOMER IS VITAL

Driven by the needs of the organization's customers, the quality improvement process recognizes the customer as being central to its purpose. Juran created a quality planning road map that was customer driven and designed to meet the needs of the organization.[97] He explained the flow process as follows:

- Identify our customers.
- Determine the needs of those customers.
- Translate those needs into our language.
- Develop product features that can optimally respond to those needs.
- Develop a process that optimally is able to produce the product features.
- Transfer the process to the operating forces.

It is important to know who the customers are, as well as to recognize their relative importance to the operation. Specific operations must be examined in some detail to identify all of the customers. Internal customers belong to the organization, either as employees or through some other relationship, such as volunteers or private contractors (for example, attending physicians). These people help produce the product: health care. External customers, such as the community, do not belong to the organization but use or purchase its goods and services or are affected by the organization in some other way. In health care, the patient is the primary external customer. Juran described customers as belonging to two groups:[97]

- The *vital few,* all of whom are of "great importance," because of the amount they buy (for example, a health maintenance organization) or because of the amount they contribute (for example, a successful surgeon who brings many patients into a hospital)
- The *useful many,* who are a relatively large number of customers, but each of whom is of only "modest importance" to the organization (for example, a patient or a staff nurse)

How does the organization discern a customer's needs? Using a simple technique, customers can be asked about their likes and dislikes either in an interview or through a written questionnaire. Indirectly, an organization can examine the products or services that customers actually use and the relative quantity that they use. In the case of a product, analysis of what is returned or discarded is helpful. Some customers may have needs that have not yet been perceived; these needs may be discovered in the details as the process is subjected to flow analysis. A pilot project can be instituted to meet the unperceived needs. If successful, the pilot program results in the identification of a particular customer need. Juran contended that customers' needs are a "moving target," not static, but requiring continuous evaluation and prioritization over time to ensure that they are met.[97]

Juran referred to the concept of replanning as a means to give direction to the retrospective analysis performed at the conclusion of a project.[97] This "Santayana Review," as Juran labeled it, reinforces positive actions and prevents the repetition of mistakes.

The Patient Was Right!

Our customer in health care, the patient, always knows the answer. As healthcare providers, we simply do not always ask the right questions. To find out why some patients sue their healthcare providers, one study evaluated patient complaints and coded them according to the quality of the physician's communication, humaneness, care and treatment, access and availability, environment, and billing. These data were compared to the number of risk management records, either incidents or lawsuits, that each of the physicians had on file. Not surprisingly, those physicians with the most complaints tended to have more risk management records.[98]

This finding tells us that it is important to systematically collect patients' evaluations of their experiences with individual practitioners. An angry patient is not necessarily responding to negligence when consulting an attorney. The real issue is medical error, for that is what ultimately will drive a lawsuit. We must look to reducing errors, rather than to placating patients.[99] Lawsuits occur one at a time. The unhappy patient is an indicator for improvement, one physician at a time.

QIT Participation

The initial selection of CQI projects that evaluate processes of direct concern to the medical staff may encourage participation. If physicians realize that CQI makes their work more effective and less frustrating, they may become willing participants in the CQI process. In one institution, for example, a CQI team that included physicians significantly decreased the time between ordering and performing diagnostic imaging scans.[100]

Team members must be clear with themselves and with others about why they are interested in the activity of a particular team. To promote individual self-awareness of these factors, the team should discuss the issue of self-interest and bias. In addition, a basic tenet of TQM holds that top management must be committed to the process.[101]

As an example, Ascension Health, a very large multicenter healthcare system, used a clinical excellence team consisting of clinical and operational leaders to oversee its safety program and affinity groups at the individual medical centers to spread the use of the developed interventional "change packages."[102] Another organization, Denver Health, a public, academic health system and Colorado's principal safety-net institution, identified quality and safety leaders to develop broad and shared improvement goals for its performance improvement program. A separate department responsible for "high-quality care" was created and given the resources to accomplish the necessary changes.[103] Strong physician leadership was built into the programs at both healthcare organizations to maximize buy-in from the clinical staff—a necessity for success.

DOING IT RIGHT

Some organizations have already distanced themselves from the competition and are setting an example for others to follow. They have embraced a top-down, bottom-up system for change similar to that employed in the Toyota Production System, Lean, and Six Sigma management and improvement systems. Two examples are Ascension Health and Kaiser Permanente.

Ascension Health

Ascension Health, the third largest healthcare system in the United States, encompasses 67 acute care hospitals in 20 states and approximately 25,000 physicians, most of whom are not employees. The organization made a strategic quality commitment in 2003 to eliminate preventable deaths by July 2008. Eight priorities for action were identified:[102]

- Reduce mortality
- Improve performance on The Joint Commission National Patient Safety Goals
- Prevent adverse drug events
- Avoid birth trauma
- Reduce incidence of pressure ulcers
- Reduce incidence of falls and falls injuries
- Reduce incidence of hospital-acquired infections
- Reduce perioperative complications

Adjusting the Institute of Medicine's reported estimates of preventable patient deaths to fit Ascension Health's experience, the organization set a goal for a reduction in avoidable deaths by 15% per year among patients not admitted for end-of-life care.[102]

A clinical excellence team, which included both clinical and operational leadership representatives, drove the initiative. The goals, strategies, and methods were approved by the board of directors, which received periodic reports on the progress and outcomes. Each hospital was expected to improve performance across all priorities, but one or two hospitals provided the leadership to develop the specific interventions for each priority called a change package. Affinity groups were formed across the system to spread the change packages within the hospitals. As part of the learning collaborative, the individual hospital performance for each priority was shared throughout the system.[102]

The results have been impressive. The company estimates that more than 5,000 patient deaths were prevented in fiscal year 2010 compared to fiscal year 2004. Its rates of neonatal mortality, birth trauma, pressure ulcer prevalence, and ventilator-associated pneumonia were significantly below the national average.[102]

In its ongoing quality journey to high reliability, Ascension Health Plans to shift its focus from the high-risk areas (priorities for action) to serious safety events (causing harm), precursor safety events (deviations reaching the patient but causing no harm), and near misses (potential events that never reach the patient).[102] The goal is to reduce serious safety events by 40% by the year 2014. The emphasis is on creating a teamwork safety culture so mistakes that are inevitable in any system will not harm the patient. The resources required are significant and include training more than 135,000 employees and caregivers.

Kaiser Permanente

Kaiser Permanente (KP) is the largest nonprofit health plan in the United States, with 8.6 million members, 35 member medical centers, and regional medical groups with approximately 15,000 physicians. KP began its quality journey by recognizing that there was considerable variation in quality, safety, efficiency, and service across its medical centers, and by realizing that it needed to measure performance consistently throughout the system. A data dashboard, known as the Big Q, containing eight measures selected in collaboration with the Institute for Healthcare Improvement, was developed in 2005; it brought together and made available the vital few performance measures that helped leaders decide whether improvement occurred over time. This key first step ensured that there was an unmistakable commitment to data transparency and that the process would be data driven.[104]

The organization's next step was to find out who was doing the best job in healthcare quality and how they did it. This benchmarking process identified five outside organizations that set the example for others in specific areas of interest. After studying these organizations, KP was able to design its performance improvement system using best practices from the benchmarked sites.[104]

KP's plan was dependent on participation by everyone from top leadership to the hourly staff workers. To help make this culture change happen, the union contract was negotiated to include performance improvement processes that featured unit-based teams (UBTs) to do the work of improvement and was called the Labor–Management Partnership. Thus everyone in the organization had a stake in quality performance and doing it better than anyone else.[105]

The performance improvement (PI) initiative focused on six core capabilities:[104]

- *Leadership priority setting,* ensuring the leadership team was engaged and working to prioritize strategy to focus on clinical, financial, employee, and patient indicators. Communication was seen as a cascading system from the very top (macro level) to the individual organizations on patient care units (micro level).
- *Systems approach to improvement*, identifying core processes, prioritizing the most important, and managing and monitoring these processes across centers. Interdisciplinary leadership team provided regular oversight.
- *Measurement capability,* which established the outcome metrics, set targets, and shared "scorecards" of the front-line units/departments across the entire organization. Performance was the priority for all centers.
- *Learning organization,* to share, learn, and spread systems and capabilities to drive performance improvement from the top down and from the bottom up.
- *Improvement capability,* which established oversight systems and an improvement

infrastructure and staff. This infrastructure unified the internal methodology for all sites, and designed and delivered the improvement curriculum for staff and physicians.

- *Culture,* which was managed for improvement by teaching staff about the mission and priorities to create a safe place to explore and learn. Operational-level leaders learned more comprehensive skills using a fellowship model. Leaders engaged in "walk-arounds" to understand operational-level priorities.

The KP approach began with a desire to reduce variation across a number of medical centers by monitoring data reflective of performance, then determining the best-in-class organizations outside KP and benchmarking them so as to design a superior quality improvement system. The success of the system was dependent on all staff embracing the quality improvement process, with a commitment from the very top leadership to do what was necessary to accomplish the change.[104]

Ultimately, all improvement happens at the customer or patient interface, the front line. The individuals at this interface can better understand the improvement process and initiatives by being engaged as participants and feeling ownership of the improvement process. The resources devoted to this initiative, including a dedicated PI staff, were considerable at KP. In a follow-up report, however, the company indicated that 22 medical centers achieved a 61% improvement over baseline in selected capabilities. KP estimated that for every $1 invested, it realized a return of $2.36. This return on investment is significant and shows the value of the thoughtful planning, implementation, and monitoring of KP's PI system.[106]

CQI AND LABOR RELATIONS

Two decisions by the National Labor Relations Board (NLRB) raise the possibility that TQM/CQI employee management teams may violate the National Labor Relations Act (NLRA) of 1935. Such a violation would occur if the TQM/CQI teams were judged to be labor organizations dominated by the employer.[107] In reality, most employee participation programs, including QITs, are problematic under the criteria set forth in the NLRA. A two-part test would have to be satisfied in any complaint of unfair labor practice: (1) The employer–employee group would have to be consistent with the definition of a labor organization and (2) it would have to be shown to be unlawfully dominated by the employer. To be considered a labor organization, the group would have to meet *all* three of the following conditions:[107] (1) Employees participate; (2) in part, the organization exists for the purposes of dealing with management; and (3) dealings concern conditions of work, grievances, labor disputes, wages, rate of pay, or hours of employment. Conditions of work can be broadly defined and would include work-related issues with which a CQI team might be concerned.

If the group is identified as a labor organization, the second part of the test is invoked: Is the group dominated by the employer? Unlawful domination exists if only one of the following conditions is met:[107] (1) An employer interferes with the labor organization's formation; (2) an employer interferes with the labor organization's administration; or (3) an employer provides the labor organization with financial and other support.

Depending on interpretation, almost any group could be considered to be in violation of any one of these three conditions. Three specific characteristics of CQI programs appear to make

them allowable.[107] First, information sharing with management is the purpose of the group. Second, employees, not management, retain the right to make decisions, by majority rule, to implement proposals. Management can participate in the decision but not control it; management cannot administer the CQI team. Third, the collective bargaining process offers an alternative solution for establishing "legal" CQI teams.

Risk managers should insist that the structure, mission, and objectives of CQI teams be reviewed and deemed allowable under the NLRA. Care must be taken to avoid even the appearance of management interference in the group process of these teams. In the early planning stages, the structure, goals, and objectives should be developed in partnership with the employees who will do the work.[108] Team members must be volunteers, not acting on behalf of other employees, and must not address employee discontent. Areas such as those involving safety and health must be approached with caution to avoid conflict with the NLRA.

Congress attempted to broaden the potential for the use of quality improvement teams in 1996, but the legislation did not survive a presidential veto. In a 2001 case involving Crown Cork and Seal, the NLRB expanded the role of teams to include employee management. The teams in question made up a management system that went beyond the bounds of traditional team management, addressing issues of plant safety, as well as issues of employee discipline, advancement, and pay. Importantly, the teams did not make proposals that management responded to with acceptance or rejection. Rather, these teams were empowered to make changes themselves. Management was represented on the teams, but did not control them or have the final decision authority.[109]

A very interesting approach to labor relations and teams, using the collective bargaining process, was undertaken at Kaiser Permanente through negotiation of its year 2005 labor agreements and inclusion within the contracts of unit-based teams. These teams represent a labor–management partnership for performance improvement throughout the KP system. The basics for proposing and participation on team projects is available to all on the LMPartnership.org website.[110] Managing performance of teams utilizes an online UBT Tracking Tool included in the 2010 National Agreement for labor (see **Box 8-8**).[111]

Box 8-8   Kaiser Permanente, Unit-Based Teams: Tracking Performance

The online education and management tools for Kaiser Permanente's UBTs are comprehensive and designed to assist team members, leaders, and sponsors to reach the objectives established for a particular team. To help teams become high performing, the 2010 National Agreement with labor requires that UBT rankings be entered into a national tracker database (UBT Tracker). This permits underachieving teams to be identified and assisted to meet goals and high-performing teams to be rewarded. Teams can view the performance of other teams to see how they compare. Teams are assessed using a five-point grading scale. Successful projects can be shared, as best practices, for others to study and use in improving their own initiatives.[111]

EFFECTIVENESS OF RISK MANAGEMENT

Risk managers may have to demonstrate the value of the services they provide.[100] Does a risk management program in health care have value? Assuming such merit exists, which programs are the most valuable? It is vital to illustrate that a risk management program materially contributes to an institution's survival and to the quality of care delivered. A study in Maryland hospitals demonstrated significantly better claims experiences in hospitals with certain risk management policies or activities.[112] In this study, one pivotal activity for the risk manager focused on regular formal education programs to teach physicians and nurses about risk management and the role of the risk manager. A key to success involved the handling of information and interventions following an adverse event. Information must get to the upper-level administration and, most importantly, to the clinical chief or chiefs as quickly as possible. Although controversial at the time, the Maryland study supported the beneficial influence of a policy to inform affected patients and families of adverse events. Investigators identified "highly productive" areas for quality review and risk management oversight in ambulatory care that included hospital discharge diagnosis, procedure codes, length of stay, and cancer staging.[113]

There is general agreement that it is important for details of clinical incidents to be shared with clinicians throughout the organization to prevent recurrence of adverse events.[72] Unfortunately, this is not always so easy when there is a companion goal to prevent litigation. Managing adverse events requires extensive analysis and planning to arrive at the best and fairest solution for all involved. Any injuries must be managed appropriately and accurate information given to the patient. Sharing knowledge about these events across the organization carries some risk and requires a planned approach as well as buy-in from all levels of leadership. Some factors relate to the potential for litigation and regulations related to the confidentiality of information, which is dependent on the specific state or jurisdiction. It is a good idea to include legal representation when setting up policies and procedures for sharing information about adverse events and open claims.

The definitive research to demonstrate conclusively that risk management makes a difference has yet to be undertaken. Given the diffuse nature of the tasks and responsibilities of risk management, as well as the lengthy tail introduced by statutes of limitation, it would be enormously expensive to design and implement a controlled study that would be relevant to this issue. More importantly, the Maryland study[112] used baseline data from a time period when risk management interventions were not so widely accepted. Even the once-controversial idea of informing patients of adverse events is now necessary if The Joint Commission accreditation or Medicare participation is expected.

The well-designed risk management program will, at the least, have the systems and the data necessary to show the history and trends in claims and adverse events that could be utilized as indicators for planned interventions. The fundamental reason why risk management is necessary is that adverse events and claims do happen.

PROGRAM EVALUATION: ISSUES AND CONSIDERATIONS

Three questions should be asked when developing a program to evaluate risk management:

- What are the areas of responsibility or functions defined for risk management within the organization?
- Which information or data are collected and available within each of these areas of responsibility or functions?
- Can this information or data be categorized and analyzed systematically to derive measures of effectiveness over time for each responsibility or function?

The evaluation process must be data driven to be consistent but the quality of the data is key to its validity and reliability. Specifically, the process must actually measure what it is defined to measure (validity) and give similar results from different users over time (reliability).

The enterprise risk management process (ERMP) is the ideal mechanism to establish the areas of interest and responsibility for the program. It can sort through the interlocking interests of the different areas and help determine data sources that are most helpful. Priority should be given to those areas or dimensions that have the highest exposure for loss or present an opportunity to increase value to the organization.

A simple flow process chart can be used to keep track of the different dimensions or measures that are anticipated for the risk management program. One example can be found on the website for the American Society for Healthcare Risk Management.[114] Risk management activities are listed along with the relevant process measures, outcome measures, and action plans. Process measures assess whether these activities are being carried out as intended. Outcome measures assess whether the program is having the impact it was designed to have. All such measures should be quantifiable, be derived from experience, describe what should happen rather than what is happening now, and be trackable. When using this self-assessment process, the risk manager first identifies the structural components of the risk management program and the necessary activities for achieving those components. A quantifiable process measure or indicator measure is then identified for each activity. In this way, a risk manager can determine whether the activity was carried out as planned. Finally, an outcome measure is formulated for the activity. This goal statement includes a quantifiable measure of the outcome of the activity if it is successful. An example flow process chart for a claims management structural component might include the following elements:[114]

- *Activity:* Set up a written claims management policy that outlines the institution's claims management process.
- *Process measure:* Senior management develops the policy and defines expectations for claim investigation and processing; this measure is reviewed at least annually.
- *Outcome measure:* Seventy-five percent or more of the claims are investigated within 24 hours of the report of the incident.
- *Review and evaluation:* Review the outcome data over time and evaluate both individual and program performance. Revise the program or expectation as needed.

The timeliness of investigation of claims can be monitored and tracked over time to ensure compliance with the policy. If the actual outcome measure does not comply with the policy statement, then the outcome being measured needs to be managed or the policy needs revision, with a new standard being established.

A similar process can be used to keep track of the different areas of emphasis in the department. For example, the number of procedures lacking appropriate informed consent should be

zero, but a chart audit may prove that this target is not being met. In the case of a short-term or periodic chart audit for the Risk Management Committee or similar body, the measures are defined and the evaluation is used to report back to the committee. Patient satisfaction measures and employee readiness for patient safety programs are other types of data sources that can be translated into activities for ongoing measures of effectiveness.

Some key data elements will be of interest for monitoring effectiveness of programs on a broader level. The experience of Kaiser Permanente in setting up its Big Q dashboard has already been mentioned.[104] Patient mortality data, claims payment data, adverse outcome occurrence information, near-miss information, malpractice and related insurance premiums, and self-insured retention limit erosion are some examples of data points that can be used for a dashboard that will draw attention to the salient issues. The dashboard is designed to give a quick summary for leadership and policy makers. Its base data must be accurate without question.

Standards as Guides

Standards are defined by the organization. It is the responsibility of each institution to determine its standards. A definition of standards begins with the corporate mission statement or a similar declaration of organizational goals or strategic objectives. To have meaning, standards must accurately reflect the company's goals. A standard must be reasonable, capable of being achieved, and measurable. In health care, specific standards may be imposed by government regulatory requirements. For example, anti-dumping provisions of the federal Consolidated Omnibus Budget Reconciliation Act (COBRA) necessitate establishing a standard and monitoring the disposition of patients arriving at the emergency department. Specific standards of clinical care as well as a community standard for care must also be considered.

Outcome measures use a standard or norm to arrive at a risk-adjusted expected value for a patient outcome.[115] This expected value is compared to actual patient outcomes to determine whether a problem exists. Outcome measurement ensures that quality has been maintained or indicates to what degree quality has been compromised. In this way, problems are identified and may be referred to quality improvement for a process and systems review. The first step is to review and confirm the accuracy of the data documenting the substandard condition. There is a tendency to assume that data must be correct because the measurements are quantitative, but, in fact, there may be problems with the measurements. The Joint Commission issued a call for collaboration in performance measurement, which it defined as "an interrelated set of process and outcome measures that, when used together, provide a meaningful performance profile of the organization to which the measures are applied."[116]

There is some concern that the quality of healthcare performance measurement may show enough variation to question its reliability. Data that are used to measure quality may not be appropriate in a particular circumstance, which in turn diminishes the value of conclusions that may be reached when using these measures. The science of measuring quality needs improvement to reduce variability and inconsistency.[117] The lesson here: Choose your measures thoughtfully.

Standards may be described either as results standards, which refer to what is accomplished, or as activity standards, which refer to the means by which something is accomplished. Outcome measures, such as patient mortality or survival, are results standards. An activity standard could specify the number of staff education sessions on basic or advanced cardiac life support for different levels of professional staff. Carroll classified more than 140 outcome indicators of patient care into 15 clinical areas for quality evaluation review.[118]

The Agency for Healthcare Research and Quality has developed quality indicators (QIs) for a broad array of conditions and makes recommendations about the data elements to collect. These "measures of health care quality make use of readily available hospital inpatient administrative data. The QIs can be used to highlight potential quality concerns, identify areas that need further study and investigation, and track changes over time."[119] The following QIs are available via free software from AHRQ and can help to identify quality-of-care events for further review:

- Prevention
- Inpatient
- Patient safety
- Pediatric

Readily available inpatient data can be used with the software. Specific information is available at the AHRQ website.[119]

Evaluation

Evaluation is the process that determines to what degree the standard was or was not met. Evaluations may be done on a regular basis, as part of the ongoing monitoring of a process, or in response to a problem within a process. In all cases, standards are assessed for compliance, and their reasonableness is reviewed. If a standard is not being met, the fault may lie with the standard rather than with individual perfor-mance. Systems problems may prevent a rea-sonable standard from being achieved. For example, even if the standard specifies that single-cut frozen section results will be avail-able to the surgeon in the operating room within a specified time period, specimen transport problems and clerical delays may prevent the surgical team from meeting that standard.

Checklists

Checklists are helpful in evaluating programs because risk managers need assurance that they have incorporated all possibilities into their risk management efforts, such as compliance with elements of the Universal Protocol to reduce the incidence of wrong-site, wrong-patient, wrong-procedure surgeries. This kind of evaluation can give the risk manager valuable and comprehen-sive feedback about specific clinical programs and allow him or her to determine whether the programs are meeting standards. Although part of the evaluation process is qualitative, the assessment may point out areas in which quanti-tative methods for monitoring are appropriate. A checklist is not a complete description, but rather identifies many components of the process.[120]

The World Health Organization's Surgical Checklist is an excellent example. It divides sur-gery into three phases: before anesthesia, before incision, and before the patient leaves the oper-ating room. Each phase requires a specific checklist to ensure that all elements of the pro-tocol have been accomplished. These items should become part of the medical record and be subject to periodic audit.[121]

Maintaining security of the records in a medical professional liability claim requires written policies and procedures, as well as methods to identify that the procedures were followed. When securing records, it is helpful to use a checklist and include the medical record as well as billing records, fetal monitoring strips, X-rays and radiology reports, photos, films, pathology slides, and any other items that may be relevant to a case (see **Box 8-9**).[122]

In the case of electronic medical records and imaging studies, it is important to understand the

---

Box 8-9   Checklist for Security of Evidence[122]

- Policy and procedure for receipt of a lawsuit include identification of persons responsible for notifying the appropriate departments to secure evidence.
- Maintain a contact list of individuals, by department, responsible for security (list to be maintained by the risk manager).
- A request form for the security of items is filled out and sent to the appropriate department.
- A procedure is in place to validate that the security form was received by the particular department and that the item was secured. A multipart form or an email system that demands return of a confirmation can be used.
- A procedure is in place to ensure that secured items are returned to the unsecured file or storage location as cases are closed.
- Each department with a security file must keep a log of secured items, which should be inventoried at least annually.
- The risk management security file should include a copy of the security forms sent to the individual departments.
- Perform a periodic audit of clinical departmental security procedures to determine their effectiveness (e.g., number of steps in the procedure, number of people responsible for the process, and adequacy of storage, retrieval, and return to storage).
- Procedures are relevant to the evidence item (e.g., the new electronic fetal monitoring and archiving system changes the process of managing fetal monitoring records).

many elements that may constitute these evidence sources. A checklist to document that these components were intact and reviewed may be an important part of the legal file.[123] If a legal "hold" is placed on a record to ensure its integrity, it is important to use a checklist to be certain all components have been included.[124] Electronic records may also contain information that was available to the provider but is not part of the patient record, such as clinical decision support, guidelines, reminders, and clinical alerts. While this information may not be released as part of the parent's record, it may become critical in a professional liability lawsuit.[125] In addition, electronic communication among clinicians could surface later in response to requests for information from the plaintiff[125] as well as audit trails of the various medical record-keeping activities. The risk manager must know the components and attributes of the records systems for the organization and be prepared to define what constitutes the patient's record.

In addition to serving as a means of internal process control, checklists can be used to encourage process involvement by a broader array of responsible individuals within the organization. Effective QI and patient safety programs require that senior leadership is closely involved with key programs. The Johns Hopkins hospital developed checklists for its executives[126] and board members[127] to document its review of the initiative for prevention of central line–associated bloodstream infections. The checklists ensure that important details are included in the review and help these senior leaders ask the right questions to encourage a successful outcome. The documents provide necessary focus on what is reported back to leadership to maintain their understanding of the success of the initiative and to create a buy-in for all results.

TOOLS FOR EVALUATION: ROOT-CAUSE ANALYSIS AND FAILURE MODE, EFFECT, AND CRITICALITY ANALYSIS

Through TJC mandates, tools have become available for the analysis and management of adverse events, including tools for root-cause analysis. The central importance of RCA for evaluation of adverse events cannot be overemphasized. Accurate information about the causes of serious events is critical for use in prevention programs. The RCA not only identifies the direct causes, such as user errors, but also brings to light the indirect causes or latent errors. As an example, TJC specifies factors that must be addressed in an RCA for a medication error, and these factors go far beyond the error of omission or commission that directly caused the mistake, to include staffing levels, orientation and training, credentialing, supervision, and physical environment, among others.[128]

One study applied RCA to healthcare errors over a 29-month period. The root causes most commonly identified were related to patient census, patient acuity, and staffing issues, primarily in nursing. Subsequent interventions focused on early response to the census/acuity/staffing issues as well as the use of constraining functions, such as removal of concentrated potassium solutions from patient care areas.[129]

The conduct of RCA has become routine in most healthcare settings, leading to a sometimes pro-forma completion process that can miss the complexity of the causes of error in a specific practice setting. The desire to find the one true root cause sometimes results in an incomplete solution.[130] The vast majority of RCA efforts specify reeducation or training as the appropriate corrective intervention. The cost of retraining and rewriting procedures as recommended by RCA can be significant,[131] but may result in little being accomplished if the larger systems problems are ignored. There is little evidence to support the position that RCA has dramatically reduced the likelihood of adverse event reoccurrence despite the fact that such analyses have been used extensively for many years. That said, RCA remains the best method, when conducted appropriately, for reviewing the causes of error.[130]

The Joint Commission now requires that healthcare organizations select one high-risk process each year and subject it, prospectively, to failure mode, effect, and criticality analysis (FMECA). The FMECA process examines the steps in the system that failed and led to the adverse outcome. Flowcharts are used, and errors at each step are rated according to their criticality or influence on the final event. Finally, solutions and redesign are planned and implemented. RCA is conducted at those steps in the process where failure is critical to the outcome.[132,133] TJC provides guidance and training on conducting RCA and FMEA; information is available on its website.[134,135] A report of root causes by event type for sentinel events is also available on the TJC website and contains valuable information about event root causes for patient safety professionals.[136]

Excellent training materials for individuals who will conduct and manage RCA and FMEA are available from the Veterans Administration as well. The fact that their development was paid for with taxpayer dollars ensures they are available without charge to all.[137,138]

EXTERNAL EVALUATION

On occasion, the risk management program will be evaluated by organizations outside the healthcare institution. These external evaluators could include The Joint Commission, insurance companies, professional organizations, government entities, and legal groups.

The Joint Commission Evaluation

As part of its accrediting procedure, TJC may examine the risk management program. TJC requires the organization to collect data about risk management activities. Risk managers need a methodology for data collection, data analysis, and data transmittal to other departments and committees. Quality, risk, and safety groups are expected to share information, with the ultimate goal being improving quality and patient safety. The Leadership Standards developed by TJC specifically address the need to share risk management activity and performance improvement initiatives directly related to these activities with the hospital's governing body and medical leadership. Aggregate data and information from risk management and these other areas must be applied to organization-wide performance improvement activities.[139]

The Joint Commission conducts unannounced visits and emphasizes the role of the National Patient Safety Goals (NPSGs) and the Core Measures to improve patient care and safety.[140] Your plan for performance improvement and risk management should include these vital elements. The care of hospitalized patients is often complex because of the severity of their illnesses and comorbid conditions, which may adversely affect mortality statistics unpredictably. Moreover, patient comprehension at discharge may not be complete even though all education activities were completed, so the rehospitalization rate may be affected. Patient mortality and rehospitalization rates are important measures of quality and should be used knowledgeably and appropriately. Despite some problems with use and evaluation of these patient safety goals and core measures, they seem to provide significant benefit for the patients.

Evaluation By Insurers/ Underwriters

The primary role of the insurance company underwriter is to act as a gatekeeper.[141] In this role, the underwriter has the greatest control over who will be given access to the protection offered by his or her insurance company.

Underwriters are concerned about credentialing, peer review, screening systems, compliance with TJC standards, pertinent regulations, and related internal evaluation mechanisms. An underwriter can evaluate the soundness of a risk management program by considering the following vital program elements:[142]

- *Commitment:* senior management involvement
- *Centralization and coordination:* a designated individual responsible for the program
- *Committee structure:* issues identified, analyzed, resolved, and monitored
- *Quality management integration:* QM and RM mutually supporting and reinforcing; mechanisms in place to share information
- *Regulatory compliance:* Medicare conditions of participation, HAC incidence, state incident reporting experience if applicable
- *The Joint Commission:* sentinel event reporting, compliance with Core Measures and NPSGs
- *Medical staff involvement:* active physician involvement
- *Informed consent:* effective in reducing claim frequency

- *Patient representation system:* handling patient complaints
- *Disposition management/discharge planning:* posthospital needs addressed (case management)
- *Incident/accident reporting:* essentially a reporting system but also very important to identify trends and to respond to adverse trends
- *Claims management:* written policy of procedures to follow after a serious incident occurs or an actual claim is filed
- *Biomedical services and medical devices:* test equipment prior to use; evaluate and remove defective equipment from service
- *Contract review:* risk manager involved in reviewing contracts
- *Educational programs:* provide education concerning risk management issues

If the healthcare institution is self-insured, a similar evaluation process can help protect the assets of the self-insured trust fund, captive insurance company, or alternate risk financing mechanism.

Claims experience is one of the most critical elements an underwriter will evaluate.[142] Underwriters want to review a minimum of five to seven years of claims experience, as well as the entire period for which coverage of prior acts is sought. Prior acts coverage insures the institution against events that occurred before the inception date of the policy. At a minimum, the risk manager should have the following information on *every* open and closed claim:[141]

- Date of loss
- Closing date
- Evaluation of the allegations
- Date of notice
- Nature of the injury

- Who was involved—insurance coverage
- Reserve evaluation or final disposition

Complicating the underwriting review process, over time, are the unpredictable changes that will take place in the legal environment, the cost of injury, expectations for patient care, and new tort opportunities. The risk manager must be well prepared for the underwriting visit each time it occurs.[143]

Benchmarking Comparisons

Benchmarking is a process whereby one organization's operation is compared to that of another, usually an organization that happens to do something better. A limited internal type of benchmarking can compare different units of the same organization to discover the "best" practices. There is no assurance, however, that any particular unit will be doing any better than any other unit. To gain the most from benchmarking, it is advisable to go outside the organization to find the best within the industry, or even outside the industry to find others that excel in similar processes.[144]

Benchmarking is a thoughtful, introspective process that goes beyond simply touring another organization. First, risk managers must know their own organizations and have an idea of what they want to accomplish. Next, organizations that are appropriate for comparison need to be identified, assessed, and compared regarding their operations. Finally, risk managers must formulate a plan to bring their operations closer to the best practices of the other organization. Evaluation and replanning must follow the implementation of any changes in the organization. In total, is not a process to be undertaken without a firm commitment in resources by upper-level management.

In health care, such external benchmarking may be difficult because organizations that are geographically close may see themselves as competitors. Internal benchmarking projects would be more likely in this setting. In one example from the litigation process,[145] individual defendants filled out questionnaires following their depositions. The questionnaires addressed the adequacy of preparation of these defendants, as well as who was most helpful at putting the individual at ease. The questionnaire also asked for suggestions on improving the process. Over time, a standard for benchmarking could be expected to develop. Another effort, involving a consortium of healthcare organizations, compared claims to organizational demographic data.[146] This comparison helped the individual organizations evaluate their claims management methods and identify areas for improvement.

Some benchmarking data sources are available commercially or through government programs. These types of data require skill in managing them to provide useful information to an organization. AHRQ offers data to the public in a number of different areas, including healthcare quality and cost.[147]

The national insurer, AON, offers a comprehensive annual report on claims and medical malpractice trends throughout the United States known as the Hospital Professional Liability and Physician Liability Benchmark Analysis.[148] This information can be used to compare your organization with national and regional developments in professional liability exposure. With this type of report, however, it is important to ask for detail about its information base. For example, not all states and jurisdictions are represented in the database. Some high-risk insurance markets may be reluctant to share information, especially when self-insured programs predominate in a region rather than commercial insurance. Although, participation in the AON project is voluntary, the resulting analysis presents useful benchmarking information for those areas covered by the report.

Kaiser Permanente used a benchmarking process to compare features from five best-in-class organizations when evaluating areas of interest for its quality improvement program. No single organization had all features of interest to KP but, using site visits and interviews, the company was able to evaluate each organization in six high-performance areas:[149]

- Leadership priority setting
- Systems approach to improvement
- Measurement capability
- Learning organization
- Improvement capacity
- Culture

KP reviewed the results and adapted the best practices to help design the organization's own performance improvement system

PRACTICE GUIDELINES

Practice guidelines, if adopted, can set a standard of care to which the practitioner will be held. These guidelines require continuous monitoring and/or evaluation to ensure that the requirements are appropriate for the clinical area, are being used properly, and are reasonable. Because such guidelines can change over time, they must be kept up-to-date. Risk managers must be aware of departures from the guidelines because of the potential liability risk exposure associated with these events. As such, practice guidelines can potentially reduce the number of medical professional liability cases

and lower the costs of settling those claims.[150] However, practice guidelines may cut in both directions. One study reviewed claims from two medical professional liability insurers and found that 17 of 259 claims used practice guidelines but that in 12 (71%) of these cases, the physician was implicated in a charge of medical "malpractice."[151]

When guidelines are implemented, they should first undergo a multidisciplinary review by the interested clinical departments, risk management team, and in-house counsel. It should be assumed that the plaintiff's counsel will review any guideline in use for that party's own purposes. Following the institution of standards for minimal monitoring during anesthesia for example, there was a decrease in anesthesia-related injuries.[150] As intended, that practice guideline appeared to lower liability exposure and resulted in reduced medical professional liability insurance premiums for anesthesiologists. The importance of using evidence-based medicine to improve health care is accepted today but review by the medical staff is critical for adoption of any new methods or guidelines.

Courts may not view guidelines formulated at the local, rather than the national, level as authoritative; thus they may be inadmissible as evidence. The court and the state, where applicable, will make this decision.[151,152]

BEST PRACTICES AND COMPREHENSIVE SOLUTIONS

Hospitals and other healthcare organizations may put together a working consensus on clinical practice for particular areas of interest. These so-called consensus best practices incorporate recognized recommendations and guidance for clinicians to use in caring for particular patient groups and disease or health conditions. Consensus best practices synthesize the recommendations of practice groups, professional societies, and government agencies such as AHRQ, and incorporate the local expectations and standards of practice to provide a roadmap for care that can be used by all clinicians in the organization. They provide a best-of-care model with an expectation for professional practice. Departures from any best practice or other standard requires written justification in the patient record indicating the reason for the departure.

PROFESSIONAL LIABILITY CLAIMS DATA _____

Without access to a voluminous database, it may be impossible to derive statistically significant conclusions from an analysis of professional liability claims data. Nevertheless, the evaluation of professional liability claims is critical. Merely the fact that a physician has a claim may mean that more claims are forthcoming[22] or that the physician's communication style is impersonal or abrupt[21] and needs an overhaul. A physician's prior claim history could reveal the existence of complaints filed with the state licensing board.[153] More importantly, professional liability claims data can be used to identify problem-prone clinical processes and suggest interventions to reduce negligence.[154]

It is important to track many different issues related to a claim. To do so, risk managers should have some form of classification scheme for the risk management issues in claims. The hallmark of a specific risk management issue is that it answers the key question: Why would we pay money on this case? Another approach is to look at issues as problems in the medical care that relate to the negative occurrence or may

adversely affect the defense of the case.[154] Risk management issues transcend the clinical fact pattern and bring together the diverse problems that we would like to prevent from reoccurring. No patient was ever harmed directly by an altered medical record, but many cases have suffered at time of trial because information in the record was changed or because portions of the record or the entire record had disappeared.[155]

Reliable claims data depend on the accuracy and completeness of the information about the claim. Nowhere is this more important than in the initial investigation. These investigations establish the fact pattern as well as the stated positions and opinions of the involved parties, witnesses, and others who have knowledge of the events. This information is best collected as soon after the incident as possible. Having reliable information, early on, permits the efficient management of the claim to the advantage of the insureds. In addition, the important risk management problems can be categorized and coded to support a risk management database. Such a data store will facilitate the identification of patterns of risk and exposure as well as clinical practice safety problems requiring intervention.

The organized and systematic approach to claims investigation is a discipline worth acquiring for any risk manager. Obtaining relevant information through document review and interview[156–159] of those involved, as well as the ability to distill this information into comprehensive, well-organized, and readable written reports[160] for internal use and for legal counsel, are skills having great value.

Targeting individual practitioners for education or sanctions based on their malpractice claims histories is problematic from a medical perspective.[161] However, the malpractice insurer may cancel a physician's insurance because of underwriting considerations, on the grounds that someone with numerous claims will be too costly for the professional liability program. At the very least, the risk manager needs to evaluate the individual claims to make sure a practitioner is not a danger to patients. For issues other than standards of care, a more thorough review is recommended. If physicians conduct the evaluation, the reviewer's knowledge of the severity of the outcome to the patient could negatively influence his or her judgment regarding the appropriateness of care.[162] It may be advisable to withhold patient outcome information from the reviewers until the quality review process is complete.

In addition to the evaluation of individual claims and discussions with the clinical director, trend data for all malpractice claims should be examined. This kind of information tracks individuals, specialties, departments, frequencies, severity of injuries, and the nature of claims. At this time, loss prevention issues can be identified. When relevant issues are involved, risk managers may direct their efforts toward education and training.

COST OF RISK

One data source that is directly related to risk management programs is the cost of risk (COR). The costs of the various risk management activities and responsibilities are estimated to determine the COR, which is then used to manage operations and monitor necessary changes identified through the ERM process. Risk can be classified into categories as follows:[163]

- *Hazard risks* are those that are generally insurable, such as property damage, directors and officers' liability, medical professional liability, and others.

- *Operational risks* are generally not insurable but present a cost to the organization, such as employee turnover, inventory management, systems processes and the cost of defensive medicine, to name a few.
- *Financial risks* affect the financial performance of an organization, such as reimbursement for care, cost of goods and services, cost of capital, and investment outcomes.
- *Strategic risks* are difficult to measure but include market share, reputation of the medical center, innovative features and programs, academic affiliation, and others.

Obviously these areas interact to influence each other. A major medical misadventure that results in negative publicity may affect the organization's ability to attract patients, to recruit new clinical staff, and to retain the staff it has. Insurance premiums could be affected as well, with an increased cost for defensive medicine being noted as well. An overall increase in the COR may occur during the period but if the program monitors these cost the positive effect of subsequent interventions can then be documented. The interest of risk management transcends the traditional role of managing liability and insurance, although those two activities are still of paramount importance for the program.

HIGH-EXPOSURE ISSUES IN HEALTH CARE
Clinical Activities

High-risk clinical activities have accumulated a history of financial loss much greater than that observed in other areas. The clinical services of obstetrics, surgery, anesthesia, and the emergency department commonly appear associated with greater severity on loss runs. Diagnostic services, such as radiology, also require close monitoring by risk management. During a clinical consultation, communication between physicians demands ongoing scrutiny.[164] Frequently, lawsuits mention the lack of informed consent. Other areas that need ongoing evaluation by risk managers include advance directives, do not resuscitate (DNR) orders, the withholding of treatment, credentialing, confidentiality and disclosure of adverse outcomes.

Monitoring

From a liability viewpoint, the monitoring of high-risk issues by risk management is a vital activity. Information on trends is particularly important for clinical areas because quality of patient care may be an issue. Procedures for monitoring whether informed consent has been obtained properly are necessary. Risk managers can track these issues through the claims and incident reporting processes. Auditing procedures also may help determine the frequency of lapses.

Medical Records

Medical records may be requested by a host of people, such as parties to lawsuits, state regulators, peer review organizations, and law enforcement agencies—and they may prove troublesome. These individuals and organizations may not be aware of, or may choose to ignore, the healthcare organizations obligation to maintain the confidentiality of the medical records.[165] Risk managers need procedures for monitoring medical record requests with respect to appropriateness and liability exposure. Two instances that should trigger risk management evaluation are requests by malpractice law firms

before a lawsuit and requests by patients who wish to review their own records. Monitoring trends in requests for medical records, particularly by law firm and by department, is a critical activity for risk managers. Tracking these trends can help identify breaches of confidentiality. Breaches may occur innocently or through intentional leaks to journalists or plaintiffs attorneys.

Electronic Health Records

Electronic health records will require a legal hold notice in the event of litigation. This will subject the entire record to review for relevant elements. Following the hold, the record must be preserved in its original state and individual access to the record will be monitored and reported. Policies must be in place to preserve records that are on hold. Failure to implement a hold subjects the case to a possible spoliation of evidence charge, which could make the case indefensible.[166] Copies of records that are released to law firms and others will be a paper copy of the treatment record only. The healthcare organization should retain copies of all documents that are released.

Health Insurance Portability and Accountability Act

HIPAA adds additional responsibilities to these obligations, and the obligations are becoming even more complex with the advent of electronic medical records. The necessity for electronic signature standards, the requirement of an unalterable record that is reliably stored, and the requirement of protection from unauthorized access[167] are just some of the important issues to consider as electronic record systems are put into widespread use.

Credentialing

A risk manager should monitor credentialing policies that might tend to exclude or deny privileges to physicians. If physicians admitting privileges are withdrawn or denied, the economic impact on their practice could be significant enough to cause them to seek compensation in court.

Withholding of Treatment

If a patient is unable to respond, the belief by a patient's family or significant others about the patient's wishes regarding resuscitation or withholding of treatment becomes an issue of paramount concern. Effective monitoring by risk management can provide an early warning that the family is in disagreement and that litigation might be contemplated.

Disclosure

Disclosure of unanticipated outcomes to patients and/or their families should be monitored by risk management. Development of policy regarding disclosure and a considered approach to the patient that includes documentation of the who, what, why, where, and when are critical activities. These events have a high probability of leading to litigation if a significant patient injury occurs.

DEPOSITION REVIEW _____

In an out-of-court setting, witnesses can be examined and can give testimony under oath before the parties in a lawsuit or their representatives. This examination process, which is called a deposition, provides an opportunity for the witnesses to tell their stories and to be questioned.

Risk managers may assist in the preparation of institutional employees for deposition.[168]

Importantly, risk managers should review depositions, or at least peruse the defense firm's summary, looking for areas of exposure. Based on such an investigation, Beckman and colleagues devised a set of questions for deposition reviews.[169] Their study examined 45 patients' depositions and classified 15 categories of "relationship issues" found in the depositions to identify problems. As perceived by the patient, these issues constituted failures in the physician–patient encounter. Physicians having specific problems in patient relationships might benefit from educational intervention. Because depositions are taken under oath, the documents often reveal information about the practitioner's involvement that was not previously understood.

Risk managers should devise a structured approach to deposition review that individualizes criteria to the particular institution and its potential problems. For example, obstetrical residents are permitted to deliver infants without an attending physician under certain circumstances. All depositions in obstetrical cases should be reviewed to validate the location of the resident and attending physicians during labor and delivery.

COMPREHENSIVE SOLUTIONS _____

No single approach to quality/performance improvement in health care works in every situation. Risk managers may assist in the development of performance improvement programs in many different disciplines. A good place to begin is those high-risk clinical areas that expose the professional liability coverage of the organization. Best practices that address clinical decision making are one component of a PI program, but other components—such as team training to encourage working in groups and simulation training to enhance performance of specific high-risk clinical tasks—are also important. Assessing the patient safety culture on the clinical care units and intervening to improve it is a good first step in the PI process.

Healthcare organizations that provide obstetrical services must consider the exposure that such care represents in terms of the medical professional liability insurance program—it sometimes accounts for 40% to 50% of the losses. Risk managers must try to reduce the incidence of adverse events and poor outcomes in obstetrics by actively supporting the development of perinatal safety initiatives along with the obstetrical clinical staff and leadership.

The comprehensive patient safety program in obstetrics reported by investigators at New York Presbyterian Hospital–Weill Cornell Medical Center (NYPWCMC) illustrates this kind of solution.[170] The hospital began with an independent review of the obstetrical department and labor and delivery by its professional liability insurance carrier. Recommendations from this review were discussed, and a comprehensive program of 22 elements was implemented over a period of about seven years from start to finish. Individual elements were added each year, culminating in the completed program.

Using a similar process, investigators at North Shore Long Island Jewish Health System (NSLIJHS) reported the results of their perinatal safety initiative (PSI) that began with a comprehensive internal review of obstetrical sentinel events, from which a multidisciplinary perinatal safety committee developed and oversaw implementation of the PSI. Their review identified for possible contributing factors for adverse events:

- Poor communication among providers
- Inadequate escalation policy to resolve conflicts in decision making
- Lack of standard clinical protocols
- Lack of standardization of interpretation of fetal heart rate (FHR) tracings

The resulting PSI program designed to address these factors was implemented over a period of two years.

Arrived at independently, the programs at NYPWCMC and NSLIJHS included some common interventions to improve perinatal safety:

- *Team training* emphasizing communication that was required of all staff and providers using either crew resource management (CRM) principles[170] or the Team STEPPS program provided through AHRQ[171]
- *Electronic medical records for obstetrics* that included templates for shoulder dystocia and operative vaginal deliveries[170] and inclusion of updated National Institute for Child Health and Development (NICHD) criteria for interpretation of FHR tracings[171]
- *Electronic fetal monitoring (EFM) education* that included either a required graded final examination on interpretation of FHR tracings and their clinical management[171] or appropriate national certification (NCC)[170]
- *Introduction and implementation of evidence-based clinical protocols and best practices* that included, among others, standardized oxytocin induction/augmentation/ stimulation protocols,[170,171] thromboembolism prophylaxis for cesarean deliveries, management of maternal hemorrhage, and a defined timetable for management of FHR abnormalities[171]
- *Obstetrical emergency simulation drills* for high-risk case scenarios

- *Multidisciplinary teaching rounds* to improve communication and patient management
- *Development of policies for escalation of concerns* by clinical staff to higher levels for resolution
- *Procedures developed for prompt reporting and systematic review of adverse events in obstetrics*

The NYPWCMC analysis of the program showed a steady decline in obstetrical sentinel events—a trend that began even before the interventions began and continued over the period of the study. The researchers acknowledge that the study is retrospective, so the impact on the obstetrical program of any single intervention or subgroup of interventions cannot be evaluated. Moreover, professional liability compensation payments declined significantly; however, because the statute of limitations is 10 years in New York, more claims from this time period could potentially develop in the future.[170]

The NSLIJHS program used weighted occurrence rates for a number of maternal/fetal and neonatal adverse outcomes to judge the success of its PSI. An overall decline in adverse outcomes was noted but, as in the NYPWCMC study, significance could not be determined for the individual interventions.[171]

It is often more effective to implement performance improvement programs in stepwise fashion to promote staff acceptance and adaptation to new methods, thereby reducing stress and error. Consolidating steps before proceeding with new ones enhances the overall process by ensuring incorporation into the work flow and reducing the complexity of any given step. In these examples, staff had time to adjust to and accept new ways of working together, which in turn improved the chance for program success.

Health care is more than clinical tasks; it is a people process that requires intervention at the level of those who practice and work in the organization. Clinical best practices are of first importance, but the staff must also be available and adequately trained. They must know how to work together through practice and understand the shared mission of the clinical department to continuously improve the quality of care. Only effective planning and leadership can make this process a success—it must be physician driven.

With so many areas in health care demanding attention, the question becomes, Where to begin? The "10 Patient Safety Tips for Hospitals" developed at AHRQ is one beginning to consider as an evidence-based short list (see **Box 8-10**).[172]

Box 8-10 Patient Safety Tips for Hospitals

The Agency for Healthcare Research and Quality has developed 10 evidence-based tips to help prevent adverse events in hospitals.[172]

1. Prevent central line–associated bloodstream infections.
2. Reengineer hospital discharges to reduce potentially preventable readmissions.
3. Prevent venous thromboembolism.
4. Educate patients about using blood thinners safely.
5. Limit shift durations for medical residents and other hospital staff if possible.
6. Consider working with a patient safety organization.
7. Use good hospital design principles to improve patient safety and quality.
8. Measure your hospital's patient safety culture.
9. Build better teams and rapid response systems.
10. Insert chest tubes safely.

WIN-WIN

A winning program for safety and performance improvement in clinical domains should use these components as a base:

- *Safety culture and readiness appraisal* using one of the available safety questionnaires for staff.[173,174]
- *Team training* to build cohesive functional groups in the clinical care areas. The success of Team STEPPS[175] is noteworthy and can be used to build a training program for all clinical and ancillary staff (see **Box 8-11**).[176–178] Implementation of a structured communication process is important for success; SBAR[179] (Situation, Background, Assessment, and Recommendation) is commonly used for this purpose.

Box 8-11   Team STEPPS

Team STEPPS, or *Strategies and Tools to Enhance Performance and Patient Safety*, is an evidence-based teamwork system designed to improve and promote communication among healthcare professionals and staff. It was originally developed by the Department of Defense and AHRQ as part of a program conducted with 19 healthcare organizations in the High Reliability Organization Network. The program was federally funded, so all training materials are free. Master trainer training programs have been offered free of charge but eligibility must first be established.

The Team STEPPS program has three phases: (1) assessment; (2) planning, training, and implementation; and (3) sustainment. It can be a lengthy process requiring support from top leadership, champions to drive it, and significant resources from beginning to end. To start the program, a readiness assessment is conducted, and it is recommended that an organization not undertake the training unless ready for the commitment.[176–178]

- *Simulation training* for development and improvement of clinical skills. Decide which areas are a priority for simulation and what you can afford. An important part of simulation training is emergency drills that pull together diverse skills to improve group performance when emergencies do occur.
- *Appropriate certification* in selected critical clinical skills, such as the interpretation of fetal monitoring tracings in obstetrics, is a critical attribute for any program.
- *Best practices for clinical management* of specific patient groups. These best practices should be arrived at through consensus-building activities of the clinical staff and leadership. When clinical best practices have been implemented in a unit, it is essential to audit compliance with the elements of this program. Sanctions should be available when best practices are ignored.
- *Electronic record systems* with computerized physician order entry. Such systems will improve the ability to communicate among providers and staff.
- *Focus on physician involvement and participation*—the glue that will hold the program together, keep it on track, and ensure improvement. Physicians need to understand their role in creating an unsafe environment in the first place and to appreciate how their leadership can right the wrongs. They must begin by listening to patients. "If invited, patients will tell us what makes them unhappy." We need to take them seriously.[180]

EVALUATION IS AN APPRAISAL

Analytical tools may assist in the identification of factors that could lead to litigation or hazards that lead to injury. TQM is a process, not a program, and must be applied to all levels of the organization. CQI is a business concept and a management technique that views quality as something dynamic that can always be improved in a continuous process of evaluation and change. No matter what the initials—TQM, CQI, CPI, or others—an evaluation follows the usual scientific method: defining the problem, collecting and analyzing data, formulating hypotheses, testing the hypotheses, and appraising the outcome before starting all over again. Enterprise risk management provides a framework to assess, evaluate, and manage the different domains of risk, thereby providing an integrated approach to risk management.

All activities that reduce the incidence of litigation are of primary concern to risk managers. Of course, existing theories and approaches created or adapted from management experiences can be blended into a risk manager's program. A predicament may emerge as risk managers initiate liability reduction activities that may affect the quality and quantity of care delivered to patients. Such conflict occurs when choices are made for economic reasons rather than for quality-of-care and patient safety improvement. The optimal solution will consider the best blend of all approaches—risk management, quality management, and patient safety.

Evaluation and change are two constants that permit an organization to reach new levels of capacity. Whether through TQM, CQI, or a combination of techniques, an organization must look at its critical processes, redefine its direction based on that review, and meet the needs of the customers utilizing its services. Performance improvement is best managed through a top-down and bottom-up approach to change, utilizing Lean management principles, and leading to high reliability throughout the organization.

The critical mass for change has already been reached through the public's awareness of the prevalence of medical errors. It is the unified program of quality, risk, and safety that will manage the future of reform in health care. Leadership at the executive and board levels is essential to redirect an organization down the path toward best-in-class performance. Providing meaningful and reliable quantitative information to the highest levels of leadership about the programs for improvement is an important aspect of this process. It is also essential to share the details of our mistakes with others who might repeat them to guarantee a safer environment for the patient. The risk manager, with appropriate legal consultation, must develop adequate information sharing mechanisms to ensure continuous improvement in healthcare quality and patient safety.

REFERENCES

1. Ober, W. B. (1992). Obstetrical events that shaped western European history. *Yale Journal of Biology and Medicine, 65*(2), 201–210.
2. Jain, V., Sebire, N. J., & Talbert, D. G. (2005). Kaiser Wilhelm syndrome: Obstetric trauma or placental insult in a historical case mimicking Erb's palsy. *Medical Hypostheses, 65*(1), 185–191.
3. Spiegel, A. D., & Kavaler, F. (1997). America's first medical malpractice crisis, 1835–1865. *Journal of Community Health, 22*(4), 283–308.
4. Mohr, J. C. (2000). American medical malpractice litigation in historical perspective. *Journal of the American Medical Association, 283*(13), 1731–1737.
5. Baker, B. R., Norton, P. G., Flintoff, V., Blais, R., Brown, A., Cox, J., … Tamblyn, R. (2004). The Canadian Adverse Events study: The incidence of adverse events among hospital patients in Canada. *Canadian Medical Association Journal, 170*(11), 1678–1686.
6. Davis, P., Lay-Yee, R., Briant, R., Ali, W., Scott, A., & Schug, S. (2002). Adverse events in New Zealand hospitals II: Preventability and clinical content. *New Zealand Medical Journal, 115*(1167), U271.

7. Zegers, M., de Bruijne, M. C., Wagner, C., Hoonhout, L. H., Waaijman, R., Smits, M., . . . vander Wal, G. (2009). Adverse events and potentially preventable deaths in Dutch hospitals: Results of a retrospective inpatient record review study. *Quality and Safety in Health Care, 18*(4), 297–302.

8. Soop, M., Fryksmark, U., Koster, M., & Haglund, B. (2009). The incidence of adverse events in Swedish hospitals: A retrospective medical record review study. *International Journal of Quality in Health Care, 21*(4), 285–291.

9. Nakajima, K., Keyes, C., Kuroyanagi, T., & Tatara, K. (2001). Medical malpractice and legal resolution systems in Japan. *Journal of the American Medical Association, 285*(12), 1632–1640.

10. Furlow, B. (2011, January 23). Japanese police investigate hospital *Acinetobacter* outbreak cover-up. *Epinewswire.* http://epinews.com/Newswire/2011/01/23/police-investigate-japanese-acinetobacter-outbreak-hospital-coverup/

11. Nagamatsu, S., Kami, M., & Nakata, Y. (2009) Healthcare safety committee in Japan: Mandatory accountability reporting system and punishment. *Current Opinion in Anesthesiology, 22*(2), 199–206.

12. Brennan, T. A., Leape, L. L., Laird, H. M,, Hebert, L., Localio, A. R., Lawthers, A. G., ... Hiatt, H. H. (1991). Incidence of adverse events and negligence in hospitalized patients. *New England Journal of Medicine, 324*(6), 370–376.

13. Thomas, E. J., Studdert, D. M., Burstin, H. R., Orav, J. E., Zeena, T., Williams, E. J., ... Brennan, T. A. (2000). Incidence and types of adverse events and negligent care in Utah and Colorado. *Medical Care, 38*(3), 261–271.

14. Baker, G. R., Norton, P. G., Flintoft, V., Blais, R., Brown, A., Cox, J., ... Tamblyn, R. (2004). The Canadian adverse events study: The incidence of adverse events among hospital patients in Canada. *Canadian Medical Association Journal, 170*(11), 1678–1686.

15. Classen, D. C., Resar, R., Griffin, F., Federico, F., Frankel, T., Kimmel, N., ... B. C. (2001). "Global trigger tool" shows that adverse events in hospitals may be ten times greater than previously measured. *Health Affairs, 30*(3), 581–589.

16. Localio, A. R., Lawthers, A. G., Brennan, T. A., Laird, N. M., Hebert, L. E., Peterson, L. M., ... Hiatt, H. H. (1991). Relations between malpractice claims and adverse events due to negligence. *New England Journal of Medicine, 325*(4), 245–251.

17. Studdert, D. M., Mello, M. M., Gawande, A. A., Gandhi, T. K., Kachalia, A., Yoon, C., ... Brennan, T. A. (2006). Claims, errors and compensation payments in medical malpractice litigation. *New England Journal of Medicine, 354*(19), 2024–2033.

18. Luzer, D. (2010, January 8). Too many law schools? *Washington Monthly.* http://www.washingtonmonthly.com/college_guide/blog/too_many_law_schools.php

19. VanDenBos, J., Rustagi, K., Gray, T., Halford, M., Ziemkeiwica, E., & Shreve, J. (2011). The $17.1 billion problem: The annual cost of measurable medical errors. *Health Affairs, 30*(4), 596–603.

20. Healthgrades patient safety release. 2008. http://www.healthgrades.com/media/dms/pdf/Health-GradesPatientSafetyRelease2008.pdf

21. Hickson, G. B., Clayton, E. W., Entman, S. S., Miller, C. S., Githens, P. B., Whetten-Goldstein, K., & Sloan, F. A. (1994) Obstetricians' prior malpractice experience and patients' satisfaction with care. *Journal of the American Medical Association, 272*(20), 1583–1587.

22. Gibbons, R. D., Hedecker, D., Charles, S. C., & Frisch, P. (1994) A random-effects probity model for predicting medical malpractice claims. *Journal of the American Statistical Association, 89*(427), 760–767.

23. Kohn, K. T., Corrigan, J. M., Donaldson, M. S. (Eds.). (1999). *To err is human: Building a safer health system.* Washington, DC: Committee on Quality of Health Care in America, Institute of Medicine, National Academy Press.

24. McDonald, C. J., Weiner, M., & Hui, S. L. (2000). Deaths due to medical errors are exaggerated in Institute of Medicine report. *Journal of the American Medical Association, 284*(1), 93–97.

25. Brennan, T. A. (2000). The Institute of Medicine report on medical errors: Could it do harm? *New England Journal of Medicine, 342*(15), 1123–1125.

26. Shojania, K., Duncan, B., McDonald, K., & Wachter, R. M. (Eds.). (2001). *Making health care safer: A critical analysis of patient safety practices.* Evidence Report/Technology Assessment No. 43; AHRQ publication 01-EO58. Rockville, MD: Agency for Healthcare Research and Quality.

27. Leape, L. L., Berwick, D. M., & Bates, D. W. (2002). What practices will most improve safety? Evidence-based medicine meets patient safety. *Journal of the American Medical Association, 288*(4), 501–507.

28. Farley, D. O., Ridgely, M. S., Mendel, P., Teleki, S. S., Damberg, C. L., Shaw, R., … Ashwood, J. S. (2009). *Assessing patient safety practices and outcomes in the U.S. health care system.* Rand Technical Report TR-725. Santa Monica, CA: Rand Corporation.

29. Burstin, H. (2009). In J. M. Corrigan (Ed.). Safe practices for better healthcare—2009 update: A consensus report. Washington, DC: National Quality Forum.

30. National Quality Forum (NQF). *Safe practices for better healthcare—2009 update: A consensus report.* Washington, DC: Author.

31. To err is human—to delay is deadly. (2009, May). Consumer's Union Safe Patient Project. http://www.safepatientproject.org/safepatientproject.org/pdf/safepatientproject.org-ToDelayIsDeadly.pdf

32. McNutt, R. A., Abrams, R., & Aron, D. C. (2002). Patient safety efforts should focus on medical errors. *Journal of the American Medical Association, 287*(15), 1997–2001.

33. Medical Event Reporting System (MERS) information. http://performancesolutions.gehealthcare.com/patient-safety/mers-event-reporting/mers-implementation-begins-journey-toward-enhancing-patient-safety.php

34. Healthcare acquired conditions. (n.d.). https://www.cms.gov/HospitalAcqCond/downloads/HACFactsheet.pdf

35. Maeda, J. L., Parlato, J., Levit, K., Andrews, R. M., & Jiang, J. (2011, June). Hospital-acquired conditions in selected community hospitals from 15 states. 2008. AHRQ Healthcare Cost and Utilization Project Statistical Brief #118. http://www.hcup-us.ahrq.gov/reports/statbriefs/sb118.pdf

36. Levinson, W., Roter, D., Mullooly, J. P., Dull, V. T., & Frankel, R. M. (1997). Physician–patient communication: The relationship with malpractice claims among primary care physicians and surgeons. *Journal of the American Medical Association, 277*(7), 553–559.

37. Carroll, J. G., & Platt, & F. W. (1998). Engagement: The grout of the clinical encounter. *Journal of Clinical Outcomes Management, 5*(3), 43–45.

38. Levinson, W., Gorawara-Bhat, R., & Lamb, J. (2000). A study of patient clues and physician responses in primary care and surgical settings. *Journal of the American Medical Association, 284*(8), 1021–1027.

39. Braddock, C. H., Edwards, K. A., Hasenberg, N. M., Laidley, T. L., & Levinson, W. (1999). Informed decision-making in outpatient practice: Time to get back to the basics. *Journal of the American Medical Association, 282*(24), 2313–2320.

40. Barry, M. J. (1999). Involving patients in medical decisions: How can physicians do better? *Journal of the American Medical Association, 282*(24), 2356–2357.

41. Roter, D. L., Hall, J. A., & Aoki, J. (2002). Physician gender effects in medical communication: A meta-analytic review. *Journal of the American Medical Association, 288*(6), 756–764.

42. Slovic, P. (1987). Perception of risk. *Science, 236,* 280–285.

43. Fullam, F., Garman, A. N., Johnson, T. J., & Hedberg, E. C. (2009). The use of patient satisfaction surveys and alternative coding procedures to predict malpractice risk. *Medical Care, 47*(5), 553–559.

44. Griffen, F. D., Stephens, L. S., Alexander, J, B., Bailey, H. R., Maizel, S. E., Sutton, B. H., & Posner, K. L. (2008). Violations of behavioral practices revealed in closed claims reviews. *Annals of Surgery, 248*(3), 468–474.

45. Bogardus, S. T., Holmboe, E., & Jekel, J. F. (1999). Perils, pitfalls, and possibilities in talking about medical risk. *Journal of the American Medical Association, 281*(11), 1037–1041.

46. Rozovsky, F. A., & Woods, J. R. (2003). *What do I say: Communicating intended or unanticipated outcomes in obstetrics.* San Francisco: Jossey-Bass.

47. Gallagher, T. H., Studdert, D., & Levinson, W. (2007). Disclosing harmful medical errors to patients. *New England Journal of Medicine, 356*(26), 2713–2719.

48. Gallagher, T. H., Garbutt, J. M., Waterman, A. D., Flum, D. R., Larson, E. B., Waterman, B. M., … Levinson, W. (2006). Choosing your words carefully: How physicians would disclose harmful medical errors to patients. *Archives of Internal Medicine, 166*(15), 1585–1593.

49. Dudzinski, D. M., Hebert, P. C., Foglia, M. B., & Gallagher, T. H. (2010). The disclosure dilemma:

Large-scale adverse events. *New England Journal of Medicine, 363*(10), 978–986.

50. Trus Biopsy Class Actions: Settlement agreement— *George Farkas v. Sunnybrook Health Sciences Centre.* Ontario Superior Court. (2010, July 13). http://reolaw.ca/pdf/sunnybrook_settlement_agreement.pdf

51. Chafe, R., Levinson, W., & Sullivan, T. (2009). Disclosing errors that affect multiple patients. *Canadian Medical Association Journal, 180*(11), 1125–1127.

52. Studdert, D. M., Mello, M. M., Gawande, A. A., Brennan, T. A., & Wang, Y. C. (2007). Disclosure of medical injury to patients: An improbable risk management strategy. *Health Affairs, 26*(1), 215–226.

53. Burroughs, T. E., Waterman, A. D., Gallagher, T. H., Waterman, B., Jeffe, D. B., Dunagan, W. C., ... Fraser, V. J. (2007). Patients' concerns about medical error during hospitalization. *Joint Commission Journal on Quality and Patient Safety, 33*(1), 5–14.

54. Berwick, D. M., Calkins, D. R., McCannon, C. J., & Hackbarth, A. D. (2006). The hundred thousand lives campaign: Setting a goal and a deadline for improving healthcare quality. *Journal of the American Medical Association, 295*(3), 324–327.

55. Consumers Union Safe Patient Project Report. (2009, May). To err is human—to delay is deadly. http://www.safepatientproject.org/safepatientproject.org/pdf/safepatientproject.org-ToDelayIs-Deadly.pdf

56. Pronovost, P., Needham, D., Berenholtz, S., Sinopoli, D., Chu, H., Cosgrove, S., ... Goeschel, C. (2006). An intervention to decrease catheter-related bloodstream infections in the ICU. *New England Journal of Medicine, 355*(26), 2725–2732.

57. MHA Keystone Center for Patient Safety and Quality: Annual report 2010. http://www.mhakeystonecenter.org/documents/2010_keystone_annual_report.pdf

58. Carroll, R. L., & Norris, G. A. (2006). Enterprise risk management in health care: The basics. In *Risk management handbook for healthcare organizations* (5th ed., Vol. 1, Chapter 1). San Francisco: Jossey-Bass.

59. *Monograph: Enterprise risk management. Part I: Defining the concept, recognizing its value.* (2006, January). Chicago: American Society for Healthcare Risk Management.

60. *Monograph: Enterprise risk management. Part II: Getting an ERM program started.* (2006, January). Chicago: American Society for Healthcare Risk Management.

61. Celona, B. D., Driver, J., & Hall, E. (2011). Value-driven ERM: Making ERM an engine for simultaneous value creation and value protection. *Journal of Healthcare Risk Management, 30*(4), 15–33.

62. Monograph: Enterprise risk management. Part III: The role of the chief risk officer. (2006, January). Chicago: American Society for Healthcare Risk Management.

63. Head, G. L., & Horn, S. (1991). *Essentials of risk management* (2nd ed., Vol. 1, pp.5, 11). Malvern, PA: Insurance Institute of America.

64. Fiesta, J. (1991). QA and risk management: Reducing liability exposure. *Nursing Management, 22*(2), 14–15.

65. Berwick, B. M. (1989). Continuous improvement as an ideal in health care. *New England Journal of Medicine, 320*(1), 53–56.

66. Berens, M. J. (2000, September 10). Nursing mistakes kill, injure thousands: Cost cutting exacts toll on patients, hospital staffs. *Chicago Tribune,* p. 1.

67. Martin, P. B., & Marder, R. J. (2001). Risk management's role in performance improvement. In R. Carroll (Ed.), *Risk management handbook for health care organizations* (pp. 801–810). San Francisco: Jossey-Bass.

68. Deming, W. D. (1986). *Out of the crisis: Massachusetts Institute of Technology Center for Advanced Engineering Study.* Cambridge, MA: MIT Press, pp. 90–92.

69. Stratton, A. D. (1991). *An approach to quality improvement that works* (2nd ed., pp. 4–5). Milwaukee: ASQC Quality Press.

70. Kim, P. S., & Johnson, D. D. (1994). Implementing total quality management in the health care industry. *Health Care Supervisor, 12*(3), 51–57.

71. Goonan, K. J. (1995). *The Juran prescription: Clinical quality management.* San Francisco: Jossey-Bass.

72. Lynn, G. F. (1991). Total quality management: A competitive strategy. *Health Care Executive, 4*(3), 1–5.

73. Speer, S. J. (2005, September). Fixing health care from the inside, today. *Harvard Business Review,* 78–91.

74. Reinertsen, J. L. (2006). Interview with Gary Kaplan. *Quality and Safety in Healthcare, 15*(3), 156–158.

75. Speer, S. J. (2009). *Chasing the rabbit: How market leaders outdistance the competition and how great companies can catch up and win.* New York: McGraw-Hill.

76. *Going Lean in health care.* (2005). IHI Innovation Series white paper. Cambridge, MA: Institute for Healthcare Improvement. www.IHI.org

77. *Principles of Lean.* (n. d.). Cambridge, MA: Lean Enterprise Institute. http://www.lean.org/whatslean/principles.cfm

78. Schillie, S. F. (n. d.). Quality improvement in healthcare. *Medscape CME Public Health and Prevention: Perspectives in Prevention from the American College of Preventive Medicine.* http://www.medscape.org/viewarticle/561651

79. Chassin, M. R., & Loeb, J. M. (2011). The ongoing quality improvement journey: Next stop, high reliability. *Health Affairs, 30*(4), 559–568.

80. Shortell, S. M., Levin, D. Z., O'Brien, J. L., & Hughes, E. F. X. (1995). Assessing the evidence of CQI: Is the glass half empty or half full? *Hospital & Health Services Administration, 40*(1), 4–24.

81. Meliones, J. N., Alton, M., Mericle, J., Ballard, R., Cesari, J., Frush, K. S., & Mistry, K. (2008, August), 10-year experience integrating strategic performance improvement initiatives: Can the balanced scorecard, six sigma, and team training all thrive in a single hospital? In: K. Henriksen, J. B. Battles, M.A. Keyes, & M. L. Grady (Eds.), *Advances in patient safety: New directions and alternative approaches. Vol. 3: Performance and tools.* AHRQ Publication No. 08-0034-3. Rockville, MD: Agency for Healthcare Research and Quality. http://www.ahrq.gov/downloads/pub/advances2/vol3/Advances-Meliones_40.pdf

82. Leavitt, H. J., & Lipman-Blumen, J. (1995). Hot groups. *Harvard Business Review, 73*(7), 109–116.

83. Jain, R., Kralovic, S. M., Evans, M. E., Ambrose, M., Simbartl, L. A., Obrosky, S. I., … Roselle, G. A. (2011). Veterans Affairs initiative to prevent methicillin-resistant *Staphylococcus aureus* infections. *New England Journal of Medicine, 364*(14), 1419–1430.

84. Headrick, L. A., & Neuhauser, D. (1995). Quality health care. *Journal of the American Medical Association, 273*(21), 1718–1720.

85. Parenti, C. M., Lederle, F. A., Impola, C. K., & Peterson, L. R. (1994). Reduction of unnecessary intravenous catheter use: Internal medicine house staff participate in a successful quality improvement project. *Archives of Internal Medicine., 154*(10), 1829–1832.

86. Young, M. J., Ward, R., & McCarthy, B. (1994). Continuously improving primary care. *Journal of Quality Improvement, 20*(2), 120–126.

87. Weingarten, S. R., Riedinger, M. S., Conner, L., Lee, T. H., Hoffman, I., Johnson, B., … Ellrodt, A. G. (1994). Practice guidelines and reminders to reduce duration of hospital stay for patients with chest pain: An interventional trial. *Annals of Internal Medicine, 120*(3), 257–263.

88. Bluth, E. I., Havrilla, M., & Blakeman, C. (1993). Quality improvement techniques: Value to improve the timeliness of preoperative chest radiologic reports. *American Journal of Roentgenology, 160*(8), 995–998.

89. Keystone Project annual report. (2010). http://www.mhakeystonecenter.org/documents/2010_keystone_annual_report.pdf

90. Joint Commission Center for Transforming Healthcare. (2010, November). *Hand hygiene project: Best practices from hospitals participating in the Joint Commission Center for Transforming Healthcare project.* Oakbrook Terrace, IL: Author. http://www.hpoe.org/resources-and-tools/resources/hand-hygiene-project.pdf

91. Joint Commission Center for Transforming Healthcare. (n.d.). *Storyboard on the Internet.* Oakbrook Terrace, IL: Author. http://www.centerfortransforminghealthcare.org/UserFiles/file/hand_hygiene_storyboard.pdf

92. Birnbaum, D. (1993). CQI tools: Sentinel events, warning, and action limits. *Infection Control and Hospital Epidemiology, 14*(9), 537–539.

93. Parisi, L. L. (1994). Implementing a CQI approach to incident reporting. *Aspen's Advisor for Nurse Executives, 9*(4), 4–5.

94. Patten, T. H. (1991). *Organizational development facilitators through teambuilding.* New York: John Wiley, pp. 157–158.

95. Longo, R. D., & Bohr, D. (1991). *Quantitative methods in quality management: A guide for practitioners.* Chicago: American Hospital Publishing.

96. Solberg, L. I., Reger, L. A., Pearson, T. L., Cherney, L. M., O'Connor, P. J., Freemen, S. L., … Bishop, D. B. (1997). Using continuous quality improvement to improve diabetes care in populations: The IDEAL model. *Joint Commission Journal on Quality Improvement, 23*(11), 581–592.

97. Juran, J. M. (1989). *Juran on leadership for quality: An executive handbook.* New York: Free Press, pp. 87–88, 90, 101.

98. Hickson, G. B., Federspiel, C. F., Pichert, J. W., & Miller, C. S. (2002). Patient complaints and malpractice risk. *Journal of the American Medical Association, 287*(22), 2951–2957.

99. Sage, W. M. (2002). Putting the patient in patient safety: Linking patient complaints and malpractice risk. *Journal of the American Medical Association, 287*(22), 3003–3005.

100. Challan, B. (1993). A risk manager's evolving experience with CQI. *Journal of Health Care Risk Management, 13*(3), 25–30.

101. Rubeor, K., Keane, V., & Cross, E. (2001). *Neonatal brachial plexus impairment program.* Annual report to Maryland Medicine Comprehensive Insurance Program, Baltimore, MD.

102. Hendrich, A., Tersigni, A. R., Jeffcoat, S., Barnett, C. J., Brideau, L. P, & Pryor, D. B. (2007). The Ascension Health journey to zero: Lessons learned and leadership perspectives. *Joint Commission Journal on Quality and Patient Safety, 33*(12), 739–749.

103. Gabow, P. A., & Mehler, P. S. (2001). A broad and structured approach to improving patient safety and quality: Lessons from Denver Health. *Health Affairs, 30*(4), 612–618.

104. Schilling, L., Chase, A., Kehrli, S., Liu, A. Y., Stiefel, M., & Brentari, R. (2010). Kaiser Permanente's performance improvement system. Part 1: From benchmarking to executing on strategic priorities. *Joint Commission Journal on Quality and Patient Safety, 36*(11), 484–498.

105. The labor–management partnership at Kaiser Permanente.(2009, March 22). http://xnet.kp.org/future/ahrstudy/032709lmp.html

106. Schilling, L., Deas, D., Jedlinsky, M., Aronoff, D., Fershtman, J., & Wali, A. (2010). Kaiser Permanente's performance improvement system. Part 2: Developing a value framework. *Joint Commission Journal on Quality and Patient Safety, 36*(12), 552–560.

107. Robinson, R. K., Fink, R. L., & Fink, L. A. (1995). Employee participation programs in the health care industry: Are they unlawful under recent labor rulings? *Hospital & Health Services Administration, 40*(1), 124–137.

108. Abrams, J. (1995). Lessening your professional liability risk. *Occupational Safety and Health, 63*(1), 35–39.

109. Crown Cork and Seal, Inc., 334 NLRB No. 92 (July 20, 2001).

110. Kaiser Permanente labor–management partnership. (n.d.). http://www.lmpartnership.org/ubt

111. Kaiser Permanente labor–management partnership: UBT Tracker. (n.d.). http://lmpartnership.org/ubt/track-performance/ubt-tracker

112. Morlock, L. L., & Malitz, F. E. (1991). Do hospital risk management programs make a difference? Relationships between risk management program activities and hospital malpractice claims experience. *Law and Contemporary Problems, 54*(2), 1–22.

113. Macnee, C. L. (1994). Penchansky R. Targeting ambulatory care cases for risk management and quality management. *Inquiry, 31*(1), 66–75.

114. Sample self-assessment tool for risk management programs and functions. (n.d.). American Society for Healthcare Risk Management. http://www.ashrm.org/ashrm/online_store/files/ASHRMselfassessmenttool-2.Sample.pdf

115. Goldfield, N., Pine, M., & Pine, J. (1995). *Measuring and managing healthcare quality procedures, techniques, and protocols.* Gaithersburg, MD: Aspen, pp. 2–3.

116. Loeb, J. M., & O'Leary, D. S. (1995). A call for collaboration in performance measurement. *Journal of the American Medical Association, 273*(18), 1405.

117. Pronovost, P. J., & Lilford, R. (2011). A road map for improving the performance of performance measures. *Health Affairs, 30*(4), 569–573.

118. Carroll, J. G. (1995). *Monitoring with indicators: Evaluating the quality of patient care.* Gaithersburg, MD: Aspen.

119. Agency for Healthcare Research and Quality. (n.d.). Quality indicators. http://www.qualityindicators.ahrq.gov/

120. Eldridge, J., & Conner, C. (2002). *Health care facilities risk management forms: Checklists and guidelines.* Gaithersburg, MD: Aspen.

121. World Health Organization. (n.d.). Patient safety checklist. http://www.who.int/patientsafety/safesurgery/ss_checklist/en/index.html

122. Acerbo-Avalone, N., & Kramer, K. (1997) Writing the investigation report. In *Medical malpractice claims investigation: A step-by-step approach.* (Exhibit 8-2). Gaithersberg, MD: Aspen, p. 155.

123. Stanyon, R. (2007). The electronic health record: Getting it all together. In *Medical malpractice claims investigation: A step-by-step approach* (chapter 3). Sudbury, MA: Jones and Bartlett.

124. Smetana, J. L. (2009). Strategies to prepare for electronic discovery in healthcare. *Journal of Healthcare Risk Management, 29*(1), 6–9, 13, 15–21.

125. Sandeep, S. M., Murtagh, L., & Mello, M. M. (2010). Medical malpractice liability in the age of electronic health records. *New England Journal of Medicine, 363*(21), 2060–2067.

126. Goeschel, C. A., Holzmueller, C. G., Berenholtz, S. M., Marsteller, J. A., Murphy, D. J., Sawyer, M., … Pronovost, P. J. (2010). Executive/senior leader checklist to improve culture and reduce central line–associated bloodstream infections. *Joint Commission Journal on Quality and Patient Safety, 36*(11), 519–524.

127. Goeschel, C. A., Holzmueller, C. G., & Pronovost, P. J. (2010). Hospital board checklist to improve culture and reduce central line–associated blood stream infections. *Joint Commission Journal on Quality and Patient Safety, 36*(11), 525–528.

128. *Minimum scope of root cause analysis for specific types of sentinel events.* (2002). Oakbrook Terrace, IL: Joint Commission on Accreditation for Healthcare Organizations.

129. Rex, J. H., Turnbull, J. E., Allen, S. J., VandeVoorde, K., & Luther, K. (2000). Systematic root cause analysis of adverse drug events in a tertiary referral hospital. *Joint Commission Journal on Quality Improvement, 26*(10), 563–575.

130. Wu, A. W., Lipshutz, A. K., & Pronovost, P. J. (2008). Effectiveness and efficiency of root cause analysis in medicine. *Journal of the American Medical Association, 299*(6), 685–687.

131. Latino, R. J. (2004). Optimizing FMEA and RCA efforts in healthcare. *Journal of Healthcare Risk Management, 24*(2), 21–28.

132. Feldman, S. E., & Roblin, D.W. (1997). Medical accidents in hospital care: Applications of failure analysis to hospital quality appraisal. *Joint Commission Journal on Quality Improvement, 23*(11), 567–580.

133. Fletcher, C. E. (1997). Failure mode and effects analysis: An interdisciplinary way to analyze and reduce medication errors. *Journal of Nursing Administration, 27*(12), 19–26.

134. The Joint Commission. (n.d.). Framework for conducting a root cause analysis. http://www.joint-commission.org/Framework_for_Conducting_a_Root_Cause_Analysis_and_Action_Plan/

135. The Joint Commission. (n.d.). FMECA worksheet. http://www.jointcommission.org/Failure_Mode_Effect_and_Criticality_Analysis_FMECA_Worksheet/

136. The Joint Commission report: Sentinel event data root causes by event type 2004 to fourth quarter 2010. (n.d.). http://www.jointcommission.org/assets/1/18/SE_RootCausesEventType2004_4Q2010.pdf

137. Veterans Administration. (n.d.). Root cause analysis. http://www.patientsafety.gov/CogAids/RCA/index.html#page=page-1

138. Veterans Administration. (n.d.). HFMEA. http://www.patientsafety.gov/SafetyTopics/HFMEA/HFMEA_JQI.html

139. Joint Commission on Accreditation of Healthcare Organizations. (1995). *Accreditation manual for hospitals. Vol. 1: Standards.* Oakbrook Terrace, IL: Author.

140. Masica, A. L., Richter, K. M., Convery, P., & Haydar, Z. (2009). Linking Joint Commission inpatient core measures and National Patient Safety Goals with evidence. *Baylor University Medical Center Proceedings, 22*(2), 105–111.

141. Barron, B. M. (1989). *How underwriters evaluate risk management effectiveness,* Presentation at the Eleventh Annual Conference of the American Society for Healthcare Risk Management of the American Hospital Association, Orlando, FL.

142. Zarrella, E. G. (1989). *How underwriters evaluate risk management effectiveness.* Presentation at the Eleventh Annual Conference of the American Society for Healthcare Risk Management, Orlando, FL.

143. Baker, T. (2005). Medical malpractice and the insurance underwriting cycle. *DePaul Law Review, 54*, 393–438.

144. Plsek, P. E. (1995). Advancing process improvement: Techniques for managing quality. *Hospital & Health Services Administration, 40*(1), 50–79.

145. Roman, K. M. (2001). Benchmarking. In R. Carroll (Ed.), *Risk management handbook for health care organizations* (3rd ed., pp. 811–836). San Francisco: Jossey-Bass.

146. Youngberg, B. J. (1998). Benchmarking in risk management. In B. J. Youngberg (Ed.), *Risk manager's desk reference* (2nd ed., pp.56–60). Gaithersberg, MD: Aspen.

147. AHRQ data sources. (n.d.). http://www.ahrq.gov/data/dataresources.htm

148. AON hospital professional liability and physician liability benchmark analysis. (n.d.). http://aon.mediaroom.com/index.php?s=43&item=1335

149. Schilling, L., Chase, A., Kehrli, S., Liu, A. Y., Stiefel, M., & Brentari, R. (2010). Kaiser Permanente's performance improvement system, Part I: From benchmarking to executing on strategic priorities. *Joint Commission Journal on Quality and Patient Safety, 36*(11), 484–498.

150. Garnick, D. W., Hendricks, A. M., & Brennan, T. A. (1991). Can practice guidelines reduce the number and costs of malpractice claims? *Journal of the American Medical Association, 266*(20), 2856–2860.

151. Hyams, A. L., Brandenburg, J. A., Lipsitz, S. R., Shapiro, D. W., & Brennan, T. A. (1995). Practice guidelines and malpractice litigation: A two-way street. *Annals of Internal Medicine, 122*(6), 450–455.

152. Mello, M. M. (2000, Fall). The role of clinical practice guidelines in malpractice litigation. *Forum*, p. 1.

153. Sloan, F. A., Mergenhagen, P. M., Burfield, B., Bovbjerg, R. R., & Hassan, M. (1989). Medical malpractice experience of physicians: Predictable or haphazard? *Journal of the American Medical Association, 262*(23), 3291–3297.

154. Kravitz, R. L., Rolph, J. E., & McGuigan, K. (1991). Malpractice claims data as a quality improvement tool. *Journal of the American Medical Association, 266*(15), 2087–2097.

155. Acerbo-Avalone, N., & Kramer, K. (1991). Identifying the medical–legal issues. In *Medical malpractice claims investigation: A step-by-step approach. (*pp. 33–38). Gaithersberg, MD: Aspen.

156. Acerbo-Kozuchowski, N., Ashton, K., Feldman, D., Schappert, J., & Joseph, V. A. (2007). Developing interview questions on specific occurrence types. In *Medical malpractice claims investigation: A step-by-step approach.* (Chapter 7). Sudbury, MA: Jones and Bartlett.

157. Guzman, J. (2007). Developing interview questions on occurrences in long-term care facilities. In *Medical malpractice claims investigation: A step-by-step approach.* (Chapter 8). Sudbury, MA: Jones and Bartlett.

158. Acerbo-Kozuchowski, N., Kassel, I., & Bernstein, P. (2007). Developing interview questions on obstetrical claims. In *Medical malpractice claims investigation: A step-by-step approach.* (Chapter 9). Sudbury, MA: Jones and Bartlett.

159. Kischak, P., & Barth, A. M. (2007). Investigating equipment related occurrences. In *Medical malpractice claims investigation: A step-by-step approach.* (Chapter 10). Sudbury, MA: Jones and Bartlett.

160. Ashton, K. (2007). Writing the investigation report. In *Medical malpractice claims investigation: A step-by-step approach.* (Chapter 12). Sudbury, MA: Jones and Bartlett.

161. Rolf, J. E., Kravitz, R. L., & McGuigan, K. (1991). Malpractice claims data as a quality improvement tool: II. Is targeting effective? *Journal of the American Medical Association, 266*(15), 2093–2097.

162. Caplan, R. A., Posner, K. L., & Cheney, R. W. (1991). Effect of outcome on physician judgments of appropriateness of care. *Journal of the American Medical Association, 265*(15), 1957–1960.

163. Colaizzo, D. A. (2006). Cost of risk. In *Risk management handbook for health care organizations*, (5th ed., Vol.3, Chapter 11). San Francisco: Jossey-Bass.

164. Gilbert, P. L. (1991). The internist as preoperative consultant: Risk assessment and management. *Mount Sinai Journal of Medicine, 58*(1), 3–8.

165. McConnell, J. C., & Praeger, A. M. (1990). Confidentiality of records maintained in a hospital setting. In L. M. Harpster & M. S. Veach (Eds.), *Risk management handbook for health care facilities* (pp. 233– 251). Chicago: American Hospital Publishing.

166. Smetana, J. L. (2009). Strategies to prepare of electronic discovery in healthcare. *Journal of Healthcare Risk Management, 29*(1), 6–9, 13, 15–21.

167. Davis, K. S., & McConnell, J. C. (2001). Data management. In R. Carroll (Ed.), *Risk management handbook for health care organizations* (pp. 115–146). San Francisco: Jossey-Bass.

168. Barton, E. L. (1990). Claims and litigation management. In L. M. Harpster & M. S. Veach (Eds.), *Risk management handbook for health care facilities* (pp. 267–294). Chicago: American Hospital Publishing.

169. Beckman, H. B., Markakis, K. M., Suchman, A. L., & Frankel, R. M. (1994). The doctor–patient relationship and malpractice. *Archives of Internal Medicine, 154*(7), 1365–1370.

170. Grunebaum, A., Chervenak, F., & Skupski, D. (2011). Effect of a comprehensive obstetric patient safety program on compensation payments and sentinel events. *American Journal of Obstetrics and Gynecology, 204*(2), 97–105.

171. Wagner, B., Meirowitz, M., Shah, J., Nanda, D., Reggio, L., Cohen, P., ... Abrams, K. J. (2011, March 1). Comprehensive perinatal safety initiative to reduce adverse obstetric events. *Journal of Healthcare Quality,* 1–10. Doi: 10.1111/j.1945-1474.2011.00134.x

172. AHRQ 10 patient safety tips for hospitals. (n.d.). http://psnet.ahrq.gov/resource.aspx?resourceID=4619

173. Sexton, B. J. (n.d.). Safety attitudes questionnaire. http://www.hret.org/quality/projects/walkrounds-saq.shtml

174. AHRQ teamwork attitudes questionnaire. (n.d.). http://teamstepps.ahrq.gov/includes/Team-STEPPS%20T-TAQ.pdf

175. Team STEPPS information and training materials. Agency for Healthcare Research and Quality. (n.d.). http://teamstepps.ahrq.gov/

176. Team STEPPS readiness assessment. (n.d.). http://teamstepps.ahrq.gov/ahrqchecklist.html

177. Team STEPPS training eligibility. (n.d.). http://teamstepps.ahrq.gov/trainingEligibility.htm

178. Team STEPPS tools and materials. (n.d.). http://teamstepps.ahrq.gov/abouttoolsmaterials.htm

179. Institute for Healthcare Improvement. (n.d.). SBAR information. http://www.ihi.org/knowledge/Pages/Tools/SBARTechniqueforCommunicationASituationalBriefingModel.aspx.

180. Hickson, G. B., & Entman, S. S. (2010). Physician's influence and the malpractice problem. *Obstetrics and Gynecology , 115*(4), 682–686.

CHAPTER 9

A Primer on Medical Malpractice

Arthur S. Friedman

Medical malpractice is controversial and sometimes complex; it affects all healthcare providers, patients, physicians, lawyers, institutions, and insurers. Reform of medical malpractice laws has long been the mantra of numerous politicians on both the national and local scenes. Although Congress recently enacted a comprehensive overhaul of medical care having seismic reverberations on the national delivery of healthcare services (the Patient Protection and Affordable Care Act and the Health Care and Education Reconciliation Act of 2010), it has not been able to muster the political will to pass legislation to correct the perceived inequities symbolized, some say, by large jury medical malpractice verdicts. The argument for reform reasons that these verdicts result in physicians leaving certain areas (e.g., obstetrics/gynecology) due to the never-ending spiral of higher malpractice premiums.

One reason for inaction on the national tort reform front is that Congress may not have the legal constitutional basis to legislate in this area. Historically, tort law has been a matter within the jurisdiction of the states.

Numerous investigative reports by the U.S. General Accounting Office (GAO) about medical malpractice related to Medicare, Medicaid, and the Veterans Administration, as well as systemic fraud in the provision of healthcare services, demonstrate the national concern with medical malpractice.

A SCIENCE OF MISTAKES

In 1984, Harvard Medical Practice Study reviewed more than 30,000 medical records from 51 New York State hospitals and found that adverse events and negligence occurred in 3.7% of hospitalizations; 2.6% of these instances caused permanent disability, and 13.6% resulted in death.[1-3] This Harvard study echoed the findings of the only other large-scale estimation of the incidence of iatrogenic injury and substandard care, the California Medical Association's Medical Insurance Feasibility Study.[4] In 1977, California researchers reported an adverse event rate of 4.6% and a negligence rate of 0.8%. Devastatingly, in the third Harvard report in the series, Localio declared: "Medical-malpractice litigation infrequently compensates patients injured by medical negligence and rarely identifies and holds providers accountable for substandard care." There is no mention of provider accountability in the case described in **Box 9-1**.

Brennan and colleagues found that certain types of hospitals have significantly higher rates of injuries because of the substandard care they deliver.[5] Furthermore, Leape et al.'s analysis[6] indicated that 67% of the adverse events were caused by nonphysician errors, not physician negligence. Leape concluded:

> Physicians and nurses need to accept the notion that error is an inevitable accompaniment of the human condition, even amongst conscientious professionals with high standards. Errors must be accepted as evidence of system flaws, not character flaws.[7]

Box 9-1

Matthew Dunn's parents brought their four-year-old son into a hospital for emergency treatment. Dunn's symptoms included fever, coughing, diarrhea, vomiting, and purple blotches on his throat. During five hours at the managed care facility, the doctor on duty examined Dunn, ordered numerous tests, and gave him Tylenol. The child's condition worsened. He was taken to a hospital, where an antibiotic was administered intravenously, but Dunn died of meningococcal infection one hour later. The doctor was sued for negligence in failing to diagnose the virus. If diagnosed, there was a small risk of death with proper treatment. A jury awarded $625,000 to the parents.[8]

In a comment related to Leape's article, Blumenthal applied total quality management and opted to redirect medical errors into "medical treasures" because the flaws were exposed and corrected.[9]

A hospital that had experienced mistakes similar to the one described in **Box 9-2** devised a plan to prevent future incidents. Administrative orders dictated that anytime surgery involved an organ or limb that comes in pairs, staff would write "NO" with a black magic marker on the organ or limb that should be left alone.[10]

Box 9-2

A Texas surgeon admitted negligently removing Benjamin Jones's healthy right lung while leaving a tumor in the left lung. Jones decided against further treatment because doctors told him he would gain a painful few months of life, at best. After his death, the family sued for wrongful death. Even though the hospital admitted no wrongdoing, a settlement gave the family $9 million. Ironically, an autopsy revealed that Jones had a good chance of beating the cancer even after the surgical mistake.[11]

A *Lancet* editorial offered advice in a similar vein.[12] What practical lesson does this "science of mistakes" have for providers? To diminish errors, attention should be paid to alterable features outside of the system. Healthcare providers should attempt to learn as much as they can about people, including how illnesses affect them and which treatments work best. "Success in bringing patients to health or relief requires the broadest possible knowledge of anything relevant to the illness."[13]

MEDICAL MALPRACTICE

In a unique theoretical approach, Senders concluded that "there are few or no 'medical errors'; there are many errors that occur in medical settings."[14] An error differs from an accident in that the error is a behavioral matter, while the accident is an unplanned event. Behavioral errors can involve a misperception, a mistake, a slip, an omission, a commission, an insertion, a repetition, or a substitution, and they may be endogenous or exogenous. Advocating "failure mode analysis," Senders advised evaluation of all incorrect actions and prevention interception. In essence, this technique demands identification of the modes of error in medical settings, prediction of the expressions of those errors, use of training and design to improve self-detection, and the interdiction of their transformation into accidents.

The National Academy of Science's Institute of Medicine (IOM) 1999 report cited studies showing that between 44,000 and 98,000 people die each year in the United States because of mistakes made by medical professionals in hospitals. Thousands of other errors are never detected, and those in nursing homes, home health care, retail pharmacies, physicians' offices, and ambulatory care centers were not included in the report.[15] The IOM said medication errors are among the most widespread and may result in deaths, permanent disability, and unnecessary suffering.

An error, whether advertent or inadvertent, is one thing, but district attorneys have sometimes escalated medical mistakes from malpractice into criminal charges. While criminal charges for a medical error are extraordinarily rare, they are not precluded by adverse determinations by state licensure or professional conduct agencies (see **Box 9-3**).

NEGLIGENCE

Negligence is a civil—as distinct from criminal—wrong and is part of the law of torts. The law of torts concerns personal wrongs providing grounds for accountability or redress, sometimes by a lawsuit. Typically, where the commission of a tort results in personal injury or harm, the injured party may then make a claim for monetary compensation. In this way, tort law permits a person who has suffered injuries or damages due to another party's wrongful actions to be compensated. Additionally, tort law

Box 9-3

- Reckless manslaughter charges were sought against an anesthesiologist who allegedly had failed to monitor vital signs and fell asleep during surgery. His eight-year-old patient died. Colorado revoked his medical license, and the boy's family accepted an out-of-court settlement. Criminal charges are still pending.[16]
- A laboratory in Oak Creek, Wisconsin, Chem-Bio Corporation, was charged with "reckless homicide" for allegedly misreading Pap smears that could have saved the lives of two women. Experts testified that the slides showed unmistakable signs of cancer. A lab technician was paid based on the number of samples analyzed. She examined 20,000 to 40,000 Pap smears each year, compared with the maximum of 12,000 samples recommended under professional standards. The estates of both victims received multimillion-dollar settlements from the laboratory and their health maintenance organization provider, Family Health Plan. The laboratory director and the technician escaped immediate charges under a deal with the prosecutors.[17]

discourages others from engaging in the same harmful conduct.

Within the field of negligence, the term "malpractice" refers to negligence as it applies to professionals such as physicians, dentists, nurses, technicians, attorneys, and accountants. "Medical malpractice" relates to professionals within the healthcare industry, to organizations that provide health care, and to the institutions in which health professionals practice, such as hospitals. An examination of the general principles of negligence provides the foundation for an understanding of medical malpractice.

Usually, negligence is defined as the failure to exercise ordinary care. But ordinary to whom? If the law set the measuring standard too high, the day-to-day conduct of most of us would, by definition, be negligent. Consequently, lawsuits would involve standards of conduct that only a small fraction of the population could ever achieve. Defendants would be held to standards that they could not possibly attain. Conversely, setting the measuring standard too low would create a situation in which the vast majority of injuries caused by "negligence" would go uncompensated, because the conduct would not have fallen below the legal standard. Therefore, the law sets the standard by which it judges the conduct of each of us based on "reasonable" person criteria. By legal definition, negligence is a failure to exercise that degree of care which a reasonably prudent person would have exercised under the same circumstances.

Does that mean that every time someone fails to exercise ordinary care, a legal cause of action for negligence is created? An answer to this puzzlement lies in the quintessential explanation of negligence in a famous 1928 decision of U.S. Supreme Court Judge Benjamin Cardozo (see **Box 9-4**).[18]

Although the New York Court of Appeals recognized that the actions of the LIRR's employees in pushing the man may have been

---

Box 9-4

Mrs. Palsgraf suffered injuries while waiting for a train, when a man carrying a package attempted to board a moving train. A Long Island Rail Road (LIRR) employee reached out from the train to pull the man in. At the same time, another employee on the platform pushed the man from behind. This pushing caused the man's package to fall on the tracks. That package contained fireworks, which exploded, causing Mrs. Palsgraf's injuries when a scale fell on her.

---

negligent, it concluded that that was not enough upon which to base liability:

> Negligence is not actionable unless it involves the invasion of a legally protected interest, the violation of a right. Proof of negligence in the air, so to speak, will not do. . . . In every instance, before negligence can be predicated on a given act, background of the act must be sought and found a duty to the individual complaining, the observance of which would have averted or avoided the injury. . . . Negligence is not a tort unless it results in the commission of a wrong, and the commission of a wrong imports the violation of a right, . . . [H]e must show that the act as to him had possibilities of danger so many and apparent as to entitle him to be protected against doing it though the harm was unintended.

In essence, negligence is founded on the relationship between the actor and the victim. That relationship must be recognized by society as establishing a legal duty between the two. This requirement that a duty exist between actor and victim may produce contrary resolutions of similar factual patterns. A person can commit a single act that inflicts identical injuries on two different victims, but negligence law may bar recovery by one of the victims, while allowing recovery by the other.

Because the law recognizes the relationship between the healthcare provider and the patient in a situation such as that described in **Box 9-5**, the professional staff have a duty to warn the patient of such a danger. Not warning the patient about that danger is considered a breach of that duty, and the conduct of the professional staff is thus negligent to her.

Box 9-5

A patient comes to the office for a scheduled appointment. She slips in a hole in the wooden floor, falls, and breaks a leg. Everyone at the office was aware of the hole but did not warn the patient.

In the scenario of **Box 9-6**, there can be no negligence. The law does not require that a burglar be warned about the hole in the floor, because there is no relationship between the actor and the victim in this case. This is not to say that there is never any duty to a stranger, or even to a lawbreaker. In this illustration, however, no duty was created.

Box 9-6

A burglar breaks into and enters the same medical office as in Box 9-5, but without permission and consent. This individual falls in the same hole in the same wooden floor and also suffers a broken leg.

In and of itself, the existence of a duty is only the condition precedent to negligence. Specifically, negligence can occur only when there is a failure, or breach, by the professional to abide by the applicable standard of conduct established by that duty. Despite the existence of the requisite relationship between the healthcare provider and the victim, not every injury caused by the provider's conduct will be the result of negligence. If a patient dies from a heart attack during an operation, his or her death may not be attributable to the surgeon's conduct; instead, the death may have resulted from the normal risks of the operation or from circumstances beyond the control of the surgeon. For the law to recognize the professional culpability, the challenged conduct must have caused the injury or at least have been a causal link in a chain of events.

Four requirements define an act as one of negligence:[19,20]

- A legally recognized relationship exists between the parties.
- The healthcare worker has a duty of care to the patient.
- The healthcare worker breached the duty of care by failing to conform to the required standards of care.
- The breach of duty was the direct cause of harm, resulting in compensable damages for the negligent actions.

Generally, damages are measured by comparing the condition of the victim before and after the injury. If the victim is a wage earner, lost wages will be a factor, as will medical expenses and the victim's pain and suffering. Those persons who earn high wages will be compensated more than the poor. Likewise, younger victims are worth more than the elderly. A slow, lingering, painful death is more valuable than an instantaneous one.

In the example in **Box 9-7**, all of the components of negligence, except an injury that produces damages recognized by the law, are present. This woman may have been scared,

Box 9-7

A hospital employee telephoned a woman that her husband had been involved in an auto accident. At the hospital, the woman was shown the X-rays of a crushed head, presumably her husband's. She was not allowed to see the body. An hour later, she saw the driver's license of the dead man. It was not her husband! She sued, but the jury found no basis for liability.[21,22]

perhaps trembling with increased anxiety, but she suffered no compensable physical harm or damages.

MEDICAL MALPRACTICE

Within the context of medical care, negligence is the improper treatment or neglect of a patient. To constitute medical malpractice, the commission or omission of an action causing the injury must arise from the exercising of professional medical judgment. Failure of a nurse to properly maintain an intravenous tube constitutes professional malpractice, whereas failure to properly supervise the patient in the bathroom is ordinary negligence. Liability for malpractice may be imposed on individual providers of medical treatment or services, such as physicians, surgeons, dentists, nurses, therapists, and technicians, as well as on the facilities where services are rendered. A clear explanation of medical malpractice emerges from a ruling in an 1898 lawsuit:

A physician and surgeon, by taking charge of a case, impliedly represents that he possesses, and the law places upon him the duty of possessing, that reasonable degree of learning and skill that is ordinarily possessed by physicians and surgeons in the locality where he practices, and which is ordinarily regarded by those conversant with the employment as necessary to qualify him to engage in the business of practicing medicine and surgery. Upon consenting to treat a patient, it becomes his duty to use reasonable care and diligence in the exercise of his skill and the application of his learning to accomplish the purpose for which he was employed. He is under the further obligation to use his best judgment in exercising

his skill and applying his knowledge. The law holds him liable for an injury to his patient resulting from want of the exercise of knowledge and skill, or the omission to exercise reasonable care, or the failure to use his best judgment. The rule in relation to learning and skill does not require the surgeon to possess that extraordinary learning and skill which belong only to a few men of rare endowments, but such as is possessed by the average member of the medical profession in good standing.[23]

One way of appreciating the issue of "duty" is to analyze the concept of foreseeability.

[T]he role of foreseeability, as it relates to duty, [is] as follows:

Foreseeability is of prime importance in establishing the element of duty, and the question of defendants' negligence, if any, must of necessity hinge on the finding of a breach of that duty. If a reasonably prudent defendant can foresee neither any danger of direct injury nor any risk from an intervening cause he is simply not negligent.

If the chief element in determining whether defendant owes a duty or obligation to plaintiff is the foreseeability of the risk then that factor will be of prime concern in every case. Further, because it is inherently intertwined with foreseeability, such duty or obligation must necessarily be adjudicated only upon a case-to-case basis. Therefore, we do not now predetermine defendants' obligations in every situation by a fixed category; no immutable rule can be established to determine the extent of that obligation for every circumstance of the future. We do, however, define guidelines that will aid in the resolution of such an issue as is presented in the instant case.[24]

THE PHYSICIAN–PATIENT RELATIONSHIP

Liability for medical malpractice is predicated on the establishment of a relationship between physician and patient. Legally, a relationship is created when there is treatment, expectation of treatment, or diagnosis for the purpose of treatment.[20] This relationship may by established by express or implied agreement. A patient may verbally agree to treatment or may do so without actually saying the words. Usually, the patient goes to the physician, a relevant interaction occurs between the parties, and there is agreement that the diagnosis, treatment, and consultation will ensure compensation. Nevertheless, the physician–patient relationship and agreement is similarly established by the treatment of an unconscious patient brought into an emergency room.

In the context of this relationship, the physician may be thought to be hired for only a specific limited purpose—to perform a preschool or camp physical examination, for example. Because of the limited nature and scope of such a physician–patient relationship, there is no duty on the physician's part to give specialized advice or treat the patient for a previously undiagnosed condition. A person seeking benefits under an insurance policy will often be sent by the insurer to a physician of the insurer's choosing, whom it pays for the purpose of conducting an independent medical examination (IME). The purpose of the IME is to substantiate the claimed injuries and the entitlement to benefits. Because no true physician–patient relationship exists,[25] the physician has only a limited duty to the person examined, at least "not to injure a patient during his physical examination."[26]

DUTY TO PERFORM PROFESSIONALLY

Medical practice deals with medical science and skills that are outside the knowledge of the ordinary or average person. Thus the standard by which conduct is measured must be altered to accommodate the specialized area of medicine. Physicians must possess the skills and knowledge that reasonably competent physicians possess—a standard comparable to the one that applies to lay people, who are legally bound to act as reasonably prudent individuals. A legal duty is imposed on physicians to use ordinary and reasonable care in the exercise of such skill and knowledge, tempered with a duty to use their best judgment. Even though physician incompetence may be easily recognizable, as in the example in **Box 9-8**, an action for liability may not ensue immediately.

Box 9-8

An anesthesiologist had physical disabilities caused by a stroke and alcoholism. His colleagues allowed him to continue practicing despite his problems. During routine back surgery, the anesthesiologist injected a 44-year-old patient with 10 to 20 times the recommended dose of a sedative. A lack of oxygen followed, and the patient suffered irreversible brain damage such that he would require 24-hour nursing care for the rest of his life. A court judgment declared the physician "an incompetent anesthesiologist," and the jury awarded $13.6 million to the patient and his family.[27]

Establishing the "reasonably competent" physician as the standard by which to measure the conduct of doctors may seem unusual. However, a comparison with the law of ordinary negligence demonstrates the wisdom of this standard. If all physicians were required to possess the skill and knowledge possessed by "excellent" doctors, 85% of the physicians would fail the test. In contrast, if the standard were the skill and knowledge of the "fair" doctor, society wold be condoning treatment and conduct that produces injuries for which there would be no compensation.

Given that medicine is an inexact science, the mere possession of the requisite skill and knowledge is not enough. Through the law, society imposes a duty on physicians to always use their best judgment. There is no liability when physicians make an error in judgment, provided they have not deviated from accepted medical practice.

At times, the line of demarcation between malpractice and an error in judgment is difficult to ascertain. Moreover, the duties to use "best judgment" and to follow "accepted medical practice" often conflict with each other. If a patient can demonstrate that the decision to follow accepted medical practice was a violation of the duty to exercise best judgment, the physician may have been guilty of malpractice.

Traditional doctrine states that a physician should be held only to that degree of skill and knowledge possessed by reasonably competent physicians within the same specific area of practice. Several courts have expanded the original restrictive definition to require that physicians must keep up with advances in their respective field, in addition to conforming to community standards. Moreover, the notion of the community or locality against which conduct will be measured is not fixed, but may fluctuate according to the nature of the particular part of the country involved.

If physicians practice as specialists, they are held to the standard of the skill and knowledge possessed by reasonably competent similar specialists. This level of skill and knowledge is greater than that possessed by general practitioners.

The law generally permits the medical profession to establish its own standard of care. Although a plaintiff in a medical malpractice case does not always require expert testimony to establish a *prima facie* case (*Benson v. Dean*, 232 N.Y. 52, 133 N.E. 125; *Meiselman v. Crown Hgts. Hosp.*, 285 N.Y. 389, 34 N.E.2d 367; *Hammer v. Rosen*, 7 N.Y.2d 376, 198 N.Y.S.2d 65, 165 N.E.2d 756), evidence that a physician conformed to accepted community standards of practice usually insulates him from tort liability (*Benson v. Dean, supra*, 232 N.Y. p. 58, 133 N.E. p. 127; Prosser, *Torts* (3d ed.), p. 168; see, also, McCoid, Liability of Medical Practitioners, 12 *Vanderbilt L.Rev.* 549, 605 ff). There is, however, a second principle involved in medical malpractice cases. Having its genesis in the reasonable man rule, this principle demands that a physician should use his best judgment and whatever superior knowledge, skill and intelligence he has (Prosser, *op. cit.*, p. 164). Thus, a specialist may be held liable where a general practitioner may not. The principle has been accepted by the Restatement of the Law of Torts (Restatement 2d, *Torts*, s 299A, comment c; s 289, subd. (b) and comment m; s 299, comment f; see, also *Harris v. Fall*, 7 Cir., 177 F. 79, 27 L.R.A.,N.S., 1174; cf. Note, *Duty of a Manufacturer to Discover Unforeseeable Common Uses of His Product,* 66 Col.L.Rev. 1190, 1192–1193). *Toth v. Community Hospital at Glen Cove,* 22 N.Y.2d 255, 262, 239 N.E.2d 368, 37, 292 N.Y.S.2d 440, 447 (N.Y. 1968).

Sources of Professional Standards

Although it is understood that healthcare professionals will be judged by standards of behavior, no universal statement of professional standards applies to every possible provider in all possible situations. In addition to the opinions of experts and the actual practices of healthcare providers, there are several sources of professional standards:

- Government statutes and regulations on licensure, certification, and professional conduct
- Standards developed by professional societies and credentialing agencies
- Voluntary accrediting agency standards such as techniques to minimize risks of infection and staffing norms for intensive care
- Administrative policies and rules of a hospital or other institution

ADDITIONAL THEORIES OF LIABILITY

Several other theories of liability are common, and risk managers should be aware of legal actions related to these theories of informed consent, strict liability, *res ipsa loquitur,* and vicarious liability.

Informed Consent

Court decisions have affirmed that a patient has the right "to determine the course of his own medical treatment" and to "decline medical treatment."[28] A physician has a duty to explain to the patient the diagnosis, the prognosis, the proposed treatment, the treatment alternatives, and the risks and benefits of each (see **Box 9-9**); these are the legal elements of informed consent.

In a lawsuit claiming lack of informed consent, the plaintiff has the burden of proving that the defendant failed to disclose material risks that would have been disclosed by a reasonable physician under similar circumstances.[29] That the treatment was medically sound is no defense. A patient still has the right to decide whether to consent to the treatment.

Box 9-9

An orthopedic surgeon performed back surgery after a patient's auto accident injury. The patient continued to have pain, so two more operations were performed. A jury found that the patient had not given informed consent to the three operations. He was not told of the possibility of surgical failure or that his pain might not be relieved. Informed of the risks, a reasonable person might have chosen to forego the surgery. There was no evidence that the surgeon had been negligent, but the patient was awarded $170,000.[30]

Strict Liability

Under normal theories of malpractice and negligence, professionals are liable if their conduct is "at fault." In the doctrine of strict liability, however, liability is assessed irrespective of fault in certain limited areas. This doctrine has its greatest impact on the sale of products. A manufacturer of a product sold on the open market ordinarily is strictly liable for any injuries caused by a defect in the item, without regard to questions of improper or negligent conduct. Because the manufacturer is in the best position to control the product and to ensure its safety, the risk of loss is viewed as another cost of doing business. Strict liability may be applicable in connection with the ingestion of pharmaceuticals, radiological diagnostic services, and the utilization of medical devices. This doctrine of strict liability has not been widely applied with respect to the mere rendition of medical services.

Res Ipsa Loquitur

Res ipsa loquitur means "the thing speaks for itself." Courts relying on this doctrine require a plaintiff to demonstrate the following four elements:[31]

- The injury would not ordinarily occur in the absence of negligence.
- The injury was caused by the actions or instrumentality within the exclusive control of the defendant.
- The injury was not due to any action on the part of the plaintiff.
- The evidence surrounding the circumstances relating to or concerning the injury was mostly within the control of the defendant.

Vicarious Liability

In medical malpractice, the doctrine of holding one person liable for the acts of another depends on the theories of agency and control. Courts have held that where two physicians jointly participate in the diagnosis and treatment of a patient, each is liable for the other's negligent treatment.[32] As opposed to the rule with respect to a partnership, membership in a professional corporation does not in itself make one physician shareholder vicariously liable for the malpractice of another physician shareholder. In the absence of supervision or control, the referral of a patient from one physician to another does not make the referring physician liable for the malpractice of the other physician.

HOSPITAL LIABILITY FOR MEDICAL MALPRACTICE

A court ruling summarized the legal responsibility of the hospital:

> Present day hospitals . . . do far more than furnish facilities of treatment. They regularly employ on a salary basis a large staff of physicians, nurses and interns, as well as administrative and manual workers, and they charge patients for medical care and treatment. . . . Certainly, the person who avails himself of "hospital facilities" expects that the hospital will attempt to cure him, not that its nurses or other employees will act on their own responsibility. . . . Hospitals should, in short, shoulder the responsibility borne by everyone else. There is no reason to continue their exemption from the universal rule of respondeat superior.[33]

Hospital liability is based on two theories: (1) *respondeat superior* and (2) ostensible agency, or agency by estoppel.

An institution may be responsible for the conduct of the physicians who practice there, as well as for its own actions. However, a hospital is an artificial entity, usually assuming a corporate form. As a corporation, a hospital cannot act except through its employees or other agents. Given this situation, the law adopts the practical approach that the employer is in the best position to control its employees, and applies liability to the employer through the doctrine of *respondeat superior*. Vicarious liability of the employer means that employers are responsible for the negligent conduct of their employees when those employees are acting on behalf of the employer. At one time, the law exempted charitable organizations from vicarious liability, but modern legal theory has eliminated that immunity.

Respondeat superior is manifest in individual employees of the hospital, such as nurses, therapists, technicians, service personnel, and other administrative personnel. Even though the nonmedical staff may not provide professional services, the hospital is liable for their conduct through the ordinary rules of negligence (see **Box 9-10**).

Box 9-10

- In November 2001, a transport stretcher carrying a Massachusetts woman collapsed, fracturing the woman's thoracic vertebra and paralyzing her. She was awarded a settlement of $1.03 million.
- In February 2000, Tennessee healthcare providers failed to monitor a ventilator patient undergoing a CT scan; the ventilator ran out of oxygen, leaving the patient in a persistent vegetative state. The verdict awarded the victim $7,366,000.
- In October 1999, inappropriate respiratory therapy resulted in the death of a 17-year-old quadriplegic in Virginia. His family was awarded a verdict of $400,000.
- In August 1998, a therapist improperly set the high-pressure alarm on a ventilator, and a Virginia man suffered a hypoxic ischemic brain injury. He was awarded a settlement of $700,000.
- The failure to provide occupational and physical therapy during an extended hospitalization caused several contractures in the patient, such that the victim required health aide assistance. The verdict in July 1998 in Washington, D.C., gave the patient $1.5 million.
- In November 1997, a woman in Florida suffered cardiac arrest during paramedic treatment. An endotracheal tube was not properly placed or was dislodged. The emergency room (ER) physician failed to correct the tube placement and brain damage resulted. The settlement was $3.6 million.[34]

A complex problem arises when hospitals contract with third parties to provide medical and other professional services. This legal situation is most commonly encountered in connection with the rendering of anesthesia, pathology, radiology, or emergency room services, as illustrated in **Box 9-11**.

Box 9-11

A plaintiff's decedent was cared for in the hospital by a physician who had a contract to operate the emergency room service. The plaintiff's lawsuit alleged negligence by the attending physician. Because the ER physician was an independent contractor, the hospital sought to escape vicarious liability. Specifically, the contract disclaimed that the hospital was the employer of the physician. An appellate court reversed the dismissal of the lawsuit by the trial court, declared the disclaimer void, and ruled that as a matter of law the physician was an employee of the hospital.[35]

The appellate court ruling in the case described in **Box 9-11** commented that the contract mandated that the physician comply with the rules of the hospital, that the physician use a fee schedule set by the agreement, and that the physician be guaranteed a minimum income. In addition, the hospital provided administrative support for the emergency room. Within these basic attributes, an employer–employee relationship existed. Perhaps seeking a broader base to establish its ruling, the court also held that the nature of the relationship of the parties barred the hospital from denying liability. This court ruling recognized that the contractual arrangement between the hospital and its physicians is transparent and invisible to the general public. In such situations, courts hold these individuals to be de facto employees. Consequently, the hospital is liable for their negligence just as if these professionals were explicitly employed by the institution. An alternative theory supporting hospital liability states that the hospital is "holding out" these professionals as if they were employees.

Although the courts have not been uniform in applying the doctrine of *respondeat superior* to these contracted services, they often identify specific indicators in determining liability: How much control does the hospital exert over the person? How does the hospital pay for the contracted services? Are the rendered services normally performed by an employee? Who owns the equipment used? Which choices are available to the patients?

This problem of contracted services may be examined from two perspectives: that of the patient and that of an objective observer. Plaintiffs who hold the hospital vicariously liable for the malpractice of its independent contractors rely on support from both perspectives. Through an examination of the factors appurtenant to the contractual relationship, the plaintiff may attempt to prove that the physician was a de facto employee or agent of the hospital. Alternatively, the plaintiff may attempt to demonstrate reliance on the fact that the physician practiced at the hospital. Because of that reliance, the patient did nothing else to verify the credentials of the physician, assuming that the hospital must have verified credentials and specified privileges for any physician who practiced within the institution.

The ostensible agency, or agency by estoppel, theory has been extended to hold the state of New York liable for the malpractice of an independent surgeon (see **Box 9-12**). After commencement of the lawsuit, the state sought to avoid liability on the grounds that the physician

was an independent contractor, not an employee, so the state could not be held vicariously liable for his negligence. Citing *Mduba v. Benedictine Hospital*, the appellate court affirmed the trial court's denial of the state's motion. Initially, the plaintiff had been examined by a state employee, who had then arranged for the surgical consultation; the consultation took place at the facility, the surgery was performed at the facility, and the surgeon was assisted by a facility nurse.

> The applicability of the doctrine [of ostensible agency or agency by estoppel] depends upon whether the plaintiff could have reasonably believed, based upon all of the surrounding circumstances, that the treating physician was provided by the defendant hospital or clinic or was otherwise acting on the defendant's behalf.

Box 9-12

An inmate at a New York State correctional facility underwent a lymph node biopsy excision after being examined by a physician's assistant. Surgery was performed by a semiretired general surgeon who rendered consultations for inmates. Following the surgery, the inmate claimed that the surgeon had committed malpractice by severing a spinal accessory nerve during the procedure.[36]

An Illinois appellate court explained the difference and interlocking nature of *respondeat superior* and apparent authority:

> In contrast to respondeat superior liability based on actual employment or agency, liability based on apparent authority may be imposed where the alleged negligence is by an independent contractor, and it is a different theory of recovery, with entirely different elements. Apparent agency is rooted in the

doctrine of equitable estoppel and is based upon the idea that "if a principal creates the appearance that someone is his agent, he should not then be permitted to deny the *371 agency if an innocent third party responsibly relies on the apparent agency and is harmed as a result." [*Oliveira ˝CBrooks v. Re/Max International, Inc.,* 372 Ill.App.3d 127, 137, 309 Ill.Dec. 889, 865 N.E.2d 252, 260 (2007) (quoting *O'Banner v. McDonald's Corp.,* 173 Ill.2d 208, 213, 218 Ill.Dec. 910, 670 N.E.2d 632, 634˝C35 (1996)].

In *Gilbert v. Sycamore Municipal Hospital,* 156 Ill.2d 511, 190 Ill.Dec. 758, 622 N.E.2d 788 (1993), the court recognized a claim for liability for negligence against a hospital founded upon apparent authority or agency where a doctor was not an employee but rather an independent contractor. The elements of this claim were as follows:

For a hospital to be liable under the doctrine of apparent authority, a plaintiff must show that: (1) the hospital, or its agent, acted in a manner that would lead a reasonable person to conclude that the individual who was alleged to be negligent was an employee or agent of the hospital; (2) where the acts of the agent create the appearance of authority, the plaintiff must also prove that the hospital had knowledge of and acquiesced in them; and (3) the plaintiff acted in reliance upon the conduct of the hospital or its agent, consistent with ordinary care and prudence. *Gilbert,* 156 Ill.2d at 524˝C25, 190 Ill.Dec. 758, 622 N.E.2d at 795. [*Williams ex rel. Beaton v. Ingalls Memorial Hosp.,* 408 Ill. App.3d 360, (2/17/11)].

As applied to contracted services, the doctrine of vicarious liability has an immediate and direct applicability to the emergency room, where patients are usually "service patients," or patients of the hospital itself (as opposed to individuals who enter the hospital only after referral from a private attending physician). However, vicarious liability also applies to physician services rendered to patients who are placed in the hospital by their private physician.

Anesthesiology is another area of practice that is likely to invoke vicarious liability. Anesthesia services are indispensable to any surgery and, as in the case of emergency room services, are typically contracted by the hospital. One anesthesiology group may provide such services, with each physician within the group having certain distinct responsibilities depending on the time and nature of the surgical procedure. An appellate court sustained a verdict against a hospital based on the alleged negligence of an anesthesiologist,[37] again relying upon the logic in *Mduba v. Benedictine Hospital.* Employing the objectivity test, the court held that a jury could, but was not required to, find the hospital vicariously liable on the basis of the degree of control exercised by the hospital over the anesthesiologist. Although the court commented that the patient was not aware of the independent status of the anesthesiology group and instead relied on the hospital, the ruling did not, as a matter of law, hold the hospital vicariously liable pursuant to the estoppel theory. In other words, the court felt that each case should be judged on its own particular facts. Logically, the courts can apply the same analytic approach to cases involving radiologists and pathologists. Points of discussion can center on the institution's control, the patient's subjective belief, or the patient's reliance on the facility. Ultimately, the court will render a policy decision based on the fact that a patient may enter a hospital through the emergency room, where the patient has no option regarding the treating physicians. That patient places the utmost trust in the institution and in the medical professionals who work there, without regard to the niceties of the financial arrangements between the hospital and those physicians. As recognized by one court,

> Having undertaken one of mankind's most critically important and delicate fields of endeavor concomitantly therewith the hospital must assume the grave responsibility of pursuing this calling with appropriate care. The care and service dispensed through this high trust, however technical, complex and esoteric its character may be, must meet standards of responsibility commensurate with the undertaking to preserve and protect the health, and indeed, the very lives of those placed in the hospital's keeping.[38]

HOSPITAL LIABILITY REGARDING STAFF PRIVILEGES

Hospitals permit doctors to perform professional services at their facilities by granting "staff privileges" that are based upon the specific training and area of practice of the individual physician. Each hospital employs a set of rules and regulations that it uses to measure and evaluate physicians for the purpose of granting or renewing privileges. In keeping with the negligence principles discussed earlier, hospitals may be liable for their negligence in affording staff privileges to incompetent physicians. "While a hospital is not responsible for the actual treatment of a patient by a private physician with staff privileges, the failure of a hospital to develop and adhere to reasonable procedures for reviewing a physician's

qualifications creates a foreseeable risk of harm thus establishing an independent duty to such patients."[39]

Using the same reasoning, liability could be assessed against any entity that negligently performs its credentialing function with the result that an otherwise ineligible physician commits malpractice. In this age of managed care, the most pertinent application of this doctrine would be the credentialing process employed by managed care entities such as health maintenance organizations.[40]

Corporate Negligence

Usually, a hospital is not liable for the negligence of its attending staff or nonemployed physicians, as it is assumed that these physicians exercise their independent judgment. Reacting to the realities of practice, however, modern theories of malpractice have developed the doctrine of corporate negligence. Under this doctrine, hospitals are liable for failing to review the credentials of their nonemployed attending physicians, or for failing to monitor the quality of care rendered by such physicians.

A rash of hospital mistakes, as described in **Box 9-13**, clearly demonstrates the magnitude of the risk manager's task in corporate negligence.

Box 9-13

- In a Michigan hospital, a surgeon removed the wrong breast during a mastectomy.
- Three incidents occurred in the same Florida hospital: (1) A patient with diabetes underwent surgery to amputate his diseased right foot; he awoke to find his left foot gone. (2) Another patient had surgery on the wrong knee. (3) A 77-year-old man died when a therapist mistakenly disconnected his ventilator.[10]

In part, the duty of a hospital to monitor the credentials and performance of physicians and other professionals practicing under its jurisdiction was established and recognized by statute and industry self-regulation. Under the federal Health Care Quality Improvement Act of 1986 (42 USC 11101-52), hospitals and other healthcare entities must review the credentials and malpractice history of all physicians who are granted admitting privileges. In a like manner, state licensure agencies and the standards of The Joint Commission detail the responsibility of hospitals to review the credentials of healthcare professionals.

Contributory Negligence

Given the existence of medical malpractice on the part of a treating physician or institution, the law requires a causal connection between the defendant's wrongful act and the plaintiff's injury. Where the condition of the patient may be severely impaired at the outset, the causal relationship between the injury and the alleged medical malpractice may be difficult to demonstrate.

Frequently, plaintiffs are guilty of some act of negligence that may have contributed to their own injury. In some jurisdictions, a jury finding that the plaintiff's own negligent actions contributed to the injury completely bars any recovery against the defendant. However, most jurisdictions allocate the damages according to the proportionate responsibility of the parties, applying the doctrine of contributory negligence.

As demonstrated in the example cited in **Box 9-14**, a jury has the right to apportion relative "blame." If overall damages were assessed at $1 million, with the plaintiff and defendant equally negligent, the plaintiff would recover $500,000 from the defendant.

Box 9-14

A patient died because the attending physician prescribed a drug that was contraindicated based on other medications the patient was taking. Evidence indicated that death was also caused by the presence of illegal substances taken voluntarily by the patient. At no point did the patient inform the physician about the use of illegal substances. A jury found that the patient's conduct made her 50% responsible for her death.[41]

LIABILITY THEORIES APART FROM MEDICAL NEGLIGENCE

Additional liability theories relevant to healthcare institutions may begin with unintentional medical negligence and proceed to intentional torts such as assault and battery, libel and slander, and invasion of privacy.

Intentional Tort or Conduct

Negligence is an unintentional tort because the actor does not intend to cause injury to the victim. In contrast, an intentional tort involves a specific action to cause harm, such as assault and battery. An intentional tort may take place when a physician performs a procedure contrary to the specific directions of the patient, or when a patient's confidential information is improperly released.

Assault and Battery

The words "assault" and "battery" are typically used together, and people perceive them as having the same meaning. In reality, battery is defined as the nonconsensual, unlawful, or wrongful physical constraint or touching of one person by another; assault is the perceived attempt at a battery. The examples in **Box 9-15** illustrate the distinction.

When a physician performs a medical procedure on a patient without consent, an action for assault and battery may be appropriate. "Any non-consensual touching of a patient's body, absent an emergency, is a battery and the theory is that an uninformed consent to surgery obtained from a patient lacking knowledge of the dangers inherent in the procedure is no consent at all."[46]

Libel and Slander

A defamatory written or printed statement is referred to as libel; slander is the speaking of such words to a third party. To be actionable, the words claimed to be defamatory must be false. If a physician discloses patient information that is not true, a defamation suit may be possible if the other elements, such as duty and damages, are provable. However, the physician may be liable under some other theory, such as contract or negligence, for the nonconsensual disclosure of truthful patient information.

Invasion of Privacy

A cause of legal action related to defamation is based on the invasion of the patient's privacy. For example, if a plastic surgeon used photographs of a patient, without the patient's consent, to advertise specialty services or procedures, the patient could sue for damages based on invasion of privacy. Typically, this situation involves the publication of "before and after" photographs.

TYPES OF DAMAGES

Courts may award different forms of compensation in successful actions against physicians, hospitals, or other healthcare providers:

- Compensatory damage awards cover economic losses for past and future medical and supportive care, or past and future loss of earnings resulting from physical impairment.
- Awards are given for pain and suffering, mental anguish, and loss of consortium, which are real and discernible but cannot be measured in economic terms.
- Punitive damage awards in excess of usual compensatory damages reflect gross negligence or deliberate wrongful intent, and are rarely granted except in the most egregious situations. In effect, they serve as an example to deter future similar conduct.

STATUTES OF LIMITATION

Statutes of limitation specify the maximum period of time after the patient's injury during which a lawsuit may be commenced, not terminated. If the lawsuit is not filed before this period expires, it is untimely and will be dismissed. The statutory period in the vast majority of states is between one and three years, but the time varies by state. For example, New York's statutory period is two and a half years. With some exceptions, the statutory period is "tolled" (deferred) during the infancy of a minor patient, and starts to run only on the patient's eighteenth birthday.

THE MOST COMMON AND MOST EXPENSIVE MALPRACTICE ALLEGATIONS

In recent years, the most frequently cited allegations in malpractice suits and the most expensive claims to settle have remained fairly constant.[47] The five most common malpractice allegations are as follows:

1. Surgery/postoperative complications
2. Failure to diagnose cancer
3. Surgery/inadvertent act
4. Improper treatment (birth related)
5. Failure to diagnose fracture or dislocation

The five most expensive settlements relate to the following allegations:

1. Improper treatment (birth-related)
2. Failure to diagnose hemorrhage
3. Failure to diagnose myocardial infarction
4. Failure to diagnose infection
5. Failure to diagnose cancer

A study of a nationwide database of 193,500 personal injury verdicts conducted by Jury Verdict Research, a firm that tracks jury awards, revealed that the average jury award in malpractice claims in the United States increased from $500,000 in 1995 to $1 million in 2000, and the national settlement median rose from $375,000 in 1995 to $500,000 in 2000. Nearly 60% of plaintiffs in medical malpractice

cases lose in front of a jury. Successful plaintiff's verdicts, however, have led to bigger awards than ever before; cases related to childbirth and cancer diagnosis have resulted in the highest jury verdicts.[48]

As of December 31, 2001, Medical Liability Mutual Insurance Company (MLMIC) insured 17,915 New York physicians. The company experienced its highest areas of loss indemnity for obstetricians (an average of $321,713), internal medicine (an average of $218,239), and general surgery (an average of $194,323):

- *Obstetrics:* 66% of cases were due to brain-damaged infants, other related injuries, and Erb's palsy.
- *Internal medicine:* 18.8% of cases were due to myocardial infarction and cardiac arrest/heart failure, 10.9% were due to colon cancer, and 9.1% were due to other related cancers.
- *General surgery:* 12.2% of cases were due to cholecystectomy; 9% to breast cancer.

The high-cost indemnity areas of the hospital for medical malpractice cases are the labor/delivery room, the ER, patients' rooms, the operating room, and the coronary care unit. General liability cases primarily concern the outcomes of slips and falls; in small hospitals this type of injury accounts for 68% of general liability cases, and in large hospitals it accounts for 80% of general liability cases.[49]

Breast, Colon, and Lu.5ng Cancer Risk Applications

Failure to diagnose breast cancer is still the main liability risk reported by the Data Sharing Project of the Physician Insurers Association of America (PIAA). This database includes more than 125,000 malpractice claims filed since 1985 and represents the insurers of 60% of all U.S. physicians. "Physical findings failed to impress the physician" was the most common reason (35%) for the delay in diagnosis; failure to follow up was a close second (31%).[50] Physicians named in breast cancer suits in 1995 included radiologists (24%), obstetricians (23%), family physicians (17%), and surgical specialists (14%). A detailed 1994 study of 500 claims found that 60% of the plaintiffs were younger than 50 years of age and that the average settlement was $307,000. PIAA advises physicians to be more aggressive in their diagnosis, especially with younger women.[51] Another PIAA study identified liability mistakes in breast, lung, and colon cancer.[52] In all three cancers, "a serious deficiency" in taking histories from patients was a major problem, as was overlooking signs of cancer in prior X-rays.

Another major problem, likely to be exacerbated when cost issues are considered, was that physicians did not order diagnostic tests in enough "suspicious" cases. In breast and colon studies, the leading cause of lawsuits was the failure or delay in ordering a specific test. "Inadequate evaluation," followed by failure to respond to an abnormal chest X-ray, was the leading cause in lung cancer suits. Failure to perform an endoscopic exam was the major reason for delay in diagnosis of colon cancer, followed closely by failure to perform a barium enema study.

Relative to breast cancer, the study suggested that providers take six precautions to avoid liability: (1) perform more careful examinations; (2) order additional studies; (3) explore complete family histories; (4) follow up after lumps are found, even if the mammogram is negative; (5) stress the importance of monthly self-examinations, particularly for women older than age 40; and (6) emphasize the importance of an annual or biennial mammogram for women older than age 40. Physicians must remember that mammograms are screening devices, not diagnostic tools. Even a fine-needle aspiration can miss the malignant tumor, and pathologists need considerable experience to interpret the aspirations.

Regarding colon cancer, physicians were urged to be more aggressive in treating younger patients. While it is uncommon for individuals younger than age 40 to have colon cancer, the probability increases after age 45. Key symptoms include bleeding, change in bowel habits, anemia, and weight loss. "Absolute indications for study include multiple polyposis, familial polyposis, ulcerative colitis, and villous adenoma. Failure to pursue a 'remote complaint' is a serious problem."[52]

The study strongly advised physicians to review prior X-ray films when considering a diagnosis of lung cancer. Regarding follow-up, the study said: "The importance of communicating the results of radiographic exams to the treating physician cannot be over-emphasized."[52]

Medication Errors

Between September 1, 1990, and December 31, 1994, 4,215 medication-related physician malpractice payments were reported to the National Practitioner Data Bank. Although 50% of the payments were less than $30,000, the mean payment was $124,998.[53] In another study based on data from 22 physician-owned professional liability insurance companies, the average settlement per case was $120,722. Analysis of the claim payment data reveals that medication error was the second most frequent and second

Box 9-16   The Most Common Medication Errors

Type of Error	Occurrence Percentage
Incorrect dosage	27
Inappropriate for medical condition	25
Failure to monitor for side effects	21
Communication failure between physician and patient	18
Failure to monitor for drug levels	13
Lack of knowledge of medication	13
Most appropriate medication not used	13
Inappropriate length of treatment	13
Failure to monitor for drug effects	12
Inadequate medical history	12
Inadequate charting	10
Failure to note allergy previously listed	10
Failure or delay in ordering laboratory test	8
Inappropriate method/site/route in administration of drug	8
Error in writing prescription	6
Patient noncompliance or error	6
Failure to read medical record	6
Pharmacy error	5
Communication failure between physician and pharmacist	4
Medication contraindicated by other medication	4
Failure or delay in reading laboratory test	4

most expensive claim against physicians. Internal medicine and family practice specialists accounted for 59.3% of all the claims and 45.8% of all the settlements. Significant injury, such as quadriplegia and brain damage, occurred in 42% of the medication errors. In 21% of the cases, the patient died, and the medication errors were a major contributing factor in death in 84.3% of the claims.[54] The causes of almost 400 drug-related claims resulting in payments of more than $5,000 are detailed in **Box 9-16**. Significantly, most of the claims involved more than one error.

Medication errors involve the interaction and communication between and among the physician, the nurse, and the pharmacist; each party may potentially commit different types of errors leading to liability. In most cases, these medication errors are preventable. Incorrect dosage is the most commonly reported medication error.

In combination, the fame of the newspaper columnist and the well-known good reputation of the treating institution brought considerable notoriety to the case described in **Box 9-17**. In addition to the disciplinary proceedings brought against physicians, nurses, and pharmacists, the inquiries initiated by The Joint Commission uncovered other areas of deficiency needing

Box 9-17

A drug overdose killed Betsy Lehman, age 39, an award-winning columnist at the *Boston Globe*. She had breast cancer and was given four times the intended dosage of a highly toxic drug during therapy at the Dana-Farber Cancer Institute. This error went unnoticed by a dozen doctors, nurses, and pharmacists. Another patient suffered heart damage after a similar drug overdose.[55]

correction to prevent further casualties. Responding to the resulting recommendations, the hospital committed $1.3 million to an education program concentrating on drug treatment protocols and appropriate medical record documentation.

"Indecipherable prescriptions are causing dangerous and costly illness" according to an American Medical Association report.[56] The cost of such errors involves liability payments as well as longer hospital stays, significant illness, or death.

Nurses should not rewrite illegible physician prescriptions or orders, because they could misinterpret the name of the drug or the dosage while copying the prescription. Additionally, the nurse could be charged with practicing medicine without a license.[57] Proper protocol requires the nurse to request clarification of all orders directly, so as to avoid misinterpretation and clinical hazards.

To avoid liability relating to the prescribing of medications, physicians should refrain from ordering unfamiliar medications, or drugs for conditions not normally handled by their own specialty. Medical record documentation should list all of the patient's current prescriptions, enumerate all known medication and other allergies, and detail discussions with the patient about his or her medications. Legible prescriptions and discussions with nurses and pharmacists are important aspects of patient care, especially in cases of unusual treatment protocols (see **Box 9-18**).[58]

To protect themselves, nurses must acknowledge suspected medication errors, report them to their supervisors and the attending physician, file an incident report, and document the event in the medical record. All adverse reactions of the patient, and

---

Box 9-18   Medication Errors

- When a Haldol prescription was 10 times the proper dosage, a man with Tourette's syndrome suffered an overdose and post-traumatic stress disorder. In a directed verdict, the jury awarded him $373,300 in November 2000.
- Owing to improper labeling of prescriptions, an overdose of prednisone caused a patient to develop avascular necrosis of the hips. The settlement amounted to $1 million (New York, June 2000).
- Magnesium sulfate was intravenously injected at eight times the prescribed dosage, leading the patient to fall into a coma for 10 weeks. The settlement was $650,000 (Illinois, December 1998).
- In a neonatal intensive care unit, an eight-pound newborn delivered by cesarean section was recuperating from corrective cardiac surgery. A missing decimal point in a prescription resulted in a tenfold overdose of intravenous potassium and the baby's death. The infant's parents filed a notice of claim for wrongful death.[33,59]

---

notification of the patient and family, should also be documented.[60]

Examining adverse drug events through a systems analysis of medication administration, investigators identified 16 major deficiencies leading to medication errors:[61]

1. Failure to disseminate knowledge about the medication
2. Failure to check the dosage and identity of the medication
3. Failure to provide the patient with information about the medication
4. Failure to accurately transcribe the medication order
5. Failure to prepare for an allergic reaction

6. Failure to track the medication order
7. Failure to communicate with all involved services
8. Incorrect use of devices
9. Lack of standardization of dosages and frequencies
10. Lack of standardization of drug distribution within a unit
11. Lack of standardization of procedures in general
12. Improper preparation of intravenous medications by nurses
13. Problems resulting from transfers or transitions of patients
14. Unresolved conflicts between providers of care
15. Problems with staffing and/or work assignments
16. Lack of feedback about adverse effects of medication errors

These failures of the healthcare system are directly linked to the most common medication errors ranked by frequency of claims.

Drug administration errors are traumatic events for nursing personnel. Nurses' self-esteem and confidence are shaken, and depending on the severity of the disciplinary process, their practice activities may change significantly.[62] The support of professional colleagues is very important, along with the appropriate measures to counteract any adverse consequences of the error. Prevention of further occurrences can be addressed through an understanding of the dynamics of the incident, in conjunction with education and discussions with all pertinent staff.

Causes of pharmacist liability have been identified by the Pharmacists Mutual Insurance Company as mechanical and intellectual.

Dispensing the wrong drug accounts for 54.9% of all such claims. More than two-thirds of the claims are for mechanical dispensing errors that can be controlled by the institution of relevant policies and procedures, prescription evaluations, careful computer entry and product handling, labeling, and dispensing. In the often complex arrangement for pharmacy services, there are several opportunities for cross-checking the appropriateness of the prescribed medication, dosage, administration orders, compounding, and preparation of admixtures and solutions.[63] If prescription legibility is the problem, direct communication with the physician and the nursing personnel who transcribe orders is essential for preventing medication errors.

In *Schroeder v. Lester E. Cox Medical Center, Inc.,* the hospital pharmacy was directly involved in a lawsuit (see **Box 9-19**).

Box 9-19

To permit arterial grafting, Irene Schroeder's doctors stopped her heart during coronary bypass surgery. A cardioplegic solution prepared in the hospital pharmacy was administered to protect the patient's heart. After the procedure, the surgeon attempted but failed to restart the heart and the patient died. A laboratory test of the cardioplegic solution revealed that it did not contain an adequate amount of dextrose, thus causing death. A jury awarded $92,000 in compensatory damages and $400,000 in punitive damages.[64]

Risk management responsibilities with regard to medication error incidents focus on diligence in reporting, documentation, and interaction with the physician–nurse–pharmacist triad to implement strategies for the future prevention of untoward events. Policies and procedures need to be continually reviewed, and incidents should be reported to the pharmacy and therapeutics committees. A comprehensive approach to this issue, with an emphasis on trending and education, is known to be successful in mitigating this risk.

Incidents cited by the U.S. Pharmacopeial Medication Errors Reporting Program reveal frequent sources of pharmacy errors—namely, confusion between opioid analgesics and drugs with similar generic names, with similar brand names, and with similar labels and packaging, as noted in **Box 9-20**.

Box 9-20   Medication Errors: Name Confusion in Drugs

- Celexa, Celebrex, and Cerebyx
- Acetozolamide and Acetazolomida
- Taxotere and Taxol
- Lamictal and Lamisil
- Roxicet and Roxaol
- Leukeran, Leucovorin and Leukine
- Zantac and Zyrtec
- Flomax and Volmax
- Adriamycin and Aredia
- Hydromorphone and morphine

More than 50% of the medication error reports are from hospital pharmacists, 4.8% from physicians, and 2.3% from nurses. Causes of these incidents include unclear and confusing packaging or labeling, suspected subpotency, and contamination. Drug administration dosage forms included injectables (35.5%), tablets (23.0%), and solutions (10.9%).[65] These manufacturing and quality control problems in the pharmaceutical industry present clear opportunities for risk management activities to reduce liability in clinical situations.

In an effort to reduce the improper use of drugs, the Food and Drug Administration has proposed that pharmacists provide patients with easy-to-understand "Medication Guides." More than 50% of Americans receiving prescriptions get no written instructions before using powerful drugs. Many patients leave healthcare facilities with prescription drugs for follow-up therapy but without written instructions. This FDA proposal would supply written patient information on drugs considered to have "serious and significant" health risks.[66]

OBSTETRICIANS UNDER FIRE

Two emerging and continuing trends have serious repercussions for both obstetricians and the patients who utilize their services: (1) the aggressive and sometimes violent activities of the anti-abortion movement and (2) the flight from practice of skilled obstetricians because of perceived risks of litigation.

One of the tactics employed by the anti-abortion movement is to institute malpractice suits against physicians who perform abortions. In the past 10 years, the Arizona Right-to-Life organization filed nine such actions. Although none resulted in a verdict against the physician, these suits had a demoralizing effect. As one doctor, who has been the object of several such suits, declared: "Even if they lose, they win." Physicians become uninsurable by carriers and their reputations are smeared.[67] In Texas, Life Dynamics, Inc., distributed pamphlets to women leaving abortion clinics listing reasons to initiate malpractice suits against their physicians.[68] Whereas previously many attorneys had refrained from instituting lawsuits involving abortions, lawyers have become increasingly active in pursuing actions on behalf of women injured during negligently performed abortions.[69] In New York State, criminal charges were lodged against one doctor whose patient died during an abortion (see **Box 9-21**).

Box 9-21

Dr. David Benjamin was sentenced to 25 years to life in prison for the murder of a 33-year-old woman who hemorrhaged from a uterine tear during an abortion.[70]

Physicians and hospitals are increasingly unwilling to endure the controversy and costs associated with the abortion debate. Thus more and more healthcare facilities are refusing to perform abortions. As a result, residents in obstetrics and gynecology will have fewer opportunities to develop the operative skills necessary to perform successful abortions, and this lack of experience will continue to pose risk problems.

The rising costs of malpractice liability insurance coverage for obstetric services have caused many physicians to stop delivering babies. Several other related factors have contributed to this situation: increases in malpractice claims against obstetric providers; fear of being sued; consolidations and closures of hospital obstetric services; issues concerning payments and Medicaid; and the daily stress of providing obstetric and gynecological services.[71]

Studies indicate that different problems arise related to obstetric practice in urban and rural areas. A California study of family practice physicians who discontinued obstetrics demonstrated that even a 25% reduction in the insurance premium was an insufficient inducement to resume obstetric services. Clearly, other issues were more of a demotivating factor than merely the cost of malpractice insurance.[72]

A review by the Washington State Physicians Insurance Exchange and Association of physicians who had discontinued obstetric practice showed that these physicians were more likely to be older, to be sole practitioners in an urban setting, and to have a higher rate of new obstetric malpractice claims. "Apparently, being named as the target of an obstetrical malpractice claim plays a significant role in the decision of some obstetricians to discontinue obstetrical practice."[73]

In essence, obstetricians are being driven out of business because of the combination of the high risk in this specialty to both the mother and the baby and the relentless pursuit of attorneys.

RISK MANAGEMENT ISSUES IN PROFESSIONAL LIABILITY LITIGATION

Certain personal and professional characteristics may be associated with providers believed to be at high or low risk of vulnerability to malpractice claims. Applying factors related to the quality of the structure, process, and outcome of patient care, statistical analysis revealed nine variables that predict high or low risk. Specifically, high risk was associated with increased age, surgical specialty, emergency department coverage, increased days away from practice, and the feeling that the litigation climate was "unfair." Low risk factors were linked to scheduling enough time to talk with patients, answering patients' telephone calls directly, feeling "satisfied" with practice arrangements, and acknowledging greater emotional distress.[74]

Are there common issues surrounding professional liability lawsuits? A survey of defense attorneys in Georgia by MAG Mutual Insurance Company identified six key areas where risk managers could make a difference.[75]

Unrealistic Patient Expectations

Approximately 88% of the lawyers stated that the patient and/or the family were surprised by the adverse outcome of medical treatment. Either they had unrealistic expectations, or they were not adequately educated regarding the course of treatment. To avoid this kind of risk, all written material, personal conversations, and telephone conversations should be documented and updated in the medical record when revised material is distributed. Defense attorneys will then know exactly what the patient was given at the time of treatment.[76]

Research has indicated that risk "appears related to patients' dissatisfaction with their physicians' ability to establish rapport, provide access, administer care and treatment consistent with expectations, and communicate effectively."[77]

No Response to Complaints

A failure by the physician to respond to the specific complaints that had instigated a patient's visit to the physician was cited by more than 80% of the attorneys. Healthcare professionals should maintain eye contact, not interrupt when the patient is talking, and observe a patient's body language. Physicians should document in the medical record that the patient's complaints were considered before a treatment was determined.

Illegible Medical Records

Nothing damages a case more than the hesitant, inarticulate efforts of physician witnesses to read their own illegible handwritten medical record notes. Nearly 77% of the lawyers identified illegibility as a significant problem, and this situation seriously inhibits the defense of a lawsuit. Incidentally, the "dictated but not read" annotation is not acceptable and has proved detrimental to the defense.

> At rest on my desk is a three-inch medical record that defies interpretation. It's part of a latent suit on alleged plastic surgical errors, and I have to send it to the surgeon who wrote the chart entries to have it transcribed...[78]

Insufficient Information in Medical Records

Not only must the information in medical records be legible, but the data should be significant and timely. Almost 70% of the lawyers claimed that information relative to medications, allergies, problems, telephone calls, and so on was missing from records and that the operative notes were written more than 24 hours after the procedure. A telephone record for each patient can document advice or prescriptions ordered directly from the pharmacy. Juries tend not be believe a physician who has no telephone log.

Comprehensive accounts are needed to describe unusual circumstances, such as a fall. The records should indicate the date, time, changes in the patient's condition, follow-up care (e.g., X-rays, laboratory data), patient or family discussions, and instructions.

Any corrections or addendums to medical records need to be made according to hospital-approved procedure (such as the word "error" or "initials"). It is not appropriate to obliterate, cross out, erase, tamper with, or otherwise change previous notes, either written or electronically entered. Often the medical record is the only evidence of the status of a patient's condition before, during, or after an event that has the potential for legal action.

No Follow-Up on Abnormal Tests

In many cases, information from diagnostic tests is not conveyed to the patient in a timely manner. Attorneys indicated that 62% of the suits involved the failure to follow up on abnormal test results. A system must exist to ensure that diagnostic reports are received, reviewed by the physician, acted upon, and placed in the record (see **Box 9-22**). A log of all diagnostic tests should be checked daily and not filed until it has been reviewed and initialed, and action, if required, has been taken.

Box 9-22   Lab Tests

Because of the late delivery of a blood sample and improper testing, there was a failure to detect spina bifida. This Washington, D.C., case resulted in a settlement of $1.1 million in August 2000.[33]

Professional Miscommunication

The opportunity for miscommunication is always present, and although miscommunication in itself may not be the proximal cause of a lawsuit, the misunderstanding may lead to errors prompting a legal action. Approximately 58% of the attorneys stated that miscommunication had occurred in many of their cases. Some common communication errors that can be remedied include the following:

- Lack of explicit directions or protocols for nursing personnel regarding when to notify the physician of a change in a patient's condition
- Inadequate communication of a patient's deteriorating condition from nursing personnel to the physician
- Failure of the covering physician to communicate to the primary physician the services provided to a patient
- Failure to communicate the degree of urgency to other healthcare personnel
- Lack of verbal communication from consultants, radiologists, or pathologists identifying an abnormality
- Reliance on the assumption that no response from the referral physician indicates that the patient's problem was resolved

These key risk factors, which have been cited in a significant number of lawsuits, can be modified through the practice of the specific risk management techniques already mentioned. Certainly, the techniques are not overly cumbersome and can decrease the likelihood of being involved in a legal action and/or increase the defensibility in court.

For an insightful and literate view of the physician–patient relationship from the perspective of a practicing doctor and teacher at Harvard Medical School, the reader is referred to "How Doctors Think" by Jerome Groobman. Dr. Groobman focuses on conditions—both procedural and human—that interfere with good communication between doctor and patient.

REFERENCES

1. Brennan, T. A., Leape, L. L., Laird, N. M., et al. (1991). Incidence of adverse events and negligence in hospitalized patients. *New England Journal of Medicine, 324*(6), 370–376.
2. Leape, L. L., Brennan, T. A., Laird, N. M., et al. (1991). The nature of adverse events in hospitalized patients. *New England Journal of Medicine, 324*(6), 377–384.
3. Localio, A. R., Lawthers, A. G., Brennan,T. A., et al. (1991). Relation between malpractice claims and adverse events due to negligence. *New England Journal of Medicine, 325*(4), 245–251.
4. California Medical Association. (1977). *Report of the Medical Insurance Feasibility Study*. San Francisco, CA: Author.
5. Brennan, T. A., Herbert, L. P., Laird, N. M., et al. (1991). Hospital characteristics associated with adverse events and substandard care. *New England Journal of Medicine, 265*(24), 3265–3269.
6. Leape, L. L., Lawthers, A. G., Brennan, T. A., et al. (1993). Preventing medical injury. *Quality Review Bulletin, 19*(5), 144–149.
7. Leape, L.L. (1994). Errors in medicine. *Journal of the American Medical Association, 272,* 1851–1857.
8. Jones, G. F. (1995, January 20). Jury awards parents $625,000 on fatal misdiagnosis of young son. *Star-Ledger* (Newark, N.J.), p. 28, col. 3.
9. Blumenthal, D. (1994). Making medical errors into "medical treasures." *New England Journal of Medicine, 272,* 1867–1868.
10. Hampson, R. (1995, March 19). Healing place or a horror? Medicial mistakes rock hospitals. *News Tribune* (Woodbridge, NJ), p. A10, col. 5.
11. Wrong lung was removed so hospital pays $9 million. (1995, April 2). *Star-Ledger* (Newark, NJ), p. 16, col. 5
12. The science of making mistakes. (1995). *Lancet, 345*(8954), 871–872.
13. Ibid.
14. Senders, J. W. (1993). Theory and analysis of typical errors in a medical setting. *Hospital Pharmacy, 28*(6), 505–508.
15. Kohn, K. T., Corrigan, J. M., & Donaldson, M. S. (Eds.). (1999). *To err is human: Building a safer health system*. Washington, DC: Institute of Medicine, National Academy Press.
16. Bayles, F. (1995, April 12). Doctors no longer sacred cows. Rash of criminal charges, indictments seen as evidence of rising public anger. *Staten Island Advance* (NY), p. A7, col. 1.
17. Lab charged with homicide for failing to detect cancer in Pap smears. (1995, April 13). *Star-Ledger* (Newark, NJ), p. 7.
18. *Palsgraf v. Long Island Rail Road*, 248 N.Y. 339, 1928.
19. King, J. H. (1986). The law of medical malpractice in a nutshell. St. Paul, MN: West, p. 9.
20. To prove a prima facie case of negligence, a plaintiff must demonstrate the existence of a duty, a breach of that duty, and that the breach of such duty was a proximate cause of his or her injuries. *Fox v. Marshall*, 88 A.D.3d 131, 928 N.Y.S.2d 317(2d Dept.), August 9, 2011.
21. Fiesta, J. (1995). Law for the nurse manager: Legal update. *Nursing Management, 26*(3), 10–11.
22. *Armstrong v. Paoli Memorial Hospital*, 633 A.2d 605, *The Citation*, February 1, 1944, 65:3:31.
23. *Pike v. Honsinger*, 155 N.Y. 201 (1898).
24. *Busta v. Columbus Hosp. Corp.*, 276 Mont. 342, 362, 916 P.2d 122, 134 (Mont., 1996).
25. *Savarese v. Allstate Insurance Company*, 287 A.D.2d 492, 731 N.Y.S.2d 226 (2d Dept. 2001).
26. *Evangelista v. Zolan*, 247 A.D. 2d 508, 669 N.Y.S.2d 325 (2d Dept. 1998).
27. Verhovek, S. H. (1994, April 9). Medical incompetence: A whispered factor in rising costs. *New York Times*, p. 8, col. 1.
28. *Matter of Storar*, 52 N.Y.2d 363, 438 N.Y.S.2d 266 (1981); see Sec. 2805-d of the New York State Public Health Law, and Sec. 4401-a of the New York State Civil Practice Law and Rules.
29. *Alberti v. St. John's Episcopal Hospital*, 116 A.D.2d 612, 497 N.Y.S.2d 701 (2d Dept. 1986).
30. No informed consent to back surgery. (1994). *American Medical News, 37*(4), 16.
31. *Fogal v. Genesee Hospital*, 41 A.D.2d 468, 344 N.Y.S.2d 552 (4th Dept. 1973).
32. *Graddy v. New York Medical College*, 19 A.D.2d 426, 243 N.Y.S.2d 940 (1st Dept. 1963).
33. *Bing v. Thunig*, 2 N.Y.2d 656, 163 N.Y.S.2d 3 (1957).
34. Healthcare Providers Service Organization. (2002). Case of the month archives, all professions. http://www.hpso.com/case/case index.lphp3

35. *Mduba v. Benedictine Hospital*, 52 A.D.2d 450, 384 N.Y.S.2d 527 (3d Dept. 1976).

36. *Soltis v. State of New York*, 172 A.D.2d 919, 568 N.Y.S.2d 470 (3d Dept. 1991).

37. *Augustin v. Beth Israel Hospital*, 185 A.D.2d 203, 586 N.Y.S.2d 252 (1st Dept. 2002).

38. *Beeck v. Tucson General Hospital*, 18 Ariz. App. 165, 500 P.2d 1153 (1972).

39. *Megrelishvili v. Our Lady of Mercy Medical Center*, 291 A.D.2d 18, 739 N.Y.S.2d 2 (1st Dept., 2002).

40. *Dykema v. King*, 959 F.Supp. 736 (D.S.C.,1997).

41. Hoffman, J. (1995, February 7). Jurors find shared blame in '84 death. *New York Times*, p. B1, col. 5.

42. *Benton v. Scroggie*, No. 93-146242, March 1994, p. 4.

43. Fiesta, J. (1995). Law for the nurse manager: Legal update. *Nursing Management, 26*(1), 30.

44. *Snyder v. Turk*, 627 N.E. 2d 1053 (Ohio Ct. of App., Aug, 19, 1993).

45. Irritated surgeon throws clamp at nurse in OR. (1995). *American Medical News, 38*(20), 22.

46. *Fogal v. Genesee Hospital*, 41 A.D.2d 468, 344 N.Y.S.2d 552 (4th Dept. 1973).

47. McCormick, B. (1995). Liability rates: Mixed signals. *American Medical News, 38*(4), 2, 31.

48. Lankarge, V. (2002, January). Soaring malpractice premiums bleed doctors, rob consumers. *Health Care News Consumer Insurance Guide*. www.heartland.org/health/jan02/malpractice.htm.

49. Robb, J. H. (2002). *Medical malpractice claims data: A 15-year review*. Presentation at 2002 MLMIC Risk Management Seminar, New York Helmsley Hotel, June 7, 2002.

50. Breast cancer leads the list of malpractice suits. (1995, June 3). *Star-Ledger* (Newark, NJ), p. 2, col. 3.

51. McCormick, B. (1995). Breast cancer still top liability risk: Cost of claims rising. *American Medical News, 38*(23), 22–23.

52. Clements, B. (1994). The most common causes of lawsuits and how you can protect yourself: Missed cancers. *American Medical News, 37*(28), 15–16.

53. Oshel, R. E. (1995). Personal communication, U.S. Department of Health and Human Services, Public Health Service, Division of Quality Assurance, National Practitioner Data Bank.

54. Crane, M. (1993). The medication errors that get doctors sued. *Medical Economics, 70*(22), 36–41.

55. Hospital official resigns over drug overdoses. (1995, May 12). *New York Times*, p. A16, col. 1.

56. Indecipherable Rx: Danger. (1995, June 13). *New York Times*, p. A22, col. 1.

57. Davino, M. (1995). Poor penmanship can create big legal risks. *RN, 58*(3), 51.

58. Clements, B. (1994). How to avoid medication errors. *American Medical News, 37*(27), 18.

59. Lambert, B. (2002, February 9). Baby dies in hospital, and parents plan to sue. *New York Times*, p. B6.

60. Parisi, S. B. (1994). What to do after a med error. *Nursing94, 24*(6), 59.

61. Leape, L. L., Bates, D. W., Cullen, D. J., et al. (1995). Systems analysis of adverse drug events. *Journal of the American Medical Association, 274*(1), 35–43.

62. Arndt, M. (1994). Research in practice: How drug mistakes affect self-esteem. *Nursing Times, 90*(15), 27–30.

63. Fitzgerald, W. L., & Roberts, K. B. (1993). Avoiding legal problems in pharmacy practice. *Drug Topics, 137*(21), 112–123.

64. LeBlang, T. R. (1993). Punitive damages. *American Druggist 209*(1), 21–22.

65. DPPR at a glance. (1995). *USP Quality Review, 47,* 1–4.

66. FDA wants pharmacists to make prescription medications user-friendly. (1995, August 24). *Star-Ledger* (Newark, NJ), p. 54, col. 1.

67. Lewin, T. (1995, April 9). Latest tactic against abortion: Accusing doctors of malpractice. *New York Times*, p. 1, col. 2.

68. Schreibman, T. (1995). Sue me, sue me. *New Woman, 25*(7), 59.

69. Shoop, J. G. (1995). Lawyers enter abortion fray on side of injured women. *Trial, 31*(2),12–14.

70. MD gets 25 years for abortion death. (1995, September 13). *Star-Ledger* (Newark, NJ), p. 5, col. 5.

71. Fondren, L. K., & Ricketts, T. C. (1993). The North Carolina obstetrics access and professional liablity study: A rural–urban analysis. *Journal of Rural Health, 9*(2),129–137.

72. Nesbitt, T. S., Arevalo, J. A., Tanji, J. L., et al. (1992). Will family physicians really return to obstetrics if malpractice premiums decline? *Journal of American Board of Family Practice, 5*(4), 413–418.

73. Rosenblatt, R. A., Weitkamp, G., Lloyd, M., et al. (1990). Why do physicians stop practicing obstetrics? The impact of malpractice claims. *Obstetrics & Gynecology, 76*(2), 245–250.

74. Charles, S. C., Gibbons, R. D., Frisch, P. R., et al. (1992). Predicting risk for medical malpractice claims using quality of care characteristics. *Western Journal of Medicine, 157*(4), 433–439.

75. Ostergard, N. (1993). Attorney survey reveals causes of litigation. *Journal of the Medical Association of Georgia, 82*(8), 414–416.

76. Ridder, W. (2000, Spring). Risk tips: Chart what you say. Risk Management Foundation of the Harvard Medical Institution. *RMF Quarterly*, 3. www.rmf-harvard.edu/publications/quarterly/spr2000/Qspr2000_ab/body.html.

77. Hickson, G. B., Federspiel, C. F., et al. (2002). Patient complaints and malpractice risk. *Journal of the American Medical Association, 287*(22), 295.

78. Ridder, W. (2000, Winter). Risk tips: Handwriting on the wall for illegible notes. Risk Management Foundation of the Harvard Medical Institution. *RMF Quarterly*, 3. www.rmfharvard.edu/publications/quarterly/win2000/Qwin2000a8body.html

CHAPTER 10

Strategies to Reduce Liability: Managing Physicians and Litigation Alternatives

Arthur S. Friedman

USING TOOLS TO REDUCE LIABILITY

Being *cognizant* of the numerous tortious events inherent in, and ancillary to, the delivery of healthcare services is qualitatively and significantly different from knowing when a negligent act will take place. Those who deal with the prevention of the tangible and emotional effects of "accidents" must both intellectually and realistically accept the fact that people will inevitably suffer injury from negligence. One of the primary responsibilities, therefore, is to establish conditions—physical and operational—that minimize the risk (and resulting injury) of a tortious act. Fortunately, those who manage that risk are armed with numerous weapons that work synergistically to reduce the chance of professional malpractice.

PROFESSIONAL PRACTICE ACTS

State legislation defines the scope of professional practice, and details the powers and functions of the regulatory board for each healthcare provider group licensed by the state. The statutory definitions delineate the scope of practice and the degree of interdependence with other practitioners, particularly physicians. State legislation uniformly grants physicians the power to diagnose and to treat patients. Lawyers frequently refer to the physician as the "captain of the ship" when care is rendered concurrently to sick and ailing patients by a number of different healthcare professionals.

Regulatory boards for each of the professions are created by statute. Legislation specifies the composition of the board, along with its duties and its broad powers to create rules and regulations for specific requirements for professional practice. A process of licensure is detailed, and can include state guidelines for mandatory continuing education and the continuous monitoring of the professionals on behalf of the public.

Professional discipline involves investigation and prosecution of allegations of profound misconduct of licensees, as well as the illegal practice of the profession by unlicensed persons. Moral character issues and health-impaired professional licensees are subject to investigation and appropriate action, such as discipline, license revocation or suspension, fines, or referrals for professional assistance.

Several categories of misconduct may trigger investigations, hearings, and possible actions against licensees:[1]

- Repeated acts of negligence
- Incompetence

- Aiding or abetting the unlicensed practice of medicine
- Failure to comply with government rules or regulations regarding the practice of medicine
- Exploitation of the patient for financial gain
- Evidence of moral unfitness to practice medicine
- Failure to maintain appropriate patient medical records
- Abandoning or neglecting a patient
- Harassing, abusing, or intimidating a patient, either physically or verbally
- Ordering excessive tests or treatments
- Unlawful use of controlled substances

Although the particular procedures for disciplining professionals may vary by jurisdiction, an inquiry is usually initiated by the receipt of a complaint. If an investigation reveals evidence of substantive (as opposed to "technical") misconduct, the involved professional will be notified of the nature of the claimed misconduct in a formal charge. At this stage in the proceeding, many cases are settled through a consent agreement. If the case is not settled, however, a hearing will be held at which the agency will be required to present proof to sustain the charges. In his or her defense, the professional can be represented by counsel and has the right to cross-examine the complainant's witnesses and to present his or her own witnesses. In cases where it is deemed that the public would be in danger if the professional continued to practice, the agency has the authority to suspend the practitioner's license immediately.

At the conclusion of the hearing by the fact-finding body, either a panel or an administrative law judge will make recommendations.

Adverse actions recommended can include revocation, suspension or limitation of the practitioner's license, probation, censure, and reprimand. There is usually at least one level of appeal within the administrative agency. A sanctioned professional may appeal the final administrative ruling in the court system, albeit with the understanding that judicial review is usually limited to whether the decision of the agency was supported by the evidence, and whether the

Box 10-1

- Mount Sinai Hospital was fined $66,000 by the New York State Health Department and suspended its live-donor liver transplant program in January 2002. Journalist Mike Hurewitz, age 57, died three days after donating part of his liver to his brother. Inadequate postoperative care was cited in his death.[2]
- The Massachusetts State Board of Registration in Medicine indefinitely suspended an orthopedic surgeon's medical license because he left an anesthetized patient with an open incision in his back in the operating room while the surgeon went to deposit his paycheck in a bank several blocks away from the Mount Auburn Hospital, where he was operating. The Board labeled him a "serious threat" to the health, safety, and welfare of the public.[3]
- The New Jersey State Board of Medical Examiners suspended the license of Dr. Jose A. Lopez when a 28-year-old mother of three died after "tummy tuck" surgery in the physician's office. Dr. Lopez was a pathologist who received plastic surgery training in Colombia. He was not board certified and had no hospital affiliations. Another of his patients was admitted to the hospital three days after liposuction because of abdominal bleeding consequent to excessive doses of lidocaine as an anesthetic. A state investigation revealed that many of Dr. Lopez's patients had suffered near-fatal infections, perforated bowels, or torn abdomens.[4]

sanctioning action taken was not arbitrary or capricious—that is, whether the penalty was disproportionate to the claimed violation. Because violations of professional conduct can lead to disciplinary sanctions and possibly malpractice lawsuits, standards and guidelines have emerged to alleviate potential problems (see **Box 10-1**).

As an example, there are 90,000 licensed physicians in the state of New York. The New York State Board for Professional Medical Conduct (OPMC) is composed of 144 physician and nonphysician lay members. OPMC statistics document that in 2010, there were 8,501 complaints received (a 33% increase over the number in 2000), and 322 licensees referred for charges (a 17% *decrease* from 2000). Disciplinary final actions against physicians include 63 surrenders, 22 revocations, 87 suspensions, 94 censures and reprimands, and 84 administrative warnings. The Commissioner of Health issued 13 summary suspensions to physicians who were declared an "imminent danger" to the public.[5]

Impaired Professionals

Health problems, disease, and disability affect healthcare professionals just as they do other members of society. However, when these medical impairments adversely affect professional judgment, patient care, collegial expectations, and social role, private and public interventions become necessary.

In a series of interviews with ill physicians, Spiro,[6] a Yale University medical school professor, found a remarkable ability for denial, continuing to practice despite pain, and reluctance to disclose their diagnosis for fear of losing professional standing. Everyone is concerned with the physiological changes that accompany aging, such as reduced visual acuity, memory lapses, depression, toxic effects of medications, and reduced functional capabilities. Additional risks to professional competence and performance are incurred with alcohol abuse, chemical dependency, and psychiatric diagnoses. Symptoms of impairment should be recognized and appropriate actions taken to help intervene with treatment, rehabilitation, and prevention of untoward professional activities. Examples of symptoms of physical impairment include the following:[7]

- Making rounds late
- Inappropriate orders
- Complaints from staff
- Frequent accidents
- Hostile behavior
- Unexplained absences
- Mood swings, arguments, and violent outbursts
- Deterioration of personal hygiene
- Multiple somatic complaints
- Excessive drinking at staff functions
- Frequent job changes or relocations
- Neglected social commitments

Prompted by a 1973 landmark article on the sick physician in the *Journal of the American Medical Association,*[8] state medical societies and licensing boards have made considerable progress in developing effective programs to identify and treat impaired physicians. Patterned after employee assistance programs (EAPs), a physician assistance committee (PAC) and program were established at the University of Maryland Medical System as a standing committee of the medical board. This PAC accepts referrals from a variety of sources, arranges for specific evaluations, refers physicians to treatment, monitors compliance, and advocates for the physician as long as there is compliance with the treatment agreement. Most of the cases the PAC sees are related to alcohol or drug dependence; approximately 20% of the cases involve psychiatric or interpersonal problems.[9]

Established in 1980, the Physician Health Committee of the Medical Society of the District of Columbia reports an 80% success rate for impaired physicians. Medical specialists using the program established by this committee include internists (15%), psychiatrists (12%), family and general practitioners (12%), and obstetricians and gynecologists (7%).[10] A program similar to Alcoholics Anonymous, the Impaired Physician Program of the Medical Association of Georgia reported that 77% of treatment outcomes for physicians recovering from substance abuse are successful.[11]

The Committee for Physicians' Health (CPH), a division of the Medical Society of the State of New York, monitors approximately 550 physicians recovering from substance abuse disorders and other psychiatric disorders. Each year, approximately 100 "new" physicians enroll in the monitoring program. In 2001, 32.7% of the newly enrolled physicians had a diagnosis of drug abuse or dependence, 22.2% had a diagnosis of alcohol abuse or dependence, 15.4% had a diagnosis of drug and alcohol abuse or dependence, 28.8% had a diagnosis of mental or emotional disorders, and 1.9% had a diagnosis of both drug/alcohol abuse or dependence and mental or emotional disorders.[12] Activities of the CPH are confidential and protected by state and federal law, and they are immune to legal challenges. CPH does not report physicians to the OPMC as long as they agree to participate, stay with the program, are helped by treatment, and do not present an imminent danger to the public. In 2010, the New York OMPC reported that out of 307 final actions, 35 involved impairment.[5]

The risks posed by impaired professionals can be extensive and potentially costly. Removal of their practices protects the public and prevents identifiable problems. However, salvaging professional careers should become an important parallel activity, with due concern given to confidentiality and reduction of the stigma that accompanies official actions against healthcare professionals.

Sexual Misconduct

The Hippocratic Oath warns, "I will come for the benefit of the sick, remaining free of all intentional injustice, of all mischief and in particular of sexual relations with both female and male persons." Physicians are not unique where sexual misconduct and harassment are concerned. These behaviors occur in all professions. In the healthcare milieu, such misconduct results from the innate power differential residing in the dependency of the patient on the professional, who exploits the opportunities.[13]

Sexual misconduct and harassment have significant harmful effects on patients, as well as ruinous consequences for the professional. Hospitals experience a three-year average of 5 rapes per year and approximately 40 other sexual assaults, according to a survey of the International Association for Healthcare Security and Safety.[14] Victims in this survey included patients and visitors; suspects included patients, employees, and one physician. Two Florida incidents are illustrative (see **Box 10-2**).

In 1990, the American Medical Association Council on Ethical and Judicial Affairs considered the sexual misconduct problem extensively and issued the following statement: "There is a

- A male nurse was witnessed raping a minor female patient at Citrus Memorial Hospital. Police charged him with "five separate counts of rape and interviewed more than 40 women who may have been victims."
- A male occupational therapy aide attacked a mentally disturbed 26-year-old female patient at Memorial Regional Rehabilitation Center. He was charged with sexual battery.[15]

long-standing consensus within the medical profession that sexual contact or sexual relations between physicians and patients are unethical."[16] The AMA Code of Medical Ethics, Opinion 8.14, affirmatively declares that "Sexual contact that occurs concurrent with the patient–physician relationship constitutes sexual misconduct." Subsumed under this ethical standard are a wide range of situations encountered in a professional's daily medical practice:

- Predatory physicians with serious personality disorders who systematically attempt to seduce patients
- Professionals who claim to use sex for therapeutic purposes
- Professionals who abuse the physical examination in an inappropriate erotic manner (see **Box 10-3**)

Box 10-3

Dr. Brij Mohan was charged with 18 allegations of professional misconduct with 6 female patients between 1991 and 1994. He fondled the breasts and genitals of female patients and asked them for sex during examinations. There were three statutory violations: abusing a patient; moral unfitness; and fraudulent practice of medicine. He admitted guilt and surrendered his license. After a year, he could apply to have his license returned.[17]

- Professionals who date patients or encourage or contribute to infatuation, intense lovesickness, or romantic situations
- Professionals who engage in sexual harassment, making erotic or suggestive remarks to patients

In 2010 in New York State, there were approximately 22 disciplinary final actions involving sexual misconduct by physicians.[5] This represents an upward trend in New York— up from 15 such actions in 2009—and may be the result of increased reporting on the part of patient-victims. There appears to be a growing trend of "zero tolerance" toward physician sexual misconduct. Physicians with these psychiatric problems or severe personality disorders are dealt with punitively by state licensing agencies and boards of professional medical conduct.

A more tolerant and compassionate attitude may be demonstrated toward physicians who experience psychiatric problems attendant to alcoholism, drug or substance abuse, and depression or organic brain disorders than toward physicians charged with sexual abuse. Physicians charged with sexual misconduct are regarded as an embarrassment to the professional community and are shunned by the mainstream. Although these physicians presumably also are psychiatrically impaired, their rehabilitation potential is viewed as poor.

FEDERATION OF STATE MEDICAL BOARDS

Many healthcare professionals have licenses to practice in several states concurrently. The Federation of State Medical Boards (FSMB), and the federal National Practitioner Data Bank help licensing boards share information across state lines concerning adverse actions taken against professionals (see **Box 10-4**).

FSMB membership consists of 70 medical boards, including allopathic, osteopathic, and composite state medical boards, plus the boards in the District of Columbia, Puerto Rico, Guam, Commonwealth of the Northern Mariana Islands, and the U.S. Virgin Islands. Through this organization, the state medical boards cooperate and share information about physicians to enhance their protection of the public and to improve the quality of care.

FSMB publishes electronically an Annual Summary of Board Actions, a compilation of disciplinary actions initiated by its member boards. The Federation Physician Data Center (FPDC) contains disciplinary actions related to physicians dating back to the 1960s. This data set is available to licensing and disciplinary boards, and government and private agencies involved in employment and/or credentialing of physicians. In 2010, the FPDC recorded 5,562 actions reported by all of the medical boards. Of these, 4,798 (85%) were prejudicial to the physician and were taken for violations involving issues such as quality of care, sexual misconduct, insurance fraud, alcohol/substance abuse, or inappropriate prescribing of controlled

substances. The disciplinary actions taken were primarily revocations, suspensions, or consent orders.

The Federation Credentials Verification Services (FCVS), established in 1996, maintains a database of physicians' core medical credentials on medical education, postgraduate training, licensing examination history, and board action history, and essentially serves as a lifetime professional portfolio. The FPDC and FCVS serve to enhance the medical licensing and disciplinary systems.[19]

Commenting on the effectiveness of the state disciplinary process, Sidney Wolfe, MD, director of the Public Citizen's Health Research Group, concluded in a report dated April 2009 that "there is considerable evidence that most boards are under-disciplining physicians," and "[m]ost states are not living up to their obligations to protect patients from doctors who are practicing medicine in a substandard manner."[20]

NATIONAL PRACTITIONER DATA BANK

On November 14, 1986, the Health Care Quality Improvement Act (HCQIA), Title W of P.L. 99-660, was signed into law. Congress was prompted to enact this legislation by the burgeoning number of medical malpractice suits, by the perceived need to improve the quality of care, and by the necessity for effective professional peer review. A major provision of this law created the National Practitioner Data Bank (NPDB), which is designed to collect comprehensive data on adverse actions taken against healthcare practitioners, malpractice payments made on their behalf, and Medicare/Medicaid exclusions of practitioners.

Four classes of adverse actions require reporting: those taken against a practitioner's license by a state medical or dental board; those taken against a practitioner's clinical privileges as a result of peer review at a hospital or other healthcare facility; those taken against membership by a professional society; and those taken by Medicare/Medicaid and the Drug Enforcement Administration (DEA), which excludes practitioners from these agencies. Indemnity is provided to peer reviewers, to individuals who provide information to the process, to hospitals relying on the information they obtain from the NPDB, and to the NPDB itself.

Insurance companies and hospitals are required to report to the Secretary of Health and Human Services (HHS) and to state licensing boards regarding medical malpractice payments resulting from court judgments or settlements. Failure to report the required information results in a civil penalty of $10,000 per claim.

From 2000 to 2009, the NPDB logged 245,818 reportable actions, involving 171,086 individual practitioners; typically approximately 80% were physicians (including MD and DO residents and interns), 10% were dentists (including dental residents), and 10% were other healthcare practitioners.[21]

According to a *Journal of the American Medical Association* study of 2005–2009 data, roughly 70% of paid outpatient claims involved death, a grave permanent injury such as brain damage, or a major injury, compared with 81% for inpatient cases. The average payment for outpatient malpractice claims was $290,000; the inpatient average payment was significantly higher, at $363,000.[22]

Hospitals are mandated to query the NPDB about all new medical staff professionals, and to do so every two years for all staff for recredentialing purposes. In 2009, there were 4,103,337 queries to the NPDB, of which 29.5% came from hospitals; 70.5% from health maintenance organizations (HMOs), preferred provider organizations (PPOs), and group practices; and 1.8% from state licensure and disciplinary boards.[21]

Malpractice report rates vary considerably among the states. These variations could reflect local factors, such as clinical practice, quality of care, size of the state, and relative number of practitioners. In addition, statutory provisions may make it either easier or more difficult for plaintiffs to sue for malpractice and obtain a payment. There are also differences among the states regarding the statute of limitations provisions governing when plaintiffs may sue, and in the burden of proof requirements. In addition, some states limit payments for non-economic damages (e.g., pain and suffering). These limits may reduce the number of claims filed by reducing the total potential recovery and the financial incentives for plaintiffs and their attorneys to file suit, particularly for children or retirees who are unlikely to lose earned income because of malpractice incidents.

According to an analysis performed by StateHealthFacts.org, an affiliate of the Kaiser Family Foundation, the median malpractice payment in the United States in 2010 was $336,437. The highest (average) payments were in Wisconsin ($1,257,938), Hawaii ($830,917), and Alaska ($708,264). The lowest (average) payments were found in West Virginia ($108,509), North Dakota ($130,000), and Kansas ($164,744).

The reporting of malpractice payments made for the benefit of medical and osteopathic interns and residents is also mandated under the HCQIA, which makes no exceptions for trainees.

Physicians and other healthcare practitioners are sent copies of all reports received by the NPDB that name them. They may submit a statement for the record and have the right to dispute the factual accuracy of the report with or without an accompanying statement.

Patient advocates want more information about their physicians and other health professionals, and have urged open access to the NPDB. Disagreeing with this position, the American Medical Association successfully has blocked consumer access and full disclosure. U.S. Representative Ron Wyden (a Democrat from Oregon), the sponsor of the original HCQIA bill, argued for consumer access: "At the very least, consumers have a right to know which healthcare provider they should avoid."[23] Similar statements by Dr. Sidney M. Wolfe, Director of the Public Citizen's Health Research Group, echo the congressman: "We believe that all information in the data bank should be available to the public—the very people it was created to protect."[24] In September 2011, the Health Resources and Services Administration (HRSA), the arm of the U.S. Department of Health and Human Services that administers the NPDB, closed public access to the version of the NPDB containing information on malpractice and other disciplinary actions against health providers because a reporter was able to identify a specific physician using NPDB information in conjunction with other public records. HRSA restored public access in November 2011 with the condition that the public user agree not to engage in the identification process that led to the closing of the public file.

To Query Is to Know

Risk managers should review the policies and procedures for credentialing, for granting clinical privileges, and for periodic recredentialing to ensure that all available professional practice data are on hand. The NPDB is an inexpensive source for supplementing data from other queries to assure the healthcare organization that practitioners are highly qualified and not apt to subject their affiliated facilities or organizations to litigation.

CLINICAL PRACTICE GUIDELINES

Clinical practice guidelines have been defined as "systematically developed statements to assist practitioners and patient decisions about appropriate health care for specific clinical circumstances."[25] There is a definite intent to influence what clinicians do so as to elevate the quality of care provided by all practitioners and to help reduce waste and abuse and improve cost-effectiveness.[26]

Guidelines Developed by Professional Groups

Typically, professional standards begin with the professional associations. Each of the medical specialty societies may develop its own standards for areas that are relevant to that specialty. Practice guidelines developed by these organizations are issued by experts including the American Medical Association (AMA), medical specialty societies, and the federal government. Step-by-step guides help local, state, and regional medical organizations to identify key attributes for practice parameters and to implement the standards.

More than 1,000 guidelines have been contributed by 180 different organizations to the National Guideline Clearinghouse (NGC), which was established in 1999. The NGC is a public resource and comprehensive database of evidence-based clinical practice guidelines. It is sponsored by the Agency for Healthcare Research and Quality (formerly the Agency for Health Care Policy and Research), in partnership with the American Medical Association and the American Association of Health Plans. The NGC's mission is to provide physicians, nurses, healthcare providers, health plans, integrated delivery systems, purchasers, and other health professionals with an accessible mechanism for obtaining objective, detailed information on clinical practice guidelines and to further such guidelines' dissemination, implementation, and use. For example, the American Society of Colon and Rectal Surgery has issued practice parameters, or guidelines, on "prevention of venous thromboembolism" and "identification and testing of patients at risk for dominantly inherited colorectal cancer." The American Academy of Child and Adolescent Psychiatry has 20 guidelines, the American Academy of Pediatrics has 42 guidelines, and the American Diabetes Association has 22 guidelines. The American Academy of Orthopedic Surgeons has developed clinical guidelines on knee surgery and ankle injury. There are 142 guidelines on neoplasms, 96 guidelines on endocrine diseases, 94 guidelines on respiratory tract diseases, and 160 guidelines on cardiovascular diseases, as well as many more.[27]

The National Comprehensive Cancer Network (NCCN) is an alliance of 17 leading cancer centers created to develop and institute clinical practice standards and research on performance outcomes. The National Oncology Outcomes Database, established by the NCCN in 1997,[28] analyzes the adherence of these centers to the practice guidelines and the outcomes that such practice achieves. The NCCN members attempt to enhance effectiveness and efficiency of care through measurement, management, and research. Their initial focus is on breast cancer, and subsequently will be on non-Hodgkin's lymphoma.

Hospitals and their medical staffs have also adopted or developed clinical practice guidelines as part of their quality improvement efforts. In addition, the American Hospital Association's Medication Safety Initiative provides information on successful practices, tools, and resources, and tracks the progress of implementation as a strategy to enhance performance and reduce errors.[29] Unfortunately, liability concerns are making some hospitals reluctant to use this new assessment tool for fear that by using it, they could be held liable for not implementing all of the safe practices recommended.[30] At the Group Health Cooperative of Puget Sound in Seattle, Washington, the implementation of two of this medical care organization's own clinical practice guidelines reduced the ordering of lipid-lowering drugs and prostate-specific antigen (PSA) testing, for a cost saving of $800,000 in the first year.[31]

Kaiser Permanente of Ohio has developed a Medical Automated Record System (MARS) to address the business and clinical needs of its system, which includes 220 physicians and 110 allied health personnel. MARS is programmed to generate reminders at the moment of care on compliance with clinical guidelines, and it tracks improvements in such areas as use of aspirin in coronary disease and use of influenza vaccines in patients older than 64 years of age.[32]

Private Initiatives

United Health Group, the second largest managed care organization in the United States, has demonstrated substantial (albeit decreasing) noncompliance of its contracted physicians with generally accepted clinical practice for treating heart attacks, high blood pressure, asthma, and recurrent heartburn (among other conditions). The company has both the information and clout to significantly impact the economic viability, of those physicians whom the company can document are consistent noncompliers. Participating physicians and other caregivers still need to demonstrate their ongoing compliance with the latest standards of practice and technological advance (through their access to evidence-based knowledge bases) to have access to the majority of United Health Group's patients.[33]

Practice guidelines in the Medical Review System of Value Health Sciences of Santa Monica, California, are used in claims processing of selected medical and surgical procedures. For its clients, this system is used to precertify hospital admissions for 34 major medical and surgical procedures, which has resulted in a decrease in the number of procedures requested after implementation, and is reported to have saved in excess of $200 million since 1990.[34]

Milliman U.S.A., a group of actuaries and healthcare consultants, has estimated that the United States could save 25% of its total healthcare costs if efficient medical practices were adopted. Unnecessary services identified by this firm included hospital days (40% to 50%), all surgery (10%), all office visits (20%), and all ancillary services (35%). Clients who utilize or subscribe to Milliman U.S.A.'s services have access to a series of guidelines that describe the best practices for treating common conditions in a variety of care settings. The purpose of these clinical tools is to assist healthcare professionals in providing quality care, while maximizing efficiency in the use of healthcare resources. The best practices represent a compilation of conclusions drawn from medical literature, practice observation, and the expert opinions of physicians, nurses, and other providers. Some guidelines are related to inpatient and surgical care, others to home care and worker's compensation.[35]

Merck, AT&T, IBM, Boeing, General Electric, American Re-Insurance Company of Princeton, General Motors, and Pepsi have joined a coalition of powerful business members that calls itself the "Leapfrog Group." Employees of these companies are steered to hospitals that have computerized physician order-entry systems, critical care–trained physicians in their intensive care units, and agreements to use "evidence-based hospital referral" systems to send patients who need complex procedures (e.g., heart surgery) to the institutions that perform them the most. The Leapfrog Group wants hospitals to make "a commitment to quality," an effort that is supported by the *Fortune 500* Business Roundtable. Over the next few years, Leapfrog members will promote the institutions that make this commitment and will hold health plans and their benefit consultants accountable for compliance with the group's practices. This initiative represents an attempt to leverage the value of huge employers behind necessary safety improvement processes while supporting employees' health.[36] The group expects healthcare providers to respond more quickly to the threat of financial losses than to any other motivation.[37]

Government Initiatives

Government organizations, such as the Agency for Health Care Policy and Research (AHCPR), create practice guidelines for use in the huge federal healthcare reimbursement programs. For example, Medicare peer review organizations have published criteria for admission as an inpatient under the Medicare program. Each criterion lists rationales for admission, relevant and nonrelevant diagnostic procedures, and discharge status rationales (see **Box 10-5**).

Box 10-5

A North Carolina state legislator's husband suffered chest pains, and the hospital diagnosed a pinched nerve. Doctors proposed a two-night stay, saying: "We can't release him. We don't have practice parameters that suggest a different strategy." Three weeks later, this legislator introduced a bill to develop parameters to reduce inappropriate care, cut costs, and boost quality.[38]

Importantly, government reviewers have used the guidelines to determine reimbursement. Medicaid has adopted the same criteria for reimbursement to its providers.

Each guideline developed by the AHCPR coves a specific disease, such as unstable angina, lower back pain, asthma, cardiac rehabilitation, and colorectal cancer screening, and discusses the most effective methods of preventing, diagnosing, and treating that condition. The financial implications of implementing these guidelines will be studied for five years by Health Economics Research of Waltham, Massachusetts, at a cost of $3.1 million.[39]

Enhancing the quality of care that Medicare patients receive was the original goal of the AHCPR guidelines, but the ultimate effectiveness is still uncertain. "If guidelines are to work, the federal government will have to develop timely and effective methods of reconciling its payment schedules with its own recommended practice standards."[40]

Several states have passed laws to support the AHCPR clinical guidelines. In 1993, California passed a law that sought to distribute information about the acute care guideline to physicians. Maryland has adopted the urinary incontinence treatment guideline that ties reimbursement to use of the guideline. Minnesota, in its Minnesota Care Act of 1992, cites adherence to these guidelines as a defense against malpractice.[38]

AHCPR guideline development aims to help physicians make better decisions and reduce ineffective and inappropriate services. Some experts argue that the guidelines do not address implementation and need to be simplified so that physicians can understand them more quickly.[41,42]

Four states (Florida, Maine, Minnesota, and Vermont) have legislated practice guidelines in an attempt to ensure a high quality of care. These laws were copied or patterned after the criteria developed by the Institute of Medicine,[43] the AHCPR, or specific state guidelines. Part of Florida's 1992 healthcare reform law requires the state's Agency for Health Care Administration to develop practice guidelines that physicians can voluntarily use as protection against medical malpractice claims. That agency plans to adopt existing standards, especially in areas of high medical utilization and high cost—for example, imaging technology, radiation treatment, and rehabilitation.

Vermont's healthcare legislation of 1992 allows state-sanctioned practice guidelines to be used as the standard of care in malpractice cases. Minnesota's 1992 healthcare reform legislation allows the state's healthcare commissioner to approve and disseminate practice guidelines to use as an absolute defense against malpractice cases for claims arising after August 1, 1993, or 90 days after the commissioner approves the guideline.

The Arkansas Patient Safety Initiative is a forum for discussion of issues, policy, data-driven studies, and dissemination of best practices to achieve quality of care. The participants include the Arkansas Medical Society, the Nurses Association, the Pharmacist Association, the Hospital Association, and the Departments of Health and Human Services, thereby ensuring a comprehensive approach with an emphasis on systems.[44]

Almost all of the states have tried to reform their malpractice litigation and defense systems to bring perspective and management to the healthcare industry. On a broader scale covering the citizens of every state, the federal government has contracted with nonprofit organizations that perform quality assessment, analysis, and improvement services. These quality improvement studies have been based on professional guidelines, utilizing aggregate data from hospitals, HMOs, and medical record reviews. Identified deficiencies are addressed at conferences and individual hospital or HMO consultations promoting best practices, with periodic reanalysis to document change.

At the Island Peer Review Organization (IPRO), a New York State agency that the federal government has contracted with to act as a quality improvement organization (QIO), projects are concerned with improving acute myocardial infarction treatment using clinical guidelines developed by the American Heart Association and the American College of Cardiology and expert consultants. They also focus on congestive heart failure evaluation and treatment, and on prevention of further transient ischemic attacks in patients with atrial fibrillation using appropriate antithrombotic, anticoagulation therapy. For HMOs, the IPRO conducts reviews of denials of care (noncoverage) and beneficiary complaints, and also performs the HEDIS audit evaluation. For contracts with QIOs to be continued by the federal government, the organizations must show improvement in the quality of care; increased use of guidelines, which involves all levels of professionals; and public education to help individuals cope with their diseases and general health.[45]

Guidelines for Worker's Compensation

To help control worker's compensation payments to employees and healthcare professionals, several states have adapted existing clinical practice guidelines or have developed their own. In Massachusetts, the Workers' Compensation Reform Act of 1991 granted the Department of Industrial Accidents authority to write guidelines that set limits on the number of reimbursable visits as well as on payments for costly tests. West Virginia's Physical Medicine Guidelines were written as regulations and are more rigorous in halting visits and controlling payments.

Under the Minnesota Medical Services Review Board parameters, providers are informed about what can be done, what is mandatory, and which therapeutic choices are appropriate. A guideline for low back pain lists the unreimbursable tests, the mandatory diagnostic modalities, and the treatment choices available, including surgery. The state's goal: "We wanted to put an end to endless treatment with passive modalities that goes on for months or years."[46]

In New York, the state's QIO is involved in the Dispute Resolution Program, which tries to intervene and bring worker's compensation issues to closure while avoiding the court system.

Mandates of Insurance Companies

Medical liability insurers are developing their own practice guidelines. While insurers offer premium discounts to physicians who voluntarily comply with the protocols, some companies require physicians to sign on as a condition of insurance. Companies across the nation are involved: Medical Insurance Company (Arizona); Medical Insurance Company (California); COPIC Insurance Company (Colorado); MAG Mutual Insurance Company (Georgia); Medical Professional Insurance Company (Massachusetts); Medical Mutual Insurance Company (Maine); Medical Assurance Company (Michigan); and Northwest Physicians Mutual Insurance Company (Oregon).[47] Will physicians regard the risk management guidelines as an unreasonable intrusion by insurers into the patient–physician relationship? A physician vice president for medical risk management of a large medical liability insurance company responds: "Physician acceptance has been nearly universal."[48]

Thomasson reports on the Participatory Risk Management Program of COPIC Insurance Company, a physician-owned and -operated medical liability company founded by the Colorado Medical Society in 1983.[48] Guidelines were developed through advisory committees and by consensus of practicing physicians. Physicians are required to comply with the established general and specialty-specific guidelines, which are attached to each new and renewal insurance application, and are expected to attend COPIC risk management seminars. Premiums are adjusted upward for adverse actions against professionals, lack of compliance to guidelines, or nonparticipation in seminars. Premiums in anesthesia and obstetrics have declined consecutively for the past four years, and the trend is expected to continue to reduce losses.

Legal Implications of Practice Guidelines

Risk managers should be aware of these practice standards, as there are legal implication for ignoring them.[49] Tort liability could increase if it is alleged that "defective" practice parameters result in harmful patient outcomes. Antitrust violations could occur if the standards are developed to protect the economic interests of specific groups of physicians. Practice parameters could also become a source of evidence in suits. Despite the legal implications, the development and implementation of practice parameters "do not appear to raise significant liability exposures for physicians, physician organizations, hospitals, payers, or other groups."[50] In court, the issue may reside in how binding the judge considers the standards to be. Codes of ethics and practice guidelines are not legal mandates.

Moniz cautions that "the movement to develop increased standards and guidelines for practice is premature" and suggests that "more studies should be done using outcome criteria in order to determine what actually does make a difference."[51] She fears the legal risks for practitioners who do not quite measure up to published standards, take reasonable shortcuts, or have differing practice styles based on region or setting. She advocates "minimalist protocols" for "safe care and *not* the maximum for ideal care."

The results of studies on the long-term benefits of clinical guidelines have not yet been published. However, sharp reductions of malpractice losses in anesthesiology have coincided with the implementation of formal written standards in that field at the Harvard Medical Institutions.[52]

Since March 1985, the Mutual Insurance Company of Arizona has required its insured anesthesiologists to sign a "preferred risk plan" and to agree to comply with underwriting requirements on patient monitoring. Similarly, the Utah Medical Insurance Association in Salt Lake City has established malpractice insurance requirements for physicians requesting coverage for obstetric care.[52]

Physician Attitudes Toward Guidelines

With the proliferation of clinical practice guidelines, is it possible for practitioners to be familiar with all the standards? Do physicians have confidence in the organizations that are creating the guidelines? What do the clinicians think about the practice parameters?

According to an AMA study, a surprising percentage of doctors are not following national guidelines that could help them treat patients better because they do not have enough information, time, or readiness to change—or enough confidence in their ability to do everything the guidelines recommend. "Despite the fact that physicians have evidence-based guidelines at their disposal for dozens of conditions, they are having similar problems across the board in implementing them in their own

practice."[53] In studies of awareness of particular guidelines, more than 10% of doctors said they simply were not aware of them. An even larger number were not familiar enough with the guidelines to follow their recommendations. In addition, individual doctors may not agree with the guidelines issued by their own peers, leading them to choose a different course of treatment. Some physicians see certain guidelines as being too oversimplified or "cookbook," not practical, a threat to their autonomy, or not completely justified by the scientific evidence.[53]

For example, factors such as lack of agreement on guidelines, lack of specific technology training, and lack of expectancy of outcome were considered barriers to guideline usage by pediatricians queried about asthma practice guidelines.[54] In an assessment of internists' familiarity with, confidence in, and attitudes about practice guidelines issued by various organizations, physicians indicated that they recognized the potential benefits of practice guidelines, but were concerned about possible loss of clinical autonomy, increased healthcare costs, decreased satisfaction with clinical practice, and legal implications in the disciplinary process.[55]

When physicians were queried about guidelines on the management of Barrett esophagus, it was discovered that there was low awareness, agreement with, and adherence to professional guidelines promulgated by the American College of Gastroenterology. Even awareness of the guidelines did not predict adherence. Among other methods, it was suggested that structuring payment incentives might help achieve optimal practice of guidelines.[56] One certainty remains: If clinical practice guidelines are to be effective, they must be accepted and followed by practitioners.

PEER REVIEW

At the heart of the peer review process is the philosophy of physicians reviewing physicians, and by extension, health professionals reviewing other like health professionals. Statutes that mandate peer review have been enacted in most states. The goal of this process is a comprehensive and equitable evaluation of medical practice to enhance the quality of care and to reduce mortality and morbidity are the goals of the process.

Participants in the peer review process are protected from lawsuits, and the law provides protection from discovery for the documents generated during the review. Legal protection ranges from complete immunity to qualified immunity, if action is taken in good faith. Peer reviewers prefer absolute immunity, given that abuses of the process could result in unwarranted damage to professional reputations if the information became public.

Rules covering document production are elucidated in peer review statutes as well. Although attorneys may not have access to the records created by peer review committees, that rule may not apply to material prepared for other purposes and used during the review. Exceptions exist for practitioners who protest disciplinary action or licensure penalties. Medical practice boards have the authority to examine peer review materials.

Confidentiality is a particularly sensitive issue in peer review procedures. Participants should be cautioned and educated about the vital nature of the peer review process. That reminder should be reinforced by risk management and quality assessment professionals.

Peer review participants have been subject to lawsuits, initiated mainly by physicians whose clinical privileges were revoked or denied. A major charge has been violation of federal antitrust legislation designed to protect free market competition (see **Box 10-6**). To remedy this situation, the Health Care Quality Improvement Act, Sections 11101 to 11152, included specific liability protection for peer review participants on or after November 14, 1986, when the act was passed. To qualify for immunity, peer review procedures must meet these requirements:

- The action must have been taken with the reasonable belief that it would improve the quality of health care.
- The physician must have been afforded adequate notice and hearing procedures, or other procedures as deemed fair to the physician under the particular circumstances.
- The action must have been taken with the reasonable belief that it was warranted by the facts known.

Box 10-6

After being faced with charges of incompetence and the potential loss of hospital privileges, a surgeon voluntarily relinquished his privileges. Subsequently, he applied for reinstatement of his privileges. His request was denied by the Medical Staff Executive Committee, and the denial was later affirmed by the Fair Hearing Committee and the Board of Governors. The surgeon sued the hospital and peer review physicians under the Sherman Antitrust Act, alleging bias in the peer review process and a conspiracy to oust him from the hospital, along with other financial issues. The district court noted that, as a matter of law, a hospital cannot conspire with its medical staff. The staff as an entity had no interest that competed with the interest of the hospital. Therefore, the surgeon could not prove conspiracy between the medical staff and the hospital; there was no concerted action by the defendants.[57]

Components of Peer Review

Peer review is conducted for six major reasons: identified quality concerns, hospital privileging decisions, group practice membership decisions, staff conduct, professional isolation, and education.[58] Peer review's critical role in patient care has been widely accepted in the medical profession. First, a major component of review is the peer evaluation of clinical judgment using written documentation, established clinical guidelines, and patient care protocols. Second, peer review evaluates technical skills not only in terms of appropriateness, but also regarding performance outcomes. Third, peer review uses practice profiles to assess resource utilization and efficiency of the care process.

Federal and state regulations, insurance companies, and voluntary agencies all use peer review within their processes of licensure or accreditation. In addition, state medical boards, nursing boards, and other regulatory bodies use peer review in investigations, on hearing panels, and as part of disciplinary proceedings.

Professional peers have been considered at times too friendly to their colleagues; at other times, they have been labeled too adversarial and vindictive. Prosecution lawyers use peers as expert witnesses to support their allegations of malpractice and misconduct. Similarly, defendants counter with their own peer experts to support their allegations. The result is a battle of experts.

Risk management strategies argue for fairness in the evaluative and support processes and attention to peer selection. Charges and allegations should be supported by documentation and peer review. Fairness also means adequate notice to the physician under review, enough time to study the facts presented, and time for discussions, hearings, and presentation of the other side of the story.

Guidelines and System Changes

The importance of "outcomes" as a measure of performance and quality of health care gives an impetus to the development of standardized criteria to be used as a baseline for clinical practice. Practice guideline development is spreading throughout the healthcare professional community—in dentistry, nursing, rehabilitation specialties, pharmacy, dietary health, long-term care, and so on. Such guidelines effectively reduce extremes and shift the focus toward quality care. Those with practices outside the norm need special attention from risk management. The defense of an unusual or allegedly distinct style that deviates from community norms usually is not very successful.

A survey of 125 academic teaching hospitals revealed that there is considerable difference in peer review, outcome monitoring, and corrective actions taken in hospitals. Peer review is generally triggered by cases where quality of care is suspected of being substandard. The survey respondents indicated a lack of consensus regarding the best peer review method, and they regarded peer review as only slightly or somewhat effective.[59]

Some approaches, however, relate directly to administrative system changes. In Michigan, a new law restricts the number of mandatory overtime hours that can be required of registered nurses (RNs). The law limits the hours of mandatory overtime that can be required of RNs to 2 hours beyond their regular shift and no more than 16 hours in 24-hour period.[60] Understaffed and overworked nursing care may increase the frequency of errors and lessen the quality of care.

Information technology is another area that has a vast potential for improvement of health, access to care, reduction of errors, and increased efficiency in delivering high-quality care. The Institute of Medicine's 1991 and 1997 reports were entirely devoted to the importance of implementing computerized medical record systems, and the 1999 report focused on patient safety recommendations and computerized physician order-entry systems. Given that medication errors account for 20% of all medical errors, the impact of such systems would be significant. Studies indicate that reminder systems and computer-assisted diagnosis and management of care improve compliance with professional guidelines. The National Quality Forum has stated that "the inadequate health information infrastructure contributes to substantial inefficiencies and waste, lost productivity, the occurrence of medical errors, and dissatisfaction with the healthcare system of both patients and practitioners."[61]

The New York Patient Occurrence Reporting Tracking System (NYPORTS) is a reporting system developed by the state's Department of Health (DOH) to which hospitals must report specific types of adverse occurrences that may or may not represent errors by the hospital. For certain types of serious adverse occurrences, hospitals are required to undertake and submit to the DOH the results of a full analysis of the occurrence. Adverse occurrences include deaths within 48 hours of admission; preoperative and unexpected deaths; and surgical cases with wrong site, procedure, or patient surgery, or retained foreign body. For 2007, New York reported 1,298 serious events. Earlier, the DOH developed guidelines that were distributed to hospitals and physicians along with possible methods of implementation to reduce such errors.[62]

In New York, some adverse events require the preparation of a root-cause analysis. In a six-month data analysis of 120 cases reported as unexpected deaths, the root causes indicated were ineffective communication (30%), policy or process (system) not carried out (24%), standard of care not met (23%), and human error (21%), among other issues.[63] It is anticipated that hospital comparisons will be made, quality improvements will be initiated, and preventable adverse occurrences and medical error will be reduced as a result of the state's efforts in this area.

The Joint Commission has expanded its interest in "sentinel events," which encompasses voluntary self-reporting of medical errors for aggregations, analysis, and reduction of the risk of future occurrences. A "sentinel event" is any unexpected occurrence involving death or serious physical or psychological injury. Root-cause analysis of these occurrences is expected to yield opportunities to alter practices to reduce the frequency and seriousness of mishaps. In one study, The Joint Commission investigated 6,782 sentinel events, affecting 6,920 patients from January 1995 through March 31, 2010. More than two-thirds of these patients died as a result of the event. The top ten most frequently reported sentinel events were as follows:

1. Wrong-site surgery
2. Suicide
3. Operative/postoperative complication
4. Delay in treatment
5. Medical error
6. Patient fall
7. Unintended retention of foreign body
8. Assault, rape, or homicide
9. Perinatal death or loss of function
10. Patient death or injury in restraints[64]

The Joint Commission introduced National Patient Safety Goals to address some of these reported occurrences. The 2003 National Patient Safety Goals are listed here:

- Improve the accuracy of patient identification
- Improve the effectiveness of communication among caregivers
- Improve the safety of using high-alert medications
- Eliminate wrong-site, wrong-patient, wrong-procedure surgery
- Improve the safety of using infusion pumps
- Improve the effectiveness of clinical alarm systems[65]

It is anticipated that The Joint commission will incorporate reviews of hospital approaches to address these goals as part of the accreditation process.

In several states where HMOs have high penetration, there have been some successful attempts to provide physicians with incentives or practices that are in accord with guidelines for prevention, diagnosis, and therapies. Where HMOs are not dominant and there are very busy physicians, such incentives may not be as effective. Some HMOs have translated provider incentives into contracts with individual physicians. Where incentives have been utilized, substantial improvement in performance has been noted, and physicians have participated in the development of incentive programs. Quality care and quality outcomes will reduce the potential for liability.

CLOSING REMARKS ON TOOLS

History teaches us that each advancement in technology brings the need for increased vigilance lest we humans become victims of our creation. The automobile no doubt provided us with greater mobility, more freedom, and other benefits. At the same time, it created its own set of negligent actions by dramatically increasing traffic fatalities.

The informational tools discussed previously certainly provide risk managers with greater information than ever before—information regarding the people who will provide healthcare services to an ever-growing population. Therein lies the trap for the unwary: Failure to properly access and *utilize* the available information creates its own set of actionable circumstances.

LIABILITY ALTERNATIVES: TORT REFORM AND NONJUDICIAL PROPOSALS

Countless physicians around the United States are experiencing skyrocketing malpractice insurance rates, making it nearly impossible for them to make a living, let alone run an office. Such hikes are forcing physicians—in particular, specialists who perform high-risk procedures on a regular basis—to curtail their practices or move to states with lower liability insurance rates in an effort to avoid debt or bankruptcy. Some doctors have lost their malpractice insurance altogether and have been forced to shut down their offices. In some areas of the country, patients have to travel to other states to be treated by specialists (see **Box 10-7**).

This crisis has raised a groundswell of demands for "tort reform." (A tort is a wrongful act or omission, not based on a contract, that causes injury to another person.) Reforms suggest changing certain legal rules, such as imposing limits on the time after an injury or its discovery in which a suit can be filed, or

Box 10-7

- The only trauma center in Las Vegas, Nevada, closed for 10 days in July 2002 after most of its surgeons resigned in protest of the high costs of medical liability and malpractice insurance, and the lack of caps on jury awards for pain and suffering. The trauma unit, at the University of Nevada Medical Center, reopened after an agreement was reached with county officials to temporarily limit the doctors' liability, and the 67 surgeons returned to work.[66]
- The American Medical Association announced in July 2002 that because of astronomical malpractice award increases, 12 states are in a medical liability crisis and 30 other states are on the brink. The AMA concluded that "the U.S. liability system has created a liability lottery, where select patients receive astronomical awards, and others suffer because of it." Congress has been urged to pass medical liability laws to avert a healthcare crisis.[67]
- Some radiologists no longer want to read mammograms because of liability concerns.[68]
- Some family physicians in Mississippi, Florida, Pennsylvania, and Texas have stopped offering obstetrics care so their insurance premiums will be lower. Obstetricians are also among those giving up obstetrics.[68]
- An Akron, Ohio, urologist decided to retire when he realized it would cost seven months of his yearly income to cover the $84,000 premium for his malpractice insurance.[69]

limiting the damages that can be awarded. These "conventional" tort reforms have been labeled pro-defendant because they limit the amounts that plaintiffs can recover, restrict the access of plaintiffs to courts, and, in effect, block the courthouse door.

An important factor underlying the impetus for tort reform may stem from physicians' fear of legal liability. The litigation process imposes large indirect costs on the healthcare system. The practice of "defensive medicine," driven by the specter of unlimited and unpredictable liability awards, not only increases patients' risk, but also adds systemic costs. One study estimated that limiting awards for non-economic damages could reduce healthcare costs by 5% to 9% without adversely affecting the quality of care. This would save $60 to 108 billion in yearly healthcare costs, with a concomitant lowering of the cost of health insurance.[70] Nevertheless, an Office of Technology Assessment study of defensive medicine and medical malpractice concluded that physicians "tend to over-estimate" their risk of being sued and that malpractice reforms would not significantly reduce the cost of defensive medicine.[71,72]

For several years now, the national political scene has resonated with a chorus of calls for "tort reform," to stem the "crisis in health care."[73] California has more than 25 years of experience with tort reform. Measured by certain indicators, its experiment has been a success. Doctors are not leaving California. Insurance premiums have risen much more slowly in the state than in the rest of the country, without any effect on the quality of care received by residents of California. Insurance premiums in California have risen by 167% over this period, while those in the rest of the country have increased 505%. This slow increase has saved California residents billions of dollars in healthcare costs and has saved federal taxpayers billions of dollars in Medicare and Medicaid programs.[74]

Traditional tort reforms within the judicial system can be classified into three types: limiting the number of lawsuits, controlling the size of awards, and limiting the access of plaintiffs to the judicial system.

Limiting the Number of Lawsuits

Reform suggestions to reduce the volume of malpractice lawsuits involve attorney fee limits, certificates of merit, pretrial screening panels, penalties for frivolous litigation, and statutes of limitations.

Attorney Fee Limits

To minimize the risk and expenditure for the plaintiff, attorneys are paid on a contingency basis. That is, the attorney receives a portion of the damages received by the plaintiff only if the lawyer wins the case. Often this amount is larger than the portion of the monetary settlement that the injured client receives. A typical contingency fee is one-third of the award, plus expenses. Some states limit the contingency percentage in cases with large monetary damage cases, but professional bar associations exert considerable political influence to thwart efforts to limit this fee arrangement.

Certificates of Merit

Before filing a suit, a plaintiff may be required to obtain an affidavit from a qualified physician or medical expert attesting that the malpractice claim has "reasonable and meritorious cause." This requirement may be a moot point in most cases, however, because law firms generally secure expert medical opinions before filing a malpractice claim.

Pretrial Screening Panels

As a prerequisite to filing a suit in court, parties may be required to submit the malpractice claim to a hearing before an impartial panel consisting of one or more attorneys and healthcare providers and, in certain states, a judge or layperson.

This panel will render a nonbinding decision on liability and sometimes damages. Parties may choose to accept the panel's findings and settle the case, or they may proceed to file a suit. In some states, the panel's findings may be entered into evidence at subsequent legal proceedings. Some states offer panels as a voluntary option.

Penalties for Frivolous Litigation

According to legal definition, a frivolous claim is one that has no hope of success. That definition is too broad, open to varying interpretations, and too vague to apply practically. A "loser pays" system, designed to prevent frivolous claims, requires the losing party to pay the winner's legal expenses. However, judge-imposed sanctions for bringing weak cases to court are seldom applied.

Statutes of Limitations

Statutes of limitations prescribe the time period after the injury in which a legal claim may be brought. Usually, the time limits are two to three years (see Box **10-8**). In cases alleging medical malpractice, this time period is measured either from the date of the negligent treatment or from the date the injury could reasonably have been discovered (the discovery rule). Some states have shortened the time period in which a claim

---

Box 10-8

After surgery in the hospital, a patient continued taking prescribed anticoagulant medication at home. One month later, she was readmitted, suffering from gastrointestinal hemorrhaging allegedly caused by inadequate monitoring of her condition. Two years and one day later, she filed a malpractice claim, but trial and appellate court rulings found the claim barred by Georgia's two-year statute of limitations.[75]

can be brought or have limited the application of the discovery rule.

Controlling the Size of Awards

Tort reform proposals may seek to impose "caps" or limits on monetary damages. Recommendations may include establishing a schedule of damages, or reducing awards by the amounts collected from other insurance coverage, restricting joint and several liability suits, and scheduling periodic payments of damages.

Caps on Damages

Damages can be economic or non-economic. Economic damages pertain to incurred and future costs arising from the injury, primarily medical and rehabilitative expenses and lost wages. Non-economic damages compensate for the pain and suffering associated with the injury, the emotional distress, and the lost enjoyment of life, or "hedonic" damages.[76] Certain states have placed caps on the non-economic amounts the jury can award or on the total of economic plus non-economic damages. States with limits of $250,000 or $350,000 on non-economic damages have average combined highest premiums of 12% to 45%, as compared to 44% in states without caps.[77]

Schedules of Damages

A schedule of damages could specify the amount of compensation for each type of negligence. For example, payment for an unnecessary surgical procedure might range from $100,000 to $300,000. Strangely enough, both plaintiffs and defendants oppose this concept. Plaintiffs fear that the schedule's limits will duplicate the law governing worker's compensation awards;

defendants believe jurors will consistently award the upper limits of any scheduled payment.

Collateral Source Offset

Some states require or permit the jury to reduce the plaintiff's malpractice award by the amount the plaintiff is entitled to receive from collateral sources, such as life, health, and disability insurance.

Restriction of Joint and Several Liability

In some jurisdictions, a winning plaintiffs has the right to collect *from each of multiple defendants* the total amount of damages. Where multiple defendants are jointly and severally liable, each tortfeasor may be required to pay the full amount. The plaintiff, however, cannot recover more than the judgment permits. Some states have eliminated joint and several liability, by seeking to apportion the damage award by the "percentage" of fault the jury assesses to each defendant. Under either system, the plaintiff is incentivized to seek out and sue other individuals and entities who may bear part of the responsibility for the plaintiff's injuries, particularly those with "deep pockets" (e.g., those having big insurance policies or substantial financial resources).

Periodic Payments of Damages

A structured award allows damages for future economic and non-economic losses to be paid over an extended period on a periodic basis, rather than in one lump sum. Defendants need not pay until the annual installment is due. However, questions do arise. What if the plaintiff dies earlier than expected? Should payments end, or should the plaintiff's estate continue receiving payments?

Limiting the Access of Plaintiffs to the System

Reform measures in this area deal with expert witness requirements, informed consent limits, and res ipsa loquitur restrictions. These proposals address the plaintiff's difficulty, or costs, of winning a lawsuit.

Expert Witness Requirements

Regulations may mandate that the expert physician witness be board certified or have meaningful experience in an area of medicine that relates to the subject of the case, which became an issue in the case described in **Box 10-9**.

Box 10-9
Expert witnesses testified that they were familiar with the term "standard of care" but not that they were familiar with the actual standard of care for interns and residents in the Detroit area. On this basis, a $1.3 million verdict to a patient's estate for negligent death was reversed.[78]

Informed Consent Limits

Did the physician provide adequate information for the plaintiff to make an informed judgment? Adequacy can be judged on the basis of whether a reasonable patient would consider the information provided adequate, or by looking at the practice of other physicians. Often, the former standard is characterized as pro-plaintiff, and some states restrict the use of this patient-oriented standard.

Res Ipsa Loquitur Restrictions

Some states restrict the use of the res ipsa loquitur doctrine in cases where the injury is obvious to nonmedical trained personnel and expert testimony of negligence is not required.

There are pros and cons for each of the tort reform proposals, and no immediate consensus on them has evolved. An illustration regarding caps demonstrates the extremes. Dr. Nancy Dickey, an AMA official, remarked that liability reform without a cap on economic damages was like "giving an aspirin where what you need is massive chemotherapy." In response, the president of Trial Lawyers of America said, "The cap is grossly unfair because it would force the most seriously injured in our society to, in effect, subsidize the wrongdoers who harm them by capping their responsibility."[76]

REMOVING MALPRACTICE LITIGATION FROM JUDICIAL SYSTEMS

Tort reform proposals to shift malpractice litigation away from the judicial system include the establishment of special administrative agencies, alternative dispute resolution mechanisms such as arbitration and mediation, and no-fault compensation for injuries. A Robert Wood Johnson Foundation grants program, Improving Malpractice Prevention and Compensation Systems, funds investigations seeking nonadversarial alternatives to malpractice litigation.[79]

Administrative Agencies

Precedents for administrative agencies to handle malpractice claims exist in worker's compensation agencies that handle occupational accident damages, in labor management agencies that mediate disputes, and in professional sports organizations that use binding arbitration entities. One AMA Specialty Society Medical Liability Project proposal recommended that state administrative agencies, consisting of consumers, lawyers, and a few physicians, handle malpractice claims.[80] Administrative agencies could adapt trial-like procedures, but would have much more leeway to avoid time-consuming pleadings. When needed, special expert panels could examine sophisticated medical evidence. Tax money would establish the administrative agencies and also compensate arbitrators, whose services are not inexpensive. Critics contend that if the agencies followed the example of the worker's compensation agencies, the monetary awards would be "notoriously stingy."[81]

Alternative Dispute Resolution: Mediation and Arbitration

Both mediation and arbitration remove procedure-bound litigation from the courtroom and place it in an informal setting where neutral intermediaries work with litigants to resolve the problem. Mediators can only attempt to negotiate agreements, as illustrated in **Box 10-10**. In contrast, arbitrators can make judgments and impose awards.

Pretrial screening panels in more than 20 states weed out nonmeritorious claims. Approximately 15 states authorize a form of voluntary arbitration. Some states allow for pretreatment arbitration agreements between physicians and patients. Supporters of alternative dispute resolution argue that this easier and less costly mechanism will open the malpractice system to thousands of people who would not otherwise file malpractice suits because the claims are too small or the court system too intimidating. Critics aver that a voluntary alternative dispute resolution system will not solve the problem because people will still sue if they are dissatisfied with the proposed settlement.[80] Given that the system does not impose a

Box 10-10

A patient suffered an adverse outcome, but believed that his physician had told him that the risk of such a result was one in 100. The doctor said he had told the patient one in 10. A Massachusetts Medical Board mediation took only 45 minutes to resolve the dispute. The doctor agreed to reimburse the patient the nominal amount for the care required because of the complication.[82]

mandate to accept the arbitration settlement, the practice lacks incentives and appears to be seldom used as an alternative.[83]

NO-FAULT PROPOSALS

Under a no-fault system, any adverse outcome would be automatically compensated without lawsuits, whether or not the outcome resulted from negligence. Some no-fault proposals promise more equitable compensation; others create mechanisms for quality control. Utah's Experiment in Patient Injury Compensation combines a no-fault system with malpractice insurance coverage.[84]

An untested no-fault proposal uses adverse medical outcomes called avoidable classes of events (ACEs) as a mechanism for determining liability for selected injuries. ACEs could be used both to promote high-quality care and to determine quickly and objectively which patients should be compensated. Because patients could be quickly compensated through a nonjudicial insurance process, ACEs are also known as accelerated compensation events.[85]

Accelerated Compensation Events

Applying compensation classification principles, the American Bar Association conducted a feasibility study of designated compensable events in 1979.[86] With a minor language change, the classification became known as accelerated compensation events.

Under the ACE system, medical experts identify categories of injuries that are generally avoidable when a patient receives good medical care. Patients experiencing an ACE would be automatically compensated through an administrative system. Compensation would be paid either by the physician's insurer or by another responsible organization. Because ACEs would not account for all claims, any ACE program would have to operate within a larger injury compensation system, which could be the existing fault-based malpractice system or an alternative fault-based approach. Non-ACE claims could be resolved through the tort system or by an alternative dispute resolution method.

Experts have developed 146 ACEs for general surgery, orthopedic surgery, and obstetrics, and the list is continuously being revised. Examples of ACEs include the following:

- Complications secondary to anticoagulant therapy in preparation for surgery
- Consequences of a misdiagnosis of breast malignancy
- Complications from failure to diagnose and treat hypoglycemia in a newborn
- Complications to infant(s) from syphilis during pregnancy that was unrecognized during prenatal care
- Complications to infant(s) from fetal distress, including brain damage, that was unrecognized or untreated during attended delivery
- Certain complications or injuries resulting from surgical procedures, including failing to remove a foreign body from the surgical site[87]

In a sample of 285 hospital obstetric claims in 24 states, the obstetric ACEs accounted for 52% of claims, with a disproportionate number of serious injury claims and paid claims involving ACEs.[88]

In claim disposition, These classes may promote predictability and consistency. These classes are developed by medical experts using epidemiological population-based concepts of "relative avoidability." In contrast, negligence is based on a lay jury's judgment. It is quite possible that the same adverse outcome will be compensated by one jury but not by another, because juries differ on whether the standard of care was met.

Enterprise Liability

In a system of enterprise liability, physicians would be immune to malpractice suits. Instead, the institution in which they practiced, or the health plan responsible for paying for the medical services provided, would assume the physicians' liability.[89] Although some hospitals and staff-model HMOs already assume such liability, few healthcare institutions are fully liable for all claims originating within their organizations.

Enterprise liability would help eliminate the costs associated with multiple-defendant suits, thereby facilitating settlement. It would promote stronger quality control within institutions and health plans, while relieving physicians of some of the psychological burdens of a malpractice suit. Institutions bearing the liability risk would have a greater incentive to evaluate physicians' performance. Institutional quality control programs may be a more effective deterrent to poor quality of care than the malpractice system, because the vast majority of patients injured as a result of negligence do not sue.[90]

Some large teaching hospitals have an arrangement known as "channeling," in which the institution and the physicians practicing in the hospital are insured under the same malpractice insurance policy. Physicians pay the hospital for the insurance, and are often required to agree to a joint defense. In return, the physicians receive favorable malpractice insurance rates and high coverage limits. Even without true enterprise liability, some of the administrative efficiencies of a joint defense already exist in these settings.

Enterprise liability could increase the number of suits, if patients feel more comfortable suing a corporate enterprise rather than an individual physician.[91] In return for no personal liability, physicians might find themselves serving as witnesses in a greater number of cases, and subject to greater scrutiny from the enterprise in which they provide care. Both no-fault and enterprise liability demonstration projects have been endorsed by the American College of Physicians.[92,93]

Other Methods

Early Offers is an innovative approach to liability that attempts to provide a new set of balanced incentives to encourage doctors to make offers quickly after an injury to compensate the patient for economic loss, and for patients to accept such offers. The system would make it possible for injured patients to receive fair compensation quickly, although providing for coverage if further losses are incurred, without the cost of litigation. Because doctors and hospitals would have an incentive to discover adverse events quickly—within 120 days after a claim is filed—to make a qualifying offer, the system would lead to prompt identification of quality problems. It may also be possible to implement an administrative form of Early Offers as an option for care provided under federal health programs.[94]

Another approach involves medical review boards. Strengthening medical review boards, which have special expertise in the technical intricacies of health care, can streamline the fact-gathering and hearing processes, make decisions more accurately, and provide compensation more quickly and predictably than the current litigation process. Incentives would be necessary for patients and healthcare providers to submit cases to the boards and to accept their judgments and decisions.

TO TORT OR NOT TO TORT

"Is lawsuit reform good for consumers?" A *Consumer Reports* article suggested that many of the proposed changes would tip the scales of justice against consumers.[95] In another criticism, feminists argued that tort reform would disproportionately hurt women and have a harsh discriminatory impact on women, children, and poor people. Others claim that caps on non-economic damages are unfair to children, the elderly, and stay-at-home mothers.[95]

Physicians argue that the medical liability system is flawed: There is no timely and adequate compensation for injured persons, negligence is not deterred, fear and distrust are promoted, healthcare providers are not given incentives to prevent and detect injuries, the physician–patient relationship is harmed, and physicians change their behavior because they are vulnerable. If physicians mainly want to avoid jury trials, alternative dispute resolution may be the most appropriate approach. If physicians are distressed when their clinical judgment is questioned, any reform that retains a fault-based system may not result in changes in physician behavior.

Medical liability reform remains uncertain in view of concurrent developments in the healthcare delivery system and in Congress.

PROACTIVE LIABILITY REDUCTION

Professional practice acts, clinical practice guidelines, and peer review seek to prevent adverse events from occurring in the first place. Tort reform and nonjudicial alternatives aim to resolve conflicts rapidly, equitably, and inexpensively after an injury occurs.

Risk managers must be comfortable developing educational programs for healthcare professionals that evolve from clinical practice guidelines and peer review findings. If administrative actions arising from regulatory professional practice acts or NPDB queries are required, risk managers must ensure that administrators are aware of their options. Regardless of the basis for proactive liability reduction activities, this area of activity can offer significant protection of the organization's financial resources.

REFERENCES _____

1. Kern, S. I. (1995). Professional misconduct categories could hold unpleasant surprises. *MSSNY's News of New York, 50*(5), 3.
2. Polygreen, L. (2002, September 7). Transplant chief at Mount Sinai quits post in wake of inquiry. *New York Times,* p. B3.
3. Surgeon who left an operation to run an errand is suspended. (2002, August 9). *New York Times,* p. A13.
4. Campbell, C. A. (2002, August 15). State suspends tummy-tuck MD's license. *Star Ledger* (Newark, NJ), p. 1.
5. New York State Department of Health Board for Professional Medical Conduct, Albany, NY.

2010 annual report, p. 14; see also *annual report 2000,* p. 15.
6. Spiro, H. M. (1993). Physician rehabilitation committee. *Straight Forward, 4*(2), 2.
7. Talbott, G. D., & Benson, E. (1990). Impaired physicians: The dilemma of identification. *Postgraduate Medicine, 68*(1), 56.
8. AMA Council on Mental Health. (1973). The sick physician: Impairment for psychiatric disorders including alcoholism and drug dependencies. *Journal of the American Medical Association, 233*(5), 664–667.
9. White, R. K., Schwartz, R. P., McDuff, D. R., & Hartmann, P. M. (1992). Hospital-based professional assistance committees: Literature review and guidelines. *Maryland Medical Journal, 41*(4), 305–309.
10. Meek, D. C. (1992). The impaired physician program of the Medical Society of the District of Columbia. *Maryland Medical Journal, 41*(4), 321–323.
11. Gallegos, K. V., Lubin, B. H., Bowes, C., et al. (1992). Relapse and recovery: Five to ten year follow-up study of chemically dependent physicians, the Georgia experience. *Maryland Medical Journal, 41*(4), 315–319.
12. Bedient, T. M. (2002, September 25). Director, Committee for Physicians' Health, Medical Society of the State of New York, personal communication.
13. Gabbad, G. O., & Nadelson, C. (1995). Boundaries in the physician–patient relationship. *Journal of the American Medical Association, 273*(18), 1445–1449.
14. The 2000 IAHSS survey: Crime in hospitals. (2001). *Journal of Healthcare Protection Management, 17*(2), 1–31.
15. Greene, J. (1994). Two arrested in hospital rapes. *Modern Healthcare, 24*(43), 33.
16. Council on Ethical and Judicial Affairs. (1991). CEJA report A–I-90: Sexual misconduct in the practice of medicine. *Journal of the American medical Association, 226*(19), 2741–2745.
17. Island MD admits sex misconduct. (1995, February 24). *Staten Island Advance* (NY), p. 1, col. 2.
18. Goldsmith, R. (2002, August 20). State rules surgeon is unfit to practice. *Star Ledger* (Newark, NJ), p. 17, col. 1.

19. www.FSMB.org

20. Public Citizen's Health Research Group. (2009, April 20). Ranking of the rate of state medical boards' serious disciplinary actions: 2006–2008.

21. National Practitioner Data Bank. (2011, September). *Combined annual report 2007, 2008 and 2009.* Washington, DC: U.S. Department of Health and Human Services.

22. Bishop, T., Ryan, A., & Casalino, L. (2011). Paid malpractice claims for adverse events in inpatient and outpatient settings. *Journal of the American Medical Association, 305*(23), 2427–2431.

23. Brinkley, J. (1994, May 29). You bet your life. Do you know the odds? *New York Times,* sec. 4, p. 4, col. 1.

24. Wolfe, S. M., & Stieber, J. (1994, June 7). Medical consumers need malpractice data. *New York Times,* p. A22, col. 4.

25. Institute of Medicine. (1990). *Clinical practice guidelines: Directions for a new program.* Washington, DC: National Academy Press.

26. Hayward, R. S., Wilson, M. C., Tunis, S. R., et al. (1995). Users' guide to the medical literature. VIII. How to use clinical practice guidelines. A. Are the recommendations valid? *Journal of the American Medical Association, 274*(7), 570–574.

27. www.guidelines.gov.ngc

28. www.nccn.org/index/wee/care/docdirection.htm

29. Berman, S. (2000). The AMA Clinical Quality Improvement Forum on Addressing Patient Safety. *Joint Commission Journal on Quality Improvement, 6*(7), 428–433.

30. Prager, L. O. (2002). Legal system could offer safety incentives. *American Medical News, 43*(22), 11:1.

31. Naughton, D. (1993). Group health cooperative puts practice guidelines into action. *Report on Medical Guidelines & Outcomes Research, 4*(6), 9–10.

32. Khoury, A. T. (1998). Support of quality and business goals by an ambulatory automated medical record system in Kaiser Permanente in Ohio. *Effective Clinical Practice, 1*(2), 78–82.

33. Couch, J. (2001, December). United Health Group's bold decision to let doctors decide: A glimpse into the future of managed care. *Industry Watch.*

34. Leavenworth, G. (1995). Quality costs less. *Business & Health, 12*(3), 6–11.

35. M&R care guidelines. (2001). Milliman USA, Inc.

36. Stewart, A. (2001, November 15). Coalition gives hospitals a to-do list. *Star Ledger* (Newark, NJ), p. 28.

37. Reducing patients' risk may lead hospitals to bow to pressure. (2001). *American Health Consultants Healthcare Risk Management, 23*(1), 1.

38. Oberman, L. (1993). States race to whip up practice guidelines: Too many cooks? *American Medical News, 36*(37), 1, 30–31.

39. AHCPR intensifies data collection efforts. (1995). *Clinical Data Management, 1*(12), 1–3.

40. Blumenthal, D., & Epstein, A. M. (1992). Physician–payment reform: Unfinished business. *New England Journal of Medicine, 326*(20), 1330–1334.

41. Gesensway, D. (1995). Putting guidelines to work: Lessons from the real world. *ACP Observer, 15*(3), 1, 28–30.

42. Gardner, J. (1994). Despite complaints, docs using practice guidelines. *Modern Healthcare, 24*(3), 36.

43. Institute of Medicine. (1992). *Guidelines for clinical practice: From development to use.* Washington, DC: National Academy Press.

44. Golden, W. E. (2001). *Implementing the safety agenda data and case-based approaches.* Arkansas Foundation for Medical Care.

45. Sheehy, T. S., et al. (2001). *Annual performance report: Island Peer Review Organization (IPRO), New York, July 31, 2000, to August 31, 2001.*

46. Workers' compensation programs climb on guidelines bandwagon. (1995). *Medical Guidelines & Outcomes Research, 6*(9), 1–3, 5.

47. Oberman, L. (1994). Risk management strategy: Liability insurers stress practice guidelines. *American Medical News, 37*(33), 1, 31.

48. Thomasson, G. O. (1994). Participatory risk management: Promoting physician compliance with practice guidelines. *Journal on Quality Improvement, 20*(60), 317–329.

49. Hyams, A. L., Brandenburg, J. A., Lipsitz, S. R., et al. (1995). Practice guidelines and malpractice litigation: A two-way street. *Annals of Internal Medicine, 122*(6), 450–455.

50. Kelly, J. T., & Toepp, M. C. (1994). Practice parameters: More than 1,500 have been developed since 1989 and more are in the works. *Michigan Medicine, 93*(3), 36–40.

51. Moniz, D. M. (1992). The legal danger of written protocols and standards of practice. *Nurse Practitioner, 17*(9):58–60.

52. Holzer, J. F. (1990). The advent of clinical standards for professional liability. *Quality Review Bulletin, 16*(2), 71–79.

53. AMA reports that many physicians do not follow guidelines [Press release]. (1999, October 19). University of Michigan. http://hdlighthouse.org/wee/care/docdiretion.htm.

54. Cabana, M. D., Ebel, B. E., et al. (2000). Barriers pediatricians face when using asthma practice guidelines. *Archives of Pediatric and Adolescent Medicine, 154*(7), 685–693.

55. Tunis, D. R., Hayward, R. S., et al. (1994). Internists' attitudes about clinical practice guidelines. *Annals of Internal Medicine, 120*(11), 956.

56. Cruz-Correa, M., Gross, G. P., et al. (2001). The impact of practice guidelines in the management of Barrett esophagus. *Archives of Internal Medicine, 161*(21), 2588–2595.

57. *Urdinaran v. Aarons* No. 99-00540 (D.N.J. September 26, 2000).

58. Wakefield, D. S., Helms, C. M., & Helms, L. (1995). The peer review process: The art of judgment. *Journal of Healthcare Quality, 17*(3), 11–15.

59. Lindrooth, R. C., Calhoun, E., et al. (2002). Peer review at teaching hospitals: Results of a national survey. *Journal of Quality Care, 1*(2), 16–19.

60. Legislation and regulatory update. (2002, March 5). Michigan Society of Healthcare Risk Management. http://216.239.37.10.../+healthcare+risk+ management.

61. Raske, K. E. (2001, July 17). Testimony on health care information technology: The essential tool for improving access to care, public health and safety. New York State Legislature, Greater New York Hospital Association.

62. New York State, Department of Health. (2005–2007). New York Patient Occurrence Reporting and Tracking System.

63. Novello, A. Walking the tightrope: Dr. Bryant Galusha Lecture Federation of State Medical Boards of the U.S. *Journal of Medical Licensure and Discipline, 87*(3), 111–115.
Faltz, L.L., Morley, J.N., Flink, E., & Dameron, P.D. (2000). The New York model: Root cause analysis

driving patient safety initiative to ensure correct surgical and invasive procedures. *News and Alert, 6.* Albany, NY: New York State Department of Health.

64. Joint Commission on Accreditation of Health Care Organizaions. (2011). Sentinel event data event type by year, 1995–Third Quarter 2011. http://www.healthleadersmedia.com/content/QUA-250699/Joint-Commission-Updates-Sentinel-Event-Statistics.

65. Joint Commission on Accreditation of Health Care Organizations. (2002). *Joint Commission announces national patient safety goals* [News release]. See http://www.jointcommission.org/standards_information/npsgs.aspx for the 2012 National Patient Safety Goals in various categories such as hospitals, ambulatory care, and office-based surguries.

66. Madigan, N. (2002, July 13). Deal on liability allows trauma center to reopen. *New York Times,* p. A7.

67. Albert, T. (2002). AMA readies for battle on tort reform. *American Medical News, 45*(26), 1:1.

68. Albert, T., & Adams, D. (2002). Professional liability insurance rates go up: Doctors go away. *American Medical News, 45*(26), 1.

69. Akron Beacon Journal (2002, January). Confronting the new healthcare crisis.

70. Kensler, D., & McClellan, M. (1996). Do doctors practice defensive medicine? *Quality Journal of Economics, 111*(2), 353–390.

71. U.S. Congress, Office of Technology Assessment. (1994). *Defensive medicine and medical malpractice.* OTA-H-02. Washington, DC: Government Printing Office.

72. Felsenthal, E. (1994, June 29). Study downplays cost of malpractice fear. *Wall Street Journal,* p. B2, col. 2.

73. Taibleson, D. (2012, February 13). For health-care, look to states for data. *Daily Iowan.* www.dailyiowan.com/201:02/13/opinions/26957.html

74. Physician Insurers Association of America testimony on National Association of Insurance Commissioners profitability by line by state, 2001. U.S. House Judiciary Committee, June 2002.

75. Anticoagulant-injuries claim barred by time. (1995). *American Medical News, 38*(6), 19.

76. Perry, C. B. (1995). Hedonic damages and cost containment of health care policy. *Trends in Health Care Law & Ethics, 10*(1–2), 119–123.

77. Office of the Assistant Secretary of Planning and Research, U.S. Department of Health and Human Services. (2002). Special update on medical liability claims. *Medical Liability Monitor.* www.medicalliabilitymonitor.com

78. Experts don't note applicable standard. (1995) *American Medical News, 38*(1), 9, 31.

79. McCormick, B. (1995). Seeking a way out. *American Medical News, 38*(1), 9, 31.

80. American Medical Association. (1988). *A proposed alternative to the civil justice system for resolving medical liability disputes: A fault-based administrative system.* Chicago: Author.

81. Rosenblum, J. (1993). *Malpractice solutions.* Knoxville, TN: Whittle Communications, p. 49.

82. Oberman, L. (1995). Board approach tries mediation over litigation. *American Medical News, 38*(9), 1, 7.

83. Shikles, J. L. (1990). Few *claims resolved through michigan's voluntary arbitration program.* CAO/HRD-91-38. Washington, DC: Government Printing Office.

84. Petersen, S. K. (1995). No fault and enterprise liability: The view from Utah. *Annals of Internal Medicine, 122*(6), 462–463.

85. Kachalia, A., & Mello, M. (2011). New directions in medical liability reform. *New England Journal of Medicine, 364,* 1564–1572.

86. American Bar Association. (1979). *Designated compensable event system: A feasibility study.* Chicago: Author.

87. Tancredi, L. R., & Bovbjerg, R. R. (1992). Creating outcomes-based systems for quality and malpractice reform: Methodology of accelerated compensation events. *Milbank Quarterly, 70,* 183–216.

88. Bovbjerg, R. R., Tancredi, L. R., & Gaylin, D. S. (1991). Obstetrics and malpractice: Evidence on the performance of a selective no fault system. *Journal of the American Medical Association, 25*(21), 2836–2843.

89. Abraham, K. S., & Weiler, P. C. (1994). Enterprise medical liability and the evolution of the American health care system. *Harvard Law Review, 108*(2), 381–436.

90. American Law Institute. (1991). *Enterprise responsibility for personal injury.* Philadelphia: Author.

91. McCormick, B. (1993). In face of doctor onslaught: Enterprise liability backers stand firm. *American Medical News, 36*(1), 35–37.

92. American College of Physicians. (1995). MICRA (Medical Injury Compensation Reform Act): New ideas for liability reforms. *Annals of Internal Medicine, 122*(6), 466–473.

93. Schmitt, R. B. (1995, March 15). Legal beat: Malpractice reform backed. *Wall Street Journal,* p. B4, col. 5.

94. Federal report endorses law professor's tort reform concept that could speed resolution of medical malpractice claims. (2002, August). University of Virginia news Service, Office of University Relations.

95. Is lawsuit reform good for consumers? (1995). *Consumer Reports, 60*(5), 312.

CHAPTER 11

Risk Management in Selected High-Risk Hospital Departments

Alice L. Epstein and Gary H. Harding

Patients seek out medical care with the hopes of clinical improvement and successful medical intervention. Specialty care brings intense physician education, knowledge, and problem solving, as well as confounding, unexpected complications.

The need to provide safe and effective patient care applies to all clinical departments. Consistent operational tenets include medical record documentation, competency of staff, and credentialing to perform the tasks necessary to care for the patient regardless of the department or medical specialty. People and technology are the fundamental underpinnings of smooth and consistent provision of services.

Ancillary departments, by definition, cross clinical lines to support the clinical specialties. Such departments, which include pharmacy, radiology, pathology, and laboratory services, are not typically the departments that have primary responsibility for the patient, but rather tend to interact with clinical specialties. Accurate and timely communication among the departments and consulting and referring physicians is essential. Shared communication and decision-making processes enhance appropriate utilization of healthcare resources.[1]

Clinical specialties bring with them unique risks and inherent liability, particularly those specialties that the medical literature and insurance data identify as posing heightened risk to patients, healthcare entities, and professionals. An analysis of physician insurance companies reported obstetric and gynecologic surgery had the most paid claims and the highest total indemnity. For indemnity payments of $1 million or more, OB/GYN surpassed all of the other medical specialties. Neurosurgery also deserves special attention, as this specialty incurred the highest average indemnity. All surgeries have similar inherent risks with the administration of anesthesia. Radiation therapy also incurred higher-than-average indemnity payments.[2] A joint study performed by a major insurance broker and risk management professional membership association included more than 90,000 claims over a 10-year period; it specifically identified obstetrics, the emergency department, and surgery as the high-risk specialties.[3] A smaller study performed by a major professional liability insurance company indicated misdiagnosis of six medical conditions—meningitis, myocardial infarction, stroke, pulmonary embolism, ectopic pregnancy, and orthopedic injury—was involved in the most frequent and most severe claims.[4] The major insurer of nurses found similar results, in that nursing specialties with the highest-paid indemnities were obstetrics, neurology/ neurosurgeons, and plastic/reconstructive surgery. The average paid indemnity against the nurses' professional liability policy was in excess of $300,000.[5]

Analysis of studies published over the past 20-plus years indicate that, although healthcare professionals have ratcheted up their personal and organizational approaches to improving patient safety and mitigating risk, there remains significant similarity in the types and rate of occurrence of serious adverse outcomes within specialty departments. While we may be more aware of the serious incidents and are better able to identify clinical problems, a significant reduction in the number of incidents has not been achieved. It would appear that individuals and society as a whole are confounded by an inconsistent and incomplete education, perceived lack of time, inattention to details and documentation, turnover, and multitasking consistently leading to competing priorities. Several professional organizations have developed tools and processes designed to influence this present-day model of decision making. Time-out and hand-off process are two examples of administrative responses geared toward helping healthcare providers slow down, deliberate their actions, and analyze potential consequences. Even with efforts such as these, there are consistent field reports of informal pushback. Professional responses include development of complaint/disease-specific templates, clinical algorithms, and staff education and reeducation. Third-party entity accreditation and certifications along with individual certifications and advance specialty training appear to have a positive impact.

As healthcare providers, we are a part of the whole; we do not practice our profession in isolation. Serious adverse clinical events result from a multitude of interacting events. While one event may trigger cascading events, the ability to identify the trigger event and subsequent events will be required to influence the frequency and severity of these adverse clinical events.

EMERGENCY DEPARTMENT

Emergency departments (EDs) care for more than 123 million patients annually in the United States, with fewer than 10% of those visits resulting in hospital admissions. Emergency medicine has a unique set of inherent risks. Between 1997 and 2007 (the most recent metrics), the total annual visits to EDs increased more than 20% while the number of EDs decreased by 5%.[6] Most patients arriving at an emergency department believe they are in a medical crisis. Based on reported data, a significant majority of patients who present to EDs are overreacting to a nonemergency situation.

ED overcrowding and a shortage of trained ED physicians and surgeons contribute significantly to problems with missed diagnosis and patients leaving prior to treatment.[7,8] Disease processes associated with the highest numbers of claims include acute myocardial infarction, appendicitis, and fractures. [2]

Standards and Guidelines

Emergency medicine professional associations abound, all of which offer guidelines and best practices to protect patient safety and improve clinical processes. Such organizations include the American College of Emergency Physicians, American College of Osteopathic Emergency Physicians, American College of Surgeons

Committee on Trauma, Emergency Nurses Association, Emergency Department Nurses Association, National Association of Emergency Medical Technicians, and the International Association of Flight and Critical Care Paramedics.

In 1986, Congress passed the Consolidated Omnibus Reconciliation Act (COBRA), which contains a section titled the Emergency Medical Treatment and Active Labor Act (EMTALA). This legislation was designed, in part, to prevent patients from being transferred solely for economic reasons. The act mandates that anyone presenting to hospital that receives Medicare reimbursement receive needed emergency medical services regardless of his or her insurance status or ability to pay. EMTALA defines an emergency medical condition as follows: "A medical condition manifesting itself by acute symptoms of sufficient severity (including severe pain) such that the absence of immediate medical attention could reasonably be expected to result in placing the health of the individual in serious jeopardy, or serious impairment to any bodily functions or serious dysfunction of any bodily part or organ."[9]

Whereas clinicians and risk managers tend to define emergencies as "life-threatening" situations, lawyers and courts may take a more liberal view. Merely the existence of an emergency department implies an implicit duty to treat any individual needing immediate attention on campus or within 250 yards of a main building. "Campus means the physical area immediately adjacent to the provider's main buildings, other areas and structures that are not strictly contiguous to the main buildings but are located within 250 yards of the main buildings, and any other areas determined on an individual case basis . . . to be part of the provider's campus."[10]

Prehospital Services

Effective response to medical emergencies requires timely identification and interaction. The more rapidly that medical intervention occurs after discovering the medical condition, the more likely that the clinical outcome will be positive. Delays prior to the patient's arrival at the ED detrimentally affect successful emergency medical or surgical interventions.

Prehospital emergency services differ significantly because of the widely varied local and state development of these systems. Emergency medical services (EMS) systems form the framework from which prehospital emergency services are delivered within the United States. The Highway Safety Act of 1966 established the Department of Transportation (DOT), which was given authority to improve EMS, including program implementation and development of standards for provider training. States were required to develop regional EMS systems, and the costs of these systems were funded by the Highway Safety Program. Programs proliferated, although standards and funding varied widely. The American College of Emergency Physicians (ACEP) developed a policy indicating that all aspects of the EMS system require the active involvement and participation of physicians, includings an identifiable physician medical director at the local, regional, and state levels.[11] Emergency medical technicians (EMTs) and paramedics who respond by ambulance to crisis situations are required by the DOT to complete an 81-hour curriculum; advanced levels of EMT training require from 280 to 1,000 hours of educational experience. Some regions in the country are fortunate to have hospital-to-field communication systems that allow online medical direction in which physicians are directly responsible for orders given to field personnel regarding specific emergency conditions.

Ambulance response services may be owned by a hospital, be owned by a governmental agency, or be privately owned. All ambulances that are part of the EMS system, regardless of ownership, are held to the same regulations and standards. Availability, response time, staff qualifications, technology, and diversion are significant risk management concerns. Clinical decisions made in the field are crucial to the patient's survival. During transport to the hospital, the patient may experience cardiac or respiratory arrest. The prehospital diagnosis may differ significantly from the ED diagnosis. Ambulances may be required to divert to a hospital that is farther away than the one originally intended due to overcrowding or understaffing of the original facility.

Department Capabilities and Staffing

The concept of categorizing EDs was first proposed by the National Academy of Sciences National Research Council in 1966 in an effort to match critically ill patients with the appropriate healthcare facility. In 1971, the American Medical Association (AMA) Commission on EMS developed the document, "Guidelines for the Categorization of Hospital Emergency Capabilities," which was published in 1973.[12] EDs vary in their specific capabilities and are identified by a "Level" designation, where Level I/Trauma Center is the most sophisticated and Level III is the most basic. A hospital can receive Trauma Center verification by meeting specific criteria established by the American College of Surgeons and passing a site review,

although individual state law provisions determine official designation as a Trauma Center. The various categories correlate with the availability of care, physician staffing, medical specialties required to be available in the hospital and on call, referral requirements, required biomedical equipment, medication availability, facility design, and support department availability.

Walk-in patients often are not aware of the capabilities of the ED they choose to access, nor are they aware of the level of services that their medical condition requires. This lack of knowledge on the part of the patient places the staff of the ED in a precarious position when treating the patient and from a legal perspective. Hospitals need to be cautious in their representation of the ED services they provide and their capabilities. Overstating capabilities without being able to deliver the services advertised can be used against the hospital when trying to defend an ED lawsuit.

Many hospitals have established off-campus emergicenters or urgicenters in an attempt to access new markets within the community, provide additional services, and reduce the patient load on the hospital ED. Risk management concerns focus on the potential—and inappropriate—public perception that these alternatives to hospital EDs are staffed and equipped to provide full emergency critical care or trauma services.

According to ACEP, EDs should be staffed by board-certified emergency care physicians and other professionals, along with on-call specialists, during all hours of operation based on the unique needs of the community and the level of emergency care offered. Often, such departments are staffed by contract physicians or residents, who may be training or "moonlighting." Not all physicians who staff EDs are necessarily board certified in emergency medicine. The hospital may not require emergency medicine board certification, but might permit the physician to serve without certification or be certified in any number of specialties including internal medicine or family practice. Specialty certifications in areas such as orthopedics and neurology may also be required based on the level of the ED. Physicians should not practice outside their scope of training or expertise, however, and are expected to contact the appropriate specialist when needed to reduce the potential for liability. Midlevel practitioners and senior-level residents are important complements in appropriate levels of ED staffing. It is important to realize that the attending physician is the primary physician responsible for the patient. Attending physicians who practice "long distance" supervision of residents, and facilities that allow such practice may experience greatly increased liability.

The nursing staff needs to be able to stabilize the patient until the physician arrives or until adequate transfer conditions and plans have been met. Advanced specialty certifications are available to nursing staff who work in EDs, including Certified Emergency Nurse, Certified Pediatric Emergency Nurse, Advanced Cardiac Life Support, and Pediatric Advanced Cardiac Life Support. A recent study indicates temporary nursing staff working in an ED are twice as likely as permanent employees to be involved in medication errors that harm patients.[14] Many hospitals have developed policies that require the on-call physician to be within 30 minutes of the hospital. Frequently the ED physician is required to cover in-house emergencies. This in-house responsibility must not compromise the availability of rapid physician response when needed by ED patients.

Hand-off communications are imperative to ensure that the staff assuming care of the patient are familiar with all aspects of the patient's condition and care rendered until the time they assume responsibility for the patient. At a change in shift or change in professionals in the emergency department, each physician should be required to update the medical record to reflect care provided, medications, and orders. The responsibility for patient care should be formally transferred.[15]

All physicians providing care in the department are under the jurisdiction of the physician-in-charge, with whom final decisions concerning admission or patient discharge should rest. As soon as it is determined that a patient's condition requires inpatient admission, the attending physician should be notified. ED physicians do not hold admitting privileges in the vast majority of hospitals. Thus it is the attending physician's responsibility to admit the patient and assume further responsibility for the patient's care, after discussing the situation with the emergency physician.

Security issues are a major concern for EDs. The Emergency Department Violence Surveillance Study collected data used to track violence toward ED nurses as well as the processes used to respond to violence. In this study, 54.4% of participants reported experiencing physical violence within a week's time period. ED workers may suffer psychological trauma and post-traumatic stress disorder because of the violent acts perpetrated in EDs.

Ideally, security personnel should be in close proximity and readily available to the ED 24 hours a day. Each entity should review the security risks and risk management issues and develop policies to minimize uncontrolled access into other sections of the hospital, to secure medications in controlled areas, and to deal with confiscated weapons. The Occupational Safety and Health Administration (OSHA) recognizes the risks of workplace violence as "an issue in EDs because of the crowded and emotional situations that can occur with emergencies. In addition, ED patients could be involved with crimes, weapons, or violence from other people that could put the ED employee at an increased risk of workplace violence." OSHA offers suggestions for minimization of these risks.[16]

Triage Process

As soon as the patient arrives at the hospital, it is the responsibility of the staff to provide clinically indicated medical services. To be able to do so and assess the patient's needs, the ED staff implement the process of *triage,* a term derived from the French word *trier,* meaning "to sort out."

The Department of Health and Human Services' Agency for Healthcare Quality and Research developed a triage tool to prioritize incoming patients and to identify those who cannot wait to be seen.[17] There are five levels of patient's condition in this triage model. Patients assessed at the most severe triage level, Level 1, require immediate attention to survive. Level 1 patients constitute approximately 1% to 3% of all ED patients. Level 2 patients are in severe distress and constitute 20% to 30% of ED patients. Level 3 patients present with a chief complaint that requires an in-depth evaluation—for example, a patient with abdominal pain. These patients make up 30% to 40% of all ED patients. Level 4 patients present with nonemergency symptoms that require an examination, laboratory test, and possibly a prescription. Level 5 patients are

often the true nonemergent cases who require an examination and prescriptions. Level 4 and Level 5 patients make up between 20% and 35% of ED volume.

Four triage decision points are critical to accurate and reliable application of triage tool. The four decision points can be reduced to four key questions for which the answers guide the user to the correct triage level:

1. Does this patient require immediate life-saving intervention?
2. Is this a patient who should not wait?
3. How many resources will this patient need?
4. What are the patient's vital signs?

The risks most commonly related to triage include the failure to determine the existence of an emergency, improper categorization of the patient's status, improper diagnosis, and failure to communicate pertinent information. In addition to receiving an initial assessment, every patient should be reassessed prior to being discharged or transferred to another facility.

Managed care insurance introduced the concepts of the physician gatekeeper, preauthorization of services, and limiting patients to the use of facilities approved by their healthcare insurance company. Decisions to assess and treat a patient should not be made on the basis of payment by third-party payers, managed care organizations, Medicaid, or Medicare. Instead, emergency care must be provided as clinically indicated by the patient's medical condition, regardless of the patient's ability to pay. Prior approval for payment purposes should not delay assessment or the provision of necessary emergency treatment.

Telephone advice and tele-diagnosis may present risk management concerns in the ED. Frequently, patients or their family members telephone the ED seeking advice on whether they should come to the ED or how they can treat an injury or illness at home. The ACEP policy statement "Providing Telephone Advice from the Emergency Department" is not supportive of this process.[18] Some emergency departments provide this service; others do not. Some hospitals respond to these calls with a set of physician-developed clinical algorithms designed to facilitate a telephone triage process to determine whether the patient should be brought to the ED. If advice is provided, a log of all calls and the advice provided should be maintained. It is important that each call end with the guidance that the caller should always report to the closest ED if he or she believes there is an emergency.

MEDICAL RECORD DOCUMENTATION AND CONSENTS

Documentation is crucial to managing risk in the ED. From point of entry into the system, through triage, assessment, physicians' orders, testing, test results, treatment, and discharge, important elements of communication need to be recorded. Although some EDs utilize free-form admission and progress notes, the majority use complaint-specific templates, which may be either paper based or computerized. Scribes are being used in crowded facilities in an effort to capture data accurately. Some hospitals use voice recognition programs for documentation; others have instituted checklists to help ensure that a particular clinical path is followed. Software programs based on emergency care clinical practice algorithms are available, as are computerized clinical protocols.

The Emergency Nurses Association, in collaboration with a multitude of professional associations with a stake in EDs, has developed a list of ED documentation metrics and definitions intended to assist in furthering patient safety and improving quality.[19] Documentation should detail the times of the following events:

- Arrival
- Offloading from the emergency vehicle
- Transfer of care from the prehospital provider
- Triage
- Placement in a treatment space
- Physician/midlevel clinician contact
- Documented decision to discharge the patient
- Decision to admit
- Admission order is documented
- ED departure

The time of the patient's arrival, departure, and tests, as well as consent to performance of procedures and tests, should be in the record. Evidence of patient education, transfer forms, and copies of discharge instructions should be maintained as well.

Whenever possible, consent for examination, treatment, and invasive procedures or tests should be obtained from the patient or an authorized individual if the patient is unable to consent. However, whenever a life-threatening emergency exists and treatment is required to save a life, consent is implied by the patient's arrival at the ED. An additional presumption is that a delay in treatment would seriously increase the hazards to health by precipitating death or a serious impairment. When treating a minor, if an emergency condition exists and the parents of the minor cannot be located, the need for consent is generally obviated. Treatment should be limited to that which is necessary to cope with the emergency. Whenever a parent or guardian provides consent via the telephone, a second hospital representative should monitor the conversation as a witness and document his or her presence in the medical record. Upon arrival at the hospital, the parent or guardian should be requested to sign the consent authorization.

A competent adult or emancipated minor who is deemed competent has the right to refuse medical and surgical treatment even if brought to the ED, unless the state can demonstrate a compelling, overriding interest. Usually, the patient's competency and strength of conviction are considered in such cases presented to the court.

Support Services

Emergency department physicians are often dependent on the analysis of diagnostic tests that are performed outside the ED. For example, electrocardiograms, when properly interpreted, reduce the number of missed diagnoses of heart attacks. Accurate interpretation of X-rays is also critical for reliable diagnoses. ED physicians have limited training in radiology but may be required to perform an initial reading of the X-ray and prescribe treatment based on their initial interpretation. A radiologist may not read/interpret the X-ray film until the following day or the following week, especially in rural facilities. Teleradiology is an alternative that provides real-time radiographic interpretations by radiologists. On occasion, the initial interpretation of the film differs from the secondary reading. Missed readings or discrepancies in film interpretation need to be documented in the medical record and brought to the attention of the emergency physician immediately. There may be a finding that will change the diagnosis and treatment plan.

Failure to communicate important medical information about a patient to the treating physician may be considered negligence, particularly if this information would have changed the physician's orders and assessment.

Departures, Discharges, and Transfers

Patients who leave the ED against medical advice or prior to medical evaluation pose special risks to the hospital. Some patients and their families may tire when faced with a lengthy wait and decide to leave before being seen by a physician. Other patients may not be pleased with the treatment they receive or may not agree with treatment plans suggested by the physician. Patients who voice their intent to leave should be advised of the possible medical and health consequences, and such conversations with the patient and the family members should be documented in the medical record. The patient should be asked to sign an AMA (discharge against medical advice) statement. If they refuse to sign, the refusal should be documented in the medical record.

Patients should be stable prior to transfer to another hospital or facility. The receiving facility must agree to the transfer in advance, and the original facility must provide the receiving hospital with medical records. Many transferring patients (for example, newborns and cardiac or psychiatric patients) require attendance by specialty-trained professionals and high-tech group or air ambulances.

A statement authorizing the transfer should be signed by the physician. It should detail the medical benefits anticipated at the receiving facility that outweigh the increased risks of transfer.

Patients discharged directly from the ED may require limited follow-up care. To reduce liability, it is recommended that written discharge instructions be given to the patient and family, and that these instructions be available in all of the most commonly used foreign languages in the service community. A nurse or the physician should review the discharge instructions with the patient prior to the patient's discharge from the ED, and a copy should be filed in the medical record. Follow-up calls should be made to patients discharged with potentially high-risk problems, such as head injury, and such calls should also be documented.

Risk Management Opportunities

Key to a successful outcome with ED services is the rapport established by the healthcare professionals in the ED with the patient and the family. Physicians should inform patients of the treatment plan and the recognized accuracy of the diagnostic tests they are to receive, identify factors that pose special risks, and discuss the options. To the extent possible, the patient and/or family should be involved in decisions regarding care. Support staff should keep family members advised of the progress of the patient and the length of time they can expect to wait. Sometimes anger expressed by a patient is secondary to the clinical situation and can be appropriately evaluated and refocused. Sometimes, however, the anger results in a lawsuit. It is important that patients be made aware that in most instances ED physicians, although working in the ED, are not hospital employees. It is advisable for the hospital to post signage indicating the physicians are not their employees and to ensure that the physicians not wear lab coats indicating that they are hospital employees.

Risk management personnel should monitor ED visits and analyze the trends in specific situations, such as complaints and dissatisfaction about present or past treatment, patients seen for a complication resulting from a previous procedure, and patients who return within 72 hours of a previous admission. Some patients may try to establish disability as a result of the injury and treatment. Other patients may make repeated visits, demanding pain medication immediately upon arrival, and may cover their drug addiction with symptoms that mimic renal colic or cardiac pain.

Risk managers have several opportunities to monitor ED services: from medical records, by specific notification by the department, or by complaints. All deaths in the ED, or within 24 hours of admission, should be investigated. Review all serious adverse patient outcomes, including attempted suicide while in the ED, medication reactions, unscheduled returns to the ED, and patient death within 24 hours of admission to the hospital.

Risk management should also monitor the ED records of patients who refuse hospitalization or treatment, of patients who leave against medical advice, and of family or patients who disappear from the waiting area.

OBSTETRICS AND NEONATOLOGY

Reviews of malpractice claims demonstrate that lawsuits related to obstetric and neonatal cases are frequently the most expensive in terms of claims settled and malpractice awards paid. With each birth it is hoped, and often expected, that the prenatal process, labor, and delivery will be uncomplicated and successful—the experience of a lifetime. Similar expectations hold true for the early hours and days of an infant's life. The physical and emotional impact of a severe injury related to a maternal or neonatal complication or injury heighten the potential for legal action.

The provision of obstetrical services is delineated by the time period relative to the delivery of the baby:

- Antepartum—care or time period before birth; includes the prenatal period
- Prenatal and antenatal (can be used interchangeably)—care or time period occurring before birth
- Perinatal—care or time period five months before and one month after birth
- Intrapartum—care or time period relating to childbirth or delivery
- Postpartum—care or time occurring in the period shortly after childbirth

Obstetrics and Neonatology Liability Risks

Claim studies of obstetric and neonatology events continue to result in the two most significant primary allegations within obstetric claims: neurological impairment to the infant and stillbirth or neonatal death. Allegations continue to include substandard care and lack of timely obstetrician presence.[19]

A medical professional liability insurance company examined 800 obstetric cases of care delivered in both the office setting and the labor and delivery unit, from prenatal management to intra-partum and postpartum care. The majority of these adverse clinical outcomes involved an attending obstetrician who performed a vaginal delivery or emergency cesarean section after a prolonged second stage of labor. The most prevalent cases in the study involved allegations of mismanagement of second-stage labor, operative vaginal deliveries, and prenatal care. Miscommunication was cited in 36% of cases; technical error and inadequate documentation were each cited in 26% of claims. An additional 15% of cases cited ineffective supervision. This type of management error became more than a sidebar to a critical physiological event. These types of documentation and communication problems seem to indicate a lack of attention to detail and to logistics.[20] Such a problem is not specific to physicians, as obstetrics leads nursing specialties in average paid indemnity claims.[3]

Infant development allegations related to the birthing process include infant neuromuscular development problems, infant death, shoulder dystocia, and brachial plexus palsy. Many of these complications are alleged to occur due to failure to recognize, and subsequent delay in treatment of, fetal distress.

Advanced medical technology has enabled physicians to save infants who may not otherwise have survived, unfortunately simultaneously providing a larger base of complications on which lawsuits can be based. The number of infants born at an early gestational age and extremely low birth weight has increased over the past 10 years, yet morbidity and mortality rates have not changed significantly since the 1990s. The National Institute of Child Health and Human Development Neonatal Research Network has been tracking these infants since 1987.[21,22] Recent reviews of data reported that 83% of infants born at 22 to 25 weeks' gestation received intensive care (consisting of mechanical ventilation). Of all study infants whose outcomes were known at 18–22 months post childbirth, 49% died, 61% died or had profound impairment, and

73% died or had impairment. Overall, 89% of infants born at 22 to 28 weeks, gestation survived more than 12 hours.

Infants at the youngest gestational ages were at greatest risk for morbidities of prematurity. Notably, 93% of the infants experienced respiratory distress. Sepsis was also diagnosed more frequently at the youngest gestational ages. Patent ductus arteriosus was diagnosed in 46% of the infants in the study. Rates of survival following the hospital delivery to discharge period increased with increasing gestational age from 6% at 22 weeks' gestation to 92% at 28 weeks. Infants born at 22 to 23 weeks had more than 3 times the risk of death compared with infants born at 28 weeks. Neonatal morbidities occurred frequently among survivors. Rates of survival with morbidity decreased from 100% at 22 weeks' gestation to 43% at 28 weeks. Infection and bronchopulmonary dysplasia were the most-frequent morbidities.

Additional factors complicate litigation surrounding obstetrics. In 1989, the American College of Obstetricians and Gynecologists (ACOG) Committee on Professional Standards decreed that hospitals with obstetric services should have the capability to begin a cesarean delivery within 30 minutes of the time that the decision is made to perform the procedure. Beginning in 1999, the Maternal–Fetal Medicine Units Network of the National Institute of Child Health and Human Development established a registry that included all cesarean births performed at the hospitals within the network. An analysis of these data indicated approximately two-thirds of all primary cesarean deliveries performed in labor for an emergency indication were commenced within 30 minutes of the decision to operate in university hospitals, yet the decision-to-incision interval appeared to

have no impact on maternal complications. Approximately 95% of infants delivered for an emergency indication beyond the 30-minute benchmark did not exhibit evidence of compromised condition at birth. Even so, allegations of not effecting cesarean delivery within 30 minutes have been cited as a common reason that obstetric malpractice claims are perceived to be indefensible. The implication is that the 30-minute interval is a requirement or standard for acceptable obstetric practice. Intrinsic to this perception is the belief that delivering within 30 minutes necessarily would prevent untoward infant outcomes. Prior studies have not shown a direct correlation, but, in fact, show similar results to this analysis.[23,24]

A seminal study involving Florida obstetricians examined the relationship between the mother's inclination to sue and the prior malpractice experience of the attending physician. A study of claims by mothers of infants who had incurred permanent injuries or had died identified numerous reasons for filing a malpractice claim: advice from knowledgeable acquaintances to file; recognition of a cover-up regarding the care of their infant; financial necessity; recognition that their child would have no future; lack of information as to why their child was injured or died; desire to seek revenge; or desire to protect others from similar harm. This same study highlighted two types of communication problems identified by the mothers: (1) their belief that some physicians had misled them and (2) a failure on the part of the physician to provide sufficient information.[25]

These studies demonstrate myriad factors that complicate the delivery process and increase a mother's inclination to sue. Clinical issues, societal issues, communication problems, and administrative support issues may all contribute in some manner to initiation of a lawsuit. While skilled caregivers are the most effective agents in managing the risk in obstetrics and neonatology, the physician–patient relationship is a prominent factor when adverse outcomes occur. Informed consent and medical record documentation must be actively monitored and maintained if litigation is to be successfully defended.

Ethical Dilemmas

Significant ethical issues must be considered in the delivery and management of high-risk infants. The concepts of right to life, quality of life, wrongful life, wrongful birth, and right to die raise religious, ethical, moral, and legal concerns to the parents, healthcare providers, and society. Whose belief system takes precedence? Is there a right or wrong answer? What happens when there is a conflict in beliefs? How much clinical information can the parents handle, and how does the healthcare provider decide what to tell the parents? To what degree and with how much vigor should physicians prolong the life of severely compromised newborns with heroic treatments? Who decides which infant receives which specialty care? Who pays for the care? Are we doing the right thing for the patient?

The physician must understand the ethical, economic, and legal dilemmas surrounding the birth and care of compromised infants. This provider's decisions are influenced by his or her own views of what is beneficial and just. The parent's, sibling's, extended family's, and society's convictions need to be reviewed in the context of the physician's convictions. Members of the family should be involved in any ethical decision-making process. Risk managers agree that parents should be provided with all the available information regarding the condition of their fetus and the potential for development. All involved caregivers should be consulted and an attempt made to achieve consensus on the ultimate decision, if possible.

ACOG and the American Academy of Pediatrics (AAP) have published multiple statements and guidelines regarding a variety of ethical topics. All documents respect the mother's right to free choice when she is capable. For example, both associations agree that fetal intervention cannot be initiated without the mother's explicit informed consent.[26]

After an initial decision on care is reached, the matter may be revisited in the event of changes in the mother's or fetus/infant's condition or in response to the expressed desires of the family members. The American Academy of Pediatrics recommends ongoing evaluation of the infant's prognosis, with treatment decisions based strictly on what will benefit the newborn. All ethical discussions and decisions regarding care of the fetus or infant should be documented in the medical record. In this situation, the clinician must fulfill three ethical obligations: (1) understanding one's own value system, (2) possessing some knowledge of ethics as a formal discipline; and (3) making the actual clinical decision and implementing it in a morally defensible way.[27,28]

Standards and Guidelines

Many professional organizations have developed clinical practice guidelines in obstetrics and neonatology: American Academy of Family Physicians (AAFP); American Academy of Pediatrics; American Institute of Ultrasound and Medicine (AIUM); American College of Nurse–Midwives; American College of Obstetricians and Gynecologists; American College of Radiology (ACR); American Pediatric Society (APS); Association of Women's Health, Obstetrics, and Neonatal Nurses; and National Association of Neonatal Nurses (NANN).

Clinical protocols, evidence-based algorithms, policies, and procedures should be reviewed on a scheduled basis and as industry standards change. Shifts in public perception and regulations should also trigger review of the aforementioned documents. Significant risk management problems can arise if practitioners are not fully aware of, and in agreement with, these policies and procedures.

Levels of Care: Institutional Capabilities

Obstetric and neonatal care services are provided in a wide range of hospital settings with varying capabilities throughout the United States. AAP and ACOG have established staffing, equipment, and support service criteria describing the classifications of the levels of care.[28]

Level I facilities provide services that are the least intensive and designed to treat low-risk mothers and their infants. Even so, a Level I facility is required to provide the following care:

- Protocol to identify and transfer high-risk patients to a higher-level facility
- Ability to perform a cesarean delivery within 30 minutes of determining the necessity for such a procedure
- Availability of blood and fresh frozen plasma
- Twenty-four-hour availability of anesthesia, radiology, ultrasound, electronic fetal heart rate monitoring, and laboratory services
- Infant and maternal resuscitation capabilities at all deliveries

- Availability of blood typing, cross-matching, and Coombs' testing
- Qualified physician or nurse–midwife present at all deliveries

In addition to meeting Level I criteria, Level II facilities must be able to manage high-risk mothers, high-risk fetuses, and small, sick neonates. A decision to transfer a high-risk or critically ill neonate to a Level III facility rests with the referring physician, in consultation with the Level III neonatologist. Level II facility staff must be able to monitor and maintain critical functions, including cardiopulmonary, metabolic, and thermal status. Staffing requirements include a board-certified obstetrician as chief of newborn services; a board-certified anesthesiologist supervising obstetrical anesthesiology; 24-hour availability of a radiologist and clinical pathologist; support staff, including a medical social worker, a physical therapist, a dietitian or nutritionist, and a respiratory therapist; and nursing staff capable of identifying and responding to obstetric complications.

A Level III facility delivers care that is more complex. In addition to meeting all Level I and II criteria, Level III facilities must provide professional staffing with experience in neonatal medicine, maternal–fetal medicine, obstetric and neonatal diagnostic imaging, advanced nursing specialties, and pediatric subspecialties. In addition, the nurse-to-patient ratio of staff is more intensive than is required in Level I or Level II facilities.

Risk managers should periodically survey their facility to document the level classification and to determine compliance of the obstetric service with the staffing, equipment, and support service requirements established by AAP and ACOG.

Except in emergency situations, and depending on the availability of healthcare providers, the family's wishes, and the condition of the mother and fetus, the prenatal care and delivery of the infant may be performed by an obstetrician, family practitioner, resident, or nurse–midwife. Credentialing and privileging of these healthcare providers should be specific to the clinical tasks they will be required to perform. In some clinical situations, the family practitioner and nurse–midwife are required to consult with or refer the case to an obstetrician. Hospitals should have policies and procedures for required consultations and referrals, as well as for precipitous deliveries. EDs should have delivery packs on hand and staff available who are trained in emergency delivery procedures and infant care.

Prenatal and Perinatal Care

Physicians agree that prenatal care is paramount to ensuring the health and well-being of the newborn. Unfortunately, not all expectant mothers avail themselves of prenatal care, perhaps because of societal pressures, perceived lack of access, lack of money, or lack of knowledge. Regardless of the reason for foregoing prenatal care, it is imperative that physicians and hospital support staff document whatever steps are taken to ensure adequate prenatal care and record the actual extent of care received by the mother. During the prenatal period, a multitude of clinical problems can develop, such as hypertension and diabetes, that may have negative effects on the mother and unborn child in the future. Physician counseling of the patient should include a discussion of the level of accuracy of diagnostic procedures and the variability of test result interpretations. Mothers should be informed as to realistic

expectations regarding morbidity, mortality, tests, and procedure limitations.

Genetic Counseling and Testing

Prenatal genetic testing generally refers to tests that are conducted during pregnancy to either screen for or diagnose a birth defect. The main goal of prenatal genetic testing is to provide families with information with which to make informed choices about pregnancy and reproduction, and to assist the physician in providing care. The U.S. Department of Health and Human Services Office on Women's Health recommends genetic testing along with other prenatal screening.[29]

Some prenatal genetic tests are screening tests. Screening tests cannot diagnose a birth defect, but only determine if the fetus has a high or low risk for a particular problem. The most commonly used tests are chorionic villus sampling, percutaneous umbilical blood sampling, and maternal serum alpha-fetoprotein testing. Screening tests may also identify pregnancies at increased risk for open neural tube defects, Down syndrome, and trisomy 18. The blood test is such a screening test and does not provide a final diagnosis. By comparison, diagnostic tests diagnose certain fetal problems such as fetal chromosome abnormalities including Down syndrome.

Genetic testing is recommended where familial history or previous obstetric history provides an indication of the potential for a problem. In the general population, the risk of delivering an infant with a serious genetic birth defect has been found to be between 3% and 5%.

Each genetic test carries identified maternal and fetal risks. Prior to genetic testing, ultrasound studies should be performed to locate the placenta, confirm gestational age, determine fetal viability, and identify multiple fetuses if present. Maternal risks for selected genetic tests include spontaneous abortion, abruptio placentae, penetration of the fetal vessels resulting in maternal hemorrhage or death, transient vaginal bleeding, and amniotic fluid leakage. Fetal risks include fetal demise, limb and oromandibular defects, intrauterine growth retardation, premature birth, and Rh isoimmunization.

Genetically at-risk mothers and their families should be given information and advice about the possible consequences of inherited disorders that may or may not be detectable, and the various options that are available for those conditions, diagnosis, management, and prevention. A full and complete informed consent should be obtained from the mother prior to genetic testing, acknowledging an understanding of the specific risks of the tests to both herself and the fetus. Infants born with unanticipated congenital abnormalities where there is no documented evidence of genetic counseling and/or testing continue to be a liability risk.

Antepartum Fetal Surveillance

The ability to monitor the clinical status of both the mother and the fetus is important in preparing for a safe delivery and ensuring the well-being of the mother and her unborn infant. Underlying medical disorders may contribute to a high-risk pregnancy. A variety of clinical risks and complications can occur during the perinatal period. Adequate assessment of the mother and fetus requires that clinicians recognize which parameters require monitoring, which techniques are most effective for doing so, and how to interpret normal, abnormal, and interference data. Appropriate equipment must be available and operating properly, and staff must be fully

trained. Mothers should be informed of the importance and risks of monitoring and should provide their consent for specific monitoring technologies.

Physicians conducting examinations and interpreting tests utilizing sophisticated biomedical equipment should be specifically evaluated for those clinical privileges. Monitoring of the clinical parameters during the antepartum and perinatal periods offers clinicians the opportunity to recognize problems early and to institute early intervention.

Establishment of the expected date of delivery (EDD) is of major importance in being able to determine the gestational age of the fetus, to evaluate fetal growth and maturity, and to plan for delivery. Additionally, medical care of ongoing medical problems or problems new to the pregnancy must be assessed through a review of the history, physical examination, and testing so that the impact on the pregnancy and the fetus is minimized.

Fetal surveillance through antepartum testing indicates the degree of fetal well-being. Results of fetal heart rate monitoring, nonstress testing, and visualization of the intrauterine contents through ultrasound/sonography studies provide the information needed for a "biophysical profile." Ultrasound/sonography is a relatively noninvasive diagnostic procedure and is one of the most widely used imaging and monitoring techniques during pregnancy. Ultrasound is performed by obstetricians, perinatologists, and radiologists, as well as by some family practitioners, to assist in determining the gestational age of the fetus at about 18 weeks, gestation, to identify fetal anomalies, to view fetal activity, to aid in amniocentesis, and to evaluate fetal growth in high-risk or suspicious situations. Standards for the use of ultrasound were developed by the American Institute of Ultrasound and Medicine, the American Academy of Pediatrics, and the American College of Radiology, but there is no mandatory training or certification for physicians who perform sonography.[30]

The nonstress test (NST) is based on the assumption that the fetal heart rate (FHR) will temporarily accelerate with fetal movement and be a good indicator of fetal autonomic function. FHR is monitored externally, and the tracing is evaluated for accelerations. Occasionally, heart rate accelerations may be induced by the use of a vibro-acoustic stimulator (VAS) to waken the healthy but sleeping fetus. Actual strips and documentation of the professional interpretation are important parts of the medical record. Blood flow studies have been used to evaluate intrauterine fetal growth, low birth weight, placental insufficiency, and severe pregnancy-induced hypertension. In addition, blood flow studies have been used to monitor Rh isoimmunization, fetal cardiac arrhythmias, and diabetes mellitus. When combined with Doppler techniques, ultrasound can measure the blood flow patterns through the vessels of the umbilical cord or the maternal artery. The NST poses no know risk to mother or baby.[31]

Documentation in the medical record of all surveillance tests can serve as a major defensive tool when a breach of standard practice is alleged. Consent forms need to be present that document the what, when, and who of testing, the results of evaluation, and monitoring outputs. Of particular importance is the medical care's responsiveness to tests and clinical evaluations indicating fetal distress and abnormalities and the interventions taken, if possible, to minimize a poor outcome for the pregnancy.

Intrapartum Period

Serious adverse events can occur during the labor and delivery stages of the process (intrapartum period). The U.S. fetal mortality rate reported in 2005 for gestations of at least 20 weeks (6.2 fetal deaths per 1,000 live births and fetal deaths) was similar to the infant mortality rate (6.9 infant deaths per 1,000 live births).[32] Intrapartum risks include the chance that labor may occur early in the pregnancy (preterm), amniotic membranes may rupture prematurely, the fetus may present in a difficult delivery position, or labor may not progress adequately or at all. Fetal heart rate monitoring and fetal blood sampling help determine the appropriate labor and delivery clinical approach.

Preterm Labor

Some mothers experience labor prior to 37 weeks' gestation, when the fetus has not had the opportunity to develop fully. In such cases, physicians must decide on the appropriate clinical course of treatment: suppression of labor, or preterm delivery if it is neither desirable nor possible to suppress labor.

Risk management considerations include policies and procedures requiring the physician to be present in the hospital during the administration of tocolytic (suppression) drugs, continuous monitoring of the mother and fetus, notification of the pediatrician or neonatologist of a potential preterm delivery, and the availability of resuscitation equipment.

Fetal Heart Rate Monitoring

Physicians evaluate the fetal heart rate to identify changes that may be associated with problems related to fetal oxygenation and placental perfusion, such as hypoxia, umbilical cord compression, tachycardia, and acidosis. The purpose of FHR monitoring is to follow the status of the fetus during labor so that clinicians can intervene if fetal distress becomes evident. Training in the interpretation of FHR patterns and the ability to understand their correlation with the fetus's condition allows the physician to institute management techniques including maternal oxygenation, amnioinfusion, and tocolytic therapy.

FHR may be evaluated effectively either by auscultation or by internal or external electronic monitoring. External fetal monitoring (EFM) that monitors FHR, the duration of uterine contractions and the interval between uterine contractions is the most commonly used method because it allows measurement of the FHR response to uterine contractions. Manual auscultation with a small, handheld Doppler device or a fetoscope is used less commonly for FHR monitoring. The ACOG guidelines include a three-tier classification system for FHR tracings:

- Category 1 FHR tracings are characterized as normal and require no specific intervention.
- Category 2 tracings are classified as indeterminate, mandating further workup, surveillance, and possibly additional tests to further evaluate fetal health.
- Category 3 tracings are characterized as abnormal and require immediate intervention, such as providing oxygen to the mother, changing her position, stopping labor stimulation, treating maternal hypotension, or initiating prompt delivery if the tracings do not return to normal.

Several types of medications used during labor and delivery may affect FHR. For example, all narcotics decrease FHR variability as well as the frequency of accelerations. The use of EFM is linked to higher rates of both vacuum and forceps operative vaginal delivery, as well as of cesarean delivery for abnormal FHR patterns and/or acidosis. Nevertheless, ACOG recommends that during labor women with high-risk conditions undergo continuous FHR monitoring. The nurse or physician should review the tracings of a patient without complications frequently approximately every 30 minutes in the first stage of labor and every 15 minutes during the second stage. The corresponding frequency for patients with complications (e.g., fetal growth restriction, preeclampsia) is approximately every 15 minutes in the first stage of labor and every 5 minutes during the second stage. [33]

Induction and Augmentation of Labor

Induction of labor refers to stimulation of uterine contractions to accomplish delivery prior to the onset of spontaneous labor. It is one of the most commonly performed obstetrical procedures in the United States. Between 1990 and 2009, the overall frequency of labor induction more than doubled, rising from 9.5% to 23.2%, and early-term (37th- and 38th-week) inductions quadrupled, rising from 2% to 8%. Reasons suggested for this increase include the availability of better cervical ripening agents, patient and clinician desire to arrange a convenient time of delivery, and concerns about the risk of fetal demise with expectant delivery near term or post term.

ACOG has established guidelines for the induction of labor prior to spontaneous onset and for augmentation of labor to improve the quality of contractions.[34] Prior to induction or augmentation of labor, it is important to determine fetal maturity and assess gestational age and the status of the cervix. Surgical induction, such as rupturing or stripping the membranes, increases the risk of infection, bleeding, fetal dislodgement, and interference with cord presentation. Medical augmentation with intravenous drugs requires careful administration with an infusion pump or controller that permits precise flow rate control. Hospital policies should address immediate availability of the delivering physician from the outset of induction or augmentation; protocols for use in fetal distress, uterine hyperstimulation, and infusion rates; and required documentation.

The Delivery

Injuries or problems that develop during the perinatal period may be present at birth in addition to specific birth-related injuries or problems. Newborn clinical injuries identified in malpractice claims as a result of vaginal delivery include newborn cardiopulmonary problems, neuromuscular developmental problems, shoulder dystocia, infant death, and Erb's palsy. Infants delivered by cesarean-section (C-section) may experience the same complications that are reported in vaginal deliveries. Cesarean-sections on demand scheduled for the convenience of either the mother or the physician have added to the risk factors to be considered. Vaginal births after cesarean (VBACs) are considered to be a safe choice for most women, but do carry some risks for both the mother and the baby. In rare cases, a cesarean scar can rupture. This event can be life threatening, causing severe blood loss in the mother and lack of oxygen for the baby.[35] Additional maternal complications with any birth process include poor maternal outcomes, such as hemorrhage, perforation, or laceration of tissue, coma, paralysis, and death.

U.S. birth statistics for 2009 report that 8.2% of all neonates were born with a low birth weight and 12.2% were born preterm.[34] Babies born before 37 completed weeks of pregnancy are called premature. The rate of premature birth has increased by 36% since the early 1980s. Premature babies are at increased risk for newborn health complications, such as breathing problems, and death. They also face an increased risk of lasting disabilities, such as learning and behavioral problems, cerebral palsy, lung problems, and vision and hearing loss. More than 70% of premature babies are born between 34 and 36 weeks' gestation. Approximately 12% of premature babies are born between 32 and 33 weeks' gestation, 10% between 28 and 31 weeks' gestation, and 6% at less than 28 weeks' gestation. An estimated 1 million fetal deaths at any gestational age occur in the United States each year. After decades of decrease, the U.S. fetal mortality rate (fetal deaths at 20 weeks' gestation or more) did not decline from 2003 to 2005.[36]

All premature babies are at risk for health problems, but the earlier a baby is born, the greater the risk for serious complications. Babies born before about 32 weeks' gestation usually are very small, and their organs are less developed than those of babies born later. Most premature births are caused by spontaneous preterm labor, either by itself or by following spontaneous premature rupture of the membranes (PROM). With PROM, the sac inside the uterus that holds the baby breaks too soon. Preterm labor is labor that begins before 37 completed weeks of pregnancy. The causes of preterm labor and PROM are not fully understood, though the latest research suggests that many cases are triggered by the body's natural response to certain infections, including those involving amniotic fluid and fetal membranes. Nevertheless, in half of all cases of premature birth, providers cannot determine why a woman delivered prematurely.[37]

Pain Management and Obstetric Anesthesia

Anesthetic and analgesic agents not only act on the mother, but may also affect the respiratory and cardiovascular status of the fetus. Anesthesia and analgesics may be administered for pain management during either a vaginal delivery or a cesarean-section. Options include intravenous analgesia and regional anesthesia, primarily epidural, for labor and vaginal delivery, and general anesthesia or spinal anesthesia for a cesarean-section.

A study using the American Society of Anesthesiologists' Closed Claim Database reviewed malpractice claims filed against anesthesiologists in obstetric cases. The most common complications were, in order of severity, maternal death, newborn brain damage, and maternal headache. Minor complications included backache, pain during anesthesia, and emotional injury. Claims involving general anesthesia were frequently associated with severe injuries and resulted in higher payments than did claims involving regional anesthesia. When obstetric anesthesia claims for injuries from 1990 to 2003 were compared to pre-1990 obstetric claims, the proportion of maternal death and newborn death/brain damage decreased, whereas maternal nerve injury and maternal back pain increased in 1990 or later claims. In 1990 or later claims, payment was made on behalf of the anesthesiologist in only 21% of newborn death/brain damage claims compared to 60% of maternal death/brain damage claims. These payments in both groups were associated with an anesthesia contribution to the

injury and substandard anesthesia care. Anesthesia-related newborn death/brain damage claims featured an increased proportion of delays in anesthetic care and poor communication compared to claims unrelated to anesthesia. Clearly, newborn death/brain damage has decreased, but it remains a leading cause of obstetric anesthesia malpractice claims over time. The authors of this study concluded that potentially preventable anesthetic causes of newborn injury include delays in anesthesia care and poor communication between the obstetrician and anesthesiologist.[38]

The primary focus of anesthesia personnel is to cater to the mother and provide pain relief. Under extreme circumstances, they may assist the neonatologist or pediatrician following the birth if their help is required or if the baby is compromised and other physicians are not available.

Obstetric anesthesia services should be supervised by an anesthesiologist or certified registered nurse anesthetist (CRNA) with special training in obstetric anesthesia. Any hospital providing obstetric services should, at a minimum, have a qualified physician or CRNA readily available, preferably within 15 to 30 minutes, in an emergency. However, it is generally recommended that 24-hour in-house anesthesia coverage be available. Qualifications for this position include the ability of the professional to manage life-threatening respiratory and cardiovascular failure, toxemia, convulsions, and aspirations.

Pre- and post-anesthesia evaluations that include both maternal and fetal status should be performed by anesthesia personnel. The decision to use a particular type of pain relief and route of administration should be discussed with the mother by the professional intending to administer the anesthesia. That discussion should include the advantages, disadvantages, and risk implications to both the mother and the fetus. Documentation of the discussion and the mother's consent to anesthesia should be reflected in the medical record.

Vaginal Delivery

Vaginal delivery is the most common route for births. Adequate staffing to care for both the newborn and the mother are required. It is preferred that a pediatrician be available for all deliveries and imperative that a pediatrician or neonatologist be present at all high-risk deliveries. Cesarean-section, infant resuscitation, and anesthesia services should also be available.

In some deliveries, labor may have to be interrupted and a C-section performed. Breech presentations are often delivered through C-section, although it has been shown that vaginal delivery may be attempted if certain obstetric criteria are met.[39]

Obstetric forceps and vacuum extractors are designed to assist in removing the fetus from the birth canal at delivery when maternal contractions are insufficient to expel the fetus. The medical literature reveals significant controversy regarding the use of these techniques. Maternal injuries associated with such adjunctive procedures range from mild abrasions to severe lacerations of the vagina, cervix, and uterus. Fetal injuries may include bruising; serious scalp, cranial, or brain injury; neurological damage; and eye injury. Litigation claims in neurologically impaired infants point to these techniques as the prima facie cause of permanent impairment, despite contrary research findings.

ACOG has made it very challenging to provide water labor or births or warm-water water immersion. Reportedly, fewer than 300 hospitals offer water births and fewer than 500 offer water labor. Proponents of this technique suggest the warm-water bathtub is more comfortable for the mother and less traumatic for the baby because it simulates the uterine environment. ACOG's Committee on Obstetric Practice addressed the issue of warm-water immersion for laboring women and for delivery of infants. The Committee felt that there were insufficient data, especially concerning rates of infection, to render an opinion on whether warm-water immersion is a safe and appropriate birthing alternative. It indicated the procedure should be performed only if the facility can be compliant with Occupational Safety and Health Act standards regarding infection. This would include the specific tub and water recirculation systems used.

Cesarean Section

Cesarean-sections are performed in response to a variety of maternal and fetal indications, including previous cesarean delivery, dystocia, breech presentation, and fetal distress. They are classified as either scheduled or emergency. The medical and legal literature suggests the decision to perform a C-section is, in large part, dependent on a physician's concerns about malpractice litigation and the mother's desire to select a birth date for the child. Every hospital should be prepared to perform an emergency C-section. Although this procedure carries surgical risks, these risks may offset infant positioning and size risks associated with vaginal delivery.

Studies indicate that the C-section rate has increased since 1965, reversing a former steady decline in use of the procedure. Approximately 1 in 3 births in the United States is now a C-section, and 26.5% of low-risk females giving birth for the first time had a cesarean birth in 2007.[40] The World Health Organization recommends that a C-section rate of 5% to 10% is associated with the best clinical outcomes for mothers and infants. The U.S. Department of Health and Human Services, through its *Healthy People* project, recommended in 2010 a C-section rate of 15%. Some members of the scientific medical community challenge the empirical or lack of evidence to support low C-section rates.

If the physician has decided to proceed with a C-section, it is generally recommended that the gestation be at term and that the mother be in active labor. An anesthesia consult should be obtained, blood should be typed and screened, fetal heart tones should be monitored immediately prior to preparation of the abdomen for surgery, infant resuscitation personnel should be in attendance, and a vaginal examination should be performed.

Vaginal Birth After Cesarean

Many pregnant women and their physicians opt for a trial of labor and a vaginal delivery even after mothers have had as many as two C-section deliveries. With a VBAC, the medical profession recognizes that the need for anesthesia may decrease, some surgical risk is eliminated, and hospital stays are shorter. ACOG has adopted the stance that attempting a VBAC is a safe and appropriate choice for most women who have had a prior cesarean delivery, including for some women who have had two previous C-sections. ACOG states, "A VBAC avoids major abdominal surgery, lowers a woman's risk of hemorrhage and infection, and shortens postpartum recovery. It may also help women avoid the possible future risks of having multiple cesareans such as hysterectomy, bowel and bladder injury, transfusion, infection, and abnormal placenta conditions (placenta previa and placenta accreta)."[41] Documented risks include those associated with any vaginal delivery, as well as uterine rupture. Should the patient and physician elect to attempt a VBAC, however, personnel and facilities for an emergency C-section should be readily available.

Neonatal Resuscitation and Management

The importance of preparation and having the capabilities to perform neonatal resuscitation is heightened by increasing numbers of premature and low-birth-weight babies. Premature newborns may be born without adequate lung function or breathing capabilities. Otherwise-healthy newborns may need external assistance to clear their breathing passages or need assistance with the first reflexive breath. These compromised infants may be apneic or gasping at delivery. Neonatal resuscitation skills are essential for all healthcare providers who are involved in the delivery of newborns. The transition from fetus to newborn requires intervention by a skilled individual or team in approximately 10% of all deliveries.

In collaboration with the American Heart Association and the American Academy of Pediatrics, the National Resuscitation Program was implemented to create infant resuscitation guidelines and to provide certification for health professionals. Its guidelines recommend that at least one person skilled in resuscitating infants be present at every delivery. This person must be capable of initiating resuscitation, including administering positive-pressure ventilation and chest compressions. Either that person or someone else who is promptly available should have the skills required to perform a complete resuscitation, including endotracheal intubation and administration of medications. It is imperative that prior to the delivery, the team be aware of who is designated to be responsible for infant intubation and resuscitation.[42]

Documentation of resuscitation efforts, meconium status, Apgar scores, umbilical cord blood test results, and the placental examination are important risk management issues in cases of compromised neonates, as their mismanagement could lead to litigation.

Apgar Scoring

The Apgar score was devised in 1952 as a simple and repeatable method for rapid assessment of the health of newborn children immediately after birth. The scoring system is still in use today in every hospital in the United States. Derived from an assessment of selected clinical parameters, the score assists the clinician in determining the degree of infant resuscitation required as well as the effectiveness, over time, of the resuscitation efforts. A quantitative score to evaluate fetal oxygenation and the potential for fetal hypoxia is derived from the following five parameters, with the maximum possible score being 10: (1) fetal breathing movement; (2) fetal body movement; (3) fetal tone, demonstrated by extension and reflexion of fetal limbs; (4) fetal heart rate, measured by a nonreactive stress test; and (5) quantitative amniotic fluid volume. A cumulative score of 7 to 10 is interpreted as a normal infant at low risk for asphyxia; a score of 4 or less strongly suggests asphyxia.[43] Many clinicians associate a low Apgar score with subsequent identification of neurological disorder, although AAP and ACOG have recommended against using the Apgar score alone as evidence of or consequent to substantial asphyxia. Additional factors that should be considered include central nervous system immaturity, maternal sedation, and congenital malformations.

Umbilical Cord Blood Acid–Base Assessment

ACOG and AAP believe that umbilical cord blood acid–base assessment is a more objective measure of the acid–base status of a newborn than is the Apgar score.[44] If a question of intrapartum asphyxia arises or a low Apgar score is recorded, the literature recommends performing cord blood sampling. In the depressed newborn, the assessment can exclude intrapartum hypoxia as the cause of the depression. Because the sample may be delayed for up to 60 minutes before testing, the 5-minute Apgar score should be determined prior to testing.

Placental Examination

An examination of the placenta can sometimes demonstrate whether an injury to the fetus, fetal maldevelopment, or birth trauma is responsible for asphyxia. In particular, a placental examination may reveal the cause of preterm labor, premature membrane rupture, fetal undergrowth, or antenatal hypoxia.[45] Although the College of American Pathologists has not changed its practice guideline since 1997,[46] several groups have examined the value of the placental examination and believe the indicators for it should be reviewed to determine whether expanding the indicators would lead to a better understanding of fetal risk.[47] Many professionals believe placental examinations can prove beneficial as a risk management tool in the handling of claims related to fetal injury.

Indications for pathological placental examinations are based on several maternal, fetal, and placental conditions. Maternal conditions include severe preeclampsia, Rh isoimmunization, substance abuse, and insulin-dependent diabetes. Fetal conditions include fetal distress, meconium staining, suspected sepsis, and seizures. Placental conditions include abruption, masses, and abnormal appearance of the placenta or cord. Saving the placenta for pathological examination when suspicion arises that something is clinically amiss can serve as a valuable risk management tactic. If clinical conditions indicate that a placenta examination may help provide answers to clinical complications, the physician should examine the placenta, document any abnormalities, and forward the placenta to the pathology department for further examination.

When a mother requests her placenta postpartum, risk management is typically concerned about the risks associated with biohazards. Some patients wish to take their placenta home and bury it in their yard to plant a tree on top of it, as a living monument to the new or lost baby. There is also a growing trend of new mothers who wish to eat their placentas during the postpartum period. The growing trend of "placentaphagia" incorporates ingestion of the dried placenta by creating "health" supplements and incorporating it into recipes. The standard practice in use in most hospitals today permits patients to pick up their placentas and take them home. However, hospital policies stipulate the placenta should be soaked in preserving chemicals and examined by the pathologist prior to release. Hence, the placentas are no longer edible, which can cause outrage among patients who planned to consume them. Accrediting and licensing bodies, however, require that pathology be evaluated prior to release.

The hospital should be prepared for patients' requests regarding their placenta and have in place a policy and procedure developed collaboratively with obstetrics, laboratory/pathology, and risk management in accordance with accrediting and licensing standards. It is probably in the best interest of the mother and the hospital to accommodate these requests and properly release the prepared and examined placenta so long as the mother signs a release acknowledging the condition of the placenta and waiver of liability. Polices and procedures should be developed in accordance with state laws and regulations regarding disposition of pathology matters, bodily remains, waste management, and blood-borne pathogen safety. Release of the placenta should be limited to healthy tissue only, as the possible need to reexamine tissue with pathology may be necessary to consider treatment of an unhealthy newborn or for litigation in the defense of the hospital, physician, or staff.

Maternal Examination Post Delivery

From a risk management perspective, it is important that following the delivery the uterus be checked for retained vaginal sponges and retained placenta fragments. Some obstetricians choose not to explore the uterus following birth, for fear of causing pain or introducing infection, and may use ultrasound for the examination. A jury may find it difficult to understand why a physical examination was not performed.

With the trend toward shortened hospital stays following a normal delivery, mothers should be advised to call immediately if they experience excessive bleeding or discomfort when at home prior to their scheduled follow-up office visit.

Family Attendance and Videotaping of Birth

Attendance of the father, significant others, and siblings has become so commonplace at births that many clinicians do not consider the act as potentially damaging in the event of a malpractice lawsuit. A video of the birth may prove to be even more harmful during court proceedings.

Most hospitals have a policy that provides guidance for staff defining when visitors attending the birth should be asked to leave the delivery room or cease filming due to the intensified need for the physician and staff to attend to the birth. This request may be viewed by the visitors as a sign that something is wrong or that the medical team is trying to cover up their actions. If hospital staff are not simultaneously filming the medical team's actions during the delivery, the visitor's version of actions taped may be all that is presented in court. Lifesaving actions crucial to the case may not be captured on the video.

Staff should be reminded that a video is a permanent record of what they say and do during the delivery and that requests to cease filming without explanation may lead to covert filming of subsequent actions. If the staff is interviewed on camera, they must understand that the words they say may be subject to misinterpretation and used against them in a court of law.

Some hospitals and physicians have considered filming deliveries as a permanent part of the medical record. This policy may not be in the best interests of the hospital in the event of an error or deviation from standard practice by the medical team. Other facilities choose to film selected parts of the delivery or take photographs. Whatever the decision, in the event that visitors and filming are permitted, information such as visitors' names and the fact that filming occurred should be entered into the medical record. If a visitor is asked to leave the delivery room and/or stop filming, this request should also be entered into the medical record.

Medical Record Documentation

Given that legal action may be initiated as far out as 21 years following the delivery in the case of an injured newborn (depending on state-specific laws), it is important that medical record documentation be accurate, objective, and complete, and provide the rationale to support all patient management decisions, including the decision not to intervene. As all hospitals move toward full implementation of electronic medical records (EMR), it is imperative that those using the EMR be involved in the selection of the obstetrics module.[48,49] Built-in prompts have been found to improve documentation.[50]

Documentation should include all consents given prior to all testing and treatment. To ensure the best continuum of care, copies of the initial history, physical findings, and laboratory data should be received by the hospital from the delivering physician soon after the first prenatal visit. At 36 weeks' gestation, the patient's prenatal care record at the hospital should be updated. If there was no prenatal care and there are indications of complications or a possibly difficult pregnancy, case management and risk management personnel should be notified to monitor the outcome of the mother and infant, as well as to facilitate subsequent follow-up. Testing or treatment refused by the mother, missed appointments, and attempts to contact the mother should be recorded as well. It is important that all events during the labor process and delivery be recorded, even if the mother has signs of early labor and is sent home to await more active labor; this record should include the physician's orders and discharge instructions given to the patient.

Fetal heart monitor tracings are considered a part of the medical record and should be filed in a manner that allows them to be retrieved easily up to 21 years after the birth. Tracings and tracing segments should be marked so that the record clearly reflects the event sequence, the physician's interpretations, and assessments. Documentation during the delivery should include the condition of the mother, fetal station, and fetal status. Detailed notes in the medical record should include the indications and rationale for the delivery method selected. All maneuvers used in vaginal delivery, including those related to breech presentation or dystocia, should be listed. A narrative labor and delivery summary note should be recorded for each delivery, especially if there are clinically significant FHR patterns, low Apgar scores, low cord pH values, dystocia, preterm deliveries, fetal demise, or a newborn with significant morbidity. All adverse events or poor outcomes should be reflected through documentation of relevant clinical facts. It is vitally important that the caregivers do not speculate in the medical record regarding a poor outcome.

Postpartum documentation should include the post-delivery examination, and clinical indicators such as wound checks, bleeding, vital signs, and pain medications. With today's shorter hospital stays for normal deliveries, there is less time for nursing interaction with the mother. Mothers deemed to be at risk for infant care and self-care problems following discharge should be identified and referred to case management. All discharge instructions, as well as planned follow-up for mothers with complications, should be documented.

Neonatal Services

Following birth, infants are admitted to a nursery. The level of nursery service depends on the condition of the infant, the desires of the pediatrician or neonatologist, the availability of beds (for example, radiant warmers, incubators, bassinets), and staffing.[51] In addition to the Level I, II, and III nurseries, many hospitals divide their nurseries into well-baby and sick-baby nurseries. Neonatal intensive care units (NICUs) are reserved for infants who are medically compromised and in need of complex medical technology and specially trained medical professionals. While providing benefits to the infants, these technologies also pose significant risk due, in part, to the compromised condition of the infant, the invasive nature of some therapies, and the sometimes inherent risks of the medical devices.

For routine births, neonatal services pose few liability risks. By comparison, with premature births, the expectation of malpractice claims is heightened. Infants with a low birth weight are biologically compromised and require time to mature and grow. Advances in science and technology have increased the ability of pediatricians and neonatologists to support tiny infants with intensive care. During this time, diagnostic evaluation of the biological status of the infant is documented; congenital malformations are detected; corrective or emergency pediatric surgery may be performed; and general support of respiration, nutrition, fluid balance, and physiological functions is provided and monitored.

Premature or otherwise-compromised infants require a significant amount of clinical support during the first few weeks after birth. Continuous observation in a therapeutic milieu with highly trained clinicians and nurses, high-tech equipment, and immediate attention to detectable alterations in status and adverse situations will reduce the potential for liability in these units. Although transient hypoxic events and intraventricular hemorrhages, pneumonitis, sepsis, ABO blood incompatibility, and excess bilirubin may not be avoidable, these conditions should be evaluated with a subsequent appropriate response.

Detailed documentation of the continuing care in regular nurseries and in NICUs is extremely important for defense in lawsuits. Daily status and changes, diagnoses, test results, consents from the parents, indicated medications and treatments, and periodic updated care plans are necessary parts of the infant's medical record.

Staff may become emotionally attached to the babies who remain in the hospital for long periods of time, sometimes for many months. Despite the best efforts and highest quality of care, deaths do occur. These serious events may be viewed by staff as personal failures and undermine their confidence in their respective professional abilities. Group discussions and opportunities for venting feelings and attitudes should be promoted to reduce staff anxiety, stress, and potential loss of experienced staff to other professional activities.

The prolonged medical attention that babies who are born prematurely or with a very low weight require to survive once discharged home raises issues related to their quality of life. Developmental delays, behavioral problems, neuromuscular deficits, mental retardation, cerebral palsy, and seizure disorders have been identified as unwanted sequelae and major contributions to the instigation of lawsuits.

When birth-related adverse events are brought to litigation, it becomes difficult to distinguish among the various contributing factors:—that is, obstetric care versus anesthesia care versus neonatal care versus the risk itself of prematurity, which may be primary. Typically, in a scattershot approach, all parties are named in the suit: hospital, obstetrician, anesthesiologist, neonatologist, pediatrician,

consultants, and other caregivers identified in the medical record. From the risk manager's point of view, every baby treated in the neonatal intensive care unit is a potential liability action.

Infant Transport

An infant's medical condition may require transport to a facility where a higher level of care is available. Level II and Level III facilities treat infants born at the respective facilities, as well as infants transferred from lower-level facilities. Infants being transported are typically medically compromised and in need of specialized support and equipment.[52]

Before transfer can occur, the sending facility must contact the receiving facility to ensure acceptance of the infant. AAP and ACOG have outlined the components of infant transport between facilities, including requirements for communications, staffing, essential equipment, vehicles, patient care, and program evaluation.[28] The referring physician is responsible for providing the receiving physician with pertinent clinical information regarding the infant. Generally, it is preferred that the maternal patient be transferred with the fetus in utero, when possible. It is important to remember that sound clinical judgment, as well as the Emergency Medical Treatment and Active Labor Act, requires that a pregnant patient not be transferred until she has been examined and stabilized and has provided consent. Transport should be ordered only if the risks of the transfer do not outweigh the risks of remaining at the original facility.

Copies of all records, tests, monitor tracings, and clinical status details of the pregnancy, labor, and delivery, as well as information related to the infant's physical examination, diagnostic tests, and therapeutic interventions, should be sent along with the patient. Transport records should include the names of the medical team members, mode of transport, time of arrival and departure from the sending hospital, and time of arrival at the receiving facility. Procedures performed en route, medications administered, and periodic vital signs should be documented, as well as the condition of the patient upon arrival at the new facility.

Risk management should review transport events and investigate any difficulties during transport or technical and professional problems en route to reduce inherent risks in these transfers.

Infant Abduction

Every infant abduction is a crisis to the hospital, physician, staff and family. There is never justification for an infant abduction. These events become media frenzies and are very difficult for a hospital to overcome from a marketing perspective. The number of infant abductions appears to be declining, in large part because of proactive security measures, educational efforts, and a shortened length of stay in the hospital.

Infant identification plays an important role in decreasing the likelihood of abductions and minimizes the potential for giving the wrong infant to the wrong mother. This process should start in the delivery room and include duplicate banding of the infant, mother, and significant other, along with the footprint, blood typing, photograph, and written assessment noting birthmarks and identifying features. If there is a need to remove the infant's identification band, it

should be replaced immediately and the incident should be documented in the medical record.

The typical characteristics of the abductor are a female with no past criminal record. Usually, the woman has convinced friends and family that she has been pregnant for the past nine months. The kidnapper typically poses as a medical caregiver and dresses in a hospital uniform. Abductions tend to occur primarily in the mother's room, followed by the nursery, pediatrics department, and other on-premises locations.

An integrated approach to designing an infant security program is recommended.[53] Hospitals should identify security problem areas, design access control systems, develop emergency procedures for responding to an abduction, and promote staff and patient education to reduce risks. Postpartum rooms and nurseries should be located behind electronically locked and alarmed doors. Only staff with a need to enter should be provided access to the codes and/or electronic keys. Some hospitals utilize closed-circuit television and electronic-alarm wrist bands. Other areas to secure include stairwells and exit doors to the maternity, postpartum, and pediatric units.

Risk management guidelines suggest discontinuing publishing the names and photos of newborns in the local newspapers. Many facilities that do offer online photos of newborns require a password for viewing that is controlled by the mother and hospital. ll staff members and physicians who have contact with infants should be required to wear a photograph identification badge at all times, which should be checked by other staff, and especially by the mother. Although a difficult public relations issue, visitor control is of paramount importance.

SURGERY AND ANESTHESIA

Surgery and anesthesia claims are often co-dependent. Although surgical procedures may technically stand on their own merits, complicating factors related to the delivery of anesthesia must be considered. One major analysis of closed claims reported that the loss rates for inpatient surgery were driven by high claim frequency, although overall claim frequency dropped over the eight-year study period. The study also indicated that in 2011 the average claim severity for inpatient surgeries was 34% higher than the average of all claims examined.[3]

The increase in the number of surgeries performed in the outpatient/ambulatory setting has resulted in examination of risk and injuries based on a study that used data from the National Practitioner Data Bank, a repository of all malpractice payments paid on behalf of practitioners in the United States. The authors reported that 3,000% more surgeries are conducted in the outpatient setting than in the hospital on an inpatient basis. Similar to other studies, they noted a decrease in the number of claims reported over the years. The number of paid malpractice claims in each setting was similar, but the average payment amount in the outpatient setting was higher than in the inpatient setting. Diagnosis-related events were the most common reason for paid claims.[54]

Surgery is a specialty with numerous subspecialties. Each subspecialty shares common risks, but all also have unique risks. The Physician Insurers Association of America (PIAA) closed claim study reported on the following surgical subspecialties: cardiovascular and thoracic surgery, general surgery, neurosurgery, gynecologic surgery, orthopedic surgery, plastic surgery, and urologic surgery. The average surgeon indemnity payments ranged from $119,000 to $323,000, with neurosurgery experiencing the highest payouts.[2]

The most frequent allegations related to surgery reported over the years are as follows:

- Unnecessary surgery
- Wrong site
- Wrong surgery
- Inappropriate procedures
- Inadvertent acts
- Injury adjacent to the treatment site
- Foreign body left in the patient
- Infection, contamination, or exposure
- Equipment malfunction or failure
- Postoperative complications
- Postoperative death

Negligence and Malpractice

Surgery and accompanying anesthesia are, by their very nature, risky. The patient has no control once the anesthesia is delivered and the surgical procedure commences. The opportunity for significant serious surgical misadventures is high. Surgical adverse events that may not seem plausible include operating on the wrong patient, operating on the wrong side of the patient, or performing the wrong procedure. Adverse events that are considered technical or physiological in nature include accidental damage to an organ or artery or hemorrhage. The CMS has decided that it will not reimburse hospitals for the care required for specific hospital-acquired conditions or events it has decided should never occur and/or for which the care of the hospital acquired condition is not reimbursable. The risk management implication of such events is that, because CMS has determined these events should never occur, they are by default construed by many as events that should be litigated. Many of the events are related to surgical misadventures:

- Surgery performed on the wrong body part
- Surgery performed on the wrong patient
- Wrong surgical procedure on a patient
- Foreign object inadvertently left in patient after surgery
- Medication error
- Air embolism
- Blood incompatibility
- Patient disability from electric shock
- Patient disability from use of contaminated drugs
- Patient disability from wrong function of a device
- Incidents whereby a line designated for oxygen intended for the patient is the wrong item or contaminated
- Patient disability from burns

Surgical Services Staff

Legally, the surgeon is considered the "captain of the ship" and works closely with his or her team to promote patient safety and provide quality services. Surgical teams may consist of general surgeons, specialty surgeons, family practice physicians, podiatrists, anesthesia personnel, nursing staff, surgical technicians and assistants, surgical and anesthesia residents, heart–lung pump technicians, and radiology technicians, to name a few. Each team member is trained to perform specific tasks. Their actions may or may not be regulated by national certification or state licensure. With the rapid advances in new surgical procedures and technologies, it is imperative that all members of the surgical team be competent and maintain their competencies. Surgeons should perform only those procedures for which they have clinical privileges as provided by the medical staff bylaws and department regulations. Risk managers recommend that surgical operating room scheduling managers be provided with the list of hospital surgeons and their approved privileges to ensure that inappropriate surgeries are not scheduled.

Sales representatives who promote new equipment and technology present a host of risk management concerns. It is important that such persons provide only technical advice and not be allowed to scrub, personally assist, or operate any equipment in the operating suite.

Preoperative Assessment

Successful surgery requires quality clinical and technical skills of the surgical team and effective preoperative assessment, treatments, and diagnostic testing that ready the patient for surgery. The preoperative assessment includes the patient's history, a physical examination, and indicated diagnostic tests completed with results reviewed. The preoperative diagnosis should be recorded in the patient's medical record prior to the first incision. Patients should be clinically prepared as best as possible before undergoing surgery. Strengthening the immune system, nutritional condition, and physiological status of the patient encourages improved postoperative outcomes. Risk factors include surgical procedure complexity, patient physiology, anesthesia, carcinoma, infection, medications, chemotherapeutic agents, and radiation.

Patient consent and patient education are important to the risk manager's ability to mitigate risk in the event of a surgical or anesthesia misadventure. Informed consent is a process, not just a document. In essence, consent forms are viewed by the court as administrative evidence that healthcare practitioners had a consent discussion with the patient, not that consent was fully achieved. A witness who signs the consent form is attesting to the signature of the patient, not to the patient's informed consent to proceed with the procedure. The consent process, which is often inter-related with patient education, is designed to ensure the patient fully comprehends what the surgical procedure and postoperative care will entail, what the expected risk and hazards are, and what the alternatives to the planned treatment are. The consent process and related patient education should be fully documented in the medical record, including the surgeon's meetings with the patient, the surgeon's and nurse's assessment of the patient's understanding of the consent, and the education provided to the patient. Patient education about what to expect as a result of the surgery, with an emphasis on the patient's responsibilities in terms of care and monitoring, can improve the preoperative preparation of the patient. Of particular interest to surgical and anesthesia personnel is the issue of whether advance directives exist and whether they are to be honored during surgical procedures or while the patient is under the influence of anesthesia. Many facilities address this dilemma through their ethics committees.

Intraoperative Risk Issues

Risk management should be notified of all unusual occurrences in surgical patients and the operating room suite, such as surgery on the wrong patient; performance of the wrong procedure; medication error; patient return to surgery for repair or removal of an organ or body part damaged in surgery or subsequently;

and unexpected patient return to surgery or unplanned readmission to hospital. No operation or procedure should be performed for which the surgeon does not have clinical privileges.

Many intraoperative issues are of high risk and pervade several surgical specialties. Such issues include anesthesia services, blood contact, implants, retained foreign bodies, and burns.

Sedation and Anesthesia

In their many forms, sedation and anesthesia remove the patient's ability to control his or her own actions—in some cases introducing paralysis of limbs, cessation of unassisted breathing, and inability to respond to pain. Responsibility for assuring quality of life, viability, and a minimum of pain remains with the surgeon, anesthesiologist, and surgical support team. Anesthesia services may be provided by anesthesiologists, by certified registered nurse anesthetists, and in some instances by general surgeons and obstetricians.

The American Society of Anesthesiologists' closed claims database was established to permit the study of anesthesia injuries so as to improve patient safety. The database includes almost 9,000 claims. Recent evaluation of the data indicates that over the past 25 years claims for surgical anesthesia have decreased. Surgical anesthesia claims with monitored anesthesia care increased in the 2000s to 10% of claims, while regional anesthesia was involved in 19%. The most common complications were death (26%), nerve injury (22%), and permanent brain damage (9%). The most common damaging events due to anesthesia in claims were regional-block–related (20%), respiratory (17%), cardiovascular (13%), and equipment-related events (10%).[56]

Because of the complex and life-supportive nature of anesthesia equipment, the Food and Drug Administration (FDA) introduced recommendations for daily and preprocedure checklists for anesthesia devices in 1986. The American Society of Anesthesiologists is currently collecting and developing a library of anesthesia machine checklists that are universal and device specific. Common elements found in the checklists include the following items:

- Emergency backup equipment
- Anesthesia machine
- Waste gas scavenging system
- Oxygen supply
- Nitrous oxide and other gases
- Oxygen pressure failure system
- Flow meters
- Warning systems
- Accessory equipment
- Machine or breathing equipment leaks
- Ventilator
- Patient suction apparatus
- Electronic monitors
- Airway pressure alarms
- Volume monitor alarms

A pre-anesthesia assessment should be based on the patient's medical, anesthesia, and medication history; an appropriate physical examination; a review of diagnostic data; and the formulation and discussion of the anesthesia plan with the patient. Patients must also be reevaluated immediately before the induction of anesthesia.

Noninvasive patient monitoring during anesthesia usually includes blood pressure, pulse, respiratory efforts, skin color, temperature, and electrocardiograms. Capnometry is used on expired gas to measure the concentration of end-tidal carbon dioxide as a reflection of patient oxygenation, whereas pulse oximetry can provide an indication of arterial oxygen saturation. Electro-encephalography (EEG) and evoked potentials, although not widely in use, have been employed as indicators of unacceptable changes in brain activity as a measure of oxygen perfusion. Invasive monitoring, such as central venous pressure, continuous arterial blood pressure, or pulmonary artery monitoring, is typically used for critically ill patients and for complex surgical procedures (for example, bypass surgery) that allow and require a more continuous method of monitoring.

If intravenous sedation (also called conscious sedation) is administered and there is no anesthesia staff present, strict protocols should be followed regarding the types of cases and clinical parameters to be monitored by nurses, and steps to be taken in the event of complications.

Universal Protocol for Preventing Wrong-Site, Wrong-Procedure, and Wrong-Person Surgery

Wrong surgery can be a devastating event to the patient and the entire surgical team. The propensity for this type of error to occur resulted in all third-party accreditation organizations requiring development of a universal protocol for all hospitals performing surgery and all ambulatory surgery centers. All accrediting bodies are specific as to how the site is to be marked.

In 1997, the American Academy of Orthopedic Surgeons established a task force to examine the subject. The task force determined that an orthopedic surgeon had a 1 in 4 chance of performing a wrong-site surgery during a 35-year career. A seminal article was published in 2006 analyzing several databases, including the National Practitioner Data Bank, the

Florida Code 15 mandatory reporting system, the American Society of Anesthesiologists' (ASA) Closed Claims Project database, and a Web-based system for collecting wrong-site data. The study results demonstrated that this type of error occurs across all specialties, with especially high numbers of such events noted in orthopedic and dental surgery. The authors estimated that 1,300 to 2,700 wrong-site errors occur annually in the United States.

'Wrong-side/wrong-site, wrong-procedure, and wrong-patient adverse events, although rare, are more common than health care providers and patients appreciate. Prevention of WSPEs requires new and innovative technologies, reporting of case occurrence, and learning from successful safety initiatives (such as in transfusion medicine and other high-risk nonmedical industries), while reducing the shame associated with these events.'[57]

In another study that same year based on wrong-site surgery cases reported to a large malpractice insurer over a 20-year period, 1 in 112,994 operations resulted in a wrong-site procedure. The reviewers found that under optimal conditions, having a universal protocol might have prevented 62% of the cases reviewed. At this time, not all of the healthcare organizations required actual marking of the surgical site. The authors concluded that while wrong-site surgery was exceedingly rare, major injury from wrong-site surgery is even rarer. They believed that the then-current site-verification protocols could have prevented two-thirds of the examined cases if used properly.[58]

Efforts to minimize and eliminate the incidence of these adverse events that seem to result from communication failures resulted in the development of universal protocols. Surgical site marking and time-out protocols are part of such a universal protocol. Marking the site is required for procedures involving right/left distinction, multiple structures (such as fingers and toes), or levels (as in spinal procedures). There are specific indications where marking is not required; they are delineated in detail by the accrediting organizations. Use of universal protocol checklists is endorsed by every surgical professional association and accrediting body.[59]

Implants

Medical implants are a significant concern in surgical liability. Implant materials have been found over the years to be in some instance incompatible with human tissue or to wear inappropriately or early. Implant materials, such as some polymers, have been alleged to contribute to systemic and local clinical complications that arise years after the implant surgery. Implantable pain pumps have broken down tissue in ways not expected by the designers or manufacturers. Implants of all types may also wear excessively, break or fracture, and be useless years after the surgery. The question of whether to remove an implant is one of great concern to the medical community. Although there are potentially serious risks to allowing the defective implant to remain in situ, there are also serious concerns about the clinical hazards of removing the implant.

The Safe Medical Devices Act (SMDA) require manufacturers to track specific medical implants from their manufacture through the distribution chain through the useful life of the device.[60] Although this requirement does not apply to hospitals, manufacturers are mandated to develop tracking systems that incorporate the hospital's ordering and implantation of the device in a patient. Currently implants and implantable devices subject to tracking include the following items:

- Glenoid fossa prosthesis
- Mandibular condyle prosthesis
- Temporomandibular joint (TMJ) prosthesis
- Abdominal aortic aneurysm stent grafts
- Automatic implantable cardioverter/defibrillator
- Cardiovascular permanent implantable pacemaker electrode
- Implantable pacemaker pulse generator
- Replacement heart valve (mechanical only)
- Implanted cerebellar stimulator
- Implanted diaphragmatic/phrenic nerve stimulator
- Implantable infusion pumps
- Silicone gel-filled breast implants
- Cultured epidermal autografts

Currently, there are no U.S. national patient-based implant registries. ECRI developed the first national implant registry in the United States in 1983 in an attempt to track patients in the event of device failure or product recalls; the registry ceased operations 6 years later due to a lack of patient participation.

It was estimated in 2000 that more than 25 million Americans carry a medical implant of some type in their bodies. Far more could be known about how these devices work and fail if they were retrieved and analyzed after they were replaced or when patients die. Considerable media attention in recent years has focused on clinical problems that may be related to implants. Breast implants, hip replacements, implantable pain pumps, and surgical mesh are only a few of the implants that have been in the headlines. This media attention has highlighted another problem in the United States—a lack of long-term data on implants. "Aside from Medicare data, no long-term clinical trials data on hip and knee devices are available from manufacturers, nor are long-term U.S. registry data available that could be used to identify complication trends with implants."[61]

Hospitals and ambulatory surgery centers should be aware of their implant tracking responsibilities. Manufacturers of all implanted devices should be contacted to ensure the implanting entity is participating in the manufacturer's tracking system. Implant recall notices should be centrally reviewed and checked for applicability and action by the implanting facility. Failure of implantable devices could have serious adverse health consequences and result in litigation against the surgeon, staff, and hospital if the proper steps in registering the implant and reacting to recalls are not taken.

Retained Foreign Bodies

Defense of cases involving a retained foreign body after surgery are very difficult to defend. Courts expect surgeons and nursing staff to be aware of which products are used during surgery as well as what is removed from the patient. In an effort to minimize the risk of leaving these items in the surgical cavity, the Association of periOperative Registered Nurses has developed recommended practices regarding sponge, sharps, and instrument count procedures.[62] If the initial and final counts are not in agreement, an X-ray of the surgical field is recommended prior to the patient's leaving the surgical table. Incorrect instrument, sponge, or sharp counts may necessitate further exploration at the surgical site.

Claims of foreign objects or material found following surgery should initiate a thorough investigation by risk management of the medical record to identify lapses in procedure and to prevent further occurrences.

Patient Burns and Pressure Injuries

During surgery, a patient may experience what appears to be a chemical or thermal burn or a pressure injury. Chemical burns may result from the fluid used to clean the surgical site prior to the surgical procedure or the adhesive conductive gel used under the dispersive electrode of an electrosurgical unit (ESU). Thermal burns may result if the patient is placed too close to a surgical light, if an operating microscope is reassembled incorrectly, or if an ESU is used. Pressure injuries, which mimic the appearance of burns, may result from sustained normal pressure during surgery, from body weight, and from external objects that reduce or impede local circulation. Vascular insufficiency may also contribute to pressure injuries. Incorrect positioning of the patient may lead to neural injuries or impairment. Additional risks are inherent in surgical patients who are elderly, who are malnourished or obese, or whose delicate skin is compromised by their basic medical status.

Because a majority of the patient's body is beneath surgical drapes and not visible to the surgical team, constant attention to placement of the patient's extremities is important. Meticulous attention to detail in positioning the patient, pressure distribution devices and padding, and careful clamping of towels may help eliminate some pressure injuries. Inspection, maintenance, and appropriate placement of electrical accessories and use of devices will reduce unintended burns and future patient discomfort. Documentation of positioning and placement of electrodes protects staff from allegations of poor practices.

Any type of patient injury, reddening of the skin, or break in skin integrity not identified prior to surgery or noticed immediately after surgery or during postoperative recuperation should be examined, treated, and documented in the medical record, as well as thoroughly investigated and reported to risk management.

Surgical Fires

Surgical fires have received significant attention during the last several years. Although surgical fires are considered rare events, they can result in serious injury, disfigurement, and death. An estimated 550 to 650 surgical fires occur in the United States each year. Serious reported patient events include second- and third-degree burns and death, primarily associated with fires occurring in the patient's airway. In 2011, the FDA launched a surgical fire prevention initiative to promote safer practices and to share fire prevention resources developed to address surgical fire factors, prevention, and response. The agency identified recommended practices to help prevent these fires, and encouraged voluntary reporting of such events to the FDA.[63]

Postoperative Recovery Care

Following surgery, patients are transported to the post-anesthesia care unit or intensive care unit for monitoring and stabilization by specially trained physicians, nurses, and ancillary staff. The patient's postoperative status should be assessed on admission to the unit and reassessed prior to discharge. Monitoring should include the patient's physiological and mental status such as vital signs and level of consciousness; pathological findings; medication, fluid, blood, or blood components administration; and unusual events or postoperative complications, as well as management of those complications.

Postoperative risk management issues concern serious adverse clinical events during transfer to the recovery area; adverse results of anesthesia; medication or transfusion reactions; cardiac or respiratory arrest or death; and postoperative neurological deficits not present on admission.

It is usually the responsibility of the anesthesia personnel to discharge a patient from the recovery room, but some facilities permit the nursing staff to use discharge criteria protocols. Such protocols are developed through the joint efforts of anesthesia, surgical, and nursing staff, and should have the approval of the medical board.

Medical Record Documentation

Medical record documentation concordant with surgical procedures requires documentation of the three stage of surgery: preoperative, intraoperative, and postoperative. The documentation of the surgical process may be the best defense a surgeon, clinical staff, and hospital have in the event they need to defend their actions following an adverse surgical event. The complexity of the surgical process is difficult to capture through documentation, but as all activities are not automatically captured through electronic means, staff and surgeons must continue to rely on their own initiation of the documentation. Surgical modules within electronic medical records are capturing much of the necessary elements of documentation.

Preoperative

- Diagnosis
- Review of the patient's history and physical status

- Advance directives
- Preoperative nursing
- Review of diagnostic test results
- Assessment of the risks and benefits of the procedure
- Need to administer blood or blood components
- Informed consent
- Pre-anesthesia documentation
- Need for additional diagnostic testing

Intraoperative

- Name of the primary surgeon and all assistants
- Anesthesia process
- Nursing interactions
- Universal precautions checklist
- Monitoring

Postoperative

- Care delivered to the patient and the patient's condition in the recovery room
- Clinical parameters monitored
- Name of the licensed, independent practitioner who is responsible for the patient
- Identification of surgeon and all staff providing direct patient care
- Operative report that includes the findings, technical procedures used, specimens removed, and postoperative diagnosis
- Surgeon's assessment of the patient's progress
- Monitoring
- Tests ordered and test results
- Dressing changes
- Medications
- Discharge plans and discharge instructions

DIAGNOSTIC IMAGING

Medical imaging is the process of creating images of the human body using various methods. Diagnostic imaging includes those techniques whereby medical images provide a basis for examining the human body so as to diagnose disease. Imaging modalities include the following methods:

- X-rays: plain film tomography
- Computed tomography (CT)
- Interventional radiography/fluoroscopy/angiography
- Ultrasound/sonography
- Magnetic resonance imaging (MRI)
- Positron emission tomography (nuclear medicine)

This chapter does not discuss the therapeutic use of radiation.

X-Rays

X-ray radiation is a portion of the electromagnetic spectrum that is not in the visible spectrum. The useful characteristic of X-ray radiation is that it absorbed and reflected differently by different tissues (e.g., bone, skin) of the body based on the density of the tissue. If the source of X-ray radiation is placed on one side of the body and a reactive film is placed on the other side of the body, a snap exposure of radiation passing through the body onto the film can provide a picture that can be analyzed. In other words, the radiation appears lighter on the image as the density of tissue increases. In the case of a broken leg, the break area can often clearly can be distinguished as opposed to the more dense intact bone on both sides of the break.

Today, the "film" is often replaced by a digital detector arrangement that collects the signal and creates a digital image. The digital image can be displayed, stored, or transmitted. X-ray with the resulting two-dimensional image is also known as plain film X-ray. Plain film X-rays are useful in many clinical disciplines. For example, chest and abdominal X-rays are routine and often used to confirm healthy morphology of the heart, lungs, and other organs, while head, chest, and limb X-rays are routinely used for determining fractures and other bone abnormalities.

X-ray radiation carries a risk of overexposure for both the patient and the clinical staff. The age of the patient, frequency of X-ray studies, and condition and age of the device contribute to the possibility of over-exposure.

Computed Tomography

Computer tomography (often referred to as CT or CAT, computed axial tomography) utilizes X-ray radiation that is coupled with collection of a series of images focused on and through a specific area of the body (such as the liver or chest), with subsequent computer reconstruction and analysis of these images. The "slices" of images are aimed through the target in multiple planes. The three-dimensional computer re-creation of the area can detect many conditions that are not apparent on a standard, two-dimensional X-ray.

CT scans are often the best diagnostic tool to rule in or rule out many diseases depending on the combination of soft and hard tissues that need to be penetrated. This modality is useful throughout the body (head, chest, abdomen, and extremities) and full body. It is used to analyze specific problems (e.g., cerebrovascular accident and trauma), to stage malignant diseases (e.g., lymphoma), and to monitor the response to therapy. As a preoperative tool, it can be used to more precisely locate and otherwise understand the characteristics of complex masses. It is used as a preventive medicine tool, for example, to monitor for colon cancer, in mammography, or for an executive physical to examine the current status of an executive's well-being. In comparison to plain film radiography, CT scans usually require exposure to higher doses of radiation because numerous slices are required to collect enough data for computer re-creation of a three-dimensional image.

As with plain film X-ray, there is the potential for over-exposure with CT scans. Computed tomography delivers a relatively high X-irradiation dose; in turn, there is a small possibility that individuals exposed to X-rays will develop cancer. Cataracts or skin burns resulting from very high levels of exposure are rare and usually associated with device failure.

Interventional Radiology (Fluoroscopy, Angiography)

Interventional radiology uses X-rays to perform in real time invasive, image-guided procedures to diagnose and treat diseases. That is, X-ray radiation in continuous use is used to show anatomy and the location and progress of a minimally invasive tool (surgical or contrast material). This modality is used in almost every organ and system. Real-time imaging of structures in motion can be augmented through injection of a radiocontrast agent to view the following structures, for example:

- Blood vessels, obstructions within them, or valves properly or improperly closing and opening

- Alimentary organs and canals to determine obstructions, structural abnormalities, or proper or improperly functioning valves; or similar aspects of any other fluid circulation or movement system.

Radiocontrast agents are typically swallowed or injected.

Interventional radiology is also useful in performing surgical procedures—specifically, implanting medical devices in specific locations to collect data, provide treatment, or provide anesthesia.

Ultrasonography

Ultrasonography utilizes non-ionizing radiation (as opposed to X-ray ionizing radiation). With this imaging technique, sound waves in the electromagnetic spectrum above the range of human hearing are channeled into the human body and are reflected back to detectors. The images are collected in real time and a computer re-creates the images for either immediate display or storage. Different frequencies of ultrasonic energy provide greater or lesser spatial resolution and/or imaging depth. Ultrasonography is useful for visualizing tendons, muscles, joints, blood vessels, and even internal organs. It can be used for interventional use (e.g., to guide needles) or to measure fluid flow (e.g., blood flowing through a blood vessel).

This technology is preferred whenever exposure to X-radiation would be undesirable (e.g., pregnancy), as it avoids exposure to ionizing radiation. The risks of long-term exposure of tissue to tissue warming or exposure of the fetus to low energy for extended periods are unknown.

Magnetic Resonance Imaging

Also called nuclear magnetic resonance imaging (NMR or NMRI), magnetic resonance imaging utilizes a magnetic field imposed upon the body to create an environment within the body that elicits real-time changes in the tissue that can be detected, recorded, and reconstructed to provide either a two-dimensional or three-dimensional image of the body. Used by itself and in conjunction with contrast media, MRI is especially useful in providing good contrast of soft tissue (e.g., in the brain, heart, muscles, and tumors).

Magnetic resonance imaging does not use ionizing radiation and there are no known harmful side effects associated with exposure to the magnetic field. The magnet field can, however, cause metallic implants/foreign bodies (e.g., pacemakers, artificial limbs, aneurysm clips, cochlear implants, prostheses) and other implanted medical devices that contain metal to move, malfunction, or increase in temperature. Loose metal objects in the room or on the patient may cause damage or injury if they are pulled toward the magnet. Dyes from tattoos or tattooed eyeliner, medication patches, or wire leads if in contact with bare skin can cause burns or skin irritation.

Positron Emission Tomography

Positron emission tomography (PET) utilizes radiopharmaceuticals administered to patients (typically injected or inhaled) for which the drug is taken up in a greater or lesser concentration by the specific tissue of interest. The radiopharmaceutical within the tissue decays over time and emits gamma radiation in a specific way. The emissions are received by a ring of detectors that ignore extraneous radiation, and the computer reconstructs an image much in the way that such reconstruction occurs in computed tomography. PET is most often used in oncology to study tumors and metastases. It is also useful in studying activity related to molecular activity (e.g., in the brain, muscles) or as the result of pharmaceuticals.

Malpractice Allegations

The most frequent diagnostic imaging allegations include incorrect diagnosis:

- Failure to diagnose
- Misdiagnoses
- Wrong diagnosis

Additional complicating factors include radiologic complications, radiologic "misses," lack of or incomplete informed consent, and over-radiation.

A recent review provided the following classification of errors in diagnostic imaging: observer errors, errors in interpretation, failure to suggest the next appropriate procedure, and failure to communicate in a timely and clinically appropriate manner.[64] Errors attributed to observer error include the following:

- Scanning error—radiologist fails to fixate in the area of the lesion
- Recognition error—radiologist fixates in the area of the lesion but fails to detect the lesion
- Decision-making error—interpretation of a malignant lesion as a normal structure
- Satisfaction of search error—diversion of the radiologist's attention from a tumor by an eye-catching but unrelated finding
- Visual perceptual error—failure to detect the abnormality because of psychophysiological factors (e.g., alertness)

- Influential perceptual error—a radiology report influences another radiologist

Errors in interpretation may occur for a number of reasons, including patient history, previous studies, and even characteristics of the room. Failure to suggest the next appropriate procedure occurs typically not because the radiologist does not know the next procedure that should follow, but rather because he or she fails to report and record it. Failure to communicate is the fourth most frequent allegation against radiologists in medical malpractice claims.

Contrast media (either ingested or injected) are used to enhance several of the imaging modalities. Exposure to such media can cause simple to severe adverse reactions, resulting in malpractice lawsuits. Different compositions of the media (e.g., low osmality versus high osmality), route of injection (e.g., extravascular versus intravascular), volume, and allergic potential affect the incidence and severity of these adverse events.

Management of Risk

Many of the risk management techniques that apply to clinical departments also apply to the management of risk in diagnostic imaging:[65]

- Staffing
- Credentialing and privileging by discipline and procedure
- Informed consent
- Staff education and training
- Adverse occurrence reporting and follow-up
- Quality control systems
- Use of and adherence to written operating and treatment policies and procedures

In addition, some risk management considerations are specific to diagnostic imaging.

Contrast media/radiopharmaceuticals, for example, can cause acute severe adverse reactions. Typically, these reactions occur within 20 minutes of injection. Risk management tactics to be implemented whenever contrast media is used include the following measures:

- Patient history includes questions about allergies to shellfish and prior history of contrast media
- Physician must be able to recognize and treat acute adverse reactions
- Treatment room stocked with basic and advanced life support monitoring equipment and drugs
- In the event of an adverse reaction, immediately discontinue contrast media administration, closely monitor the patient until the symptoms have stabilized or resolved, and assess the patient's airway, breathing, and circulation (ABCs).

Radiation Exposure

The basic premise of controlling radiation exposures follows the acronym ALARA: as low as reasonably achievable.[66] With respect to diagnostic imaging, ALARA means taking every reasonable effort to keep the exposures to ionizing radiation as far below the dose limits as practical given the clinical purpose for which the test is undertaken, taking into account the state of technology and the economics of improvements in relation to benefits and safety. There are three elements in decreasing radiation dose:

- Decrease the time of exposure
- Increase the distance of the patient and staff from the radiation source
- Use proper shielding

Patient safety can be enhanced by asking related questions prior to making a decision to use diagnostic imaging or a specific modality.

- Is the procedure necessary for making an accurate diagnosis?
- Is there a risk to not having the procedure?
- Could alternative procedures accomplish the same goal with no or lower exposure and without other mitigating risks?
- Is the patient's situation likely to result in the procedure being inconclusive, requiring a further diagnostic imaging procedure and resultant increase in exposure?
- Would it be more efficacious to perform the procedure more likely to result in the desired outcome first?

REFERENCES

1. Hannemann-Weber, H., Kessel, M., Budych, K., Schultz, C. (2011) Shared communication processes within healthcare teams for rare diseases and their influence on healthcare professionals' innovative behavior and patient satisfaction. *Implementation Science 6*, 40. http://www.implementationscience.com/content/pdf/1748-5908-6-40.pdf

2. Physician Insurers Association of America. (2011). Data sharing reports: Claim trend analysis, risk management review, and semiannual reports. Rockville, MD: Author.

3. *Hospital and physician professional liability benchmark analysis.* (2011). Chicago, IL

4. CNA HealthPro. (2008). *Emergency department liability: Sound risk control strategies can reduce misdiagnosis.* Chicago, IL: VantagePoint (08:3), CNA. http://www.cna.com/vcm_content/CNA/internet/Static%20File%20for%20Download/Risk%20Control/Network%20Security/emergencydepartmentliabilitysoundriskcontrolstrategiescanreducemisdiagnosis.pdf

5. CNA HealthPro. (2011). *Understanding nurse liability, 2006–2011: A three-part approach.* Chicago, IL: Claim Study, CNA. http://www.cna.com/vcm_content/CNA/internet/Static%20File%20for%20Download/Risk%20Control/Medical%20Services/UnderstandingNurseLiability,2006-2010-AThree-PartApproach-11-2011.pdf

6. Centers for Disease Control and Prevention, National Center for Health Statistics. (2008). National Hospital Ambulatory Medical Care Survey: 2008 emergency department summary tables. http://www.cdc.gov/nchs/data/ahcd/nhamcs_emergency/nhamcsed2008.pdf

7. American College of Emergency Physicians. (2011). *How overcrowding affects your access to emergency care.* Dallas: Author. http://www.acep.org/Content.aspx?id=25906&terms=overcrowding

8. American College of Emergency Physicians. (2011). *Emergency department waiting times.* Dallas: Author. http://www.acep.org/Content.aspx?id=25908&terms=waiting

9. CFR 489.24, Special responsibilities of Medicare hospitals in emergency cases. http://ecfr.gpoaccess.gov/cgi/t/text/text-idx?type=simple;c=ecfr;cc=ecfr;idno=42;region=DIV1;q1=489;rgn=div5;sid=095f8200c4ce87894318de7a63502ffb;view=text;node=42%3A5.0.1.1.7#42:5.0.1.1.7.2.14.5

10. CFR 413.65, Requirements for a determination that a facility or an organization has provider-based status. http://edocket.access.gpo.gov/cfr_2005/octqtr/pdf/42cfr413.65.pdf

11. American College of Emergency Physicians. (2005). *Medical direction of emergency medical services.* Dallas: Author. http://www.acep.org/Content.aspx?id=29570&terms=prehospital%20director

12. American Medical Association. (1973). *Recommendations of the Conference on the Guidelines for the Categorization of Hospital Emergency Capabilities.* Chicago, IL: Author.

13. Emergency Nurses Association, Institute for Emergency Nursing Research. (2011). *Emergency Department Violence Surveillance Study.* Des Plaines, IL: Author. http://www.ena.org/IENR/Documents/ENAEDVSReportNovember2011.pdf

14. Pham, J.C., Andrawis, M., Shore, A,D., Fahey, M., Morloch, L., & Pronovost, P.J. (2011, July/August). Temporary ER staff linked to more medication errors. *Journal of Healthcare Quality.*

15. Farhan, Brown, R., Vincent, C., & Woloshynowych, M. (2011, December 28). The ABC of handover: Impact on shift handover in the emergency department. *Emergency Medicine Journal.*

16. U.S. Department of Labor, Occupational Safety and Health Administration. (2012) Emergency department eTool. http://www.osha.gov/SLTC/etools/hospital/er/er.html#workplaceviolence

17. U.S. Department of Health and Human Services, Agency for Healthcare Research and Quality. (2012). Emergency Severity Index (ESI): A triage tool for emergency department care. http://www.ahrq.gov/research/esi/esi1.htm

18. American College of Emergency Physicians, (2006). *Providing telephone advice from the emergency department: Policy statement.* Dallas: Author. http://www.acep.org/content.aspx?id=29658

19. Emergency Nurses Association, (2011). *Consensus statement on definitions for consistent emergency department metrics,* Des Plaines, IL: Author. http://www.ena.org/media/PressReleases/Documents/07-13-11_DefinitionsED_Metrics.pdf

20. Clark, S. L., Belfort, M. A., Dildy, G. A., & Meyers, J. A. (2008). Reducing obstetric litigation through alterations in practice patterns. *Obstetrics and Gynecology, 112,* 1279–1283.

21. CRICO. (2010). *Annual benchmarking report malpractice risks in obstetrics.* Cambridge, MA: Author. http://www.rmf.harvard.edu/~/media/Files/_Global/KC/PDFs/2010_OB_report1.pdf

22. De Jesus, L., Generic Database Subcommittee, NICHD Neonatal Research Network. *Risk factors for post-discharge mortality among extremely low birth weight infants (ELBW).* Presented to the Pediatric Academic Societies, Vancouver, Canada, May 1–4, 2010.

23. Stoll, B. J., et al., NICHD Neonatal Research Network. (2010). Neonatal outcomes of extremely preterm infants from the NICHD Neonatal Research Network. *Pediatrics, 126*(3), 443–456. http://pediatrics.aappublications.org/content/126/3/443.full.pdf

24. Bloom, S. L., (2006). Decision-to-incision times and maternal and infant outcomes. *Obstetrics & Gynecology, 108*(1), 6–11.

25. Hickson, G., Clayton, E. W., Githens, P. B., & Sloan, F. A. (1992). Factors that prompted families to file medical malpractice claims following perinatal injuries. *Journal of the American Medical Association, 268*(11), 1359–1363.

26. American College of Obstetricians and Gynecologists. (2011, August). Committee opinion 501: *Maternal–Fetal intervention and fetal care centers.* Washington, DC: Author. http://www.acog.org/~/media/Committee%20Opinions/Committee%20on%20Ethics/co501.pdf?dmc=1&ts=20120304T2148424362

27. AAP Committee on Fetus and Newborn. (2007). Noninitiation or withdrawal of intensive care for high-risk newborns. *Pediatrics, 119*(2), 401–403.

28. American Academy of Pediatrics (AAP) & American College of Obstetricians and Gynecologists. (2007). *Guidelines for Perinatal Care.* (6th ed.).

29. U.S. Department of Health and Human Services, Office on Women's Health. (n.d.). Prenatal testing. http://www.nlm.nih.gov/medlineplus/prenataltesting.html

30. American Institute of Ultrasound in Medicine. (2007). *AIUM practice guideline for the performance of obstetric ultrasound examinations.* Laurel, MD: Author. http://www.aium.org/publications/guidelines/obstetric.pdf

31. U.S. Department of Health and Human Services, National Institutes of Health. (2010). Fetal heart monitoring. http://www.nlm.nih.gov/medlineplus/ency/article/003405.htm

32. American Academy of Pediatrics, Clinical Reports. (2011). Standard terminology for fetal, infant, and perinatal deaths. *Pediatrics, 128*(1), 177–181. http://aappolicy.aappublications.org/cgi/content/full/pediatrics;128/1/177

33. American College of Obstetrics and Gynecology. (2009, July). *Practice bulletin 106: Fetal heart rate monitoring.* Washington, DC: Author.

34. Centers for Disease Control, and prevention. (2011, November 3). Births: Final data for 2009. *National Vital Statistics Reports, 60*(1). http://www.cdc.gov/nchs/data/nvsr/nvsr60/nvsr60_01.pdf

35. American College of Obstetricians and Gynecologists. (2010, August). *Practice bulletin 115: Vaginal birth after previous cesarean delivery.* Washington, DC: Author.

36. Centers for Disease Control and Prevention. (2009, April). The challenge of fetal mortality. NCHS Data Brief 16. http://www.cdc.gov/nchs/data/databriefs/db16.htm

37. March of Dimes Foundation. (2010, April). *Premature birth.* White Plains, NY: Author. http://www.marchofdimes.com/baby/premature_indepth.html

38. Davies, J. M., (2009). Liability associated with obstetric anesthesia: A closed claims analysis. *Anesthesiology, 110*(1),131–139.

39. American College of Obstetrics and Gynecology, Committee on Obstetrics Practice. (Reaffirmed 2010). *Committee Opinion 340: Management of breech presentation.* Washington, DC: Author. http://www.acog.org/~/media/Committee%20Opinions/Committee%20on%20Obstetric%20Practice/co340.pdf?dmc=1&ts=20120304T1904399401

40. U.S. Department of Health and Human Services. (n.d.). Healthy people, 2020: Maternal, infant and child health. http://healthypeople.gov/2020/topicsobjectives2020/objectiveslist.aspx?topicId=26

41. American College of Obstetrics and Gynecologists. (2010, July 2). Ob gyns issue less restrictive VBAC guidelines [News release]. http://www.acog.org/About_ACOG/News_Room/News_Releases/2010/Ob_Gyns_Issue_Less_Restrictive_VBAC_Guidelines

42. American Heart Association. (2010). Neonatal resuscitation: 2010 American Heart Association guidelines for cardiopulmonary resuscitation and emergency cardiovascular care. *Pediatrics, 126*(5), e1400–e1413. http://pediatrics.aappublications.org/content/126/5/e1400.full.pdf+html

43. Finster, M., Wood, M. (2005). The Apgar score has survived the test of time. *Anesthesiology, 102*(4), 855–857. http://www.ncbi.nlm.nih.gov/pubmed/15791116

44. American College of Obstetrics and Gynecology, Committee on Obstetric Practice, & American Academy of Pediatrics, Committee on Fetus and Newborn. (2006, reaffirmed 2010). *ACOG/AAP Committee Opinion 348: Umbilical cord blood gas and acid–base analysis.* Washington, DC: ACOG. http://www.acog.org/Resources_And_Publications/Committee_Opinions/Committee_on_Obstetric_Practice/Umbilical_Cord_Blood_Gas_and_Acid-Base_Analysis

45. American College of Obstetrics and Gynecology, Committee on Obstetric Practice. (2009). Management of stillbirth: Practice bulletin 102. *Obstetrics and Gynecology, 113,* 748–761.

46. Langston, C., Kaplan, C., Macpherson, T., Manci, E., Peevy, K., Clark, B. et al. (1997). Practice guideline for examination of the placenta developed by the placental pathology practice guideline task force of the

College of American Pathologists. *Archives of Pathology and Laboratory Medicine, 121,* 449–476.

47. Curtin, W. M., (2007). Pathologic examination of the placenta and observed practice. *Obstetrics and Gynecology, 109*(1), 35–41.

48. Dagroso, D., Williams, P. D., Chesney, J. D., Lee, M., Theobans, E., & Enberg, R. N., (2007, winter). Implementation of an obstetrics EMR module: Overcoming user Dissatisfaction. *Journal of Healthcare Information Management, 21*(1). http://www.himss.org/content/files/jhim/21-1/15_OC_Implement.pdf

49. Lagrew, D. C. Jr. (2008). Voluntary physician adoption of an inpatient electronic medical record by obstetrician-gynecologists. *American Journal of Obstetrics and Gynecology, 198*(6), 690.e1–690.e5; discussion 690.e5–690.e6.

50. Haberman, S., Feldman, J., Mehri, Z. O., Markenson, G.C., Coher, G.W., & Minkoff, H. (2009). Effect of clinical-decision support on documentation compliance in an electronic medical record. *Obstetrics and Gynecology, 114*(2 Pt 1), 311–317.

51. American Academy of Pediatrics, Committee on Fetus and Newborn. (2004, reaffirmed May 1, 2011). Levels of neonatal care: Policy statement. *Pediatrics, 114*(5), 1341–1347. http://aappolicy.aappublications.org/cgi/content/full/pediatrics;114/5/1341

52. Karlsen, K. A., Trautman, M., Price-Douglas, W., & Smith, S. (2011). National survey of neonatal transport teams in the United States. *Pediatrics, 128*(4), 685–691.

53. Hiner, J., Pyka, J., Burks, C., Pisegna, L., & Gador, R. (2012). Preventing infant abductions: An infant security program transitioned into an interdisciplinary model. *Journal of Perinatal and Neonatal Nursing, 26*(1), 47–56.

54. Bishop, T. F., Ryan, A. M., & Casalino, L.P. Paid malpractice claims for adverse events in inpatient and outpatient settings. *Journal of the American Medical Association, 305*(23), 2427–2431. Corrected on June 23, 2011.

55. Griffen, F. D. (2007). ACS closed claim study reveals critical failure to communicate. *Bulletin of the American College of Surgeons, 92*(1), 11–16.

56. Metzner, J., Posner, K. L., Lam, M. S., & Damino, K. B. (2011). Closed claims' analysis. *Best practices Research in Clinical Anaesthesiology, 25*(2), 263–276.

57. Seiden, S. C., & Barach, P. (2006). Wrong-side/ wrong-site, wrong-procedure, and wrong-patient adverse events: Are they preventable? *Archives of Surgery, 141*(9), 931–939.

58. Kwaan, M. R., Studdert, D. M., Zinnes, M. J., & Gawande, A. A. (2006). Incidence, patterns, and prevention of wrong-site surgery. *Archives of Surgery, 141*(4), 353–357; discussion 357–358.

59. CNA HealthPro. (2011). Surgical safety: Twelve strategies to reduce error and complication rates. *VantagePoint, 2.* http://www.cna.com/vcm_content/ CNA/internet/Static%20File%20for%20Download/ Risk%20Control/Medical%20Services/ SurgicalSafety-TwelveStrategies.pdf

60. U.S. Food and Drug Administration. (2010, April 30; current as of February 2012). Medical devices advice: Comprehensive regulatory assistance postmarket requirements: Medical device tracking. http://www.fda. gov/MedicalDevices/DeviceRegulationandGuidance/ PostmarketRequirements/MedicalDeviceTracking/ default.htm#link_2

61. ECRI Institute, Health Technology Assessment Info Service. (2012, February 1). *Joint ventures: Collecting registry data on patient-reported outcomes.* Plymouth Meeting, PA: Author.

62. Association of periOperative Registered Nurses. (2012). *Perioperative standards and recommended practices: recommended practices for prevention of retained surgical Items.* Denver: Author.

63. U.S. Food and Drug Administration. (2011, October 13). Medical device safety, FDA safety communication: Preventing surgical fires. http://www.fda.gov/ MedicalDevices/Safety/AlertsandNotices/ ucm275189.htm

64. Pinto, A. (2010). Spectrum of diagnostic errors in radiology, *World Journal of Radiology, 2*(10), 377–383. http://www.wjgnet.com/1949-8470/full/v2/ i10/377.htm

65. CNA Financial. (2010). Diagnostic imaging: Sound policies help reduce test-related risks. *InBrief, 1.* Chicago, IL. http://www.cna.com/vcm_content/ CNA/internet/Static%20File%20for%20Download/ Risk%20Control/Medical%20Services/ DiagnosticImaging-SoundPoliciesHelpReduceTest-relatedRisks2010-1.pdf

66. Code of Federal Regulations, Title 10, Section 20.1003 (10 CFR 20.1003). May 21, 1991. Amended November 16, 2005.

CHAPTER 12

Risk Management for Infection Control Programs

George Allen and Michael H. Augenbraun

INTRODUCTION

In the United States and other countries throughout the world, the goal of infection control programs is to prevent the transmission of infections to patients, visitors, and healthcare personnel. In the United States, infection control programs are required by federal agencies such as the Occupational Safety and Health Administration (OSHA) and the Centers for Medicaid and Medicare Services (CMS), by accrediting bodies such as The Joint Commission (TJC), and by state, city, county, and local departments of health for hospitals and other healthcare institutions. The infection control program in healthcare settings includes procedures for determining the risk of transmission of infectious agents to patients, personnel, visitors, and the institution, as well as enforcement of procedures and protocols to manage this risk. The leadership of the healthcare institution—specifically, the board of directors, chief executive officer, medical director, and other members of the executive team—is responsible for implementing the infection control functions in the institution.

Specific federal laws such as OSHA Bloodborne Exposure Standard[1] require employers of personnel who may come in contact with blood and other potentially infectious materials of patients as part of their job function to provide training for those employees to prevent exposures; to institute policies and procedures to require those employees to use barriers and personal protective equipment, and to provide the appropriate personal protective equipment and vaccination against hepatitis B infection free of charge to those employees, all in an attempt to prevent the transmission of blood-borne infections to those employees.

Healthcare-associated infections (HAIs), defined as infections that occur in patients while they access healthcare institutions for care, are known not only to be one of the leading causes of death in the United States,[2] but also to result in needless suffering and expense. In 2002, there were approximately 1.7 million HAIs and 99,000 deaths from this cause in the United States.[3] According to the Centers for Disease Control and Prevention (CDC), 20% of HAIs are preventable, and approximately 1 out of every 20 hospitalized patients contracts an HAI.[4] The overall annual direct medical costs of HAIs to U.S. hospitals are believed to range from $28.4 billion to $45 billion, with the potential for saving as much as $31.5 billion by effectively managing the risk for infections and preventing 70% of those infections.[5]

Infections in hospital personnel are generally associated with unprotected exposure to the blood and the bodily fluids of other individuals, particularly patients. Such infections that can occur in staff members include infections caused by viruses (**Box 12-1**), bacteria (**Box 12-2**), fungi (**Box 12-3**), parasites (**Box 12-4**) and prions (**Box 12-5**).

Infections in patients are generally associated with the use of medical devices whose primary function is to help patients achieve an optimal level of wellness and/or to facilitate their recovery from identified medical conditions. However, such devices bypass the natural defense mechanisms of the patient, which otherwise serve as the first line of defense in humans for preventing the invasion of invading microorganisms. These devices include the following:

- Vascular catheters that can cause bloodstream infections (BSI)
- Urinary catheters resulting in urinary tract infections (UTI)
- Ventilators—devices that help patients to breathe—resulting in ventilator-associated pneumonias (VAP)
- Surgical site infections (SSI) as a result of surgical procedures

---

Box 12-1

Viruses are obligate intracellular parasites that can replicate only inside living cells. They range in size from 20 nm to 1,000 nm (1 mm) in diameter and come in many different shapes. Viruses are composed of a nucleic acid (DNA or RNA) genome, a protein coat (capsid), and sometimes a lipid envelope. Common viruses that personnel in hospitals may come in contact with and that result in infection include adinovirus; AIDS virus (HIV); common cold virus; cytmegalovirus; enterovirus; Epstein-Barr virus; hepatitis A, B, C, D, E, F, and G viruses; herpes simplex virus; herpes zoster virus; influenza virus; norovirus; parainfluenza virus; rotavirus; rubella virus; and varicellazoster virus.

Box 12-2

Pathogenic bacteria are single-cell microorganisms. Some are obligate pathogens that depend on the host for some of their key nutrients but live outside host cells, whereas others are obligate intracellular parasites that require some nutrients or enzymes found only inside host cells. Bacteria have a circular DNA genome and enzyme systems. They range in size from 100 nm to 5 mm, and are classified by thier shape (rod/bacillus, sphere/coccus, or spiral/spirillum) and by the structure of their cell walls (gram positive or gram negative). They reproduce by binary fission, with each cell giving rise to two identical daughters. Common bacteria include *Staphylococcus*, *Streptococcus*, *Escherichia coli*, *Salmonella*, *Shigella*, and *Neisseria*.

Box 12-3

Fungi are eukaryotic organisms that have a lipid bilayer plasma membrane. Their genetic material is DNA. They may be unicellular (yeast) or multicellular (filamentous fungi), or they may exist in both forms (dimorphic fungi). Most pathogenic fungi are opportunistic, meaning that they cause disease only when the immune system of the host is weakened. Common fungi include *Candida* species, *Aspergillus* species, *Fusarium*, *Trichosporon*, and *Malassezia* species.

Box 12-4

Parasites are microorganisms or macroorganisms that need to satisfy their vital nutritional requirements by feeding off of certain host tissues or body fluids that contain the specific biochemicals that the parasite needs. Parasitic worms (helminthes) are macroscopic, ranging in size from 0.3 mm to 25 m long. There are parasites for every single tissue of the human body. Common parasitic diseases include malaria, ascaris, hookworms, whipworms, filarial worms, and schistosomes.

Box 12-5

Arion is an abnormal transmissible agent, believed to be a microscopic protein particle similar to a virus but lacking in nucleic acid. Prion diseases comprise a group of animal and human brain diseases that are uniformly fatal and often characterized by a long incubation period. Conditions thought to be caused by prions include bovine spongiform encephalopathy (BSE), mad cow disease, variant Creutzfeldt-Jakob disease (vCJD), Gerstmann-Straussler-Scheinker syndrome, fatal familial insomnia, kuru, chronic wasting disease (CWD), and scrapie.

INFECTION RISK IN HEALTHCARE SETTINGS

Infection hazards are naturally concentrated in healthcare institutions. Infection control risk management is a proactive process that identifies risks, assesses those risks for frequency and severity, eliminates those that can readily be eliminated, and minimizes those that cannot be eliminated. Infection risk management procedures are simple procedures. Principal among such procedures are enforcing compliance with hand hygiene recommendations for all levels of personnel, including requiring hand hygiene before and after every patient contact and whenever hands are visibly soiled (**Box 12-6**); the use of isolation procedures (**Box 12-7**); and the use of vaccines (**Box 12-8**). This chapter outlines the risk for the development and transmission of some of the most frequently encountered categories of infections, reviews some of the recent outbreaks of infections in healthcare institutions, and discusses the infection control risk management procedures that should be implemented to prevent such infection exposures and outbreaks.

Box 12-6   Hand Hygiene

Hand hygiene is one of the most important ways to prevent the spread of infections. Healthcare providers should practice hand hygiene at key points in time to disrupt the transmission of microorganisms to patients, including before patient contact; after contact with blood, body fluids, or contaminated surfaces (even if gloves are worn); before invasive procedures; and after removing gloves (wearing gloves is not enough to prevent the transmission of pathogens in healthcare settings). Hand hygiene consists of hand washing with soap and water or use of an alcohol-based hand sanitizer before and after patient contact and after contact with the immediate patient care environment.

HAND RUB (FOAM AND GEL)

1. Apply to the palm of one hand (the amount used depends on specific hand rub product).
2. Rub the hands together, covering all surfaces, focusing in particular on the fingertips and fingernails, until dry. Use enough rub to require at least 15 seconds to dry.

HAND WASHING

1. Wet the hands with water.
2. Apply soap.
3. Rub the hands together for at least 15 seconds, covering all surfaces, focusing on the fingertips and fingernails.
4. Rinse under running water and dry with a disposable towel
5. Use the towel to turn off the faucet.

Source: http://www.cdc.gov/handhygiene/training.html

Bloodstream Infection Risk

Vascular catheters are tubes that are inserted directly into the patient's veins, to allow for easier delivery of medications, blood, or nutrition.

Box 12-7

UNIVERSAL PRECAUTIONS/STANDARD PRECAUTIONS

- All patient contact.
- Wash hands before and after patient contact. Use personal protective equipment (PPE) when contact with mucous membranes and all body fluids except sweat is anticipated—fluid-resistant gown, mask, mask with face shield or goggles.

RESPIRATORY AIRBORNE PRECAUTIONS (COLOR CODED BLUE)

- Diseases known to be transmitted via the airborne route—TB, varicella zoster.
- Single room—Airborne infection isolation room with negative pressure or portable HEPA filter.
- Wash hands before and after patient contact. N95 respirator required for TB; fluid-resistant gown *only* is to be worn when performing procedures where soiling is anticipated.

DROPLET PRECAUTIONS (COLOR CODED GREEN)

- Diseases known to be transmitted via respiratory droplets.
- Invasive meningiococcal disease, pertussis, H1N1.
- Single room preferred; can cohort. Maintain spatial separation of 3 feet.
- Wash hands before and after each patient contact. Surgical mask is required (N95 respirator required for H1N1); fluid-resistant gown *ONLY* is to be worn when performing procedures where soiling is anticipated.

CONTACT PRECAUTIONS (COLOR CODED ORANGE)

- Patients with multi–drug-resistant pathogens including MRSA, VRE, ESBL, or *C. difficile*, or with diseases known to be transmitted by direct contact or indirect contact with contaminated objects.
- Single room preferred; can cohort. Maintain spatial separation of 3 feet. Cohort a patient with *C. difficile* only with another patient with *C. difficile*.
- Wash hands before and after each patient contact; gowns are worn for close contact (touching patient, or patient care equipment, transporting patient, assigned for in-room patient observation). Fluid-resistant mask/ face shield and fluid-resistant gown are worn when performing procedures where splashing and soiling is anticipated.

Source: Siegel, J. D., Rhinehart, E., Jackson, M., Chiarello, L., & Healthcare Infection Control Advisory Committee. (2006). Management of multidrug-resistant organisms in healthcare settings.

http://www.cdc.gov/hicpac/pdf/guidelines/MDROGuideline2006.pdf

A central catheter or line is defined as an intravascular catheter that terminates at or close to the heart or in one of the great vessels (aorta, pulmonary artery, superior vena cava, inferior vena cava, brachiocephalic veins, internal jugular veins, subclavian veins, external iliac veins, common iliac veins, femoral veins, and in neonates, the umbilical artery/vein). It is used for infusion, withdrawal of blood, or hemodynamic monitoring. In the intensive care unit (ICU), these catheters are particularly important for patient care, but they can sometimes become infected. Such infections are dangerous, and potentially lethal. These so-called central line–associated bloodstream infections (CLABSI) are defined as bacteremia/fungemia in a patient with an intravascular catheter with at least one positive blood culture obtained from a peripheral vein, clinical manifestations of infection (i.e., fever, chills, and/or hypotension), and no apparent source for the bloodstream infection except the catheter.[6] Each year in the United States, an 80,000 CLABSIs occur, resulting in as many as 28,000 deaths among patients in ICUs.[7] Bloodstream infections are usually serious infections typically causing a prolongation of hospital stay, increased cost, and risk of mortality.

CLABSI can be prevented through proper management of the central line. Careful precautions must be taken to avoid introducing harmful bacteria into patients when inserting the central catheter and when using it to administer medications or monitor patients. Consequently, research-based infection control risk management procedures can decrease or eliminate the number of central line–associated bloodstream infections. Healthcare providers should follow specific guidelines for catheter insertion:

- Use sterile barrier technique.
- Use proper hand hygiene.
- Use chlorhexidine for disinfecting the skin.
- Avoid the femoral (groin) insertion site.

Once the central line has been inserted, healthcare providers must manage it properly:

- Monitor the insertion site.
- Use recommended sterile techniques.
- Scrub the hub or port when entering the catheter to deliver medication.
- Monitor the patient and remove catheters when they are no longer needed.

The Association for Professionals in Infection Control and Epidemiology has campaigned for a culture of zero tolerance for HAIs, and infection preventionists are implementing

The following elements should be considered when designing a facility-specific insertion checklist.

- Data field columns—lists items completed or done with reminder, and rationale for deviation from procedure.
- Before insertion section—includes information regarding site assessment, bundle elements completed, and full body drape in place.
- During procedure section—include documentation of maintenance of a sterile field, maximal sterile barriers, and drape change if contaminated.
- After procedure section—document the following action: site cleansed with antiseptic agent; sterile gauze or transparent dressing applied; placement verified; facility-specific practices applied, such as a securement device, a chlorhexidine-impregnated sponge or dressing, or lot number of the catheter.
- Physician competence requirement statement—include a statement noting the requirement that physicians or intravenous team inserters must be credentialed to place central lines or the number of acceptable attempts prior to calling in another clinician.
- Procedure note—integrate the physician documentation into the checklist by including site selection, insertion status, type of anesthesia, insertion site, the number of lumens, reason for line, type of line, and the number of attempts to pass the needle.
- Signature section—document the names of the inserting clinician, supervising clinician, and nurse.

Source: Beyond the bundle: Reducing the risk of central line–associated bloodstream infections. (2010, March 18). *Pennsylvania Patient Safety Advisory 7* (suppl 1).

https://www.ecri.org/Documents/PA_PSRS/2010.3_Supplement.pdf

this philosophy for CLABSI by bundling evidence-based practices generally using checklists (**Box 12-9**) when central catheters are being inserted and maintained. The use of a checklist ensures and documents compliance with aseptic technique—the principal infection risk management strategy for preventing CLABSI.

Risk for Transmission of HIV

For healthcare workers, exposure to the blood and certain body fluids of patients, particularly through needlestick injuries and cuts, is the primary mechanism for the transmission of human immunodeficiency virus (HIV) in the healthcare setting. The risk of healthcare workers getting HIV on the job is very low, especially if they carefully follow universal precautions (i.e., using protective practices and personal protective equipment to prevent HIV and other blood-borne infections.) Through December 2001, there were 57 documented cases of occupational HIV transmission to healthcare workers in the United States, and no confirmed cases have been reported since 1999.[8]

HIV is spread from one person to another through sex and blood-to-blood contact. The virus attacks the immune system, and a person develops acquired immunodeficiency syndrome (AIDS) when his or her immune system becomes so damaged that it can no longer fight off diseases and infections. Current blood tests for HIV are more than 99% accurate. However, it usually takes from a few weeks to a few months after a person becomes infected for enough antibodies to develop to be detected in a blood test. For this reason, if someone was infected recently, the test may not yet show that the person is infected. This fact is important because it points to an important infection control risk management strategy to prevent transmission to healthcare workers—namely the implementation of universal or standard precautions when caring for all patients.

It is important to remember that casual, everyday contact with an HIV-infected person does not expose healthcare workers or anyone else to HIV. For healthcare workers on the job, the main risk of HIV transmission is through accidental injuries from needles and other sharp instruments that may be contaminated with the virus. This risk is small, estimated to be less than 0.5% from a needlestick, a figure based on the findings of several studies of healthcare workers who received punctures from HIV-contaminated needles or were otherwise exposed to HIV-contaminated blood. However, healthcare workers should assume that the blood and other body fluids from all patients are potentially infectious. For this reason, they should routinely use protective barriers:

- Wear gloves and/or goggles when anticipating contact with blood or body fluids.
- Immediately wash their hands and other skin surfaces after contact with blood or body fluids.
- Carefully handle and dispose of sharp instruments during and after use.
- Use safety devices properly; such devices have been developed to help prevent needlestick injuries and are now readily available.

Additionally, every healthcare institution should have policies and procedures to offer and provide post-exposure prophylaxis (PEP) as recommended by the Centers for Disease Control and Prevention (CDC) to employees who sustained a needlestick or other mucous membrane exposure to a patient's blood or body fluid. The CDC guidelines outline a number of considerations in determining whether healthcare workers should receive PEP and in choosing the type of PEP regimen. For most

HIV exposures that warrant PEP, a basic four-week, two-drug regimen is recommended. For HIV exposures that pose an increased risk of transmission based on the infection status of the source and the type of exposure, a three-drug regimen may be warranted. Special circumstances, such as a delayed exposure report, unknown source person, pregnancy in the exposed person, resistance of the source virus to antiviral agents, and toxicity of PEP regimens, are also discussed in the CDC guidelines.[9]

Pneumonia Infection Risk

Pneumonia is inflammation of the lung, most often caused by infection with bacteria, viruses, or other organisms. Occasionally, inhaled chemicals that irritate the lungs can cause pneumonia. Healthy individuals usually can fight off pneumonia infections. By comparison, people who are sick, including those who are recovering from the flu (influenza) or an upper respiratory illness, have a weakened immune system, which makes it easier for bacteria to grow in their lungs.

Hospital-acquired pneumonia is an infection of the lungs contracted during a hospital stay. This type of pneumonia tends to be more serious, because patients in the hospital already have weakened defense mechanisms, and the infecting organisms are usually more dangerous than those encountered in the community. Hospital patients are particularly vulnerable to pneumonia caused by gram-negative bacteria and staphylococci. Ventilator-associated pneumonia (VAP) is a highly lethal form of pneumonia contracted by patients on ventilators in hospitals and long-term nursing facilities.

Pneumonia often mimics the flu, beginning with a cough and a fever. Symptoms can vary depending on age and general health. The signs and symptoms of pneumonia may include the following:

- Fever
- Lower-than-normal body temperature in older people
- Cough
- Shortness of breath
- Sweating
- Shaking chills
- Chest pain that fluctuates with breathing (pleurisy)
- Headache
- Muscle pain
- Fatigue

Ventilator-associated pneumonia is the most common infection found in ICUs, accounting for 47% of the total infections in ICU[10]; 25% of all healthcare-associated infections involve VAP, with an estimated 5 to 10 VAP cases occurring per 1,000 hospital admissions and 9% to 27% of intubated patients developing this disease, with an attributable mortality of 33%.[11,12] In addition, VAP contributes to increased morbidity due to length of stay on mechanical ventilation and hospital stay[13] and increasing hospital costs.[14,15] In the United States, VAP can cost approximately $40,000 per case, presenting as 300,000 new cases annually.[14]

The main risk factor for VAP is the length of stay on mechanical ventilation, which increases colonization of the upper airways and stomach by pathogenic germs, further predisposing the patient to micro aspiration— which seems to be the pathophysiology for VAP.[16] Stomach colonization by pathogenic bacteria as a source of pneumonia is related to multiple factors: the inappropriate use of antibiotics; use of prophylaxis for stress ulcers; the

patient lying in the supine position; the severity of disease, including hemodinamic instability and the use of vasopressors; and the use of continuous sedation as well as parenteral nutrition.

Recognizing the risk factors for VAP is the first step in implementing suitable measures for its prevention and management. Infection preventionists, in their efforts to prevent VAP, work to ensure that evidence-based recommendations to prevent the development of VAP are implemented:

- Compliance with hand hygiene by all staff caring for the patient on a ventilator.
- Using the semi-recumbent positioning— that is, elevating the heads of ICU patients' beds between 30 and 45 degrees.
- Providing sedation vacation and weaning assessment. The sooner patients are extubated, the lower their risk of developing VAP. To ensure that patients are extubated as soon as possible, time sedation vacations— a six- to eight-hour daily period when sedating drugs are withheld, as appropriate—to mesh with daily spontaneous breathing trials and extubation-readiness assessment.
- The use of oral versus nasal feeding tubes. A growing body of evidence suggests that oral tubes may be better than nasal tubes in preventing VAP because oral tubes reduce sinusitis, a condition that is associated with the development of VAP in some patients.
- Stress ulcer prophylaxis.
- The use of selective digestive tract decontamination.
- The use of continuous subglottic secretion removal. Several trials support the benefits of using endotracheal tubes that continuously drain these secretions. That includes relatively new tubes that are fitted with

separate dorsal lumens above the cuff and allow for easier suctioning.

- The use of targeted oral hygiene with use of oral chlorhexidine gluconate washes.[17]

Additionally, infection preventionists may use bundled evidenced-based strategies to prevent CLABSI. **Box 12-10** provides an example of a VAP bundle that can easily be implemented to reduce the potential for patients on ventilators to develop VAP in healthcare settings.

Risk for Tuberculosis

Personnel in healthcare settings are also at risk for the development of pneumonia and other lower respiratory tract infections. The chief pathogen of concern for healthcare workers is tuberculosis (TB). Tuberculosis is a disease caused by *Mycobacterium tuberculosis*. These bacteria usually attack the lungs, but can attack other parts of the body such as the kidney, spine, and brain. If not treated properly, TB disease can be fatal.

Tuberculosis is spread from person to person through the air. The general symptoms of TB disease include feelings of sickness or weakness, weight loss, fever, and night sweats. The symptoms of TB disease of the lungs also include coughing, chest pain, and coughing up of blood; symptoms of TB disease in other parts of the body depend on the area affected.

Staff in healthcare settings, as an infection control risk management strategy, must maintain a high index of suspicion for TB when a patient come to the emergency room or is being admitted to the hospital with these signs and symptoms. Such a patient must be immediately placed on airborne isolation; staff must use personal protective equipment (PPE)—a special mask—to prevent themselves and other individuals from being exposed to the TB bacteria; and medical follow-up and evaluation must be instituted for staff and others who have been exposed to a patient with TB disease if the patient was not isolated or the appropriate PPE was not being used.

Airborne isolation requires the patient to be placed and cared for in an airborne infection isolation room (AIIR). Such rooms are built with special ventilation, negative air pressure, and a minimum of 12 air changes per hour. This configuration prevents contaminated air laden with TB bacteria from rushing out into the corridor when the patient sneezes, coughs, speaks, or sings, thereby potentially exposing individuals walking by, as they will breathe in the contaminated air and become infected with TB.

Staff caring for the patient must wear a special mask—a N95 respirator mask that has filters to screen out the TB bacteria. Personnel must be fit-tested and certified to wear this respirator. The goal is to create a good seal with the face and the mask so as to prevent the wearer from breathing in the TB bacteria when caring for the patient.

If a patient was not placed into isolation and later found to have TB, anyone who came in contact with him or her, including staff members, is at risk for being infected with the TB bacteria. These individuals will be required to have medical follow-up, including testing 10 weeks after the exposure to determine if they are now infected or have converted their skin test (PPD test). If they have never been infected with TB, their TB skin test history prior to the exposure will be negative. A positive PPD skin test indicates that the individual has been exposed to the TB bacteria and is infected. He or she is not infectious, however, and cannot transmit the bacteria to anyone else at this point. Individuals who are PPD negative at baseline will require a PPD test 10 weeks after the exposure; they are said to have converted if the PPD test reads as positive at that point. They will be offered prophylaxis in the form of medication (usually isoniazid) for 3 to 6 months as there is a possibility they will develop TB disease later in their lifetime. Only when a person has TB disease can he or she transmit TB to others.

In general, TB remains a serious public health problem, particularly with the increase in multidrug-resistant (MDR TB) and extensively drug-resistant TB (XDR TB) strains of TB. Multidrug-resistant TB is TB that is resistant to at least two of the best anti-TB drugs—isoniazid and rifampicin, which are considered first-line drugs and are used to treat all persons with TB disease. Extensively drug-resistant TB is a relatively rare type of MDR TB; it is defined as TB that is resistant to isoniazid and rifampin, as well as to any fluoroquinolone and at least one of three injectable second-line drugs (i.e., amikacin, kanamycin, or capreomycin). Thus XDR TB is resistant to first-line and second-line drugs, so patients are left with treatment options that are much less effective.[18]

A total of 11,181 TB cases were reported in the United States in 2010, for a rate of 3.6 cases per 100,000 population. This rate represents a decline of 3.9% from 2009 and the lowest rate recorded since national reporting began in 1953. However, the national goal of TB elimination (defined as less than 0.1 case per 100,000 population) by 2010 has not been achieved. Although TB cases and rates have decreased among foreign-born and U.S.-born persons, foreign-born persons and racial/ethnic minorities continue to be the groups more likely to present with TB in the United States:

- In 2010, the TB rate among foreign-born persons in the United States was 11 times greater than that among U.S.-born persons.
- TB rates among Hispanics, non-Hispanic blacks, and Asians were 7, 8, and 25 times greater, respectively, than those among non-Hispanic whites and among U.S.-born racial and ethnic groups.
- The greatest racial disparity in TB rates was for non-Hispanic blacks, in whom the rate was 7 times greater than the rate for non-Hispanic whites.[19]

Consequently, although the prevalence of TB is on the wane, healthcare workers must continue to maintain a high index of suspicion as the primary infection prevention risk management strategy. When patients are being admitted to hospitals, they should immediately isolate those individuals with signs and symptoms suggestive of TB until TB is ruled out.

MULTIDRUG-RESISTANT PATHOGENS: AN EMERGING INFECTION RISK THREAT

Mitigating the risk for the transmission of infections in patient, personnel, and visitors is a critical component of infection control programs.

The specialized personnel in hospitals and healthcare facilities who manage the infection control programs generally include a physician who functions as the hospital epidemiologist and chairperson of the Infection Control Committee as well as registered nurses or microbiologists—the infection preventionists—who conduct surveillance and put into operation the institution-wide plan for preventing the transmission of infection in patients, personnel, and visitors. In recent years, efforts to prevent transmission of infections have become more robust because of escalating media attention coupled with the emergence and increasing prevalence of multidrug-resistant organisms (MDROs).

MDROs are defined as microorganisms (primarily bacteria) that are resistant to one or more classes of antibiotics, resulting in infections that are difficult to treat or for which no antibiotics are effective. They include methicillin-resistant *Staphylococcus aureus* (MRSA), vancomycin resistant enterocci (VRE), certain gram-negative bacteria including those producing extended spectrum beta-lactamases (ESBLs), and organisms that are resistant to multiple classes of antimicrobial agents, including *Escherichia coli, Klebsiella pneumoniae*, strains of *Acinetobacter baumannii, Sternotrophomonas maltophilia, Burkholderia cepacia*, and *Ralstonia pickettii*.[20]

In addition, the emergence of *Clostridium difficile* has highlighted the risk of transmission of infections in healthcare settings, as this bacterium forms spores, is difficult to eradicate from the environment, and is not killed by the disinfectant solutions generally used in healthcare settings. Moreover, the now widely available alcohol-based hand hygiene products are not effective against this spore forming bacteria. *C. difficile* is a gram-positive anaerobic bacillus that produces two exotoxins: toxin A and toxin B. It is a common cause of antibiotic-associated diarrhea. Diseases that result from *C. difficile* infections include pseudomembranous colitis, toxic megacolon, perforations of the colon, and sepsis. Clinical symptoms include watery diarrhea, fever, loss of appetite, nausea, and abdominal pain/tenderness. The risk for infection with *C. difficile* increases in patients who had antibiotics as part of their treatment regimen, gastrointestinal surgery/manipulation, long length of stay in healthcare settings, a serious underlying illness, immunocompromising conditions, or who are at an advanced age.

Enzyme immunoassays can detect toxin A, toxin B, or both. Tissue culture cytotoxicity assay detects toxin B only. *C. difficile* toxin is very unstable: It degrades at room temperature and may be undetectable within 2 hours after collection of a stool specimen. False-negative results occur when specimens are not promptly tested or kept refrigerated until testing can be done, which in turn may delay procedures to prevent transmission.

C. difficile is shed in feces. Any surface, device, or material (e.g., commodes, bathing tubs, and electronic rectal thermometers) that becomes contaminated with feces may serve as a reservoir for the bacteria's spores. *C. difficile* spores are transferred to patients mainly via the hands of healthcare personnel who have touched a contaminated surface or item. The infection can usually be treated with an appropriate course of antibiotics including metronidazole or vancomycin. After treatment, repeat *C. difficile* testing is not recommended if the patient's symptoms have resolved, as patients may remain colonized.

C. difficile–associated disease can be prevented by the following measures:

- The judicious use of antibiotics
- The implementation of contact isolation for patients known or suspected to be infected with *C. difficile*
- Strict attention to hand hygiene with soap and water before and after every patient contact
- Cleaning the environment with a sodium hypochlorite solution, as the *C. difficile* spores are resistant to the most commonly available disinfectants generally used in healthcare institutions

OUTBREAKS IN HEALTHCARE SETTINGS

Hospitals and healthcare institutions generally have data on the baseline incidence of hospital-acquired infections, which enables them to easily identify abnormal levels or outbreaks when they occur. An outbreak may be defined as an increase in the occurrence of infections with reference to the recorded baseline infection rate. Additionally, it may be identified based on cases of infection that are clearly associated in time and place. In essence, an outbreak encompasses an incident in which two or more individuals (including patients, healthcare workers, or visitors) are experiencing a similar illness that is linked in time or place, a greater than expected rate of infection compared with the usual background rate for the healthcare institution, or a single case of a certain rare disease such as diphtheria, botulism, rabies, or polio. Although outbreaks represent only approximately 10% of cases of infection acquired in hospital, any major increase in the number of cases is evidence that an infection has begun to spread and is beginning to pose a possible serious threat to other patients, staff, and visitors.

General daily surveillance performed by infection preventionist staff on behalf of the infection control program in the institution is the mechanism used to identify outbreaks. Reasons for outbreaks vary widely. On rare occasions, outbreaks are associated with intrinsic contamination of supplies used for healthcare delivery including intravenous solutions, feeding solutions, skin cleansing solutions, antiseptics, and disinfectants. Most often, however, infection outbreaks can be traced to the following sources:

- Noncompliance with prudent infection control practices such as hand hygiene, isolation techniques and procedures, and aseptic and sterile technique
- Environmental sanitation
- Contaminated equipment or supplies
- Inadequate cleaning of equipment
- Recommended vaccination such as the annual influenza vaccination to prevent influenza
- Hepatitis B vaccination to prevent hepatitis B infection

Several outbreaks are worth highlighting. In 1989, six patients in a Texas pediatric facility were found to have *Burkholderia cepacia* infection or pseudo-infection. Three of patients were determined to have peritonitis (infection of the peritoneal fluid), one had pseudo-peritonitis, and two had pseudo-bacteremia. Epidemiological studies revealed one risk factor for peritonitis with *B. cepacia*—namely, the performance of peritoneal dialysis in the dialysis unit with use of one lot of povidone-iodine used to clean the site before peritoneal dialysis. This lot of povidone-iodine was later found to be intrinsically contaminated. Blood cultures yielded *B. cepacia* after nurses wiped the tops of blood culture bottles with the povidone-iodine solution before inoculation. *B. cepacia* was cultured from three povidone-iodine containers used at the hospital and from four containers of the same lot obtained from other healthcare facilities in Texas and California. The investigation demonstrated that intrinsic contamination of povidone-iodine solution with *B. cepacia* can result in infections in addition to colonization and/or pseudoinfection.[21]

Another outbreak of infection with *B. cepacia* was found to be due to intrinsically contaminated ultrasound gel in an Australian hospital; obstetric patients were the victims in this instance. Nonsterile ultrasound gel became contaminated due to manufacturing procedures and also during usage of opened bottles. A cluster of eight clinical cases of vaginal colonization (one clinically proved to be colpitis) with *B. cepacia* was recognized. When the cluster came to attention, a microbiological investigation of the environment, including surfaces, equipment, and ultrasound gels from different manufacturers, was initiated. Isolates from three different patients and four isolates of ultrasound gel bottles (two opened and two sealed) were investigated by pulsed-field gel electrophoresis (PFGE) to clarify clonality and source. Environmental specimens revealed no growth of *B. cepacia*, but the four bottles from the incriminated manufacturer (two opened, bottles and two sealed bottles, all belonging to the same batch) were highly contaminated with *B. cepacia*. These isolates and the isolates from the three patients showed the same genotype pattern by PFGE.[22]

At seven months, outbreak of healthcare-associated *B. cepacia* bacteremia involving children in a pediatric hospital was identified. The first 4 cases occurred in a 31-bed neonatal intensive care unit (NICU). Three weeks later, in the 18-bed gastroenterology intensive care unit of the same institution, a 16-month-old child developed *B. cepacia* bacteremia. Later, in the 22-bed pediatric intensive care unit, 2 additional cases of bacteremia with *B. cepacia* were identified. Epidemiologic and environmental studies were conducted to identify the source and route of infection; all were negative. Subsequent investigations focused on a commercially prepared lipid emulsion that was frequently used in both wards, and with which the same bottle was sometimes used for several patients in the NICU. Ten randomly chosen bottles of this product were cultured and found to be negative. As cases continued to be identified, 50 bottles of the product were chosen randomly for culture. After removing the plastic flip-off caps, a drop of condensation was noted on top of the stoppers of 25 bottles. Cultures yielded *B. cepacia* in two cases. The manufacturer was notified and a total of 50 bottles stored in the manufacturing plant after autoclaving were examined; *B. cepacia* was found in the stopper of one of the bottles. The bacterium was subsequently found in the autoclave cooling water and in residual water remaining inside the autoclave after the sterilization cycle. A retrospective investigation was launched, and 4 additional cases were identified. The product was recalled and production was halted until the problem was solved.[23]

Another outbreak involving intrinsic contamination with *B. cepacia* occurred in two major hospitals affiliated to the National Guard. The investigation revealed positive cultures from used and freshly opened, multidose albuterol nebulization bottles. Subsequently, four different batches of multidose albuterol nebulization proved to be contaminated with *B. cepacia*. Between May 2003 and March 2004 a total of 2,121 inpatients and

318 outpatients from one hospital were exposed to the albuterol nebulization, and a total of 283 inpatients and 34 outpatients were exposed at the other hospital. Fifty-two patients from both hospitals were found to have at least one positive culture with *B. cepacia*.[24] **Box 12-11** provides additional information on the bacterium *B. cepacia*.

In August 2005, the CDC was notified of a *Ralstonia* species outbreak among pediatric patients receiving supplemental oxygen therapy with the Vapotherm 2000i, a reusable medical device that delivers humidified, warmed oxygen via nasal cannula and that is widely used by neonatal clinicians in hospitals in the United States. Nationally, *Ralstonia mannitolilytica* was confirmed in 38 patients aged 5 days to 7 years; 35 (92%) of the patients were exposed to the Vapotherm 2000i before recovery of the organism. Pulsed-field gel electrophoresis showed related *R. mannitolilytica* strains from isolates sent from 18 hospitals in 12 states. A Vapotherm machine reprocessed with a protocol proposed by the manufacturer grew *Ralstonia* spp. after 7 days of simulated use. In December 2005, Vapotherm recalled the 2000i.[25]

On November 14, 2007, a nurse working at an outpatient infusion center in Texas contacted the CDC because 5 patients with cancer who were having infusion therapy at the center were hospitalized and found to have *Serratia marcescens* (SM) bloodstream infections over a one-week period. Subsequently, on December 6, 2007, clinicians in Chicago notified the CDC about an outbreak of SM bloodstream infections among patients who were receiving supplies from a local home care company. On January 14, 2008, clinicians at another referral cancer center in Texas reported an outbreak of SM bloodstream infections. Investigation of these outbreaks led to the identification of

---

Box 12-11

GENERAL INFORMATION ABOUT *B. CEPACIA*

Burkholderia cepacia is the name of a group or "complex" of bacteria that can be found in soil and water. *B. Cepacia* bacteria are often resistant to common antibiotics.

POPULATIONS SUSCEPTIBLE TO *B. CEPACIA* INFECTION

B. cepacia poses little medical risk to healthy people. However, people who have certain health problems such as weakened immune systems or chronic lung diseases (particularly cystic fibrosis) may be more susceptible to infections with *B. cepacia*. *B. cepacia* is a known cause of infections in hospitalized patients.

SYMPTOMS OF *B. CEPACIA* INFECTION

The effects of *B. cepacia* on people vary widely, ranging from no symptoms at all to serious respiratory infections, especially in patients with cystic fibrosis.

TRANSMISSION OF *B. CEPACIA* INFECTION

Trasmission of *B. cepacia* from contaminated medicines and devices has been reported. *B. cepacia* can also be spread to susceptible persons by person-to-contact, contact with a contaminated surface, and exposure to *B. cepacia* in the environment.

Source: Centers for Disease Control and Prevention. (n.d). *Burkholdieria cepacia* in healthcare settings.

http://www.cdc.gov/HAI/organisms/bCepacia.html#al

---

a multiple-state outbreak of SM bacteremia associated with the use of contaminated prefilled heparin and isotonic sodium chloride solution (saline) syringes manufactured by a single company. Twenty-one of the 101 patients treated at the Texas chemotherapy infusion center developed SM infections. Five cases were identified at the referral center in Texas who had exposure to the same lot number of heparin flushes, and an additional 18 cases were identified among patients who had not been exposed to heparin flush but were exposed to prefilled saline syringes from the same company that supplied the prefilled heparin syringes. A total of 162 cases of SM bloodstream infections from nine states were identified among patients at facilities using prefilled heparin and/or saline syringes made by the same company. A U.S. Food and Drug Administration (FDA) inspection of the company revealed that it was not in compliance with quality system regulations, resulting in intrinsic contamination of the prefilled syringes.[26]

Between June 1990 and February 1993, the CDC conducted investigations at seven hospitals because of unusual outbreaks of bloodstream infections, surgical-site infections, and acute febrile episodes after surgical procedures. Sixty-two case patients were identified, 49 (79%) of whom underwent surgery during the outbreak period. The investigation found that only exposure to propofol, a lipid-based anesthetic agent, was significantly associated with the postoperative complications at all seven hospitals. In six of the outbreaks, an etiologic agent (*Staphylococcus aureus, Candida albicans, Moraxella osloensis, Enterobacter agglomerans,* or *Serratia marcescens*) was identified, and the same strains were isolated from the case patients. Although cultures of unopened containers of propofol were negative, at two hospitals cultures of propofol from syringes currently in use were positive. At one

hospital, the recovered organism was identical to the organism isolated from the case patients. Interviews with and observation of anesthesiology personnel documented a wide variety of lapses in aseptic techniques. It was concluded that with the increasing popularity and use of lipid-based medications, which can support rapid bacterial growth at room temperature, strict aseptic techniques are essential during the handling of these agents to prevent extrinsic contamination and dangerous infectious complications.[27]

In April 2001, an infection preventionist at a large community hospital suspected an outbreak as she noted an increase in the frequency of isolation of *Candida parapsilosis* strains from cultures of blood and central vascular catheter tips from adult inpatients. Twenty-two cases of bloodstream infection with *C. parapsilosis*—15 confirmed and 7 possible—were identified. The factors associated with this outbreak included hospitalization in the intensive care unit and receipt of total parenteral nutrition. Samples for surveillance cultures were obtained from healthcare workers' hands, central venous catheter insertion sites, and medical devices. Twenty-six percent of the healthcare workers surveyed demonstrated hand colonization with *C. parapsilosis*, and one hand isolate was highly related by PFGE to all case-patient isolates. It was concluded that this outbreak of *C. parapsilosis* bloodstream infections in adults resulted from an interplay of host, environment, and pathogen factors, all related to poor infection control practices. Recommendations for control measures focused on improving compliance with hand hygiene and basic infection control recommendations.[28]

Another large outbreak deemed to be entirely preventable because of poor infection control practices involved the transmission of hepatitis C, a blood-borne viral infection. In 2008, an outbreak of hepatitis C in the state of Nevada was traced to poor infection control and injection practices in two ambulatory endoscopy clinics. The investigation conducted by the CDC and the Nevada State Health Division Bureau of Licensure and Certification included the notification of approximately 63,000 former patients of potential exposure to hepatitis C and other infectious diseases, and found more than 100 people who had developed hepatitis C as a result of their exposure in the endoscopy clinics. Additional, inspections of 28 Nevada ambulatory surgery centers for compliance with Medicare standards revealed 64% had serious problems, primarily in infection control.[29]

MANAGEMENT OF RISK

Given that infections acquired in healthcare institutions in patients, visitors, and healthcare employees will undoubtedly continue to occur and that infection outbreaks due to intrinsic contamination or extrinsic factors are likely, infection preventionists must embrace a philosophy of zero tolerance and work to educate personnel and the public about strategies to reduce the likelihood of such events.

Risks of malpractice litigation because of infections that cause death or disability are reduced by the following:

- Early identification of infection
- Prompt diagnosis
- Appropriate treatment
- Consultations with infectious disease specialists
- Contact with the infection control program of the institution

- Continuous monitoring of the patient's progress
- Concern for staff caring for the patient

Infection control risk management involves the following measures:

- Compliance with hand hygiene recommendations
- Compliance with basic aseptic practices
- Isolation precautions
- Simple infection prevention strategies, such as covering the nose and mouth with a tissue when coughing or sneezing
- Taking vaccinations for preventable diseases

It also involves maintaining a high index of suspicion when multiple similar cases are noted—outbreaks—necessitating epidemiologic investigations and the expertise of the city, state, and CDC.

REFERENCES

1. Occupational Safety and Health Administration. (1991). Occupational exposure to bloodborne pathogens: Final rule. 56 *Fed. Reg.* 64, 175–182, 29 C.F.R. pt 1910.1030.
2. Department of Health and Human Services. (n.d.). HHS action plan to prevent healthcare-associated infections: Executive summary. http://www.hhs.gov/ash/initiatives/hai/2-hai-plan-exec-summ.pdf
3. Klevens, R. M., Edwards, J. R., Richards, C. L., Horan, T. C., Gaynes, R. P., Polluch, D. A., & Cardo, D. M. (2007). Estimating healthcare-associated infections and deaths in US hospitals. *Public Health Reports, 122,* 160–166.
4. Centers for Disease Control and Prevention. (n.d.). Health care associated infections: The burden. http://www.cdc.gov/HAI/burden.html.
5. Centers for Disease Control and prevention. (n.d.). The direct medical cost of healthcare associated infections in U.S. hospitals and the benefit of

prevention. http://www.cdc.gov/HAI/pdfs/hai/Scott_CostPaper.pdf

6. Appendix A, CDC guideline. (2002). *Morbidity and Mortality Weekly, 51*(RR10), 27–28.

7. Provonost, P., Needham, D., Berenholtz, S., Sinopoli, D., Chu, H., Cosgrove, S., . . . Goeschel. (2006). An intervention to decrease catheter-related bloodstream infection in the ICU. *New England Journal of Medicine, 355*(26), 2725–2732.

8. Centers for Disease Control and Prevention. (2011, February). HIV/AIDS surveillance report, 2009. Vol. 21. http://www.cdc.gov/hiv/surveillance/resources/reports/2009report/index.htm

9. Centers for Disease Control and Prevention. (n.d.). Occupational HIV transmission and prevention among health care workers. http://www.cdc.gov/hiv/resources/factsheets/hcwprev.htm

10. Vincent, J. L., Bihari, D. J., Suter, P. M., Bruining, H. A., White, J., Nicolas-Chanoin, M. H., . . . Hemmer, M. (1995). The prevalence of nosocomial infection in intensive care units in Europe: Results of the European Prevalence of Infection in Intensive Care (EPIC) Study. EPIC International Advisory Committee. *Journal of the American Medical Association, 274,* 639–644.

11. Heyland, D. K., Cook, D. J., Griffith, L., Keenan, S. P., & Brun-Buisson, C. (1999). The attributable morbidity and mortality of ventilator-associated pneumonia in the critically ill patient. The Canadian Critical Trials Group. *American Journal of Respiratory Critical Care Medicine, 165,* 1249–1256.

12. Chastre, J., & Fagon, J.Y. (2002). Ventilator-associated pneumonia. *American Journal of Respiratory Critical Care Medicine, 165,* 867–903.

13. Papazian. L., Bregeon, F., Thirion, X., Gregoire, R., Saux, P., Denis, J. P., . . . Gouin, F. (1996). Effect of ventilator-associated pneumonia on mortality and morbidity. *American Journal of Respiratory and Critical Medicine, 154,* 91–97.

14. Rello, J., Ollendorf, D. A., Oster, G., Vera Llonch, M., Bellm, L., Redman, R., & Kollef, M. H. (2002). Outcomes scientific Advisory Group, Epidemiology and outcomes of ventilator-associated pneumonia in a large US database. *Chest 122,* 2115–2121.

15. Warren, D. K., Shukla, S. J., Olsen, M. A., Kollef, M. H., Hollenbeak, C. S., Cox, M. J., . . . Fraser, V. J. (2003). The outcome and attributable cost of ventilador associated pneumonia among intensive care unit patients in a suburban medical center. *Critical Care Medicine, 31,*1312–1137.

16. Cook, D. J., & Kollef, M. H. (1998). Risk factors for ICU acquired pneumonia. *Journal of the American Medical Association, 279,* 1605–1606.

17. Darves B. Seven strategies to prevent VAP: a look at the evidence. Today Hospitalist. May 2005. Accessed November 25, 2011 from: http://todayshospitalist.com/index.php?b=articles_read&cnt=262

18. Centers for Disease Control and Prevention. (n.d.). Tuberculosis. http://www.cdc.gov/tb/publications/factsheets/drtb/mdrtb.htm

19. Centers for Disease Control and Prevention. (2011). Trends in tuberculosis—United States, 2010. *Morbidity and Mortality Weekly, 60*(11), 333–337. http://www.cdc.gov/mmwr/preview/mmwrhtml/mm6011a2.htm

20. Siegel, J. D., Rhinehart, E., Jackson, M., Chiarello, L., & the Healthcare Infection Control Advisory Committee. (2006). Management of multidrug-resistant organisms in healthcare settings, 2006. http://www.cdc.gov/hicpac/pdf/guidelines/MDROGuideline2006.pdf

21. Panilio, A. L., Beck-Sague, C. M., Siegel, J. D., Anderson, R. L., Yetts, S. Y., Clark, N. C., . . . Jarvis, W. R. (1992). Infections and pseudoinfections due to povidone-iodine solution contaminated with *Pseudomonas cepacia. Clinical and Infectious Disease, 14*(5), 1078–1083.

22. Hell, M., Abel, C., Albrecht, A., Wonja, A., Chmelizek, G., Kern, J. M., . . . Apfalter, P. (2011). *Burkholderia cepacia:* outbreak in obstetric patients due to intrinsic contamination of nonsterile ultrasound gel. *BMC Proceedings, 5* (suppl.6), 075. http://www.biomedcentral.com/content/pdf/1753-6561-5-s6-o75.pdf

23. Doit, C., Loukil, C., Ferroni, A., Fontan, J. E., Bonacorsi, S., Bidet, P., . . . Bingen, E. Outbreak of *Burkholderia cepacia* bacteremia in a pediatric hospital due to contamination of lipid emulsion stoppers. *Journal of Clinical Microbiology, 42*(5), 2227–2230.

24. Balkhy, H. H., Cunningham, G., Francis, C., Almuneef, M. A., Cunnigham, G., Stevens, G., . . . Daniel, D. (2005). A National Guard outbreak of *Burkholderia cepacia* infection and colonization secondary to intrinsic contamination of albuterol nebulization solution. *Amercian Journal of Insection Control, 33,* 182–188.

25. Jhung, M. A., Suneshine, R. H., Noble-Wang, J., Coffin, S. E., St. Jhon, K., Lewis, F. M., . . . Srinivasan, A. (2007). *Pediatrics, 19*(6); 1061–1068

26. Blossom, D., Noble-Wang, J., Su, J, Por, S., Chemaly, R., Shams, A., . . . Srinivasan, A. (2009). Multistate outbreak of *Serratia marcescens* bloodstream infections caused by contamination of prefilled heparin and isotonic sodium chloride solution syringes. *Archives of Internal Medicine, 169*(18), 1705–1711.

27. Bennett, S. N., McNeil, M. M., Bland, L. A., Arduino, M. J., Villanino, M. E., Perrotta, D. M., . . . Jarvis, W. R. (1995). Postoperative infections traced to contamination of an intravenous anesthetic, propofol. *New England Journal of Medicine, 333,* 147–154

28. Clark, T. A., Slavinski, S. A., Morgan, J., Lott, T., Arthington-skaggs, B. A., Brandt, M. E., . . . Hajjeh, R. A. (2004). Epidemiologic and molecular characterization of an outbreak of *Candida parapsilosis* bloodstream infections in a community hospital. *Journal of Clinical Microbiology, 42*(10), 4468–4472.

29. Outbreak of hepatitis C at outpatient surgical centers: Public health investigation report. (2009, December). Southern Nevada Health District Outbreak Investigation Team, Las Vegas. http://www.southern-nevadahealthdistrict.org/download/outbreaks/final-hepc-investigation-report.pdf.

CHAPTER 13

Risk Management in Psychiatry

Amy Wysoker

Risk management in psychiatry poses unique and diverse issues for health professionals and for the institutions providing mental health services. These services could be rendered in a specialty facility, in a small unit in a general hospital, in scattered ambulatory centers, or in private offices. A newspaper article highlighted the unique character of the liability concerns in a psychiatric setting (see **Box 13-1**).

Box 13-1

A psychiatric patient, Gary C. Badger, swallowed pens, coat hanger pieces, metal strips, knives, television antennas, and radio batteries. He had surgery five times to remove material from his stomach. Badger filed suit, claiming that those responsible for his care negligently allowed him access to ingestible objects.[1]

This situation challenges practitioners to offer the safest, most therapeutic care possible to the patient while minimizing obvious and not-so-obvious risks. Psychiatric areas of concern to risk managers include: informed consent; the right to treatment; the right to refuse treatment; clinical risks in psychiatry such as psychopharmacology; electroconvulsive therapy (ECT), suicide, seclusion and restraints, elopement and wandering, discharge and after-care planning, and child and adolescent psychiatry; confidentiality and stigma; and high-risk incidents such as violence, illicit substance use, and sexual misconduct.

INFORMED CONSENT

Unless declared incompetent by the courts, psychiatric patients have the right to select their treatment regimen, as do all other types of patients. Psychiatrists in institutional settings are responsible for evaluating the individual's ability to comprehend the situation and for providing all necessary information. Practice guidelines and professional standards specify each psychiatric discipline's responsibility.[2]

In cases where the patient exhibits psychotic symptomatology, the difficulty is obvious. However, the legal system requires that as much information as necessary be provided to the patient. In legal cases, the courts look for medical record documentation of informed consent throughout the course of treatment.

Competency is a legal term and is determined in the judicial system. *Decision-making capacity* is a clinical term and comprises the ability to make a meaningful, informed decision about participation in treatment or research. It is task specific.[3–5] Although patients may be experiencing psychotic symptoms, some may be able to make decisions about their care.

Other patients exhibiting psychotic symptomatology may not be able to make such decisions. Depression, with its symptoms of hopelessness and apathy, and other illnesses can also affect decision-making ability.[6,7] Wirshing and colleagues found that when adequate informed consent procedures were established, the subjects were able to understand and retain critical components of the information.[8] Carpenter and colleagues concluded that although people with schizophrenia may have difficulty with the cognitive demand of the informed consent process, in many situations educational interventions can correct these difficulties.[9] In another study, most of the psychiatric patients were able to provided consent; however, one in five people with schizophrenia had a significantly decreased capacity to do so.[10]

Four legal criteria standards define when a patient can be considered competent to consent to treatment: the patient must be able (1) to communicate a choice, (2) to understand the applicable information about the planned treatment and the various options for treatment, (3) to recognize their clinical situation, and (4) to manipulate information rationally.[11]

The MacArthur Competence Assessment Tool—Treatment (MacCAT-T) provides a structured method for clinicians to assess patients' competence to make treatment decisions.[12–17] The American Psychiatric Association (APA) has also formulated guidelines for assessing decision-making capacities.[18] Vellinga and colleagues reviewed the available instruments to assess decision-making capacity.[19]

Notably, difficulties obtaining informed consent in schizophrenia remain despite the various assessment tools available.[20] Dunn and Jeste reported that deficits in patients' understanding of informed consent may be related to the consent materials, and that education interventions could correct these deficiencies.[21] Wirshing, Sergi, and Mintz studied the use of a brief educational video to facilitate the informed consent process for both medical and psychiatric treatment research; their findings indicated the video was an effective teaching tool.[22] Another study also indicated that multimedia consent might be a valuable adjunct to traditional written informed consent for research with people with schizophrenia.[23] Another concern with schizophrenia research is the fluctuating nature of the patient's capacity and the search for ways to address these issues as well as the use of surrogate consent.[24] Surrogate decision making for treatment issues should be based on what is called "substituted judgment," which means the decision should be based on what the patient would have done if able to do so. If this is not known or if no surrogate is available, then the "best interest" standard is used. Although a difficult concept to define, it is based on "what would most people choose in this situation." This decision should not be left to one person; rather, a decision-making process involving two or three additional people is recommended. Additionally, utilization of the ethics committee is advised.[5] Risk managers need to be cognizant of these issues as they assist the mental health practitioner.

Although the primary provider may legally delegate the informed consent process to other healthcare providers, he or she is still accountable for ensuring that adequate consent has been obtained. Risk management departments may choose to prohibit this procedure to avert another layer of liability.[25]

Galen discussed explaining to the patient the importance of self-disclosure in the therapeutic process.[26] At the onset of treatment, the patient's understanding of the risks of withholding information from professionals and the benefits of cooperating with the therapist should be ascertained. In the event of subsequent self-injury, appropriate documentation can reduce liability.

Implementing informed consent within the practice of psychotherapy is an issue for therapists to address in their practices.[27,28] Risk managers can review the pertinent liability variables using a model for obtaining informed consent for long-term psychotherapy. This model focuses on six areas that therapists should cover with patients: (1) the diagnostic model used and the recommendation for treatment; (2) the potential risks and benefits of treatment; (3) alternative treatment options, including less expensive short-term approaches; (4) explanation of the necessity for psychotherapy; (5) restrictions of insurance coverage; and (6) plans for evaluating the patient's response to treatment.[29] A summary of statutes, regulations, and cases relating to informed consent and psychotherapy is available to therapists and risk managers.[30]

Informed Consent and Research

Informed consent procedures involving research with psychiatric subjects must be adhered to with diligence, as illustrated in **Box 13-2**.

Box 13-2
A ruling by the National Institutes of Health declared that researchers at the University of California at Los Angeles (UCLA) had not adequately obtained informed consent from schizophrenic patients. Subjects in the study were withdrawn from their neuroleptic medications. Although consent forms had been obtained from subjects or family members, sufficient information outlining the potential risks of discontinuing medication had not been provided.[31]

Research guidelines adhere to the general informed consent requirements but are more expansive. The U.S. Department of Health and Human Services provides the specific elements that need to be included in consent forms for research.[32] Meanwhile, the National Bioethics Advisory Commission (NBAC) report titled *Ethical and Policy Issues in Research Involving Human Participants* is a document guiding research endeavors.[33,34] Some basic principles to be covered are summarized here:

- A statement that the study involves research
- An explanation of the purpose of the research
- The duration of the subject's participation
- A description of the study procedures
- An explanation of any experimental aspect
- An explanation of foreseeable risks or discomforts that may result
- A description of the benefits that may be expected
- A discussion of alternative procedures or treatments available
- A statement that confidentiality will be maintained
- Who can be contacted for information
- Who can be contacted if a research-related injury occurs
- A statement that participation is voluntary
- A statement that the patient can withdraw from the study at any time without penalty or loss of benefits to which she or he would be entitled without consenting to the research

Risk managers in psychiatry need to be well versed in the guidelines in the document addressing research with vulnerable populations.[33,35,36] In cases where the risk–benefit ratio is increased and the mental capacity of a patient is not certain, the inclusion of third-party consent is crucial.[37] When vulnerable populations are included in research, the appropriateness of using them should be shown.[38] Indeed, many states have convened task forces to address research with vulnerable populations and have promulgated state guidelines for such studies to ensure these patients' protection.[39, 40] Researchers need to provide the subject with information about all the necessary components of the research protocol for informed consent, consider employing a third-party consent person, and have all consent forms completed prior to embarking on the proposed project.[41]

Additional helpful resources for mental health researchers and risk managers include the American Psychiatric Association Task Force's report on research ethics.[42] and Mental Health America's "Position Statement 26: Participant Protections in Psychiatric Research."[43] A decisional framework is also available for mental health practitioners involved in research to assist in the evaluation of category of risk.[44]

Research with Children

Mental health research with children brings out additional concerns. According to human subject research children are defined as "persons who have not attained the legal age for consent to treatments or procedures involved in the research, under the applicable law of the jurisdiction in which the research will be conducted."[45] Given the sensitive nature of research with children, it is crucial for researchers and risk managers to be knowledgeable about the relevant laws. Children are unable to provide informed consent, but they may be able to give their assent, which means they agree to participate. Institutional review boards (IRBs) need to determine whether the child is able to assent to the research; if so, assent must be obtained. Additional protection is outlined for IRBs when approving research for children and is available through the Office for Human Research Protections (OHRP) website.[46]

Hooper, Smyth, and Roberts discuss how research on children and adolescents is ethically justified.[47] They address nine domains that should be considered:

- Scientific merit and design
- Expertise, commitment, and integrity
- Risks and benefits
- Confidentiality
- Participant selection and recruitment
- Informed consent and decisional capacity
- Incentives
- Institution and peer/professional review
- Data presentation

Risk managers can monitor the research process with these domains in mind.

RIGHT TO TREATMENT

In *Wyatt v. Stickney*,[48] the court stated that all involuntarily hospitalized people with mental illness or mental retardation have the right to a psychologically and physically humane setting. A sufficient number of qualified staff to administer active therapeutic treatment and an individualized treatment plan constitute the rights of treatment. If these legally defined standards are not met, patients need to be discharged unless they choose to remain at the facility voluntarily. As increasing numbers of patients are discharged from inpatient mental health facilities, a related liability arises. Supposedly, the patients are discharged to receive follow-up ambulatory care at treatment sites in the community. Who is responsible if the community treatment centers are not available? What happens if the released patients inflict harm on themselves or on others?

Right to the Least Restrictive Alternative

After evaluating an individual's needs in terms of providing care that permits maximum freedom, the patient is entitled to the right to the least restrictive alternative.[49] *Dixon v. Weinberger*[50] affirmed that right.

"Restrictive" has six conceptual dimensions: (1) *structural* refers to the type of setting; (2) *institutional* relates to the procedures set forth for operating the institution and the degree of patient involvement; (3) *enforcement* concerns the consequences of rule breaking; (4) *treatment* pertains to the type of treatment modalities provided; (5) *psychosocial atmosphere* applies to status differences between employees and patients and the level of authority provided; and (6) *patient characteristics* refers to the ability of patients to participate in their care related to their diagnosis.[51] Following through on these concepts allows patients to receive treatment in the least restrictive setting relative to their clinical needs. Caregivers must know the available referral sources when formulating treatment plans.

Recent court cases have brought clarification in questionable situations. *In re Turnbough*,[52] the court confirmed a lower court's decision to appoint a guardian to make decisions for a 24-year-old woman with cerebral palsy and bipolar disorder who was unable to make appropriate decisions for her own self-care. It was found that a nursing home was the least restrictive environment for this woman.

However, in *Salcido v. Woodbury County*,[53] the court determined that a patient with dementia should receive treatment in a psychiatric facility due to the individual's abusive and inappropriate behaviors rather than receiving care in a nursing home. Each case is decided on the individual needs of the patient based on what is determined to be the least restrictive setting in which to best treat that individual.

Right to Treatment and the Closure of Psychiatric Facilities

In response to consumer groups advocating for less hospitalization and more supportive community services, changed laws, and restricted payments from the federal government, most states have deinstitutionalized their mental health systems. Data from the National Institute of Mental Health Strategic Plan indicate that approximately 13 million American adults (1 in 17) suffer from serious mental illness.[54] In this country, during the past four decades 93% of state psychiatric hospital beds have been eliminated.[55] In 1999, a Department of Justice report claimed that approximately 16% of the total U.S. jail and prison population has a serious mental illness (see **Box 13-3**).

Box 13-3
One day last month Jesus Portelles, stripped naked and, convinced that demons had entered his body, used the broken edge of a plastic spoon to carve open his stomach. By the time the guards at the Dade County, Miami, Florida jail could unlock his cell door and grab him, his guts were spilling out. But the demons stayed.[63]

This amounts to approximately 300,000 persons, which is four times the number of people in state psychiatric hospitals.[56,57] Data from 2004–2005 indicate similar findings.[57–59] Additionally, approximately one-third of the U.S. homeless population has schizophrenia or bipolar disorder.[57,59,60] A recent phenomena reported by librarians in a survey in 2009 is that libraries have become "unintended shelters" for the mentally ill; libraries are viewed by such persons as a safe heaven to protect them from violence and living on the streets.[61] The closure of state psychiatric hospitals, along with the realization that persons with psychiatric illnesses are not getting the treatment they need and may, as a consequence, become part of the penal system, has drawn additional attention to the care (or lack thereof) of the psychiatrically ill in the United States. Approximately 3.6 million Americans older than 18 years of age (40% of those with schizophrenia and 51% of those with bipolar)go untreated.[60,62] Failure to treat has devastating results, as the following data for the United States demonstrate:

- Homeless: 200,000
- Incarcerated: 319,000
- Homicides: 10% of total number (1,600 per year)
- Suicides: 6,000
- People with schizophrenia—impairment of insight (anosognosia): 50%
- People with bipolar disorder—impairment of insight: 40%

The return of the state psychiatric hospital and a community health system that provides humane, individualized, coordinated care with appropriate funding would provide options for treatment. But will communities be accepting of such facilities, and will additional services and monies be available?

Right to Treatment: Involuntary Outpatient Treatment

"Involuntary outpatient treatment represents an effort to provide more suitable care for patients who, in the present system, are either overconfined or undertreated."[64] Geller delineated clinical guidelines that must be met in sequential order to ensure a right to treatment.[64] Patients must

1. Verbalize a desire to live in the community.
2. Have previously been unsuccessful in living in the community.
3. Show evidence of competency to understand the stipulations of their involuntary community treatment.
4. Have the ability to comply with the involuntary community treatment plan.
5. Have prescribed treatment plans that demonstrate effectiveness when used properly with the identified patient.
6. Be capable of administration in the outpatient system.
7. Be monitorable by the outpatient treatment agencies providing the prescribed treatments and enforcing their compliance.
8. Have public inpatient systems integrated into the community plan and supporting outpatient involuntary community treatment.
9. Not be dangerous while complying with the prescribed outpatient treatment.

Legislation for involuntary outpatient treatment has become a major focus in the United States throughout the past years. Forty-four states have enacted some form of legislation for involuntary outpatient commitment,[65] known as mandatory outpatient treatment, assisted outpatient treatment (AOT), or involuntary commitment, to name a few terms. Some states also have named their laws in memory of a person killed by the act of a mentally ill person, such as New York's Kendra's Law and California's proposed Laura's Law.[66] The Treatment Advocacy Center, an organization dedicated to eliminating barriers to the treatment of severe mental illness, provides updates on the status of all state laws for involuntary outpatient treatment and provides a model law for implementation.[65,67,68] Miller believes that the community practitioner must be involved in the treatment goals prior to the outpatient order.[69]

The controversy surrounding mandatory outpatient treatment remains at the forefront of psychiatric care. Studies have indicated that AOT is effective and results in increased treatment compliance. Decreased hospitalization rates, decreased homelessness, and reduced violence, arrests, and victimization have also been shown to be associated with such treatment.[65] This issue will continue to be addressed by patient rights advocates, civil libertarians, practitioners, and family groups. In particular, challenges to the laws on involuntary outpatient treatment will continue to occur (see the Right to Refuse Treatment" section). Potential lawsuits for mandating treatment, as well as for not initiating treatment, are a concern. Risk managers need to be involved in knowing and understanding the laws and staying current on them. Risk managers need to educate practitioners on the legal implications of their actions and advise them accordingly.

Right to Treatment and "Medical Necessity"

Managed care raises key questions about insurance coverage—namely, who should be covered and for how long? In the United States,

physician-ordered "medical necessity" services stimulate the reimbursement system. Sabin and Daniels discuss three models of medical necessity: the normal function model, the capability model, and the welfare model.[70] For a model to be useful, basic criteria should be considered and these questions answered: Does the model make distinctions that the public and the clinicians regard as fair? Can it be administered in the real world? Does the model lead to results that society can afford? Sabin and Daniels concluded that the normal function model best met these criteria for three reasons. First, society recognizes that mental illness should be treated to relieve suffering. Second, professional guidelines, such as the *Diagnostic and Statistical Manual of Mental Disorders (DSM-IV)*,[71] provide an accepted means to diagnose the mentally ill. Third, the normal function model allows society to determine the scope of insurance coverage—that is, how much it will pay.

However, the right to treatment and the reimbursement requirement of defined "medical necessity" pose potential conflicts with this model. Individuals requiring a certain type of psychiatric treatment may be unable to secure the care they need. A comprehensive reform of psychiatric care has been recommended, changing the definition of medical necessity from an acute care model to one that covers both care for acute episodes and long-term care for chronic conditions. Long-term care might help mentally ill persons avoid future acute episodes.[72]

Right to Treatment and Insurance Coverage

Over the years many states have instituted laws to mandate increased mental health coverage in insurance plans. Timothy's Law, enacted in 2007 in New York State, is one such law.[73] In addition to individual states legislation, the Mental Health Parity and Addiction Equity Act, a federal law, went into effect in January 2011.[74] Nevertheless, studies indicate the public lacks knowledge of this important federal mandate. Risk managers need to be knowledgeable about their respective state laws and the details of the federal law.

The Affordable Care Act of 2010[75] will bring significant changes to facilitate the treatment of mental illness in the coming years. In 2014, insurance carriers will not be able to denial coverage for substance abuse or mental illness as a "preexisting condition," nor can they raise premiums for their coverage. Prior to 2014, insurance can be provided under the new "preexisting condition insurance plan." In 2014, however, services for substance use and mental disorders will become part of the "essential benefits package." These services must be covered by certain plans including any insurance offered through the "Exchanges and Medicaid" system.

Right to Treatment and Psychiatric Advance Directives

Additional right-to-treatment issues pertain to the use of a psychiatric advance directive (PAD). The PAD is a legal document that outlines patients' wishes for treatment. Written when patients are able to make decisions, these documents provide mental health professionals with their treatment choices, if they relapse and are not able to contribute to decision making at the time. Preferences for hospitalization, medications, psychiatrist, electroshock treatment, outpatient treatment, and other preferences can be written in the PAD. PADs can be revoked or

changed when patients are not experiencing an acute episode.[76–78]

There are many issues related to the use of PADs as reported by patients. Studies have indicated that mental health providers' lack of knowledge about or failure to see the importance of the PAD, creating the PAD, and obtaining the document during a crisis acts as a barrier to these directives, use. Appointing a surrogate to facilitate patients' wishes in a crisis has also been suggested.[79–83] State-by-state information on PADs is available online at the National Resource Center on Psychiatric Advance Directives.[84] Mental health professionals must become knowledgeable about PADs, and risk managers need to monitor and facilitate their use. By doing so, patient preferences are honored, which in turns decreases decreasing liability issues.

In combination, the closing of psychiatric hospitals, the reduced availability of psychiatric beds, the changes in the reimbursement system, a reformed healthcare system, and the need to ensure patient rights are protected may cause right-to-treatment problems. As these changes occur, the courts will be asked to provide clarification. New definitions of the right to treatment need to be formulated as treatment modalities and insurance benefits change.

RIGHT TO REFUSE TREATMENT

All patients, including the mentally ill, have the right to refuse treatment. In psychiatric care, this right may be complicated by the competency status of the patient. A patient may have a diagnosable mental illness, yet still be competent to make decisions about treatment preferences. In addition, the right to refuse treatment is affected by whether the patient's status as an inpatient is voluntary or involuntary and, more recently, by whether outpatient treatment is mandated. Some states employ a full-time legal advocate who is responsible for ensuring that patients secure their legal rights.

Right to Refuse Psychotropic Medications

Commonly, the right to refuse treatment involves the refusal to take psychotropic medications. In *Rogers v. Okin,*[85] the court concluded that psychiatric patients have the right to refuse psychotropic medications unless such refusal poses a threat of danger to themselves or to others. Administration of medications against the will of a patient is permissible only in emergencies and only if the patient is a danger to self or to others. Policies should contain procedures for personnel to follow when patients refuse psychotropic medications or a danger to self or others.

General guidelines for nursing personnel in emergency situations should include the following information:

- Which interventions have been attempted prior to the emergency
- An explanation given to the patient of why he or she is a danger to self or others
- Procedures for informing the appropriate healthcare practitioner (i.e., psychiatrist)
- Documentation of the first three elements in the patient chart

In instances where medication is clinically indicated, but is not required for an emergency, court orders may be obtained to facilitate drug administration. Before seeking a court order, it is imperative that treatment personnel attempt a medication education regimen. Education should be provided over a period of time so that

the patient can gradually comprehend what is being taught and then make an informed decision. These interventions need to be documented in the patient's record. If education proves unsuccessful, a court order may be pursued.

Risk managers need to verify that the mental health team understands the legality of a court order when one is obtained. The judge's order needs to be included in the patient's medical record prior to administering the medication. The court order should state the length of time the medication can be given and state that, if refused, the medication can be administered intramuscularly (IM). The latter point must be clearly mentioned in the court order or the IM medication cannot be given. Individual state laws need to be reviewed by risk managers for other specific legal requirements, and staff need to be educated and policies consistent.

Right to Refuse Involuntary Hospitalization

In psychiatry, the right to refuse treatment includes the right to refuse involuntary court-ordered hospitalization. Two basic legal rights provide rationales for a person's right to refuse psychiatric hospitalization: freedom of thought and the right to live and conduct one's life as long as it does not interfere with the rights of others.[86]

The authority that states have to institute involuntary commitment is based on their *parens patriae* power and their police power. *Parens patriae* allows states to intercede in the lives of persons who are unable to care for themselves, including people with mental disabilities, so as to protect them. Police power, in contrast, is intended to protect society from potential harm; it is utilized to commit mentally ill persons whose conditions pose harm to others. Unlike in dealings with criminal defendants, police power commitments can be used to detain or confine a mentally ill person without any proof of a violation of criminal law. In some states, the prediction of dangerous behavior—even without evidence that the individual has previously committed a harmful act—could lead to commitment.

A variety of liability issues may arise from the right to refuse treatment, as illustrated by the Billie Boggs case (see **Box 13-4**).

Box 13-4

Billie Boggs, a 40-year-old homeless black woman, panhandled on New York's fashionable Upper East Side for money to buy food. A mental health team decided to forcibly hospitalize her because they determined she was mentally ill and unable to care for herself. On her behalf, the New York Civil Liberties Union brought suit, claiming she was not mentally ill, she was not dangerous, and her rights were being violated. Mass media reported on the battle, thereby bringing public attention to the problem of the homeless mentally ill.[87]

False imprisonment is confining an individual without the legal authority to do so. Lawsuits have been brought claiming false imprisonment of mentally ill persons, such as in *Arthur v. Lutheran General Hospital, Inc.*[88] In this case, the patient was hospitalized involuntarily after he refused voluntary admission. The courts found that the patient should not have been held without a physician certification indicating the patient was a danger to others. In another case, *Wingate v. Ridgeview Institute, Inc.*,[89] a patient voluntarily admitted himself to a alcohol rehabilitation program and then changed his mind and was held against his wishes; the court found in favor of the patient. The legal

standard for involuntary commitment is "grave danger of serious harm or death of the person or another." If a patient does not meet this standard, he or she should not be held. Courts have ruled in opposition to the patient and in favor of the institution when it has been shown that the patient did meet the standard and was in need of protection and treatment.[25] It is important to remember that all patients have the legal right to request in writing their wish for discharge if they did not wish, or no longer want, to remain in the facility voluntarily. The hospital needs to document their reasons and testify in court as to why patients' wishes should not be respected. In such cases, patients have a right to have legal representation and to present their own reasons. A judge then makes the final decision.

Institutions need to establish procedural guidelines for their staff to follow when it is clinically necessary to hospitalize patients against their wishes. Adherence to this protocol protects the patient's rights while minimizing the institution's liability. To avoid risk, documentation of the process must be evident in the patient's chart.

Right to Refuse Involuntary Outpatient Treatment

The laws mandating involuntary outpatient treatment are being challenged in the courts and continue to need close watching. The various laws enacted provide patient protection and allow for patients to be part of the decision-making process, as well as to appeal decisions. Issues relating to patients' refusals to adhere to outpatient treatment plans after they have been mandated and subsequent interventions (i.e., hospitalizations) also bring new liability concerns. All laws that have been challenged have been considered constitutional. However, in a recent New York Court of Appeals case, *In the Matter of Miguel M.*,[90] the court ruled the Privacy Rule described in the Health Insurance Portability and Accountability Act (HIPAA) "prohibits the disclosure of a patient's medical records to a State Agency that requests them for use in a proceeding to compel the patient to accept mental health treatment, where the patient has neither authorized the disclosure nor received notice of the agency's request for the records."

This finding may be considered a setback for assisted outpatient laws. The court did state the following caveat:

> We emphasize that it is far from our purpose to make the enforcement of Kendra's Law difficult. It may often be possible to avoid all disclosure problems by getting the patient to authorize the disclosure in advance; surely many mentally ill people will, while they are under proper care, recognize that disclosure is very much in their own interest. When there is no advance authorization, patients who are given notice that their records are being sought often may not object; when they do object, their objections may often be overruled. We hold only that unauthorized disclosure without notice is, under circumstances like those present here, inconsistent with the Privacy Rule.

Results of this ruling can be taken into consideration when PADs are created (see the "Right to Treatment and Psychiatric Advance Directives" section). Having PADs in place can significantly help with involuntary outpatient mandates if discussed and documented when patients can make decisions for themselves. As such, patients' preferences can be honored if they become ill and relapse.

Box 13-5

Hundreds of emails released by Prima Community College show school officials investigated the troubled young man in the months before he shot Representative Gabrielle Giffords and 17 others in January, killing six. The emails depict a student with serious emotional problems whose strange behavior upset those around him. More disruptions eventually prompted administrators to suspend [Jared] Loughner from school.[92]

Tragedies such as the Virginia Tech massacre in 2007 and the Tucson killings in 2011 have brought to light the difficulties in treating the mentally ill and protecting the public. In both cases, the accused had a history of untreated mental illness (see **Box 13-5**). The Treatment Advocacy Center's mission is "dedicated to eliminating barriers to the timely and effective treatment of severe mental illness"[91]; it is but one organization dedicated to advocating for involuntary treatment laws and educating the public and professionals about their usage. Risk managers working in healthcare institutions subject to outpatient commitment laws need to stay abreast of court rulings and their legal implications.

CLINICAL RISKS IN PSYCHIATRY

There are unique clinical risks associated with the practice of psychiatry, such as the side effects of psychopharmacology, the use of electroconvulsive therapy, patient suicide, the use of restraints, patients who elope or wander, aftercare planning, and therapy for children and adolescents. Each clinical risk has liability issues that apply regardless of the location of the treatment site.

Psychopharmacology and Side Effects

Psychotropic medications are instrumental in the treatment of individuals with psychiatric conditions. Until recently, the prescription of medications has been the sole domain of the physician. "Over the years, nurse practice acts changed to allow nurse practitioners and states like New Jersey, clinical nurse specialists, to obtain prescriptive privileges."[93,94] Furthermore, managed care has broadened the use of nonphysician prescribers, if allowed by state law. Institutions need to incorporate these changes into their policies along with procedures to ensure patient safety.

Prior to the initiation of therapy, patients must be informed of the benefits and risks and agree to the treatment plan. They must be part of the decision-making process. Unfortunately, despite the success of psychotropic medications, many patients develop severe side effects such as extrapyramidal symptoms (EPS), which comprise a variety of neurological disturbances. To lessen the symptomatology, practitioners may alter the dosage, switch to a different antipsychotic drug, or prescribe an antiparkinsonian drug to reverse the side effect.[95] To reduce the potential for liability, it is important that the approach taken and the rationale for the intervention be documented.

Approximately 20% of patients receiving long-term treatment with neuroleptic medications develop tardive dyskinesia with long-term EPS.[96] These disturbances may include abnormal involuntary movements such as tongue writhing, tongue protrusion, chewing motions, lip smacking, choreiform finger movements, and abnormal limb and trunk movements (see **Box 13-6**).

Administration of the Abnormal Involuntary Movement Scale (AIMS), which scores the presence of tardive dyskinesia, is recommended for all patients receiving antipsychotic medications.[95,96] The Extrapyramidal Symptom Rating Scale is another tool to assess symptoms of parkinsonism, akathisia, dystonia, and tardive dyskinesia resulting from psychotropic medications to treat the mental disorder.[98]

In 1992, an American Psychiatric Association (APA) task force report on tardive dyskinesia recommended regular examinations of patients treated with psychotropic medications at least every three to six months. In addition, the APA report recommended that informed consent be documented by a progress note rather than by consent forms.[99,100]

In the prescription of medications, risk management strategies include monitoring the prescribing practitioner's dosages to ensure that the patient is not accumulating an excessive dose over long periods of time. Nursing personnel are instrumental in monitoring the patient's response to medication and in reporting the reaction to the prescribing practitioner. The risks and benefits of neuroleptic medications, as well as of alternative treatments, must be explained to the patient and family.[101] The Tardive Dyskinesia Center's mission is to assist families of patients who experience the negative effects of antipsychotic medication, inclusive of legal action. Communication among mental health providers is imperative to minimize the negative consequences of medication, promote the health of the ill, and avoid liability.[102]

Lacro et al. describe the use of informed consent forms to ensure patient involvement in treatment decisions and to reduce liability.[103] However, there is controversy regarding the appropriate means of documenting informed consent, such as forms versus record charting. Some states require a written consent form outlining the information. Practitioners and risk managers should check their state laws for legislative mandates.

Electroconvulsive Therapy

Electroconvulsive therapy (ECT) has undergone periods of use, abuse, neglect, and reevaluation as a treatment modality. With this modality, a low-voltage alternating current of electricity is sent to the brain to produce a therapeutic effect for the treatment of clinical depression. ECT is indicated for severe cases of clinical depression or manic episodes. Generally, it is applied following a nonresponsive treatment course of antidepressive/antipsychotic medication, for those patients with medical conditions preventing the use of medications, and for patients in need of a rapid response. Risk managers have many resources at their disposal for determining when ECT should be considered an option for treatment, anesthesia considerations, as well as the role of the nurse in the procedure, and the

treatment of accompanying side effects.[104–109] The American Psychiatric Nurses Association's Position Statement of ECT provides guidance to nursing personnel participating in ECT.[110] Liability guidelines for the use of ECT include the following:[111]

- Secure proper informed consent.
- Do a comprehensive medical examination.
- Follow emergency management procedures.
- Provide for adequate patient supervision during and after the procedure.
- Review the privileging process of those professionals allowed to conduct the ECT treatment.

The negative connotations that have plagued ECT over the years and the possibility of side effects need to be clarified. Patients' opposition to ECT is frequently based on lack of knowledge. In addition, refusal of treatment may be based on inaccurate information. Informed consent needs to be provided in clear language, explaining the reasons for ECT, alternative treatments, and the benefits and risks associated with the procedure. The patient and family need to be informed of when, where, and by whom the procedure will be administered and the approximate number of treatments expected. The patient and family need to understand that they will be kept informed of the progress during the treatment and that they may terminate the treatment at any time. If the patient is too ill to make decisions and provide informed consent, a court-appointed guardian (usually a family member) needs to be assigned and consent obtained from the guardian before any treatment can begin.[112] Strict adherence to guidelines minimizes the physician's and the institution's liability risk.

Suicide

The National Institute of Mental Health's latest statistics on suicide were reported in 2007. At that time suicide was the tenth leading cause of death for all Americans. A total of 34,598 deaths, for a rate of 11.3 suicide deaths per 100,000 people, was reported. It was also estimated that 11 attempted suicides occurred per each suicide death. For males, suicide was the seventh leading cause of death; it was the fifteenth leading cause of death for females. From ages 15 to 24, suicide was the third leading cause of death. In this population, more males died of suicide than females. Elderly persons (age 65 and older) have a higher suicide rate than the general population. Non-Hispanic whites, American Indians, and Alaska natives have the highest rates for ethnic groups.[113] These staggering statistics indicate an area of possible increased lawsuits if suicidal individuals in these age groups are not identified early on in the healthcare field. If they are properly identified and referred for treatment, their mental health practitioners need to be aware of the increased risk of suicide in these populations.

The Joint Commission, the organization that accredits hospitals, instituted in 1995 the reporting of "sentinel events":

> A sentinel event is an unexpected occurrence involving death or serious physical or psychological injury, or the risk thereof. Serious injury specifically includes loss of limb or function. The phrase, "or the risk thereof," includes any process variation for which a recurrence would carry a significant chance of a serious adverse outcome. Such events are called "sentinel" because they signal the need for immediate investigation and response.[114]

The rate of inpatient suicides, which include suicides at the facility as well as those occurring within 72 hours post discharge, as reported to The Joint Commission from 1995 through November 2010 as sentinel events, varied from 4 in 1996 to a high of 103 in 2008, but feel to 67 to November 2010. Additional data reports indicate that suicide has ranked among the top five most frequently reported sentinel events, although it is not always specific to a psychiatric facility; suicide sentinel events may also occur in general hospital units, emergency departments, and home care and long-term care facilities. The Joint Commission does highlight that reporting is voluntary and suggests caution when interpreting these statistics because they do not adequately report the true number of suicides. However, the numbers do indicate a potential liability that risk managers need to take seriously.[115,116] In New York, a report entitled "Incident Reports and Root Cause Analyses 2002–2008: What They Reveal About Suicides" provides a comprehensive discussion about the 122 suicides reported to the Office of Mental Health during this time period.[117] This report is helpful to all risk managers, as it offers an analysis and accompanying recommendations.

The responsibility to monitor or supervise patients has always been higher in inpatient facilities than when patients live in the community, given that there is more control over patients in such institutions (see **Box 13-7**). Guido provides a review of relevant court cases in which families sued for compensation for wrongful death due to suicide.[25] In *Hooper v. County of Cook*,[118] the family was awarded $1,212,000. In this case, the patient was exhibiting psychotic behavior and a plan of care was instituted. However, one-to-one observation was not implemented, and the patient was found hanging by her hospital gown in the bathroom. The courts found that hospital personnel in this case did not provide reasonable care; it was their duty to protect suicidal patients from their own inflicted self-harm. In another case, *Reid v. Altieri,*[119] a patient was not hospitalized after seeking treatment. The court decided that the hospital was liable because the patient had an actual plan and healthcare personnel should admit a patient in these circumstances. *In re Baptist Hospitals of Southeast Texas,*[120] the court found a hospital liable for a patient's denial of suicide thoughts, ruling that patients cannot be relied on if they are exhibiting psychotic symptomology. Other court cases, however, have not found the hospitals liable if hospital staff did follow standards of care (*Soderman v. Smith,*[121] *Kinchen v. Gateway Community Service Board*[122]) despite patients successfully committing suicide. They claimed the outcome was not the key issue, but rather the interventions initiated. The standard of care is the ultimate deciding factor: Did mental health professionals and staff follow standards of care?

Box 13-7

A 12-year-old boy was able to hang himself while a patient at a New Hampshire psychiatric hospital, despite expressed suicidal ideation and prior suicidal gestures. The family settled the lawsuit before trial for a confidential amount.[123]

Silverman reviewed inpatient standards of care and the suicidal patient and delineated 10 areas that need standards of care for the treatment of the suicidal patient:[124]

1. Therapeutic contract
2. Treatment planning
3. Comprehensive evaluation
4. Therapeutic milieu
5. Hospital policies and procedures
6. Hospitalization risks and benefits
7. Watch procedures and protocols
8. Clinical risk management and judgment
9. Psychopharmacological agents
10. Discharge and aftercare planning

In November 2010, The Joint Commission published a follow-up report to its 1998 "Sentinel Event Alert" on preventing inpatient suicides.[125] As this alert addresses various patient settings—not just psychiatric units—it is crucial that all risk managers are knowledgeable about this document and that the organization's administration imparts the information in it to all staff.

Tishler and Reis[126] discuss issues related to preventing inpatient suicide, thereby avoiding a sentinel event. Janofsky[127] discusses improving observation practices and the related difficulties. A review of the Agency for Healthcare Research and Quality's National Guideline Clearinghouse refers to a practice guideline entitled "Assessment and Care of Adults at Risk for Suicidal Ideation and Behavior" developed by the Registered Nurses Association of Ontario (2009), which is specifically valuable to nursing personnel. The American Psychiatric Association has an excellent resource document entitled *Safe MD: Practical Applications and Approaches to Safe Psychiatric Practice*, which has a comprehensive chapter on suicide entitled "Safe Passage Through Suicide Risk: Navigating the Failure Modes."[128] All risk managers and mental health professions should be knowledgeable about content of this document—it is extremely important.

Alleged failures to meet standards of care with suicidal inpatients can be classified in terms of foreseeability and causation related to the responsibilities and roles of the clinician, the inpatient staff, and the hospital's administration. A primary intervention for hospitalized suicidal patients is staff observation and monitoring, or 15- or 30-minute checks. These interventions often provide a false sense of security for the institution, however, as patients may still inflict self-injury. Institutions should periodically evaluate their suicide watch policies. In reality, there may not be enough staff to provide the necessary observation, and when staff-to-patient ratios approach inappropriate levels, liability increases.

Psychiatric care provided by or reimbursed by managed care entities brings additional concerns to the treatment of the suicidal patient (see **Box 13-8**). Inpatient care needs to be justified, and therapists are confronted with dilemmas between cost containment and clinical indications. In recent years, the number of lawsuits against psychiatrists and managed care organizations relating to outpatient suicide has increased. The courts have decided that a physician's duty of care should not be determined by fiscal considerations. As protection against liability, therefore, practitioners repeatedly appeal denials for additional treatment from managed care companies.[129] Rissmiller has described factors complicating cost-containment decisions in the treatment of suicidal patients.[130] Suicide assessment techniques identified a larger number of patients at high risk for hospitalization, but only a small number actually successfully committed suicide. Psychiatrists who fear a lawsuit if a patient commits suicide may recommend preventive hospitalization to decrease their own possible professional liability. However, inpatient treatment should be reserved for those patients who have made serious attempts at suicide and for those who are at high risk because of other factors. Suicidal patients

should be committed to a treatment network allowing for movement between inpatient care, day hospitals, and outpatient care depending on their symptomatology. The roles and responsibilities of healthcare workers in regard to suicidal patients are summarized in **Box 13-9**.

Box 13-8

A patient of a managed care program was denied certification of additional hospitalization. This patient was discharged and subsequently committed suicide. A court ruled that the treating physician has the responsibility to appeal for an extension of benefits if the patient requires further treatment. All such physician efforts on behalf of the patient need to be documented.[131]

Discharge and Aftercare Planning

Litigation risks associated with discharge of mentally ill persons relate to the appropriateness of the discharge and the follow-up treatment of all psychiatric patients, with a specific emphasis on the suicidal patient. Staff members need to provide instructions about medication and follow-up appointments, and to incorporate the patient's and family's full compliance and adherence to aftercare recommendations in the plan of care. Plans and rationales need to be documented in the patient's medical record and discharge summary.

The HIPAA Privacy Rule[132] allows the sharing of information among health providers if this information is pertinent to the patient's care. Mental health personnel should not assume and share information simply because HIPAA permits this sharing, however. This point is very important in all aspects of treatment, including discharge and aftercare planning. Providers must first explore in therapy/counseling sessions why

Box 13-9 Professional Roles and Responsibilities Regarding Suicidal Patients[124]

	Responsibilities		
	Clinician	**Inpatient Staff**	**Hospital Administration**
Foreseeability	1. Correctly diagnose the patient. 2. Properly anticipate future behavioral difficulties.	1. Properly communicate suicidal risk among staff. 2. Appraise changes in suicidal risk.	1. Properly inform staff of suicidal risk. 2. Correctly predict future behavior.
Causation	1. Arrange for protection against harm. 2. Regulate, supervise, observe, and restrain the patient. 3. Establish a safe, secure, and protective environment. 4. Dispense therapy associated with suicidal behaviors. 5. Abide by written orders. 6. Properly document clinical decisions. 7. Enhance staff communications. 8. Maintain patients in the hospital. 9. Furnish adequate postdischarge plans. 10. Arrange for postdischarge care.	1. Appraise changes in the patient's condition.	1. Ensure a protective environment. 2. Design and maintain a safe and secure facility. 3. Eliminate all dangerous means of assisting suicidal behavior from the patient's access.

it is important to share the information with aftercare facilities, which specific information will be shared, and why (the rationale). All aspects of this conversation need to be documented in the medical record. Patient treatment is based on confidentiality and trust; without this trust, treatment may be hindered. It is very important for risk managers to oversee staff and continually educate them about the importance of these issues to avoid litigation.

Seclusion and Restraint

The use of restraints and seclusion for the management of violent behavior are controversial and vehemently debated issues in psychiatry. Mental health advocacy groups actively monitor the use of these treatment modalities and voice their views to professionals and legislators. In 1998, *The Hartford Courant* reported a large number of deaths occurring from the inappropriate use of restraints in psychiatric facilities. It was noted that approximately 50 to 150 deaths from the inappropriate use of restraints or seclusion methods occur each year in the United States. Because reporting of such incidents has not been mandatory, data collection on this topic continues to be a problem.[133] Federal legislation governing the use of seclusion and restraints followed on the heels of such reports, as the Hartford newspaper story, and in 1999 the Health Care Financing Administration (HCFA; now known as the Centers for Medicaid and Medicare [CMS] provided guidelines as to how agencies need to comply with the federal rule regulating the use of these modalities in psychiatric facilities. The Children's Health Act of 2000 further expanded on patient rights and established national standards governing the use of seclusion and restraints in all psychiatric facilities for children and youth that receive federal funds.[134] Risk managers should specifically refer to Title XXXII, Provisions Relating to Mental Health, Sections 3206 through 3209, as they relate to seclusion and restraints.

In January 2007, following public comment on the 1999 Patients' Rights Condition of Participation (CoP) Interim Rule, the Final Rule was implemented; it states the current criteria to be followed. Risk managers, hospital administrators, and all mental health practitioners working in these settings should be knowledgeable of the requirements of the Hospital Conditions of Participation in Medicare and Medicaid Programs: Patients' Rights Rule, 42CFR Part 482.[135] The State Operations Manual Appendix A, Survey Protocol—Regulations and Interpretive Guidelines for Hospitals, is an excellent source for familiarizing oneself with the specifics of the requirements.[136] Some of the major points in the Final Rule are summarized here:

- All patients have the right to be free from physical or mental abuse, and corporal punishment. All patients have the right to be free from restraint or seclusion, of any form, imposed as a means of coercion, discipline, convenience, or retaliation by staff. Restraint or seclusion may be imposed only to ensure the immediate physical safety of the patient, a staff member, or others, and must be discontinued at the earliest possible time.
- Revised definition of restraint and seclusion:
  - Restraint is any manual method, physical or mechanical device, material, or equipment that immobilizes or reduces the ability of apatient to move his or her arms, legs, body, or head freely; or a drug or medication when it is used as a restriction to manage the patient's behavior or restricts the patient's freedom of movement and is not a standard treatment or dosage for the patient's condition.
    - A restraint does not include devices, such as orthopedically prescribed devices, surgical dressings or bandages, protective helmets, or other methods that involve the physical holding of a patient for the purpose of conducting routine physical examinations or tests, or to protect the patient from falling out of bed, or to permit the patient to participate in activities without the risk of physical harm (this does not include a physical escort).
  - Seclusion is the involuntary confinement of a patient alone in a room or area from which the patient is physically prevented from leaving.
    - Seclusion may be used only for the management of violent or

self-destructive behavior that jeopardizes the immediate physical safety of the patient, a staff member, or others.

- The rule applies to the use of restraint, the use of seclusion, and the simultaneous use of restraint and seclusion regardless of patient location.
- Restraint or seclusion may be used only when less restrictive interventions have been determined to be ineffective to protect the patient, a staff member, or others from harm.
- The type or technique of restraint or seclusion used must be the least restrictive intervention that will be effective to protect the patient, a staff member, or others from harm.
- The use of a restraint or seclusion intervention should be reflected in the patient's plan of care or treatment plan based on an assessment and evaluation of the patient.
- The use of restraint or seclusion must be in accordance with the order of a physician or other licensed independent practitioner who is responsible for the care of the patient and implemented in accordance with safe and appropriate restraint and seclusion techniques.
- Orders for the use of restraint or seclusion must never be written as a standing order or on an as-needed basis (PRN).
- The attending physician must be consulted as soon as possible if the attending physician did not order the restraint or seclusion.
- Each order for restraint or seclusion used for the management of violent or self-destructive behavior that jeopardizes the immediate physical safety of the patient, a staff member, or others may be renewed only in accordance with the following limits for up to a total of 24 hours:

(1) 4 hours for adults 18 years of age or older;
(2) 2 hours for children and adolescents 9 to 17 years of age; or
(3) 1 hour for children under 9 years of age; and

- After 24 hours, before writing a new order for the use of restraint or seclusion for the management of violent or self-destructive behavior, a physician or other licensed independent practitioner who is responsible for the care of the patient must see and assess the patient.
- Each order for restraint used to ensure the physical safety of the nonviolent or non-self-destructive patient may be renewed as authorized by hospital policy.
- Restraint or seclusion must be discontinued at the earliest possible time, regardless of the length of time identified in the order.
- The condition of the patient who is restrained or secluded must be monitored by a physician, other licensed independent practitioner, or trained staff who have completed the training criteria.
- Physician and other licensed independent practitioner training requirements must be specified in hospital policy. At a minimum, physicians and other licensed independent practitioners authorized to order restraint or seclusion by hospital policy in accordance with state law must have a working knowledge of hospital policy regarding the use of restraint or seclusion.
- When restraint or seclusion is used for the management of violent or self-destructive behavior that jeopardizes the immediate physical safety of the patient, a staff member, or others, the patient must be seen face-to-face within 1 hour after the initiation of the intervention by (1) a physician

or other licensed independent practitioner or (2) a registered nurse or physician assistant who has been trained in accordance with the requirements specified in this section.

- The patient must be seen face-to-face within 1 hour after the initiation of the intervention to evaluate

(1) The patient's immediate situation;
(2) The patient's reaction to the intervention;
(3) The patient's medical and behavioral condition; and
(4) The need to continue or terminate the restraint or seclusion.

- If the face-to-face assessment is conducted by a trained registered nurse of physician assistant, they must consult with the attending physician or other licensed independent practitioner who is responsible for the care of the patient as soon as possible after the completion of the 1-hour face-to-face evaluation.
- Simultaneous restraint and seclusion use is permitted only if the patient is continually monitored
  - Face-to-face by an assigned, trained staff member; or
  - By trained staff using both video and audio equipment. This monitoring must be in close proximity to the patient.
- When restraint or seclusion is used, there must be documentation in the patient's medical record of the following:
  - The 1-hour face-to-face medical and behavioral evaluation if restraint or seclusion is used to manage violent or self-destructive behavior;
  - A description of the patient's behavior and the intervention used.

- The patient's condition or symptom(s) that warranted the use of the restraint or seclusion.
- The patient's response to the intervention(s) used, including the rationale for continued use of the intervention.

The patient has the right to safe implementation of restraint or seclusion by trained staff. The hospital must require appropriate staff to have education, training, and demonstrated knowledge based on the specific needs of the patient population. Details of the requirements are to facilitate the standards described previously and are specified in the rules and regulations [standard (f)] for risk managers and hospital administration.

Reporting requirements of deaths from seclusion and restraints have been expanded since the Interim Rule was published and can also be located in the documents identified earlier. The detailed list of directives is mandatory and risk managers must ensure they are carried out if a death occurs.

Sheridan concluded that behaviors precipitating restraint included verbal threats, threats with an object to be used as a weapon, and physical aggression.[137] These behaviors occurred more frequently in relation to external situations, such as conflict with staff, as opposed to internal psychiatric symptoms. An important finding was that patients viewed conflict with staff as the event most likely to lead to the use of restraints.

Klinge found that staff believed that medication should be used first, followed by seclusion, and finally by restraints.[138] Higher-educated staff felt that other professionals, not only physicians, should be able to order seclusion and restraints, but they also indicated that these modalities are overused. Finally, gender was associated with different views: Female staff commented that patients gained attention from the use of restraints and seclusion, while male staff considered such treatment a negative experience.

Betemps, Somoza, and Buncher examined hospital characteristics, patient diagnosis, and staff reasons related to the use of seclusion and restraints.[139] Geographic location was the only hospital characteristic associated with the use of seclusion and restraints. Facilities in the Pacific and mid-Atlantic areas used these modalities significantly less than institutions in other geographic areas. Patients with schizophrenic disorders were restrained more often than people with other diagnoses. Staff reasons for the use of restraints and seclusion fell into six major categories; in order of frequency they are (1) protection of the patient and others, (2) patient agitation, (3) physical violence, (4) verbal violence, (5) psychotic or delusional episode, and (6) intoxicated behavior.

Seclusion and restraints are interventions administered by nursing personnel. Many authors have addressed seclusion and restraints in the nursing literature. Larue et al.[140] provide an in-depth analysis of factors influencing decisions on the use of seclusion and restraint. Stokowski[141] offers answers to psychiatric nurses' questions about the use of seclusion and restraints. Some of these questions relate to which situations seclusion should be used versus restraints; which alternative interventions can be used to avoid either use; how to de-escalate a person in crisis; how to work with staff to reduce the use of seclusion and restraint; and how to deal with staff shortages.

The National Alliance on Mental Illness (NAMI) has taken the following position: "De-escalation techniques and debriefings should be used after each restraint and seclusion incident." It is important for mental health personnel to ask patients during the assessment phase which types of interventions they would choose if the need is indicated; this preference should guide treatment. De-escalation techniques and debriefings are crucial after an incident to learn about and improve patient care and prevent future episodes. In a study conducted in Australia, Needham and Sands[142] studied post-seclusion debriefing and concluded that the intervention was not conducted on a consistent basis; thus these authors recommended a post-seclusion debriefing framework.

Hellerstein, Staub, and Lequesne[143] implemented a program to decrease the number of patients in restraints and reduce the amount of time spent in restraints without an increase in negative outcomes. The interventions included staff education, such as identifying patients at risk and implementing interventions to decrease escalation; use of a coping survey to assess patient preferences for handling their agitation; and decreasing initial time in restraint from 4 to 2 hours before obtaining a new order.

Pollard, Yanasak, Rogers, and Tapp[144] found that despite staff resistance, organizational and leadership commitment could change practices on a psychiatric unit, resulting in reduced use of seclusion and restraint. Sclafani and colleagues[145] initiated a consultant service that facilitated a team-based approach, resulting in a decrease in the use of restraints through specific intervention plans.

Muralidharan and Fenton[146] reviewed the literature, comparing different intervention strategies (excluding pharmacological and seclusion and restraints) such as behavioral contracts, observational levels, staff–patient ratios, and de-escalation techniques, and found their use was not supported by clinical trials. Clinical practice utilizing such measures persists, even though it is not based on research findings. Sailas and Fenton[147] reviewed the literature and found no controlled studies that evaluated the use of seclusion or restraints, although there were reports of negative effects during the use of these interventions. They concluded that alternative interventions need to be developed and that the continued use of seclusion and restraints needs to be examined.

Comfort rooms are an interesting new preventive tool being explored and implemented in mental health settings. The New York State Office of Mental Health defined a comfort room as follows:

A tool that is used to prevent the use of restraint and seclusion

- To be used at will and not forced upon individuals
- To be used when necessary to avoid episodes of restraint and seclusion—not as a reward for good behavior or a privilege that is taken away as a punishment (unless the individual is unable to use the room safely)
- To be used before the onset of aggressive/uncontrolled behavior[148]

A comfort room is *not*

- An alternative to restraint and seclusion
- A seclusion room
- A time-out space
- A punishment or reward
- To be used after an individual has already lost control of his/her behavior[148]

This preventive tool may bring its own risk management challenges, healthcare personnel need to ensure it is used as intended and not used when it should not be.

The literature, although nonconclusive, provides guidance on restraint and seclusion to nursing and other mental health professionals. It is important for nursing personnel to follow the competences outlined in the American Nurses Association's *Scope and Standards of Psychiatric Mental Health Nursing*[149] as well as The American Psychiatric Nurses Association's (APNA) *2007 Position Statement on the Use of Seclusion and Restraint* (original, 2000; revised, 2007) and the *Seclusion and Restraints Standards of Practice* (2000; revised 2007).[150] These documents provide the nurse with guidance on the level of care to be delivered. Risk managers need to be familiar with these documents and create environments where one can practice accordingly and ethically. The *Safe MD* document also has a chapter on reducing risk in the management of aggressive patients that provides a wealth of information for staff and risk managers.[151]

As noted previously, there are many issues related to seclusion and restraints and patient safety. The use of restraints and seclusion is, therefore, a source of potential liability. In *Hanson v. Hospital of Saint Raphael,*[152] a patient with a history of self-harm was admitted to the hospital after a self-inflicted injury; the individual was placed in restraints and medicated involuntarily to prevent additional harm. The courts found that the patient had no grounds for a lawsuit in this case. However, each case is decided on based on its specifics and personnel's adherence to the standards of care. Without proper administration and supervision, restraints may restrict body movement in such a way as to seriously harm the patient. Institutional policies must guide personnel regarding the use of restraints and seclusion. Federal and state laws and the dictates of The Joint Commission provide the specifics for adherence. Guidelines need to specify indications for the use of restraints and seclusion, permissible forms of restraint, ways to initiate restraints and seclusions, procedures to safely administer these treatments, written orders, time limits, monitoring care, physical care requirements, and documentation requirements.[153] Case conferences should review and evaluate the necessity and appropriateness of restraint applications. Alternatives and future interventions need to be formulated on the basis of the new information and in consultation with the patient. Documentation of, and the rationale for, all interventions must be evident in the medical record.

Elopement and Wandering

Psychiatric hospitals are caught a blind between ensuring patient rights and initiating security measures to prevent patient elopement and wandering, leaving the premises without authorization, and straying within the facility (see **Box 13-10**). This is not an uncommon liability risk.

Box 13-10

Greystone Park Psychiatric Hospital in New Jersey reported that a patient who was housed in a locked ward, but who had grounds privileges, escaped and took the bus to the local mall.[154]

Three cases provide such evidence. In *Estate of Hollan v. Brookwood Medical Center*,[155] a psychiatric patient was on a supervised outing with other patients on an outside deck at the facility. He was able to elope, and fell to his death. The court found in favor of the family, were awarded $12,000. The courts found in *Hofflander v. St. Catherine's Hospital*[156] that if a facility does not take reasonable measures to prevent a patient from elopement when evidence indicated the possibility, it is liable for neglect of a vulnerable person. Conversely, in *Ball v. Charter Behavioral Health*,[157] the court ruled if there was no foreseeable action evident to staff and a patient elopes, the facility is liable.[25]

Allowing patients the opportunity to walk outside the facility is certainly a valued therapeutic intervention. However, if staffing is not sufficient to guarantee safety for patients and staff escorts, the therapeutic goal is not accomplished. Administrators and staff need to comply with the law. Policies need to address both therapy and safety issues. If not, danger results and liability increases. *Safe MD* provides an excellent chapter on elopement; it is a must for all risk managers and mental health professionals.[158]

The National Association of State Mental Health Program Directors Research Institute (NASMHPD) collects and analyzes data submitted to it (the most recent data are from 1999–2010). Its member organizations chose measures that are relevant to them. One such measure is elopement, which indicates the concern that psychiatric facilities have about this possibility, and the need for risk managers to take notice.[159]

The scenario described in **Box 13-11** raises questions about the ease with which a patient can leave a facility and how patient is screened upon return. When patients are initially admitted to an institution, their private property is carefully checked. If patients elope and then return, however, they may not go through a similar check of their property. To prevent harm to patients and staff, there must be procedures in place for dealing with elopement returns.

Box 13-11

Daniel Alvarez, a patient at Brooklyn State Hospital in New York state, escaped and roamed the city for 12 hours. He returned at dawn after a night of drinking, was searched, and was placed back with the other patients. Later that day, another patient died after Alvarez stabbed him four times in the chest with a knife he had obtained while free. As a result of this incident, three top executives at the hospital were demoted and transferred.[160,161]

Although patients may be classified as violent or homicidal when they first come to the unit, these symptoms may diminish or disappear after treatment. Policies should explain who is eligible for random access to the grounds or to the community. Patients with a history of violence need special attention (see **Box 13-12**).

Box 13-12

Like many patients at Napa, Massey had a pass that allowed him to wander on the grounds unsupervised. He allegedly cornered Gross [a female psychiatric technician] between a couple of buildings, attacked her, stuffed dirt into her mouth—which kept her from screaming—and strangled her.[162]

Child and Adolescent Psychiatry

Risk management in child and adolescent psychiatry is a concern to hospitals and treating practitioners. Related malpractice cases have increased, and the statute of limitations for filing a claim is significantly longer than that for adult patients. Child protection laws and the legal mandates for reporting suspected child abuse or neglect are readily cited in malpractice

litigation. Additionally, an area of increased liability deals with negligent evaluations for child custody and child sexual abuse allegations.[163] In some states, reregistration for professional licensure requires a continuing education child abuse course to keep practitioners knowledgeable about the salient issues.

While hospital administration must provide a protective environment for all patients, special emphasis is placed on the needs of children and adolescents (see **Box 13-13**). In most states, a minor is considered to be any individual who is younger than age 18 and is deemed legally incompetent, so that consent for treatment must come from parents or guardian. Exceptions include minors seeking treatment for drug abuse, consent for contraception, and treatment for psychiatric reasons.[49] The legal rights of children must be protected, yet treatment should be provided when clinically indicated and legally sanctioned. To provide guidelines for practitioners, risk managers must be knowledgeable about applicable state statutes.

Box 13-13

"The Justice Department focused on New York because of people like Darryl Thompson, an emotionally disturbed 15-year-old who died after being pinned face down on the floor at the infamous Tryon Residential Center. A federal investigation found that children in the system were often brutally punished for minor offenses like laughing too loud or sneaking an extra cookie."[164] A settlement will provide decent psychiatric care at the state's four youth prisons.

Children can be admitted to a psychiatric hospital against their will. If a parent authorizes the child's admission, it is considered a voluntary admission. Safeguards instituted over the years are meant to protect children when the parent's decision may not be in their best interest. Many states have modified their statutes by lowering the age required for consent, by requiring consent of the child, or by having a court hearing if the child continues to object to hospitalization.[49]

Information in medical records concerning children must be entered in a manner that protects the child as well as the confidentiality of parents. To facilitate a trusting relationship, the child or adolescent must be able to share with the therapist without fear that this information will be shared with parents. Therapists are advised to make it clear to their patient and parents what is considered confidential and what is not. Documentation of these discussions should be placed in the medical record.[165] Written objective information based on observed behaviors must omit the opinions or attitudes of the observer.[166]

Pediatric patients are even more vulnerable than the adult psychiatric population because of growth and developmental patterns. In this age group, sexual identity is being established and tested, and acting out is common. Institutional policies should mandate a dress code, room limitations, visiting hours, and interventions regarding seductive behaviors. Setting firm limits and maintaining consistency among staff are crucial. Policies should also specify which interventions are available for the children to voice their feelings and concerns around these issues.

A new area of concern is the increased number of children receiving psychiatric medications. Questions are being raised about the informed consent process and about the information being provided on the long-term effects of children being on medications and alternative therapies. The potential for lawsuits has increased as more attention has been placed on the diagnosis and psychopharmacological management of children with psychiatric disorders. The FDA has published many black-box warnings concerning adverse reactions and side effects from psychotropic medications. Moreover, the long-term effects of these medications are unknown and as such are associated with greater liability concerns. Risk managers and practitioners need to be aware of the potential liability involved in treating children with psychiatric disorders, and provide patients with the most current information, options for treatment, risks, and benefits. This information should be clearly provided in consent forms, and practitioners should document the process used to inform the family members of their choices.

Faille, Clair, and Penn[165] provide a detailed discussion of additional risk management concerns in the child and adolescent population. The Association of Child and Adolescent Psychiatric Nurses' (ACAPN) *Position Statement on the Rights of Children in Treatment Settings* is another resource to risk managers and health practitioners.[167] Children and adolescents are a vulnerable population who need extra oversight by risk managers.

CONFIDENTIALITY AND STIGMA

Stigmatization of people with mental disorders has persisted throughout history... It deters the public from seeking, and wanting to pay for, care. In its most overt and egregious form, stigma results in outright discrimination and abuse. More tragically, it deprives people of their dignity and interferes with their full participation in society.[168]

This comment made by the Surgeon General pinpoints the stigma of mental illness that affects individuals using therapeutic services.

Although strides are being made to change the public's view of mental illness, there is a long way to go. Therefore, the stigma of mental illness places special emphasis on the need for confidentiality. Unauthorized release of medical information is a breach of confidentiality and raises ethical and legal concerns that place the mental healthcare professional in a precarious situation. As an aid in providing treatment, family members may be questioned to gather relevant information. Although professionals may obtain information from others, they must make a distinct effort not to disclose personal information shared by the patient. There is a distinction between getting information and respecting the patient's right to privacy. Frequently, this is a delicate balancing act that requires concentrated attention.

Patient and mental health professional confidentiality enhances the therapeutic relationship. Patients should have the opportunity to share freely and to work through their concerns. Perceived threats of breach of confidentiality may compromise the therapeutic relationship. If a patient refuses to allow the mental health professional to communicate with others, the therapist must respect the patient's wishes, despite the inability to obtain needed information. A common breach of confidentiality, however, is the discussion of patients in public areas where others are able to hear. Risk managers need to remind all personnel, through continuing education, of the inappropriateness of careless conversation and subsequent legal implications. Another issue of confidentiality relates to photographs of patients. Many times pictures are taken in milieu groups or recreational activities

in psychiatric settings. The courts in *Cedars Healthcare Group, Ltd., v. Freeman*[169] ruled that removing names does not suffice, as the person may be recognized in the picture. Facilities must be very cognizant of photographing patients and educate the staff (i.e., recreational and activity personnel) as to the ramifications of violating patient confidentiality in this way. Hospital policy would need to outline appropriate procedures based on legal protocol.

Continuity of care is imperative and requires referrals to various treatment facilities and resources. For the mental health professional to disclose information, the patient needs to understand what is involved and agree to release the data. Patients must be informed as to who will receive the data and why it is necessary to share the information. Explanations should pinpoint what information is necessary to share, how it will be used, and when the information will be provided to the other sources. A signature on a release form should be obtained and secured in the chart.[49]

Institutions must be responsive to the risk issues of confidentiality. Medical records data involve unique problems regarding the right to privacy and confidentiality. Because of the sensitive nature of the data, psychiatric informational material must be protected using reliable security measures. The Privacy Rule, as required by the HIPAA,[170] provides additional federal regulations that protect the privacy of medical records. Risk managers need to become fully knowledgeable about all relevant laws.

Privileged Communication

Privileged communication is a legal term applicable in court proceedings. It prevents information shared by a patient with certain persons from being disclosed in court. The person or institution that obtains the information is bound by law not to disclose it to any third party. State laws generally hold that communications between clients and attorneys, husbands and wives, patients and physicians, and clergy and parishioners are confidential.[49, 171] The U.S. Supreme Court decision in *Jaffe v. Redmond*[172] determined that psychotherapis–client confidentiality privileges exist in civil and criminal federal courts under the Federal Rules of Evidence.[173] However, exactly who is considered a psychotherapist has not been clearly defined by the court.[174] Professionals must check their individual state laws to clarify the legal dictates of privileged communication.

Although states grant professionals the privileged communication right, specified exemptions to that privilege exist. The most common exceptions include the following situations:[49, 175]

- When the courts order an examination
- When civil commitment is sought by the therapist
- When child abuse is suspected
- When the patient brings a defense of mental illness into the litigation proceedings
- When the patient presents a danger to others

Duty to Protect/Warn

In *Tarasoff v. Regents of the University of California* (see **Box 13-14**), the court established as an exception to privileged communication the "duty to protect" when a patient presents a danger to others. Additional court cases have supported this decision (*Evans v.*

Benson,[176] *DeJesus v. United States Department of Veterans Affairs*,[177] *Stewart v. North Coast Center*[178]). One of the differentiating factors is that there needs to be a "clearly identifiable victim who is a family member or someone known to the patient"; if this victim is identifiable, then the mental health provider must report to law enforcement officers and if feasible to the specific persons.[25(p.412)] To guide mental health professionals, risk managers should advise their institutions to incorporate pertinent legal definitions into their polices and procedures.

Box 13-14

Tatiana Tarasoff's parents sued the University of California, claiming that a therapist in the university's counseling center knew that his client was threatening to kill their daughter. Their daughter was not warned of the possible danger and was killed. Her parents won the case, and subsequently most states accepted the concept of "duty to protect."[179]

An algorithm proposed by Felthous[180, 181] helps clinicians make critical decisions regarding hospitalization and disclosures to protect others; however, it should not replace clinical judgment. Four questions are of utmost importance:

- Is the patient a danger to others?
- Is this danger due to mental illness?
- Is the danger imminent?
- Is the danger targeted at specific individuals?

Approximately 1,770 children in the United States died in 2009 from abuse and neglect. The Child Abuse Prevention and Treatment Act (CAPTA), which was amended in 2003 by the Keeping Children and Families Safe Act of 2003 defined child abuse and neglect as "any recent act or failure to act on the part of a parent or caretaker which results in death, serious physical or emotional harm, sexual abuse or exploitation; or an act or failure to act which presents an imminent risk of serious harm." All states, the District of Columbia, and all U.S. territories have some type of statute identifying those professionals who are mandated to report child maltreatment, along with the specifics regarding such reporting. The National Child Abuse and Neglect Data System (NCANDS) provides an annual analysis of the data collected on child abuse and neglect.[182]

In addition, elder abuse is a growing concern. Every year, thousands of elderly persons are abused, neglected, and exploited by family members. In response, all 50 states have passed some type of elder abuse prevention laws. Although the laws and definitions differ, each state has enacted reporting systems.[183] The U.S Administration on Aging's, National Center on Elder Abuse website provides a current list of the various states laws and resources.[184] To reduce their liability risk, professionals need to know their respective state laws and procedural responsibilities for both child and elder abuse and neglect.

HIGH-RISK INCIDENTS

Given that psychiatric treatment deals with emotions, high-risk incidents may be triggered by the volatility of events in the patient's life. These high-risk incidents could involve violence, the use of illicit drugs, or sexual misconduct. Risk managers should be prepared to reduce potential liability of such high-risk areas of concern.

Violence and the Mentally Ill

There is much debate among professionals and mental health advocacy groups regarding the belief that those with mental illness are more prone to be violent than the rest of the population. Earlier professional studies indicated, that an association does exist between mental illness and the likelihood of being involved in violent incidents.[185] Approximately 10% to 20% of hospital patients physically assaulted others prior to their hospitalization.[186,187] (See **Box 13-15**). Blomhoff and colleagues[188] found that the only discriminating demographic was that the violent group experienced more violence in the family of origin. A history of previous violence by the patient was the best single predictor of violence. Numerous recent studies have found that noncompliance with treatment, inclusive of medication noncompliance, as well as a lack of awareness of his or her illness increases a person's violent behavior.[189,190]

> ### Box 13-15
>
> According to a report mandated by the federal government, patients at Napa committed 75 physically aggressive acts against staff in a single six-month period ending in early 2009. In the same period one year later, there were nearly four times as many assaults. The report also shows that patient-on-patient aggression more than doubled during that same time.[162]

The MacArthur Community Violence Study, based on the findings of Steadman and colleagues, reached the following conclusions regarding people discharged from psychiatric hospitals and the incidence of community violence:[191,192]

- "People discharged from psychiatric hospitals" is not a homogeneous category regarding violence.
- Those persons without a substance abuse diagnosis are involved in significantly less community violence than people with a co-occurring substance abuse diagnosis.
- Those persons without symptoms of substance abuse have about the same prevalence of violence as other people living in their communities who do not have symptoms of substance abuse.
- People with symptoms of substance abuse (those discharged from the hospital and nonpatients) have a higher incidence of violence than those without symptoms of substance abuse. Those discharged from a psychiatric hospital have a higher prevalence of violence than others in the community.

In their study, McNiel and Binder found that the symptom patterns of assaultive patients differed from those of nonassaultive patients.[193] Krakowski and Czobor noted that transient violence occurred primarily as a result of paranoid delusions and probably was a symptom of acute decompensation.[194] Chronic, repetitive patterns of violence were related to neurological impairment.

Torrey, a leader in obtaining treatment for the chronically ill psychiatric patient, believes that without treatment the mentally ill do have a higher prevalence of violence.[195] Torrey addressed three predictors of violent behavior in a subgroup of patients with serious mental illness: medication noncompliance, a history of violent behavior, and concurrent drug and alcohol abuse.[196] He recommended the following steps to decrease violence by the seriously mentally ill:

- Involuntary hospitalization
- Involuntary medication
- Allowing outpatients to remain in the community only if they comply with treatment and take medication
- Releasing individuals with serious mental illness into the community only if they are monitored to ensure oral medication compliance

Investigators have described a decision tree to guide judgments about pharmacological and behavioral treatments of aggression. These decisions depend on where the patient encountered difficulty during the course of the disorder.[197]

Davis outlined individual, situational, and structural factors affecting violence in psychiatric inpatients.[198] Individual variables included drug abuse, stage of illness, psychosis, and a history of violence. Situational factors included staff inexperience, provocative incidents, management's ability to tolerate violence, staff attitudes and behavior, overcrowding, and lack of privacy. Structural factors included changes in mental health policies that make "dangerous" a criteria for hospitalization and a shortage of treatment facilities in the community. Davis claimed that violence is the result of an interaction between the various types of factors and is not simply an extension of individual pathology.

Monahan outlined guidelines to assist in preventing violence and reducing the risk of civil liability.[179] These guidelines address five domains: (1) risk assessment, (2) risk management, (3) documentation, (4) policy, and (5) damage control. The MacArthur Risk Assessment Study developed an actuarial model called the multiple iterative classification tree (ICT) to predict violence in the community in patients who were recently discharged from psychiatric facilities. Further study of the model concluded that the tool might be useful for decision making among practitioners in acute care psychiatric facilities.[199–201] Despite having these tools with specific indicators to guide their clinical practice, it remains difficult to determine with any certainty the potentially violent patient.[202,203]

When patients verbally or otherwise express violent intentions, mental health professionals must be aware of their responsibilities. The Treatment Advocacy Center provides the following statistics from the Department of Justice:

> [S]pouses killed by spouse—12.3 percent of defendants had a history of untreated mental illness; of children killed by parent—15.8 percent of defendants had a history of untreated mental illness; of parents killed by children—25.1 percent of defendants had a history of untreated mental illness; and of siblings killed by sibling—17.3 percent of defendants had a history of untreated mental illness.[60]

On these occasions, healthcare workers are exempted from the responsibility of privileged communication. The duty to protect prevails if criteria are met. (See the "Duty to Protect/Warn" section). Additionally, mandatory involuntary outpatient laws provide treatment to people with a history of violence and should be used accordingly. Mental health professionals and risk managers need to understand the complexities involved with determining risk of violence, understand relevant laws, and provide support and education to decrease potential liability both in the facility and for discharge planning.

Violence in the Institution

Violence directed toward staff and other patients is a continuous problem needing institutional attention. "Overwhelmingly, the facilities where risk of assault was highest were psychiatric hospitals."[204] The unfortunate death of a mental health counselor allegedly by a psychiatric patient is evidence of this continuous problem (see **Box 13-16**)

Box 13-16

A 27-year-old mentally ill man was arrested in January 2011 after allegedly killing Stephanie Moulton, a 24-year-old female mental health counselor at a group home in Revere, Massachusetts, where he was a patient, and dumping her body in Lynn, Massachusetts. A judge ruled that the patient was not competent to stand trail and ordered that he be held at Bridgewater State Hospital. In April 2011, her family filed a wrongful death suit.[205,206]

Nursing personnel are in the best position to assess the potentially violent patient and to intervene accordingly before an outbreak of violence occurs. It is their responsibility to protect both their patients and themselves from acts of violence. Institutions are liable for acts of violence directed at one patient by another patient. Patients are in facilities to be treated, not to incur physical harm as a result of another patient's illness. However, hospital administrators must provide the nursing personnel and other staff with adequate resources to provide protection for themselves and for the patients they care for. Neglecting proper staffing patterns and violence education protection, to name a few interventions, increases the rate of violence and the liability risk to the facility. The Joint Commission[207] has addressed the importance of preventing violence in the healthcare setting and has added this unfortunate occurrence to its list of sentinel events.

What can nurses and other members of the mental healthcare team do to prevent violence in a psychiatric unit? Gould discussed seven practical ways to reduce levels of violence in a psychiatric ward:[208]

- Provide areas for patient privacy.
- Establish good facilities that value the patients.
- Provide a comfortable and reasonably decorated environment.
- Allow patients to be partners in their care.
- Listen to patient requests and respond accordingly.
- Have a continuity of staff who work well as a team.
- Provide clear leadership to the unit.

Gadon, Johnstone, and Cooke[209] conducted a systematic review of the literature on situational variables and institutional violence. Their findings identified the following risk factors: "security level, amount of time spent with patient, staff position, times of high interaction among patients and staff, vulnerable times such as shift changes, areas where there is high traffic and increased opportunities for interaction, and a well managed establishment that includes policy consultation aimed at a range of staff levels."

Situational factors related to staff characteristics—especially having a sense of humor, establishing clear boundaries with clients and respecting the clients being served.

Moylan and Cullinan[210] found an increase in severity of injuries since 1996. Eighty percent of the nurses of a sample of 110 nurses were assaulted. Of that number, 65% were injured and 26% were seriously injured. These authors also noted that those nurses who were injured actually decided to restrain patients later in their aggression than those who were not injured.

Lu, Wang, and Liu[211] conducted a survey in Taiwan of psychiatric nurses' reactions to being assaulted on an inpatient unit. Feeling sore in the area hit, anger, and fear of the patient who assaulted them were the most common reactions. These researchers, also found less severe reactions to the assault with older age, greater duration of occupational experience, and more social support.

In a study by Ryan and Porter, 61 nurses were asked about being attacked by their patients.[212] In addition to experiencing a variety of feelings such as helplessness, anger, shock, and disbelief, the nurses felt that they should have done something to prevent the attack. Lanza found that nurses were hesitant to share their responses to such attacks.[213,214] They seemed to blame themselves for not being able to do anything to prevent the attack.

Controversy exists as to whether staff members may file charges against patients who intentionally assaulted them. Phelan supports the idea of prosecuting psychiatric patients for assault.[215] New York's Violence Against Nurses Act[216] is an example of one state law that makes it a felony to assault a registered nurse or licensed practical nurse while he or she is working. In addition to criminal prosecution, civil cases can be brought forward in such circumstances.

The American Psychiatric Nurses Association's *Workplace Violence 2008 Position Statement* provides a comprehensive review of the problem and provides recommendations for prevention.[217] The American Nurses Association also provides detailed information on workplace violence, inclusive of state statutes.[218] These resources are important documents for risk managers. Institutions need to consider patient violence against staff to be a potential source of liability and ensure that environments are safe.

Availability of Illicit Substances

Illicit substance use in psychiatric facility units has become a pervasive problem. Family members, visitors, and staff may all be sources of illicit drugs, and many facilities have an underground drug source. Use of these substances further complicates the therapeutic process. Policies and guidelines need to state explicit rules that apply to illicit substance use in a unit. Random drug screening procedures and the right to screen for drugs need to be developed in a written statement readily available to staff and patients.

Frequently, illicit substance use in psychiatric units is met with disapproval and disgust. It is easy to forget that substance abuse is an illness. Professionals may view illicit drug use in an inpatient unit as a punitive matter and punish the patient. Although automatic discharge following noncompliance with rules may be indicated, liability issues regarding such discharge may surface. However, liability risk decreases as long as decisions are made on the basis of clinical judgments and are documented accordingly.

Professional Sexual Misconduct

Psychiatric mental health professionals must be cognizant of the ramifications of possible alleged sexual conduct and misconduct (see **Box 13-17**). Gutheil and Gabbard examined the concept of boundaries and boundary violations in clinical practice.[219] Three principles underlined the relationship among boundaries, boundary crossings, boundary violations, and sexual misconduct:

- Sexual misconduct usually starts with relatively minor boundary violations, such as last name to first name, personal conversation during sessions, some body contact such as pats on the shoulder, and trips outside the office, and ends ultimately in sexual intercourse.
- Not every boundary crossing or violation leads to or represents evidence of sexual misconduct.
- Fact finders, including juries, ethics committees, licensing boards, and professional organizations, usually believe that the presence of boundary violations or crossings is presumptive evidence of, or supports allegations of, sexual misconduct.

Box 13-17

It had all the trappings of a made-for-television movie: a prominent psychiatrist, a patient with multiple personalities, and allegations of sex. In fact, lawyers often referenced Hollywood during the sexual misconduct trial of Dr. Ronald Malave, who was found innocent of charges that he had sex with a woman who has as many as a dozen distinct personalities. But a DeLand, Florida, courtroom is a far cry from the studios of Tinseltown. Attorneys for both Malave and his accuser say the case should serve as a cautionary tale for mental health professionals and their patients.[220]

Boundary issues that clinicians need to be knowledgeable of include role; time; place and space; money; gifts, services, and related matters; clothing; language; self-disclosure and related matters; and physical contact. Although guidelines are helpful, the context of the clinical situation must be emphasized. At times, crossing a boundary may be harmless, because clinical judgment dictates the course of action. If such is the case, there must be written documentation of the rationale. Under no circumstances is a sexual relationship between a mental health professional/therapist and a patient a boundary that may be violated. From a risk management approach, a handshake is the only permissible form of physical contact.

Zur provides a comprehensive discussion of the self-disclosure in psychotherapy.[221] Knowledge of the four types of self-disclosure—deliberate, unavoidable, accidental, and patient initiated—is important for mental health therapists to recognize and as such avoid in their practice. Gabbard reports the more isolated the professional's practice is, the greatest of risk of a boundary violation.[222] He not only recommends that regular consultation be part of one's practice, but also stresses how crucial this aspect is.

To prevent boundary violations of a sexual nature, Epstein[223] and Simon[224] developed an exploitation index providing therapists with a list of questions to answer to monitor their own behavior and to act as a warning indicator of boundary violations. Risk managers can use the index for educational purposes to promote open discussion and self-awareness of boundary issues. Education is the key to the prevention of boundary violations. All healthcare professions should incorporate professional conduct issues in their educational programs, and risk managers must continue the educational process.[223–225]

Staff–Patient Sexual Misconduct

In the claim described in **Box 13-18**, the hospital was sued for not following its own policies and for not conducting an adequate employee background check. The male employee in this case had been dismissed from previous employment after pleading guilty to a similar sexual assault charge. Furthermore, the prior employer was sued by the hospital for not providing accurate information on a reference. Administrators must be observant of employee hiring policies, conduct background checks, and adhere to legislative requirements.

Box 13-18

A 22-year-old female ex-patient sued a hospital after being sexually assaulted by a male employee who had attended her while she was an inpatient. Because of her past self-destructive behaviors, the patient's physician had prescribed one-to-one observation. According to hospital policy, the observer should have been of the same sex. However, in this case the observer was a male employee.[226]

Lawsuits highlight the need for risk managers and hospital administrators to be diligent in preventing sexual abuse and assault among their employees. In one case, a worker in a psychiatric facility was sentenced to prison time for assaulting adolescent patients (see **Box 13-19**); in another case, a staff member and another patient were accused of sexual abuse of a 14-year-old. Another court ruled that a hospital has a duty to protect patients from harm, especially when vulnerable (see **Box 13-20**).

Box 13-19

Investigators uncover "credible evidence" of sexual assault at Bronx Children's Psychiatric Center. It is alleged the boy was exposed to "sexual abuse, sodomy, assault and violence" and the hospital is accused of failing to supervise the staff.[227]

Box 13-20

A 13-year-old patient with a history of sexual acting out repeatedly told staff she was going to have sex with a specific male nursing supervisor. During her hospitalization, she was accompanied by this supervisor to an area in the hospital and had sexual intercourse in the bathroom. The staff member was arrested, convicted, and sentenced to prison.[228]

Screening staff to identify individuals who may engage in sexual misconduct is very difficult and makes risk management strategies demanding. An interpretation of psychological testing, verbal language, or body language cues might indicate potential employees at high risk to engage in sexual misconduct and allow for appropriate intervention. Such evaluative techniques, however, are fraught with possible errors and potential risk liability. Accordingly, educational programs to help staff understand patient dynamics and sexual conduct may be the prudent approach.

FRAUD AND ABUSE

Fraud and abuse in psychiatry should not be overlooked by risk managers. In a competitive healthcare market, the desire for—and retention of—patients is a high priority. In the early 1990s, cases investigating fraudulent billing began. In 1991, Texas Senate hearings on complaints from patients brought attention to fraudulent and abusive psychiatric treatment and billing practices. In a settlement, National Medical Enterprises provided $2.6 million in free psychiatric services, paid millions in free psychiatric services, and paid the state $1.1 million to reimburse the investigative costs.[229] A subsequent federal investigation uncovered allegations against psychiatric hospitals throughout the nation, including the following charges:[230]

- Charging exorbitantly and billing for services never rendered
- Engaging in overly aggressive and deceptive advertising and marketing
- Holding voluntary patients against their will without medical justification
- Unnecessarily hospitalizing patients instead of using outpatient care

- Paying kickbacks or bounties for the delivery of patients to treatment facilities

At the time, investigators found specific instances of violations in several states.

In Wisconsin, a hospital paid kickbacks for patient referrals, billed for services never provided, and included billing days when the patient was not hospitalized. In Georgia, the vice president of a psychiatric hospital chain was indicted for filing false Medicare hospital cost reports.

The Medicare Fraud Strike Force established in March 2007 has charged more than 1,000 defendants with fraud costing more than $2.3 billion. Its operations are now part of the Health Care Prevention and Enforcement Action Team (HEAT), which was established in May 2009, as a joint initiative between the Department of Justice and the Department of Health and Human Services. The team's goal is prevention of fraud and enforcement of anti-fraud laws throughout the county (see **Box 13-21**). The Affordable Health Care Act has provided additional tools and resources to facilitate the goals of the team.[231]

Box 13-21

Psychiatrist Alan Gumer pleaded guilty to his role in in a $200 million scheme in which American Therapeutic Corporation (ATC), a Miami-based company of mental health clinics, falsely billed Medicare. Dr. Gumer signed false medical evaluations that qualified the patients for costly group therapy psychiatric mediation to individuals so it appeared they needed the group treatment. Millions of dollars in kickbacks were paid by ATC in support of the scheme, in which Medicare beneficiaries received unnecessary services and ATC billed the federal government for these services. Gumer could receive 10 years in prison and was fined $250,000.[232]

According to the Centers for Medicaid and Medicare Services,[233] the most common Medicaid frauds include the following offenses:

- Billing for "phantom patients" who did not really receive services
- Billing for medical services or goods that were not provided
- Billing for old items as if they were new
- Billing for more hours than there are in a day
- Billing for tests that the patient did not need
- Paying a "kickback" in exchange for a referral for medical services or goods
- Charging Medicaid for personal expenses that have nothing to do with caring for a Medicaid client
- Overcharging for healthcare services or goods that were provided
- Concealing ownership in a related company
- Using false credentials
- Double-billing for healthcare services or goods that were provided

The government has also brought action against facilities receiving federal funding and providing substandard conditions. A recent case involved the pharmaceutical company AstraZeneca, which was charged with illegally marketing its antipsychotic medication Seroquel (see **Box 13-22**). Reimbursement is intended not just for services provided, but for quality care. Likewise, individual insurance companies are monitoring for fraud and have instituted legal action when appropriate.

To prevent allegations of fraud and/or abuse, risk managers in healthcare facilities should be sure that all employees are cognizant of the institution's referral, treatment, and billing practices. Self-monitoring procedures to eliminate possible fraud and abuse are a necessity. Risk management can curtail possible fraud, such as that depicted in Box 13-21.

Box 13-22
AstraZeneca was required to pay $520 million to settle a fraud case for illegally marketing Seroquel, an antipsychotic drug, for uses not approved as safe and effective by the FDA. As a result of the company's actions, false claims for payments were submitted to federal insurance programs. The federal government will receive $301,907,007 from the civil settlement and the state Medicaid and District of Columbia will share up to $218,092,993 of the civil settlement.[234]

At the same time, adhering to Medicaid and Medicare regulations can be daunting, be confusing, and not necessarily constitute intent to fraud.[235] Risk mangers need to assist professionals and facilities in clarifying confusing regulations and preventing billing errors. Fraud and abuse compromise the care rendered to patients. Professionals need to be alert to fraud and abuse by their colleagues, and initiate

Box 13-23
A Missouri psychiatrist was charged with being involved in "upcoding," or billing for work not performed. He spent approximately 5 minutes or less with patients and billed Medicaid for 20 minutes. In a related civil settlement, he agreed to pay $830,329 and be excluded from the Medicare program. His former employer agreed to reimburse the U.S. government an additional $865,812 for his false charges to Medicare.[236]
A Tennessee psychologist was sentenced to 18 months in prison for submitting false and fraudulent claims to Medicaid and Medicare programs. He created a billing scheme to defraud the federal government for claims not provided and that were known to him to be false, totaling $3 million.[237]

appropriate professional and legal remedies in such cases (see **Box 13-23**).

PSYCHIATRIC CONCERNS ARE EVERYWHERE

Awareness of the unique potential risk when treating patients with psychiatric problems is not intended to produce paranoia among mental health professionals. Rather, practitioners must be enlightened about occupational realities. With current treatment modalities, patients with mental illness can be cared for in acute care facilities. Even if the facility has a small number of psychiatric beds, the risk manager must be alert to the distinctive potential for liability risks. Only when therapists are informed can optimal care be provided to the patients. In addition, being knowledgeable about risk liabilities protects professionals and institutions while they tend to their patients.

REFERENCES

1. Rile, B. (1995, February 4). Mental patient sues institutions, says workers let him eat objects. *Star-Ledger* (Newark, N.J.), p. 7, col. 1.

2. Teich, C. (1994). Risk management in the psychiatric setting. In B. Youngberg (Ed.), *Risk management desk reference* (pp. 445–454). Gaithersburg, MD: Aspen.

3. Leo, R. J. (1999). Competency and the capacity to make treatment decisions: A primer for primary practitioners. *Primary Care Companion to the Journal of Clinical Psychiatry, 5,* 131–141.

4. University of California, San Diego. (2002). Decision making capacity guidelines. UCSD Human Research Protections Program. http://irb.ucsd.edu/decisional.shtml.

5. Orr, R. D. (2004, March 10). Center for Bioethics and Human Dignity. Competence, capacity, and surrogate decision-making. http://cbhd.org/content/competence-capacity-and-surrogate-decision-making.

6. Wysoker, A. (2000). Informed consent: The ultimate right. *Journal of the American Psychiatric Nurses Association, 6,* 100–102.

7. Appelbaum, P. S., Grisso, T., Frank, E., O'Donnell, S., & Kupfer, D. (1999). Competence of depressed patients for consent to research. *American Journal of Psychiatry, 156,* 1380–1384.

8. Wirshing, D. A., Wirshing, W. C., Marder, S. R., Liberman, R. P., & Mintz, J. (1998). Informed consent: Assessment of comprehension. *American Journal of Psychiatry, 155,* 1508–1511.

9. Carpenter, W. T. Jr., Gold, J. M., Lahti, A. C., Queern, C. A., Conley, R. S., Bartko, J. J., . . . Appelbaum, P. S. (2000). Decisional capacity for informed consent in schizophrenia research. *Archives of General Psychiatry, 57,* 533–538.

10. Informed consent among people with schizophrenia. (2002, July). *American Journal of Psychiatry.*

11. Appelbaum, P. S., and Grisso, T. (1988). Assessing patients' capacities to consent to treatment. *New England Journal of Medicine, 319*(25), 1635–1638.

12. Grisso, T., Appelbaum, P. S., & Hill-Fotouhi, C. (1997). A clinical tool to assess patients' capacities to make treatment decisions. *Psychiatric Services, 48,* 1415–1419.

13. Grisso, T., Appelbaum, P. S., & Hill-Fotouhi, C. (1998). *A clinical tool to assess patients' capacities to make treatment decisions: The MacArthur Competence Assessment Tool treatment.* Sarasota, FL: Professional Resource Press.

14. Grisso, T., Appelbaum, P. S., Mulvey, E. P., & Fletcher, K. (1995). The MacArthur Treatment Competence Study II: Measures of abilities related to competence to consent to treatment. *Law and Human Behavior, 19,* 127–148.

15. Grisso, T., & Appelbaum, P. S. (1995). The MacArthur Treatment Competence Study III: Abilities of patients to consent to psychiatric and medical treatments. *Law and Human Behavior, 19,* 149–174.

16. MacArthur Research Network on Mental Health and the Law. (2001). The MacArthur Treatment Competence Study. http://macarthur.virginia.edu/treatment.html

17. MacArthur Research Network on Mental Health and the Law. (2004, May). The MacArthur Treatment Competence Study: Executive summary. http://www.macarthur.virginia.edu/treatment.html

18. American Psychiatric Association Official Actions. (1998). Guidelines for assessing the decision making capacities of potential research subjects with cognitive impairment. *American Journal of Psychiatry, 155,* 1649–1650.

19. Velllinga, A., Smit, J. H., van Leeuwen, E., van Tilburg, W., & Jonker, C. (2004). Instruments to assess decision-making capacity: An overview. *International Psychogeriatrics, 16,* 397–419. doi: 10.1017/S1041610204000808

20. Author: Dunn, L. B., Palmer, B. W., Appelbaum, P. S., Saks, E. R., Aarons, G. A., & Jeste, D. V. (2007). Prevalence and correlates of adequate performance on a measure of abilities related to decisional capacity: Differences among three standards for the MacCAT-CR in patients with schizophrenia. *Schizophrenia Research, 89*(1), 110–118. doi: 10.1016/j.schres.2006.08.005

21. Dunn, L. B., & Jeste, D. V. (2001). Enhancing informed consent for research and treatment. *Neuropsychopharmacology, 24*(6), 595–607.

22. Wirshing, D. A., Sergi, M. J., & Mintz, J. (2005). A videotape intervention to enhance the informed consent process for medical and psychiatric treatment research. *American Journal of Psychiatry, 162*(1), 186–188. doi: 10.1176/appi.ajp.162.1.186

23. Jeste, D. V., Palmer, B. W., Golshan, S., Eyler, L. T., Dunn, L. B., Meeks, T., . . . Appelbaum, P. (2009). Multimedia consent for research in people with schizophrenia and normal subjects: A randomized controlled trial. *Schizophrenia Bulletin, 35*(4), 719–729. http://schizophreniabulletin.oxfordjournals.org/content/35/4/719.full

24. Appelbaum, P. (2006). Decisional capacity of patients with schizophrenia to consent to research: Taking stock. *Schizophrenia Bulletin, 32*(1), 22–25.

25. Guido, G. W. (2010). *Legal and ethical issues in nursing* (5th ed.). Upper Saddle River, NJ:Pearson.

26. Galen, K. D. (1993). Assessing psychiatric patients' competency to agree to treatment plans. *Hospital & Community Psychiatry, 44*(4), 361–363.

27. Beahrs, J. O., & Gutheil, T. G. (2001). Informed consent in psychotherapy. *American Journal of Psychiatry, 158*(1), 4–10.

28. Campbell, T. W. (1999). Issues in forensic psychology: Psychotherapy malpractice. http://www.campsych.com/malpractice.htm

29. Wenning, K. (1993). Long-term psychotherapy and informed consent. *Hospital & Community Psychiatry, 44*(4), 364–366.

30. Saks, E. R. (2011). *Informed consent to psychoanalysis: The law, the theory, and the data.* University of Southern California Law School. University of Southern California Legal Studies Working Paper series: Paper 75. http://law.bepress.com/usclwps/lss/art75

31. US researchers fail to get informed consent. (1994). *British Medical Journal, 308*(6931), 739.

32. U.S. Department of Health and Human Services. (2002). Human subject protections. http://os.dhhs.gov

33. National Bioethics Advisory Commission. (2001). *Ethical and policy issues in research involving human participants.* Bethesda, MD: Author. http://www.bioethics.gov

34. U.S. Department of Health and Human Resources, U.S. Food and Drug Administration. (2009). CFR. Title 21. Subpart B—Informed Consent of Human Subjects. http://www.accessdata.fda.gov/scripts/cdrh/cfdocs/cfcfr/CFRSearch.cfm?CFRPart=50&showFR=1&subpartNode=21:1.0.1.1.19.2

35. National Bioethics Advisory Commission. (1998). Research involving persons with mental disorders that may affect decisionmaking capacity. www.bioethics.gov

36. American Association on Mental Deficiency. (1998). Center for the Study of Ethics in the Professions, Illinois Institute of Technology. American Association of Mental Deficiency statement on the use of human subjects for research, adopted May 1969, verified on April 21, 1998. http://www.iit.edu/departments/csep/PublicWWW/codes

37. American Association on Mental Deficiency, Legislative and Social Issues Committee. (1977). *Consent handbook.* Special publication no. 3. Washington, DC: Author.

38. Morgan, G. A., Harmon, R. J., & Gliner, J. A. (2001). Ethical problems and principles in human research. *Journal of the American Academy of Child and Adolescent Psychiatry, 40*(10), 1231–1233.

39. Advisory Work Group on Human Subject Research Involving Protected Classes. (1998). *Recommendations on the oversight of human subject research involving the protected classes.* Albany: Department of Health, State of New York.

40. *Final report of the Attorney General's Research Working Group*. (1998). Baltimore: Office of the Maryland Attorney General.

41. Heinssen, R. K., Perkins, D. O., Appelbaum, P. S., & Fenton, W. S. (2001). National Institute of Mental Health Workshop: Informed consent in early psychosis research. *Schizophrenia Bulletin, 27*(4), 571–584.

42. American Psychiatric Association. (2006). Ethical principles and practices for research involving human participants with mental illness. *Psychiatric Services, 57*, 552–557. doi: 10.1176/appi.ps.57.4.552

43. Mental Health America. (2007). Position statement 26: Participant protections in psychiatric research. http://www.mentalhealthamerica.net/go/position-statements/26

44. Yanos, P. T., Stanley, B. S., & Greene, C. S. (2009). Research risk for persons with psychiatric disorders: A decisional framework to meet the ethical challenge. *Psychiatric Services.* doi: 10.1176/appi.ps.60.3.374

45. U.S. Department of Health and Human Resources. (n.d.). Research with children-45 CFR 46.402(a). Special protections for children as research subjects. http://www.hhs.gov/ohrp/

46. U.S. Department of Health and Human Resources. (n.d.). Office of Human Subject Protections (OHRP). http://www.hhs.gov/ohrp/

47. Hoop, J. G., Smyth, A. C., & Roberts, L.W. (2008). Ethical issues in psychiatric research on children and adolescents. *Child and Adolescent Psychiatric Clinics of North America, 17*(1), 127–148.

48. *Wyatt v. Stickney*, 344 Fed. Supp. 373 (1972).

49. Keglovits, J. (1992). Legal issues and clients' rights. In K. S. Wilson & C. R. Kneisel (Eds.), *Psychiatric nursing* (pp. 930–952). Redwood City, CA: Addison-Wesley.

50. *Dixon v. Weinberger*, 405 Fed. Supp. 974 (1975).

51. Garritson, S. H. (1983). Degrees of restrictiveness in psychosocial nursing. *Journal of Psychosocial Nursing, 21*(12), 9–16.

52. *In re Turnbough*, 34 S.W.3d 225 (Mo.App., 2000).

53. *Salcido v. Woodbury County*, 119 F.Supp.2d 900 (N.D Iowa, 2000).

54. U.S. Department of Health and Human Services, National Institutes of Health, & National Institute of Mental Health. (2008). National Institute of Mental Health Strategic plan. NIH Publication No. 08-6368. http://www.nimh.nih.gov/about/strategic-planning-reports/nimh-strategic-plan-2008.pdf

55. Hospital closures and the Medicaid IMD Exclusion. (n.d.). www.psychlaws.org/Hospital/Closure/Index.htm

56. Fact sheet: Criminalization of Americans with severe mental illnesses. (n.d.). www.psychlaws.org

57. Torrey, E. F., Kennard, A. S., Eslinger, D., Lamb, R., & Pavle, J. (2010, May). More mentally ill persons are in jails and prisons than hospitals: A survey of the states. http://www.treatmentadvocacycenter.org/storage/documents/final_jails_v_hospitals_study.pdf

58. The shortage of public hospital beds for mentally ill persons: A report of the Treatment Advocacy Center. (2008, March). http://www.treatmentadvocacycenter.org/storage/documents/the_shortage_of_publichospital_beds.pdf

59. Treatment Advocacy Center. (2011). Deinstitutionalization. http://www.treatmentadvocacycenter.org/a-failed-history

60. Treatment Advocacy Center. (2011). Consequences of non-treatment. http://www.treatmentadvocacycenter.org/problem/consequences-of-non-treatment

61. Treatment Advocacy Center. (2009–2010, winter). Public libraries: Unintended shelters. Catalyst. http://www.treatmentadvocacycenter.org/storage/documents/winter_2009.pdf

62. Treatment Advocacy Center. (2011). Fast facts. http://www.treatmentadvocacycenter.org/problem/fast-facts-

63. Clary, M. (2002, July 11). The snake pit: The county jail is one of the largest psychiatric facilities in Florida. *Miami News Times.* www.miaminewtimes.com.

64. Geller, J. (1990). Clinical guidelines for the use of involuntary outpatient treatment. *Hospital & Community Psychiatry, 41*(7), 749–755.

65. Treatment Advocacy Center. (2011). Assisted outpatient treatment: Backgrounder. http://www.treatmentadvocacycenter.org/solution/getting-involved/471-assisted-outpatient-treatment

66. New York Mental Hygiene Law §9.31 (c) §9.01 (c) §9.60 (c).

67. Treatment Advocacy Center (TAC) model law for assisted treatment. (2000). Arlington, VA. www.psychlaws.org

68. Treatment Advocacy Center. (2011). Treatment Advocacy Center model law. http://www.treatmentadvocacycenter.org/legal-resources/tac-model-law

69. Miller, R. D. (1999). Coerced treatment in the community. *Psychiatric Clinics of North America, 22*(1), 183–194.

70. Sabin, J. E., & Daniels, N. (1994). Determining "medical necessity" in mental health practice. *Hastings Center Report, 24*(6), 5–13.

71. American Psychiatric Association, Committee on Nomenclature and Statistics. (1994). *Diagnostic and statistical manual of mental disorders* (4th ed.). Washington, DC: Author.

72. Ford, W. E. (2000). Medical necessity and psychiatric managed care. *Psychiatric Clinics of North America, 23*(2), 309–317.

73. New York State Insurance Department. (n.d.). Timothy's Law: Information about mental health parity. http://www.ins.state.ny.us/timothy.htm

74. U.S. Department of Health and Human Services, Centers for Medicare and Medicaid Services. (2011). The Mental Health Parity and Addiction Equity Act of 2008. https://www.cms.gov/Health InsReformforConsume/04_TheMentalHealth ParityAct.asp#TopOfPage

75. U.S. Department of Health and Human Services. (2010, August 19). The Affordable Care Act & mental health: An update. http://www.healthcare.gov/news/blog/mentalhealthupdate.html

76. Wysoker, A., Agrati, G., Collins, J., Marcus, P., & Thelander, B. (2004, December). Legal and ethical considerations: Mandatory outpatient treatment. *Journal of the American Psychiatric Nurses Association, 10*, 247b–253.

77. Geller, J. (2000). The use of advance directives by persons with serious mental illness for psychiatric treatment. *Psychiatric Quarterly, 71*(1), 1–13.

78. Mental Health Treatment Preference Declaration Act, Illinois Stat. Public Act 86-1190. (1990).

79. Scheyett, A., Kim, M., Swanson, J., & Swartz, M. (2007). Psychiatric advance directives: A tool for empowerment and recovery. *Psychiatric Rehabilitation Journal, 31*(1), 70–75.

80. Srebnik, D. S., & Russo, J. (2007). Consistency of psychiatric crisis care with advance directive instructions. *Psychiatric Services.* doi: 10.1176/appi.ps.58.9.1157

81. Appelbaum, P. (2006). Commentary: Psychiatric advance directives at a crossroads—When can PADs be overridden? *Journal of the American Academy of Psychiatry and the Law, 34*, 395–397.

82. Van Dorn, R.A., Swanson, J. W., Swartz, M. S., Elbogen, E., Ferron, J. (2008). Reducing barriers to completing psychiatric advance directives. *Administration and Policy in Mental Health and Mental Health Services Research, 35*(6), 440–448. doi: 10.1007/s10488-008-0187-6

83. Swartz, M. S., Swanson, J. W., Van Dorn, R. A., Elbogen, E. B., & Shumway, M. (2006). Patient preferences for psychiatric advance directives. *International Journal of Forensic Mental Health, 5*(1), 67–81.

84. National Resource Center on Psychiatric Advanced Directives. (n.d.). State by state info. http://www.nrc-pad.org/content/view/282/83/

85. *Rogers v. Okin,* 478 F. Supp. 1342 (1979).

86. Stuart, G. W. (1995). Legal context of psychiatric nursing care. In G. Stuart & S. J. Sundeen (Eds.), *principles and practice of psychiatric nursing,* (pp. 171–197). St. Louis: Mosby.

87. Brooks, A. (1988). Law and ideology in the case of Billie Boggs. *Journal of Psychosocial Nursing and Mental Health Service, 26*(7), 22–25.

88. *Arthur v. Lutheran General Hospital, Inc.,* 692 N.E.2d 1238 (Ill App., 1998).

89. *Wingate v. Ridgeview Institute, Inc.,* 504 S.E.2d 714 (Ga. App., 1998).

90. *Miguel v. Barron,* New York Court of Appeals, 2011 NY Int. 78, May 10, 2011, No. 76.

91. Treatment Advocacy Center. (2011). Who we are and what we do. http://www.treatmentadvocacycenter.org

92. Goldstein, S. (2011, May 21). Feds alerted to Gabrielle Giffords shooter three months before Tucson massacre. *NYDailyNews.com.*

93. New York State Education Department. (1993). *Nursing handbook.* Albany: NYSED, pp. 24–27.

94. Certification of nurse practitioners/clinical nurse specialists. (1993). *New Jersey Register* (Trenton, NJ), pp. 2829–2833.

95. Laraia, M. T. (1995). Psychopharmacology. In G. Stuart & S. J. Sundeen (Eds.), *Principles and practice of psychiatric nursing* (pp. 663–701). St. Louis: Mosby.

96. Feltner, D. E., & Hertzman, M. (1993). Progress in the treatment of tardive dyskinesia: Theory and practice. *Hospital & Community Psychiatry, 44*(1), 25–33.

97. Malinconico, J. (1995, April 2). $700,000 to settle big suit: County paid up to avoid bigger losses. *News Tribune* (Woodbridge, NJ), p. A17, col. 1.

98. Chouinard, G., & Margolese, H.C. (2005). Manual for the Extrapyramidal Symptom Rating Scale (ESRS). *Schizophrenia Research, 76*(2), 247–265.

99. American Psychiatric Association. (1992). *Tardive dyskinesia: A task force report*. Washington, DC: Author, pp. 217–226, 231–251.

100. Benjamin, S., & Munetz, M. R. (1994). Community mental health center practices related to tardive dyskinesia screening and informed consent for neuroleptic drugs. *Hospital & Community Psychiatry, 45*(4), 343–346.

101. McElroy, E., Conn, V., & Huff, B. (1994). Persons experiencing the effects of mental disorders: What psychiatric nurses need to know about medication management: The family perspective. In *Psychiatric mental health nursing psychopharmacology project* (pp. 59–61). Washington, DC: American Nurses Publishing.

102. Tardive Dyskinesia Center. (n.d.). http://www.tardivedyskinesia.com/

103. Lacro, J. P., Sewell, D. D., Warren, K., et al. (1994). Improving documentation of consent for neuroleptic therapy. *Hospital & Community Psychiatry, 45*(2), 176–178.

104. Baghai, T. C., & Moller, H. J. (2008). Electoconvulsive therapy and its different indications. *Dialoques Clinical Neuroscience, 10*(1), 105–117.

105. Fitzsimons, L. M., & Mayer, R. L. (1995). Soaring beyond the cuckoo's nest: Health care reform and ECT. *Journal of Psychosocial Nursing and Mental Health Services, 33*(12), 10–13.

106. Kellner, C. (2010). ECT today: The good it can do. *Psychiatric Times.* http://www.psychiatrictimes.com/electroconvulsivetherapy/content/article/10168/1665079

107. Kellner, C. (2011). Electroconvulsive therapy: The second most controversial medical procedure. *Psychiatric Times, 28*(1). http://www.psychiatrictimes.com/display/article/10168/1793704

108. Kelly, K. G., & Zisselman, M. (2000). Update on electroconvulsive therapy (ECT) in older adults. *Journal of the American Geriatrics Society, 48*(5), 560–566.

109. Mayo, C., Kaye, A. D., Conrad, E., Baluch, A., & Frost, E. (2010). Update on anesthesia considerations for electroconvulsive therapy. *Middle East Journal of Anesthesiology, 20*(4), 493–498.

110. American Psychiatric Nurses Association. (2011). APNA position statement: Electroconvulsive therapy. http://www.apna.org/i4a/pages/index.cfm?pageid=4448

111. American Psychiatric Association. (2001). *A task force report on the practice of electroconvulsive therapy: Recommendations for treatment, training and privileging* (2nd ed.). Washington, DC: Author.

112. American Psychiatric Association. (1996). Electroconvulsive therapy (ECT). http://ww.psych.org/public_info/ ect~1.cfm

113. National Institute of Mental Health. (2010). Suicide in the U.S.: Statistics and prevention. http://www.nimh.nih.gov/health/publications/suicide-in-the-us-statistics-and-prevention/index.shtml

114. The Joint Commission. (2011). Sentinel event. http://www.jointcommission.org/sentinel_event.aspx

115. The Joint Commission. (2011). Topic library item: Sentinel events trends reported by year. Suicide events reviewed by The Joint Commission. Sentinel event data: Event type by year: 1995–fourth quarter 2010. http://www.jointcommission.org/assets/1/18/Event_Type_by_Year_1995-4Q2010(v2).pdf

116. The Joint Commission. (2010, November 17). A follow-up report on preventing suicide: Focus on medical/surgical units and the emergency department. Issue 46. http://www.jointcommission.org

117. New York State Office of Mental Health. (2009, June). Incident reports and root cause analyses 2002–2008: What they reveal about suicides. http://www.omh.ny.gov/omhweb/statistics/suicide_incident_rpt/

118. *Hooper v. County of Cook*, 2006 WL. 1319458 (Ill. App., May 15, 2006).

119. *Reid v. Altieri*, 2007 WL 750596 (Fla. App., March 14, 2007).

120. *In re Baptist Hospitals of Southeast Texas*, 2006 WL 2506412 (Tex. App., August 31, 2006).

121. *Soderman v. Smith*, 2007 WL 2389564 (Super. Ct. Sacramento Co. Cal., July 13, 2007).

122. *Kinchen v. Gateway Community Service Board*, 2006 WL 3803014 (11th Cir., December 28, 2006).

123. Medical malpractice cases: Inpatient suicide. (2002). Abramson, Brown and Duga. www.arbd.com/bases/mm.inpasuic.html

124. Silverman, M. M., Berman, A. L., Bongar, B., et al. (1994). Inpatient standards of care and the suicidal patient. Part II: An integration with clinical risk management. *Suicide and Life-Threatening Behavior, 24*(2), 152–169.

125. The Joint Commission. (1998, November 6). Sentinel event alert. Inpatient suicides:

Recommendations for prevention. Issue. http://www.jointcommission.org

126. Tishler, C. L., & Reis, N. S. (2009). Inpatient suicide: Preventing a common sentinel event. *General Hospital Psychiatry, 31*(2), 103–109.

127. Janofsky, J. S. (2009). Reducing inpatient suicide risk: Using human factors analysis to improve observation practices. *Journal of the American Academy of Psychiatry and the Law, 37*(1), 15–24.

128. American Psychiatric Association. (2009). *Safe MD: Practical applications and approaches to safe psychiatric practice. Safe passage through suicide risk: Navigating the failure modes.* http://www.psych.org/Departments/QIPS/Downloads/SAFEMD.aspx

129. Slovenko, R. S. (1999). Malpractice in psychotherapy: An overview. *Psychiatric Clinics of North America, 22*(1).

130. Rissmiller, D., Steer, R., Ranieri, W., et al. (1994). Factors complicating cost containment in the treatment of suicidal patients. *Hospital & Community Psychiatry, 45*(8), 782–788.

131. Doctors study why elderly are so prone to suicide. (2002, July 23). Associated Press. www.cnn.com/2002/HEALTH/07/023/elderly.suicide.ap/index.html

132. U.S. Department of Health and Human Services. (n.d.). The Health Insurance Portability and Accountability Act of 1996 (HIPAA) privacy and security rules. Health information privacy. http://www.hhs.gov/ocr/privacy/

133. The Surgeon General's call to action to prevent suicide. (1999). http://www.surgeongeneral.gov/library/calltoaction/fact1.htm

134. The Children's Health Act of 2000: A summary. Title XXXII—provisions relating to mental health. http://www.samhsa.gov/legislate/Sept01/child-health_title32.htm

135. 1999 Patients' Rights Condition of Participation (CoP) Interim Rule, the Final Rule 42CFR Part 482. *Federal Register*/Vol.71, No. 236/Friday, December 8, 2006/Rules and Regulations. United States Department of Health and Human Services, Centers for Medicare and Medicaid Services. (2011). 42 CFR Part 482, Medicare and Medicaid Programs; Hospital Conditions of Participation: Patients' Rights; Final Rule.

136. State operation manual: Appendix A. Interpretative guidelines—hospitals. www.hcfa.gov/pubforms/07_som/somap_a_171_to_196.htm

137. Sheridan, M., Hourion, R., Robinson, L., et al. (1990). Precipitants of violence in a psychiatric inpatient setting. *Hospital & Community Psychiatry, 41*(7), 776–780.

138. Klinge, V. (1994). Staff opinions about seclusion and restraint at a state forensic hospital. *Hospital & Community Psychiatry, 45*(2), 138–141.

139. Betemps, E. J., Somoza, J., & Buncher, R. (1993). Hospital characteristics, diagnoses, and staff reasons associated with use of seclusion and restraint. *Hospital & Community Psychiatry, 44*(4), 367–371.

140. Larue, C., Dumais, A., Ahern, E., Bernheim, E., & Mailhot, M. P. (2009). Factors influencing decisions on seclusion and restraint. *Journal of Psychiatric and Mental Health Nursing, 16*(5), 440–446. doi: 10.1111/j.1365-2850.2009.01396.x

141. Stokowski, L. (2007). Alternatives to restraint and seclusion in mental health settings: Questions and answers from psychiatric nurse experts. *Medscape Nurses News, Nursing Perspectives.* http://www.medscape.com/viewarticle/555686

142. Needham, H., & Sands, N. (2010). Post-seclusion debriefing: A core nursing intervention. *Perspectives in Psychiatric Care, 46*(3), 221–233. doi: 10.1111/j.1744-6163.2010.00256.x

143. Hellerstein, D. J., Staub, A. B., & Lequesne, E. (2007). Decreasing the use of restraint and seclusion among psychiatric inpatients. *Journal of Psychiatric Practice, 13*(5), 308–317.

144. Pollard, R., Yanasak, E. V., Rogers, S. A., & Tapp, A. (2007) Organizational and unit Factors contributing to reduction in the use of seclusion and restraint procedures on an acute psychiatric inpatient unit. *Psychiatric Quarterly, 78*(1), 73–81. doi: 10.1007/s11126-006-9028-5

145. Sclafani, M. J., Humphrey, F. J., Repko, S., Haeng, D. S., Wallen, M. C., & DiGiacomo, A. (2008). Reducing patient restraints: A pilot approach using clinical case review. *Perspectives in Psychiatric Care, 44*(1), 32–39. doi: 10.1111/j.1744-6163.2008.00145.x

146. Muralidharan, S., & Fenton, M. (2006). Containment strategies for people with serious mental illness. *Cochrane Database of Systematic Reviews, 3*, CD002084. doi: 10.1002/14651858.CD002084.pub2

147. Sailas E. E. S., & Fenton, M. (2000). Seclusion and restraint for people with serious mental illnesses.

Cochrane Database of Systematic Reviews, 1, CD001163. doi: 10.1002/14651858.CD001163

148. New York State Office of Mental Health. (2009). Comfort rooms: A preventative tool used to reduce the use of restraint and seclusion in facilities that serve individuals with Mental illness. http://www.omh.state.ny.us/omhweb/resources/publications/comfort_room/

149. American Nurses Association. (2010). *Nursing: Scope and standards of practice.* Washington, DC: Author.

150. American Psychiatric Nurses Association. (2007). Seclusion and restraint position statement. http://www.apna.org/i4a/pages/index.cfm?pageid=3729

151. American Psychiatric Association. (2009). *safe MD: Practical applications and approaches to Safe psychiatric practice. Aggression: Reducing risk in the management of aggressive patients.* http://www.psych.org/Departments/QIPS/Downloads/SAFEMD.aspx

152. *Hanson v. Hospital of Saint Raphael,* 2007 WL. 2317825 (Conn. Super., July 20, 2007).

153. Johnson, V. P. (1994). Psychiatry. In *Risk management handbook for health care facilities* (pp. 165–176). L. M. Harpster & M. S. Veach. (Eds.), Chicago: American Hospital Publishing.

154. Ragonese, L. (2002, August 2). Another Greystone patient escapes on a public bus. *Star-Ledger* (Newark, NJ), p. 32, col. 1.

155. *Estate of Hollan v. Brookwood Medical Center,* 2007 WL 912202 (Ala. Cir. Ct., February 15, 2007).

156. *Hofflander v. St. Catherine's Hospital,* 635 N.W.2d 13 (Wis. App., 2001); confirmed 2001 WL 21499928 (Wisconsin, July 1, 2001).

157. *Ball v. Charter Behavioral Health,* WL 2422866 (La., App., August 23, 2006).

158. American Psychiatric Association. (2009). *Safe MD: Practical applications and approaches to safe psychiatric practice. Elopement: A primer on safety and prevention.* http://www.psych.org/

159. National Association of State Mental Health Program Directors Research Institute, Inc. (1999–2010). National public rates: Elopement rate. Behavioral healthcare performance measurement system. http://www.nri-inc.org/reports_pubs/2010/National_Public_Rates.pdf

160. McKinley, J. C. (1994, November 25). 3 officials are demoted after slaying at mental hospital. *New York Times,* p. B5, col. 1.

161. Harpaz, B. J. (1995, January 7). Pataki fires deputy mental health commissioner. *Staten Island Advance* (New York), p. A3, col. 1.

162. Jaffe, I. (2011, April 7). At California mental hospitals, fear is part of the job. National Public Radio.

163. Guyer, M. J. (1990). Child psychiatry and legal liability: Implications of recent case law. *Journal of American Academy of Child Adolescent Psychiatry, 29*(6), 958–962.

164. Editorial: Injustice for children. (2010, July 16). *New York Times,* Opinion Pages.

165. Faille, L., Clair, M., & Penn, J. (2007). Special risk management issues in child and adolescent psychiatry. *Psychiatric Times, 24*(8).

166. Wagner, K. D., Pollard, R., & Wagner, R. F. Jr. (1993). Malpractice litigation against child and adolescent psychiatry residency programs, 1981–1991. *Journal of American Academy of Child Adolescent Psychiatry, 32*(2), 462–465.

167. Association of Child and Adolescent Psychiatric Nurses. (n.d.). Practice parameters: Child and adolescent inpatient psychiatric treatment. http://www.ispn-psych.org/html/white_papers.html

168. U.S. Department of Health and Human Services. (1999). Introduction and themes, Chapter 1: The roots of stigma. www.surgeongeneral.gov/library/mentalhealth/chapter1/sec1.html

169. *Cedars Healthcare Group, Ltd., v. Freeman,* 2002 WL 31466407 (Fla.App., November 6, 2002).

170. U.S. Department of Health and Human Services. (2002). Modifications to the standards for privacy of individually identifiable health information—final rule. http://www.hhs.gov/news/press/2002pres/20020809a.html

171. Levy, R., & Rubenstein. (1996). *The rights. People with mental disabilities: The authoritative ACLU guide to the rights of people with mental illness and mental retardation.* Carbondale, IL: American Civil Liberties Union.

172. *Jaffe v. Redmond,* 64 U.S.L.LW 4491 (1996). *Jaffe v. Redmond,* U.S. 1 (1996).

173. Ciccone, J. R. (1999). The United States Supreme Court and psychiatry in the 1990s. *Psychiatric Clinics of North America, 22*(1), 197–211.

174. 20 Rev.Litig. 1 (2000).

175. Wysoker, A. (2001). Confidentiality. *Journal of the American Psychiatric Nurses Association, 7*, 57–58.

176. *Evans v. Benson*, 2007 WL 1299261 (Iowa, May 4, 2007).

177. *DeJesus v. United States Department of Veterans Affairs*, 2007 WL 454726 (3rd.Cir., March 14, 2007).

178. *Stewart v. North Coast Center*, 2006 WL 1313098 (Ohio App., May 12, 2006).

179. Monahan, J. (1993). Limiting therapist exposure to Tarasoff liability. *American Psychologist, 48*(3), 242–250.

180. Felthous, A. R. (1999). The clinician's duty to protect third parties: Forensic psychiatry. *Psychiatric Clinics of North America, 22*(1), 49–60.

181. Felthous, A. R. (2001). Introduction to this issue: The clinician's duty to warn or protect. *Behavioral Sciences & the Law, 19*(3), 321–324. doi: 10.1002/bsl.445

182. U.S. Department of Health and Human Services, Administration for Children and Families, Administration on Children, Youth and Families, Children's Bureau. (2010). Child maltreatment 2009. http://www.acf.hhs.gov/programs/cb/stats_research/index.htm#can

183. Administration on Aging. (2000). Elder abuse prevention. http://www.aoa.dhhs.gov/factsheets/abuse.html

184. U.S. Department of Health and Human Services, National Center on Elder Abuse, Administration of Aging. (2011). http://www.ncea.aoa.gov/ncearoot/Main_Site/index.aspx

185. Mulvey, E. (1994). Assessing the evidence of a link betwen mental illness and violence. *Hospital & Community Psychiatry, 45*(7), 663–962.

186. Otto, R. K. (1992). Prediction of dangerous behavior: A review and analysis of "second generation" reports. *Forensic Reports, 5*, 103–138.

187. Staznickas, K. A., McNiel, D. E., & Binder, R. L. (1993). Violence toward family caregivers by mentally ill relatives. *Hospital & Community Psychiatry, 44*(4), 385–387.

188. Blomhoff, S. B., Seim, S., & Friis, S. (1990). Can prediction of violence among psychiatric inpatients be improved? *Hospital & Community Psychiatry, 41*(7), 771–775.

189. Elbogen, E. B., Van Dorn, R. A., Swanson, J. W., Swartz, M. S., & Monahar, J. (2006). Treatment engagement and violence risk in mental disorders. *British Journal of Psychiatry, 189*, 354–360.

190. Alia-Klein, N., O'Rourke, T., Goldstein, R. Z., & Malaspina, D. (2007). Insight into illness and adherence to psychotropic medications are separately associated with violence severity in a forensic sample. *Aggressive Behavior, 33*(1), 86–96.

191. MacArthur Research Network on Mental Health and the Law. (2002). The MacArthur Community Violence Study. http://macarthur.virginia.edu/violence.html

192. Steadman, H., Mulvey, E., Monahan, J., Robbins, P., Appelbaum, P., Grisso, T., . . . Silver, E. (1998). Violence by people discharged from acute psychiatric inpatient facilities and by others in the same neighborhoods. *Archives of General Psychiatry, 55*, 393–401.

193. McNiel, D. E., & Binder, R. L. (1994). The relationship between acute psychiatric symptoms, diagnosis,and short-term risk of violence. *Hospital & Community Psychiatry, 45*(2), 133–137.

194. Krakowski, M. I., & Czobor, P. (1994). Clinical symptoms, neurological impairment, and prediction of violence in psychiatric inpatients. *Hospital & Community Psychiatry, 45*(7), 700–705.

195. Briefing paper: Violence and severe untreated mental illness. (Updated 2002, June). Treatment Advocacy Center. http://www.psychlaws.or/default.htm

196. Torrey, E. F. (1994). Violent behavior by individuals with serious mental illness. *Hospital & Community Psychiatry, 45*(7), 653–662.

197. Corrigan, P. W., Yudofsky, S. C., & Silver, J. M. (1993). Pharmacological and behavioral treatments for aggressive psychiatric inpatients. *Hospital & Community Psychiatry, 44*(2), 125–132.

198. Davis, S. (1991). Violence by psychiatric inpatients: A review. *Hospital & Community Psychiatry, 42*(6), 585–589.

199. Monahan, J., Steadman, H., Appelbaum, P., et al. (2000). Developing a clinically useful actuarial tool for assessing violence risk. *British Journal of Psychiatry, 176*, 312–319.

200. Monahan, J., Steadman, H., Silver, E., et al. (2001). *The MacArthur study of mental disorder and violence.* New York: Oxford University Press.

201. Monahan, J., Steadman, H. J., Robbins, P. C., Appelbaum, P., Banks, S., Grisso, T., ... & Silver, E. (2005). An actuarial model of violence risk assessment for persons with mental disorders. *Psychiatric Services, 56*(7), 810–815.

202. Monahan, J., & Steadman, H. J. (1994). Toward a rejuvenation of risk assessment research. In *Violence and mental disorder: Developments in risk assessment* (pp.1–17). J. Monahan & H. Steadman. (Eds.), Chicago: University of Chicago Press.

203. Steadman, H., Monahan, J., Appelbaum, P. S., et al. (1994). Designing a new generation of risk assessment research. In *Violence and mental disorder: Developments in risk assessment* (pp. 297–318). J. Monahan & H. Steadman. (Eds.), Chicago: University of Chicago Press.

204. Sullivan, C., & Yun, C. (1995). Workplace assaults on minority and mental health care workers in Los Angeles. *American Journal of Public Health, 85*(7), 1011–1014.

205. Anderson, T., & Wen, P. (2011, January 20). Employee allegedly killed by client at Revere mental health facility. *Boston Globe.* Boston.com

206. Family of slain Peabody social worker files wrongful death suit. (2011, April 21). PeabodyPatch.org

207. The Joint Commission. (2010, June 3). Sentinel event alert: Preventing violence in the health care setting. Issue 45. http://www.jointcommission.org/sentinel_event_alert_issue_45_preventing_violence_in_the_health_care_setting_/

208. Gould, J. (1994). The impact of change on violent patients. *Nursing Standard, 8*(19), 38–40.

209. Gadon, L., Johnstone, L., & Cooke, D. (2006) Situational variables and institutional violence: A systematic review of the literature. *Clinical Psychology Review, 26*(5), 515–534.

210. Moylan, L. B., & Cullinan, M. (2011) Frequency of assault and severity of injury of psychiatric nurses in relation to the nurses' decision to restrain. *Journal of Psychiatric and Mental Health Nursing, 18.* doi: 10.1111/j.1365-2850.2011.01699.x

211. Lu, C. H., Wang, T. F., & Liu. C. Y. (2007). Psychiatric nurses' reactions to assault upon them by inpatients: A survey in Taiwan. *Psychology Republic, 100*(3), 777–782.

212. Ryan, J., & Porter, E. (1989). The assaulted nurse: Short-term and long-term responses. *Archives of Psychiatric Nursing, 3*(6), 323.

213. Lanza, M. L. (1983). The reactions of nursing staff to physical assault by a patient. *Hospital & Community Psychiatry, 34*(1), 44–47.

214. Lanza, M. L. (1984). A follow-up study of nurses' reactions to physical assault. *Hospital & Community Psychiatry, 35*(5), 492–494.

215. Phelan, L., Mills, M., & Ryan, J. (1985). Prosecuting psychiatric patients for assault. *Hospital & Community Psychiatry, 36*(6), 581–582.

216. New York State Nurses Association. (2010). Violence against nurses law takes effect Nov. 1. www.nysna.org

217. American Psychiatric Nurses Association. (2008). Workplace violence: APNA 2008 position statement: Executive summary. http://www.apna.org/i4a/pages/index.cfm?pageid=3786

218. American Nurses Association. (2011). Workplace violence. www.nursingworld.org

219. Gutheil, T., & Gabbard, G. O. (1993). The concept of boundaries in clinical practice: Theoretical and risk management dimensions. *American Journal of Psychiatry, 150*(2), 188–196.

220. Haun, M. (2002, April 27). Acquittal draws attention to rarity of sexual misconduct by psychiatrists. *The Daytona Beach News-Journal.*

221. Zur, O. (2010). Self-disclosure and transparency in psychotherapy and counseling: To disclose or not to disclose, this is the question. from http://www.zurinstitute.com/selfdisclosure1.html

222. Ibid.

223. Epstein, R. S. (2002). Post-termination boundary issues. *American Journal of Psychiatry, 159*(5), 877–885.

224. Simon, R. I. (1999). Therapist–patient sex: From boundary violations to sexual misconduct. Forensic psychiatry. *Psychiatric Clinics of North America, 22*(1), 31–47.

225. Gabbard, G. O., & Nadelson, C. (1995). Professional boundaries in the physician–patient relationship. *Journal of the American Medical Association, 273*(18), 1445–1449.

226. Spoto, M. (1994, November 18). Expatient sues hospitals after sexual assault. *Star-Ledger* (Newark, NJ), p. 42, col. 3.

227. Marzulli, J. (2010, January 28). Investigators uncover "credible evidence" of sexual assault at Bronx Children's Psychiatric Center. *New York Daily News.* NYDailyNews.com

228. *Unnamed Patient v. Unnamed Private Psychiatric Hospital,* 2007 WL 1765189 (Sup Ct. Los Angeles Co. Cal., May 30, 2007).

229. Johnsson, J. (1995). Feds expand fraud investigation. *American Medical News, 38*(20), 3, 27–28.

230. Baine, D. P. (1993). *Psychiatric fraud and abuse.* HRD-93-92. Washington, DC: Government Accounting Office, p. 3.

231. HHS Secretary Sebelius, U.S. Attorney General Holder kick-off first regional health care fraud prevention summit in Miami, Florida. (2010, July 16). http://www.hhs.gov/news/press/2010pres/07/20100716a.html

232. United States Department of Justice, Office of Public Affairs, (2011, June 30). Miami-area psychiatrist pleads guilty for role in $200 million Medicare fraud scheme. http://www.justice.gov/opa/pr/2011/June/11-crm-871.html

233. U.S. Department of Health and Human Services, Centers for Medicare and Medicaid Services. (2005, December 14). Most common Medicaid rip offs and fraud schemes. http://www.cms.gov/FraudAbuseforConsumers/04_Rip_Offs_Schemes.asp

234. Pharmaceutical giant AstraZeneca to pay $520 million. (2010, April 27). U.S. Department of Health and Human Services. http://www.hhs.gov/news/press/2010pres/04/20100427a.html

235. Ibid.

236. St. Louis psychiatrist admits lying to FBI in Medicare probe. *St. Louis Business Journal,* (2010, October 12). http://www.bizjournals.com/stlouis/stories/2010/10/11/daily17.html?surround=etf&ana=e_article

237. United States Department of Justice, Western District of Tennessee, (2011, March 21). United States District Court sentences psychologist for false billings to Medicaid and Medicare. http://www.justice.gov/usao/tnw/news/2010/2010JUN28Semrau.html

CHAPTER 14

Telemedicine

Gary H. Harding and Alice L. Epstein

It's an interesting world in which today's generation lives. Clinicians who have been in the workforce for 20 to 50 years or longer can recall the days when "telemedicine" for health care consisted of a nurse calling a physician or support service on the rotary dial telephone. The conversation was then recorded with handwritten notes in the patient's paper medical chart, capturing the sense of the need for and the results of the conversation.

In contrast, a newly graduated healthcare professional today is expected to have significant experience with remote wireless telephones, telemetry, mobile applications (apps), and computer applications that transform the communication device into a medical device, provide a view of patient data (e.g., images) from a patient thousands of miles away, and reproduce administrative or medical record information about all aspects of the patient's care and billing. Some clinicians have embraced the technology and changes as they have occurred, while others have stubbornly placed personal and sometimes field of influence roadblocks in the way of acceptance of the technology and changes, and still others have "gone along for the ride" somewhere in the middle, grasping what they can when they can.

Regardless of where we might find ourselves on this today, technology advances are inevitable and deemed by the federal government to both improve the quality of health care and control the cost.[1] It is important for healthcare providers to take a three-pronged approach to telemedicine:

- Accept new technology with enthusiasm.
- Embrace change and contribute to it.
- Maintain a healthy degree of skepticism and be vigilant in identifying and addressing risks that may heretofore been non-issues.

These three approaches are not inconsistent with one another and are the very basic ingredients for success.

The good news is that healthcare clinicians are, in general, a uniquely inquisitive and motivated group who have a high degree of ability to succeed in this realm of technology. Control of the inherent risks requires understanding what the technologies are, how the technology is used, who the users and recipients of information are, and the value of the information derived from the technology. The risk manager and user of the information should plan for and anticipate problems and potential adverse events.

TELEMEDICINE DEFINED

Put succinctly, telemedicine is the collection and communication of healthcare information—specifically, clinical information as opposed to administrative information—over a distance via telecommunication and/or information systems from one site to another.[2] For the purposes of this chapter, the discussion of telemedicine does not encompass telemetry within the same facility. It also does not include physician billing systems or remote dictation of medical notes. Moreover, a clinician's use of a wireless laptop to conduct an online medical literature search related to analysis of a current patient's possible condition is not part of the discussion.

Telemedicine is primarily a twentieth- and twenty-first-century technological advance. Predecessors to the societal and technological development can be found in telegraphic auditory signals (Morse code) and radio communications from fixed locations to ambulances or helicopters.

The terms "telehealth," "m-health," and "e-health," are not the same as "telemedicine" and should not be used interchangeably with the latter term.[3] The former terms typically include broad, more diverse activities other than clinical care, such as medical education, patient education, research, and administrative aspects of health information technology. Various information media may confuse these terms and inappropriately use them interchangeably. Careful attention to the reported activity versus actual definition is recommended. This chapter deals primarily with telemedicine and only occasionally touches on telehealth, m-health, or e-health.

Although the American Telemedicine Association defined telemedicine as the "use of medical information exchanged from one site to another via electronic communication to improve patients' health status," it includes "medical education" (continuing medical education [CME]) and "consumer medical and health information"—nonclinical services that have no direct effect in improving an individual patient's health status. This chapter recognizes the position of the primary professional association dealing with telemedicine and includes discussions of the following services:

- Patient consultation service
- Specialist referral service
- Remote patient monitoring service
- Consumer medical and health information service and social media

An alternative means of categorizing telemedicine is to view how the actual process occurs and contributes to health care:

- Store and forward
- Remote monitoring
- Interactive service in real time

According to one study, 90% of physicians routinely use a smartphone during their workday to access medically related information.[4] Another study predicts that by 2015, 30% of the world's smartphone users will use mobile health apps—a 5% increase from 2011.[5]

In this chapter, the alternative means of categorizing telemedicine are periodically identified within the "Telemedicine Services" review to demonstrate how these categories may be utilized independently or in combination within a service. Data and patient information privacy and security, and resultant breaches of them, will not be discussed in this chapter. Vigilance to maintain privacy of patient information is paramount to the success of all telemedicine programs.

TELEMEDICINE SERVICES _____

The paradigm and taxonomy of telemedicine is in a continual state of development. Although the American Telemedicine Association is actively developing and improving both, they are not always in accordance with the systems used by the major stakeholders, including American National Standards Institute, ASTM International (formerly known as American Society for Testing and Materials), U.S. Department of Health and Human Services, U.S. Food and Drug Administration, and Health Resources and Services Administration Office of Rural Health Policy for the Advancement of Telehealth.[6] The categories described within this chapter follow commonly accepted practice, but are not all-inclusive or exhaustive.

Patient Consultation

Patient consultation entails an exchange of medical data between the patient and a remote physician. Uses include a patient in a remote clinic, for example, where a "live visual and audio feed" of the patient is provided to the physician for the purpose of diagnosis and treatment. In the event a physician is not available on-site (e.g., in a rural clinic staffed primarily by nurses), this service allows the clinician on-site to draw upon the clinical training and experience of a more experienced healthcare provider whenever a question arises or a more complex diagnosis or prescription is needed. Rural healthcare providers who operate in low population densities find online and remote patient consultation particularly useful. Where low population densities exist, exposure to a wide variety and large number of disease entities is unlikely, so providers may not have opportunities to gain experience diagnosing and treating

such diseases. Generating the financial resources to support full-time, high-level medical professionals is also unlikely in this setting. Hence, availability of patient consultation services is an improvement to the quality of care in underserved rural areas.

Studies have shown that patients have the ability to recall important components of both face-to-face and telephone consultations—perhaps reflecting the familiar, less anxiety-provoking environment of primary care.[7]

Further, while quite difficult to measure, the overall cost of health care may be reduced by telemedicine patient consultation because the need for the patient to travel long distances to receive diagnostic tests is reduced and therapeutic treatments can occur earlier in the process, thereby reducing morbidity.

It is important to note that Medicare reimbursement for telehealth is currently limited. To qualify for reimbursement, specific requirements must be met regarding the location of the patient, the professional provided the telemedicine services, and the type of services provided.[8]

Specialist Referral Service

Physicians and advanced practice clinicians may need to consult a specialist from another discipline to gain additional insight into the clinical findings or to confirm (or rule out) a diagnosis. Historically, physicians accomplished this type of consultation by communicating with a physician of known expertise in the hallway of the hospital, by mail or telephone, or by sending the patient in person to meet with the specialist. This process could be slow, costly, and dangerous for the patient, or result in lack of communication or miscommunication. Today, the treating physician can set up a "live" Internet video teleconference where the patient, the treating physician, and the consulting specialist are in the same "virtual room" at the same time. The treating physician, or even the patient, can send vital diagnostic information (e.g., images, ECGs) to the consulting specialist, who may be better prepared and trained to perform an accurate analysis of the information. There is even a Health Insurance Portability and Accountability Act (HIPAA)–compliant mobile messaging smartapp that allows physicians to find and communicate with each other.

Major medical specialties that utilize telemedicine to provide consultations include radiology, dermatology, ophthalmology, psychology/psychiatry, pain management, cardiology, rehabilitation, and pathology. These specialties represent a mix of fields in which treatment is highly dependent on images and data (e.g., radiology, pathology, cardiology), while others (psychiatry, pain management, and rehabilitation) are dependent on intense patient interaction.[9–11]

Radiology makes great use of Internet technology through which diagnostic images, including plain-film X-rays, CT, PET, MRI, and other images, taken in locations across the globe, are sent to a consulting specialist in another location for analysis. The process includes the normal image collection device (e.g., the X-ray machine) and typically relies on a computer sending system, a transmission system (e.g., DSL, Internet), and a computer receiving system.

Remote Patient Monitoring

Remote patient monitoring uses medical devices to collect patient data and send these data to a remote location for expert analysis. This service has been in use for more than 20 years. Examples include collection of patient vital signs such as ECG or respiratory effort over lengthy periods. Examples include Holter monitoring (long-term collection of ECG data) and apnea monitoring (long-term collection of breathing effort and heart rate data) to identify adverse clinical events occurring in the daily life of an at-home patient. With this service, the patient is attached to a medical monitoring device through electrodes to collect and store data over a lengthy period. Once the data collection period is complete, the data are transmitted through an online or telecommunication modem to a center for expert interpretation. Staff at the center may then perform computer-assisted analysis of the data and provide recommendations either directly to the patient or to the patient's physician.[12]

This service is also being used for monitoring of blood glucose, fetal condition, blood pressure, weight, hemoglobin, and other related home healthcare services. Essentially, as long as a patient is connected to a medical device that can monitor a specific vital sign or other clinical parameter, there is no technologic barrier to those data being forwarded in real time, daily, or less frequently to the remote location for analysis.[13]

Consumer Medical and Health Information and Social Media

Consumer medical and health information services use the Internet as a vehicle for consumers (e.g., patients) to gain information about specific health topics or to share information with one another. Numerous websites are dedicated to consumer education, some of which are provided by federal and state governments, public health departments, pharmaceutical companies, disease-specific associations, commercial enterprises, healthcare systems/

hospitals, and even individuals with no training or creditable expertise.[14]

Social media is, by definition, a group of Internet-based applications that builds on the ideology and technological foundations of the World Wide Web, and that allows the creation and exchange of user-generated content (UGC).[15] Social media and blogs sponsored by all of those sources noted previously provide the public and clinicians with the opportunity to communicate individual experiences to one another.[16] The public's ability to obtain detailed healthcare information outside the historical doctor–patient relationship (e.g., support, education) has many positive aspects, and there is a certain therapeutic value to sharing experiences and resources with others in a similar position.[17] However, the potential for misinformation, misinterpretation of information, and unintentional/ unexpected public release of sensitive, otherwise confidential, and protected information is a major drawback of such exchanges.

Telenursing

Telenursing programs at the primary care level include disease management, prescription refill monitoring, medication and symptom management, lab test and results monitoring, and patient education.[18,19]

Managed care organizations and healthcare plan insurers are continually seeking ways to decrease emergency department and primary care physician utilization. Inroad in this sense made in accountable care organizations and patient-centered medical homes are forecasted to be growth opportunities for telemedicine. Telemedicine is also well positioned to meet the fundamental objectives of increasing patient satisfaction, creating a patient-centered system

through care coordination, and reducing costs even though current Medicare regulations do not allow for reimbursement of such services.[20]

Nurse advice telephone systems have been commercially available since 1987 with the founding of Ask-A-Nurse. As the provision of basic health care is moving away from the specialized physician and out of the acute care facility to outpatient or home services, nursing professionals are moving to the forefront of direct patient care and monitoring. The use of telemedicine to connect patient and nurse makes sense, especially in rural, remote, or low-population-density locations. State-specific Nurse Practice Acts may or may not specifically address telemedicine, but the Nurse Practice Acts and state regulations do address what constitutes nursing practice. Delegation of medical acts is defined by state-specific medical regulations, but may or may not address telemedicine.

Telepharmacy

Prescription services, medication fulfillment and delivery, medication monitoring, and medication management make up the complex offerings within telepharmacy. State regulations and state Boards of Pharmacy are primarily responsible for the regulation of the practice of telepharmacy. These regulations vary tremendously with respect to what is legally permissible in each state in which the telepharmacy is located, where the prescribing physician is located, and where the patient is located.[21]

One scenario places a licensed pharmacist at a central pharmacy site; that individual supervises a registered pharmacy technician at a remote telepharmacy through the use of videoconferencing technology. The technician prepares the prescription drug. The pharmacist communicates face-to-face in real time with the technician and the patient through audio and video computer links. Licensed pharmacists provide traditional pharmacy services, including drug utilization review, prescription verification, and patient counseling to a remote site via telepharmacy technology.

Telepharmacy in rural hospitals is well positioned to improve medication safety, according to a study by the Upper Midwest Rural Health Research Center.[22] While useful for traditional activities such a drug dispensing, drug therapy monitoring, and patient consultation, telepharmacy is expected to become more essential to identifying undesirable potential individual patient drug interactions and monitoring formulary compliance.

Access to pharmacists and pharmacy information is subject to similar constraints as access to clinical healthcare providers, information, and education. The ability for pharmacists to remotely provide their services makes the availability and use of telemedicine essential. U.S. House of Representatives and Senate versions of the Online Pharmacy Safety Act of 2011 have been introduced to Congress, and the final bill is expected to pass in late 2012; it will clarify the limits of telepharmacy.

Some Internet and mail-order pharmacies provide only medication ordering and prescription fulfillment services. A recent study of 60 online pharmacies found that those evaluated did not provide an adequate level of security for the consumers' personal data, with the majority of flaws being cross-site scripting or old versions of software that had not been updated.[23] More than 96% of online pharmacies operate illegally, according to the National Association of Boards of Pharmacy (NABP). As of December 31, 2011, NABP had assessed 8,789 Internet drug outlets selling prescription medications and found 96.21% of them to be out of compliance with state and federal pharmacy laws and practice standards.[24]

Telerehabilitation

Rehabilitation following injury or illness, whether physical or other functional or cognitive impairment (e.g., due to stroke, auditory injury or illness, brain or nervous system injury), often takes a lengthy period of time. Historically, rehabilitation was provided on an inpatient basis or as an outpatient through repeated visits to a clinic. Many times, the patient graduated to home self-care with periodic visits to a facility for determination of progress between visits. For those persons with disabilities or constrained by long travel times or costs, rehabilitation according to standard protocols might be difficult. Telemedicine, however, allows the rehabilitation specialist to perform clinical assessments and institute or modify clinical therapy.

As in many basic and specialized healthcare areas, making a diagnosis or changing treatment in rehabilitation is highly dependent on what the patient tells the provider and what the clinician sees and hears. For example, the rehabilitation specialist can use telemedicine to determine how a patient with speech impairment is progressing, using the patient consultation service to visualize and hear the patient in real time. Perhaps the specialist may be able to keep closer tabs on the patient's progress, or lack thereof, by more frequent interactions than scheduled clinic visits might allow.

An evaluation of 61 Australian telerehabilitation studies that involved 12 clinical categories found 71% of the telerehabilitation applications were successful. The reported outcomes for 51% of the applications appeared to be clinically significant. The authors concluded that telerehabilitation shows promise in many fields, but compelling evidence of its benefits and impact on routine rehabilitation programs is still limited.[25]

Emergency Telemedicine

Sometimes referred to as teletrauma, the use of telemedicine in emergency medicine from the first point of patient contact via the emergency department (ED) and throughout the continuum into critical care is an essential component of an effective emergency management system (EMS). Telemedicine services are essential to everyday ED practice in many ways—from the ability for nonclinical first responders (e.g., the user of an automated external defibrillator [AED] to respond to a person who has suffered a cardiac event) or even patients themselves (e.g., a patient with an implantable pacemaker) to use medical devices to determine the onset of a life-threatening or otherwise dangerous event and immediately pass this information along to a healthcare professional, to the emergency response crew being able to forward essential patient data at the scene or in transit to a higher-level professional, to the Level 1 facility emergency department seeking the expertise of the Level 3 facility professionals.

While historically, professional emergency responders depended on radio and telephone connections, the public had no access to the emergency management system's specialized radios and lacked the skills and experience necessary to ascertain many important signs or symptoms to pass along to healthcare professionals on the telephone—except perhaps that the person was not breathing and they could not feel a pulse. Telemedicine—whereby an easily attached medical device measures the important patient vital signs, the responder-specific important labels or, better yet, automatically transmits the data to the remote location, and subsequently may even provide life-saving treatment—is a vast improvement in responding to and treating potentially life-threatening events in a timely manner. Where time is of the essence, as it is in life-threatening events occurring outside the healthcare facility, telemedicine makes a difference.[26]

Smartapps are also appearing on the scene. One example allows the EMS provider to record a log of critical events with a time stamp. The provider can record vitals, interventions, take notes, and then email them to a higher-level professional.

RISK MANAGEMENT TACTICS

Telemedicine includes a mix of clinical and technological risks. The clinical risk regularly occurring in both standard inpatient and outpatient care remains prevalent in telemedicine and is complicated by the additional systems and personnel required for use of telemedicine. Due to the relative newness of application of telemedicine in many areas both clinical and administrative, risk expertise is not as voluminous as in many areas. Adding to the difficulty in precisely identifying and quantifying all of the risks potentially associated with telemedicine are the following issues:

- A lack of large-scale, randomized, controlled, clinical trials

- Variability of state regulations
- A lack of significant case law
- A lack of significant claims studies focusing on the topic

Risk management requires the identification of priorities. Telemedicine entails a vast array of risk management concerns. Risk management involvement and review are most effective when the decision to implement telemedicine technology is being considered. Highly specific and individualistic risk management techniques and applications may be necessary, although use of system techniques that a facility routinely applies to new or emerging technologies may be helpful. Departmental experts to be consulted in addition to the risk manager should include the clinical departments affected, nursing, biomedical engineering, information technology, communications, facility engineering, and ancillary support departments expected to interact with the technology.

Clinical Care Risks

Telemedicine used in a clinical specialty does not eliminate the inherent risks of that specialty's provision of care. For example, failure to diagnose and misdiagnosis are recognized risks inherent in radiology. Whether performed through interpretation of a hard-copy image at a facility or remotely via telemedicine, a radiologist can fail to diagnose or misdiagnose a patient based on the data provided. Similarly, a cardiologist examining an ECG, whether straight from the monitor and printer or remotely viewed on a smartphone, can fail to diagnose an event properly or provide a misdiagnosis.

Proficiency in using telemedicine as a conjunctive aid to clinical practice is not a foregone conclusion for clinicians. For example, while a radiologist might have years of experience examining images on film, it is a valid concern that the same level of expertise may not be present when viewing the image on a tablet computer screen or, for that matter, a smartphone screen. It is important that those making use of and contributing to telemedicine be formally credentialed and privileged to participate in telemedicine. It is also important to ensure that those using or contributing to telemedicine maintain their licenses to practice.

Generally, if the risk is inherent to the clinical specialty as described elsewhere in this text without the use of telemedicine, it remains inherent to the clinical specialty even with the use of telemedicine.

Complications in patient care can arise from the following sources:

- Patient noncompliance without the knowledge of the clinician
- Patient misinterpretation or inability to relate the patients's conditions to the tele-clinican
- Inability of the patient to recall or understand directions and instructions
- Clinician misinterpretation of data
- Medication errors

Clinical Care Risk Recommendations

Clinical risk management and patient safety requirements should always be applied to telemedicine services. Clinical protocols for telemedicine should be equal to or higher than the protocols in place for the same clinical service, regardless of where or how care is delivered. When examining inpatient and outpatient clinical service risk management practices, the risk manager must ensure that the modifications take into consideration the unique properties of telemedicine as applied in the individual system. Ensure that all clinicians involved with the telemedicine program are properly licensed, credentialed, and privileged. Ensure the management and documentation of necessary education, training, orientation, and continuing education.

Pay attention to details in developing, capturing, and memorializing standard operating procedures, and individual deviations from these procedures, throughout the telemedicine system.

Define consent and the consent process to include telemedicine. Include and allow individual deviations where necessary or desirable, but define the deviations.

Develop an adverse event identification, reporting, and response program that ensures the complete participation of the telemedicine program.

Refine the quality improvement, patient safety, and risk management programs to capture, include, and analyze the activities and data of telemedicine participants.

Administrative Risks

As in all clinical practice, there must be an evaluation of the clinical aspects of quality improvement, patient safety, and risk management. Is the use of telemedicine adding to or detracting from the quality of care, or is it increasing or decreasing the morbidity and mortality? Along with credentialing, privileging, and licensing risks, other recognized administrative risks include the following:

- Lack of, inappropriate, incomplete, or non-adherence to operational policies and procedures (e.g., the opportunity for significant inconsistencies among remote providers of telemedicine services serving a facility)

- Lack of consistent quality improvement, patient safety, and risk management programs, systems, analysis, and action between telemedicine users and the facilities with which they interact (e.g., consider the increased complexity of individual satellite providers adhering to consistent program requirements for not one facility, but among and consistent with each facility to which they consult)

- Lack of, inconsistent, or incomplete contracts for services, facilities, resources, or responsibilities

- Lack of, inconsistency or incompleteness of the definition of the provider–patient relationship (e.g., risk of assertions of patient abandonment)

- Failure to obtain informed consent (e.g., a specialist using telemedicine prescribes treatment, but that treatment is actually carried out in the patient care location without either party obtaining and documenting informed consent from the patient)

- Training and competencies (e.g., the remote location misinterprets the fetal heart rate recording and, as a result, provides improper treatment or fails to provide treatment)

- Integration of telemedicine into workflow (e.g., needed therapy does not occur in a timely manner because initiation of a consult or analysis is delayed)

- Communication and chain of command (e.g., the primary responsibility for care of a specific patient)

- Documentation (e.g., the specialist using telemedicine provides a prescription, but the issuance and patient use of that prescription are not translated to those with primary responsibility for the patient and a medication error with sequalae results)

- Adverse event notification (e.g., an adverse event recognized by one location or the other occurs, but is not transmitted to the other location, which may then repeat the error on the same or another patient unnecessarily)

Another risk deserves special attention—jurisdiction. If the patient is in one location and the specialist is in another location, where does the jurisdiction lie? If the patient injury results in Texas, but the treatment plan or misdiagnosis occurred in France (or Washington, Minnesota, or New York), which country or state law has jurisdiction? As no clear case law specifically related to telemedicine exists, each litigated case may make new case law, with the question of specific outcomes unassured and unassurable.

Administrative Risk Recommendations

Use accepted practices to perform a needs analysis and to identify system requirements with specificity throughout each and every "telemedicine system."

Define in the contract and/or by policy and procedure what constitutes a provider–patient relationship—and adhere to that definition.

Perform a contracts analysis to determine what contracts for telemedicine services should include.

Determine and memorialize jurisdiction—for example, in the event of a lawsuit, "the law of the state of [insert state] will be used." In addition to providing some guidance to what parties have agreed to, advantages from a risk treatment perspective may arise from prospectively, and in writing, placing the jurisdiction in one locale versus another.

Ensure that all environments within the telemedicine program are ethical and legal.

Technological Risks

Telemedicine gives rise to questions about how the technology (equipment and methods) can be implemented safely to meet the goals of telemedicine. A review of technology systems failure demonstrates that as the number of technological implements and actions increase, the potential for and number of failures likewise increase. Recognize that currently the following conditions prevail:

- Few clinical reviews exist in telemedicine and no large, random analysis has been performed.
- Systems in use vary dramatically by device(s) and by method(s).
- No standardization exists to which systems and methods must adhere.

Risk generally rises as the number of devices in the treatment line increases, but no definitive study has been performed to indicate that this is the case in telemedicine. Indeed, the area of technical risk in telemedicine is in its infancy. Identification and minimization of risk associated with telecommunication systems (including interactive systems) are not in their infancy, however, and the system risks identified therein have direct application to telemedicine.

The basic technical risks of telemedicine to clinical care are threefold:

- Equipment and function do not meet the need.
- If equipment and function meet the need, performance does not.
- Derived data are or become corrupt or unlawfully shared.

Technology and methods need to faithfully reproduce the provider–patient–data interfaces. Sometimes that means an electrical signal (e.g., a vital sign) needs to be faithfully reproduced. At other times, it may mean an image, a patient skin color, motion or sound, or thoughts are faithfully reproduced. The accuracy of this reproduction is critical because the factor is essential to proper diagnosis and treatment even in the inpatient and outpatient environments. This issue becomes compounded when a medical device is created by using a standard mobile telecommunications platform (e.g., a smartphone), attaching a front-end sensor from a manufacturer or distributor other than the smartphone manufacturer, and controlling the hardware using a mobile platform application designed by a second or third manufacturer or distributor. Questions arise about (1) whether the specifications and performance of this "medical device" are both safe and comparable to the medical device manufactured by a recognized medical device manufacturer, and (2) who is liable for a failure. While the U.S. Food and Drug Administration (FDA) appears to have examined the first issue as it relates to a mobile platform application, it is questionable whether a clear avenue to liability for the smartphone, front-end, or application manufacturer would exist. Would the home or clinical user or the prescriber be liable for application design, use, and resulting clinical outcome?

It is important to note and to discuss applications that are currently in use, approved for use, and expected to increase through smartphones, tablet computers, personal digital assistants, or similar mobile platform receiving, sending, and viewing systems. Use and innovation are expanding so rapidly that FDA recently published draft guidance for mobile medical applications and noted its intent to "apply its authority" to this area.[27]

Assume the technology and methods *do* meet the need. But what if a link in the system is subject to periods of inability to use it (e.g., smartphone outage, inability to send or receive large files) whether because of device failure, software problems, or "an act of God"? If a telemedicine system is "unreasonably" susceptible to failure, redundant or backup systems are most probably required, although they may not be in place.

HIPAA requires secure control of patient-related information. The federal requirement that all medical records in the United States be converted into the electronic format by 2014 has to be an important consideration in the implementation of telemedicine. As mobile platforms and applications expand, so are breaches of data security. If a breach of financial data, confidential phone message information, or sensitive company research and development is now considered an everyday occurrence, it stands to reason that breaches of sensitive medical information are not far behind and, of course, have already occurred. Actual and potential future differences in federal and state requirements for data control and security and the associated risks can be identified and, therefore, subjected to analysis for risk treatment and minimization.

Essential risks to be addressed include the following issues:

- Equipment availability and function
- Safe environment
- Data generation, access, storage, archiving, and retrieval
- Lack of system redundancies and backup, and lack of an intrusion detection and response system

- Failure of software/hardware bridges and interfaces
- Data breach, disclosure, and regulatory notification
- Electronic discovery and variations between federal and state rules

Technological Risk Recommendations

Use available professionals to perform a needs analysis, system specification, and analysis of responses to request for proposals for systems to be used in the telemedicine program.

Once system hardware and software have been configured, perform a simulated pre-use test to ensure that both hardware and software are performing properly. Ensure that recognized risks and important aspects of the system faithfully reproduce all the characteristics of the provider–patient–data triad necessary to perform the intended functions.

Develop and institute a periodic maintenance and performance procedure to ensure that the telemedicine system continues to perform properly and adequately. Ensure that systems are in place to encourage users of the telemedicine system to report idiosyncrasies, problems, failures, or other concerns to a centralized reporting and analysis system.

If all or a portion of a telemedicine system can be viewed as a "medical device," a "mobile platform or application," or other system subject to standard, requirements, or guidelines, examine the system or portion to assure that it complies with these protocols.

Carefully, carefully, carefully, and with expertise, evaluate the data security program throughout the system. Periodically and routinely, evaluate the behavior of the users of the telemedicine system to ensure they understand and are adhering to data protection methods.

Identify newly recognized existing or potential routes of data corruption and address them.

Ensure redundant systems are in place for critical connectivity and that appropriate redundant clinical video and exam equipment is available for critical clinical encounters and clinical functions.

Consumer Medical and Health Information Services and Social Media Risks

Participation in and support of consumer medical and health information services carries some risk, though substantial case law in this area is currently lacking. The use of social media to share this information further compounds the risk. Two basic edicts are important to support and understand: (1) sharing medical information, experience, and support in the public domain has merit; and (2) misinformation from nonexperts is prevalent and to be expected. Participation in consumer medical and health information services requires a willingness to consider the potential value of perspectives and experiences of patients and providers, as well as a willingness to apply a healthy degree of skepticism when assessing the correctness of information.

Increasing the complexity by having a clinician participate in social media, a healthcare system, or other corporation actively participating in and soliciting customer interactions via social media or an entity promoting unproven and unsubstantiated treatments/therapy can create problems that are more complex. The reality is that some information is supportable in fact and some is patently absurd, yet given credence in the social media. Differentiating between the two unfortunately can be beyond the education and training of the public, and other factors (e.g., mistrust or fear of medical professionals, personal fears of disease, hopes of a miracle) can influence decision making.[28]

Also, there is the possibility of unlawful release of patient-specific information where a "controlled access" database really is not controlled or where whisper-down-the-lane occurs and sensitive information initially shared between two necessary entities finds its way to a third, fourth, or open entity for access by potentially millions of people (e.g., if it goes "viral"). Some corporations now require individuals to share access to their social media pages as part of the pre-employment process, and no clear case law has been established in U.S. courts indicating that such practice is a violation of privacy. Consider the risk that arises, for example, if the individual who has recommended an applicant for a job is also a social media participant and that participant has shared with the job applicant that he or she is currently seeking employment elsewhere or undergoing mental health counseling.

Social media also pose a risk to clinicians who use social media to serve their patients. Just as a patient may not understand, misinterpret, or misuse clinical advice, a user of telemedicine-provided advice via social media might do so as well.

Consumer Medical and Health Information Services and Social Media Risks

Review the U.S. Department of Health and Human Services' *General Guidance for Utilization of New and/or Social Media* (www.hhs.gov/web/policies/webstandards/socialmedia.html).

Develop a consumer health education and social media plan that includes the following elements:[29]

- Policies and procedures governing use
- Social media definition, scope, and limitations
- Privacy and confidentiality requirements
- Rules of use and behavior
- Identification and rules for organization-hosted sites and non-organization-hosted sites
- Copyright laws
- Proprietary information
- Conflict of interest
- Disclaimer
- Best practices
- Education and training requirements as applicable to individual and all staff
- Crisis plan

REFERENCES

1. U.S. Department of Health and Human Services, Office of the National Coordinator for Health Information Technology. (2012). Improving patient care. http://healthit.hhs.gov/portal/server.pt/community/healthit_hhs_gov__home/1204

2. American Telemedicine Association. (2012). *Telemedicine defined.* Washington, DC: Author. http://www.americantelemed.org/i4A/pages/index.cfm?pageid=3333

3. American Telemedicine Association. (2012). *Telemedicine/telehealth terminology.* Washington, DC: Author. http://www.americantelemed.org/files/public/abouttelemedicine/Terminology.pdf

4. Bulletin Healthcare. (2011, March 16). *Physician mobile use grows 45%; Apple® dominates Android™ and Blackberry®.* Reston, VA: Author. http://www.bulletinhealthcare.com/PressReleases/MobileData.pdf

5. research2guidance. (2012, January 12). *Mobile health market report 2011–2016: The impact of smartphone applications on the mobile health industry.* Berlin, Germany: Author.

6. Bashshur, R., Shannon, G., Kawpinski, E., & Grigsby, J. (2011). The taxonomy of telemedicine. *Telemedicine and e-Health, 17*(6), 484–494.

7. McKinstry, B., Watson, P., Elton, R., Pinnock, H., Kidd, G., Meyer, B., . . . Sheikh, A. (2011). Comparison of the accuracy of patients' recall of the content of telephone and face-to-face consultations: An exploratory study. *Postgraduate Medical Journal, 87*(1028), 394–399.

8. Center for TeleHealth and eHealth Law. (2012, February). Medicare reimbursement checklist: Telehealth originating site facility fee. Washington, DC: Author. http://ctel.org/wp-content/uploads/2012/02/Medicare-Reimbursement-Checklist-Telehealth-Originating-Site-Facility-Fee-2012-February-2012.pdf

9. McGeary, D. D., McGeary, C., & Gatcher, R. (2012, February 5). A comprehensive review of telehealth for pain management: Where we are and the way ahead. *Pain Practice.*

10. Kumar, S., Wang, E. H., Pokabla, M., & Noecker, R. (2012, February 3). Teleophthalmology assessment of diabetic retinopathy fundus images: Smartphone versus standard office computer workstation. *Telemedicine Journal of Electronic Health, 18*(2), 158–162.

11. Brand, J., & Mckay, D. (2012, January 31). Telehealth approaches to obsessive–compulsive related disorders. *Psychotherapy Research, 22*(3), 306–310.

12. Pekmezaris, R., Mitzner, I., Pecinkar, K. R., Nouryan, C. N., Lesser, M. L., Siegel, M., & Swiderski, J. W. (2012, January 27). The impact of remote patient monitoring (telehealth) upon Medicare beneficiaries with heart failure. *Telemedicine Journal of Electronic Health, 18*(2), 101–108.

13. Bui, A. L., & Fonarow, C. G. (2012). Home monitoring for heart failure management. *Journal of the American College of Cardiology, 59*(2), 97–104.

14. North, F., Ward, W. J., Varhey, P., & Tulledge-Sheitel, S. M. (2012, February 24). Should you search the Internet for information about your Acute symptom? *Telemedicine Journal of Electronic Health.*

15. Kaplan, A. M., & Haeniein, M. (2010). Users of the world, unite! The challenges and opportunities of social media. *Business Horizons, 53*(1).

16. Ford, E. W., Huerta, T. R., Schilhavy, R. M., & Mennchemi, N. (2012). Effective US health system websites: Establishing benchmarks and standards for effective consumer engagement. *Journal of Healthcare Management, 57*(1), 47–64, discussion, 64–65.

17. Neiger, B. L., Thacheray, R., Var-Wagersen, S. A., Harson, C. L., West, J. H., & Barnes, M. D. (2012). Use of social media in health promotion: Purposes, key performance indicators, and evaluation metrics. *Health Promotion Practices, 13*(2), 159–164.

18. Vinson, M. H., McCallum, R., Thornton, D. R., & Champagne, M. T. (2011). Design, implementation, and evaluation of population-specific telehealth nursing services. *Nursing Economics, 29*(5), 265–272.

19. Naditz, A. (2009). Telenursing: Front-line applications of telehealthcare delivery. *Telemedicine Journal of Electronic Health, 15*(9), 825–829.

20. Roop, E. S. (2011). Can telehealth reduce costs? *For the Record, 23*(22), 14. http://www.fortherecord-mag.com/archives/120511p14.shtml

21. Casey, M. M, Sorerson, T. D., Elins, W., Knudson, A., & Gregg, W. (2010). Current practices and state regulations regarding telepharmacy in rural hospitals. *American Journal of Health-System Pharmacy, 67*(13), 1085–1092. http://www.baxa.com/resources/docs/research/AJHPCurrentStateRegulationsfor TelepharmacyJuly2010.pdf

22. Casey, M., et al. (2008, December). Implementation of telepharmacy in rural Hospitals: Potential for improving medication safety. Final Report #8. Upper Midwest Rural Health Research Center. http://www.uppermidwestrhrc.org/pdf/report_telepharmacy.pdf

23. Kuzma, J. (2011). Web vulnerability study of online pharmacy sites. *Informatics for Health and Social Care, 36*(1), 20–34.

24. National Association of Boards of Pharmacy. (2012, January). Internet drug outlet identification program progress report for state and federal regulators, January 2012. Mount Prospect, IL: Author. http://www.nabp.net/programs/assets/IDOI_Report_01-12.pdf

25. Hailey, D., & Roine, R. (2011). Evidence of benefit from telerehabilitation in routine care: A systematic review. *Journal of Telemedicine and Telecare, 17*(6), 281–287.

26. Grossmann Zamora, R. J., Sorondo, B., Holmberg, R., & Bjorn, P. (2011). Telemedicine consultation for emergency trauma: The 130 million square foot trauma room. *Bulletin of the American College of Surgeons, 96*(6). http://www.facs.org/fellows_info/bulletin/2011/zamora0611.pdf

27. Food and Drug Administration. (2011, July 21). *Draft guidance for industry and Food and Drug Administration staff: Mobile medical applications: Draft Guidance.* p. 29.

28. CNA Financial Corporation. (2010). Social media liability: Effective strategies to minimize risk. *Alert Bulletin, 6.* http://www.cna.com/vcm_content/CNA/internet/Static%20File%20for%20Download/Risk%20Control/Medical%20Services/EffectiveStrategiestoMinimizeRisk.pdf

29. American Hospital Association Society for Healthcare Strategy and Market Development. (2011). *Emerging media handbook.* Chicago, IL: Author.

PART 3

Managing Risks in Other Healthcare Venues

CHAPTER 15

Risk Management in Ambulatory Care Settings

Karen E. Benker

INTRODUCTION

The steady migration of clinical services out of hospitals into more cost-efficient outpatient settings raises new challenges in risk management. Ambulatory care managers and clinical leaders need to assess the vulnerabilities of their sites and plan effective strategies to limit risks, especially if they are not subject to accreditation. Risks in ambulatory care include harm to patients, visitors, and staff, and also include harm to the financial life of the healthcare organization. Of all paid malpractice claims, a greater number now come from the ambulatory or joint ambulatory–inpatient setting than those from the inpatient setting alone, as shown in **Table 15-1**.[1] With an average payment of nearly $300,000, these claims can easily threaten the survival of an ambulatory practice, whether in primary care or one of the subspecialties.

Table 15-1 Paid Malpractice Claims by Setting, 2009[1]	
Setting	**Percentage of All Claims**
Outpatient	43.1%
Outpatient and inpatient	9.4%
Inpatient	47.6%

The special needs for risk management in the ambulatory setting spring largely from its differences from the inpatient setting. In the inpatient setting, specially trained professionals manage care and have access to the patient 24 hours a day during a highly concentrated treatment episode. They document their work in a common medical record, often an electronic health record (EHR) that offers decision support for standards of care and drug selection. Moreover, the team members have routine protocols for the transfer of responsibility from one person to the next. A risk management department and compliance office continually ensure that patient safety issues receive attention and that staff members follow all legal and regulatory requirements. While the physician fundamentally makes all major clinical decisions, a multidisciplinary team ensures adherence to the treatment plan. The patient remains mostly passive throughout this process.

In the current ambulatory care setting, however, a physician typically sees the patient only briefly at irregular intervals spread out over months or years. In these offices, employees often have a lower level of training than hospital staff and informally perform a variety of tasks, from scheduling appointments, collecting copayments, and taking phone messages to recording vital signs. The coordination with providers scattered among other sites takes place through written referrals carried by the patient or sent through the mail. The array of providers involved with one patient document their activities in separate record systems, often on paper, scattered among individual sites. Most importantly, the patient and the family are in control of seeking care, carrying out the treatment plan, and coordinating care with other providers.

ASSESSMENT OF THE PRACTICE SETTING

Normally, the first step in ambulatory care to managing the risks of harm to patients and to the practice is to assess the risks by examining facts about the specific site. In the past, this assessment began with an examination of reports of errors. Error reporting, however, proved unreliable and inadequate. In many cases, only incomplete anecdotal information was available, and both physicians and staff often kept errors secret. Another model of assessing potential harm relied on the study of bad outcomes. Again, information was often incomplete or available only after serious harm had already occurred.

The modern model for managing risks relies on a total assessment of the practice setting to identify potential flaws in the system that could create harm. This model rests on three core principles:

- A culture of safety
- Good employment practices
- Ethical business practices

A Culture of Safety

The seminal report by the Institute of Medicine, *To Err Is Human*,[2] spurred investigation into the best techniques for minimizing harm to patients.

Drawing heavily on the advancements in the science of airline safety, researchers soon established that the key element was the fostering of a new practice environment—a "culture of safety." The key to this approach is the recognition that human errors are inevitable. In the complex healthcare environment, everything cannot always go as planned. Instead of punishing people who make errors, in this model errors and near-misses become the basis of looking for ways to strengthen the system of care so that errors are less likely to occur.

The culture of safety has four key features:

- Psychological safety
- Active leadership
- Transparency
- Fairness

Psychological safety reflects the freedom and encouragement that all people have to bring up their concerns and the earned trust they have that their concerns will be received with respect and careful consideration as a basis for change. Each person in the practice, as well as each patient and family member, receives praise for asking questions and suggesting possible problems. As examples, the nurse may suggest without fear of punishment that some patients do not really understand the explanations that the physician is giving. A medical assistant may report that he was using the wrong-size cuff for taking blood pressures. A housekeeper may report that he accidentally unplugged the refrigerator when waxing the floors.

In each case, others welcome the report, which then becomes the basis of a discussion of the impact of that event and of ways to prevent similar events in the future. Experience has shown that trust builds as staff first begin to report on equipment problems, then on near-misses or errors in the work of others, then on their own near-misses or errors, and finally on their own violations of policy. While it may seem naïve to believe that this transformation can occur, in fact, it is the basis of airline safety. One airline found that half of self-reported errors by technicians involved violation of procedures. Once that fact emerged, it was clear that technicians had had to use "work-arounds" to deal with a dysfunctional system of procedures.[3] The solution was to create a functional system of procedures, rather than to punish the technicians for violating procedures. A similar situation might emerge in a community clinic, where clerical staff acknowledge that they do not follow the official policy of advising patients to come 20 minutes early for their appointments because they realize that the physicians are always at least 30 minutes behind schedule and the reception area becomes crowded with frustrated patients if they come early or on time. The solution is to remove bottlenecks to the productivity of the physicians.

Active leadership uses the key skills of sharing information, inviting other team members to contribute their expertise, making oneself approachable, and creating an environment in which all staff are comfortable in expressing their concerns. Each person in authority in the ambulatory setting offers praise and thanks for staff who come forward with concerns. If the lead physician listens attentively and gratefully to feedback from low-ranking staff about patients' expressions of frustration with the failure to return phone calls, then a tone is set for active commitment to the change. The active leader starts with the assumption that if anyone says there is a problem, then there is a problem until proved otherwise.

Transparency means that problems are not hidden: "Sunlight is the best disinfectant." Problems are openly discussed so that the organization can learn from them to improve the system of care. Individual staff members may stand up and say, "I almost gave the wrong vaccine today. It could happen to you, too. Let's figure out how to prevent this error from happening." Transparency also means that the patient and family receive an explanation of any errors that occurred, along with an apology and an expressed commitment to learn from the error to prevent it from happening again. Many hospitals have begun the practice of active disclosure to the media when a patient suffers a major preventable harm with an explanation of the investigation that will take place and a commitment to preventing similar occurrences in the future.

Fairness is described this way by the Agency for Healthcare Research and Quality:

> A just culture recognizes that individual practitioners should not be held accountable for system failings over which they have no control. A just culture also recognizes many individual or "active" errors represent predictable interactions between human operators and the systems in which they work. However, in contrast to a culture that touts "no blame" as its governing principle, a just culture does not tolerate conscious disregard of clear risks to patients or gross misconduct (eg, falsifying a record, performing professional duties while intoxicated).[4]

People know they are accountable for their behaviors, but the response differs depending on the source of their error. Fairness means that the housekeeper will not be punished for accidentally unplugging the refrigerator. He was just trying to do the right thing—wax the floor. At the same time, people realize that if their error stemmed from a malicious intent or reckless disregard of safety, then they have done something unacceptable. David Marx classifies behaviors with the potential to harm patients into three categories:[5]

- Human error: inadvertently doing the wrong thing
- At-risk behavior: intentionally choosing to do something risky without perceiving the heightened risk
- Reckless behavior: consciously choosing to put others in harm's way

He then advises the responses from the organization for each type of error (See **Table 15-2**).

For example, in one case a nurse may unintentionally use an insulin syringe instead of a tuberculin syringe to give a skin test. Both types of syringes look alike and were stored together. An urgent phone call distracted the nurse while she was preparing to implant the skin test. In that situation, the solution is a better way to store the syringes and a better way to reduce staff multitasking. In another case, the nurse may use the insulin syringe knowing that it is different from the tuberculin syringe, but not believing that the difference is important. In that situation, the nurse needs education and more awareness of the clinical environment. In a third case, the nurse may have flagrantly made the same mistake repeatedly with no regard for the patient's legitimate need for a reliable tuberculosis (TB) test. In that situation, punitive action is warranted.

Good Employment Practices

When the team of personnel who diagnose and prescribe in the outpatient setting expands to include physician assistants and nurse practitioners, the employer or supervisor of these colleagues has specific risks. Under the principle of vicarious liability, the physician or the

Table 15-2   Managerial Response to Patient Safety Risks

Type	Response	Approach
Human Error	Changes in	Console
Inadvertent action: slip, lapse, mistake	–Processes	
	–Procedures	
	–Training	
	–Design	
At-Risk Behavior	Removing incentives for at-risk behavior	Coach
A choice: risk believed justified or not recognized	–Creating incentives for healthy behaviors	
	–Increasing situational awareness	
Reckless Behavior	Manage through	Punish
Conscious disregard of unreasonable risk	–Remedial action	
	–Punitive action	

owners of a practice may be held legally responsible for the actions of these employees. The patients may sue under the principle of negligent supervision. The severity of injury in negligent malpractice claims can be very high, with more than one-fourth involving death of the patient.[6] In Massachusetts, a patient sued a primary care physician because a nurse practitioner in his practice missed a diagnosis of cervical cancer when she failed to perform a Pap test appropriately two years in a row. Both times the result came back as "insufficient quantities," but there was no follow-up to obtain an adequate specimen.[7]

The greatest risk occurs when nonphysicians exceed their legally authorized duties. Many small practices employ medical assistants to perform a wide array of clerical and clinical tasks. Legally permitted activities by medical assistants, however, vary widely by state. South Dakota requires that medical assistants register with the state and undergo a background check. New York prohibits medical assistants from performing triage or administrating medications by any route. Maine, by comparison, permits medical assistants to perform any invasive procedure, including the administration of injections as long as it is "under the direct control" and "in the immediate presence" of a physician. Nevertheless, in all states, the employer and the immediate supervisor can be held liable for the adverse outcomes of the medical assistant. This risk is magnified if the nonphysician does not have on record valid credentials and licenses.

The physician employer is also at risk from inappropriate actions of other personnel in the ambulatory care setting. Breaches of patient confidentiality are a common problem. Inadvertent release of confidential information may occur through casual off-duty conversations, overheard discussions between doctor and patient, faxed communications, and poorly protected computerized records. Employees of an ambulatory practice may also use confidential patient information for criminal purposes (see **Box 15-1**).

These cases do serious damage to the reputation of the healthcare organization as a whole. Any criminal or abusive behavior by an employee toward a patient, such as cursing or sexualized touching, also exposes the employer to risk, especially if documentation is lacking of appropriate background checks prior to hiring.

Box 15-1

- A phlebotomist in Seattle used patient information fraudualently to obtain four credit cards in a patient's name.[8]
- A front desk clerk in Florida sold patient information on more than 1,000 patients, which was then used to generate $7 million in fraudulent Medicare claims.[9]

In addition to risks of lawsuits from patients, the ambulatory care physician or manager must attend closely to fair employment practices in payment, benefits, hiring, and firing. Employees who believe that they have been treated unfairly can create serious problems for the practice. The whistleblower law protects an employee who reports the employer for alleged fraudulent billing.

A team of well-trained and well-supervised employees is essential both to provide excellent, safe patient care and to lower risks to the financial stability of the ambulatory setting from lawsuits. As noted earlier, everyone in the setting should be encouraged and rewarded for speaking up about potential dangers, near-misses, or outright mistakes in patient care. Regular staff meetings should also include discussions of "What if...?": What if we lost electrical power over a weekend? What if an employee had a needlestick injury? The more the entire enterprise is oriented toward planning for prevention, the more successful the practice will be in minimizing risk.

Part of developing a high-performing team is hiring the right people for the right jobs. Hiring the neighbor's teenage daughter as the receptionist because she has a nice telephone voice and will work for minimum wage is usually a bad business decision. The policy and procedure manual should have clear job descriptions, including required training, experience, and skills. The hiring process should be fair and well documented. There should be full documentation of education, previous positions, criminal record check, immunizations, TB status, certifications, and current licenses. Previous employers and people submitting recommendations should be interviewed by telephone to explore any gaps in the résumé or areas of concern. Some private employers routinely ask the prospective employee to consent to a credit check as a mark of responsibility and stability. Some states permit urine drug screens for healthcare workers. No one—whether as a paid worker or as a volunteer—should be allowed to perform any task on-site until fully vetted.

To capitalize on this extensive investment in hiring the right person, the practice's management must devote time to orientation and training. This initial period should guarantee that the new staff member becomes familiar with the following aspects of the ambulatory care practice:

- The vision and mission of the practice
- Employee rights under federal and state laws

- The code of ethics and business conduct
- Duties and benefits
- The Health Insurance Portability and Accountability Act (HIPAA)
- Telephone and computer security
- The culture of safety

All employees should receive periodic performance reviews and constructive feedback to facilitate their progressive development. Management should review credentials annually to ensure that each employee is current with all requirements. On a regular, appropriate basis, all employees should receive refresher minicourses in patient safety, compliance with antifraud regulations, policies and regulations on confidentiality, serving patients with low health literacy, serving difficult patients, and other topics identified as relevant to the practice.

Ethical Business Practices

The successful ambulatory care practice will have an active program to prevent fraud and abuse. If the practice outsources its billing and collections, it is important to realize that federal law requires that any Medicare funds be deposited directly into the bank account of the practice—not the account of the billing service. Federal law also prohibits kickbacks for referrals, routinely waiving Medicare copayments, or charging Medicare patients 15% or more than the Medicare fee schedule. In addition, state laws may apply. In Illinois, for example, the state medical practice act prohibits percentage-based billing as a form of fee-splitting; percentage-based billing creates an incentive for the billing service to code higher levels of services than were actually provided. To protect the practice from charges of fraud, the following steps are essential:

- Provide clear documentation of the diagnosis and services provided.
- Promptly return any overpayments (within 60 days).
- Verify the identity of any patient to whom you extend credit, because in a case of identify theft you would be collecting your fee illegally from the patient whose identify was stolen.
- Order durable medical equipment (DME) only on the basis of face-to-face evaluation of the patient.

In addition, the Patient Protection and Affordable Care Act requires that all healthcare providers and suppliers establish a compliance program that contains core elements set by the Department of Health and Human Services in consultation with the Office of the Inspector General (OIG). These elements are outlined here:[10]

1. Written policies and procedures: At least annually, audit your coding, contracts, and care; keep your policies up-to-date and user-friendly.
2. Compliance professionals: Assign one person to serve as compliance officer, and provide extra training and backup consultants as needed.
3. Effective training: Involve every employee and keep documentation of their successful learning.
4. Effective communication: Solicit feedback openly with posters from all employees and patients; protect their confidentiality or anonymity.
5. Enforcement of standards: When issues arise, take and document corrective action.
6. Prompt response: Do not equivocate; deal with problems as they arise.

The OIG maintains an active surveillance of insurance claims to Medicare, Medicaid, and the State Children's Health Insurance Program under the anti-kickback statute known as the Stark law. Under this law, the following practices are illegal:

- Specific types of joint venture arrangement: Forbidden joint venture arrangements usually involve a physician referring patients to an entity with which he or she, or an immediate family member, has a financial relationship (i.e., referrals to a laboratory, pharmacy, or durable medical supply company owned by a spouse or family member).
- Routine waiver of Medicare Part B copayments and deductible: Routine waivers of Medicare copayments would create an unfair market advantage over competing medical practices. Medicare does allow a physician to waive copayments for individual patients on the basis of financial hardship.
- Hospital incentives to referring physicians: The Stark law forbids a hospital from renting medical office space to a referring physician at less than market rates (because the hospital hopes to capture the physician's business). Another example is a hospital incentivizing physician's to limit services to Medicare or Medicaid patients in their care to maximize the hospital's financial margin under the diagnosis-related group (DRG) payment system.
- Prescription drug marketing practices: One fraudulent prescription drug marketing scheme sought to provide frequent-flier airline mileage to physicians who completed a new-patient questionnaire each time they prescribed a specific drug.

- Arrangements for the provision of clinical laboratory services: It is forbidden for a clinical laboratory to provide expensive gifts in exchange to sending patients for tests.

The OIG also aggressively prosecutes for fraud those physicians who bill for services that were not provided. Fraudulent billing practices come under the federal False Claims Act, passed during the Civil War to deal with widespread corruption by suppliers to the Union Army.[11] Subsequent amendments extended coverage to Medicare and Medicaid reimbursements (see **Box 15-2**).

Less flagrant types of billing fraud are the focus of attention of Medicare and Medicaid insurance carriers. The government provides to the carriers a list of typical coding profiles by region and by specialty. Carriers review the billing of each practice carefully to assess whether providers are up-coding or down-coding visits. If a given practice has a profile with higher codes than are typical, an audit may reveal a systematic practice of overstating the complexity of the visit for the sake of a higher reimbursement. The carrier may then refer the matter to the OIG, which may demand high retroactive penalties based on the percentage of over-coding in a sample of bill. In one case, the electronic software of community health center incorrectly submitted higher codes. The practice spent several years in negotiations to resolve the issue and had to pay back a substantial sum. In other cases, practices have outsourced coding and billing to companies that charge a percentage of collections or of gross claims. This arrangement creates a financial incentive for the billing company to inflate claims, a clear form of billing fraud. *Regardless of who submits the bill, the practice is legally responsible for the accuracy of the bill.* The practice may pay heavy fines for errors or fraud committed by others.

> **Box 15-2**
>
> In 2011, the FBI made predawn raids in Miami, Brooklyn, Tampa, Chicago, Baton Rouge, Houston, Dallas, and Los Angeles and arrested more than 100 doctors, nurses, therapists, and healthcare company executives for requesting reimbursement from the government for medical services never performed and pharmaceuticals not provided.[12]

HIGH-RISK AREAS

Several high-risk areas in the clinical ambulatory setting deserve special attention:

- Missed diagnoses
- Medication risks
- Infectious risks
- Communication
- Documentation

Missed Diagnoses

The malpractice claims for outpatient care highlight the major risks to patient safety. A recent review of more than 4,000 cases in which insurance companies made malpractice payments on behalf of physicians revealed the following pattern of leading adverse events:[1]

- Diagnostic: 46%
- Treatment/medication: 30%
- Surgical: 14%

The Physician Insurers Association of America (PIAA)—the insurance industry trade association representing medical professional liability insurance companies—reports that the most common diagnostic error was failure or delay in diagnosing cancer, particularly cancer of the breast,[13] lung,[14] and colorectum.[15] Diagnostic errors were not only the most common, but also the most expensive claims.

- The typical breast cancer patient with a missed or delayed diagnosis was a premenopausal woman who presented with a mass for which the physician failed to obtain a tissue diagnosis.
- Medical records of 67% of the patients with a missed diagnosis of lung cancer contained no history of exposure to known carcinogens, and the treating physician often failed to compare chest X-rays with previous available films.
- Medical records of 62% of the patients with a missed diagnosis of colorectal cancer did not have a notation regarding a family history of the diseases.

Other commonly missed diagnoses include myocardial infarctions with atypical presentations,[16,17] acute abdomen,[6,18] stroke,[19] and infection.[5]

One in-depth look at 307 closed malpractice claims from four insurance companies in which a patient alleged a missed or delayed diagnosis provides a closer look at the problems.[5] Most of the errors occurred in primary care physicians' offices. The mean interval between when the diagnosis could reasonably have been made until it was actually made was 465 days. The key breakdowns in delayed diagnoses of cancer were as follows:

- Failure to order an appropriate diagnostic test: 59%
- Failure to interpret a diagnostic test correctly: 46%
- Failure to record an appropriate history or physical exam: 23%
- Failure to refer: 18%
- Provider did not receive test results: 16%

Other studies not based on malpractice claims have shown equally disturbing results.

Box 15-3

A 45-years-old New Jersey woman in 2008 received a $2 million settlement for delayed diagnosis of stage 4 breast cancer by biopsy. She had made four separate visits to her physician over the previous two years complaining of the painful lump.[20]

A review of 105 abnormal Pap smears at 11 clinics found that in 45% there was no documentation of appropriate follow-up.[21] A review of more than 500 patients with colorectal cancer[22] found that one-third had at least one missed opportunity to make an earlier diagnosis, with a mean of 4.2 missed opportunities. The most common deficits were persistent failure to work up an iron-deficiency anemia, a positive fecal occult blood test, or rectal bleeding. In another one-third of cases, the primary care physician ordered the diagnostic work-up, but was never aware that the test was not performed (see **Box 15-3**).

Several strategies help minimize missed diagnoses by focusing on specific points in the diagnostic process. The first point is in the routine care of asymptomatic patients. The key strategy is to document a baseline history that would identify the patient who is at risk for specific conditions—for example, a history of smoking or a family history of early colon cancer. A standard complete history form that the patient and the provider together fill out and review on the first visit to the practice is the best protection against this lapse.

Routine flags or flowcharts in the ongoing medical record for periodic screening tests that are due, such as mammograms and annual fecal occult blood tests, also help the busy clinician manage ongoing care. The ambulatory practice that does not yet have an EHR should consider using formatted pages and flowcharts for preventive care.

A medical practice can uniformly order screening and other standard preventive measures with these steps:

- Have the provider or a staff member review each chart before each visit to highlight needed screening and immunizations.
- If the clinician delays testing until a chronic condition such as diabetes, is under better control, then a clear note in the record helps document the reason for delay and includes a plan for a return visit to address the need.

The extra time required to set up such a system of documentation pays off in a higher level of care that conforms to practice standards (see **Box 15-4**).

The next key point in terms of the risk of missing a diagnosis is the failure of the physician to work up a problem presented by a patient. Recall that the largest proportion of malpractice payments for a missed diagnosis of breast cancer occurred in premenopausal women with a lump and normal mammography. This lapse may take the form of performing a cursory examination for what appears a minor complaint and then failing to see the patient on an urgent basis if he or she calls complaining of worsening symptoms. What appeared to be a localized furuncle on Thursday can be a rapidly spreading methocillin-resistant *Staphylococcus aureus* (MRSA) cellulitis on Saturday. The staff person who is responsible for answering the phone needs specific instructions to inform the provider anytime a patient calls repeatedly or expresses worsening symptoms.

Another point for focus occurs when the patient does not complete the screening or diagnostic test. High-functioning EHRs can generate alerts for the provider when an ordered test or referral report does not appear by a given date. Ambulatory care sites without an EHR need to maintain a tickler file of all tests and referrals, with a daily review being undertaken to identify results that have not returned on time. While a medical assistant or other staff member may review the tickler file daily, the licensed practitioner who ordered the test must document the appropriate follow-up plan in the patient's chart. Patients who do not complete work-ups are liability risks. The documentation in the chart should show that the provider has communicated the appropriate urgency and potential consequences of failing to follow through on needed tests.

The next point of focus in avoiding a missed diagnosis occurs when the specialist to whom a patient is referred does not send back a timely and detailed report with recommendations. Primary care physicians report that they receive only three out of every five reports from specialists to whom they have referred a patient. One measure for improving patient safety and for lowering liability risk to the referring physician is to establish a network of reliable colleagues who do return reports promptly. Another approach is to work within professional associations and with local third-party payers to seek integrated data-sharing systems that lower this risk. Meanwhile, the ambulatory care site must document in the patient's chart the steps taken to obtain findings from all referrals.

An additional point of focus is failure to follow up on an abnormal or equivocal test result. The EHR or laboratory printout may flag the abnormality, but it is the responsibility of the practitioner to review and initial each day all test results, to identify those that require follow-up, to document a plan in the medical record, and to add a note with a follow-up date in a tickler file or in the EHR.

These routines require the typical provider to review hundreds of data points each day. One study estimated that the average primary care physician processes more than 900 tests each week.[23] Processing requires not only reviewing the result, but also making appropriate decisions, and documenting this activity in both the chart and a tickler file. Each practice has to design reliable routines, including using ancillary staff, standard forms, and/or the EHR, to minimize the clerical responsibilities of the physician. Most physicians find they need to set aside protected time each day to handle reviewing and following up on abnormal, equivocal, or missing test results.

The final point of focus in missing a diagnosis occurs when the physician does not notify the patient of test results and of steps that he or she needs to take. One effective approach is the creation of a standard form letter preprinted with the most common tests and columns for check marks as "within normal limits," "slightly abnormal," and "abnormal," with space for comments and follow-up instructions.

Medication Risks

A PIAA report showed that the single most common basis for malpractice claims (5%) is harm to a patient because of a medication error.[24] These errors include prescribing the wrong dosage, prescribing a drug to which the patient has a known allergy, failing to monitor for side effects, and failing to provide clear instructions. In nearly two-thirds of the PIAA claims for fatal drug allergies, the medical record documented the existence of the allergy. A prospective survey in four primary care practices found that one in four patients developed an adverse drug event in the three months

following a medical visit.[25] Half of these events were either preventable (e.g., the wrong dosage) or ameliorable (e.g., the physician knew about but ignored side effects). Older patients, especially those with several comorbidities, are at special risk related to medications. One study focusing on a cohort of more than 30,000 Medicare enrollees found that one-fourth of the events were preventable, for example, by close monitoring or by avoiding known drug–drug interactions.[26] These preventable events were often life-threatening or fatal. The fatal adverse outcomes included fatal bleeding, hypoglycemia, digitoxicity, and anaphylaxis.

Another study,[27] based on analysis of data from the National Electronic Injury Surveillance System, found that 100,000 elderly patients suffer adverse drug events each year severe enough to require emergency hospitalization. Half occur in individuals 80 years or older. Four types of medication accounted for two-thirds of these hospitalizations: warfarin, insulin, oral antiplatelet agents, and oral hypoglycemic agents. In 56% of the cases, the person was taking five or more medications. Most of the events came from unintentional overdoses, including more than 95% of those involving warfarin or oral hypoglycemics. A recent study of how well patients interpreted medication labels found major gaps in their understanding of standard instructions such as "for external use only."[28]

The keys to minimizing risks of harm to a patient from a medication allergy, side effect, drug–drug interaction, or unintentional overdose are good documentation and good communication with the patient or caregiver. At the initial patient visit, the routine form must document any history of any drug allergy or reaction. The chart must also contain a full list of all medications, vitamins, homeopathic remedies, and over-the-counter products used with specific questions asked about eye drops, nasal sprays, inhalers, patches, lotions, and suppositories with dosage and frequency. It is also worthwhile to ask specifically what the patient uses for intermittent pain (e.g., aspirin, ibuprofen, acetaminophen) and for seasonal colds (e.g., dextromethorphan, antihistamines). This information provides an opportunity of advising patients and caregivers about potential adverse effects of these common medications. A standard informational handout on medication safety with specific alerts for this patient and documenting this counseling help prevent future problems. Each subsequent visit should be viewed as an occasion to update the medication list and any interim drug allergies or adverse events.

A standard form with clear printed instructions and warnings should accompany each prescription given to a patient to supplement the common difficulties with reading labels on medication. The medical record should clearly display in a flowchart the names, doses, and date of each prescription. No one should refill medications without reviewing the medical record and adding an entry. Telephoned prescriptions may be risky; faxed or electronically submitted copies with clearly legible drug name and dose are safer.

The elderly require special attention in the ambulatory care setting to minimize their risk of adverse drug effects. The provider must carefully note any changes in medication from other providers and check for any potential drug–drug interactions. Software on personal handheld electronic devices or within the EHR commonly alert providers to these possible

risks. Older patients are more likely to have lower literacy levels, impaired vision and hearing, and difficulty opening medication containers—all factors that put them at higher risk for not taking medications as prescribed. In addition, the older patient requires periodic mental status evaluation, particularly of short-term memory, to assess the risk of accidentally taking repeated doses. Involvement of the caregiver in education, risk assessment, and safety planning is often necessary. Many useful medication organizers and reminders are also available for home use, such as vibrating pill boxes and automatic timed dispensers. The elderly person who lives alone is at special risk, and a home assessment by a visiting nurse or other trained professional is often helpful in developing and implementing a safe plan of care. The frail elderly often have difficulty remembering and traveling to and from medical appointments. If the practice includes a high proportion of elderly patients, the setting may wish to establish a home-visiting program by the physician or nurse practitioner. In-home medical monitoring is especially appropriate if the patient is on warfarin or hypoglycemics because of the need for frequent blood tests. The patient's chart should include a flowchart with these serial blood test results for easy reference.

Children are also at higher risk of harm from medication errors. The correct dose changes with the ages and stages of development; complicated calculations are often necessary; and precise dose measurement is often important. Parents and other caregivers need clear instructions, including procedures for contacting the practice site in case the child's status does not improve.

Infectious Disease Risks

The shift of many invasive procedures from the hospital to the ambulatory care setting has dramatically increased the risk of spread of infections in this new setting. More than 30 outbreaks of hepatitis B or C alone, infecting 448 persons, have centered on out-of-hospital care settings.[29] Vulnerable patient groups, such as cancer patients undergoing chemotherapy, are at special risk of acquiring dangerous infections.

Box 15-5

The Nevada Sate Board of Medical Examiners suspended the medical licence of a urologist for reusing a needle guide intended for single use to perform prostate biopsies or implant gold seed radiation implants. Because of the potential risk of acquiring hepatitis B, hepatitis C, or HIV, 101 patients received letters advising testing and follow-up.[30]

Serious risks in infection control in the ambulatory setting are common (see **Box 15-5**):

- The Georgia State Department of Public Health traced an outbreak of blood infections in 10 patients to a hematology–oncology practice, where staff used a single needle and syringe to withdraw medication and diluents from multidose bottles and to inject chemotherapy agents into different bags of fluid.[31]
- The Centers for Disease Control and Prevention (CDC) identified an outbreak in a pain clinic of eight cases of severe methicillin-susceptible *Staphylococcus aureus* (MSSA) infections linked to the reuse of syringes with multidose vials.[32]

- The Texas Department of State Health Services identified the source of an outbreak of abscesses in 25 patients at an allergy clinic as improper cleansing of the skin before injection.[33] Staff had diluted the topical antiseptic with nonsterile water.
- An ambulatory care practice in Colorado had to recall dozens of patients for testing for HIV, hepatitis B, and hepatitis C after a medical assistant incorrectly used the same syringe with a fresh needle to inject flu vaccine into infants and toddlers.[34]

In the investigation of most of these cases, staff demonstrated in mock injection procedures egregious errors in infection control because of lack of appropriate training.

Staff, as well as patients, may be at risk from infections in the ambulatory care setting. Risks from needlestick injuries or from exposure to patients with active tuberculosis have been recognized for many years. In addition, staff may become carriers or develop infections in other ways. A recent outbreak of boils in eight staff members in the outpatient practices of a cancer center was linked to one patient with community-acquired methicillin-resistant *Staphylococcus aureus* (CA-MRSA).[35] Because MRSA can be life threatening and can be transmitted by asymptomatic carriers to family members, staff need policies and procedures to protect them from this risk.

The CDC publishes authoritative documents to assist ambulatory sites in preventing infections.[36,37] The following key areas are covered:

- Infection prevention education and training
- Occupational health

- Surveillance and disease reporting
- Hand hygiene
- Personal protective equipment
- Injection safety
- Respiratory hygiene/cough etiquette
- Environmental cleaning
- Reprocessing of reusable medical devices
- Sterilization of reusable instruments and devices
- High-level disinfection of reusable instruments and devices

The CDC material offers clear models of administrative policies and facility practices as well as routines for periodic observations of personnel performance. The manager of an ambulatory care site needs, in addition, to become familiar with local regulations in areas such as disposal of medical waste, mandated reporting of accidents and conditions, and post-exposure prophylaxis for HIV.

In all practices, the prevention and control of CA-MRSA is of growing importance. Children and adolescents are at special risk of a small break in the skin becoming contaminated by this bacterium in the general environment, especially during sports. Common scenarios in sports include a minor abrasion becoming infected from a towel or a wrestling mat. The infected site can rapidly develop into a life-threatening infection. Parents and athletes should receive printed educational material on the importance of not sharing towels, razors, and athletic gear and of washing and covering all breaks in the skin. Any suspect lesion should be drained, cultured, and covered. The patient should receive printed instructions to keep the area covered and to seek medical care immediately if the lesion worsens. The clinical area where treatment is provided should be thoroughly disinfected immediately.

Small practices may find it helpful to hire a consultant to perform an annual review of infection control procedures and to recommend needed revisions.

Communication Issues

Breakdown in communication about test results led to a $70 million increase in malpractice claims from 1991 to 2010. These failures accounted for 4% of malpractice lawsuits and 7% of legal costs.[38] The most common errors were failing to tell the patient the results, giving the patient the wrong results, or failing to notify the referring clinician of the results. A 1996 report survey of more than 250 primary care physicians in an academic medical center and 21 suburban practices found that as many as one-third had no reliable method of assuring receipt of the results of all tests ordered.[39] One-third also reported they did not always notify patients of abnormal results, usually because the patient was expected to return to the clinic soon. Only one-fourth reported having a reliable method for identifying patients overdue for follow-up.

On a typical day, a primary care physician may have hundreds of separate test results to review. A survey of 262 primary care physicians and residents in the Boston area using electronic health records found they spent an average of 74 minutes per day managing test results; only one-third had a system to detect if a patient had missed completing a test. Few had systems in place to guarantee that each test result was received and followed up on appropriately.[23] In another study, primary care physicians reported that they received only three out of every five reports from specialists to whom they had referred a patient.[40]

Communication issues involving the telephone are especially important in ambulatory settings. Because ambulatory care physicians rely heavily on the telephone for communication with patients, breakdowns can be disastrous. A detailed look at 32 closed malpractice cases involving telephone communication found this frequency of the following serious errors:[6]

- No or poor documentation of the call: 88%
- Faulty triage, usually because of taking an incomplete history over the phone: 84%
- Failure to respond to repeated calls for the same problem: 44%
- Dropped messages or delayed response because of lack of policies and procedures for managing calls: 38%

The basis for the legal actions was failure to diagnose or negligent treatment. Fourteen of the 32 patients died. The nonfatal outcomes alleged included perforated bowel, cerebral palsy, brain damage, and amputation. Of the 32 cases, only 60% resulted in a payment to the plaintiff, with an average indemnity of more than $500,000.

Communicating with patients by distributing printed material is also important in ambulatory care. New patients should receive an attractive welcome booklet in large type written with the appropriate literacy level and language. The booklet should spell out all the key points about the practice, including 24-hour contact information, reimbursement policies, and methods by which patients may make complaints (see **Box 15-6**). Because the patient and family will be responsible for carrying out the plan of care, the practice likewise benefits from having printed information sheets available as appropriate for the patient

---

Box 15-6 Contents of a Patient Education Booklet

Mission, vision, and values of the practice

Hours of care

Holiday schedule

Procedures for urgent or emergent contact after hours

Brief description of the roles of staff

HIPAA rights

Other rights of patients

Rights of adolescent patients

Responsibilities of patients
- Keeping/rescheduling appointments
- Financial arrangements
- Notifying of changes in address and other personal information

Advance directives

Patient complaint procedures

---

population that cover key points of taking specific medications or following therapeutic dietary regimens. These become the framework for educating patients on a face-to-face basis as helpful reminders at home.

All staff should routinely ask patients if they have any questions or concerns. Some practices routinely survey their patients to measure satisfaction and to solicit suggestions for improvement of care. Managers should also routinely ask staff for suggestions on increasing patient satisfaction and improving services.

Communication with difficult patients is especially important. Patients who miss appointments or do not adhere to treatment plans are at risk for poor health outcomes that may result in malpractice claims. The physician or a skilled staff member should explore with the patient and family any barriers to keeping appointments or to following medical advice. Common reasons, which patients may be reluctant to disclose, are difficulty in understanding verbal explanations or in reading printed material, lack of money for medications or diagnostic testing, and overwhelming stresses at home or on the job. To the extent reasonable, the team should tailor the treatment plan to the patient's capacities and help the patient mobilize help from personal networks, such as family or friends, or from formal sources, such as social services. The medical record should document the reasons for tailoring the treatment plan and the steps taken to assist the patient. The special attention to these needs can change a "problem patient" into a grateful collaborator in his or her own care.

Inevitably, some patients will not be satisfied with the services that the practice provides and will persistently ignore medical advice or miss appointments. These patients remain at risk for poor health outcomes that may trigger malpractice claims. If a patient complains about medical care received, the physician should personally call or meet with the patient. Patients appreciate the chance to share their perspective fully with a respectful listener. They may move from angry frustration to valued collaborator in their own care. Of course, some patients have very difficult personalities. The classic article by James Groves[41] gives valuable advice for maintaining an effective relationship with such patients.

When a patient persists in disrupting the ambulatory care environment, a written contract between patient and practice can spell out specific behavior that each agree to do. For example, the patient may be asked to agree to come on time for scheduled appointments, refrain from disruptive behavior in the reception area, and speak courteously to all staff. The physician may agree, in turn, to call the patient the day after each visit for a brief follow-up on symptoms.

Either the patient or the physician has the legal right to terminate the relationship. (Special considerations may apply if the patient is in a managed care organization.) To the extent possible, the relationship should end on a cordial note. The physician does not need to give a reason for terminating the relationship. However, the patient must receive both adequate notice (usually 15 to 30 days) and assistance in transferring records. The physician should provide a copy of the medical record directly to the new physician, rather than to the patient. In case of emergency until the transfer occurs, the physician must be available for care. The notification to the patient should include a review of the patient's medical needs, medications, and behavioral advice. The notice should go out by certified mail with return receipt requested. The receipt and a copy of the letter along with a brief note remain in the patient's chart. The appointment clerk needs to be aware not to schedule another appointment with this patient.

Respectful boundaries help prevent miscommunication. Patients who know that they are respected and valued participate more completely in their care, including asking more questions, expressing doubts, revealing reluctance to carry out a prescribed treatment regimen, and following through on testing and treatment decisions. To help guarantee excellent relationships with patients, the office procedure and personnel management manuals should spell out how patients will get greeted, how the reception area will be maintained, how appointments will be scheduled to minimize waiting, how patient privacy and confidentiality will be maintained, how follow-up appointments will be scheduled, and how reminder phone calls and follow-up phone calls will be scripted. The office procedure manual should include a standard form to capture the full medical history at the first visit. The form should also document how the patient prefers to receive test results (e.g., phone, fax, email, postal mail), emergency contact information, and any special alerts such as orders of protection or avoidance of leaving messages on the home phone.

Another aspect of maintaining respectful relationships with patients involves avoiding any behavior that might be misconstrued as sexual misconduct. The following general recommendations apply to establishing respectful boundaries:

- Take the sexual history while the patient is fully clothed.
- Explain ahead of time the reason for examining the breasts, lower abdomen, genital area, or rectum.
- Provide appropriate gowns and allow the patient to change in privacy.
- Have a chaperone present for both male and female patients when the genitals or rectum will be examined. Unless the patient requests, do not let a family member be the chaperone so that the patient may speak freely about sexual matters. Document the name of the chaperone in the chart. If the patient asks that no chaperone be present, document that fact in the chart.
- Be available to speak with the patient after she or he is fully dressed and the chaperone is not present.
- Avoid joking or suggestive language.
- Educate yourself and your staff about the cultural concerns of specific religious or ethnic groups in your community.
- Demonstrate acceptance and respect for members of sexual minorities (gay, lesbian, bisexual, and transgender). Ask

transgender patients if they prefer to be addressed as a man or a woman.
- Do not agree to see patients privately after hours. Do not suggest or engage in romantic or sexual relationships with patients.

Poor communication with other providers can create major risks. A study of nearly 50,000 malpractice claims against primary care physicians for negligence showed that in the outpatient setting, poor communication between providers could be disastrous.[6] In more than half of the claims, the patient died. Severe damage was also common, where the researchers defined "high severity" as leading to significant permanent, major permanent, or grave injury.

A different aspect of communication problems arises when a physician is seeing a patient as a consultant for the benefit of a third party— for example, in a pre-employment physical or worker's compensation case. The law considers the primary duty of the physician to be to the party paying for the examination, but there is a limited duty to the patient. Contracts in which the third-party payer exempts or forbids the physician from communicating results to the patient are unethical and leave the physician open to a malpractice suit. When a serious potential problem is discovered, the physician must at a minimum inform the patient that follow-up is needed and must stress the appropriate level of urgency. Providing more information, including the potential diagnosis, creates a legal physician–patient relationship with a duty of care, but it is often the ethical and legally safest course to follow.

Physicians who do consult under contract with third-party payers face other potential conflicts of interest and special legal risks. For example, the examining physician must hold confidential any information offered by the patient that is not directly related to the reason for the examination. Likewise, the physician may not engage in discussions with the third-party payer about the patient that are not discoverable by the patient, but may discuss only the contents of the report issued. Legal advice should be sought prior to entering into any agreements with employers or insurance companies.

Documentation

Good documentation is essential to managing risk in the ambulatory setting. Documentation in patients' medical records should include all the key clinical data, especially the reasoning of the physician for the decisions made. In addition, record should indicate the advice and education provided to the patient and family. In the same way that informed consent for a procedure is necessary, many practices also ask for a signed refusal of a strongly indicated recommendation—for example, for a diagnostic colonoscopy. The record should also have notations for missed or cancelled appointments with appropriate follow-up and notations of phone calls. If the phone conversation takes place when the record is not available, a written note should be created immediately either electronically or on paper; the information should be added to the record as soon as possible the next day. No entry should ever be erased or covered up in the record. If an error is made at the time of writing, the mistake should be crossed out with a single line, dated, and initialed by the writer. The correct entry can be added below the erroneous data. If an early entry later proves incorrect—for example, the patient recalls a family member who had early colon cancer—the practitioner can go back to the original

family history and add in the margin "See entry [date]" with signature and date.

Medical records and appointment logs may be kept indefinitely as a protection in case of a lawsuit in the future. Paper records can be scanned electronically and kept in a compact form. Most risk managers, however, advocate keeping the paper records in storage indefinitely.

As the Affordable Care Act takes full effect, more and more practices will convert to use of an electronic medical record (EHR). Most physicians find the following EHR features promote good patient care and efficient use of data:

- Templates for full histories
- Immediate access to evolving standards and guidelines for practice
- Automatic date and time on all entries
- Automatically updated medication record
- E-signatures (making an entry inalterable)
- Alerts to known allergies, drug–drug interactions, and screenings needed
- Ability to graph longitudinally key clinical indicators, such as blood urea nitrogen (BUN) or weight
- Electronic prescribing
- Alerts to missing and abnormal test results
- Ability to mark reports as reviewed
- Simplified referrals
- Integration with other medical records and other systems

Preliminary work suggests that use of an EHR reduces the risk of paid malpractice claims.[42] Other studies show that management of abnormal test results remains a problem, even with an EHR.[43,44] Part of the problem seems to be "alert overload"—physicians receive so many signals from the software that they ignore all but the most urgent. A survey of users of the

EHR found that only 41% were satisfied with their ability to manage test results.[23] The improvements in EHR design that they would most like were as follows:

- Prioritization of tests results with the abnormal reports presented first
- Letter-writing capabilities with predefined texts
- A warning when a patient missed a test

Ambulatory practices that are not yet using an EHR will have many options to buy an effective system that meets their specific needs.

OFFICE MANAGEMENT

Each ambulatory care setting will benefit from having clear, regularly updated policies and procedures that help maintain high standards of patient care and that lower the risk of legal suits from patients or employees. This content fits well into the policy and procedure manual that covers all aspects of the management of the setting. A typical manual begins by explaining the mission, vision, and values of the practice setting. Although the organizational framework varies according to the specific needs of the setting, the following sections are commonly found within a manual:

- Administration
- Personnel
- Records
- Infection control
- Risk management
- Quality management

Each section has content especially relevant to risk management. Some of the most important topics to include are outlined here.

Administration

This section should clearly describe organization of the setting:

Hours of care
Holiday schedule
Procedures for urgent or emergency contact after hours
HIPAA
Patient rights
Treatment rights of adolescents
Patient responsibilities
Policy on missed appointments
Patient complaint procedures
Transfer of care to other provider
Consent forms for treatment and procedures
Policies and consent forms for treating minors
Forms for advance directives
Telephone policies (see **Box 15-7**)

Box 15-7   Telephone Policies

- Documentation of all messages on telephone log and in medical record
- Management of all telephone messages
- Procedures on triage of patient calls
- Policy on reminder calls for appointments
- Policy on prescription refills by telephone

Personnel

This section clarifies all issues of hiring, supervision, standards, discipline, rights, and training of employees (see **Boxes 15-8** through **15-10**).

- Hiring
- Application form for employment
- Policies on references
- Verification of valid licenses, certificates, and hospital privileges (as appropriate)
- Verification of identity

Box 15-8   Hiring Policies to Consider

Routine checks:
- Practitioner databases
- Criminal records
- Credit rating
- Drug screening

Box 15-9   Topics for Employee Training

- HIPAA
- Compliance
- Policies and procedures on communications with patients
- Policies on documentation and integrity of medical records
- Policy on complaints from patients
- Mandatory reporting requirements in state
- Infection control
- Emergency and disaster preparedness
- Communication with low-literacy patients
- Communication with patients with limited English proficiency
- Communication with hearing-impaired patients
- Cultural sensitivity
- Culture of safety
- Reporting of adverse events and near-misses
- Accident prevention

- Mandated immunizations and TB testing
- Compliance with employment laws
  - Equal Employment Opportunity (EEO)
  - Americans with Disabilities Act (ADA)
  - Family and Medical Leave Act (FMLA), if there are 50 or more employees
  - Fair Labor Standards Act (FLSA)
  - Occupational Safety and Health Administration (OSHA) regulations
- Job descriptions with explicit performance standards and identified supervisor
- Dress standards, including use of nametag with job title

- Specific documentation of delegation of services to physician assistants and nurse practitioners in conformity with state regulations
- Employee complaint/grievance policies
- Periodic review of licenses, certificates, and hospital privileges
- Policy on workplace violence
- Disciplinary procedures
- Employee training and education, including dates, specific topics, sign-in sheets, and post-event evaluation of learning.

Box 15-10   OSHA Regulations in Ambulatory Care[45]

- Blood-borne pathogens
- Hazard communication
- Exit routes
- Electrical safety
- Reporting occupational injuries and illnesses
- Display of OSHA poster
- Ionizing radiation

Records

This section of the policy and procedure manual describes policies and procedures for patient health records and for mandated logs at the setting, including the maintenance, storage, and archiving of paper records and the backup of electronic records. Of special importance is a clear policy and procedure regarding documentation of all missed appointments and actions taken in the patient record and documentation of receipt and communication of all test results.

Other important information is maintained in administrative logs. In addition, the setting needs to keep records of the minutes of staff and committee meetings and of fire drills or other emergency preparedness activities.

Box 15-11   Routine Logs

- Treatment logs
- Procedure logs
- Appointment logs
- Controlled substances logs
- Equipment checks

Infection Control

This section describes the policies and procedures in place to allow personnel to provide safe care and to assess systematically adherence to infection prevention practices through periodic direct observation. Some key elements are highlighted here:

- Hand hygiene
- Personnel protective equipment
- Injection safety
- Respiratory hygiene/cough etiquette
- Environmental cleaning
- Sterilization of reusable instruments and devices
- High-level disinfection of reusable instruments and devices (e.g., for endoscopy)

Risk Management

In this section, the manual should describe routine policies needed cover these issues:

- Routine records of self-assessment for potential fraud, lapses in confidentiality, adverse patient outcomes, and legal suits
- The compliance plan and compliance officer as required by the OIG

In addition, even a small practice benefits from having a clear plan for risk management. Usually, the plan specifies that a multidisciplinary risk management committee reviews at least annually the following data:

- Incident identification and reporting, including near-misses and sentinel events
- Methods of assuring the current and ongoing competency of staff
- Results of investigation of the adverse outcomes, near-misses, and sentinel events

A sentinel event in ambulatory care, as defined by The Joint Commission, is "an unexpected occurrence involving death or serious physical or psychological injury, or the risk thereof." In other words, a sentinel event sends a signal or warning that immediate attention is needed. The event is not necessarily the result of error, but its seriousness demands close investigation.

Box 15-12   Examples of Sentinel Events

- Any patient death, paralysis, coma, or other major permanent loss of function associated with a medication error
- A patient fall that results in death or major permanent loss of function as a direct result of the injuries sustained in the fall
- A patient abduction from the organization where he or she receives care, treatment, or services
- Assault, homicide, or other crime resulting in patient death or major permanent loss of function

The investigation involves a root-cause analysis (RCA) to clarify what happened and why. The RCA aims to arrive at a preventive solution, if possible, for the sentinel event. A variety of standard methods for conducting a RCA exist. Whatever the method used, the written minutes of the committee should document the discussion and the action steps taken to prevent a reoccurrence of the adverse event. The documented activities of an on-site risk management committee are helpful not only in improving the quality of patient care but also in defending against malpractice claims by demonstrating a thoughtful and consistent attention to a high quality of care.

Quality Management

It is valuable for each practice to have a quality improvement committee that conducts periodic peer review of charts. Such a committee may review five to ten randomly selected charts to assess how well the practice is meeting a particular standard of care—for example, for good control of diabetes or for screening for colorectal cancer. This activity creates an incentive for ongoing improvement. Practices that use an EHR are able to generate reports on these items readily and may be eligible for a higher rate of reimbursement of "meaningful use" of the EHR. Keeping a record of the activities of this committee and the trends in key indicators is helpful in case of audits or litigation.

SUMMARY

Ambulatory health care is rapidly evolving into a larger sector of the healthcare system with a high-tech, complex environment that presents many challenges to patient safety and to compliance with laws on business practice. The successful ambulatory practice has a robust risk management plan to assess and minimize risks to patients and to the practice. Excellent materials are available in the public domain to guide in the development of the plan and its implementation.

REFERENCES

1. Bishop, T. F., & Casalino, R. A. (2011). Paid malpractice claims for adverse events in inpatient and outpatient settings. *Journal of the American Medical Association, 305*(23), 2427–2431.
2. Institute of Medicine. (1999). *To err is human: Building a safer health system.*
3. GE-Healthcare. (2010). Is your culture ready for event reporting? Part 1.
4. Patient safety network glossary. http://psnet.ahrq.gov/popup_glossary.aspx?name=justculture
5. Marx, D. (2007). Patient safety and the just culture. *The Just Culture Community.*
6. Phillips, R. L. Jr., Dovery, S. M., Fryer, G. E. Jr., Miyoshi, T. J., Green, L. A. (2004). Learning from malpractice claims about negligent, adverse events in primary care in the United States. *Quality and Safety in Health Care, 13*, 121–126.
7. Massachusetts Medical Society. (2011). Failure to properly supervise nurse practitioners and physician assistants.
8. Wash, W. D. (August, 2004). *United States v. Gibson*, No. CR04–374RSM, 2004 WL 2188280.
9. DeWaal, I. C. S. (2007). Successfully prosecuting health insurance portability and accountability act medical privacy violations against noncovered entities. *U.S. Attorneys Bulletin, 55*(4), 10–16.
10. Health Insurance Portability and Accountability Act. 45CFR Parts 160, 162, & 164. U. D. o. H. a. H. Services. *Federal Register.* 164.308.
11. The False Claims Act. All About Qui Tam. http://www.all-about-qui-tam.org/fca_history.shtml
12. Miami Herald (2011). Feds make Medicare fraud sweeps in Miami, nationwide. February 17, 2011.
13. Physician Insurers Association of America. (2002). Breast cancer study. Cited in MedRisk e-Learning Services, Risk Management Consult.
14. Physician Insurers Association of America. (2005). Lung cancer study. Cited in MedRisk e-Learning Services, Risk Management Consult.
15. Physician Insurers Association of America. (2008). Colon cancer study. Cited in MedRisk e-Learning Services, Risk Management Consult.
16. Gandhi, T. K., Thomas, E. J., Puopolo, A. L., Yoon, C., Brennan, T. A., & Studdert, D. M. (2006). Missed and delayed diagnoses in the ambulatory setting: a study

of closed malpractice claims. *Annals of Internal medicine, 145*(7), 488–496.

17. Brown, T. W., Kelen, G. D., & Levy, F. (2010). An epidemiological study of closed emergency department malpractice claims in a national database of physician malpractice insurers. *Academic Emergency Medicine, 17*(5).

18. Rusnak, R. A., & Fastow, J. S. (1994). Misdiagnosis of acute appendicitis: Common features discovered in cases after litigation. *American Journal of Emergency Medicine, 12*(4), 397–512.

19. Physician Insurers Association of America. (2008). Risk management review: Neurology.

20. Blume Gold Fader Berkowitz Donnelly Fired & Forte (2011). $2 million settlement: Failure to timely diagnose and treat breast cancer. Retrieved from http://www.njatty.com/articles/cases/cf06.htm

21. Chen, E. T., Elder, N. C., & Hickner, J. (2010). Crossing the finish line: Follow-up of abnormal test results in a multisite community health center. *Journal of the National Medical Association, 102*(8), 720–725.

22. Singh, H., Petersen, L. A., Collins, C., Petersen, N. J., Shethia, A., & El-Serag, H. B. (2009). Missed opportunities to initiatve endoscopic evaluation for colorectal cancer diagnosis. *American Journal of Gastroenteralogy, 104*(10), 2543–2554.

23. Poon, E. G., Sequist, T. D., Murff, H. J., Karson, A. S., & Bates, D. W. (2004). "I wish I had seen this test result earlier!". Dissatisfaction with test result mangement systems in primary care. *Archives of Internal Medicine, 164*, 2223–2228.

24. Physicians Insurers Association of America. (2000). PIAA Data sharing system.

25. Gandhi, T. K., Borus, J., Seger, A. C., Peterson, J., Burdick, E., Seger, D. L., . . . Bates, D. W. (2003). Adverse drug events in ambulatory care. *New England Journal of Medicine, 348*(16), 1556–1564.

26. Gurwitz, J. H., Harrold, L. R., Rothschild, J., Debellis, K., Seger, A. C., Cadoret, C., . . . Bates, D. W. (2003). Incidence and preventability of adverse drug events among older persons in the the ambulatory setting. *Journal of the American Medical Assoiction, 289*(9), 1107–1116.

27. Budnitz, D. S., Shehab, N., & Richards, C. L. (2011). Emergency hospitalizations for adverse drug events in older Americans. *New England Journal of Medicine, 365*(21), 2002–2012.

28. Wolf, M. S., Bass, P. F., Curtis, L. M., Lindquist, L. A., Webb, J. A., Bocchini, M. V., . . . Parker, R. M. (2010). Improving prescription drug warnings to promote patient comprehension. *Archives of Internal Medicine, 170*(1), 50–56.

29. Thompsson, N. D., Moorman, A. C., & Holmberg, S. D. (2009). Nonhospital health care-associated hepatitis B and C virus transmission: United States, 1998–2008. *Annals of Internal Medicine, 150*(1), 33–39.

30. Nevada State Board of Medical Examiners. Case No. 11-12859. Retrieved from http://www.medboard.nv.gov/Discipline/Kaplan—Michael.htm

31. Abe, K., Sunenshine, R., Noble-Wang, J., Cope, J., Jensen, B., & Srnivasan, A. (2007). Outbreak of *Burkholderia cepacia* bloodstream infection at an outpatient hematology and oncology practice. *Infection Control and Hospital Epidemiology, 28*(11), 1311–1313.

32. Radcliff, R., Briscoe, J., Gupta, R., Fosheim, G., McAllister, S. K., Jensen, B.,. . . Patel, P. P. (2011). Severe methicillin-susceptible *Staphylococcus aureus* infections associated with epidural injections at an outpatient pain clinic. *American Journal of Infection Control.*

33. Hocevar, S. N., Williams, M., Pascoe, N., O'Connel, H., Jensen, B., Hatch, M., & MacCanell, T. (2010). *Allergy injection-associated* Mycobacterium *abscessus outbreak—Texas, 2009.* Infectious Diseases Society of America, 48th Annual Meeting, Vancouver.

34. Dickinson, C. (2011). Children told to be tested for HIV after flu vaccine reused. TV Broadcast, 9NEWS Evenings. Denver, CO. 9News.com

35. Kassis, C., Raad, I. I., Perego, C. A., Dvorak, T., Hulten, K. G., Frenzel, E.,. . . Chemaly, R. F. (2011). Outbreak of community-acquired methicillin-resistant *Staphyloccus aureus* skin infection among health care workers in a cancer center. *American Journal of Infection Control, 39*(2), 112–117.

36. U.S. Department of Health and Human Services. (2011). *CDC guide to infection prevention in outpatient settings: Minimum expectations for safe care.* 16.

37. U.S. Department of Health and Human Services. (2011). *CDC infection prevention checklist for outpatient settings: Minimum expectations for safe care.* 16.

38. Gale, B. D., Davidson, S. J., & Juran, D. C. (2011). Failure to notify reportable test results: Significance

in medical malpractice. *Journal of the American College of Radiology, 8*(11); 776–779.

39. Boohaker, E. A., Uman, J. E., & McCarthy, B. D. (1996). Patient notification and follow-up of abnormal test results: A physician survey. *Archives of Internal Medicine, 156*(3), 327–331.

40. O'Malley, A. S. (2011). Referral and consultation communication between primary care and specialist physicians. Ibid. *171*(1), 56–65.

41. Groves, J. E. (1978). Taking care of the hateful patient. *New England Journal of Medicine, 298*(16), 883–887.

42. Virapongse, A., Shi, P., Jenter, C. A., Volk, L. A., Kleinman, K., Sato, L., & Simon, S. R. (2008). Electronic health records and malpractice claims in office practice. *Archives of Internal Medicine, 168*(21), 2362–2367.

43. Singh, H., Sittig, D. F., Espadas, D., Khan, M. M., & Petersen, L. A. (2010). Notification of abnormal lab test results in an electornic medical record: Do any safety concerns remain? *American Journal of Medicine, 123*(3), 238–244.

44. Singh, H., Vu, M. S., Rao, R., Khan, M. M., & Petersen, L. A. (2007). Communication outcomes of critical imaging results in a computerized notification system. *Journal of the American Medical Informatics Association, 14*(4), 459–466.

45. OSHA. Compliance assistance quick start: Health care industry. Retrieved from https://www.osha.gov/dcsp/compliance_assistance/quickstarts/health_care/index_hc.htm

CHAPTER 16

Risk Management in Long-Term Care Institutions and Services

Kathie McDonald-McClure

INTRODUCTION

In 2010, individuals age 65 and older made up 13% of the total U.S. population.[1] Among all the states, Florida had the highest percentage of seniors (17.2%), while Alaska had the lowest percentage (7.6%).[2,3] Seniors are predicted to account for 16.5% of the U.S. population in 2020 as a direct result of the aging "baby boomer" generation.[4] The first of the "baby boomers" (those born between 1946 and 1964) turned age 65 in 2011, and the aging of this cohort will lead to dramatic growth in the number of older Americans. In turn, by 2020, an estimated 12 million older Americans will require care by a long-term care provider.[5]

Long-term care providers serve individuals who require nursing, support for activities of daily living, or custodial care for extended periods of time due to chronic, multiple health problems and functional disabilities.[6] Additionally, long-term care providers provide post-acute care for those who need treatment or rehabilitation to completely recover or regain independence.[7] Several options of care are available depending on a patient's needs and independence, including nursing homes, community-based services, home health care, and hospice. People typically develop long-term health care needs as they age, so the predicted

increase in the size of the elderly population presages significant challenges for the long-term care provider community.

The increase in need for long-term care also is placing significant pressure on both private and government financial resources. In 2005, spending for nursing homes and home care was $206.6 billion.[8] Almost 70% of these expenditures was funded through Medicare and Medicaid, 7% by health insurance, 18% through out-of-pocket expenses by families, and 5% from other sources. This excludes the costs of unpaid family caregivers and lost wages of family members while taking care of their relatives. By 2009, the cost to the Medicare and Medicaid programs for nursing home and home health care had quadrupled from 2005, with expenditures by Medicare reaching $502.3 billion and Medicaid reaching $373.9 billion.[9]

TYPES OF LIABILITY CLAIM COSTS

Like the rising costs of long-term care, the costs of general and professional liability insurance for long-term care providers have been increasing over the last few decades. This trend reflects increases in both the number of lawsuits and the size of awards. Insurance for long-term care facilities also has become more expensive as many insurance writers have withdrawn from the business. The increased costs of maintaining commercial liability insurance have forced some nursing homes to close or to operate without insurance, both of which have caused certain long-term care professionals to question the well-being and quality of care for elderly people.[10]

The 2011 long-term care actuarial analysis conducted by AON from data available as of 2010 indicated that, while the frequency of long-term care claims has decreased since 2005, the severity of such claims has increased, resulting in a higher average loss per paid claim. The average loss rate per occupied long-term bed for 2010 was $1,390. The average ultimate size of each long-term claim increased from $125,000 in 2005 to $153,000 in 2010. In terms of frequency, falls with injury accounted for most losses (27%), followed by pressure ulcers or wounds (17%), adverse responses to procedures (11.4%), unknown causes (22.7%), and other causes (21.9%), such as elopement, assault, abuse, neglect, adverse drug reactions, and injuries unrelated to falls.[11]

In terms of claim dollars by claim type, pressure ulcers and wounds accounted for the largest percentage of claim dollars at 28.7%, with their high average claim size being $264,843. By comparison, the more frequent claim type, falls with injury, accounted for 22.5% of the total claim dollars, with an average of $131,104 paid per claim. Although elopements occur far less often than pressure ulcers and other injuries, they are financially more costly than all other claim types, with an average claim size of approximately $300,000.[11]

Long-term care claims are also affected by substantive tort reform. States that have implemented such reform have legislatively capped non economic damages at $500,000 or less. In 2010, in states with substantive tort reform, the average loss rate per occupied bed was $1,200, and claim frequency in such states has been decreasing since 2003. States without substantive tort reform, by comparison, had an average loss rate of $1,540 per occupied bed and a claim frequency that has remained stable at a higher rate than that found in states with reform.[11]

Risk management in long-term care requires continuous identification of situations, policies, or practices that have the potential to cause financial loss. The goal of risk management is to develop and implement strategies to remove or minimize these risks. In developing a loss control strategy, it is important to consider the various factors that contribute to liability claims in long-term care, including the demographics of the long-term care patient that the provider should be prepared to address, the long-term care type category into which the provider falls, and the regulatory enforcement environment within which the long-term care provider operates.

DEMOGRAPHICS OF INDIVIDUALS NEEDING LONG-TERM CARE

Potential sources of liability risk for long-term care include the patient's or resident's own physiology or medical diagnosis, the care provider, the type of care the individual receives, and the environment in which the individual receives his or her care. As people age, they become more susceptible to chronic illness or functional difficulties.[12] A 2007 study on the health of older Americans found that 80% of Americans age 65 and older have at least one chronic health problem, with the treatment of chronic conditions accounting for almost 95% of healthcare expenditures.[13] As people move into their eighties and nineties, the results of physiological aging substantially increase the probability of needing additional, regular assistance with day-to-day activities.[14] In 2004, approximately 85% of all nursing home residents 65 and older required assistance in three or more activities of daily living, such as bathing, dressing, eating, transferring from bed to chair, and using the toilet.[15]

In addition to being prepared to give assistance with activities of daily living, long-term care providers must be prepared to address a resident's medical problems. Primary medical diagnoses of nursing home residents fall into three major categories: circulatory system disorders (23.7% at admission), mental disorders (16.4% at admission), and nervous system disorders (14% at admission).[15] Aging brings on declines in immune response (making the elderly more susceptible to infection), thermal response, renal and pulmonary function, and glucose tolerance. Physiological changes of aging can significantly affect the absorption, distribution, metabolism, and clearance of drugs, thereby affecting drug therapy in the elderly.[16,17]

Individuals in long-term care settings also need greater protection in minimizing accidents. In some cases, their mental health may suffer as they age, leading to wandering or forgetfulness.

Documentation in the medical record of admission status, periodic appraisals of physical health and mental status and the potential deteriorations identified previously, and all important events and incidents is critical for both the care of the patients and the protection of the facility. These age-related risks, along with related liability exposure and risk management strategies, are addressed in greater detail in specific subsections later in this chapter.

TYPES OF LONG-TERM CARE PROVIDERS

Long-term nursing care is provided in a variety of settings today, ranging from 3-bed, privately owned adult residential care homes, to 20-bed units in acute care hospitals, to 1,200-bed government-operated institutions. In 2004, there were more than 16,100 nursing facilities and 1.7 million beds in the United States, which had an occupancy rate of 86.3%.[15] Of U.S. residents age 65 and older, 1,317,300 were living in nursing homes in 2004.[18] Nearly three-fourths of nursing home residents were women, and approximately half were 85 and older.[18] The average length of stay was 835 days, which is expected to decrease as home care services and subacute care become more readily available.[19]

Subacute care, which can have varying definitions, is generally considered a step above skilled nursing home care, while not quite rising to the level of acute hospital care. It is often an option for people who do not require further hospitalization but are not well enough to return to a nursing home or to home. With this type of care, a resident receives therapy or treatment for a specific illness or injury until he or she is able to return home or to a wing of the facility that provides less intensive care.[20,21]

Another type of long-term care is home and community-based care. Home and community-based care can include a wide range of services in the individual's home (e.g., physical, psychosocial, case management, personal care, homemaker, chore services, respite care, transportation, telephone reassurance and friendly visiting, home-delivered meals).[22] The availability of such care has gradually increased because many elderly and chronically ill people prefer to remain in their own homes. Based on

2000 U.S. Census data, an estimated two-thirds of individuals who receive long-term care live in the community rather than in an institutional setting.[23]

Finally, a form of home care that has garnered increased recognition over the last decade is hospice care. The focus of these services is on comfort care, not on curing an illness. It is provided by a team of specially trained professionals and caregivers who care for the "whole person," including his or her physical, emotional, social, and spiritual needs. Hospice care is most often provided in the home, although it can be provided on a temporary basis in an institutional setting, and is generally available only for individuals who are terminally ill with a life expectancy of six months or less.[24]

LONG-TERM CARE REGULATORY ENFORCEMENT: QUALITY OF CARE

This chapter focuses on nursing homes because of the availability of more liability risk data and because a significant factor in the heightened liability for nursing homes is the fact that nursing homes have been highly regulated. However, many of the risk and liability issues for nursing homes have just as much applicability to the other long-term care settings described earlier, particularly with the passage of the Patient Protection and Affordability of Care Act (PPACA), which was signed into law on March 23, 2010.[25] The PPACA gave the Center for Medicare & Medicaid Services (CMS) more tools with which to aggressively enforce provider compliance with healthcare fraud, waste, and abuse laws. This increased enforcement is expected to reveal more deficiencies across the span of long-term provider types, and

particularly among providers for which there is evidence of unchecked fraud and abuse, including home health and hospice. Of particular concern is that federal and state fraud and abuse enforcement efforts are increasingly including civil and criminal prosecutions for substandard quality of care, "worthless services," and the failure to meet the regulatory conditions of participation in the Medicare program. Evidence of this step-up in quality of care enforcement can be seen in United States Attorney Offices across the United States.[26,27] (See **Box 16-1**.)

> ### Box 16-1
>
> - A U.S. Attorney claimed that a nursing home violated the False Claims Act by billing Medicare and Medicaid $16 million for inadequate care, including failure to follow physicians' orders, failure to treat wounds and pressure sores, failure to update resident care plans, and failure to monitor blood sugar levels of diabetic residents.[26]
> - The California Department of Social Services revoked the license of a residential care facility, and the facility's owners faced police and district attorney criminal investigation into financial and physical abuse after one resident died and two were hospitalized.[28]

Oversight of nursing homes is split between federal and state authorities.[29] Nursing homes are licensed by the state in which the facility is located and, therefore, are subject to certain state requirements for maintenance of the facility's license. Each state establishes its own definition of a nursing home, licensing requirements, and regulations.

A 1986 Institute of Medicine study found that many nursing home residents were being abused, neglected, and given inadequate care. As a result, in 1987, the Federal Nursing Home Reform Act, which was part of the Omnibus

Budget Reconciliation Act (OBRA '87), was passed. OBRA '87 significantly affected nursing home standards by establishing a Residents' Bill of Rights and requiring nursing homes to meet minimum standards of care to receive Medicare and Medicaid reimbursement.[30] CMS (formerly known as the Health Care Financing Administration [HCFA]), an agency of the U.S. Department of Health and Human Services (DHHS), is responsible for establishing these standards. State agencies, under a contract with CMS, are responsible for determining whether the facility meets these standards, while CMS surveyors often do a comparative survey to check the adequacy of the state agency inspection of the facility.[29]

In July 1998, President Bill Clinton announced a nursing home quality initiative to strengthen the oversight of nursing homes and to levy strong penalties against nursing homes that failed to meet the Medicare and Medicaid standards. In response, DHHS, through HCFA, phased in key provisions to strengthen nursing home inspection systems. In addition, DHHS issued new instructions to the states to strengthen their nursing home inspections and to take tougher enforcement actions against poor performers.

Each regulatory body has its own schedule of on-site facility inspections and reviews of administrative policies, operations, finances, professionals' credentials, and medical and nursing care services.[31] Close attention should be paid to the necessary documentation of patient care conferences, meetings of the board of directors, medical staff meetings, adverse incidents, and committees on medical records, infection control, and safety. Site inspection reports are given to the facility, which then has the opportunity to correct the deficiencies and

avoid sanctions.[32] To encourage nursing home compliance, sanctions may be imposed for unmet requirements, including fines, denial of reimbursements, required training, monitoring, or termination from Medicare and Medicaid programs.[33] (See **Box 16-2**). State agencies that inspect facilities propose sanctions, and CMS then reviews and imposes them.[33] A facility may appeal the cited deficiency through informal dispute resolution, before an administrative law judge, or before the DHHS Department Appeals Board.[33] If the appeal is successful, the sanction may be reduced or rescinded.[32]

Box 16-2

Medicare sanctions include the following options:

- Civil monetary penalty (CMP), in which a home must pay a fine for each day or incidence of noncompliance
- Denial of payment for new admissions (DPNA), in which Medicare and Medicaid payments may be denied for new residents
- In-service training, in which the facility must train its employees on a specific issue
- Plan of correction, in which CMS develops a plan that the facility must follow within a certain period of time
- State monitoring by an on-site monitor to ensure compliance and goal achievement
- Temporary management, in which a manager appointed by the state steps in with the power to hire, fire, and make changes as necessary
- Termination, where the facility is deemed ineligible to receive Medicare or Medicaid payments

Of these penalties, fines are the most common. Through the appeal processes, however, facilities can avoid having to pay the fines by correcting the problem.[33] This, in turn, can lead to a "yo–yo"–type action, in which facilities constantly are in and out of compliance.

The written site inspection report is called a statement of deficiencies and plan of correction. The statement of deficiencies is a detailed report of the nursing facility's perceived failure(s) to meet Medicare and Medicaid standards. The facility lists its proposed plan of correction in a column next to each stated deficiency. Plaintiff attorneys often seek to admit the statement of deficiencies into evidence in jury trials, arguing that the failure to comply with the cited standards constitutes proof of alleged negligent care that led to a resident's injuries, decline in physical or mental health, or death. The plaintiff attorney also may seek to use the defendants' plan of correction as an admission of wrongdoing by the nursing home. Accordingly, the facility should state at the beginning of its plan of corrections that the submitted plan is not intended to be an admission by the facility of any liability or wrongdoing. The facility may be well advised to seek legal counsel before submitting a plan of correction for serious deficiencies, particularly if a liability claim is likely.

LONG-TERM CARE LIABILITY FOR FALSE OR DECEPTIVE MARKETING

Risk managers should be involved with monitoring the institution's marketing activities, which can also create liability risks. Importantly, plaintiff attorneys in a negligent care lawsuit will attempt to use the marketing materials as evidence of the high-quality care that the facility failed to provide. Similarly, nursing facilities, assisted living, and other long-term care providers may be liable to residents or patients, or may be forced to pay substantial fines, if it is determined that they have falsely advertised their services or the results of their services.[34] Facilities that knowingly make misleading or false

representations are at risk for a deceptive trade practice lawsuit and possible penalties of triple damages, all attorneys' fees, and costs. Because this type of action is not based on professional negligence, malpractice insurance may not cover it.

To reduce the risk of advertising liability:

- *Do* limit information in your brochures to verifiable facts about the facility and the care rendered to patients.
- *Do* use factual statements about accommodations, programs, services, and admission procedures.
- *Do* review brochures with regard to state deceptive trade practice statutes and consumer protection laws.
- *Do* review and revise older brochures still in circulation.
- *Don't* use words that imply guarantees such as "promise" or "ensure."
- *Don't* use absolute phrases that may be misleading or could be used against the facility in the event that there is a less than optimal outcome for a resident, such as "state-of-the-art facility," "the most secure accommodations," or "programs are designed to allow each resident to return to independent living."
- *Don't* indicate approval for specialized programs until the approval has been officially secured.

Retain all marketing material in accordance with the organization's document retention policy and any state law requirements. Keep a record of the precise dates during which each piece of marketing material was in use, which could help to protect the facility in the event of litigation that involves which promises were made and when. Include admission packets in your review of marketing materials to ensure consistent messaging and avoidance of potentially misleading, false, or overly zealous marketing statements.

LIABILITY RISKS ASSOCIATED WITH AGING

Decreased Cognition and Sensory Risks

Physiological aging is universal and progressive as one accumulates chronic disorders and disabilities. Elderly people's weakened immune systems and slower responses can certainly be traced to aging. With aging, there is a decrease in brain weight, accompanied by a change in the proportion of gray to white matter, which may affect an individual's cognitive abilities. A person's memory worsens because the number of cells decreases. Age-related changes also affect sight, hearing, taste, touch, and smell, as well as physiological patterns and abilities.[35] The decreased cognitive and sensory abilities, in turn, influence the ability to complete daily living activities unaided.[36]

Fall Risks

As an individual ages, bone density and strength decrease, making the individual prone to fractures.[35] Falls are the leading cause of injuries for elderly people,[37] with one-third of elderly adults falling every year.[38] The most common resultant injuries are to the head and fractures of the wrist, spine, and hip. "The cost of falls among older people is enormous because of the resulting high death toll, disabling conditions, and recovery in hospitals and rehabilitation institutions."[39] The United States spends an estimated $20 billion annually for the treatment of elderly post-fall injuries. Of the 380,000 hip fractures in 2008, each costing an average of $37,000, 90% were a result of falling. "Approximately 25 percent of hip fracture patients make a full recovery, 40 percent require a nursing home admission, 50 percent will be dependent on a cane or a walker, and 20 percent will die in one year."[39]

While older people are understandably nervous about falling, it is possible that their fears make them more likely to fall.[40] Studies have identified factors, besides medical illness, affecting falls in nursing homes. Hill et al.'s study interviewed nursing staff who had witnessed at least one resident fall. The study identified three broad themes with several categories contributing to the risk of falls. First, the person may contribute to his or her risk of falling due to changes in health status, decline in functional abilities, or behavioral or personality changes. Second, the nursing home environment may increase this risk through design safety errors such as unreachable call buttons, limited space leading to clutter, obstacles blocking the residents, equipment misuse such as not locking wheelchairs or using them as walking devices, and staff organization. Hill et al.'s study indicated that falls were more likely when a facility is understaffed because nurses are not able to monitor the residents as effectively. Third, interactions may lead to falls, such as high-risk activities. Falls are more likely to occur during changes of shift and meal times, with the highest percentage of falls occurring between 6 and 8 P.M. when everyone is finishing dinner and preparing for bed.[41]

One review examined the correlation between falls and medication, finding that side effects including dizziness, motor impairment, or cognitive changes may increase the risk of falling. Psychotropic drugs were also strongly associated with falls. In addition to the type of drug prescribed, the dosage and use of multiple medications influenced the risk of falling.[42]

Another review analyzed studies conducted to reduce falls in long-term care facilities. Several studies tested the effects of exercise on falling, determining that courses combining different types of exercise (e.g., balance, strength/resistance, endurance, and flexibility) achieved a significant reduction in the rate of falls. Where only one type of exercise was used, balance or functional training reduced the rate of falls, but other types of exercise by themselves did not. Some surgeries also affected fall rates. Cardiac pacemakers reduced fall rates. Cataract surgery in the first eye reduced fall rates, although surgery in the second eye did not. The review found that home safety interventions did not reduce fall rates.[43]

These findings indicate that a variety of factors affect the likelihood of a fall. Systematic evaluation of adverse events in each nursing home should help facilities identify and correct these factors to reduce the risk. Generally, risk factors for falls can be modified through exercise, a review of medication profiles, elimination of medications that may increase the risk of falling, and the use of environmental safety devices such as hand rails.

Medication Risks

Elderly people often take several different medications. Combined with general frailty and functional decline, they are very susceptible to adverse drug events (ADEs).[44] Adverse drug events are a result of adverse drug reactions or medication errors in prescription or administration. Severe illness or taking multiple medications at the same time can increase the possibility of an ADE. Nursing home residents as a group are particularly vulnerable because they are often ill or taking many medications.[45] It may be difficult to identify whether an ADE has occurred, however, because symptoms can be nonspecific, such as a fall or general cognitive impairment.[44]

The results of a Massachusetts study suggested that 350,000 ADEs occur yearly in the national nursing home population, with more than half being preventable. The study indicated that 20,000 fatal or life-threatening ADEs occur each year, of which as many as 80% were preventable. A study conducted by the same researchers three years later revealed that as many as 1.9 million ADEs occur in the United States each year, 40% of which were preventable.[46]

Inappropriate dosages, adverse drug reactions, omissions, incorrect administration or prescription of medications, and polypharmacy create medication risks for a resident. These factors can also predispose residents to other risks that have serious effects, such as falls. To avoid common—and often preventable—problems, long-term care facilities must develop procedures to recognize drug-related effects quickly, to ensure accurate and safe prescription and dispersal of medications, and to monitor a resident who is on medications.

Infection Control Risks

The incidence of infection increases dramatically with age because an older person's immune system is considered to be more compromised than that of a younger person.[36] A recent study indicated that 15% of U.S. nursing facilities were cited for deficiencies in infection control. Infections are responsible for nearly 400,000 deaths each year. In one study conducted by the University of Pittsburgh

Graduate School of Health, being short-staffed was associated with the facility's receipt of an infection control citation. The researchers expressed a concern that overworked or rushed staff might overlook infection control measures, such as hand washing.[47]

Infection control programs in nursing homes and facilities are mandated by a variety of oversight-oriented organizations. To participate in Medicare, for example, a nursing facility must have an infection control program. The program must establish methods to investigate infections, to prevent the spread of disease, and to accommodate employees who have communicable diseases.[48] The Occupational Safety and Health Administration (OSHA) also regulates infection control in nursing homes. Nursing facilities must follow the industry standards in 29 C.F.R. 1910 *et seq.* Twenty-five states have established additional OSHA-approved plans.[49] Finally, government and private agencies also have focused on preventing infection, including the Association for Practitioners in Infection Control, the American Geriatrics Society, and the federal Centers for Disease Control and Prevention (CDC). State and local standards governing nursing homes and facilities vary depending on the location.

Infection control risks arise when there are inadequate preventive measures or lack of enforcement of measures in place: hand washing; proper sharps disposal; monitoring and control of staff and visitors who may bring infectious diseases into the facility; isolation of residents when indicated; wearing gloves, goggles, and gowns when caring for infectious patients; moving and repositioning patients who are bedridden or always in wheelchairs; and education of staff in infection control policies.[50] When these safety procedures are not followed, the facility may be found liable for injuries to employees or residents.

Under the 1987 Omnibus Budget Reconciliation Act (OBRA) legislation, HCFA (renamed CMS) developed an outcome-oriented survey process. That process aimed to ensure that residents received the highest quality of care while maintaining the highest obtainable level of functioning. Through the OBRA regulations, the required infection control committee was replaced with a newly mandated quality assessment committee that was given a broader scope of responsibility. CMS has since emphasized the need to control and prevent infection in long-term care facilities. Each facility must design an infection control program that meets the following criteria:

- Investigates, controls, and prevents infections in the facility
- Decides which procedures, such as isolation, should be applied to an individual resident
- Maintains a record of incidents and corrective actions related to infections[50]

Risk managers in nursing homes and facilities should develop programs that exceed the minimum standard of care. Development, implementation, and ongoing evaluation of written infection control policies and procedures can foster a well-informed, well-educated, and well-trained staff to protect residents and staff from infection and liability.

Pressure Ulcer Risks

Skin also becomes more fragile with the aging process, making the elderly more susceptible not only to bruises and cuts but also to pressure ulcers.[35] Pressure ulcers are also known as bed sores, pressure sores, and decubitus ulcers. They are generally found on the elbow, heel, hip, shoulder, back, and back of the head. An estimated 11% of nursing home residents had pressure ulcers in 2004. State and federal regulatory agencies view pressure ulcers as an indicator of potentially deficient quality of care.[51] Even when pressure ulcers are unavoidable,[52] their presence presents a high risk of exposure from both a regulatory and liability claim standpoint. Pressure ulcers were responsible for 17% of the distribution of long-term care claims in 2010 and accounted for 28.7% of the dollar distribution, making them the most costly incidents, with the exception of elopement, at an average of $264,843 per claim.[11] Nursing home negligence claims based on the development of a resident's pressure ulcer have resulted in multimillion-dollar verdicts. (See **Box 16-3**.)

Risks in Caring for Patients with Dementia

A failure to make appropriate care provisions for an individual with dementia who then suffers an injury, often from a fall, can lead to significant liability risk. (See **Box 16-4**.) The term "dementia" describes several symptoms that affect a person's intellectual and social functions.[54] Although Alzheimer's disease is the most common cause of dementia in older people, various other causes are possible, including hereditary diseases and physical injuries.[55] Currently, an estimated 5.3 million Americans are affected by Alzheimer's disease.[56] In some persons, unfamiliar environments or changes in their environments may trigger exaggerated reactions, unusual sexual behaviors, wandering or accidents, including falls. Older adults also experience sleep pattern changes that result in more frequent, and longer, periods of nocturnal waking as compared to those of younger adults. Older adults with mild to moderate organic brain syndrome exhibit "sundowning," or sundown syndrome, which involves behavioral changes that begin in the early evening and range

---

Box 16-3

A jury in Polk County, Florida, awarded $114 million (including $100 million in punitive damages) to the estate of a female resident who was placed in a nursing home for rehabilitation to regain her strength so that she could return home. Within two weeks of her admission, the resident fell and experienced a closed head trauma. Afterward, the resident developed multiple pressure ulcers (including one with a very deep wound to the bone); allegedly became malnourished, dehydrated, and overmedicated; and developed contractures. The plaintiff introduced evidence that the nursing home company's focus was on expansion and growth, and not on resident care. Former caregivers, including the staff coordinator, a certified nurse assistant, and a nurse, all testified about terrible conditions, including short staff and inadequate supplies. The plaintiff's expert testified that the resident's injuries were the result of poor treatment that led to her death.[53]

Box 16-4

A jury in Fayette County, Kentucky, rendered a verdict for $1,027,473 (including $1 million for pain and suffering) for a female nursing home resident who had Alzheimer's disease, among other conditions, and was found on an unlocked storage room floor with serious multiple fractures and cuts to her head and face. The plaintiff claimed that the nursing home staff failed to adequately supervise her. The resident had gone missing for a short period and a search then ensued, whereupon the staff found her in the storage room. The nursing home's defense was that care was exemplary in that the staff had implemented an appropriate care plan and carefully observed the resident every 30 minutes. The plaintiff countered that the real criticism was not of the nurses but of the "powers-that-be behind the scenes that made decisions that affect patient care." The claim for punitive damages was not allowed.[58]

from disorientation to nighttime wandering to hallucinations.[57]

Individuals with dementia often place themselves in dangerous situations, making their safety a major liability risk. Many people with dementia have additional behavioral problems that their caregivers must accommodate, including wandering, delusions, refusal of care, and aggression.[59] Dementia and age-related behavioral changes, which are often the root of a liability claim, are some of the most difficult and challenging for long-term care providers to address.

Because dementia is such a common occurrence with nursing home residents, with an estimated 60% to 80% of residents in 2005 having some form of dementia, long-term care providers need policies to protect these residents. Providers must address the dementia patient's unique needs for controlled levels of stimulation, personalized structure of daily events based on an individualized care plan, and provision of verbal and visual guides to assist residents as they move from one activity to another.[59] Care for these individuals must be planned, monitored, and adjusted to accommodate their cognitive impairments. Program design should strive to eliminate chemical and physical restraints and should include appropriate policies and procedures and proper documentation of restraints, when used. Comprehensive orientation, support, and education of staff working with the special care that individuals with dementia need are essential in minimizing risk. These measures can help protect residents from potential injury and the facility from claims of abuse and substandard care.

Elopement and Wandering Risks

As stated previously, individuals with dementia often pose a heightened risk for wandering and elopement, creating many difficulties for the long-term care provider and often exposing the provider to extremely costly lawsuits. Two types of wandering are distinguished: (1) goal directed, in which the resident appears to be searching for something, and (2) non-goal directed, where the resident wanders aimlessly. Of even greater concern is that people who wander are at a risk to "elope"—that is, to leave the long-term care facility unsupervised—increasing the potential for harm. Elopement can be goal or non-goal directed. Discovering that a resident has eloped is a daunting experience for the caregivers and the family. Those who elope may be disoriented and unprepared to navigate unfamiliar outdoor landscapes.[60,61] (See **Box 16-5**.)

Box 16-5
A resident in Massachusetts eloped from a nursing facility in the middle of the night. She was later found dead in a puddle of water near the nursing home. State officials found that the facility had not taken precautions to prevent these types of occurrences and fined the nursing home $20,000.[62]

Elopement lawsuits against long-term care providers, particularly nursing homes, result in some of the highest per-claim costs, estimated to be near $300,000. Fortunately, the incidence of elopement is relatively small in comparison to other claims.[11] Even so, no long-term care provider can afford to be without a risk management plan that aims to reduce resident elopement. When the individual who has eloped is disoriented or suffers from dementia, the potential for an adverse outcome increases. Elopement has ended in hypothermia, accidents involving cars, and death. Once an individual has been missing for more than 24 hours, the risk of death or injury increases dramatically.[60]

At admission, the long-term care provider should evaluate the individual's mental capacity and his or her propensity for wandering. If the individual has wandered or eloped before, or if he or she has had recent cognitive or behavioral changes, the assessment should reflect those events and take steps to safeguard the individual. As part of a risk management plan, nursing homes and assisted living facilities should develop an elopement limitation plan and familiarize all staff with it. The facility should identify those residents at risk of elopement and notify staff of this possibility. Because physical and chemical restraints are usually inappropriate to control residents with wandering tendencies, facilities should use other means to monitor residents, such as regularly checking on them or using electronic tags that notify staff if a resident steps too close to an exit.[60,61]

Disguising exits may also hinder a resident's flight; however, facilities should be careful not to violate fire safety procedures in doing so.[61] Efforts to make the resident feel comfortable also may reduce the urge to leave the building.[60] In the event that a resident does leave, the facility must take immediate steps to locate him or her, notifying the police and even the media if necessary.[60] Finally, a long-term care facility should communicate with residents' families to explain facility policies and procedures aimed at addressing wandering behavior and elopement risk issues, which may prompt families to provide information that can help reduce the risk for a resident.

Restraint Risks

Although the 2011 AON report[11] did not specifically identify restraints as a liability risk, adverse outcomes after an inappropriate use of restraints can prompt a liability claim. A physical restraint is "any manual method or physical or mechanical device, material, or equipment attached or adjacent to the resident's body that the individual cannot remove easily which restricts freedom of movement or normal access to one's body." These items include "leg restraints, arm restraints, hand mitts, soft ties or vests, lap cushions, and lap trays," as well as bed rails, Velcro, and placement of a mobile chair in a position where a resident cannot freely move or get up. Chemical restraints are drugs "used for discipline or convenience and not required to treat medical symptoms."[63]

The use of restraints to control behavior in individuals in long-term care facilities has significantly decreased over the last 20 years. In 1991, an estimated 21% of residents were restrained.[64] By 2007, only 5.5% were restrained.[65] Risks of restraints include injury from falls, accidental death by strangulation, contractures, pressure sores, anxiety, social isolation, and functional decline.

Patient autonomy is a concern when using physical restraints. One of the provisions in the 1987 OBRA legislation mandates that "[t]he resident has the right to be free of, and the facility must ensure freedom from, any restraints imposed or psychoactive drug administrations for the purpose of discipline or convenience, and not required to treat the resident's medical symptoms." These regulations require documentation for restraint use as well as informed consent. Even so, if a resident needs emergency treatment or unexpectedly exhibits violent behavior, restraints may be used to protect the safety of the resident and others.[63]

A risk manager's restraint reduction program must keep medical, nursing, and administrative staff informed of Food and Drug Administration (FDA) product alerts regarding safety issues with restraining devices. FDA bed rail alerts, for example, warn of entrapment and death risks that result when an individual gets trapped between the bed rail and bed mattress.[66,67] The restraint reduction program also should require development and adoption of written policies and procedures addressing the use of restraints. If a policy permits restraints, it should clearly address how evaluations are conducted, including the maximum time between observations and appropriate documentation in the medical record. The policy should conform to CMS standards.

Therapy and Dietary Services Risks

Not every service is directly related to medical needs or provided by employees of a long-term care facility. Other services or service groups can add further risks and potential harm that must be reviewed and addressed. For example, long-term care facilities are required to provide certain dietary services.[68] The facility must employ qualified dieticians, prepare palatable and nutritious meals, and ensure proper sanitary conditions in the preparation and distribution of food.[68] The facility faces liability risks from improper handling of food or sanitation procedures, use of outdated foods, lack of training or lack of documentation of the training of feeders, lack of documentation of prescribed therapeutic diets, or failure to meet each patient's nutritional needs. Lack of proper nutrition and appropriate hydration, based on the resident's needs and medical conditions, may expose a resident to other risks, such as the exacerbation of diabetes or a cardiac condition, the spread of infectious diseases, or the development, or delayed healing, of pressure ulcers related to malnourishment, or dehydration. (See **Box 16-6**.) Facilities and other long-term care providers should consider the resident's or patient's personal assessment and plan of care in preparing food selections.

Box 16-6
A Hopkins County, Kentucky, jury awarded $42.75 million (including $40 million for punitive damages) to the spouse of a 92-year-old nursing home resident suffering from multiple comorbidities, including cancer and stroke, who died within nine days of admission from alleged dehydration and malnutrition. The resident also had infections and bed sores. The state protective services investigated and substantiated the neglect allegations. The plaintiff claimed that he simply failed to get enough water through his feeding tube to survive during his short stay. The nursing home's defense focused on the resident's age and significant preexisting conditions (prostrate cancer, renal problems, stroke, malnutrition, pleural effusions) and on evidence that nurses followed all doctor orders regarding water flushes.[69]

Another common service that an outside group often provides is therapy. Many therapeutic technologies such as electrical stimulation, heat applications, hot water, and plaster casting may cause burns, scarring, and deformities if used incorrectly, opening up a facility to liability claims.[70] Utilization of occupational therapy, physical therapy, and therapeutic recreation resources each has associated risks for long-term care patients and residents. (See **Box 16-7**.) Staff education in each therapeutic area should be emphasized to alert staff to the potential hazardous risks of their respective professions and the need to document treatments, incidents, and adverse events.

Disaster Planning and Fire Safety

Disasters can occur both inside and outside the facility, and long-term care facilities are required to prepare plans to deal with both possibilities.[72] Written plans must exist that include

A paraplegic patient in Tennessee who was receiving physical therapy fell from her wheelchair while unattended. This 22-year-old had made great progress during her first month of training, which increased her self-esteem and hope for the future. However, after the accident caused a fractured femur, she experienced severe major depression and great emotional distress about the loss of opportunity and independence. She received a case settlement of $140,000.[71]

simulation drills.[72] Fires are a serious safety concern, especially as residents of long-term care facilities are unlikely to be able to quickly evacuate. Facilities must comply with the Life Safety Code of the National Fire Protection Association, install battery-operated smoke alarms, and install a sprinkler system.[73] Facilities also must have an emergency power system sufficient to light entrances, maintain life support systems, and maintain fire protection devices.[73]

Environmental factors, such as hurricanes, tornados, floods, electrical power failures, or explosions, may also affect healthcare facilities. Hurricane Katrina, which hit New Orleans in August 2005, caused flooding and loss of electricity in healthcare facilities across the affected area, and resulted in the drowning of 35 residents of one suburban nursing home and the prosecution of its owners for negligent homicide (they were acquitted).[74]

Internal building disasters include power failures, bombs and explosions, fires, collapsing walls or floors, elevator mishaps, or catastrophes in the parking areas. Individual patients have created threatening situations by smoking in bed or in bathrooms and by lighting themselves or furniture on fire.

Physical damage to the facility engenders repair costs, although that expense may be mitigated by appropriate insurance coverage. Other potential losses include reduced revenue if patient bed space is lost for any period of time. Liability estimates should include these factors along with the potential harm to patient, employee, visitor, or community services.

Risk management activities involve ensuring the training and effectiveness of staff in responding to disasters and fires, as well as the availability and functional status of equipment needed to respond to each type of situation. Disaster and fire safety plans should document drills and the testing and readiness of necessary equipment. Insurance coverage concerning the premises, restoration and equipment replacement, and business interruption should be reviewed.

ELDER ABUSE AND VIOLENCE

Elder abuse has drawn governmental and media attention over the past decade as evidenced by the passage of the Elder Justice Act of 2009 (EJA), which was passed under ACA and became effective March 23, 2010.[75] Elder abuse consists of physical abuse, sexual abuse, psychological abuse, financial exploitation, neglect, or any combination thereof.[76] A number of risk factors have been associated with elder abuse, including physical impairment, mental health problems, cognitive impairment, and lack of adequate social support.

It is difficult to identify how many instances of elder abuse occur in any given year, partially because incidents are either not reported or not investigated when they are reported. Residents may fear retaliation for reporting abuse either from their abusers or from the nursing home staff. If a facility does not have a clear policy on handling a report of abuse, it may take several days post-report before an incident is investigated. Some family members to whom the residents report the abuse do not believe them. Further, failing memories exacerbate difficulties in punishing abusers because a witness or victim might not be able to remember enough details after the initial report. Some victims may even pass away before a trial or disciplinary hearing could occur.

Under state law, alleged elder abuse is typically reported to a state's Adult Protective Services, an agency that investigates and arranges protection for victims. Reporting, however, varies widely by state as a matter of state law. Some states place a duty on everyone to report abuse, whereas others require that only certain professionals do so.[76]

The EJA's reporting requirements, literally read, are broader than most state requirements, in that every employee, owner, operator, manager, agent, or contractor has a duty to report a reasonable suspicion of abuse, neglect, or exploitation to law enforcement authority and to the DHHS Secretary.[75] There is not yet a national Adult Protective Services data system that tracks abuse and neglect reports across the United States; ACA mandates the formation of an Advisory Board on Elder Abuse, Neglect, and Exploitation to make recommendations on methods for the most effective coordinated national data collection.

Elderly residents are not the only victims of violence in the nursing homes. Residents themselves may verbally or physically assault the staff, due to paranoia, reduced capacity, dementia, or other medical issues. Residents have bitten, kicked, punched, used their canes as weapons, and deliberately rammed their wheelchairs into staff. Violent behavior also occurs between residents over trivial, but heated arguments such as which TV show to watch.

Long-term care facilities should have procedures to address alleged and actual abuse in their homes, including implementation of appropriate policies and procedures to meet the EJA's reporting requirements. Where appropriate, long-term care providers should notify Adult Protective Services and law enforcement of suspected abuse, as well as take other protective or preventive measures to ensure the continuing safety of patients, residents, and staff.

RISKS POSED BY EMPLOYEES AND RISKS POSED TO EMPLOYEES

Employee risks arise out of administrative failure to comply with federal equal employment opportunity practices, failure to properly screen applicants before hiring, failure to check credentials of professionally licensed personnel, and failure to prevent work-related injuries. Signed into law in 1994, the federal Violent Crime Control and Law Enforcement Act permitted states to conduct national criminal background checks of current or prospective employees of federally assisted long-term care facilities.[77] Although this act was to have enabled national— as opposed to state—criminal checks on employees when requested,[77] long-term care providers must rely on their state to gain access to the national database—specifically, the National Crime Information Center (NCIC)—and there is still no singular system to ensure that a background check conducted in one state will pull in all relevant data for all 50 states and the federal enforcement agencies. As previously mentioned, the EJA recognized deficiencies in the current background check systems and commissioned a committee to make recommendations for a national data collection system for abuse, neglect, and exploitation.

In spite of federal legislation encouraging background checks, a report by the DHHS revealed that 92% of nursing facilities had at least one employee with a criminal history. Half of these employees had five or more convictions. Although many of the convictions were for crimes against property, convictions for crimes against persons were also noted. Other than a mandate to check state abuse registries, no federal requirement currently mandates that long-term care facilities must check potential employees' criminal records. Although 10 states do require a national FBI check and 33 require state criminal record checks, the remainder do not specifically address this issue.[78] A long-term care facility cannot employ someone who has committed abuse or neglect of a patient. Unfortunately, this mandate does not provide enough protection because records do not always indicate whether the victim was a long-term care resident. Additionally, some homes do not conduct background checks for those hired in housekeeping or food services, despite the fact that these employees will interact with residents.[79]

In response to increasing concerns about the safety of elderly people, ACA has set aside money and established a framework to enable states to develop national background checks. The deadline to submit grant proposals was June 30, 2011.[80] Kentucky recently received a $3 million grant that would enable the state to scan fingerprints to use in background checks, as opposed to the current "name-based background checks."[81]

Although employees may pose some risks to their patients, long-term care employees are also vulnerable. Workplace risks faced by these individuals include long-term physiological effects, violence, and blood-borne pathogens.[82] Ergonomics has also become a major focus point for OSHA, which instituted ergonomics guidelines for nursing homes on March 13, 2003. These guidelines are designed to prevent musculoskeletal disorders. OSHA's four-pronged approach emphasizes providing guidelines, enforcement, research, and outreach and assistance. OSHA identified five goals: protecting workers, identifying and creating solutions for problems related to resident movement, identifying and creating solutions for problems related to lifting residents, training, and providing additional information.[83]

FALSE CLAIMS RISKS AND MANDATORY COMPLIANCE PROGRAMS

Long-term care providers also should ensure that a compliance program is in place to audit and monitor claims for reimbursement submitted to governmental and private third-party payers, particularly Medicare and Medicaid. Inaccurate or inappropriate claims, including claims not supported by caregiver documentation in the patient chart, can lead to federal and state civil and criminal penalties under the federal False Claims Act, as well as under similar state false claims laws. Multimillion-dollar fines and penalties against healthcare providers are regularly pursued, along with prison sentences, by federal and state enforcement authorities across the United States, particularly for therapy or other care that was not medically necessary, that was not documented, or that was never provided.[84-86] The DHHS Secretary, the DHHS Office of Inspector General, and the Department of Justice work together with state Medicaid Fraud Control Units, and even with private, commercial payers, to investigate, apprehend, and punish those who commit Medicare or Medicaid fraud.[86]

Medicare provides its beneficiaries with brochures advising them how to detect fraud by comparing their processed claim statements to the services they actually received.[87] Complaints from Medicare beneficiaries and their families frequently focus on unnecessary, overpriced services, on services not provided, or on nonexistent (phantom) employees. These allegations, in turn, are the target of inquiries by the federal and state enforcement authorities and can be fodder for plaintiff lawyers in a negligent care case. No matter what triggers the investigations, they typically reveal overcharges and charges for nonexistent services. (See **Box 16-8**).

Box 16-8

Examples of letters from beneficiaries and their families and nursing home administrators:[88]

- "I am writing you concerning a bill that was charged to my mother who was a patient at . . . nursing home in . . . North Carolina. At the time of this speech therapy, my mother was 95 years old and could not communicate with anyone so how they could give her speech therapy is beyond me . . . They were paid $2,550 for doing nothing."
- "Documentation is enclosed regarding two . . . residents who questioned the charges billed to Medicare by [a rehabilitation agency] . . . In one case a 98 year old who has used a hearing aid for years is evaluated for hearing rehab potential 'at no charge,' the therapist told the nurses. Regardless, $450 is an outrageous charge for a hearing test."

Moreover, employing individuals who falsely represent that care was given, falsely code a claim for a higher level of care than can be supported, falsify medical records, or otherwise engage in activity that leads to a false Medicare or Medicaid claim could damage the long-term care provider's goodwill, reputation in the community, and relationships with prospective clients and with regulatory agencies.[89] It is not only critical that providers have a robust compliance program to adequately educate staff about unlawful and ethical conduct so as to reduce false claims risks, but such programs will become mandatory under PPACA for nursing homes effective March 23, 2013, and for other providers on later dates to be prescribed by DHHS.[90,91]

SUBACUTE CARE RISKS

Many long-term care facilities have created subacute care units to accommodate patients who previously received rehabilitation or skilled medical care in an acute care hospital. Generally considered a transitional phase, subacute care is designed to return patients to independent living quickly and to save money by decreasing the time spent in acute care. Subacute care is a relatively new field that focuses on patients who need assistance after a serious illness or injury, but who do not necessarily need the full services of a hospital. Initially designed to follow acute hospitalization, this type of care is now also used in place of it. Subacute care has another benefit as well: It provides residents with greater choice in picking the type of community best suited to their needs. As a lower-cost alternative to acute care, these services are attractive to residents.

Hospitals were the first to develop subacute care options, but nursing homes soon realized they needed a share of this new care type if they were to remain competitive. Despite its benefits, subacute care creates new risks for long-term care facilities. Most importantly, regulation of subacute care is not clear. Although such care is subject to OSHA, EEOC, and FMLA regulations, among others, it is less clear whether subacute providers are bound by all other nursing facility regulations.[92]

Subacute units may be subject to different licensing requirements than nursing facilities, and staff also must be trained to handle subacute issues.[92] Exposure to lawsuits may increase because by nature, subacute patients are expected to recover enough to return to independent living. Thus they expect to see significant and noticeable improvements. Patients may be younger, again raising expectations of measurable success rates. These factors can lead to unmet expectations, which often give rise to lawsuits.

Because the needs of subacute care patients may be more similar to those of acute care patients than to those of long-term care facility residents, depending on the type of care being delivered in the subacute unit and the goals for such care, facilities may want to mirror some of the practices of acute care as well as to comply with the standards required by the facility's license and Medicare enrollment type. Professionally established standards of care should be recorded in documentation similar to the forms and checklists utilized in acute care facilities. Having adequate staff who are well trained and well aware of the needs of post-acute residents can help cut back on lawsuits. Facilities providing subacute care should implement the following measures:

1. A comprehensive resident care program specifying employee supervision
2. Direction by the physician or specialist clinician in concert with the medical director to assure regulatory compliance
3. A specific program management process
4. Case management with quality control

5. Criteria targeting the specific care needs of a patient population identified through market research
6. Individualized resident care plans developed by a team of specialists in the targeted area of care
7. Facility enhancement to meet subacute care needs
8. Care with measurable outcomes aimed at returning individuals to the community

A key risk management strategy in avoiding claims is ensuring client satisfaction. The subacute care area is challenging in that regard because expectations may be high, particularly if the goal is to restore patients to a state where they are able to return to an independent lifestyle. If this process takes a long time or cannot be completed due to medical complications, patients might assume that the facility is to blame. Further, the shorter duration of care limits the development of long-term relationships with residents and families, which could also affect client satisfaction.

HOME HEALTHCARE RISKS

Home health care has become a popular alternative for individuals who do not need full-time care or medical attention and prefer to age in place.[93] Home healthcare agencies may provide services either directly or through subcontracting, and patients receive these services in their own homes. Medicare is the largest payer for home health care, accounting for nearly 41% of payments in 2009.[94] Between 2002 and 2006, Medicare spending for home health care increased by 44%.[95] If a person meets Medicare's qualifications for home health services, he or she may choose a Medicare-certified home health agency that has agreed to accept Medicare's approved payment rate.[96] Despite the conveniences of home health care, it carries a variety of risks, both for the patient and for the providers, which must be taken into consideration.

Liability risks in home health care include meeting regulatory and voluntary standards, patient management, informed consent for care and termination, product and equipment failure, patient and employee safety, and employee hiring and training. Administrators and risk managers must recognize home healthcare liability risks and develop procedures to mitigate these risks. Home healthcare companies are by no means immune from liability claims. (See **Box 16-9**.)

Box 16-9

A jury in Walker County, Georgia, awarded $9,502,683 ($4 million for pain and suffering, $5.5 million for wrongful death) to the family of a 51-year-old resident of an assisted living facility with cerebral palsy, who died after developing multiple infected decubitus ulcers. The award was assessed against the assisted living facility, its owner, and the home healthcare company. The family claimed that it hired home healthcare to provide weekly medical treatment to the resident and that the assisted living facility was to provide "around-the-clock" care.[97]

One area of concern is that providers may contract or subcontract with agencies to deliver specialized services. As a consequence, Individual employees may not be under the direct supervision and control of the home health agency. When a contract for home healthcare services is prepared with another agency, risk managers should seek to transfer the liability risk to the contractor agency and "hold harmless" the home health agency. Moreover, these

other agencies must be held accountable for written reports on the patient's condition and for compliance with the physician's treatment plan.

Who Receives Home Health Care?

In 2008, an estimated 3.3 million Medicare beneficiaries received home healthcare services.[98] Medicare paid $16.5 billion for these services. This expenditure is up significantly from 1999, when Medicare spent an estimated $3.6 billion on home health.[99] In 2007, 68.7% of these patients were older than age 65, and approximately 64% were women. The average duration of home health services is 315 days. On any given day in 2007, almost 1.5 million people were receiving home healthcare services.[98] The increase in home health services reflects DHHS and CMS goals to keep individuals in their homes for as long as possible.

The most common primary reasons for admission to home healthcare programs were diabetes (10.1%), heart disease (8.8%), malignant neoplasm (3.9%), obstructive pulmonary diseases (3.4%), hypertension (3.3%), and cerebrovascular disease (3.3%). Approximately 84% of these patients had trouble with at least one of the activities of daily living, which include bathing, dressing, transferring, eating, and using the toilet. Moreover, 50.5% of these patients had four or five limitations.[98] Home healthcare patients are generally homebound, and for Medicare to cover their costs, patients must be unable to leave the house unassisted.[100]

To begin receiving home healthcare services, a patient's doctor must order the services. The home healthcare agency and the doctor then create a plan of care, including which services the patient needs and how often. The plan of care must be reviewed at least every 60 days, which is the length of an incident of care.[96]

Regulation of Home Health Care

Public and voluntary regulatory mechanisms ensure the quality of home healthcare services. Provider agencies must be licensed by the individual states[101] and afterward may be certified by a combination of entities: Medicare or Medicaid; the Community Health Accreditation Program (CHAP), a subsidiary of the National League for Nursing (NLN); or The Joint Commission.

Agencies receiving Medicare reimbursement must meet the standard of care defined by Medicare regulations as to the specific services that will be reimbursed. Patients are eligible for Medicare reimbursement only if they meet the following requirements: They are homebound; they need skilled nursing on a part-time basis or require speech, physical, or occupational therapy; they are under the care of a doctor; and a doctor establishes and regularly reviews their plan of care.[95] Federal law guides eligibility and standards for home health services, although states are allowed to use additional criteria to determine who receives such services.[102]

Additional regulatory mechanisms have emerged to cover the growing industry. In 1986, the American Nurses Association published standards for home health nursing practice.[103] Two years later, the Joint Commission on Accreditation of Healthcare Organizations (JCAHO, now The Joint Commission) issued its standards and began accrediting voluntary home healthcare organizations.[104] In 1988, HCFA (now CMS) proposed that freestanding home healthcare agencies accredited by the NLN and the hospital-based agencies accredited by JCAHO be deemed to have also met Medicare certification requirements.

Within the past few years, Medicare and Medicaid payments for home healthcare have sparked debate. CMS is responsible for minimizing improper payments for home health services, which are paid per episode of care. Each payment is based on the national average cost, which is then adjusted to take into consideration the severity of the patient's condition and the extent of required services. This system was updated and refined at the beginning of 2008 to make payments more accurate.[104] In July 2011, CMS announced additional changes that, if finalized, are intended to promote even greater efficiency.[105] Medicare fraud in the home health industry could be contributing to increased costs for Medicare. Fraud includes providing services that were not necessary or billing for services and equipment that were never provided.[106]

Patient Management Risks in Home Care Settings

Risk identification and reduction in home health care must begin with the home health agency assessing the patient's healthcare needs and ability to participate in care. The environment in which the care will be delivered should be assessed for safety—especially for fire hazards. Fires are particularly dangerous for the elderly because they are unable to react as quickly, may be on medicines that affect their cognitive abilities, or may be alone and unable to seek help.[107] If a patient is on oxygen, there is an even greater risk of serious injury or death due to oxygen's highly flammable nature, especially if the patient smokes.[108]

To safeguard against allegations of abandonment, agreements with patients should include how and when services may be terminated and should identify the conditions for substitution of regular staff with equally quali-fied staff. Agencies should also ensure that the appropriate level of healthcare provider is assigned to the patient. Not only must the appro-priate provider be selected, but that provider must also be properly trained and supervised while rendering the necessary care.

Informed Consent Risks

Generally, patients must formally consent before the start of any procedure or treatment, including home health care. An unanswered dilemma is "who" is obligated to obtain and document consent before a home healthcare patient receives treatment. Home health care challenges the historical tradition, supported by ethics and law, that only physicians can obtain and document a valid informed consent by the patient. "To date there are no cases on the obligation of home health care staff that have come to trial. Nor has it been identified whether consent obtained by a nonphysician is valid."[109]

Home healthcare risk managers need to be attentive to the inherent potential risks related to informed consent and develop a policy to sys-tematically mitigate this risk. At the time of the informed consent process, the home healthcare nurse can review everything in the event the physician missed something. This process is extremely important in relation to the Patient Self-Determination Act and implementation of the healthcare proxy so that patients and fami-lies may fully exercise their rights under this law, and refuse treatment with full knowledge of the consequences if they so wish. Home health-care agencies need to develop and implement appropriate policies to notify patients of their rights within state law to safeguard adherence to

the patient's wishes in the area of these advance directives.

Termination of Care Risks

Under ACA, effective January 1, 2011, Medicare requires that all Medicare patients have a face-to-face encounter with a physician or certain nonphysician practitioners within 90 days before or within 30 days of the initial start of home health care for a matter related to the need for home health services. If this face-to-face encounter does not occur within the pre-scribed time, then the home health agency can terminate care, but should provide a written notice to the patient of the reason for termina-tion before the termination takes effect. The National Association of Home Care (NAHC) has developed a notice letter for purposes of this type of termination.[110]

Other grounds for terminating home healthcare services include problems in the delivery of care or services, nonparticipating patients or families, patients too sick to remain in the home, abusive patients and families, and insufficient resources to cover the cost of care.[109] Agencies must be familiar with state regulations regarding the discharge of patients. Termination of care should be outlined in the patient's service contract.

When it is anticipated that care will be ter-minated for any reason before the end of the contracted period, adequate notification must be given to the patient, family, and other caregivers, including (1) when services will terminate, (2) where continued services should be obtained, and (3) how any records will be forwarded to the new agency or made available.[111] State licensure statutes and regulations may stipulate additional requirements for termination of home health care. Any decision by the patient or family to terminate services must be documented. Policies and procedures for termination of services can help agencies protect themselves from allegations of abandonment—a situation in which a professional relationship is terminated without affording the patient reasonable notice or opportunity to find a replacement. For example, terminating home care services to keep costs low may give rise to a claim of abandonment.[112]

Within agency policies and procedures, the issue of patient and family nonparticipation or noncompliance in regard to the physician's plan of care must be addressed. Consistent nonparticipation may be an indication that a pediatric or elderly patient is being neglected or abused by the family, friends, or other caregivers.

Incident Reporting

Adverse incidents will probably occur in providing in-home care to patients. Home healthcare agencies should facilitate reporting any incident representing a risk exposure to the agency by establishing a format for collecting information as well as a time frame for reporting based on the magnitude of the incident. Incidents that may fall outside of the staff's responsibilities, such as dangerous or unsanitary conditions in the home or abusive patients and family members, should be included in the report as well; it is better for staff to over-report than to neglect to report adverse incidents.

Home healthcare employees provide a variety of medical and nonmedical care, including the following services: blood pressure, temperature, and respiration readings; skin care; catheter care; colostomy and other "ostomy" care; dressing changes; administration of medications; assistance with exercise;

monitoring durable medical equipment and devices; and assistance with activities of daily living. Each of these tasks may enhance the opportunity for an adverse incident or occurrence. In addition, those providers who provide relief or continued care may not appear in the home in a timely manner so that staff may depart after completion of their shift. All incidents need to be investigated, documented, and communicated to the patient and/or family members to reduce dissatisfaction with the care plan and services, or with the assigned staff. Personal property of patients or family also may be broken or damaged, and there may be theft allegations.[113] (See **Box 16-10**.)

Box 16-10

A home healthcare nurse allowed an air conditioner repair man into the home as scheduled. In casual conversation, the repair man asked about the patient and the patient's medications. Although she had given no information, the nurse felt uncomfortable and went to telephone the police. Before she could do so, however, the patient needed care. While she was busy, the repair man rushed out of the house. In checking, the nurse found that the patient's narcotics were missing.[114]

Staff need patient information files in the home that include emergency and nonemergency telephone numbers, as well as emergency plans. Personnel also need to know how to modify the home to prevent accidents, increase bed mobility, position the patient to prevent skin deterioration, transfer patients, safely use bathroom equipment, administer medication, and use technical devices. The healthcare provider and staff must develop these plans in communication with the patient and family to ensure quality and safe care.

Falls in the Home Healthcare Population

It is difficult to pinpoint the exact cause of falls in the home healthcare population. Some of the causes will be similar to those falls in nursing home facilities, including physiological weakness, confusion, and medication effects. Home healthcare providers should evaluate the fall potential of patients and develop prevention strategies. Such strategies may include minimizing environmental risks, teaching or reteaching adaptive behaviors, and reducing accompanying risk factors such as changes in visual acuity. Careful assessment of the patient's home and necessary remedial intervention can help to decrease liability risk that may arise out of a patient injury.

High-Technology Home Health Care: Product and Equipment Failure

Modern medical technology coupled with advances in healthcare delivery has enabled patients to receive complex care at home. Yet with each high-technology activity an agency adds to its services, the risk of liability increases. Greater utilization of high-technology home health care may also reflect the provision of care to a younger population, whose members may be more capable of operating these devices. In terms of legal remuneration for damages as a result of negligence, these younger people generally receive higher monetary awards based on longevity. As this younger population becomes more prevalent in home health care, there will be increased risks to agencies.

The federal Safe Medical Device Act of 1990 clarified specific applications to home healthcare organizations. At the time of its passage, people were concerned that it would be difficult to determine when equipment or technology was having an adverse effect on patients.[115] A mini-hospital set up in the home may involve the use of a variety of sophisticated medical equipment and products, which may be difficult to monitor. Such high-technology equipment may include dialysis units, infusion therapy, phototherapy, apnea monitors, respiratory volume ventilators, gaseous oxygen, massage, and heating and cooling mattresses or pads.

Advances in telecommunications and computer technologies also have applications in home care: electronic devices for measuring patient physiological processes; electronic devices for administering or monitoring oxygen, drug, and other therapies in the home; personal emergency response systems to monitor smoke or fire, or to signal police or ambulance; and video-phones for direct visualization and communication. Home healthcare agency employees need to notice potential problems with the various types of equipment being used by their patients. In turn, agencies need to carefully select and use responsible equipment vendors and train employees in the responsible use of such equipment. In addition, agencies should develop policies on troubleshooting equipment, equipment maintenance and replacement, and emergency action plans in the event of equipment malfunction or failure.

Home Healthcare Employees

In 2008, an estimated 958,000 employees worked in the U.S. home health industry.[94] Home healthcare agencies are exposed to a multitude of diverse risks surrounding the hiring, employing, or contracting for professional and allied home healthcare providers. Agencies are particularly vulnerable regarding liability for the actions of their employees or contractors. Simply put, the employees provide care "in the field," away from the consistent watchful supervision of supervisors and administrators. Thus agencies must pay special attention to their hiring policies and procedures to help mitigate this aspect of employee-related risk. (See **Box 16-11**.)

Box 16-11

The nurse caring for multimillionaire tobacco heiress Doris Duke in her mansion was arrested and charged with stealing $439,000 in valuables from Duke and five others.[116]

There are no standard requirements that background checks be done on employees in home health care.[117] Indeed, in 2009, proposed requirements for background checks met with opposition in California.[118] Negligent hiring, however, can be lethal, because without regular supervision, employees have almost complete autonomy in the field. Sussman and Siegel recommend the following documentation for hiring new applicants:[119]

- Applicant interview that includes a review of employment history and an assessment of skills
- Verification of legally accepted permission to work, such as citizenship, residency, or working visa
- Verification of health clearance, including immunization, TB, and hepatitis B status

- Assessment of current license or certification status
- Evidence of state and/or agency requirements, such as infection control training and CPR certification
- Verification of malpractice insurance
- Applicant's permission to check references
- Background check through public records for criminal convictions or reports of patient abuse (mandated by the federal Violent Crime Control and Law Enforcement Act of 1994)

Toward this end, home healthcare agencies must develop clear job descriptions for personnel that indicate responsibilities as well as limitations. Staff must be highly qualified, dedicated, and reliable. Home healthcare agencies must assess and supervise the work of all caregivers through periodic field visits and communication with patients and families. Data must be documented and plans developed and implemented where a need for improvement is identified. Ongoing performance evaluations of staff are fundamental to patient safety. Documentation should specify objective recommendations for continuous staff development and detail plans for improvement, along with implementation and time frames for expected results.

Organizations must comply with all federal, state, and local laws and regulations regarding employee reimbursement. Employee wages and hours worked must be recorded in accordance with the regulatory mandates. Because of the nature of the industry, employee reimbursement practices in home healthcare agencies are being scrutinized by federal and state audits regarding minimum wages, overtime, and record keeping. (See **Box 16-12**.)

A patient recruiter for a home health agency in Miami, Florida, pleaded guilty to involvement in a fraud scheme. The facility for which he recruited patients billed Medicare for expensive and unnecessary services, many of which were never provided. The recruiter also provided kickbacks and falsified reports of beneficiaries.[120,121]

Negligence Related to Failure to Instruct

Under a number of state laws, employers can be held liable for the actions of their employees, regardless of whether the actions are in keeping or even contrary to their job description. A U.S. Supreme Court ruling found that an entity's failure to properly train its personnel can be considered "deliberate indifference" and can result in charges of negligence and civil actions.

Home health care relies on staff to provide care and anticipates the participation of the patient, family, and significant others in maintaining the continuity of care between the provider's visits. Even though teaching is not reimbursable, the home healthcare provider's ability to train the staff and those who will provide this interim care is critical to control risks. Such training should be documented, with the documentation signed by the patient and/or caregiver, and kept in the patient's record. Training patients, employees, family members, and other caregivers cannot be a one-time educational requirement, especially when high-technology equipment is being used.

Safety of Employees

Home healthcare employees may encounter liability risks related to their own safety, including threats, physical assault, and mugging.[122] One of the major problems for home healthcare workers is that they are in unfamiliar environments and probably far from assistance and other support. Employees must be acutely aware of hazards in the environment and safeguard themselves. Potential hazards include toxic substances within the house, infections, violence, and threats.[123] Animal hair, cigarette smoke, dust, vermin, and other unsanitary conditions are frequently reported dangers to both patients and healthcare employees.[124] Each home visited is a separate worksite with all the normal safety concerns of the healthcare industry involved, but it may be impossible to satisfy them in each individual site.[124] Home healthcare organizations need to have policies and procedures regarding the safety of workers in the community and the use of security escorts in unsafe neighborhoods. There should be an ongoing program to develop community relationships and to assess the community to ensure employee safety.

Two major areas of concern are injury from lifting or transferring patients and injury from sharps. To prevent physical injury, employees must learn safe transferring, lifting, and positioning techniques. These are similar to the concerns and recommendations that OSHA has in place for nursing home facilities.[82,83,125] The difficulty is that homes are not necessarily designed for people in need of medical assistance. Moreover, home healthcare employees do not have access to equipment or other assistance in these tasks, making moving patients even more difficult for them.

Sharps injury or exposure to other bodily fluids is a huge safety concern. Due to the increasing range of services offered through home health care, more sharp medical devices, such as needles, lancets, and intravenous systems, are being used in nonhospital and nursing home facilities.

Many patients self-inject medications or test their glucose levels with lancets. These sharps are disposed of in household trashcans as opposed to specially designed containers, and the possibility for injury increases as a result. Many infections are passed through exposure to bodily fluids, and any used sharps have the potential to infect a nurse or aide if they are pierced. Clutter, lack of space, and unsanitary conditions contribute to sharps injuries, both in using and disposing of sharps. Although sharps with safety devices are available, nurses and aides report that they are more difficult to use or take longer.[126]

Employees must be aware of the extent of the home healthcare agency's insurance coverage in the event of an injury. Already expansive, employee activities in home health care are continually increasing. Agencies must regularly review all insurance policies to identify and safeguard against gaps in coverage. Does the insurance coverage apply if employees perform a task outside of their job description, such as taking a patient's child to school after the employee's assigned working hours? (See **Box 16-13**.)

Independent Contractor Versus Employee

Home healthcare agencies are subject to federal Internal Revenue Service (IRS) investigations and to liability for misclassification of home healthcare providers. Liability for misclassification of an employee as an independent contractor could include repayment of all associated taxes with interest, civil fines up to $500,000, and criminal charges resulting in up to five years in prison. It is not clear exactly where the line between an independent contractor and an employee is drawn. The IRS has

---

Box 16-13

Question: Can home health aides recover benefits for injuries incurred in an accident that occurs when going from their home to their job assignments?

Answer: Employees probably cannot receive worker's compensation benefits if they are hurt while traveling from or to their home from a job site. However, there are many times when employees who are injured during travel may receive worker's compensation, such as when they are traveling at the express wish of their employer, when the travel benefits the employer, or when the employee is injured while driving a company vehicle. Worker's compensation laws vary from state to state, so check with your worker's compensation carrier for the law applicable to specific facts.

---

indicated that the distinction "depends on the facts of each case."[127] According to the IRS, "[t]he general rule is that an individual is an independent contractor if the payer has the right to control or direct only the result of the work and not what will be done and how it will be done."[127] An employee, in contrast, is controlled by the employer and can be told how a given activity will be done.[128] Prudent home health care organizations should apply the "right of control" test and use IRS definitions to determine the employment classification of home healthcare workers to minimize liability risks.

HOSPICE CARE

In 2009, Medicare paid almost $12 billion for hospice care, compared to $2.9 billion for such care in 2000. Although many have praised the service for providing medical support to dying patients, others are concerned that the services are being abused. Hospice is designed for terminal care, and Medicare has announced that it will not pay more than six months worth of hospice care unless a doctor or nurse practitioner examines the patient and determines that he or she is still terminal. Although the median duration for hospice use is only 17 days, there are enough cases where people have been in hospice for four or five years to indicate that the system is flawed.[129]

In 2007, 1,045,100 patients were discharged from hospice care. The most common reason, by far, for discharge was death, accounting for 84.3% of cases. The remainder were discharged because their condition had stabilized or because they were entering inpatient facilities. Women remained in hospice longer than men. Approximately 42.8% of admissions were due to malignant neoplasm; 11.1% were admitted for heart disease, 6.6% for dementia, and 4.7% for obstructive pulmonary diseases. Almost all patients received skilled nursing services, and many received bereavement services, medical social services, and spiritual services.[93]

Risk exposure in hospice care to some extent mirrors the liability risks in home health care and long-term care facilities. Nevertheless, the purpose of hospice is different from that of long-term care. Symptom control—specifically, pain management—is critical to patient care. Home administration of controlled substances to alleviate pain, such as morphine, is a definite risk exposure. Hospice care agencies must minimize the risk of potential diversion of controlled substances by staff, family members, significant others, or anyone else who may enter or be in the household. Policies and procedures for the administration of controlled substances must comply with federal and state laws regarding storage, administration, discarding of unused medication, and documentation.

GROWING INDUSTRY, GROWING RISKS

Because the need for long-term care increases with age, especially after age 85, demand for care can be expected to increase as the baby boomer generation ages. Medical advances also may increase the need for long-term care, as people live longer and, therefore, survive long enough to develop age-related disabilities, such as Alzheimer's disease, or simply need more help due to weakened physiological and cognitive abilities. The availability of informal, unpaid caregivers, such as family and neighbors, will also affect the demand for public long-term care services. Greater geographic dispersion of families, smaller family sizes, and the large percentage of women who work outside the home may continue to strain the capacity of informal caregiving. In the short term, large numbers of caregivers in the baby boomer generation may ease the strain. As baby boomers themselves grow older, however, they may have fewer family members to care for them. Some states are increasingly emphasizing home- and community-based services and constraining costly institutional care as they seek more efficient or cost-effective ways to organize and prioritize services.

Serving the needs of the elderly and disabled is a growing industry. As home care agencies and hospices are faced with declining revenues from Medicare and demands from managed care plans to reduce utilization and resources, professional liabilities may increase. However, with appropriate attention to admissions for care, care management, and policies for discharge and termination, potential risks can be minimized.

REFERENCES

1. Howden, L. M., & Meyer, J. A. (2011, May). Age and sex composition: 2010. 2010 U.S. Census Briefs. http://www.census.gov/prod/cen2010/briefs/c2010br-03.pdf

2. Florida. (n.d.). http://quickfacts.census.gov/qfd/states/12000.html

3. Alaska. (n.d.). http://quickfacts.census.gov/qfd/states/02000.html

4. U.S. Government Accountability Office. (2002). Long-term care: aging baby boom generation will increase demand and burden on federal and state budgets. GAO-02-544T.

5. America's Health Insurance Plans. (2004). Guide to long-term care insurance. http://publications.usa.gov/USAPubs.php?PubID=5879

6. What is long-term care? (n.d.). http://www.medicare.gov/longtermcare/static/home.asp

7. Alliance for Quality Nursing Home Care. (2009). Trends in post-acute and long-term care. http://www.aqnhc.org/www/file/AQNHC_Care_Context_914%20Updated.pdf?phpMyAdmin=HzHnhISAGxbugH-niVxYkWiXQq0

8. Georgetown University Long-Term Care Financing Project. (2007, February). National spending for long-term care: Fact sheet. http://ltc.georgetown.edu/pdfs/natspendfeb07.pdf

9. Centers for Medicare & Medicaid Services. (n.d.). National health expenditures. https://www.cms.gov/nationalhealthexpenddata/downloads/highlights.pdf

10. Weinberg, A. D., & Levine, J. M. (2008, September 5). Clinical areas of liability: Risk management concerns in long term care. *Annals of Long Term Care*. http://www.annals oflongtermcare.com/article/3564

11. AON. (2011). 2011 long term care: General liability and professional liability actuarial analysis. http://www.ahcancal.org/about_ahca/Documents/2011_Long_Term_Care_Actuarial_Analysis_FINAL.pdf

12. Charbel. (2011, May 24). Health promotion and disease prevention. *Drugswell blog*. http://drugswell.com/wowo/blog1.php/2011/05/24/health-promotion-and-disease-prevention?page=2

13. Merck Institute of Aging and Health. (2007). *The state of aging and health in America 2004.*

14. 2010 annual quality report. (2010). http://www.ahcancal.org/quality_improvement/Documents/2010QualityReport.pdf

15. The national nursing home survey: 2004 overview. (2009, June). *Vital and Health Statistics Series, 13*(167), Figure 4: Percentage of nursing home residents, by number of activities of daily living dependencies.

16. Wiggins, S. A. (n.d.). Implications of physiologic aging. (Developed in part with the American Geriatrics Society Syllabus for Geriatric Medicine in Clinical Practice.) Landon Center of Aging, KU Medical Center. http://www2.kumc.edu/coa/Education/AMED900/ClinicalImplicationsofPhysiologicAging.htm#Outline

17. Dorshkind, K., & Swain, S. (2009, August). Age-associated declines in immune system development and function: Causes, consequences, and reversal. *Current Opinion in Immunology, 21*(4), 404–407. doi:10.1016/j.coi.2009.07.001. http://www.ncbi.nlm.nih.gov/pmc/articles/PMC2742656/

18. The national nursing home survey: 2004 overview. (2009, June). [Note 15]. Page 17, Table 5: Number, percent distribution, and rate per 10,000 population of nursing home residents, according to sex, race, and geographic region, by age at time of interview.

19. The national nursing home survey: 2004 overview. (2009, June). [Note 15]. Page 19, Table 7: Number and percent distribution of nursing home residents, according to length of time since admission in days, by selected resident characteristics.

20. What is subacute care? (2008, January 1). *McKnight's Long-Term Care and Assisted Living News*. http://www.mcknights.com/what-is-subacute-care/article/104134/

21. Subacute care. (n.d.). Mayo Clinic Health System. http://www.mayohealthsystem.org/mhs/live/page.cfm?pp=locations/serviceoutput.cfm&orgid=FSH&nav=Ser&id=13515300000000467

22. Clark, R. F. (1996, August 21). *Home and community-based care: The U.S. example.* Office of the Assistant Secretary for Planning and Evaluation, U.S. Department of Health and Human Services.

23. American Geriatrics Society. (n.d.). Community based care: Aging in the know. http://www.healthinaging.org/agingintheknow/chapters_ch_trial.asp?ch=14

24. Centers for Medicare & Medicaid Services. (2011, August). Medicare hospice benefits. http://www.medicare.gov/Publications/Pubs/pdf/02154.pdf

25. Public Law 111-146 (2010).

26. Honeycutt Spears, V. (2011, July 19). U.S. Attorney says nursing home's "worthless" care led to deaths, injuries; inadequate care cited in 5 deaths. *Lexington (KY) Herald Leader.* WLNR 17774841.

27. Federal prosecutors ask for help in pursuing nursing home cases. (2011, March 9). *Lexington (KY) Herald Leader.* http://www.kentucky.com/2011/03/08/1662820/federal-prosecutors-ask-for-help.html

28. Death at Woodlake senior facility sparks inquiry. (2011, April 27). *Visalis Times-Delta* (Visalia, CA). WLNR 8162364.

29. U.S. Government Accountability Office. (2010 April 28). *Nursing home understatement update.* GAO-10-434R).

30. Certification and compliance: Nursing homes. (n.d.). https://www.cms.gov/CertificationandComplianc/12_NHs.asp

31. About nursing home inspections. (n.d.). http://www.medicare.gov/Nursing/aboutinspections.asp?language=English

32. State operations manual: Appendix PP: Guidance to surveyors for long term care facilities. (2011, January 7). http://www.cms.gov/manuals/Downloads/som107ap_pp_guidelines_ltcf.pdf

33. U.S. Government Accountability Office. (2007). *Nursing homes: Efforts to strengthen federal enforcement have not deterred some homes from repeatedly harming residents.* GAO-07-241.

34. False advertising: Deceptive marketing practices = real liability. (2009). *AlertBulletin.* http://www.cna.com/vcm_content/CNA/internet/Static%20File%20for%20Download/Risk%20Control/Medical%20Services/FalseAdvertisingDeceptiveMarketingPracticesRealLiability.pdf

35. Aging: What to expect. (n.d.). http://www.mayoclinic.com/health/aging/HA00040

36. Smith, P. W., Bennett, G., Bradley, S., Drinka, P., Lanterbach, E., Mart, J. & Steveson, K. (2008, July). SHEA/APIC guideline: Infection prevention and control in the long-term care facility. AJIC Special Communication. http://www.apic.org/Content/NavigationMenu/PracticeGuidance/APIC-SHEA_Guideline.pdf

37. Boyd, R., & Stevens, J. A. (2009). Falls and fear of falling: Burden, beliefs and behaviours. *Age and aging, 38,* 423.

38 Costs of falls among older adults, (n.d.). http://www.cdc.gov/HomeandRecreationalSafety/Falls/fallcost.html

39. Fall prevention facts. (n.d.). http://orthoinfo.aaos.org/topic.cfm?topic=A00101

40. Span, P. (2010, September 1). Fear of falling. *New York. Times New Old Age Blog.* http://newoldage.blogs.nytimes.com/2010/09/01/fear-of-falling-2/

41. Hill, E. E., Nguyer, T., Shaha, M., Werzel, J., DeForge, B., & Spellbning, A. (2009, October 27). Person–environment interactions contributing to nursing home resident falls. *Residential Gerontologic Nursing, 2,* 287. www.ncbi.nlm.nih.gov/pmc/articles/PMC3042855/

42. Riefkohl, E. Z., Bieber, H., Burlingane, M., & Lowerthal, D. (2003, November). Medications and falls in the elderly: A review of the evidence and practical consideration. *P&T Community, 38*(11). http://www.ptcommunity.com/ptjournal/fulltext/28/11/PTJ2811724.pdf

43. Cameron, I. D., Murray, G., Gillespie, L., Robertson, M., Hill, K., Cumming, R., & Kerse, N. (2010). Interventions for preventing falls in older people in nursing care facilities and hospitals (review). *Cochrane Library,* 17. http://www.cochranejournalclub.com/preventing-falls-in-nursing-care-facilities-and-hospitals/pdf/CD005465_full.pdf

44. Hamilton H. J., Gallagher, P., & O'Mahony, D. (2009, January 28). Inappropriate prescribing and adverse drug events in older people. *BMC Geriatrics, 9,* 5. http://www.biomedcentral.com/1471-2318/9/5

45. U.S. Government Accountability Office. (2000). *Adverse drug events: The magnitude of health risk is uncertain because of limited incidence data.* GAO/HEHS-00-21.

46. Gurwitz, J. H., Field, T., Judge, J., Rochon, P., Harrold, L., Cadoret, C., . . . Bates, D. (2005). The incidence of adverse drug events in two large academic long-term care facilities. http://www.amjmed.com/article/S0002-9343(04)00718-1/fulltext

47. Castle, N. Co., Wagner, L., Ferguson-Rome, J., Mer, A., & Handler, S. (2011). Study finds infection control violations at 15 percent of U.S. nursing homes. http://www.apic.org/AM/Template.

cfm?Section=Featured_News_and_Events&CONTEN
TID=17918&TEMPLATE=/CM/ContentDisplay.cfm

48. 42 C.F.R. § 483.65 (2011).

49. Nursing homes & personal care facilities. (n.d.).
http://www.osha.gov/SLTC/nursinghome/index.html

50. CMS manual system: Revisions to Appendix
PP—"Interpretive guidelines for long-term care facilities," Tag F441. (2009, July 20). http://www.cms.
gov/transmittals/downloads/R51SOMA.pdf

51. Park-Lee, E., & Caffrey, C. (2009, February).
Pressure ulcers among nursing home residents:
United States 2004. http://www.cdc.gov/nchs/data/
databriefs/db14.pdf

52. Stokowski, L. A.(2010, February 5). In this corner:
The unavoidable pressure ulcer. *Medscape Today
News.* http://www.medscape.com/viewarticle/715969

53. Estate of Juanita Amelia Jackson v. Briar Hill, Inc., et al.,
11 FJVR 2-32, 2010 WL 5781222 (Fla. Cir. Ct. July 20,
2010).

54. Dementia. (n.d.). http://www.mayoclinic.com/health/
dementia/DS01131

55. Dementia: Hope through research. (n.d.). http://www.
ninds.nih.gov/disorders/dementias/detail_dementia.htm

56. Dementia/Alzheimer's disease. (n.d.). http://www.cdc.
gov/mentalhealth/basics/mental-illness/dementia.htm

57. Sundowner syndrome. (n.d.). *Sundownerfacts:
A Sundowner's Syndrome Resource.* http://sundown-
erfacts.com/sundowners-syndrome

58. *Hendrix v. Cambride Place*, 09-4416, Kentucky Trial
Court Review, 15 K.T.C.R. 11 (November 2011).

59. Wilkins, C. H. (2005, November). Diagnosis and
management of dementia in long-term care. *Annals
of Long-Term Care, 13*(11), http://www.aging.ufl.
edu/files/pdf/resources/dementialongterm.pdf

60. Boltz, M. (2006, September/October). Wandering
and elopement: A comprehensive approach. *Assisted
Living Consult.* http://www.assistedlivingconsult.
com/issues/02-05/ALC02-05_Elopement.pdf

61. Connell, B. R. (2003, April). Why residents wander
and what you can do about it. *New York Times.* http://
findarticles.com/p/articles/mi_m3830/is_4_52/
ai_100204753/

62. Massachusetts nursing home fined for elopement
death. (2011, May 31). http://www.aboutnursing-
homeneglect.com/2011/05/elopement-death-fine/

63. 42 C.F.R. § 483.13(a).

64. Appleby, J., & Gillum, J. (2009, February 16). Fewer
care facilities use restraints for elderly residents. *USA
Today.* http://www.usatoday.com/news/nation/2009-
02-16-nursing-home-restraints_N.htm

65. Use of physical restraint in nursing homes cut by half
in 8 years. (2010, July 14). *AHRQ News and
Numbers.* Rockville, MD: Agency for Healthcare
Research and Quality. http://www.ahrq.gov/news/nn/
nn071410.htm

66. FDA Hospital Bed Safety Workgroup. (2003, April).
*Clinical guidance for the assessment and implemen-
tation of bed rails in hospitals, long term care facilities, and home care settings.*

67. Bed-rail entrapments still a serious problem. (2008,
July 24). *McKnight's Long-Term Care News &
Assisted Living.* http://www.mcknights.com/bed-rail-
entrapments-still-a-serious-problem/article/112809/

68. 42 C.F.R. § 483.35.

69. *Offutt v. Harborside Healthcare*, 2010 WL 579073
(Ky. Cir. Ct. 4th Judicial Cir. Hopkins Co., November
16, 2010).

70. Smith, C. (2008, May 12). Liability & lawsuits in
geriatrics, http://occupational-therapy.advanceweb.
com/Article/Liability-and-Lawsuits-in-Geriatrics.
aspx

71. Paraplegic physical reconditioning patient falls from
wheelchair while unattended—fractured femur with
depression. (n.d.). http://www.hpso.com.../casespro-
findex.php3

72. 42 C.F.R. § 483.75(m).

73. 42 C.F.R. § 483.70.

74. Nossiter, A. (2007, September 8). Nursing home owners acquitted in deaths. *New York Times.* http://www.
nytimes.com/2007/09/08/us/nationalspecial/08nursing.
html

75. The Patient Protection and Affordable Care Act
(PPACA), H.R. 3590, Subtitle H, Elder Justice Act of
2009, PPACA § 6701.

76. U.S. Government Accountability Office. (2011). Elder
justice: stronger federal leadership could enhance
national response to elder abuse. GAO-11-208.

77. 42 U.S.C. § 5119a.

78. Pear, R. (2011. March 2). Study finds criminal pasts
of nursing home workers. *New York Times.* http://
www.nytimes.com/2011/03/03/us/03nursing.html

79. Violent Crime Control and Law Enforcement Act of
1994, Pub. L. No. 103-3355.

80. CMS national background check program. (n.d.).
https://www.cms.gov/SurveyCertificationGenInfo/
04_BackgroundCheck.asp

81. Governor Beshear's Communication Office. (2011, June 22), Kentucky to implement more stringent criminal background checks for caregivers. http://governor.ky.gov/pressrelease.htm?PostingGUID={EB818BE0-074F-4762-A798-B1BDF874E8AC}

82. Nursing home eTool. (n.d.). http://www.osha.gov/SLTC/etools/nursinghome/index.html

83. Ergonomics guidelines announce for nursing home industry. (2003, March 13). http://www.osha.gov/pls/oshaweb/owadisp.show_document?p_id=10129&p_table=NEWS_RELEASES

84. Schoofs, M. (2011, May 14). Medicare fraud nets guilty plea. *Wall Street Journal.* http://online.wsj.com/article/SB10001424052748704681904576321621961413458.html

85. Malove, R. D. (2011, July 1). Brooklyn physical therapy workers plead guilty to $3.4 million fraud. http://www.healthcarefraudblog.com/2011/07/brooklyn_physical_therapy_work.html

86. Medicare fraud strike force charges 111 individuals for more than $225 million in false billing and expands operations to two additional cities. (2011, February 17). http://www.hhs.gov/news/press/2011pres/02/20110217a.html

87. Fraud & abuse. (n.d.). http://www.medicare.gov/navigation/help-and-support/fraud-and-abuse/fraud-and-abuse-overview.aspx

88. U.S. Government Accountability Office. (1995). Medicare: Tighter rules needed to curtail overcharges for therapy in nursing homes. GAO/HEHS-95-23.

89. Lundstrom, M. (2011, September 18). Falsified patient records are untold story of California nursing home care. *Sacramento Bee.* WLNR 18558998.

90. PPACA §§ 6401 and 6402.

91. The Patient Protection and Affordable Care Act of 2010 ("PPACA") includes mandatory compliance and ethics program requirements for nursing home providers. (2011, April). *ABA Health eSource, 7*(8). American Bar Association. http://www.americanbar.org/newsletter/publications/aba_health_esource_home/aba_health_law_esource_1104_rosenbaum.html

92. Pratt, J. R. (2009). *Long term care: Managing across the continuum (3rd ed.).* Sudury, MA: Jones and Bartlett.

93. Home health care and discharged hospice care patients: United States, 2000 and 2007. (2011, April 27). http://www.cdc.gov/nchs/data/nhsr/nhsr038.pdf

94. Basic statistics about home care. (2010). http://www.nahc.org/facts/08HC_stats.pdf

95. U.S. Government Accountability Office. (2009). *Medicare: Improvements needed to address improper payments in home health.* GAO-09-185.

96. Medicare and home health care official booklet. (n.d.). http://www.medicare.gov/publications/pubs/pdf/10969.pdf

97. *Teresa Tucker v. Travis Thompson d/b/a Country Crossing Assisted Living and Hutcheson Home Health Care,* JAS GA Ref. No. 259787WL, 2011 WL 1527630 (Ga. State Ct., March 6, 2011).

98. Goldberg, J., Johnson, M., Pajerowski, W., Tanamor. M., & Ward, A. (2011, January 11). Home health study report https://www.cms.gov/HomeHealthPPS/Downloads/HHPPS_LiteratureReview.pdf

99. Home health care information registry. (n.d.). http://www.calregistry.com/inhome/hhealth/htm

100. U.S. Government Accountability Office. (2004). *Medicare home health: Payments to most freestanding home health agencies more than covered their costs.* GAO-04-359.

101. Certification and compliance: Home health-providers.(n.d.). https://www.cms.gov/CertificationandComplianc/06_HHAs.asp

102. Smith, G., Keefe, J., Carpenter, L., Doty, P., Kennedy, G., Buswell, B.,... Williams, L. (2000, October). Understanding medicaid home and community services: A primer, (Chapter 3). George Washington University, Center for Health Policy Research. http://aspe.hhs.gov/daltcp/reports/primer.htm#Chap3

103. Friedman, Y. (2006). Mapping the literature of home health nursing. *Journal of the Medical Librarians Association.* http://www.ncbi.nlm.nih.gov/pmc/articles/PMC1463031/

104. Joint Commission standards. http://www.jointcommission.org/standards_information/standards.aspx

105. CMS proposes 2012 Medicare home health payment changes. (2011, July 5). http://healthnewsdigest.com/news/health%20care%20reform0/CMS_Proposes_2012_Medicare_Home_Health_Payment_Changes.shtml

106. Operator of two home health care businesses indicted in alleged $20 million Medicare fraud scheme. (2011, June 29). http://www.fbi.gov/chicago/press-releases/2011/operator-of-two-home-health-care-businesses-indicted-in-alleged-20-million-medicare-fraud-scheme

107. Home safety for the elderly: Fire safety and burn precautions. (n.d.). http://www.aginghomehealth-care.com/home-safety-for-the-elderly.html

108. Burn injuries due to cigarette-related residential fires. (2004, September 24). http://www.ok.gov/health/documents/Cigarette_HouseFires2004.pdf

109. Documentation, training protect hospital from risk in home care. (1993). *Hospital Risk Management, 15*(11), 164–167.

110. NAHC model notice of termination of care (version 2). (n.d.). http://www.nahc.org/regulatory/PPS2011-Docs/5NoticeTermination.doc

111. 42 U.S.C. 395bbb.

112. OIG compliance program guidance for home health agencies, (1998, August 7). Office of Inspector General, Department of Health and Human Services. *Federal Register, 63*(152), 42410, 42414.

113. Home health aide arrested for $30k theft from family. (2011, July 1). http://www.mycentraljersey.com/article/20110701/NJNEWS/110701004/Home-health-aide-arrested-30K-theft-from-family

114. *Warding off thieves.* (1994). *24,* 28–29.

115. Alder, H. C. (1993). Safe Medical Devices Act: Management guidance for hospital compliance with the new FDA requirements. *Hospital Technology and Sevices.* http://www.ncbi.nlm.nih.gov/pubmed/10129209

116. Duke nurse charged with robbing heiress. (1995, October 10). *Star-Ledger.* p.14.

117. Copple, B. (2007, December 3). Does your home health company run background checks? http://michiganhomecare.wordpress.com/2007/12/03/does-your-home-health-company-run-background-checks/

118. Bailey, E. (2009, October 28). Planned background checks for in-home healthcare workers are criticized. http://articles.latimes.com/2009/oct/28/local/me-home-care28

119. Sussman, M. L., & Siegel, P. J. (1991). Assessing an agency's risk. *Caring, 10*(9), 42–45, 67–68.

120. Patient recruiter for Miami health care agency pleads guilty in $25 million Medicare fraud scheme. (2011, July 21). http://www.justice.gov/opa/pr/2011/July/11-crm-952.html

121. Berens, M. J. (2010 December 12). Bed brokers scramble to cash in: Referral companies charge adult homes hefty fees to steer seniors to them; most never check facilities for quality. *Seattle Times.* WLNR 24751061.

122. Nadwairski, J. A. (1992). Inner-city safety for home care providers. *Journal of Nursing Administration, 22*(9), 42–47.

123. Gershon, R., Pogorzelsha, M., Qureshi, K., Stone, P., Carton, A., Samar, S., ... Sherman, M. (2008). Home health care patients and safety hazards in the home: Preliminary findings. http://www.ncbi.nlm.nih.gov/pubmed/21249854

124. Gershon, R. (2008, October). Household-related hazardous conditions with implications for patient safety in the home health care sector. *Journal of Patient Safety.* http://www.ahrq.gov/downloads/pub/advances2/vol1/Advances-Gershon_88.pdf

125. Ergonomics for the prevention of musculoskeletal disorders. OSHA 3182-3R 2009. http://www.osha.gov/ergonomics/guidelines/nursinghome/final_nh_guidelines.pdf

126. Quinn, M. (2009). Sharps injuries and other blood and body fluid exposures among home health care nurses and aides. *American Journal of Public Health* (Suppl). http://ajph.aphapublications.org/cgi/reprint/99/S3/S710.pdf

127. Independent contractor defined. (n.d.). http://www.irs.gov/businesses/small/article/0,,id=179115,00.html

128. Employee (common-law employee). (n.d.). http://www.irs.gov/business/small/article/0,,id=179112,00.html

129. Rau, J. (2011, June 27). Concerns about costs rise with hospices' use, *New York Times.* http://www.nytimes.com/2011/06/28/health/28hospice.html

CHAPTER 17

Risk Management in Office-Based Surgery

Jean G. Charchaflieh

THE GROWTH OF OFFICE-BASED SURGERY

Office-based surgery (OBS) is an invasive procedure that requires general anesthesia, and deep or moderate sedation, and that is performed in a doctor's office that is not part of a hospital or an ambulatory surgical center (ASC).

OBS can be considered one of the oldest forms of practice in medicine. Over time, technological advances in medicine shifted the practice of surgery from individual physician's offices to large medical centers that have operating rooms (OR) that are much better equipped with devices, staffed with personnel, and supported with ancillary services than what can be available in a physician's office. This pattern of concentrating surgical and invasive procedures into large medical centers made economic and practical sense. As this pattern of practice became the norm, regulation of hospital practices was undertaken by state and federal agencies, and regulation of physicians' surgical and other procedural practices was provided by hospitals in the form of clinical privileges that were requested by the physician and granted by the medical board of the hospital.

In the last quarter of the twentieth century, technological advances that decreased the invasiveness of surgical procedures, along with economic incentives, led to a shift of surgical and invasive procedures from the hospitals OR to free-standing (not part of hospital) ASCs. In turn, regulations for licensing, operation, and physicians' practices in ASCs were introduced by state and federal agencies. The same trend of technological advances and economic incentives that led to the shifting of invasive procedures from hospital-based ORs to ASCs led to rerouting of some of the minimally invasive procedures from hospitals and ASCs to physicians' offices and a new pattern of practice labeled office-based surgery emerged.

The two main technological advances that facilitated the migration of surgical procedures from the hospital and the ASC to the OBS setting were (1) decreased invasiveness of surgical procedures and (2) decreased invasiveness of anesthetic procedures due to the introduction of intravenous anesthetic drugs (propofol) and minimally invasive airway management devices (laryngeal mask airway [LMA]).

Decreased invasiveness of surgical procedures provide many advantages:

- Decreased duration of procedure
- Decreased blood loss
- Decreased need for deep levels of anesthesia
- Decreased stress response
- Decreased postoperative pain

Surgical technological advances that have decreased the invasiveness of surgical procedure and are commonly employed in OBS are outlined in **Box 17-1**.

Box 17-1   Surgical Technological Advances That Decrease the Invasiveness of Surgical Procedure
• Use of video scopes to approach body cavities for diagnosis and therapeutic interventions instead of open surgical approaches • Use of an endovascular approach to blood vessels for diagnosis and therapeutic intervention (angioplasty) instead of open extravascular approaches • Use of laser, radiofrequency, or cold temperatures (cryoablation) for lesion ablation instead of surgical excision of lesions • Use of micrographic devices and approaches (i.e., Mohs micrographic skin surgery)

Intravenous anesthetic drugs eliminate the need for bulky, expensive anesthesia machines; scavenging systems to eliminate waste anesthetic gases; and treatment kits for malignant hyperthermia (when succinylcholine is also eliminated). Propofol, the intravenous anesthetic drug, is particularly suitable for OBS because of the following characteristics:

• Fast onset and short duration of action, allowing for rapid induction of anesthesia, accurate titration during the maintenance phase of anesthesia, and rapid emergence from anesthesia
• Decreased sense of hangover, better sense of mental clarity, and mild euphoric effect upon recovery
• Antiemetic properties, in contrast to the emetic properties of inhalational anesthetic agents

The LMA is also particularly suitable for OBSs:

• It allows for manual insertion without the use of a rigid laryngoscope or other insertion devices.
• It permits insertion without use of neuromuscular-blocking drugs (NMBDs), which eliminates inherent risks associated with NMBDs, including the malignant hyperthermia-triggering risk linked to succinylcholine.
• The LMA's proximal positioning above the vocal cords provides less stimulation during maintenance of anesthesia, requiring less anesthetic depth and allowing faster and smoother emergence from anesthesia.

One disadvantage that emerges with increased safety and ease of a procedure is that it invites physicians who are not quite familiar with it to venture into performing the procedure (**Box 17-2**).

Box 17-2   Minimally Invasive Procedures Performed in the OBS Setting
Minimal invasive vitrectomy[1] Blepharoplasty under local anesthesia[2] Liposuction for body contouring and lipoharvesting[3] Adenotonsillectomy[4] Laryngeal steroid injection for vocal cord scar[5] Flexible videolaryngoscopy with transoral vocal fold injection for dysphagia[6] Laryngeal laser surgery[7] Laser ablation of glottal papillomatosis and dysplasia under local anesthesia[8] Endoscopic injection laryngoplasty[9] Laser-assisted uvulopalatoplasty for snoring an obstructive sleep apnea (OSA)[10] Soft palate implants for OSA[11] Multilevel (tongue and palate) radiofrequency tissue ablation for OSA[12] *(continues)*

Thermoplastic mandibular advancement
  devices[13]
Cryoablation of breast fibroadenomas[14,15]
Diagnostic breast ductoscopy[16]
Ultrathin esophagogastroduodenoscopy (u-EGD)
  by family practice physicians[17]
Sigmoidoscopy[18]
Diagnostic and operative micro-laparoscopy[19]
Single-puncture laparoscopy sterilization with
  local anesthesia[20]
Flexible hysteroscopy without anesthesia[21]
Hysteroscopic sterilization[22]
Ablation of submucous uterine myomas[23]
Endometrial ablation[24]
Radiofrequency interstitial tumor ablation (RITA)
  of prostate cancer[25]
Transurethral needle ablation (TUNA) of benign
  prostatic hyperplasia (BPH)[26]
Transurethral radiofrequency (RF) collagen for
  stress urinary incontinence (SUI)[27]
Needle arthroscopy of the knee with synovial
  biopsy sampling[28]
Arthroscopic synovectomy of the wrist[29]
Mohs micrographic skin surgery (MMS)[30]
Endovenous radiofrequency ablation of
  varicose veins[31,32]
Endovenous laser surgery for varicose veins[33]
Needle biopsy of the thyroid[34]

Box 17-3   Administrative/Economic Factors in the Shift of Procedures to OBS

- Decreased costs for the patient, doctor, and insurer
- Increased scheduling ease for the patient and doctor
- Increased privacy for the patient
- Decreased risk of nosocomial infection
- Increased operational efficiency
- Increased consistency of nursing personnel

Technological advances in surgery and anesthesia were coupled with administrative/economic factors that favored shifting procedures away from hospital and ASCs and toward OBS facilities (**Box 17-3**).

Regulation of OBS occurred on a voluntary basis or through state mandates. The federally funded Medicare program did not allow a facility fee for procedures performed in an OBS facility, as it did for procedures performed in a hospital or an ASC; therefore, it did not actively participate in regulating the practice of OBS. Application of a facility fee can double the cost of a procedure. For example, an inguinal hernia repair performed in a hospital can

cost $2,237, compared to $895 in an OBS facility, with the difference in cost being mainly due to the hospital's facility fee.[35] Despite providers' inability to collect a facility fee for a procedure performed on an OBS basis from medicare, the decrease in overhead cost and increased efficiency seem to offset this fee differential and maintain the advantage of shifting procedures from hospitals and ASCs to OBS facilities.

The growth of OBS occurred not only through shifting of procedures from hospitals and ASCs to OBS facilities, but also through the development of new procedures that were practiced mainly in OBS facilities. Given that there is no requirement to report OBS procedures at either the state or federal level, it is difficult to determine the precise number of OBS procedures that are performed. Available estimates suggest that this number is in the tens of millions per year, with an annual growth rate of approximately 2%.

The decreased invasiveness and increased safety of surgical and anesthetic procedures allowed many physicians to expand the scope of their practice. In turn, the traditional boundaries between surgical and medical specialties in general and between specific specialties began eroding. The process of obtaining clinical privileges from hospitals' medical boards was traditionally a limitation on which procedures a physician was privileged to perform in the hospital. In an OBS facility, however, in most cases the scope of practice of a physician was limited only by the physician medical license, which essentially grants the physician the privilege of the practice of medicine and surgery in its broadest term. Unfortunately, some physicians expanded the scope of their practice in OBS beyond their competence, with occasionally disastrous consequences (**Box 17-4**).

Box 17-4   Egregious Unsafe Practices in OBS

- In 1993, in Queens, New York, a physician who had been barred from surgery at a hospital because of incompetence and who had previously had his license suspended for "sewing the wrong parts of a woman's anatomy together" performed a mid-trimester abortion that led to the death in his office of a 33-year-old woman.[36]
- Singer Claudio Martell died during enhancement procedures on his chin, cheeks, torso, and penis.[37]

SOURCES OF RISK IN OBS

Sources of risk in OBS, both to the healthcare provider and to the consumer, are many. Some are similar to those encountered in hospital settings or ASCs, while others are more prominent in OBS settings.

Informed Consent and Breach-of-Contract Issues

Data from malpractice insurance claims indicate that the majority (67%) of claims stemming from lipoplasty—a procedure that is performed almost exclusively on an OBS basis—are due to informed consent or breach-of-contract issues. The overall industry norm for this category of claims is 26%. These findings might indicate that expectations, clarity of information, and disclosure are particularly important for lipoplasty procedures, and for cosmetic procedures in general.[38]

Bleeding, Thromboembolism, and Infections

Several studies of adverse events (AEs) in plastic and cosmetic OBS have identified the three main causes of AEs and deaths:[39–42]

- Bleeding (hematoma formation)
- Thromboembolism (deep vein thrombosis and pulmonary embolism)
- Infections

The reported rate of AEs was approximately 3 per 1,000 procedures, and the reported rate of death was approximately 2 per 100,000 procedures.[39–40] Data from Mohs micrographic skin OBS procedures indicate that the AE rate is in the range of 1%, including cases of intraoperative bleeding.[43]

Perforation of Viscus and Drug Toxicity

Studies of liposuction OBS procedures show that, in addition to the three previously mentioned causes of AE and death, leading causes of death include perforation of the abdomen or viscus and medication toxicity. The reported rate of serious adverse events (SAEs) in OBS was approximately 7 per 10,000,[44] and the death rate was approximately 19 per 100,000.[45]

Interference with Pacemakers or Implantable Cardioverter–Defibrillators Due to the Use of Electrosurgery Units

Electrosurgery unit (ESU) devices, also known as electrocautery, are used both for tissue cutting and cauterization of bleeding vessels. Use of a unipolar ESU device can interfere with the function of an implantable pacemaker or an implantable cardioverter–defibrillator (ICD), leading to serious complications such as reprogramming of a pacemaker, firing of an ICD, asystole, bradycardia, tachyarrhythmia, and depletion of battery life of a pacemaker.[46] Use of bipolar ESU devices practically eliminates the risk of interference with pacemakers and ICDs.

Anesthetic Complications

The American Society of Anesthesiologists' Closed Claims Project (ASA CCP) allows closed claims that are provided on a voluntary basis by insurance companies (approximately 30% of all U.S. companies participate) to be examined and analyzed by volunteer members of the ASA CCP. The project has been ongoing since the mid-1980s. In its most recent review in June 2011, it had 8,954 claims.[47]

ASA CCP data show that during the 2000s, anesthesia-related claims stemming from OR locations have decreased, while those stemming from non-OR locations, including pain management, have increased. The most common types of claims involved regional anesthesia (19%), chronic pain management (18%), and monitored anesthesia care (MAC, 10%). The most common injuries were death (26%), nerve injury (22%), and permanent brain damage (9%). The most common damaging events were regional-block-related (20%), respiratory (17%), cardiovascular (13%), and equipment-related events (10%).

Common locations where non-OR procedures are performed include gastroenterology (GI) suites, cardiac catheterization and electrophysiology labs, emergency rooms (ER), and lithotripsy, radiology, and magnetic resonance imaging (MRI) suites. Compared to OR claims, non-OR claims were more likely to involve older and sicker patients, emergency procedures, and MAC; to result in respiratory complications and death; and to be judged as being preventable by better monitoring.[48]

Lessons learned from examining the characteristics of anesthetic complications in remote locations outside the OR can be used to avoid similar anesthetic complications in OBS. The predominant lesson is the importance of vigilance in the monitoring and management of respiratory function (both ventilation and oxygenation).[49] Substandard care, preventable by better monitoring, was implicated in the majority of claims associated with death.

Lapses in Infection Control Practices

Infectious complications rank high as problems associated with OBS, and lapses in infection control practices can be a major contributor to such complications. Heightened infection control practices, including jewelry restrictions, alcohol hand scrubs, and sterile gloves, gowns, and towels, have been shown to decrease infectious complications rates in one OBS practice from 2.5% to 0.9%.[50]

Data from the center for Medicare & Medicaid Services (CMS) indicate that lapses in at least one category of infection control are encountered in 67.6% of ASCs, while lapses in three or more infection control categories are encountered in 17.6% of ASCs. The most common problems are encountered in the categories of handling of single-dose vials (SDV, 28.1%), reprocessing of equipment (28.4%), and blood glucose monitoring equipment (46.3%).[51] CMS requires ASCs and OBS facilities to observe infection control practices in five categories—hand hygiene, injection safety and medication handling, equipment reprocessing, environmental cleaning, and handling of blood glucose monitoring equipment. Lapses in infection control practices pose risks for both patients and staff, and lead to citations of noncompliance with regulatory agencies and accrediting organizations.

Infectious risks to healthcare workers include exposure to blood-borne pathogens such as hepatitis B virus (HBV), hepatitis C virus (HCV), and human immunodeficiency virus (HIV).[52] The following techniques can minimize such risks:

- Using universal precautions (protective measures applied with all patients)
- Organization of the surgical field
- Consideration of alternative treatments in high-risk patients
- Safe handling, transferring, and disposal of sharps
- Working without using sharps
- Protection from backspray injuries

Complications Due to Preexisting Medical Conditions

Preexisting medical conditions may present particular risks to patients undergoing surgery on an ambulatory basis, such as in OBS settings (**Box 17-5**).[53]

Box 17-5   Complications Due to Preexisting Medical Conditions

Condition	Associated Risk of Adverse Event
Hypertension or being elderly	Intraoperative minor cardiac AEs
Obesity	Intraoperative minor respiratory AEs and postoperative respiratory AEs
Smoking or asthma	Postoperative respiratory AEs
Postoperative nausea and vomiting	Postoperative prolonged stays
Age older than 85 years, significant comorbidity, or hospital admissions in past 6 months	Higher rates of hospital admission

Obesity and obstructive sleep apnea (OSA) are emerging as particular risks for postoperative respiratory complications. Patients with OSA may require prolonged monitoring in the postoperative period, which may exclude them from having procedures on an outpatient basis, including OBS. There is a continuing need for a reliable method to assess the severity of OSA and translate this assessment of severity into practice recommendations, ranging from suitability of the patient and procedure for OBS to postoperative management. The American Society of Anesthesiologists (ASA) has developed clinical practice guidelines (CPG) focused on the safety of performing a procedure on an outpatient basis (ASC or OBS) in patients with increased risk for OSA.[54] Further studies evaluating the impact of OSA on OBS and recommendations for best practices are needed.

Complications Due to Incorrect Surgical Procedure

Incorrect surgical procedure events (wrong patient, side, site, procedure, or implant) can occur in any practice setting. Data from the Veterans Health Administration (VHA) medical centers indicate that incorrect surgical procedure events occur equally frequently in OR sites and in non-OR sites such as interventional radiology suites.[55] The most common root cause for such events is lack of standardization of clinical processes. Suggested actions to decrease such events include root-cause analysis, policy changes, and team training.[56]

The data from the VHA study are consistent with data from the New York Patient Occurrence Reporting and Tracking System (NYPORTS), which indicate that the most common causes of incorrect surgical procedure events are failure in communication, poor team dynamics, poor team orientation and training, ignoring available information, failure of site marking and of performing the time-out process, and time pressure.[57] Data from The Joint Commission (TJC) indicate that 41% of incorrect surgical procedure events occur in orthopedic procedures,[58] with orthopedic problems having one of the highest rates of migrating from hospital settings to ACSs and OBS facilities.[59]

Complications Causing Unplanned Hospital Admission after OBS

Procedural complications are the most common cause of unplanned hospital admission after OBS. Data from American Association for the Accreditation of Ambulatory Surgical Facilities (AAAASF)–accredited OBS facilities indicate that the unplanned hospital admission rate for OBS ranges from 0.3% to 0.03%.[60–62]

Data from the national Medicare database indicate an overall unplanned hospital admission after OBS rate of 0.4%, which is lower than that for procedures performed in hospital outpatient departments (OPDs). The Medicare data also indicate that OBS populations are relatively healthier, younger, and more prosperous than those who undergo procedures in hospital OPDs.[63]

Data from the New York State Department of Health (NYS DOH) show that the most common AEs after OBS procedures are unplanned transfer to a hospital (43% of total reports) and unplanned admission to a hospital within 72 hours after an OBS procedure (41% of total reports).[64] The type of OBS procedures most frequently associated with AEs were endoscopy procedures (colonoscopy and upper endoscopy—47% of total reports), and the second most common type of procedures associated with AEs were end-stage renal disease–related procedures (15% of total reports).

Death Due to OBS Procedures

Information about death due to OBS procedures is limited both by the sparse amount of data and by the controversy about analyzing the existing data. The controversy arises both from the numerator (which deaths should be counted as OBS-related deaths) and from the denominator (the total number of OBS procedures that should be considered in analyzing OBS-related deaths) used to calculate the death rate. Such debate can result in significant differences in estimates of rates of death in association of OBS procedures. For example, based on selecting two different denominators for OBS procedures, two groups of investigators analyzing Florida data calculated two significantly different rates of death for OBS procedures—9.2 versus 0.4 per 100,000 procedures.[65,66]

In some instances, the numerator (number of deaths) exists without a denominator (total number of OBS procedures). Data from NYS DOH showed a total of 22 deaths (defined as death within 30 days of undergoing an OBS procedure) over a 10-month period (January–September 2008). Almost two-thirds of the reported deaths occurred in patients having procedures for end-stage renal disease (ESRD). The second most common procedure type associated with death was endoscopy (colonoscopy and upper endoscopy—18% of total reported deaths).

Comparisons Between OBS, ASCs, and Hospitals

It is difficult to determine, based on available data, whether a certain site of practice (hospital versus ASC versus OBS facility) is safer than another. Inherent bias in selection of procedure, patient, and provider, plus differences in definition of study parameters, data sources, and analyses, are likely to confound such comparisons. A major methodological challenge in outcome studies of OBS is the calculation of event rates, as in many cases the denominator—the total number of OBS procedures—is unknown. Event rates are easier to calculate for procedures performed in outpatient departments of hospitals or in ASCs because databases recording the total number of procedures performed have been established.

In most states, the State Ambulatory Surgery Databases (SASD) of the Agency for Healthcare Research and Quality's (AHRQ) Healthcare Cost and Utilization Project (HCUP) capture more than 100 variables on each healthcare encounter. In addition, the National Survey of Ambulatory Surgery routinely issues statistical reports on OPDs and ASCs. Medicare and commercial insurance databases also provide extensive data from OPDs and ASCs. There is no state or federal standard reporting of activities in OBS facilities, however. The only organization that requires OBS facilities to maintain a log of all invasive procedures, except those performed under only local anesthesia, and to report all adverse events is the accrediting agency AAAASF.

Despite these limitations, a few studies have compared rates of complications in procedures performed on an outpatient versus inpatient basis. They found no difference in relation to widely performed surgical procedures such as hernia repair and laparoscopic cholecystectomy.[67,68]

Operating Room Fires

Over the last decade, the incidence of OR fires has increased. In 2003, the estimated rate of OR fires was 100 per year.[69] In 2010, that number increased to 550 to 650 incidents per year.[70]

Data from the ASA CCP show that burn injury is a particular risk for procedures performed under monitored anesthesia care, where burns account for 20% of total claims, compared to their 2.2% rate for all claims.[71] Burn injuries lead to disability in 6% of cases and death in 1% of patients. Common features of OR fires include the following:

- Surgery performed on the face, neck, and tonsil (78% of surgical fires)
- Use of ESU (68%) and laser equipment (13%)
- Use of supplemental oxygen that crates an oxygen-enriched atmosphere (74%)
- Use of alcohol-based surgical site preparation solutions

During OR fires, both patients and OR personnel are at risk of burn injury as well as smoke inhalation injury. For a fire to occur, three elements must be present: fuel, an oxidizer, and heat (ignition source). Eliminating or minimizing the role of any of these three elements would eliminate or minimize the risk of fire. The American Society of Anesthesiologists has developed a practice advisory on the prevention and management of operating room fires.[72] The Anesthesia Patient Safety Foundation (APSF) has also created an algorithm for the prevention and management of surgical fires that is supported by many national patient safety organizations and is available in a video format from the organization's website.[73,74]

RISK MANAGEMENT IN OBS

Legal Requirements

Legal requirements of operating an OBS practice should be in place dependent on the state requirements.

Naming Designation of an OBS Practice

Physicians operating an OBS should avoid the words "center" or "clinic" in naming their OBS practice, as these words are reserved for ACSs licensed to collect facility fees from private, state, and federal insurance carriers. The use of the words "center" and "clinic" in naming an OBS practice might bring allegations of misrepresentation—namely, that such a name is used to illegally collect facility fees reserved for licensed ACSs.

Corporate Designation of an OBS Facility

The OBS practice should be owned and operated as a professional entity (e.g., a professional corporation [PC], a professional limited liability corporation [PLLC], or a limited liability partnership [LLP]) that does not share fees with a general business corporation (e.g., a limited liability corporation [LLC] or an incorporation [Inc]). This is essential to avoid two allegations: (1) engaging in illegal fee splitting with a lay entity and (2) violating the Corporate Practice of Medicine Doctrine (CPMD), which prohibits a lay entity from employing medical professionals, and allows only a professional entity to employ healthcare professionals. Violating the CPMD can involve professional and criminal allegations that apply to both the employer and the employee. A nurse employed by a general corporation can be guilty of sharing fees with the corporation, which is both a criminal and professional violation, and unauthorized practice of medicine, which is a criminal violation. A physician owner of a practice that violates the CPMD can be charged with professional and criminal violations. The CPMD aims to protect the public from a business relationship that could place constraints upon professional judgment, unduly limit professional practice, invade the professional integrity of the professional, or permit the business to make professional decisions.

Referral to an OBS Facility

The Stark II Federal law prohibits physicians from making referrals to an entity in which they, or a family member, has a financial interest. This restriction may have implications for physicians practicing in more than one location with different ownership of practice facilities.

Contracts Between Physicians and Hospitals

Most contracts between hospitals and physicians contain exclusive noncompetition clauses. The terms of such clauses might prevent a physician from practicing in an OBS facility within a certain geographic area relative to the hospital during or after the physician's employment by the hospital.

Healthcare Authority Requirements

Healthcare authority requirements for OBS practice should be followed. Some states apply their existing ASC regulations to OBS practices. Most states, however, have created regulations specific to OBS. State policies regulating OBS practice range from loose guidelines to extensive regulations, or a combination of regulation and guidelines. Aspects of regulation include the following points:

- Facility accreditation by a nationally recognized independent accrediting organization
- Personnel requirements for education, training, licensing, board certification, hospital privileges, and scope of practice
- Patient selection in terms of age limit or physical status as classified by the American Society of Anesthesiologists
- Procedure selection in terms of limits on duration, expected blood loss, and certain body sites (e.g., brain, large vessels)
- Tracking and reporting adverse events

Accrediting Organizations' Standards

Three accrediting organizations are recognized by most states for accrediting OBS facilities: the Accreditation Association for Ambulatory Health Care (AAAHC), the American Association for the Accreditation of Ambulatory Surgical Facilities (AAAASF), and The Joint Commission (TJC).

The AAAHC was the first organization to accredit ambulatory care sites, beginning in 1979 with a focus originally on community health centers. It accredits more than 1,500 healthcare facilities across the United States.

The AAAASF began in 1980 as the American Association for Accreditation of Ambulatory Plastic Surgery Facilities, which was created by the American Society of Plastic and Reconstructive Surgeons to set a high standard of care in the private offices of plastic surgeons. The organization changed its name in 1992 to AAAASF based on requests for accreditation from other surgical specialties. Originally, AAAASF accredited only offices owned by surgeons, but it has recently expanded to offer accreditation for office endoscopy and other non-surgical practices. Facilities also have the option of undergoing a somewhat more rigorous level of accreditation to meet Medicare standards. AAAASF has accredited more than 1,000 ambulatory surgery facilities nationwide. It requires accredited facilities to maintain a log of all invasive procedures, except those performed under only local anesthesia, and to report all adverse events via an online AE reporting system.

TJC developed its OBS services in 2001 in response to the national regulatory trend for accreditation. TJC emerged in 1951 (as the Joint Commission for the Accreditation of Healthcare Organizations [JCAHO]) as a collaboration of the American College of Physicians, the American Medical Association, the Canadian Medical Association, and the American College of Surgeons to improve hospital care. In 1975, it established an ambulatory heathcare accreditation and has gradually branched out to accredit other organizational forms of health care, including international organizations.

The three accrediting organizations maintain similar standards:

- Physicians must be board qualified or eligible or otherwise proven competent.
- Physicians must have local hospital privileges for procedures they will perform as OBS.

- Facilities have detailed plans for evaluating, educating, monitoring, and discharging patients.
- Facilities have detailed safety and maintenance requirements for the physical site and equipment.
- Facilities must comply with existing regulations, including reporting adverse events.

Professional Societies' Clinical Practice Guidelines

The clinical practice guidelines (CPG) developed by professional societies should be adopted when applicable. Examples include the following guidelines:

- American College of Surgeons (ACS): *Statement on Patient Safety Principles for Office-Based Surgery.*[75]
- American Society of Anesthesiologists (ASA): *Guidelines for Office-Based Anesthesia.*[76]
- Centers for Disease Control and Prevention (CDC): *Guide to Infection Prevention for Outpatient Settings.*[77]
- Federation of State Medical Boards (FSMB): *Report of the Special Committee on Outpatient (Office-Based) Surgery.*[78] FSMB represents 70 medical licensing and disciplinary boards, and its OBS guidelines represent input from accrediting organizations, professional societies, and governmental agencies (**Box 17-6**).
- American Gastroenterological Association (AGA): *Standards for Office-Based Gastrointestinal Endoscopy Services.*[79]
- American College of Obstetricians and Gynecologists (ACOG): Presidential Task Force on Patient Safety in the Office Setting.[80]

Box 17-6   Organizations Represented in the FSMB Guidelines for OBS

- American Association for Accreditation of Ambulatory Surgery Facilities
- The Joint Commission
- Accreditation Association for Ambulatory Health Care
- Institute for Medical Quality
- American Society of Anesthesiologists
- American Association of Nurse Anesthetists
- American College of Surgeons
- American Academy of Dermatology
- American Medical Association
- American Osteopathic Association
- Anesthesia Patient Safety Foundation
- Health Care Financing Administration

- American Society of Plastic Surgeons (ASPS): Committee on Patient Safety. This group has published evidence-based practice advisories on many topics, including liposuction,[81] malignant hyperthermia,[82] blood dyscrasias,[83] obstructive sleep apnea and obstructive lung disease,[84] patient assessment and prevention of pulmonary side effects,[85] and patient selection and procedures in ambulatory surgery.[86]

Management Practices

Management practices that are effective and efficient should be established.

Personnel Management

The OBS facility should maintain written policies describing personnel credentialing and required competencies according to requirements of federal, state, accrediting, and reimbursement agencies. This may include professional licensure; residency and fellowship training; board certification or eligibility; privileges to perform equivalent procedures at a local hospital or an ASC facility; continuing medical education (CME) certification; Basic Life Support (BLS), Advanced Cardiac Life Support (ACLS), and Pediatric Life Support (PALS) certification; infection control certification; and Health Information Portability and Accountability Act (HIPAA) training certification.

A medical director for the facility should be identified, and the organizational structure, lines of authority, responsibilities, accountability, and supervision of personnel described.

The facility should document that individuals administering anesthesia are licensed, qualified, and working within their scope of practice. It should also document that practitioners intending to produce a certain level of sedation have the capacity to rescue patients from deeper levels of sedation.

Facility Management

The OBS facility should have written policies for handling emergencies such as surgical fires, general fires, power outages, weather disasters, and cardiopulmonary arrest. These policies should cover issues of personnel, equipment, and procedures.

A written transfer agreement should exist with a reasonably convenient hospital where OBS physicians have admitting privileges or where they can arrange transfer of care for the patient. All information relevant to patient care should be readily available at time of transfer.

Medical Records Management

The OBS facility should consider use of an electronic medical record system. It should maintain accurate and legible patient medical records that contain pre-, intra-, and post-procedure information and abide by HIPAA laws.

The medical record system should document the performance of procedure-specific checklist. It should also document that the primary care provider was informed of the procedure results and the patient's status.

Quality Management

There should be a quality management process that tracks and identifies trends related to patient outcomes, including deaths, cardiopulmonary events, anaphylaxis, adverse drug reactions, infections, postoperative complications and hospital admissions, medication errors, and results of patient satisfaction surveys. When required, adverse events should be reported to the respective state's regulatory agencies and accrediting organization.

Communication with Patients

The OBS facility should provide information to patients, or prospective patients, that describes the facility's scope of services, contact information, the billing process, and a list of patient rights and responsibilities. Patient education should be performed to provide patients with procedure-specific education that covers the preoperative, intraoperative, and postoperative periods, with the opportunity to ask questions plus written instructions for the postoperative period.

Safe Clinical Practices

Preoperative Practices

Patient selection includes patient screening and assessment for suitability for an OBS procedure using regulating agencies' requirements and guidelines developed by accrediting and professional organizations. Particular risk groups include patients at extremes of age as well as patients with obstructive sleep apnea, obesity, pacemakers and implantable cardiac defibrillators (ICDs), chronic obstructive pulmonary disease (COPD), end-stage renal disease, and epilepsy.

Preoperative patient assessment should include a medical history and physical examination (H&P); ordering and reviewing appropriate diagnostic testing (labs, imaging studies, EKGs) and consultant evaluations; and developing a patient assessment and plan (A&P) of care for the preoperative, intraoperative, and postoperative periods. If state law requires supervision of a certified registered nurse anesthetist (CRNA), an anesthesiologist or a physician assuming the responsibility for supervision of the CRNA must perform the preoperative assessment.

Procedure selection should include assessing the duration of the procedure (should be less than 6 hours), the complexity of the procedure including expected blood loss (should be less than 500 mL), and suitability for discharge home after the procedure. When possible, a less invasive approach to performing the procedure should be selected. This approach may require staging of the procedure to allow for use of a minimally invasive method.

The physician performing the procedure must also conduct a comprehensive informed consent discussion with the patient (or his or her representative) that covers the necessity, appropriateness, and risks of the proposed procedure; treatment alternatives, including no treatment; and the patient's acknowledgment that his or her questions, if any, were answered. The individual responsible for supervising the administration of the anesthesia must conduct a comprehensive informed consent discussion with the patient (or his or her representative) that covers the necessity, appropriateness, and risks of the proposed anesthetic plan; treatment alternatives, including no anesthesia; and the patient's acknowledgment that his or her questions, if any, were answered.

Finally, operative site marking is important: The operative physician should mark the site of surgery while the patient is fully alert.

Intraoperative Practices

If supervision of a CRNA is required by state law, then an anesthesiologist or a physician assuming the responsibility for supervision of the CRNA must prescribe the anesthesia, supervise the administration of anesthesia, and be available for diagnosis, treatment, and management of anesthesia-related complications or emergencies.

Patient monitoring should be performed according to the patient's condition and level of sedation. Monitoring should be continuous and recorded manually or electronically. When moderate sedation is administered, the healthcare professional who is monitoring the patient can assist the practitioner who is performing the procedure with interruptible tasks. When deep sedation or general anesthesia is administered, the healthcare professional who is monitoring the patient should be dedicated to patient monitoring and administration of the anesthesia and should not participate in the procedure.

Monitoring during moderate sedation should include assessment of ventilation, oxygenation, heart rate (HR), and blood pressure (BP). Ventilation is monitored most effectively using an exhaled CO_2 detection method (capnography). Capnography is mandatory when direct observation of ventilation and access to the patient airway are not readily available. This technique has been shown to alert practitioners to respiratory depression and apnea before hypoxemia develops.[87] Oxygenation is monitored using pulse oximetry, which provides continuous assessment of both oxygenation (O_2 saturation) and heart rate. Blood Pressure should be measured manually or automatically at intervals according to patient condition and stability but not at intervals exceeding 10 minutes. Monitoring of an electrocardiogram (EKG) may be indicated based on the patient's condition, the type of anesthesia (general), and the performed procedure; it provides information about heart rate, heart rhythm, and acute ischemic cardiac events.

Supplemental oxygen should be provided to prevent and treat hypoxia. This intervention should be applied judiciously using the least invasive method. A nasal cannula is suitable for most patients. In addition, a means of delivering oxygen by positive-pressure ventilation (PPV) should be readily available at the procedure site. An Ambu bag is a self-inflating bag that allows PPV with the use of a mask or other airway device such as an endotracheal tube or laryngeal mask airway. Supplemental oxygen is not without risk, including the possibility of supporting OR fires and delaying detection of apnea, and it should not be used if it is not needed to prevent or treat hypoxia.

Medications and solutions that are used both in the sterile field and for sedation or anesthesia should be labeled with both the name and the concentration of the drug. Emergency medications should be available in the procedure room.

Resuscitation medications, equipment, and capabilities must be readily available and accessible in the suite where the procedure is being performed (**Box 17-7**).

Warming devices should be available for procedures that are expected to be more than 2 hours in duration or cover more than 20% of the patient's total body surface area (TBSA).

Box 17-7 Emergency Equipment and Drugs

Defibrillator
Monitoring equipment for EKG, BP, HR, O_2 saturation, and CO_2 detection
High-flow oxygen source
Ambu-bag with face mask
Suction source with Yankauer suction catheter
Laryngoscope
Endotracheal tubes with stylets
Laryngeal mask airways
Oral and nasal airways
Face masks and nasal cannulas
Latex allergy cart
Warming blankets and fluid warmers
IV catheters and IV fluids
Atropine
Epinephrine
Amiodarone
Lidocaine
Sodium bicarbonate
Calcium chloride
Dextrose 50%
Naloxone and flumezanil
Metoprolol
Furosemide
Hydralazine
Nitroglycerine
Ephedrine
Phenylephrine
Albuterol
Methylene blue
Intra-lipids

A time-out process (a checklist) before the procedure starts should be conducted by the whole operative team (surgery, nursing, and anesthesia) to verify the following:

- Patient identity by two different means (e.g., name, medical record number, DOB) and from two different sources (e.g., patient chart and ID band)
- Procedure to be done

- Procedure side and site
- Patient position
- Availability of special equipment and materials (e.g., blood)
- preoperative antibiotics to be administered, if any

The Institute for Safety in Office-Based Surgery (ISOBS) used its own acronym (ISOBS) to create a safety checklist for OBS that was adapted from the World Health Organization (WHO) surgical safety checklist (**Box 17-8**).

Postoperative practices

If supervision of a CRNA is required by state law, then an anesthesiologist or a physician assuming the responsibility for supervision of the CRNA must prescribe postanesthesia medications and supervise postanesthesia care.

A staff member trained in postoperative care must stay with the patient until the patient is recovered to baseline mental status.

The physician supervising the postoperative care must be available until the patient has been discharged home.

At least one person with training in advanced resuscitative techniques (ACLS or PALS) must be immediately available until all patients are discharged.

The patient can be discharged once physician-defined discharge criteria are met.

Box 17-8

Safety Checklist for Office-Based Surgery
from the Institute for Safety in Office-Based Surgery (ISOBS)

Introduction Preoperative encounter; with practitioner and patient	**Setting** Before patient in procedure room; with practitioner and personnel	**Operation** Before sedation/analgesia; with practitioner and personnel*	**Before discharge** On arrival to recovery area; with practitioner & personnel	**Satisfaction** Completed post-procedure; with practitioner and patient
Patient **Patient medically optimized for the procedure?** ☐ Yes ☐ *No, and plan for optimization made.* **Does patient have DVT risk factors?** ☐ *Yes, and prophylaxis plans arranged.* ☐ *No* *Procedure* **Procedure complexity and sedation/analgesia reviewed?** ☐ Yes **NPO instructions given?** ☐ Yes **Escort and post-procedure plans reviewed?** ☐ Yes	**Emergency equipment check complete (e.g. airway, AED, code cart, MH kit)?** ☐ Yes **EMS availability confirmed?** ☐ Yes **Oxygen source and suction checked?** ☐ Yes **Anticipated duration ≤ 6 hours?** ☐ Yes ☐ *No, but personnel, monitoring and equipment available*	**Patient identity, procedure, and consent confirmed?** ☐ Yes **Is the site marked and side identified?** ☐ Yes ☐ *N/A* **DVT prophylaxis provided?** ☐ Yes ☐ *N/A* **Antibiotic prophylaxis administered within 60 minutes prior to procedure?** ☐ Yes ☐ *N/A* **Essential imaging displayed?** ☐ Yes ☐ *N/A* *Practitioner confirms verbally:* ☐ **Local anesthetic toxicity precautions** ☐ **Patient monitoring (per institutional protocol).** ☐ **Anticipated critical events addressed with team.** ☐ **Each member of the team has been addressed by name and is ready to proceed.**	**Assessment for pain?** ☐ Yes **Assessment for nausea/vomiting?** ☐ Yes **Recovery personnel available?** ☐ Yes *Prior to discharge:* *(with personnel and patient)* **Discharge criteria achieved?** ☐ Yes **Patient education and instructions provided?** ☐ Yes **Plan for post-discharge follow-up?** ☐ Yes **Escort confirmed?** ☐ Yes	**Unanticipated events documented?** ☐ Yes **Patient satisfaction assessed?** ☐ Yes **Provider satisfaction assessed?** ☐ Yes

This checklist is not intended to be comprehensive. Additions and modifications to fit local practice are encouraged. *Adapted from the WHO Surgical Safety Checklist.
© 2010 Institute for Safety in Office-Based Surgery (ISOBS), Inc – All Rights Reserved – www.isobs.org

These criteria should include stable vital signs within the range of the preoperative baseline level, responsiveness and orientation within the preoperative baseline level, voluntary movement within the preoperative baseline level, controlled pain, and minimal nausea and vomiting.

Written, procedure-specific, uniform postoperative patient instructions and education should be provided for the patient when awake enough. These instructions should cover pain management, postprocedure diet, medications, and activities; identify follow-up appointments; and provide an emergency phone number. The name of a covering physician should be provided in case of a scheduled absence in the postoperative period of the physician who performed the procedure. Appropriate "hand-off communication" should be performed between physicians.

A responsible adult must escort the patient home if the patient received moderate sedation, deep sedation, regional anesthesia, or general anesthesia.

A written emergency plan should be in place, including written protocols for the timely and safe transfer of the patient to a hospital within a reasonable proximity when needed.

A postoperative telephone interview should be designed to gather specific data about patient outcome and satisfaction.

INCREASING ROLE OF OFFICE-BASED SURGERY

Rates of OBS continue to grow due to overall satisfaction on the part of the patients and practitioners with such surgery. While this growth is taking place, efforts to enhance safety of OBS should be maintained. Risks of complications, death, and transfer to hospital appear to be small when appropriate OBS procedures are performed on suitable patients by competent physicians in a quality OBS facility. In general, factors that have been shown to affect physician competence include volume (number) of performed procedures, training, and experience. Patient factors that have been shown to increase risk of AEs in hospitals or ASCs include advanced age, severe systemic illness (ASA class of 3 or greater), and presence of HIV, cancer, peripheral vascular disease, or cardiovascular disease. Procedure factors that have been shown to increase the risk of AEs in hospitals or ASCs include urologic procedures, sinus surgery, open neck surgery, pandendoscopy (esophago-gastro-duodenoscopy [EGD] and colonoscopy), prolonged surgery, and use of general anesthesia. Factors that have been associated with increased patient satisfaction include increased age and recall of postoperative instructions.[88] Factors that have been associated with increased patient dissatisfaction include age younger than 10 years, anxiety, pain, vomiting, and being awake during the procedure.

REFERENCES

1. Gualtieri, W. One-port pars plana vitrectomy (by 25-G micro-incision). (2009, April). Graefe's *Archive for Clinical and Experimental Ophthalmology*, *247*(4), 495–502.
2. Harley, D. H., & Collins, D. R. Jr. (2008, January). Patient satisfaction after blepharoplasty performed as office surgery using oral medication with the patient under local anesthesia. *Aesthetic Plastic Surgery*, *32*(1), 77–81.
3. Sasaki, G. H. (2011, January). Water-assisted liposuction for body contouring and lipoharvesting: Safety and efficacy in 41 consecutive patients. *Aesthetic Surgery Journal*, *31*(1), 76–88.
4. Gravningsbråten, R., Nicklasson, B., & Raeder, J. (2009, February). Safety of laryngeal mask airway and short-stay practice in office-based adenotonsillectomy. *Acta Anaesthesiologica Scandinavica*, *53*(2), 218–222.

5. Mortensen, M. (2010, December). Laryngeal steroid injection for vocal fold scar. Current Opinion in *Otolaryngology & Head and Neck Surgery*, *18*(6), 487–491.

6. Andrade Filho, P. A., Carrau, R. L., & Buckmire, R. A. (2006, September-October). Safety and cost-effectiveness of intra-office flexible videolaryngoscopy with transoral vocal fold injection in dysphagic patients. American *Journal of Otolaryngology*, *27*(5), 319–322.

7. Koufman, J. A., Rees, C. J., Frazier, W. D., Kilpatrick, L. A., Wright, S. C., Halum, S. L., & Postma, G. N. (2007, July). Office-based laryngeal laser surgery: A review of 443 cases using three wavelengths. *Otolaryngology Head and Neck Surgery*, *137*(1), 146–151.

8. Zeitels, S. M., Franco, R. A. Jr., Dailey, S. H., Burns, J. A., Hillman, R. E., & Anderson, R. R. (2004, April). Office-based treatment of glottal dysplasia and papillomatosis with the 585-nm pulsed dye laser and local anesthesia. *Annals of Otology, Rhinology, and Laryngology*, *113*(4), 265–276.

9. Song, P. C., Sung, C. K., & Franco, R. A. Jr. (2010). Voice outcomes after endoscopic injection laryngoplasty with hyaluronic acid stabilized gel. *Laryngoscope*, *120*, Suppl 4: S199.

10. Han, S., & Kern, R. C. (2004, August). Laser-assisted uvulopalatoplasty in the management of snoring and obstructive sleep apnea syndrome. *Minerva Medica*, *95*(4), 337–345.

11. Goessler, U. R., Hein, G., Verse, T., Stuck, B. A., Hormann, K., & Maurer, J. T. (2007, May). Soft palate implants as a minimally invasive treatment for mild to moderate obstructive sleep apnea. *Acta Otolaryngol*, *127*(5), 527–531.

12. Steward, D. L. (2004, December). Effectiveness of multilevel (tongue and palate) radiofrequency tissue ablation for patients with obstructive sleep apnea syndrome. *Laryngoscope*, *114*(12), 2073–2084.

13. Friedman, M., Pulver, T., Wilson, M. N., Golbin, D., Leesman, C., Lee, G., & Joseph, N. J. (2010, July). Otolaryngology office-based treatment of obstructive sleep apnea-hypopnea syndrome with titratable and nontitratable thermoplastic mandibular advancement devices. *Otolaryngology Head and Neck Surgery*, *143*(1), 78–84.

14. Kaufman, C. S., Littrup, P. J., Freman-Gibb, L. A., Francescatti, D., Stocks, L. H., Smith, J. S., . . . Simmons, R. (2004, June). Office-based cryoablation of breast fibroadenomas: 12-month follow-up. *Journal of the American College of Surgeons*, *198*(6), 914–923.

15. Kaufman, C. S., Littrup, P. J., Freeman-Gibb, L. A., Smith, J. S., Francescatti, D., Simmons, R., . . . Henry, C. A. (2005, September-October). Office-based cryoablation of breast fibroadenomas with long-term follow-up. *Breast Journal*, *11*(5), 344–350.

16. Dooley, W. C., Francescatti, D., Clark, L., & Webber, G. (2004, October). Office-based breast ductoscopy for diagnosis. *American Journal of Surgery*, *188*(4), 415–418.

17. Wilkins, T., & Gillies, R. A. (2004, November–December). Office-based ultrathin esophagogastroduodenoscopy in a primary care setting. *Journal of the American Board of Family Practice*, *17*(6), 438–442.

18. Hilsabeck, J. R. (1983, May). Experience with routine office sigmoidoscopy using the 60-cm flexible colonoscope in private practice. *Diseases of the Colon & Rectum*, *26*(5), 314–318.

19. Almeida, O. D. Jr., & Val-Gallas, J. M. (1998, November). Office microlaparoscopy under local anesthesia in the diagnosis and treatment of chronic pelvic pain. *Journal of the American Association of Gynecologic Laparoscopy*, *5*(4), 407–410.

20. Miller, G. H. (1997, January-March). Office single puncture laparoscopy sterilization with local anesthesia. *Journal of the Society of Laparoendoscopic Surgeons*, *1*(1), 55–59.

21. Bradley L. D., & Widrich, T. (1995, May). State-of-the-art flexible hysteroscopy for office gynecologic evaluation. *Journal of the American Association of Gynecologic Laparoscopy*, *2*(3), 263–267.

22. Levie, M. D., & Chudnoff, S. G. (2006, March-April). Prospective analysis of office-based hysteroscopic sterilization. *Journal of Minimally Invasive Gynecology*, *13*(2), 98–101.

23. Glasser, M. H., & Zimmerman, J. D. (2003, November). The HydroThermAblator system for management of menorrhagia in women with submucous myomas: 12- to 20-month follow-up. *Journal of the American Association of Gynecologic Laparoscopy*, *10*(4), 521–527.

24. Laberge, P. Y., Sabbah, R., Fortin, C., & Gallinat A. Assessment and comparison of intraoperative and

postoperative pain associated with NovaSure and ThermaChoice endometrial ablation systems. *Journal of the American Association of Gynecologic Laparoscopy*, *10*(2), 223–232.

25. Shariat, S. F., Raptidis, G., Masatoschi, M., Bergamaschi, F., & Slawin, K. M. (2005, November). Pilot study of radiofrequency interstitial tumor ablation (RITA) for the treatment of radio-recurrent prostate cancer. *Prostate*, *65*(3), 260–267.

26. Berardinelli, F., Hinh, P., & Wang, R. (2009, September). Minimally invasive surgery in the management of benign prostatic hyperplasia. *Minerva Urologica Nefrologica*, *61*(3), 269–289.

27. Wells, W. G., & Lenihan, J. P. Jr. (2007, June). Use of in-office anesthesia during non-surgical radiofrequency collagen denaturation for stress urinary incontinence. *Current Medical Research & Opinion*, *23*(6), 1279–1284.

28. Baeten, D., Van den Bosch, F., Elewaut, D., Stuer, A., Veys, E. M., & De Keyser, F. (1999). Needle arthroscopy of the knee with synovial biopsy sampling: Technical experience in 150 patients. *Clinical Rheumatology*, *18*(6), 434–441.

29. Wei, N., Delauter, S. K., Beard, S., Erlichman, M. S., & Henry, D. (2001, October). Office-based arthroscopic synovectomy of the wrist in rheumatoid arthritis. *Arthroscopy*, *17*(8), 884–887.

30. Cook, J. L., & Perone, J. B. (2003, February). A prospective evaluation of the incidence of complications associated with Mohs micrographic surgery. *Archives of Dermatology*, *139*(2), 143–152.

31. Dietzek, A. M. (2007, September-October). Endovenous radiofrequency ablation for the treatment of varicose veins. *Vascular*, *15*(5), 255–261.

32. Roland, L., & Dietzek, A. M. (2007, September). Radiofrequency ablation of the great saphenous vein performed in the office: tips for better patient convenience and comfort and how to perform it in less than an hour. *Perspectives in Vascular Surgery and Endovascular Therapy*, *19*(3), 309–314.

33. Oh, C. K., Jung, D. S., Jang, H. S., & Kwon, K. S. (2003, November). Endovenous laser surgery of the incompetent greater saphenous vein with a 980-nm diode laser. *Dermatologic Surgery*, *29*(11), 1135–1140.

34. Wang, C., Vickery, A. L. Jr., & Maloof, F. (1976, September). Needle biopsy of the thyroid. *Surgery, Gynecology, & Obstetrics*, *143*(3), 365–368.

35. Schultz, L. (1994, July-September). Cost analysis of office surgery clinic with comparison to hospital outpatient facilities for laparoscopic procedures. *International Surgery*, *79*(3), 5.

36. Belkin, L. (1993, July 16). Hospital says it barred doctor in abortion death. *New York Times.*

37. 'Dr. Lips' Guilty of Killing Patient. (1994, June 1). *Miami Herald.*

38. Bruner, J. G., & de Jong, R. H. (2001, April 15). Lipoplasty claims experience of U.S. insurance companies. *Plastic and Reconstructive Surgery, 107*(5), 1285–1291.

39. Keyes, G. R., Singer, R., Iverson, R. E., McGuire, M., Yates, J., Gold, A., & Thompson, D. (2004, May). Analysis of outpatient surgery center safety using an internet-based quality improvement and peer review program. *Plastic and Reconstructive Surgery, 113*(6), 1760–1770.

40. Keyes, G. R., Singer, R., Iverson, R. E., McGuire, M., Yates, J., Gold A, ... Thompson D. (2008, July). Mortality in outpatient surgery. *Plastic and Reconstructive Surgery, 122*(1), 245–250; discussion 251–253.

41. Byrd, H. S., Barton, F. E., Orenstein, H. H., Rohrich, R. J., Burns, A. J., Hobar, P. C., & Haydon, M. S. (2003, August). Safety and efficacy in an accredited outpatient plastic surgery facility: A review of 5316 consecutive cases. *Plastic and Reconstructive Surgery, 112*(2), 636–641; discussion 642–646.

42. Blake, D. R. (2008, September-October). Office-based anesthesia: Dispelling common myths. *Aesthetic Surgery Journal, 28*(5), 564–570; discussion 571–572.

43. Cook, J. L., Perone, J. B. (2003, February). A prospective evaluation of the incidence of complications associated with Mohs micrographic surgery. *Archives of Dermatology, 139*(2), 143–152.

44. Housman, T. S., Lawrence, N., Mellen, B. G., et al. (2002, November). The safety of liposuction: Results of a national survey. *Dermatolgic Surgery, 28*(11), 971–978.

45. Grazer, F. M., & de Jong, R. H. (2000, January). Fatal outcomes from liposuction: Census survey of cosmetic surgeons. *Plastic and Reconstructive Surgery, 105*(1), 436–446; discussion 47–48.

46. El-Gamal, H. M., Dufresne, R. G., & Saddler, K. (2001, April). Electrosurgery, pacemakers and ICDs: A survey of precautions and complications

experienced by cutaneous surgeons. *Dermatologic Surgery, 27*(4), 385–390.

47. Metzner, J., Posner, K. L., Lam, M. S., & Domino, K. B. (2011, June). Closed claims' analysis. *Best Practice & Research Clinical Anaesthesiology, 25*(2), 263–276.

48. Metzner, J., Posner, K. L., Domino, K. B. (2009, August). The risk and safety of anesthesia at remote locations: The U.S. closed claims analysis. *Current Opinion in Anaesthesiology, 22*(4), 502–508.

49. Metzner, J. I. (2010). Risks of anesthesia at remote locations. *ASA Newsletter, 74*(2), 17–18.

50. Martin, J. E., Speyer, L. A., & Schmults, C. D. (2010, October). Heightened infection-control practices are associated with significantly lower infection rates in office-based Mohs surgery. *Dermatologic Surgery, 36*(10), 1529–1536.

51. Schaefer, M. K., Jhung, M., Dahl, M., Schillie, S., Simpson, C., Llata, E., . . . Perz, J. F. (2010, June). Infection control assessment of ambulatory surgical centers. *Journal of the American Medical Association, 303*(22), 2273–2279.

52. Alghamdi, K. M., & Alkhodair, R. A. (2011, January-February). Practical techniques to enhance the safety of health care workers in office-based surgery. *Journal of Cutaneous Medicine and Surgery, 15*(1), 48–54.

53. Lermitte, J., & Chung, F. (2005, December). Patient selection in ambulatory surgery. *Current Opinionsn in Anaesthesiology, 18*(6), 598–602.

54. Gross, J. B., Bachenberg, K. L., Benumof, J. L., Caplan, R. A., Connis, R. T., Coté, C. J., . . . American Society of Anesthesiologists Task Force on Perioperative Management. (2006). Practice guidelines for the perioperative management of patients with obstructive sleep apnea: A report by the American Society of Anesthesiologists Task Force on Perioperative Management of Patients with Obstructive Sleep Apnea. *Anesthesiology, 104*, 1081–1093.

55. Neily, J., Mills, P. D., Eldridge, N., Dunn, E. J., Samples, C., Turner, J. R., . . . Bagian, J. P. (2009, November). Incorrect surgical procedures within and outside of the operating room. *Archives of Surgery, 144(11)*, 1028–1034.

56. Neily, J., Mills, P. D., Eldridge, N., Carney, B. T., Pfeffer, D., Turner, J. R., . . . Bagian, J. P. (2011, July

18). Incorrect surgical procedures within and outside of the operating room: A follow-up report. *Archives of Surgery, 146*(11), 1235–1239.

57. Faltz, L. L., Morley, J. N., Flink, E., & Dameron, P. D. H. (2010). The New York model: Root cause analysis driving patient safety initiative to ensure correct surgical and invasive procedures. In: K. Henriksen, J. B. Battles, M. A. Keyes, & M. L. Grady (eds.), *Advances in Patient Safety: New Directions and Alternative Approaches (Vol. 1: Assessment).* Rockville, MD: Agency for Healthcare Research and Quality.

58. (2009, November). New Joint Commission center to take on wrong-site surgery. *Operating Room Management, 25*(11), 1, 6.

59. Howell, B. (2006). Is competition the answer? A health care policy question. Health Care Association of New York.

60. Blake, D. R. (2008, September-October). Office-based anesthesia: Dispelling common myths. *Aesthetic Surgery Journal, 28*(5), 564–570; discussion 571–572.

61. Morello, D. C., Colon, G. A., Fredricks, S., Iverson, R. E., & Singer, R. (1997, May). Patient safety in accredited office surgical facilities. *Plastic and Reconstructive Surgery, 99*(6), 1496–1500.

62. Bitar, G., Mullis, W., Jacobs, W., et al. (2003, January). Safety and efficacy of office-based surgery with monitored anesthesia care/sedation in 4778 consecutive plastic surgery procedures. *Plastic and Reconstructive Surgery, 111*(1), 150–156; discussion 7–8.

63. Fleisher, L. A., Pasternak, L. R., Herbert, R., & Anderson, G. F. (2004, January). Inpatient hospital admission and death after outpatient surgery in elderly patients: importance of patient and system characteristics and location of care. *Archives of Surgery, 139*(1), 67–72.

64. Morley, J. (2008, October 2). Office-Based Surgery, Presentation to the State Hospital Review and Planning Council. Albany, NY: New York State Department of Health.

65. Vila, H. Jr., Soto, R., Cantor, A. B., & Mackey, D. (2003, September). Comparative outcomes analysis of procedures performed in physician offices and ambulatory surgery centers. *Archives of Surgery, 138(9)*, 991–995.

66. Venkat, A. P., Coldiron, B., Balkrishnan, R., et al. (2004, December). Lower adverse event and mortality rates in physician offices compared with ambulatory surgery centers: A reappraisal of Florida adverse event data. *Dermatological Surgery, 30*(12 Pt 1), 1444–1451.

67. Mitchell, J. B., & Harrow, B. (1994, May). Costs and outcomes of inpatient versus outpatient hernia repair. *Health Policy, 28*(2), 143–152.

68. Gurusamy, K., Junnarkar, S., Farouk, M., & Davidson, B. R. (2008, February). Meta-analysis of randomized controlled trials on the safety and effectiveness of day-case laparoscopic cholecystectomy. British *Journal of Surgery, 95*(2), 161–168.

69. Commission, T. J. (2003, June). Preventing surgical fires. Sentinel Event Alert, 24(29).

70. Heller, A. (2010, January). OR fires more common than once believed. *Anesthesiology News, 63*(1).

71. .Bhananker, S. M., Posner, K. L., Cheney, F. W., Caplan, R. A., Lee, L. A., & Domino, K. B. (2006, February). Injury and liability associated with monitored anesthesia care: A closed claims analysis. *Anesthesiology, 104*(2), 228–234.

72. American Society of Anesthesiologists Task Force on Operating Room Fires, Caplan, R. A., Barker, S. J., Connis, R. T., Cowles, C., de Richemond, A. L., . . . Wolf, G. L. (2008, May). Practice advisory for the prevention and management of operating room fires. *Anesthesiology, 108*(5), 786–801; quiz 971–972.

73. APSF newsletter (Winter 2012). 26(3), 41–43.

74. Prevention and Management of Surgical Fires (video) (2010). ASPF. Retrieved from http://www.apsf.org

75. The American College of Surgeons. (2003, March 17). Statement on Patient Safety Principles for Office-based Surgery Utilizing Moderate Sedation/Analgesia, Deep Sedation/Analgesia, or General Anesthesia. ACS/AMA coordinated consensus meeting on office-based surgery. Retrieved from http://www.facs.org

76. The American Society of Anesthesiologists. Guidelines for Office-Based Anesthesia. Retrieved from http://www.asahq.org

77. Centers for Disease Control and Prevention. Guide to Infection Prevention for Outpatient Settings. Retrieved from http://www.cdc.gov/

78. Federation of State Medical Boards Report of the Special Committee on Outpatient (Office-Based) Surgery. Retrieved from http://www.fsmb.org/pdf/2002

79. American Gastroenterological Association. (2001, August). The American Gastroenterological Association standards for office-based gastrointestinal endoscopy services. *Gastroenterology, 121*(2), 440–443.

80. Erickson, T. B., Kirkpatrick, D. H., DeFrancesco, M. S., & Lawrence, H. C. III. (2010, January). Executive summary of the American College of Obstetricians and executive summary of the American College of Obstetricians and Gynecologists Presidential Task Force on Patient Safety in the Office Setting: Reinvigorating safety in office-based gynecologic surgery. *Obstetrics & Gynecology, 115*(1), 147–151.

81. Haeck, P. C., Swanson, J. A., Gutowski, K. A., Basu, C. B., Wandel, A. G., Damitz, L. A., . . . ASPS Patient Safety Committee. (2009, October). Evidence-based patient safety advisory: Liposuction. *Plastic and Reconstructive Surgery, 124*(4 Suppl), 28S–44S.

82. Gurunluoglu, R., Swanson, J. A., Haeck, P. C., & ASPS Patient Safety Committee. (2009, October). Evidence-based patient safety advisory: Malignant hyperthermia. *Plastic and Reconstructive Surgery, 124*(4 Suppl), 68S–81S.

83. Haeck, P. C., Swanson, J. A., Schechter, L. S., Hall-Findlay, E. J., McDevitt, N. B., Smotrich, G. A., . . . ASPS Patient Safety Committee (2009, October). Evidence-based patient safety advisory: Blood dyscrasias. *Plastic and Reconstructive Surgery, 124*(4 Suppl), 82S–95S.

84. Haeck, P. C., Swanson, J. A., Iverson, R. E., Lynch, D. J., . . . ASPS Patient Safety Committee. (2009, October). Evidence-based patient safety advisory: Patient assessment and prevention of pulmonary side effects in surgery. Part 1. Obstructive sleep apnea and obstructive lung disease. *Plastic and Reconstructive Surgery, 124*(4 Suppl), 45S–56S.

85. Haeck, P. C., Swanson, J. A., Iverson, R. E., Lynch, D. J., & ASPS Patient Safety Committee. (2009, October). Evidence-based patient safety advisory: Patient assessment and prevention of pulmonary side effects in surgery. Part 2. Patient and procedural risk factors. *Plastic and Reconstructive Surgery, 124(4 Suppl)*, 57S–67S.

86. Haeck, P. C., Swanson, J. A., Iverson, R. E., Schechter, L. S., Singer, R., Basu, C. B., . . . ASPS Patient Safety Committee. (2009, October). Evidence-based patient safety advisory: Patient selection and procedures in ambulatory surgery. *Plastic and Reconstructive Surgery*, *124*(4 Suppl), 6S–27S.

87. Vargo, J. J., Zuccaro, G. Jr., Dumot, J. A., et al. (2002). Automated graphic assessment of respiratory activity is superior to pulse oximetry and visual assessment for the detection of early respiratory depression during therapeutic upper endoscopy. *Gastrointestinal Endoscopy*, *55*, 826–831.

88. Coyle, T. T., Helfrick, J. F., Gonzalez, M. L., Andresen, R. V., & Perrott, D. H. (2005, February). Office-based ambulatory anesthesia: Factors that influence patient satisfaction or dissatisfaction with deep sedation/general anesthesia. *Journal of Oral and Maxillofacial Surgery, 63*(2), 163–172.

INDEX

Boxes, figures, and tables are indicated by *b*, *f*, and *t* following the page number.

guideline clearinghouse, 279
indecipherable prescriptions, 262
malpractice liability, 289*b*
online guidelines, 117
pay-for-posting, 48
physician's adherence to guidelines, 284
sexual misconduct problems, 274–275
social media use, 116
Specialty Society Medical Liability Project, 292–293
*American Medical Response of Connecticut v. National Labor
   Relations Board* (2010), 76
American National Standards Institute, 411
American Nurses Association (ANA), 384, 393, 468
American Osteopathic Association, 157
American Pediatric Society (APS), 313
American Psychiatric Association (APA), 364, 366, 374, 377,
   384, 385
American Psychiatric Nurses Association (APNA), 375,
   384, 393
American Society for Bioethics and Humanities (ASBH), 146
American Society for Healthcare Risk Management
   (ASHRM), 9, 217
American Society for Testing and Materials (ASTM), 411
American Society of Anesthesiologists (ASA), 319, 485, 486,
   488–489, 491
American Society of Colon and Rectal Surgery, 279
The American Society of Healthcare Risk Managers, 98
American Society of Plastic and Reconstructive
   Surgeons, 490
American Society of Plastic Surgeons (ASPS), 491
Americans with Disabilities Act of 1990 (ADA)
   AIDS as disability, 68
   bipolar disorder as disability, 81
   compliance, 444
   conflicts with, 30, 30*b*
   HIV discrimination, 146
American Telemedicine Association, 410, 411
ANA (American Nurses Association), 384, 393, 468
Ancillary departments, 301
Anesthesia. *See also* Surgery
   complications, 133, 485
   intravenous drugs, 481, 482
   obstetric, 319–320
   practice guidelines, 283, 284
   vicarious liability, 255
Anesthesia Patient Safety Foundation (APSF), 489
Angiography, 337
Antenatal, defined, 310
Antepartum, defined, 310
Antepartum fetal surveillance, 315–316
Anti-fraud activities, 52
Anti-kickback provisions, 73
Antitrust laws, 283, 285, 285*b*
AON (national insurer), 224–225, 450, 460
AOT (assisted outpatient treatment), 368–369
APA (American Psychiatric Association), 364, 366, 374, 377,
   384, 385
APEs. *See* Adverse patient events

Apgar scoring, 322
APNA (American Psychiatric Nurses Association), 375,
   384,393
Apologies, 107–110, 427
APOs (adverse patient occurrences), 13
Appointment logs, 442
Appraisal evaluation, 232–233
APS (American Pediatric Society), 313
APSF (Anesthesia Patient Safety Foundation), 489
Arbitration, 75, 293, 293*b*
Arion, defined, 347*b*
Arizona Right-to-Life, 264
Arthur v. Lutheran General Hospital, Inc. (1998), 372
ASA (American Society of Anesthesiologists), 319, 485, 486,
   488–489, 491
ASBH (American Society for Bioethics and Humanities), 146
ASC (ambulatory surgical center), 481
Ascension Health system, 212–213
ASHRM (American Society for Healthcare Risk
   Management), 9, 217
Asian population, 101
Ask-A-Nurse, 413
ASPS (American Society of Plastic Surgeons), 491
Assault, 257–258, 258*b*. *See also* Violence and violence
   prevention
Assent to research, 366
"Assessment and Care of Adults at Risk for Suicidal Ideation
   and Behavior" (Registered Nurses Association of
   Ontario), 377
Assisted outpatient treatment (AOT), 368–369
Association for Professionals in Infection Control and
   Epidemiology, 349, 457
Association of Child and Adolescent Psychiatric Nurses'
   (ACAPN), 387
Association of Women's Health, Obstetrics, and Neonatal
   Nurses, 313
ASTM (American Society for Testing and Materials), 411
At-risk behavior, 428, 428*t*
Attorney fee limits, 290
Augmentation of labor and delivery, 317–318
Authorities having jurisdiction (AHJ), 156
Automobile liability, 131
Autonomy, 140–141, 141*b*
Aviation/aircraft liability, 131
Avoidable classes of events (ACEs), 293
Awards (liability), 258, 291

B
Baby boomer generation, 481
Baby Doe regulations, 138, 148
Baby K court decision (1992), 149, 152
Background checks, 77, 395, 429, 463–464, 472
Ball v. Charter Behavioral Health (2006), 385
Baptist Hospitals of Southeast Texas, In re (2006), 377
Barriers
   communications, 97
   guideline usage, 284

I

IAQ (indoor air quality), 43, 176–177, 177*b*
ICD (implantable cardioverter-defibrillator), 485
ICRA (infection control risk assessment), 179
ICT (multiple iterative classification tree), 391
Identify theft, 431
IHI (Institute for Healthcare Improvement), 103, 200
Illicit substances, 394
ILSMs (interim life safety measures), 179
IME (independent medical examination), 249
IM (intramuscular) administration of medication, 371
Immigrants, undocumented, 142
Immigration Reform and Control Act of 1986, 61
Immunity from liability, 46, 285
Immunizations, 349*b*, 444
Impaired Physician Program of the Medical Association of Georgia, 274
Impaired professionals, 273–274
Implantable cardioverter-defibrillator (ICD), 485
Implantable pacemaker, 485
Implanted medical devices, 38
Implicit standards, 29
Implied contracts, 64
Improvement capability, 214
Improvement score (value-based purchasing), 50
Improving Malpractice Prevention and Compensation Systems, 292
Incident identification, 18, 445
Incident prevention, 20–21
Incident reporting
    ambulatory care, 445
    do's and don'ts, 12–13
    home healthcare, 470, 470*b*
    Medicare, 3
    process, 18–19, 197–199
    state-mandated, 19
    systems for, 11–13, 12*b*
"Incident Reports and Root Cause Analyses 2002–2008: What They Reveal About Suicides," 376
Incident review and evaluation, 20
Incinerators, medical waste, 41
Incivility, 78–79*b*, 78–81, 79*t*
Incorrect surgical procedure events, 487
Independent contractor vs. employee, 474
Independent medical examination (IME), 249
Indoor air quality (IAQ), 43, 176–177, 177*b*
Induction of labor, 317–318
Infants. *See also* Obstetrical services
    abduction of, 159*b*, 167, 327
    development allegations, 310
    ethical issues, 148–150, 312
    resuscitation and management, 321–323
    transport, 326–327
    treatment for, 148–149
Infection control certification, 492
Infection Control Committee, 355
Infection control during construction, 179

Infection control programs, 345–362
    bloodstream risk, 347–350
    healthcare settings outbreaks, 356–360
    healthcare settings risk, 347–354
    HIV transmission risk, 350–351
    multidrug-resistant pathogens, 354–356
    office-based surgery, 485–486
    overview, 345–347, 346–347*b*
    pneumonia risk, 351–353
    policy and procedures, 445
    risk management measures, 360, 456–457
    tuberculosis risk, 353–354
Infection control risk assessment (ICRA), 179
Infectious disease risks, 437–438, 437*b*
Infectious waste management, 162–163, 163*b*
Influential perceptual errors, 339
Information sharing, 45, 205
Information systems. *See* Computer systems
Information theft, 156, 170–171, 170–171*b*, 172*b*. *See also* Health Insurance Portability and Accountability Act of 1996 (HIPAA)
Informed consent
    electroconvulsive therapy, 375
    ethical issues, 144–145
    forms vs. record charting, 375
    HIV-infected physicians, 68
    home healthcare, 469
    liability issue, 251*b*
    limits to, 292
    managing expectations, 198
    office-based surgery, 484
    Patient's Bill of Rights, 45
    policy, 105–106
    telemedicine, 417
Injuries and illnesses
    employee's, 132
    medical, 193–197, 193*b*
    medication-related, 3–4
    personal, 156
    reduction in, 200
    workplace violence and, 393
Inpatient prospective payment system (IPPS), 49, 111
In re. See name of party
In-service training, 453*b*
Institute for Healthcare Improvement (IHI), 103, 200
Institute for Healthcare Improvement VAP Bundle, 353*b*
Institute for Safety in Office-Based Surgery (ISOBS), 495, 495*b*
Institute of Medicine (IOM)
    Crossing the Quality Chasm, 5, 47
    electronic medical records, 287
    health literacy, 104
    medical error reduction, 195–196
    medical mistakes, 245
    nursing homes, 452
    To Err Is Human: Building a Safer Health Care System, 3, 48, 159, 194, 426